The Christian Theology Reader

Praise for previous editions of *Christian Theology: A Reader*

"In a time when Christians are increasingly ignorant of our own traditions, McGrath's efforts in his *Introduction* and this *Reader* are most welcome. Those who have found his *Introduction* a significant resource will undoubtedly also want to use his companion set of readings. Its great strength is the breadth of figures and topics treated, and we can hope that students who become acquainted with the riches in these brief selections will want to return to engage the primary sources in their fullness. Such engagements could offer an important sign of hope for Christianity's future."

L. Gregory Jones, Duke University, North Carolina

"This anthology of extracts from primary sources will prove extremely useful for teaching historical and systematic theology. It is essential that students use primary sources, and a compromise has to be reached between undue expectations and snippets which are too brief to help. In the light of the author's introductions, the quotations are sufficiently substantial to be useful, yet remain within a compass which is realistic for undergraduate or theological college needs. I shall place it high on my book-lists for students."

Anthony C. Thiselton, University of Nottingham

"*The Christian Theology Reader* brings the best primary sources to the theological inquirer."

Gabriel Fackre, Andover Newton Theological School

Also by Alister E. McGrath from Blackwell Publishing

Christian Theology: An Introduction, 4th edn (2007)
Christianity: An Introduction, 2nd edn (2006)
The Blackwell Companion to Protestantism (edited with Darren C. Marks, 2003)
The Intellectual Origins of the European Reformation, 2nd edn (2003)
A Brief History of Heaven (2003)
The Future of Christianity (2002)
Christian Literature: An Anthopology (edited, 2000)
Reformation Thought: An Introduction, 3rd edn (1999)
Christian Spirituality: An Introduction (1999)
Historical Theology: An Introduction (1998)
The Blackwell Encyclopedia of Modern Christian Thought (1995)

For a complete list of Alister E. McGrath's publications from Blackwell Publishing, visit our website at www.blackwellpublishing.com/mcgrath

The Christian Theology Reader

Third Edition

Edited by

Alister E. McGrath
University of Oxford

BLACKWELL PUBLISHING
350 Main Street, Malden, MA 02148-5020, USA
9600 Garsington Road, Oxford OX4 2DQ, UK
550 Swanston Street, Carlton, Victoria 3053, Australia

First edition published 1996 by Blackwell Publishing Ltd
Second edition published 2001 by Blackwell Publishing Ltd
Third edition published 2007 by Blackwell Publishing Ltd

3 2008

Library of Congress Cataloging-in-Publication Data

The Christian theology reader / edited by Alister E. McGrath.—3rd ed.
p. cm.
Includes bibliographical references and index.
ISBN 978-1-4051-5358-4 (pbk. : alk. paper)
1. Theology, Doctrinal—Popular works. I. McGrath, Alister E., 1953–

BT77.C47 2007
230–dc22
2006001999

A catalogue record for this title is available from the British Library.

Set in 10/12pt PhotinaMT
by SPi Publisher Services, Pondicherry, India
Printed and bound in Singapore
by Fabulous Printers Pte Ltd

The publisher's policy is to use permanent paper from mills that operate a sustainable forestry policy, and which has been manufactured from pulp processed using acid-free and elementary chlorine-free practices. Furthermore, the publisher ensures that the text paper and cover board used have met acceptable environmental accreditation standards.

For further information on
Blackwell Publishing, visit our website:
www.blackwellpublishing.com

Contents

Mission Statement

This book aims to introduce you to the key ideas, personalities, and schools of thought within Christian theology by direct engagement with original theological texts. It assumes that you know virtually nothing about the subject. It provides 361 readings, drawn from 233 different sources, spread throughout the two thousand years of Christian history, each illustrating a key doctrine, point of view, intellectual development, or theological landmark. It encourages you to engage actively with these texts by providing each of these readings with

- an *introduction*, which sets the reading in its context;
- a brief *commentary*, which explains some key issues and helps you to understand the significance of the reading;
- a set of *study questions*, which will help you assess how well you have understood the text, and encourage further interaction with it.

After you have worked through this book, you will be able to achieve the following *objectives*:

- read and understand more advanced works of theology, including works by major theologians and works about major theologians or areas of theology;
- make sense of lectures and talks dealing with Christian theology;
- make informed contributions to debates and discussions in churches, universities, seminaries, and colleges;
- give accurate and reliable introductory presentations to church and student audiences on many aspects of Christian thought.

Preface

Christian theology is one of the most fascinating and rewarding subjects it is possible to study. The rich theological tradition of Christianity has taken root in virtually every part of global culture, and given rise to some of the most creative and important reflection in the history of human thought. To study this is to do more than gain insights into the Christian gospel; it is to understand more about human culture itself. For, as its influence has spread, Christianity has not demanded that cultures should fall into line with its precepts; from the outset, Christianity has taken root within existing cultures, and thus set in motion a rich and dynamic process of interaction between the ideas and values of the gospel and those already present in a given culture.

The motives for the study of Christian theology vary enormously. Some wish to study it in order to prepare themselves for some form of Christian ministry. Others undertake it in order to deepen their grasp and appreciation of their faith. Others are curious outsiders, wondering what Christianity has to say on various issues. Yet for every ten people who would like to begin the serious study of theology, there are probably six or seven who find the task to be impossible, due to the lack of a reliable and intelligible introduction to its themes. There are many such introductions available; the problem is that they make what often turns out to be hopelessly unrealistic demands of their readers. They assume too much knowledge on the part of those who use them, and fail to take the trouble to introduce and explain ideas, debates, and terms.

It was the widespread recognition of this need which led to the development of *Christian Theology: An Introduction*, which was first published in 1994 and is now about to enter its fourth edition. This work evolved in response to over a decade's experience of teaching theology in the United Kingdom, North America, and Australia, and was rigorously tested against its intended readership to ensure that it was as comprehensive and intelligible as possible. The widespread adoption of this work suggests that it has achieved at least some of its goals. This work incorporates many features to ensure that the study of theology is presented in an accessible and interesting manner.

Nevertheless, the approach adopted in the *Introduction* placed limits upon the amount of primary source material which could be cited. It is invaluable to have the basic themes, debates, and personalities of Christian theology introduced by a skilled and unbiased commentator. Yet this can only lay a foundation for interacting with these themes, debates, and personalities *by reading and interacting with original texts*. The idea of creating a linked reader was considered at an early stage in the planning of the *Introduction* itself, in order that appropriate texts could be identified from the outset. This made it possible to identify the nature and extent of difficulties encountered by students, so that the correct level of explanation could be established. Indeed, extracts from some of the seminal texts thus identified were incorporated into the *Introduction* itself. However, limitations upon space and the consistent emphasis upon explanation within this earlier work restricted the amount of citation possible.

This latest edition of the *Reader* makes available a series of more than 360 seminal texts of Christian theology, drawn from more than 230 different sources throughout the two thousand years of Christian history, arranged on a broadly thematic basis, to allow its users to engage directly with the intellectual richness of the Christian tradition. (A "source" here means an individual theologian, irrespective of how many of that theologian's writings are excerpted, or a confessional document such as the Council of Trent or the Heidelberg Catechism.) Every attempt has been made to ensure that the work is broadly representative, chronologically and intellectually, of the two thousand years of sustained critical reflection within western Christianity. Readings are provided from every century of Christian thought after the closing of the New Testament. The readings are drawn from a wide variety of theological genres – works of systematic theology, conciliar pronouncements, confessions of faith, catechisms, sermons, biblical commentaries, poems, hymns, and letters. On rare occasions, readings are drawn from non-Christian sources (such as Karl Marx), where the author or current of thought which she or he represents has had a significant impact on Christian theological reflection.

The emphasis upon explanation, characteristic of the *Introduction*, has been carried over into this *Reader*. Within the limits of the space available, every effort has been made to explain the importance of each reading, identify its context and key features, and alert the reader as to what to look out for in reading the text. To allow easy correlation with the *Introduction*, the *Reader* is divided into 10 chapters which reflect the basic structure of the earlier work. However, the *Reader* can be used as a free-standing resource, without any need to consult the *Introduction*.

This *Reader* aims to make available a collection of texts likely to be of interest to those beginning the study of Christian theology, or deepening an existing knowledge. The texts chosen belong to two categories. In the first place, there are seminal texts which represent landmarks in Christian thinking on certain subjects. These texts represent the statement of ideas or the development of arguments which have had a considerable impact, or which illustrate aspects of major debates within the Christian tradition. These texts are often quite brief. I have seen no pressing reason for quoting extended passages simply for the sake of doing so. The reader will thus find regular citation from such landmark writers as Irenaeus, Clement of Alexandria, Origen, Tertullian, Augustine, Thomas Aquinas, Martin Luther, John Calvin, F. D. E. Schleiermacher, Karl Barth, and Karl Rahner. Despite this focus on classic texts, however, a substantial proportion of the sources for this *Reader* date from the twentieth century, ensuring that classic and modern writings are both fairly and fully represented.

In the second place, texts published after 1950 have often been selected on the basis of the lucidity or convenience of their discussion of highly complex questions. Often, these texts act as surveys of a broad field on the part of an informed writer, or as statements of a general theological position or trend – such as feminism, postliberalism, or evangelicalism. These texts tend to be more extended, in that it is the discussion of the questions under consideration, as much as the ideas which are actually defended, which will be of interest to readers. The discipline of Christian theology includes a substantial commitment to dialogue with the past tradition, as well as with its living representatives. Besides illustrating approaches and ideas from the recent past and present, these more extended texts allow readers to gain an appreciation of the importance of interaction with the past in theology. They are all included here to allow the reader to sample and appreciate the great richness and diversity of modern Christian theology.

This book is a reader in Christian theology, not in church history. This is not a collection of texts for the church historian. There are many documents of historical importance – such as the Toleration Edict of Galerius (April 311) – which have limited theological relevance. The texts have been chosen on the basis of the known needs of those studying Christian theology at seminary, college, or university level. Church history is a separate discipline, requiring its own collections of texts, many of which are currently available to interested readers. Nor is this book a specialist reader, focusing on one historical period, or a single writer, theological school, or geographical region. The work is intended to act as a general introduction to the great tradition of doing theology within a Christian context, in order to encourage its readers to take matters further.

Sadly, there is not space to include all the texts which one might hope to include in a work of this sort. If it is of any interest, the 361 readings finally selected were chosen from a group of 1,250 possible candidates, identified on the basis of literature searches and evaluated on the basis of first-hand classroom testing. In preparation for the third edition of this work, a wide process of consultation was undertaken to ensure that the work was as useful as possible; this has led to the addition of some new material. Detailed consultation with users on how the work might be improved has led to the incorporation of additional texts, including extracts from works by two leading medieval theologians omitted from earlier editions – Bonaventure and Duns Scotus – as well as increased representation of Catholic, Orthodox, and women writers, particularly during the twentieth century.

Despite these new and welcome additions, an enormous amount of important material has still had to be omitted. Time and time again, pressure on space has forced me to set to one side texts which many readers will feel ought to have been included, or to give only a brief extract from a text which some will feel merits fuller citation. I apologize for these shortcomings, of which I am only too painfully aware. The omission of any particular theologian must not in any way be understood to imply that this theologian has made an insignificant contribution to the development of Christian theology. It is hoped that, as future editions of this work emerge, it will prove possible to incorporate a greater selection of more recent writings, in addition to those now included in the third edition.

It is the firm intention of the author and publisher to make this volume as useful and helpful as possible in the long term. The structure of the work has been designed to make inclusion of additional or alternative texts possible in later editions without major disturbance of its existing form. Both the author and publisher are committed to responding to end-user evaluation in improving and extending the work in the future. If you have any comments which might be helpful in this ongoing process of revision and improvement of the present edition of this volume or *Christian Theology: An Introduction*, you are invited to send them in writing to the publishers.

Alister E. McGrath
Oxford University

Approaching the Readings

Each text in this reader follows a common pattern, as follows:

Each text is identified by a *number*, which allows cross-reference to texts within this *Reader*. This number allows the chapter within which the reading occurs, and the location of that reading within the chapter, to be identified. Thus "4.10" (Gregory of Nazianzus on Apollinarianism) designates the 10th reading within chapter 4, dealing with the person of Jesus Christ.

This is followed by a concise statement of the *author and theme* of the reading. For example, the title "Thomas Aquinas on the Principle of Analogy" (1.10) allows the reader to identify both the author of the piece and its broad theme. The readings have been grouped thematically over 10 chapters, and are arranged chronologically within chapters. Augustine's views on the church are thus found before those of Luther. Once more, it must be emphasized that a reading allocated to one chapter may well prove to be of relevance in other contexts. Basic biographical and bibliographical details concerning each author cited will be found in the major section "Details of Theologians" (pp. 683–701). Note that the list of authors is cross-referenced to the readings, so that looking up "Augustine" will immediately identify all readings from this important author included in this work.

This is followed by an *introduction* to each reading, which provides background information to the text, and allows its importance to be appreciated. In most cases, the introduction will be brief; in others, a more extended introduction is required to ensure that the full significance of the text in question is understood. The introduction may draw attention to matters such as the date of writing of the text, as well as its original language, information concerning technical terms, other writers referred to in the text, or points of possible difficulty. A full glossary of theological terms is also provided at the end of the work. The introduction ends by referring the reader to other related texts of interest within the *Christian Theology Reader*, where this seems appropriate.

The *text* itself then follows, translated into English where necessary. Extended texts have occasionally been abridged, to allow the exclusion of material which was judged not to be of critical importance to the point under discussion. The exclusion of material is indicated in the standard manner, using ellipsis as follows: [. . .]. Where the original text is not in English, and the reader might benefit from knowing, for example, the original Latin term or phrase being translated, this term will be included in italic type in parentheses. For example, the reading based on Martin Luther's 1539 treatise *On the Councils and the Church* makes reference to "this holy Christian people (*dis Christlich heilig Volck*)"; the reading here includes a contemporary English translation of this significant phrase, with the early modern German original indicated, where this might be helpful to some readers. Those readers who do not need to know the original terms need not pay attention to this information.

This is followed by a *commentary*, which is intended to help the reader appreciate the importance of the text, to draw attention to some of its specific features, and to explain any points of particular difficulty.

A series of *study questions* then follows, designed to help the reader engage with the text. These ensure that the text has been properly understood and that its significance has been appreciated.

The chapter in which the text is located concludes with a list of helpful *works for further reading*, allowing you to take the topic further if you wish to.

The *source* of the text is identified in a later section of the work, for the benefit of readers who wish to study the text in its original context or language, or, where material has been omitted, who wish to examine the passage intact. Where possible, this reference is given to precise line numbers or page columns; if this is not possible, the page number alone is provided. Where material has been taken from copyright material, appropriate acknowledgment is provided. In the case of classic pieces, care has been taken to ensure that references are given to the best critical editions available.

To the Student: How to Use this Work

This book has been written primarily with the needs of two groups of people in mind: those who are studying it by themselves, and those who are being taught it as part of a seminary, college, or university course.

Studying by Yourself

If you are studying theology by yourself, please read what follows carefully.

1 You are strongly recommended to purchase the companion volume *Christian Theology: An Introduction*, and use it alongside this *Reader*. It will provide you with a substantial amount of background material which you will find invaluable in making sense of the readings. In particular, you should read the four chapters dealing with "landmarks," which will help you understand more about the history of Christian theology and some of the key theologians who you will encounter at first hand in this *Reader*. You are also recommended to read this textbook's chapter relating to the topic you wish to study, which will help you set the reading in its full context. If you do not wish to use this additional resource, then read the short section entitled "The Development of Christian Theology: An Historical Overview" (pp. xxvii–xxxiii), which will help you get a sense of the historical backdrop to the ideas you will be exploring.

2 The texts in this *Reader* are arranged *thematically* by chapter and *chronologically* within each chapter. It is recommended that you adopt a thematic approach and work your way through each chapter, noticing the way in which later writers often draw on or engage with the ideas of their predecessors – even if they do not always draw attention to this fact. The introduction to each of the chapters also provides some guidance on thematic studies. There is no need to study the chapters in the order in which they are presented; start with whatever general theme seems most interesting to you. Knowledge of other chapters is not presupposed; where readings from other chapters might be relevant, these are noted.

3 Try using the following approach in relation to each reading.

- i Make sure that you can identify the author. When did the author live? In which part of the world was he or she based?
- ii Spend a little time thinking about the work from which the reading is taken. What kind of a work is it? For example, is it academic, polemical, pastoral, popular? Who is the author writing for?
- iii Note any points of importance identified in the introduction.
- iv Now read the text itself. This book has generous margins, to encourage and enable you to annotate the readings and scribble notes. Note any important phrases used. Try to summarize the passage, noting the flow of the argument and any assumptions which seem to be especially important.
- v Now close the book and see if you can summarize the reading. The more information you can retain, the better. In particular, try to recall the main points of any arguments used. Your summary will vary from one reading to another, depending on its length and complexity. However, the kind of summary that you are aiming to produce will take the following forms:

1.7 In his *Proslogion*

Anselm of Canterbury argues for the existence of God like this. He defines God as being "that than which nothing greater can be thought." He then points out that the idea of God is not as great as the reality of God. So if we agree on this definition of God, and can think of God, God must exist.

8.19 In *The Babylonian Captivity of the Church*

which Luther wrote in 1520, he argues that the Lord's Supper (which he refers to as either "the Mass" or "the sacrament of the altar") is like a testament, for three reasons. First, because it is about an inheritance. Second, because it identifies heirs. And third, because it proclaims the death of the testator.

This kind of exercise will help you test your own understanding of the passage, and also enable you to make the best possible use of the information for yourself.

Being Taught by Someone Else

If you are using this *Reader* as part of a taught course, whoever is directing the course will explain the way in which you are to use this book. This will generally take the form of directing you to read, summarize, and comment on certain passages. You may find that the explanatory material will thus be unnecessary, on account of the guidance and input that will be provided for you. However, experience suggests that you will benefit considerably from the additional material provided. You may also like to try using the approach recommended for those studying theology by themselves, which may be a helpful supplement to what your instructor recommends.

Preparing Talks?

The book will also be of service to those preparing talks, sermons, or addresses on key themes of Christian theology, who wish to incorporate source material into the lecture, or interact with a leading representative of a position under examination. For example, the following topics, among many others, could easily be addressed on the basis of this *Reader*.

- The role of tradition in Christian theology (see readings 2.2, 2.5, 2.10, 2.19, 2.22, 2.25, 2.28, 2.33, 2.34, 2.47, 2.50).
- The place of icons in the Reformed tradition (for example, see 1.14: The Heidelberg Catechism on Images of God; 3.39: Jacques Ellul on the Theology of Icons).
- What can we know of God from nature?
- Christian approaches to other faiths
- What does it mean to say that we are "created in the image of God"?
- Some themes in the theology of Martin Luther.

To the Teacher: How to Use this Book

The basic idea behind this book is to make your task as a teacher as rewarding and stimulating as possible, by setting before students a wide variety of interesting texts, along with campus-tested explanatory material. It is designed to save you trouble and effort, and allow you to do some creative and exciting things with your students and the texts, rather than have to spend endless hours of classroom time on very basic explanations and comments.

This collection of readings has been designed to be as useful as possible to teachers of theology at every level. You will find the following information useful for helping your students get the most out of the texts.

1 The texts have been selected to give continuous and comprehensive coverage of all major theological debates over the last two thousand years of Christian history. More than 230 different sources have been used. In preparing for the third edition of this work, extensive research was undertaken to identify which texts are likely to be most useful to those teaching courses in Christian theology. This has resulted in a significant expansion of the range of readings offered.
2 The contents of this book can be mastered without the need for any input on your part. Every explanation which this book offers has been classroom-tested on student audiences, and refined until students reported that they could understand the points being made without the need for further assistance. If you set students the assignment of reading a collection of named texts, you can realistically expect them to have grasped their basic features and themes before you begin to take them further and deeper.
3 The book aims to encourage students to interact with the original texts of Christian theology. Most teachers report that students find themselves intimidated by this interaction, partly because they are worried that they will not be able to make sense of what they read. This work aims to build student confidence by offering several layers of assistance, all of which have been tested on student audiences – and modified where necessary – to make sure that they work.
4 Each of the 361 readings is provided with an *introduction*, a *commentary*, and a set of *study questions*. These have been written as clearly as possible, and students

should find that they have been given enough assistance to be able to approach a text with confidence, and make sense of what they read. You may find it helpful to read the section entitled "To the Student: How to Use this Work," which will give you an idea of how students are being encouraged to approach these texts.

5 The work is theologically neutral; it does not advocate any denominational agenda. Thus the work will help your students *understand* Barth (or Aquinas or Augustine or Luther), but it will not ask them to *agree* with Barth (or Aquinas or Augustine or Luther). The book aims to put you, the teacher, in the position of interacting with the classic resources of the Christian tradition, on the basis of the assumption that your students, through reading and reflecting on the texts contained in this book, will have a good basic understanding of the issues, and have had the experience of engaging directly with the original texts, rather than reading about them at second hand.

6 Although this work is ideally suited as a companion volume to *Christian Theology: An Introduction*, it can be used on its own, or as a companion to other introductions to Christian theology.

7 There is a website linked to this text and its companion volume *Christian Theology: An Introduction*, which is now entering its fourth edition. It is the intention of both the author and publisher to use this site to provide updated bibliographies, additional teaching materials, and other material which it is hoped will be of use to all those teaching theology. A useful list of relevant reading material, much published in the last 15 years, is provided at the end of each chapter, and a list of additional readers is to be found at the end of the work. It is intended that the website will provide an expanded and continually updated collection of materials of use to both teachers and students.

The Development of Christian Theology: An Historical Overview

This reader brings together a substantial number of readings drawn from the first two thousand years of Christian theology. Theology is "talk about God"; Christian theology is "talk about God" from a Christian perspective. Engaging with these readings is one of the best ways of understanding how Christians have tried to express their faith, develop its ideas, and weave its themes together into a systematic whole. Each reading is accompanied by an introduction, comment, and study questions, designed to make this process of engagement as straightforward, interesting, and profitable as possible.

To get the most out of these readings, however, it is important to have an overview of the main features of the development of Christian theology. If you are using this reader alongside its companion volume, *Christian Theology: An Introduction*, you will find that this provides you with a detailed road map which will allow you to get the most from this collection of readings. It will help you make much more sense of what you read, and allow you to appreciate the context in which they were written. The four introductory chapters provide a survey of historical theology. The following four chapters deal with issues of sources and interpretation, dealing with material covered in the first two chapters of this reader. The remaining chapters present a detailed engagement with the major themes of Christian theology, providing an in-depth introduction to the readings.

However, not all will want to make use of this specific introduction to Christian theology. For those not using this companion volume, this brief section will give you something of a panoramic view of the main landmarks of this process of development, and identify readings that will help you understand some of its features. While this can only highlight some of the many themes of Christian theology (passing over many topics, debates, schools of thought and topics that fully deserve discussion), it will nevertheless help readers to get their bearings in the midst of this vast landscape of ideas.

For the sake of convenience, historians of Christian thought tend to break its first two thousand years down into more manageable sections. While everyone has their own views about how best to divide Christian history, many use a framework which looks something like this.

The Apostolic Period

The first hundred years is often referred to as the *apostolic* period. This is the period during which the works now included in the New Testament were written. During this time, Christianity was spreading throughout the Mediterranean region and beyond. The missionary journeys of St Paul, described in the Acts of the Apostles, are an excellent example of this activity. This reader does not include readings from the New Testament, as this document is so readily accessible.

The Patristic Period

This is followed by the *patristic* period, which is usually held to begin about the year 100. There is no firm agreement about when this period ended: some scholars suggest it ends in the fifth century, while others extend it by at least two centuries. The Council of Chalcedon (451) marked a landmark in Christian thinking, especially over the identity of Jesus Christ, and is seen by many writers as bringing this important period of theological development to a close. The unusual word "patristic" derives from the Greek word *pater* ("father"), and designates a group of writers who are often collectively known as the "fathers of the church." (Sadly, there were very few women among them.) The readings include selections from all the major writers of this period – such as Irenaeus of Lyons, Clement of Alexandria, Origen, the Cappadocian fathers, Athanasius, and Augustine of Hippo.

The patristic period witnessed important theological explorations of the relation of faith and classical culture, clarifying the place of the Bible in Christian theology (including establishing the New Testament canon), the identity of Jesus Christ, the doctrine of God (including the Trinity), the doctrine of the church, and the relation of grace and free will. All of these are well represented in this reader. In what follows, we will look at each of them in a little more detail.

Faith and classical culture

As Christianity expanded in its first centuries, it moved from a Palestinian context into the Greek-speaking world of the eastern Mediterranean, establishing a presence in the great cities of Alexandria and Antioch. It also began to grow in the western Latin-speaking Roman Empire, including North Africa. This raised the question of how Christianity related to ideas already present in this region – for example, classic philosophy (1.1-4).

The place of the Bible

One of the most important achievements of the patristic period was establishing which books dating from the apostolic period were to be regarded as "canonical" or "biblical" (2.1). Considerable attention was also paid to the question of how the Bible was to be interpreted (2.3-4, 2.6, 2.8), and especially the role of tradition in combating unorthodox interpretations of the Bible (2.2, 2.5, 2.10). During this period, "creeds" began to emerge as communally accepted and authorized summaries of the Christian faith (1.5-6; 2.7).

The identity of Jesus Christ

The patristic period saw clarification of the identity and significance of Jesus as being of the utmost importance. Where was he to be placed on a theological map? The period witnessed growing acceptance of the "two natures" doctrine, along with exploration of how best to make sense of Jesus Christ being both divine and human. The Arian and Nestorian debates were of particular importance in clarifying this matter. These debates are widely regarded as being of critical importance, and they are well represented in this collection (4.1-16).

The doctrine of God

Classical Greek philosophy already had its ideas about what "God" was like. One of the most important tasks of Christian theology was to differentiate the Christian idea of God from its philosophical rivals (3.1). Many early debates concentrated on what it meant to say that God was creator (3.4-5), the role of the Holy Spirit (3.10, 3.15, 3.17-19), or how the existence of evil was consistent with a good God (3.2, 3.6, 3.14). However, the most significant discussions concerned the doctrine of the Trinity – the distinctively Christian idea of one God in three persons. How was this to be understood (3.3, 3.9, 3.11-13, 3.16, 3.20)?

The doctrine of the church

Patristic writers initially paid relatively little attention to the doctrine of the church (7.1-3), tending to focus attention on developing a coherent understanding of the sacraments (8.1-6). The Donatist controversy of the fourth century forced the western church to reconsider the nature of the church (7.5-6), and who was authorized to administer the sacraments (8.7-8). These debates would break out once more during the Reformation period.

The doctrine of grace

Although the Greek-speaking church made significant contributions to early Christian reflections on human nature and grace (6.1, 6.5-7), the most sustained engagement with these issues took place within the western church, largely as a result of the

Pelagian controversy (6.11-21). This debate, initially involving Pelagius and Augustine of Hippo, is well represented within this reader, on account of its intrinsic interest.

The Middle Ages

The Middle Ages, or medieval period, is regarded as extending from the end of the patristic era to about the year 1500. This long period was immensely creative culturally, and productive theologically, producing theological classics such as Peter Lombard's *Four Books of the Sentences* and Thomas Aquinas's great thirteenth-century work, the *Summa Theologica*. Peter Lombard's medieval theological textbook was the subject of many commentaries, which used its material to develop increasingly sophisticated theological ideas. The reader includes selections from Peter Lombard's classic text (8.15, 10.12), as well as some of the major commentaries on its themes (6.28-30). A number of extended extracts from Aquinas's *Summa Theologica* will help readers understand and appreciate its distinctive style (1.9-10, 3.24, 4.22, 5.17). The readings include extracts from all the major writers of this period – such as Anselm of Canterbury, Thomas Aquinas, Bonaventure, Duns Scotus, and William of Ockham.

Among the many issues to be explored in detail during this period were the relation between faith and reason, how to interpret the Bible, and the theology of the sacraments. Alongside this, there was continuing exploration of issues debated during the patristic period, such as the relation of grace and free will.

Faith and reason

The Middle Ages saw new attention being given to a whole range of issues concerning the relation of faith and reason, theology and philosophy. One reason for this was the emergence of universities in western Europe, particularly the University of Paris. The debates over whether God's existence could be proved (1.7-9, 1.11) or the grounds of the incarnation (4.21-2, 5.16) are good examples of this concern.

Biblical interpretation

The rise of the monasteries led to a new interest in the correct interpretation of the Bible. The constant use of the Bible in corporate worship and private devotion raised important questions about how the Bible was to be understood and applied (2.11-13).

The institution of the church

The rise of the papacy raised increasingly important questions about the church and its sacramental system. Major issues debated during the Middle Ages included the definition of a sacrament (8.14-15), and the vexed question of how Christ could be present in the Eucharist (8.10-13, 8.16). The growing political power of the church raised important theological questions about the relation of church and state (7.8, 7.10).

The relation of grace and free will

In many ways, medieval theology can be seen as an extended commentary on Augustine's theology. It is therefore not surprising that issues concerning grace and human freedom should emerge as important at this time (6.26, 6.29-30).

The Reformation and Post-Reformation Period

The sixteenth century marked a period of radical change in the western church. This period of *reformation* witnessed the birth of Protestantism, through writers such as Martin Luther and John Calvin. Certain theological debates became especially heated around this time, especially the place of the Bible in theological reflection, the doctrine of the church, and the question of what it is necessary to do in order to be saved. The Catholic Church also went through a period of reformation around this time, with the Council of Trent setting out the definitive Catholic position on issues of importance at this time. Many scholars also include the seventeenth century in this period, arguing that this represents the Protestant and Catholic consolidation of the developments that began in the previous century. It was during this century that Christians emigrated to North America, and began to establish that region as a major player in theological debates.

A number of significant theological developments take place during this period, most of which relate to Protestantism. Two new styles of theological texts make their appearance, both generally (though not exclusively) associated with Lutheranism and Calvinism respectively – Melanchthon's *Loci Communes* ("Commonplaces") and Calvin's *Institutes* (1.13, 2.17-18, 6.35-8, 8.21). The "Catechism," with its distinctive "question and answer" format, became of major importance at this time in theological education; this reader includes extracts from two of the most celebrated: Luther's *Lesser Catechism* (8.20) and the Heidelberg Catechism (1.14).

The reader includes extracts from all the major theological writers of the period – such as Martin Luther, Huldrych Zwingli, John Calvin, and Roberto Bellarmine – as well as drawing on important confessional documents, such as the Council of Trent. The theological debates of this period were often intense, and sometimes ferocious, focusing especially on the interpretation and authority of the Bible, the nature of the church, and the doctrine of grace. In each case, Protestants and Catholics found themselves adopting very different positions.

The authority of the Bible

A major debate between Protestants and Catholics concerned whether, in the first place, the Bible had an authority independent of that of the church; and in the second, whether the Bible could be interpreted without the guidance of the church (2.19-23,

2.25, 2.28). Alongside these specific debates, there was continued discussion over methods for the interpretation of Scripture (2.14-15).

The church

Three major debates concerning the church became of particular importance around this time. In the first place, what were the marks of the true church? Was the church defined by institutional, historical continuity with the past – or by the faithful preaching of the gospel (7.12-20). Second, how many sacraments were there? Protestants tended to identify only two gospel sacraments; the Catholic Church recognized seven (8.17). Third, in what sense, if any, was Christ present at the Eucharist? The Catholic church maintained its commitment to the specific doctrine of transubstantiation, while various viewpoints emerged within Protestantism (8.18-19, 8.22-3, 8.28).

The doctrine of grace

The Protestant reformation brought a new emphasis to the idea of "justification by faith," which was strongly resisted by Catholicism (6.32-5, 6.38-9). Later Pietist writers also expressed concern over certain ways of formulating this doctrine, which they considered detrimental to personal holiness (6.45-6, 6.48). A further debate broke out within Protestantism over predestination, focusing on the teaching of John Calvin on this matter (6.36, 6.40, 6.43).

The Modern Era

The period since about 1800 is often referred to as the "modern era." This was a period of considerable instability in western Europe, especially following the French Revolution of 1789, and later through the rise of Marxism in eastern Europe in the twentieth century. Despite these anxieties, it was a period of remarkable theological creativity throughout western Europe and North America. In addition, a growing Christian presence in Africa and Asia during the twentieth century led to an increasing interest in developing "local theologies" in these new regions. These local theologies would be grounded in the Christian tradition, but sensitive to their local situations. Although this reader cannot hope to document the emergence of these distinctive theologies outside the west, there is no doubt that this has been a development of major importance, which will become increasingly significant in the twenty-first century.

A wide range of theological issues came to the fore during the modern period. Many traditional issues continued to be debated, including the relation of faith and reason (1.19-22), the authority and interpretation of Scripture (2.33-6, 2.44-7), the doctrine of the Trinity (3.31, 3.35-6, 3.40, 3.43), the identity of Christ (4.32, 4.34, 4.37, 4.40), the grounds of redemption (5.24-35), and the nature of the church (7.21-30). In most cases, these debates were shaped by the concerns of the Enlightenment, which stressed the importance of reason, and was generally suspicious of theological arguments involving an appeal to church tradition or divine revelation. A number of additional issues began to emerge as characteristic of this period. In what follows, we shall note some of these new debates.

A growing awareness of the existence of other religions led to a new interest in clarifying the relationship of Christianity and other faiths. This issue has been discussed to a far greater extent, and with far greater intensity, in the twentieth century than in any previous period of history (9.4-12). It is for this reason that most of the readings in this section are of such recent origin.

The rise of rationalism within western culture led to a critique of a number of aspects of traditional Christian theology. The most important of these was the rise of the "historical Jesus movement" as a result of the belief that there was a massive gap between an essentially simple, rational "Jesus of history," and the church's rather more complex "Christ of faith" (4.29-31, 4.33, 4.36, 4.41). As rationalism began to lose its influence in the early twentieth century, Christian theology began to rediscover the idea of revelation (2.39-42), and to regain confidence in the doctrine of the Trinity as a means of expressing the distinctive identity of the Christian God (3.36, 3.38, 3.40). Although many in the nineteenth century were critical of the idea of dogma (1.23), the concept has once more emerged as significant (1.34).

A final factor of importance has been the growing realization of the importance of issues raised by feminist writers, who have pointed out the need to explore further issues relating to the traditional use of male language about God (3.41, 3.42), the maleness of Christ as the central figure of the Christian faith (4.38-9), or essentially masculine approaches to biblical interpretation or theological concepts (2.45, 6.55-6).

This brief survey of theological history can only identify, in a very cursory and unsatisfactory manner, some of the great themes to have been explored and debated during Christian history. It is hoped that it will help you appreciate and begin to engage with the readings collected in this volume.

Acknowledgments

In producing this work I have incurred debts of many kinds. It is my privilege to be able to acknowledge them.

This book had its origins in a course I taught at Drew University, Madison, NJ, in the fall of 1990, while I was serving there as Ezra Squire Tipple Visiting Professor of Historical Theology. How, I wondered, could I get my graduate students to enjoy sixteenth-century theology – the course that I had been assigned to teach? Eventually, I developed the approach that underlies this book: I would get them to interact with carefully chosen texts. I would begin the seminar by setting out the background to the text – introducing the author, the context, and the ideas, and then allow students to explore the text interactively, raising questions and making points. It worked well. On my return to Oxford, I continued the process, gradually expanding the range of texts. This collection of readings is the result of that long process of trial and error.

I owe an enormous amount to my students at Oxford University, on whom much of the material contained in this *Reader* was tested over a period of nearly 10 years. They patiently suffered my expositions and explanations of key texts in a series of seminars and lectures, just as I patiently listened to their difficulties and questions. The first edition of this work also owed much to discussions with faculty and students at Princeton Theological Seminary, McGill University, Wheaton College, Drew University, Westminster Theological Seminary, Regent College, Vancouver, Moore College, Sydney, and Ridley College, Melbourne. The mutual sharing of experiences, frustrations, and approaches did much to enable me to plan the first edition of this work.

I have subsequently benefited substantially from the experience of those who used the first and second editions in their classrooms and who made invaluable suggestions for its further improvement. The author and publisher also wish to thank the following for their invaluable guidance in expanding and revising the work for this new edition: Jose Abraham, Neil D. Anderson, Vincent E. Bacote, A. Barnes, Stephen D. Benin, Frank W. Buckner, William D. Buhrman, Charlene P. E. Burns, A. B. Caneday, Harold Carl, Karen L. Carr, Sung Wook Chung, D. Coakley, Richard Collins, W. Cranford, Lisa W. Davison, Marianne Ferguson, Christopher Fisher, June-Ann Greeley, Barry Harvey,

Thomas Harvey, Arne Hassing, Sally Holt, T. L. Holtzen, Neil Hudson, Richard J. Jones, Warren A. Kay, Nathanael King, Kari Kloos, Bill Lanning, Gerard Mannion, Tom McCall, Darren J. N. Middleton, Keith Graber Miller, William Miller, Isabel Mukonyora, Mike Parrott, David Ratke, Kurt Richardson, Nelson Rivera, Greg Robertson, William Rodriguez, James B. Sauer, David Schultz, James L. Schwenk, Stephen Shoemaker, Steven Simpler, Patrick T. Smith, Ewan Stewart, J. Michael Thigpen, Richard F. Wilson, Norman Wirzba, and Daniel K. Wong.

The editor and publishers are grateful to the following for permission to reproduce copyright material.

1.15 John Locke, pp. 314–15 from P. H. Nidditch, *An Essay Concerning Human Understanding*. Oxford: Clarendon Press, 1975. Copyright © 1975. Reprinted by permission of Oxford University Press.

1.20 Søren Kierkegaard, pp. 182–3 from *Unscientific Postscript*, David F. Swenson and Walter Lowrie. Princeton, NJ: Princeton University Press, 1941. Copyright © 1941 by Princeton University Press, 1968 renewed. Reprinted by permission of Princeton University Press.

1.24 Karl Barth, "Theology," pp. 39–57 from *God in Action*. Edinburgh: T & T Clark (now Continuum), 1936.

1.25 Ludwig Wittgenstein, pp. 31–2 from *Philosophical Investigations*. Oxford: Blackwell Publishing, 1968. Copyright © 1968 by Blackwell Publishing. Reprinted by permission of Blackwell Publishing Ltd.

1.26 Ludwig Wittgenstein, pp. 82–6 from G. H. von Wright, *Culture and Value*, Peter Winch. Oxford: Blackwell Publishing, 1980. Copyright © 1980 by Blackwell Publishing. Reprinted by permission of Blackwell Publishing Ltd.

1.27 Vladimir Lossky, pp. 27–8 from *The Mystical Theology of the Eastern Church*. London: James Clarke, 1957. Copyright © 1957. Reprinted by permission of James Clarke and Co/Lutterworth Press.

1.29 Paul Tillich, pp. 59–64 from *Systematic Theology*, 1. Chicago: University of Chicago Press, 1951. Copyright © 1951. Reprinted by permission of The University of Chicago Press.

1.30 Sallie McFague, pp. 32–4 from *Models of God: Theology for an Ecological Nuclear Age*. Philadelphia: Fortress Press, 1987. Copyright © 1987 by Fortress Press. Reprinted by permission of Augsburg Fortress.

1.31 Gustavo Gutiérrez, pp. 9–12 from *A Theology of Liberation*, second edition. Maryknoll, NY: Orbis Books, 1988. Copyright © 1988. Reprinted by permission of Orbis Books and SCM Press.

1.32 Brian A. Gerrish, p. 175 from *The Old Protestantism and the New: Essays on the Reformation Heritage*. Chicago: University of Chicago Press, 1982. Copyright © 1982. Reprinted by permission of The University of Chicago Press.

1.33 George Lindbeck, pp. 22–5, 38–9, 47–8 from *The Nature of Doctrine*. Philadelphia: Westminster Press, 1984. Copyright © 1984 by George A. Lindbeck. Reprinted by permission of Westminster John Knox Press.

1.34 Dumitru Staniloae, pp. 81–3 from *The Experience of God: Orthodox Dogmatic Theology*. Brookline, MA: Holy Cross Orthodox Press, 1998. Copyright © 1998. Reprinted by permission of Holy Cross Orthodox Press.

2.29 Philip Jakob Spener, pp. 87–9 from T. G. Tappert, *Pia Desideria*, T. G. Tappert. Philadelphia: Fortress Press, 1964. Copyright © 1964 by Fortress Press. Reprinted by permission of Augsburg Fortress.

2.30 Nicolas Ludwig von Zinzendorf, pp. 40–1 from *Nine Public Lectures on Important Subjects in Religion*. Iowa City: University of Iowa Press, 1973. Copyright © 1973. Reprinted by permission of Wipf and Stock Publishers.

2.31, 6.47 and 10.17 Jonathan Edwards, pp. 61, 69, 109, 134 from Perry Miller, *The Images of Divine Things*. New Haven, CT: Yale University Press, 1948.

2.41 Karl Barth, pp. 191, 193–4 from *Church Dogmatics*, I(1). Edinburgh: T & T Clark (now Continuum), 1975. Copyright © 1975. Reprinted by permission of the publisher, The Continuum International Publishing Group.

2.42 Emil Brunner, pp. 55–8 from *The Christian Doctrine of Creation and Redemption: Dogmatics Vol. 2*. London: Lutterworth Press, 1952. Copyright © 1952. Reprinted by permission of James Clarke and Co/Lutterworth Press.

2.43 Rudolf Bultmann, pp. 151–5 from *History and Eschatology*. Edinburgh: Edinburgh University Press, 1957.

2.44 Karl Rahner, pp. 371, 373–7 from *Foundations of the Christian Faith: An Introduction to the Idea of Christianity*, William V. Dych. New York: Crossroad, 1978. English translation Copyright © 1978 by The Crossroad Publishing Company. Reprinted by permission of the publisher.

2.45 Phyllis Trible, "Feminist Hermeneutics and Biblical Studies," pp. 116–18 from *Christian Century* 3–10 February, 1982. Copyright © 1982 by *Christian Century*. Reprinted with permission from the February 3–10, 1982, issue of the *Christian Century*. Subscriptions: $49/yr, from P.O. Box 378, Mt. Morris, IL 61054, 1–800–208–4097.

2.47 John Meyendorff, pp. 7–8 from *Living Tradition: Orthodox Witness in the Contemporary World*. Crestwood, NY: St Vladimir's Seminary Press, 1978. Copyright © 1978. Reprinted by permission of St. Vladimir's Seminary Press, 575 Scarsdale Road, Crestwood, NY 10707.

2.48 J. I. Packer, pp. 80–2 from *God has Spoken*, second edition. London: Hodder & Stoughton, 1979.

2.49 Thomas F. Torrance, pp. 151–4 from *The Trinitarian Faith*. Edinburgh: T & T Clark (now Continuum), 1988. Copyright © 1988. Reprinted by permission of the publisher, The Continuum International Publishing Group.

3.26 Julian of Norwich, pp. 151, 174, 176 from *Revelations of Divine Love*, Clifton Wolters. Harmondsworth: Penguin, 1958. Copyright © 1952 by Clifton Wolters. Reprinted by permission of John Wolters.

3.32 Karl Barth, pp. 28–9 from *The Epistle to the Romans*. Oxford: Oxford University Press, 1933. Copyright © 1933. Reprinted by permission of Oxford University Press, Inc.

3.35 Leonardo Boff, pp. 156–8 from *Trinity and Society*. Tunbridge Wells: Burns & Oates. Copyright © 1986. Reprinted by permission of Orbis Books.

3.36 Robert Jenson, "The Triune God," pp. 87–92 from C. E. Braaten and R. W. Jenson, *Christian Dogmatics*, 1. Philadelphia: Fortress Press, 1983. Copyright © 1983 by Fortress Press. Reprinted by permission of Augsburg Fortress.

3.37 Hans Küng, pp. 530–3 from *The Incarnation of God*. Edinburgh: T & T Clark (now Continuum), 1987. Copyright © 1987. Reprinted by permission of the publisher, The Continuum International Publishing Group.

3.38 Eberhard Jüngel, p. 13 from *God as Mystery of the World*. Edinburgh: T & T Clark (now Continuum), 1999. Copyright © 1936. Reprinted by permission of the publisher, The Continuum International Publishing Group.

3.39 Jacques Ellul, pp. 102–6 from *The Humiliation of the Word*. Grand Rapids: Eerdmans, 1985. Copyright © 1981 by Editions du Seuil. English translation Copyright © 1985 by William B. Eerdmans Publishing Co. Originally appeared in French as *La parole humilée*. Reprinted by permission of Georges Borchardt, Inc, for Editions du Seuil.

3.40 Walter Kasper, pp. 267–9 from *The God of Jesus Christ*, M. J. O'Connell. London: SCM Press, 1983. Copyright © 1983. Reprinted by permission of SCM-Canterbury Press Ltd and Crossroad Publishing.

3.41 Paul Jewett, pp. 323–5 from *God, Creation and Revelation*. Grand Rapids: Eerdmans, 1991. Copyright © 1991 by Wm. B. Eerdmans Publishing Co, Grand Rapids, MI. Used by permission of the publisher.

3.42 Anne Carr, "Feminist Theology," pp. 223–4 from A. E. McGrath, *Blackwell Encyclopaedia of Modern Christian Thought*. Oxford: Blackwell Publishing, 1993. Copyright © 1994 by Blackwell Publishing. Reprinted by permission of Blackwell Publishing Ltd.

3.43 Sarah A. Coakley, "Persons in the 'Social' Doctrine of the Trinity: A Critique of Current Analytic Discussion," pp. 123–5 from Stephen T. Davis, Daniel Kendall, and Gerald O'Collins, *The Trinity: An Interdisciplinary Symposium on the Trinity*. Oxford: Oxford University Press, 2002. Copyright © 2002. Reprinted by permission of Oxford University Press.

3.34 Richard Swinburne, pp. 126–31 from *The Coherence of Theism*. Oxford: Oxford University Press, 1977. Copyright © 1977. Reprinted by permission of Oxford University Press.

4.33 Ernst Troeltsch, pp. 134–9 from *Religion in History*, James Luther Adams and Walter F. Bense. Edinburgh: T & T Clark (now Continuum), 1991. Copyright © 1991. Reprinted by permission of the publisher, The Continuum International Publishing Group.

4.34 Dorothy L. Sayers, pp. 32–5 from *Creed or Chaos?* London: Methuen, 1947. Copyright © 1947 by Dorothy L. Sayers. Reprinted by permission of David Higham Associates.

4.35 Paul Tillich, pp. 113–14 from *Systematic Theology*, 2. Chicago: University of Chicago Press, 1978. Copyright © 1978. Reprinted by permission of The University of Chicago Press.

4.36 and 5.32 Wolfhart Pannenberg, pp. 22–5, 38–9, 47–8 from *Jesus - God and Man*, Philadelphia: Westminster Press, 1968. Copyright © 1968, 1977 by The

Westminster Press, Reprinted by permission of Westminster John Knox Press and SCM-Canterbury Press.

4.37 Thomas F. Torrance, pp. 87–91 from *The Ground and Grammar of Theology*. Charlottesville: University Press of Virginia, 1980. Copyright © 1980. Reprinted by permission of the publisher, The Continuum International Publishing Group.

4.38 Rosemary Radford Ruether, pp. 127–30 from *Sexism and God-Talk: Towards a Feminist Theology*. Boston: Beacon Press, 1983. Copyright © 1983. Reprinted by permission of SCM-Canterbury Press Ltd.

4.39 Daphne Hampson, pp. 50–2 from *Theology and Feminism*. Oxford: Blackwell Publishing, 1990. Copyright © 1990 by Daphne Hampson. Reprinted by permission of the author.

4.40 Morna D. Hooker, "Chalcedon and the New Testament," pp. 86–8 from Sarah Coakley and David A. Pailin, *The Making and Remaking of Christian Doctrine*. Oxford: Clarendon Press, 1993. Copyright © 1993. Reprinted by permission of Oxford University Press.

4.41 N. T. Wright, pp. 4–8 from *Jesus and the Victory of God*. London: SPCK, 1996. Copyright © 1996 by Fortress Press. Reprinted by permission of Augsburg Fortress and SPCK/Sheldon Press.

5.29 Gustaf Aulén, pp. 17–22 from *Christus Victor: An Historical Study of the Three Main Types of the Idea of the Atonement*. London: SPCK, 1931. Copyright © 1931 by The Society of the Sacred Mission. Reprinted by permission.

5.30 Vladimir Lossky, "Redemption and Deification," pp. 97–8 from *In the Image and Likeness of God*. Crestwood, NY: St Vladimir's Seminary Press, 1974. Copyright © 1974. Reprinted by permission of St. Vladimir's Seminary Press, 575 Scarsdale Road, Crestwood, NY 10707.

5.31 Bernard Lonergan, pp. 8–13 from *The Collected Works of Bernard Lonergan: 6 - Philosophical and Theological Papers, 1958–1964*. Toronto: University of Toronto Press, 1996. Copyright © 1996. Reprinted by permission of University of Toronto Press.

5.34 Dorothee Soelle, pp. 162–4 from *Suffering*. Philadelphia: Fortress Press, 1975. Copyright © 1975 by Fortress Press. Reprinted by permission of Augsburg Fortress.

5.35 Colin E. Gunton, pp. 62–5 from *The Actuality of Atonement*. Edinburgh: T & T Clark (now Continuum), 1988. Copyright © 1988. Reprinted by permission of the publisher, The Continuum International Publishing Group.

6.50 Emil Brunner, pp. 346–51 from *The Christian Doctrine of God: Dogmatics, Vol, 1*. London: Lutterworth Press, 1949. Copyright © 1949. Reprinted by permission of James Clarke and Co/Lutterworth Press.

6.52 Emil Brunner, pp. 109 from *Truth as Encounter*, Second edition. London: SCM Press, 1964. Copyright © 1964. Reprinted by permission of SCM-Canterbury Press and Westminster John Knox Press.

6.53 Reinhold Niebuhr, pp. 256–9, 266–7 from *The Nature and Destiny of Man*, 1. New York: Macmillan, 1941. Copyright © 1941. Reprinted by permission of Westminster John Knox Press.

6.54 Pope Paul VI, "Pastoral Constitution on the Church in the Modern World, Gaudium et Spes," from *Vatican website*, 24083. www.vatican.va/archive/hist_councils/ ii_vatican_council/documents/vatii_cons_19651207_gaudium-et-spes_en.html, 1965.

6.55 Daphne Hampson, pp. 121–4 from *Theology and Feminism*. Oxford: Blackwell Publishing, 1990. Copyright © 1990 by Daphne Hampson. Reprinted by permission of the author.

6.56 Mary Hayter, pp. 87–92 from *The New Eve in Christ*. London: SPCK, 1987. Copyright © 1987 by Wm. B. Eerdmans Publishing Co, Grand Rapids, MI. Reprinted by permission of Wm. B. Eerdmans Publishing Co, and SPCK/Sheldon Press.

7.25 Yves Marie Joseph Congar, pp. 111–13 from *Lay People in the Church: A Study for a Theology of the Laity*, revised Donald Attwater. London: Cassell, 1965. Copyright © 1965. Reprinted by permission of the publisher, The Continuum International Publishing Group.

7.27 John D. Zizioulas, pp. 257–9 from *Being as Communion: Studies in Personhood and the Church*. Crestwood, NY: St Vladimir's Seminary Press, 1985. Copyright © 1985. Reprinted by permission of St. Vladimir's Seminary Press, 575 Scarsdale Road, Crestwood, NY 10707.

7.28 Leonardo Boff, pp. 11–15 from *Ecclesiogenesis: The Base Communities Reinvent the Church*. Maryknoll, NY: Orbis Books, 1986. Copyright © 1986. Reprinted by permission of Orbis Books.

7.29 Avery Dulles, p. 185 from *The Catholicity of the Church*. Oxford: Clarendon Press, 1985. Copyright © 1985. Reprinted by permission of Oxford University Press.

7.30 Stanley Hauerwas, pp. 91–2 from *A Community of Character: Toward a Constructive Christian Social Ethic*. Notre Dame, IN: University of Notre Dame Press, 1981. Copyright © 1981 by University of Notre Dame Press. Reprinted by permission of the publisher.

8.32 Edward Schillebeeckx, pp. 108–19 from *The Eucharist*. London: Sheed & Ward (now Continuum), 1968. Copyright © 1968. Reprinted by permission of the publisher, The Continuum International Publishing Group.

8.33 World Council of Churches, "Baptism, Eucharist and Ministry", pp. 2–3 from *Faith and Order Paper 111*. Geneva: World Council of Churches, 1982. Copyright © 1982 by World Council of Churches. Reprinted by permission of WCC Publications.

8.34 Alexander Schmemann, pp. 224–7 from *The Eucharist: Sacraments of the Kingdom*. Crestwood, NY: St Vladimir's Seminary Press, 1988. Copyright © 1988. Reprinted by permission of St. Vladimir's Seminary Press, 575 Scarsdale Road, Crestwood, NY 10707.

8.35 Rowan Williams, pp. 203–4 from *On Christian Theology*. Oxford: Blackwell Publishing, 2000. Copyright © 2000 by Blackwell Publishing. Reprinted by permission of Blackwell Publishing Ltd.

8.36 Pope John Paul II, "Evangelium Vitae," from *Vatican website*, 38436. www.vatican.va/edocs/ENG0141/_index.htm, 2005.

9.5 C. S. Lewis, "Is Theology Poetry?," pp. 15–16 from *C. S. Lewis Essay Collection*. London: Collins, 2000. Copyright © C. S. Lewis Pte. Ltd. Extract reprinted by permission of The C. S. Lewis Company.

9.6 Karl Rahner, pp. 115–34 from *Theological Investigations*, 5. New York: Crossroad, 1966. Copyright © 1966. Reprinted by permission of The Copyright Clearance Center, www.copyright.com

9.8 Clark H. Pinnock, pp. 64–9 from *A Wideness in God's Mercy*. Grand Rapids: Zondervan, 1992. Copyright © 1992 by Clark H. Pinnock. Reprinted by permission of The Zondervan Corporation.

9.9 John Hick, pp. 82–7 from *The Second Christianity*. London: SCM Press, 1983. Copyright © 1983 by John Hick. Reprinted by permission of the author.

9.10 C. S. Song, pp. 109–13 from *Third-Eye Theology: Theology in Formation in Asian Settings*, Revised. Maryknoll, NY: Orbis Books, 1990. Copyright © 1990 by C. S. Song. Reprinted by permission of the author.

9.11 John B. Cobb, Jr, "Beyond Pluralism," pp. 81–4 from G. D'Costa, *Christian Uniqueness Reconsidered: The Myth. of a Pluralistic Theology of Religions*. Maryknoll, NY: Orbis Books, 1990. Copyright © 1990. Reprinted by permission of Orbis Books.

9.12 Lesslie Newbigin, pp. 159–61 from *The Gospel in a Pluralist Society*. Grand Rapids: Eerdmans, 1989. Copyright © 1989 by Wm. B. Eerdmans Publishing Co, Grand Rapids, MI. Reprinted by permission of Wm. B. Eerdmans Publishing Co. and SPCK/Sheldon Press.

10.19 Rudolf Bultmann, "New Testament and Mythology," pp. 1–16 from H. W. Barstch, *Kerygma and Myth*. London: SPCK, 1953. Copyright © 1953 by SPCK Publishing. Reprinted by permission of SPCK/Sheldon Press.

10.20 Helmut Thielicke, pp. 44–7 from *Theological Ethics*, 1. Grand Rapids: Eerdmans, 1966. Copyright © 1966 by Wm. B. Eerdmans Publishing Co, Grand Rapids, MI. Used by permission of the publisher.

10.21 Richard Bauckham, "Jürgen Moltmann," pp. 298–300 from D. F. Ford, *The Modern Theologians*, 2 vols. Oxford: Blackwell Publishing, 1989. Copyright © 1989 by Blackwell Publishing. Reprinted by permission of Blackwell Publishing Ltd.

10.22 Hans Urs von Balthasar, pp. 176–7 from *Mysterium Paschale*. Edinburgh: T & T Clark (now Continuum), 1990. Copyright © 1990. Reprinted by permission of the publisher, The Continuum International Publishing Group.

10.23 Gabriel Fackre, pp. 223–5 from *The Christian Story: A Narrative Interpretation of Basic Christian Doctrine*, Revised. Grand Rapids: Eerdmans, 1984. Copyright © 1984 by Wm. B. Eerdmans Publishing Co, Grand Rapids, MI. Used by permission of the publisher.

10.24 Philip E. Hughes, pp. 404–7 from *The True Image: The Origin and Destiny of Man in Christ*, Grand Rapids: Eerdmans, 1989. Copyright © 1989 by Wm. B. Eerdmans Publishing Co, Grand Rapids, MI. Used by permission of the publisher.

10.25 Kathryn Tanner, pp. 108–10 from *Jesus, Humanity and the Trinity: A Brief Systematic Theology*. Minneapolis: Fortress Press, 2001. Copyright © 2001 by Fortress Press. Reprinted by permission of Augsburg Fortress.

Every effort has been made to trace copyright holders and to obtain their permission for the use of copyright material. The publisher apologizes for any errors or omissions in the above list and would be grateful if notified of any corrections that should be incorporated in future reprints or editions of this book.

Editor's Note

Because not all lecturers or students will use the material in the chapter order of this book, the text occasionally repeats important source and explanatory information. This allows the student to have enough essential background information within a particular chapter to make sense of the chapter topic, without having to refer to other chapters in order to understand it. Experience has shown that students prefer to have such information immediately accessible, rather than to have to search it out elsewhere within the book.

1

Getting Started: Preliminaries

Introduction

Starting to study Christian theology involves exploring a whole range of issues. Some of these center on the identity and characteristics of theology itself. For example, what is theology? And how did it develop? How does it relate to other areas of life, such as philosophy or culture? How does our way of talking about God relate to our everyday language? To what extent – and in what ways – can the existence of God be proved?

The present chapter provides readings which explore all of these issues, some in depth. The following general themes are especially recommended for study.

1 The patristic debates over the relation of philosophy and theology. The early church witnessed an especially interesting and important discussion of the extent to which theology should interact with secular philosophy.

The Patristic Debate on the Relation of Philosophy and Theology

2 Since the Middle Ages, Christian theology has found itself dealing with the issue of whether God's existence can be proved. A number of approaches have been set forward, particularly by Anselm of Canterbury and Thomas Aquinas. Exploring this debate is an excellent way of engaging with some issues of fundamental theological importance.

Can God's Existence be Proved?

1.7	Anselm of Canterbury's Proof for the Existence of God
1.8	Gaunilo's Reply to Anselm's Argument
1.9	Thomas Aquinas on Proofs for the Existence of God
1.11	William of Ockham on Proofs of God's Existence
1.16	René Descartes on the Existence of God
1.17	Blaise Pascal on Proofs for the Existence of God
1.19	Immanuel Kant on Anselm's Ontological Argument
1.22	John Henry Newman on the Grounds of Faith
1.26	Ludwig Wittgenstein on Proofs for the Existence of God

3 A third area of considerable interest is the way in which theology makes use of language and imagery, including the question of whether theological language is analogical or metaphorical in character. The following readings introduce these important themes.

Theological Language and Images

1.10	Thomas Aquinas on the Principle of Analogy
1.14	The Heidelberg Catechism on Images of God
1.25	Ludwig Wittgenstein on Analogy
1.29	Paul Tillich on the Method of Correlation
1.30	Sallie McFague on Metaphor in Theology
1.32	Brian A. Gerrish on Accommodation in Calvin's Theology
3.39	Jacques Ellul on the Theology of Icons
4.20	John of Damascus on the Incarnation and Icons

4 A fourth area of much theological interest in the last two centuries concerns the nature of dogma. Is this simply a hangover from the past? Or does it play a continuing role in contemporary theological reflection? The following readings represent a variety of approaches, each with its own distinctive emphasis.

The Nature of Dogma

1.23	Adolf von Harnack on the Origins of Dogma
1.33	George Lindbeck on Postliberal Approaches to Doctrine
1.34	Dumitru Staniloae on the Nature of Dogma
2.38	Charles Gore on the Relation of Dogma to the New Testament

1.1

Justin Martyr on Philosophy and Theology

In his two apologies for the Christian faith, written in Greek at Rome at some point during the period 148–61, Justin Martyr (c.100–c.165) sets out a vigorous defense of Christianity in which he seeks to relate the gospel to secular wisdom. Justin has an especial concern to relate the Christian gospel to the forms of Platonism which were influential in the eastern Mediterranean region at this time, and thus stresses the convergence of Christianity and Platonism at a number of points of importance. In particular, Justin is drawn to the pivotal concept of the "Logos" (the Greek term means "word"), which plays a key role in both Platonic philosophy and Christian theology – for example, see John 1: 14, which affirms that "the Word became flesh, and dwelt among us." A central theme in Justin's defense of the Christian faith is the idea that God has scattered "the seeds [*spermata*] of the Logos" throughout the world before the coming of Christ, so that secular wisdom and truth can point, however imperfectly, to Christ. See also 1.2, 1.3, 1.4.

We have been taught that Christ is the firstborn of God, and we have proclaimed that he is the Logos, in whom every race of people have shared. And those who live according to the Logos are Christians, even though they may have been counted as atheists – such as Socrates and Heraclitus, and others like them, among the Greeks. [...] Whatever either lawyers or philosophers have said well, was articulated by finding and reflecting upon some aspect of the Logos. However, since they did not know the Logos – which is Christ – in its entirety, they often contradicted themselves. [...] Whatever all people have said well [*kalōs*] belongs to us Christians. For we worship and love, next to God, the Logos, who comes from the unbegotten and ineffable God, since it was for our sake that he became a human being, in order that he might share in our sufferings and bring us healing. For all writers were able to see the truth darkly, on account of the implanted seed of the Logos which was grafted into them. Now the seed and imitation [*mimēma*] of something which is given on the basis of a person's capacity to receive it is quite different from that thing itself, of which the communication and imitation are received according to the grace of God.

Comment

Note how Justin argues that Jesus Christ *is* the Logos. In other words, the foundational philosophical principle of the Platonic system, according to Justin, is not an abstract idea which needs to be discovered by human reason, but something which has been made known to humanity in a specific form. What the philosophers were seeking has been made known in Christ.

It follows that all true human wisdom derives from this Logos, whether this is explicitly recognized or not. Justin argues that philosophical contradictions and tensions arise through an incomplete access to the Logos. Full access to the Logos is now possible, however, through Christ.

Justin then asserts that all those who honestly and sincerely act according to what they know of the Logos can be reckoned as being Christians, including Socrates. It thus follows that what is good and true in secular philosophy can be accepted and honored by Christians, in that it ultimately derives from the Logos, whether this is explicitly recognized or not.

Questions for Study

1 Why do you think Justin wanted to stress the convergence of Christianity and Platonism?
2 What Christian attitude to secular philosophy results from Justin's understanding of the Logos?
3 What difficulties arise from the assertion that the pagan philosophers Socrates and Heraclitus can be regarded as Christians?

1.2

Clement of Alexandria on Philosophy and Theology

The eight books of Clement of Alexandria's *Stromata* (the word literally means "carpets") deal at length with the relation of the Christian faith to Greek philosophy. In this extract from the *Stromata*, originally written in Greek in the early third century, Clement (c.150–c.215) argues that God gave philosophy to the Greeks as a way of preparing them for the coming of Christ, in the same way as he gave the Jews the law of Moses. While not conceding that philosophy has the same status as divine revelation, Clement goes beyond Justin Martyr's suggestion that the mere seeds of the Logos are to be found in Greek philosophy. See also 1.1, 1.3, 1.4.

Thus until the coming [*parousia*] of the Lord, philosophy was necessary to the Greeks for righteousness. And now it assists those who come to faith by way of demonstration, as a kind of preparatory training [*propaideia*] for true religion. For "you will not stumble" (Proverbs 3: 23) if you attribute all good things to providence, whether it belongs to the Greeks or to us. For God is the source of all good things, some directly (as with the Old and the New Testaments), and some indirectly (as with philosophy). But it might be that philosophy was given to the Greeks immediately and directly, until such time as the Lord should also call the Greeks. For philosophy acted as a "custodian" [*epaidagōgei*] to bring the Greeks to Christ, just as the law brought the Hebrews. Thus philosophy was by way of a preparation, which prepared the way for its perfection in Christ.

Comment

It is clear that Clement is concerned to explore the ways in which Greek philosophy can be thought of as preparing the way for the gospel. Clement argues that the Old Testament prepared the way for the Jewish people to receive the Christian faith; Greek philosophy, he argues, served a similar function for the Greeks.

Clement clearly regards philosophy as having a continuing positive role for Christians. It has not been made irrelevant by the coming of Christ; it remains a way by which sincere and truth-loving people can make their way to faith. Christ is seen as the perfection and fulfillment of philosophy, just as he is also to be seen as the perfection and fulfillment of the Old Testament.

Questions for Study

1 Read the following verse from Paul's Letter to the Galatians: "Now before faith came, we were confined under the law, kept under restraint until faith should be revealed. So that the law was our custodian until Christ came, that we might be justified by faith" (Galatians 3: 23–4). The Greek word here translated as "custodian" is the same word that Clement uses to refer to the role of philosophy. There is no doubt that Clement intended his readers to pick up on this parallelism. What points does Clement hope to make? You may find it helpful to begin by asking what role Paul appears to assign to the law in this Galatians passage, and then compare this with the role assigned to philosophy by Clement.

2 "Christ is Logos and Nomos." This summary of the relation of Christ to both Greek philosophy and the Old Testament is often encountered in the literature, and was first proposed by the noted German historian of Christian thought Adolf von Harnack. "Logos" is, as we have seen, the Greek word for "word," and has important overtones for Platonic philosophy. "Nomos" is the Greek word for "law," and picks up on the important role assigned to the law in the Christian faith by Paul. So what points are made by the statement "Christ is Logos and Nomos"? And why would writers such as Clement or Justin want to make such points in the first place?

3 The New Testament often identifies two broad audiences for the gospel: "Jews and Greeks." Read the following brief extract from Paul's First Letter to the Corinthians. "For Jews demand signs and Greeks seek wisdom, but we preach Christ crucified, a stumbling block to Jews and folly to Gentiles, but to those who are called, both Jews and Greeks, Christ the power of God and the wisdom of God" (1 Corinthians 1: 22–4). In what way does Clement develop and extend Paul's concerns?

1.3

Tertullian on the Relation of Philosophy and Heresy

The Roman theologian Tertullian (c.160–c.225) was noted for his hostility toward the inappropriate intrusion of philosophy into theology. Philosophy, he argued, was pagan in its outlook, and its use in theology could only lead to heresy within the church. In his *de praescriptione haereticorum* ("On the Rule of the Heretics"), written in Latin in the first years of the third century, Tertullian sets up a celebrated contrast between Athens and Jerusalem, symbolizing the tension between pagan philosophy and the revelation of the Christian faith. Tertullian's basic question concerned the relation of Christian theology with secular philosophy, especially Platonism. The Greek city of Athens was the home of the Academy, an institution of secular learning founded by Plato in 387 BC. For Tertullian, Christian theologians inhabited a completely different mental world to their pagan counterparts. How could there be a dialogue between them? See also 1.1, 1.2, 1.4.

For philosophy provides the material of worldly wisdom, in boldly asserting itself to be the interpreter of the divine nature and dispensation. The heresies themselves receive their weapons from philosophy. It was from this source that Valentinus, who was a disciple of Plato, got his ideas about the "aeons" and the "trinity of humanity." And it was from there that the god of Marcion (much to be preferred, on account of his tranquility) came; Marcion came from the Stoics. To say that the soul is subject to death is to go the way of Epicurus. And the denial of the resurrection of the body is found throughout the writings of all the philosophers. To say that matter is equal with God is to follow the doctrine of Zeno; to speak of a god of fire is to draw on Heraclitus. It is the same subjects which preoccupy both the heretics and the philosophers. Where does evil come from, and why? Where does human nature come from, and how? [...] What is there in common between Athens and Jerusalem? between the Academy and the church? Our system of beliefs [*institutio*] comes from the Porch of Solomon, who himself taught that it was necessary to seek God in the simplicity of the heart. So much the worse for those who talk of a "Stoic," "Platonic" or "dialectic" Christianity! We have no need for curiosity after Jesus Christ, nor for inquiry [*inquisitio*] after the gospel. When we believe, we desire to believe nothing further. For we need believe nothing more than "there is nothing else which we are obliged to believe."

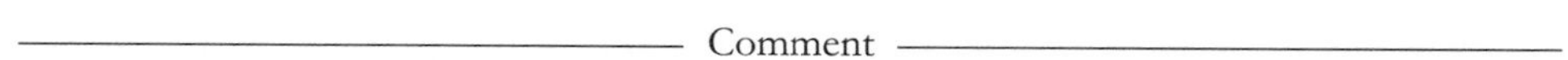

Comment

Athens and Jerusalem are here contrasted: the former is the home of pagan philosophy, the latter of divine revelation, culminating in Christ. The "Academy" is a specific reference to the Platonic school of philosophy at Athens, rather than a more general reference to what would now be known as the "academic" world (although this modern English word derives from the name of Plato's school). Note how Tertullian argues that it is a simple matter of historical fact that heresies seem to derive their ideas from secular philosophy. This, in his view, is enough to raise very serious questions concerning the use of philosophy in theology.

Many of the heresies that Tertullian mentions are forms of Gnosticism. In particular, he makes reference to the second-century writer Marcion, who was excommunicated in the year 144. According to Marcion, Christianity was a religion of love, which had no place whatsoever for law. The Old Testament relates to a different God from the New; the Old Testament God, who merely created the world, was obsessed with the idea of law. The New Testament God, however, redeemed the world, and was concerned with love. For Marcion, the purpose of Christ was to depose the Old Testament God (who bears a considerable resemblance to the Gnostic "demiurge," a semidivine figure responsible for fashioning the world) and replace this with the worship of the true God of grace.

Tertullian's basic thesis is that secular philosophies contain core ideas which ultimately are inconsistent with the Christian faith. If these philosophical systems are used as the basis of Christian theology, a serious tension will result, which could lead to the erosion of Christian integrity.

Questions for Study

1 Tertullian and Justin Martyr (1.1) both make reference to the pagan philosopher Heraclitus. Summarize their differing attitudes to him. How would you account for these differences?
2 What does Tertullian mean by the following question: "What is there in common between Athens and Jerusalem? between the Academy and the church?"
3 Tertullian is a Latin-speaking theologian, based in the western Mediterranean region; Justin and Clement were both Greek-speaking, based in the eastern Mediterranean region. Does this observation have any relevance to their attitudes to philosophy?

1.4

Augustine on Philosophy and Theology

In this extract from *de doctrina Christiana* ("on Christian doctrine"), originally written in Latin around 397, Augustine of Hippo (354–430) deals with the relation between Christianity and pagan philosophy. Using the exodus from Egypt as a model, Augustine argues that there is no reason why Christians should not extract all that is good in philosophy, and put it to the service of preaching the gospel. Just as Israel left behind the burdens of Egypt, while carrying off its treasures, so theology can discard what is useless in philosophy, and exploit what is good and useful. See also 1.1, 1.2, 1.3.

If those who are called philosophers, particularly the Platonists, have said anything which is true and consistent with our faith, we must not reject it, but claim it for our own use, in the knowledge that they possess it unlawfully. The Egyptians possessed idols and heavy burdens, which the children of Israel hated and from which they fled; however, they also possessed vessels of gold and silver and clothes which our forebears, in leaving Egypt, took for themselves in secret, intending to use them in a better manner (Exodus 3: 21–2; 12: 35–6). [...] In the same way, pagan learning is not entirely made up of false teachings and superstitions. [...] It contains also some excellent teachings, well suited to be used by truth, and excellent moral values. Indeed, some truths are even found among them which relate to the worship of the one God. Now these are, so to speak, their gold and their silver, which they did not invent themselves, but which they dug out of the mines of the providence of God, which are scattered throughout the world, yet which are improperly and unlawfully prostituted to the worship of demons. The Christian, therefore, can separate these truths from their unfortunate associations, take them away, and put them to their proper use for the proclamation of the gospel. [...] What else have many good and faithful people from amongst us done? Look at the wealth of gold and silver and clothes which Cyprian – that eloquent teacher and blessed martyr – brought with him when he left Egypt! And think of all that Lactantius brought with him, not to mention Marius Victorinus, Optatus and Hilary of Poitiers, and others who are still living! And look at how much the Greeks have borrowed! And before all of these, we find that Moses, that most faithful servant of God, had done the same thing: after all, it is written of him that "he was learned in all the wisdom of the Egyptians" (Acts 7: 22).

Comment

Note how Augustine adopts a critical yet positive attitude to philosophy. It asserts some things which are true, and others which are false. It cannot be totally rejected on the one hand; on the other, neither can it be uncritically accepted. It is important to note that Augustine is affirming that Christians are free to make use of philosophical ideas, which can be detached from their pagan associations. It must be remembered that, until the conversion of the Roman emperor Constantine, pagan culture was strongly hostile to Christianity, and encouraged its persecution and oppression. Augustine's argument is that philosophical ideas can be extricated from their historical associations with the pagan culture which persecuted earlier generations of Christians. Although this persecution had ended nearly a century before Augustine's time, it was still an important theme in Christian thinking. Augustine's approach allowed a more positive attitude to be adopted to the ideas and values of secular culture.

Notice how Augustine appeals to a series of distinguished Christians who were converted to Christianity from paganism, yet were able to make good use of their pagan upbringing in serving the church. Cyprian is of especial importance for Augustine, in that Cyprian had been martyred by the Romans in the third century.

Questions for Study

1 Augustine makes use of a number of biblical passages in making his points. What is the specific point of the reference to the Israelites leaving Egypt? And what is the importance of the "gold and silver" to Augustine's argument? Note how these commodities are things that are mined, rather than created. Does the fact that they are extracted from the ground, rather than fashioned by human hands, affect Augustine's argument in any way?
2 Augustine declares that Moses himself was "learned in all the wisdom of the Egyptians." What biblical passage is this based upon? And what role does this observation play in Augustine's argument?
3 Augustine's attitude to secular philosophy could be described as one of "critical appropriation." How does this compare with those adopted by Justin, Clement, and Tertullian?

1.5

The Nicene Creed

The Nicene creed is widely regarded as the basis of orthodox Christianity in both the eastern and western churches. The word "creed" derives from the Latin term *credo* ("I believe"), with which many creeds open. Although the focus of this specific creed is primarily Christological, its importance relates to its function as a "rule of faith" within the churches. As part of its polemic against the Arians, the Council of Nicea (June 325) formulated a short statement of faith, based on a baptismal creed used at Jerusalem. This creed was intended to affirm the full divinity of Christ against the Arian understanding of his creaturely status, and includes four explicit condemnations of Arian views, as well as its three articles of faith. As the full details of the proceedings of Nicea are now lost, we are obliged to rely on secondary sources (such as ecclesiastical historians, and writers such as Athanasius and Basil of Caesarea) for the text of this creed. Note that the translation provided here is of the Greek original, rather than of the Latin version of Hilary of Poitiers. Note also that the term "Nicene creed" is often used as a shorter way of referring to the "Niceno-Constantinopolitan creed," which has a significantly longer discussion of the person of Christ, and also makes statements concerning the church, forgiveness, and eternal life. See also 1.6, 2.7, 2.23, 4.6, 4.7.

We believe in one God, the Father, the almighty [*pantocrator*], the maker of all things seen and unseen.

And in one Lord Jesus Christ, the Son of God; begotten from the Father; only-begotten – that is, from the substance of the Father; God from God; light from light; true God from true God; begotten not made; being of one substance with the Father [*homoousion tō patri*]; through whom all things in heaven and on earth came into being; who on account of us human beings and our salvation came down and took flesh, becoming a human being [*sarkōthenta, enanthrōpōsanta*]; he suffered and rose again on the third day, ascended into the heavens; and will come again to judge the living and the dead.

And in the Holy Spirit.

As for those who say that "there was when he was not," and "before being born he was not," and "he came into existence out of nothing," or who declare that the Son of God is of a different substance or nature, or is subject to alteration or change – the catholic and apostolic church condemns these.

Comment

It is clear that this creed is specifically directed against Arius's position, which can be summarized in the following manner.

1 The Son is a creature, who, like all other creatures, derives from the will of God.
2 The term "Son" is thus a metaphor, an honorific term intended to underscore the rank of the Son among other creatures. It does not imply that Father and Son share the same being or status.
3 The status of the Son is itself a consequence not of the *nature of the Son*, but of the *will of the Father*.

Each of the specific condemnations in the text is directed against a fighting slogan of the Arian party.

The use of the phrase "being of one substance with the Father [*homoousion tō patri*]" is especially important. During the Arian controversy of the fourth century, debate came to center upon two terms as possible descriptions of the relation of the Father to the Son. The term *homoiousios*, which means "of similar substance" or "of like being," was seen by some as representing a judicious compromise, allowing the close relationship between Father and Son to be asserted without requiring any further speculation on the precise nature of that relation. However, the rival term *homoousios*, "of the same substance" or "of the same being," eventually gained the upper hand. Though differing by only one letter from the alternative term, it embodied a very different understanding of the relationship between Father and Son; namely, that the Son was identical with the Father in terms of their being or existence – or, to put this more formally, that the Son was ontologically identical with the Father. This affirmation has since come to be widely regarded as a benchmark of Christological orthodoxy within all the mainstream Christian churches, whether Protestant, Catholic, or Orthodox.

Questions for Study

1. This creed focuses on the identity of Christ, and especially his relation to God the Father. Why is this? Why is there relatively little material relating to other aspects of the Christian faith? You might like to compare this creed with the later Apostles' creed (1.6) to appreciate this point.
2. What is the point at issue in the discussion over whether the Son is *homoiousios* or *homoousios* with the Father? Is it important?
3. What does this creed mean when it asserts that Christ is "God from God; light from light; true God from true God"?

1.6

The Apostles' Creed

The document known as the Apostles' creed is widely used in the western church as a succinct summary of the leading themes of the Christian faith. Its historical evolution is complex, with its origins lying in declarations of faith which were required of those who wanted to be baptized. The 12 individual statements of this creed, which seems to have assumed its final form in the eighth century, are traditionally ascribed to individual apostles, although there is no historical justification for this belief. During the twentieth century, the Apostles' creed has become widely accepted by most churches, eastern and western, as a binding statement of Christian faith, despite the fact that its statements concerning the "descent to hell" and the "communion of saints" (here printed within square brackets) are not found in eastern versions of the work. See also 1.5, 2.7, 2.23.

1. I believe in God, the Father almighty, creator of the heavens and earth;
2. and in Jesus Christ, his only [*unicus*] Son, our Lord;
3. who was conceived by the Holy Spirit and born of the Virgin Mary;
4. he suffered under Pontius Pilate, was crucified, dead and buried; [he descended to hell;]
5. on the third day he was raised from the dead;
6. he ascended into the heavens, and sits at the right hand of God the Father almighty;
7. from where he will come to judge the living and the dead.
8. I believe in the Holy Spirit;
9. in the holy catholic church; [the communion of saints;]
10. the forgiveness of sins;
11. the resurrection of the flesh [*resurrectio carnis*];
12. and eternal life.

Comment

Note how the document is traditionally divided into 12 affirmations, each of which is linked with an apostle.

The credal statements are brief, and nonpolemical. It is interesting to compare this with the Nicene creed (1.5), which is concerned to counter Arian ideas, and thus explicitly condemns such teachings. The Apostles' creed avoids such polemics and does not have the same Christological preoccupation found in the Nicene creed.

The brevity of the credal affirmations reflects the origins of this creed as a statement of faith which would be made at the time of an individual's baptism. There are many examples of Christian works from the patristic period which provide expansions and explanations of these statements, such as Cyril of Jerusalem's catechetical lectures.

Questions for Study

1 How do you account for the differences in format and content between the Nicene and Apostles' creeds?
2 Why do you think that this creed has become increasingly important in ecumenical discussions between Christian denominations in recent decades?
3 There is no mention made in this creed of the sources of Christian beliefs, such as the idea of revelation, or the important place of the Bible in the Christian life. Why not?

1.7

Anselm of Canterbury's Proof for the Existence of God

In his *Proslogion*, written in Latin around 1079, Anselm of Canterbury (c.1033–1109) offers a definition of God as "that than which no greater thing can be thought" (*aliquid quo maius cogitari non potest*). He argues that, if this definition of God is correct, it necessarily implies the existence of God. The reason for this is as follows. If God does not exist, the idea of God remains, yet the reality of God is absent. Yet the reality of God is greater than the idea of God. Therefore, if God is "that than which no greater thing can be thought," the idea of God must lead to accepting the reality of God, in that otherwise the mere idea of God is the greatest thing which can be thought. This, however, contradicts the definition of God on which the argument is based.

Therefore, Anselm argues, given the existence of the idea of God, and the acceptance of the definition of God as "that than which no greater thing can be thought," the reality of God necessarily follows. Note that the Latin verb *cogitare* is sometimes translated as "conceive," leading to the definition of God as "that than which no greater thing can be conceived." Both translations are perfectly acceptable. See also 1.8, 1.19.

This [definition of God] is indeed so true that it cannot be thought of as not being true. For it is quite possible to think of something whose non-existence cannot be thought of. This must be greater than something whose non-existence can be thought of. So if this thing (than which no greater thing can be thought) can be thought of as not existing, then, that very thing than which a greater thing cannot be thought is not that than which a greater cannot be thought. This is a contradiction. So it is true that there exists something than which nothing greater can be thought, that it cannot be thought of as not existing.

And you are this thing, O Lord our God! So truly therefore do you exist, O Lord my God, that you cannot be thought of as not existing, and with good reason; for if a human mind could think of anything greater than you, the creature would rise above the Creator and judge you; which is obviously absurd. And in truth whatever else there be beside you may be thought of as not existing. So you alone, most truly of all, and therefore most of all, have existence: because whatever else exists, does not exist as truly as you, and therefore exists to a lesser degree.

Comment

This approach is often referred to as the "ontological argument." (The term "ontological" refers to the branch of philosophy which deals with the notion of "being.") Anselm himself does not refer to his discussion as an "ontological" argument.

It is important to note that the *Proslogion* is really a work of meditation, not of logical argument. In the course of this work Anselm reflects on how self-evident the idea of God has become to him and what the implications of this might be. We must be careful not to present Anselm as setting out to offer a foolproof argument for the existence of God, which he clearly did not intend to do.

The crux of Anselm's point is this: the *idea* of something is inferior to its *reality*. It therefore follows, according to Anselm, that the idea of God as "that than which nothing greater can be conceived" contains a contradiction – because the reality of God would be superior to this idea. In other words, if this definition of God is correct, and exists in the human mind, then the corresponding reality must also exist.

Questions for Study

1 Anselm offers a very specific definition of God as the basis of his argument. But where does this definition come from?
2 Does the idea of something imply its existence? We shall consider this question further in 1.8.

3 Anselm's argument is set in the context of a sustained meditation on the nature of God, rather than a logical analysis of the nature of God's being. How important is the context of Anselm's argument to the form it takes?

1.8

Gaunilo's Reply to Anselm's Argument

In this response to Anselm's argument for the existence of God (see 1.7), written at some point in the late eleventh century, the Benedictine monk Gaunilo argues that the mere *idea* of something – whether a perfect island or God – does not guarantee its existence. Being able to conceive something does not imply that it is really there. This document is sometimes referred to as "The Reply on behalf of the Fool," a reference to the fool who denied the existence of God in Scripture (Psalm 14: 1). See also 1.7, 1.19.

To give an example. People say that somewhere in the ocean there is an island which, because of the difficulty (or rather the impossibility) of finding that which does not exist, some have called the "Lost Island." And we are told that it is blessed with all manner of priceless riches and delights in abundance, far more than the Happy Isles, and, having no owner or inhabitant, it is superior in every respect in the abundance of its riches to all those other lands that are inhabited by people. Now, if someone were to tell me about this, I shall easily understand what is said, since there is nothing difficult about it. But suppose that I am then told, as though it were a direct consequence of this: "You cannot any more doubt that this island that is more excellent than all other lands truly exists somewhere in reality than you can doubt that it is in your mind; and since it is more excellent to exist not just in your mind but in reality as well, therefore it must exist. For if it did not exist, any other land existing in reality would be more excellent than it, and so this island, already conceived by you to be more excellent than others, will not be more excellent." I say in response that if anyone wanted to persuade me in this way that this island really exists beyond all doubt, I should either think that they were joking, or I should find it hard to decide which of us I ought to think of as the bigger fool: I myself, if I agreed with them, or they, if they thought that they had proved the existence of this island with any certainty, unless they had first persuaded me that its very excellence exists in my mind precisely as a thing existing truly and indubitably and not just as something unreal or doubtfully real.

Comment

There is, according to Gaunilo, an obvious logical weakness in Anselm's "argument" (although it must be stressed that Anselm does not really regard it as an argument in the first place). The weakness can be understood as follows. Imagine, Gaunilo suggests, an island, so lovely that a more perfect island cannot be conceived. By Anselm's argument, that island *must* exist, in that the reality of the island is necessarily more perfect than the mere idea.

In much the same way, someone might argue that the idea of a hundred dollar bill seems, according to Anselm, to imply that we have such a bill in our hands. The mere idea of something – whether a perfect island or God – thus does not guarantee its existence.

The response offered by Gaunilo is widely regarded as exposing a serious weakness in Anselm's argument. It may, however, be pointed out that Anselm is not so easily dismissed. Part of his argument is that it is an essential part of the definition of God that God is "that than which nothing greater can be conceived." God therefore belongs to a totally different category than islands or dollar bills. It is part of the nature of God to transcend everything else. Once the believer has come to understand what the word "God" means, then God really does exist for him or her. This is the intention of Anselm's meditation in the *Proslogion*: to reflect on how the Christian understanding of the nature of God reinforces belief in his reality. The "argument" does not really have force outside this context of faith, and Anselm never intended it to be used in this general philosophical manner. For Anselm, the issue is that of the internal consistency of faith, not its capacity to demonstrate its ideas in the public arena.

Questions for Study

1 Summarize in your own words the point which is made by Gaunilo in the idea of the "Lost Island."

2 Anselm argued that Gaunilo had not entirely understood him. The argument which he set out in the *Proslogion* did not, he insisted, involve the idea that there is a being that is, as a matter of fact, greater than any other being; rather, Anselm had argued for a being so great that a greater one could not even be conceived. How would you respond to Anselm's counterargument?

3 In the light of Gaunilo's criticism, can any further use be made of Anselm's reflections on the existence of God?

1.9

Thomas Aquinas on Proofs for the Existence of God

In this famous discussion, the great scholastic theologian Thomas Aquinas (c.1225–74) sets out five ways in which the existence of God may be demonstrated. Although these cannot be regarded as "proofs" in the strict sense of the word, Aquinas regards them as demonstrating the consistency of Christian theology with what is known of the world. The "Five Ways" do not include the argument set out by Anselm earlier, which we considered at 1.7 and 1.8. The *Summa Theologiae* ("The Totality of Theology"), which Aquinas began to write in Latin in 1265 and left unfinished at the time of his death, is widely regarded as the greatest work of medieval theology. Note that the Latin term *motus* can be translated "motion" or "change." The first of Aquinas's arguments is normally referred to as the "argument from motion"; however, it is clear that the *motus* in question is actually understood in more general terms, so that the term "change" is more appropriate as a translation. See also 1.7, 1.8, 1.11, 1.16, 1.17.

Whether God's Existence Can Be Demonstrated

There are two types of demonstration. There is demonstration through the cause, or, as we say, "from grounds," which argues from cause to effect. There is also demonstration by means of effects, following the order in which we experience things, arguing from effect to cause. Now when an effect is more apparent to us than its cause, we come to know the cause through its effect. Even though the effect should be better known to us, we can demonstrate from any effect that its cause exists, because effects always depend on some cause, and a cause must exist if its effect exists. We can therefore demonstrate that God exists from what is not evident to us on the basis of effects which are evident to us. [. . .]

Whether God Exists

The existence of God can be proved in five ways. The first and most obvious proof is the argument from change [*ex parte motus*]. It is clearly the case that some things in this world are in the process of changing. Now everything that is in the process of being changed is changed by something else, since nothing is changed unless it is potentially that towards which it is being changed, whereas that which changes is actual. To change something is nothing else than to bring it from potentiality to actuality, and a thing can be brought from potentiality to actuality only by something which is actual. Thus a fire, which is actually hot, makes wood, which is potentially hot, to be actually hot, thus changing and altering it. Now it is impossible for the same thing to be both actual and potential in the same respect, although it may be so in different respects. What is actually hot cannot at the same time be potentially hot, although it is potentially cold. It is therefore impossible that, in the same manner and in the same way, anything should be both the one which effects a change and the one that is changed, so that it should change itself. Whatever is changed must therefore be changed by something else. If, then, whatever is changing it is itself changed, this also must be changed by something else, and this in turn by something else again. But this cannot go on forever, since there would then be no first cause to this process of change, and consequently no other agent of change, because secondary things which change cannot change unless they are changed by a first cause, in the same way as a stick cannot move unless it is moved by the hand. We are therefore bound to arrive at a first cause of change which is not changed by anything, and everyone understands that this is God.

The second way is based on the nature of an efficient cause. We find that there is a sequence of efficient causes in the observable world. But we do not find that anything is the efficient cause of itself. Nor is this possible, for the thing would then be prior to itself, which is impossible. But neither can the sequence of efficient causes be infinite, for in every sequence the first efficient cause is the cause of an intermediate cause, and an intermediate cause is the cause of the ultimate cause, whether there are many intermediate causes, or just one. Now when a cause is taken away, so is its effect. Hence if there were no first efficient cause, there would be no ultimate cause, and no intermediate cause. But if there was an infinite regression of efficient causes, there would be no first efficient cause. As a result, there would be no ultimate effect, and no intermediate causes. But this is plainly false. We are therefore bound to suppose that there is a first efficient cause. And everyone calls this "God."

The third way is from the nature of possibility and necessity. There are some things which may either exist or not exist, since some things come to be and pass away, and may therefore exist or not exist. Now it is impossible that all of these should exist at all times, because there is at least some time when that which may possibly not exist does not exist. Hence if all things were such that they might not exist, at some time or other there would be nothing. But if this were true there would be nothing in existence now, since what does not exist cannot begin to exist, unless through something which does exist. If nothing had ever existed, it would have been impossible for anything to begin to exist, and there would now be nothing at all. But this is plainly false, and hence not all existence is merely possible. Something in things must be necessary. Now everything which is necessary either derives its necessity from somewhere else or does not. But we cannot go on to infinity with necessary things which have a cause of their necessity, any more than with efficient causes, as we proved. We are therefore bound to suppose something necessary in itself, which does not owe its necessity to anything else, but which is the cause of the necessity of other things. And everyone calls this "God."

The fourth way is from the gradation that occurs in things, which are found to be more good, true, noble and so on, just as others are found to be less so. Things are said to be more and less because they approximate in different degrees to that which is greatest. A thing gets hotter and hotter as it approaches the thing which is the hottest. There is therefore something which is the truest, the best, and the noblest, and which is consequently the greatest in being, since that which has the greatest truth is also greatest in being. [. . .] Now that which most thoroughly possesses the nature of any genus is the cause of all that the genus contains. Thus fire, which is most perfectly hot, is the cause of all hot things. [. . .] There is therefore something which is the cause of the being of all things that are, as well as of their goodness and their every perfection. This we call "God."

The fifth way is based on the governance of things. We see how some things, like natural bodies, work for an end even though they have no knowledge. The fact that they nearly always operate in the same way, and so as to achieve the maximum good, makes this obvious, and shows that they attain their end by design, not by chance. Now things which have no knowledge tend towards an end only through the agency of something which knows and also understands, as in the case of an arrow which requires an archer. There is therefore an intelligent being by whom all natural things are directed to their end. This we call "God."

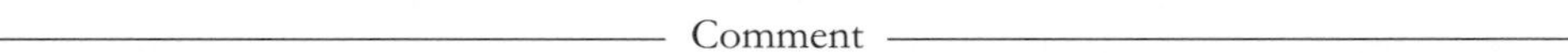

The first way begins from the observation that things in the world are in motion or change. The world is not static, but is dynamic. Examples of this are easy to list. Rain falls from the sky. Stones roll down valleys. The earth revolves around the sun (a fact, incidentally, unknown to Aquinas). This, the first of Aquinas's arguments, is normally referred to as the "argument from motion"; however, it is clear that the "movement" in question is actually understood in more general terms, so that the term "change" is more appropriate as a translation at points. Aquinas argues that everything which moves is moved by something else. For every motion, there is a cause. Things don't just move – they are moved by something else. Now each cause of motion must itself have a cause. And that cause must have a cause as well. And so Aquinas argues that there is a whole series of causes of motion lying behind the world as we know it. Now unless there are an infinite number of these causes, Aquinas argues, there must be a single cause right at the origin of the series. From this original cause of motion, all other motion is ultimately derived. This is the origin of the great chain of causality which we see reflected in the way the world behaves. From the fact that things are in motion, Aquinas thus argues for the existence of a single original cause of all this motion – and this, he concludes, is none other than God.

The second way begins from the idea of causation. In other words, Aquinas notes the existence of causes and effects in the world. One event (the effect) is explained by the influence of another (the cause). The idea of motion, which we looked at briefly above, is a good example of this cause-and-effect sequence. Using a line of reasoning similar to that used above, Aquinas thus argues that all effects may be traced back to a single original cause – which is God.

The third way concerns the existence of contingent beings. In other words, the world contains beings (such as human beings) which are not there as a matter of necessity. Aquinas contrasts this type of being with a necessary being (one who is there as a matter of necessity). While God is a necessary being, Aquinas argues that humans are contingent beings. The fact that we *are* here needs explanation. Why are we here? What happened to bring us into existence? Aquinas argues that a being comes into existence because something which already exists brought it into being. In other words, our existence is caused by another being. We are the effects of a series of causation. Tracing this series back to its origin, Aquinas declares that this original cause of being can only be someone whose existence is necessary – in other words, God.

The fourth way begins from human values, such as truth, goodness, and nobility. Where do these values come from? What causes them? Aquinas argues that there must be something which is in itself true, good, and noble, and that this brings into being our ideas of truth, goodness, and nobility. The origin of these ideas, Aquinas suggests, is God, who is their original cause.

The fifth and final way is sometimes referred to as the "teleological" argument. Aquinas notes that the world shows obvious traces of intelligent design. Natural processes and objects seem to be adapted with certain definite objectives in mind. They seem to have a purpose. They seem to have been designed. But things don't design themselves: they are caused and designed by someone or something else. Arguing from this observation, Aquinas concludes that the source of this natural ordering must be conceded to be God.

Questions for Study

1 Does Aquinas really regard these five lines of thought as "arguments"? If not, how would you describe them?

2 Why is the idea of an infinite regression of causes impossible? Aquinas clearly assumes that this is the case, and his arguments seem to depend on the validity of the assumption. Thus the argument from motion only really works if it can be shown that the sequence of cause and effect stops somewhere. There has to be, according to Aquinas, a Prime Unmoved Mover. Does Aquinas succeed in demonstrating this point?

3 Do the arguments set out above lead to belief in only *one* God? The argument from motion, for example, could lead to belief in a number of Prime Unmoved Movers. There seems to be no especially pressing reason for insisting that there can only be one such cause, except for the fundamental Christian insistence that, as a matter of fact, there is only one such God. What would Aquinas say in response? And what of his critic, William of Ockham (1.11)?

4 Notice how often Aquinas concludes his discussion with words such as: "and everyone agrees that this is 'God.' " But is he right? For example, can the "Prime Unmoved Mover" be directly equated with the Christian God?

1.10

Thomas Aquinas on the Principle of Analogy

One of the issues which Thomas Aquinas discusses in his *Summa Theologiae* (see 1.9) is the way in which language about God works. The critical question is whether language which is used to refer to God – as in the phrases "God is righteous" or "God is wise" – bear any relation to the same words, when used to refer to human beings – for example, in the phrase "Socrates is wise." The basic idea that Aquinas explores is that these words are used analogously in these different contexts. Although they are used with different meanings, there is a clear relationship between them, reflecting in part the fact that the created order bears the likeness of its creator. See also 1.25, 1.27, 1.29, 1.30.

Are Words Used Univocally or Equivocally of God and Creatures?

It is impossible to predicate anything univocally of God and creatures. The reason for this is that every effect which is less than its cause does not represent it adequately, in that the effect is thus not the same sort of thing as the cause. So what exists in a variety of divided forms in the effects exists simply and in a unified way in the cause – just as the simple power of the sun produces many different kinds of lesser things. In the same way, as we said earlier, the many and various perfections in creatures pre-exist in God in a single and unified form.

So the perfection of words that we use in speaking of creatures differ in meaning, and each of them signifies a perfection which is distinct from all the others. Thus when we say that a man is wise, we signify his wisdom as something distinct from other things about him – such as his essence, his powers, or his existence. But when we use this word in relation to God, we do not intend to signify something distinct from his essence, power, or existence. When the word "wise" is used in relation to a human being, it so to speak delimits and embraces the aspect of humanity that it signifies [*quodammodo circumscribit et comprehendit rem significatum*]. This, however, is not the case when it is used of God; what it signifies in God is not limited by our meaning of the word, but goes beyond it. Hence it is clear that the word "wise" is not used in the same sense of God and a human being, and the same is true of all other words, so they cannot be used univocally of God and creatures.

Yet although some have said that this is mere equivocation, this is not so. If it were the case, we could never argue from statements about creatures to statements about God – any such argument would be rendered invalid by the fallacy of equivocation. But we know, both from the teachings of the philosophers who prove many things about God and from the teaching of St Paul, who says, "The invisible things of God are made known by those things that are made" (Romans 1: 20), that this does not happen. We must say, therefore, that words are used of God and creatures according to an analogy, that is a certain proportion, between them [*nomina dicuntur de Deo et creaturis secundum analogiam, id est, proportionem*].

We can distinguish two kinds of analogical uses of words. First, there is the case of one word being used of several things because each of them has some proportion to another. Thus we use the word "healthy" in relation to both a diet and a complexion because each of these has some order and proportion to "health" in an animal, the former as its cause, the latter as its symptom. Secondly there is the case of the same word used because of some proportion – just as "healthy" is used in relation to both the diet and the animal because the diet is the cause of the health in the animal.

In this way some words are used neither univocally nor purely equivocally of God and creatures, but analogically [*analogice, et non aequivoce pure neque pure univoce*]. We cannot speak of God at all except on the basis of creatures, and so whatever is said both of God and creatures is said in virtue of a certain order that creatures have in relation to God [*ordo creaturae ad Deum*] as their source and cause in which all their perfections pre-exist.

This way of using words lies somewhere between pure equivocation and simple univocity. The word is neither used in the same sense, as in the case of univocation, nor in totally different senses, as with equivocation. The several senses of a word which is used analogically signify different relations to something, just as "health" in a complexion means a symptom of health and in a diet means a cause of that health. [. . .]

Are Words Predicated Primarily of God or of Creatures?

[. . .] All words used metaphorically in relation to God apply primarily to creatures and secondarily to God. When used in relation to God they signify merely a certain likeness between God and the creature [*nihil aliud significant quam similitudines ad tales creaturas*]. When we speak of a meadow as "smiling," we only mean that it is seen at its best when it flowers, just as people are seen at their best when they smile, according to a similarity of proportion [*secundum similitudinem proportionis*] between them. In the same way, if we speak of God as a "lion," we only mean that he is mighty in his deeds, like a lion. It is thus clear that, when something is said in relation to God, its meaning is to be determined on the basis of the meaning it has when used in relation to creatures.

This is also the case for words that are not used metaphorically, if they were simply used, as some have supposed, to express God's causality. If, for example, "God is good" meant the same as "God is the cause of goodness in creatures," the word "good," as applied to God, would have contained within its meaning the goodness of the creature. "Good" would thus apply primarily to creatures and secondarily to God.

But it has already been shown that words of this sort are said of God not just causally, but also essentially [*causaliter, sed etiam essentialiter*]. When we say "God is good" or "God is wise," we do not simply mean that God causes wisdom or goodness, but that these perfections pre-exist supremely in God. We conclude, therefore, that from the point of view of what the word means it is used primarily of God and derivatively of creatures, for what the word means – the perfection it signifies – flows from God to the creature. But from the point of view of our use of the word we apply it first to creatures because we know them first. That, as we have mentioned already, is why it has a way of signifying what is appropriate to creatures.

Comment

In this major analysis of the way in which the created order mirrors its creator, Aquinas points out that speaking about God involves using words that normally apply to things in the everyday world. So how do these two different uses relate to each other? Aquinas draws a distinction between the "univocal" use of a word (where the word means exactly the same thing whenever it is used) and the "equivocal" use (where the same word is used, but with different meanings. Thus the word "bat" is used univocally when it is used to refer to a vampire bat and a long-eared bat, in that the word refers to a nocturnal flying animal with wings in each case. But the word "bat" is used equivocally when the same word is used to refer to both a nocturnal flying animal with wings, and a piece of wood used to strike a ball in baseball or cricket. The word is the same; the meaning is different.

In this important passage, Aquinas argues that words cannot be used univocally to refer both to God and humanity. The word "wise" does not mean the same in the statements "God is wise" and "Solomon is wise." The gulf between God and humanity is too great for the word to mean the same. Yet the word is not used equivocally, as if it referred to something totally different. There is a relation between its use to refer to God, and its use in human contexts. The word "wise" is used *analogously*, to mean that divine wisdom is not identical to, nor totally different from, human wisdom. There is "an analogy, that is a certain proportion, between them."

Questions for Study

1 What does Aquinas want us to understand by the phrase "God is a lion"?
2 "When used in relation to God [words] signify merely a certain likeness between God and the creature." Locate this statement within the text. What does Aquinas mean by this? And how is this related to his doctrine of creation?
3 "When we say 'God is good' or 'God is wise,' we do not simply mean that God causes wisdom or goodness, but that these perfections pre-exist supremely in God." Locate this statement within the text. What does Aquinas mean by it? And how does this help establish the relationship between the statements "God is wise" and "Solomon is wise"?

1.11

William of Ockham on Proofs of God's Existence

William of Ockham (c.1285–1347), one of the most significant later medieval theologians, made important contributions to the long-standing debate about whether God's existence could be proved. Some of his most significant arguments concern the unity (or unicity) of God – in other words, whether there is a single, unique entity which is God, rather than a class of beings known as gods. Or, to put this another way, can it be shown that there is only one God – not a multiplicity of gods – and that this God is the same as that proclaimed by the Christian church? Ockham's important answer is that the belief that there is a god (and possibly many gods) can be sustained by reason – but the belief that there is *only one God* is a matter of faith.

In traditional scholastic manner, Ockham begins by setting out his question, then identifying arguments that might seem to point to a positive response, before raising objections to this. He then sets out his own answer in greater detail. See also 1.9, 1.17, 1.26.

Question 1: *Can it be proved by natural reason that there is only one God?*

That it can be proved: for there is only one world, so there is one ruler (Aristotle, *Metaphysics*, Book XII); but it can be proved by natural reason that there is one such world, according to Aristotle in the first book *On the heavens*. Therefore, it can be proved, by natural reason, that there is one ruler; but this is God; therefore, etc.

Against this: an article of faith cannot be proved by evidence; but it is an article of faith that there is one such God; therefore, etc.

Concerning this question, I shall first consider what is meant by the name "God"; secondly I shall respond to the question.

Article 1

Concerning the first point, I say that this name "God" can have various descriptions. One is that "God is some thing more noble and more perfect than anything else besides him." Another is that "God is that than which nothing is more noble and more perfect."

Article 2

Conclusion 1

Concerning the second point, I say that if we accept "God" according to the first description, then it cannot be demonstratively proved that there is only one God. The reason for this is that it cannot be evidently known that God, accepted in this sense of the term, exists. Therefore it cannot be evidently known that there is only one God. The consequence is obvious. The antecedent is proved in this way: the proposition "God exists" is not evident by itself, since many doubt it; nor can it be proved from propositions known by themselves, since in every argument something that is open to doubt or is based upon faith will be assumed; nor is it known by experience, as is manifest.

Conclusion 2

Secondly I say that, if it could be evidently proved that God, as God is accepted to be, exists, then the unity of God could be evidently proved. The reason for this is the following: If there were two Gods, let us call them *A* and *B*, then on the basis of our description God *A* would be more perfect than anything else, therefore God *A* would be more perfect than God *B*, and God *B* would be more imperfect than God *A*. But God *B* would also be more perfect than God *A*, because according to our assumption God *B* would be God. Consequently God *B* would be more perfect and more imperfect than God *A*, and God *A* than God *B*, which is clearly a contradiction. If, therefore, it could be evidently proved that God, as God is accepted to be, exists, then the unity of God could be evidently proved.

Conclusion 3

Thirdly I say that the unity of God cannot be evidently proved if we accept "God" according to this second description. Yet this negative proposition, "The unity of God cannot be evidently proved," cannot be proved demonstratively either, because it cannot be demonstrated that the unity of God cannot be evidently proved, except by resolving the arguments to the contrary, just as it cannot be demonstratively proved that the stars make up an even number, nor can the Trinity of Persons be demonstrated. Yet even these negative propositions – "It cannot be demonstrated that the stars make up an even number" and "The Trinity of Persons cannot be demonstrated" – cannot be evidently proved.

Conclusion 4

It must be understood, however, that it can be demonstrated that God exists, if we accept "God" according to the second description set out earlier. For otherwise we could go on *ad infinitum*, if there were not a certain one among those things which exist to which nothing is prior or more perfect. But from this it does not follow that it can be demonstrated that there is only one such being. But this we hold by faith.

Comment

Ockham is clearly concerned that earlier attempts to demonstrate God's existence – such as Aquinas's "Five Ways" – either assume their outcomes, or fail to demonstrate that only one God exists. For example, there is no logical reason why Aquinas's argument from motion should not lead to the conclusion that there could be several unmoved movers, were it not for the assumption, based on the specific beliefs of the Christian tradition, that there is only one such God. Ockham succeeds in clarifying the argument, demonstrating that there is no logical reason to believe that there is only one God. This, he concludes, must be recognized to be an article of faith, not a legitimate conclusion of unaided human reason.

Questions for Study

1 Summarize the second point of Ockham's argument in your own words. Do you agree with him? What are the implications of this argument for earlier arguments of this nature?
2 Summarize the third point of the argument in your own words. To what extent is it dependent on what definition of "God" is used?
3 What conclusions do you think Ockham would like us to draw about the relationship of Christian faith and unaided human reason?

1.12

Martin Luther on the Theology of the Cross

In 1518 the German reformer Martin Luther (1483–1546) defended a series of theses in a disputation at Heidelberg, in which he set out the basic features of the "theology of the cross." Of particular importance is the idea that theology involves a response to the "rearward parts of God" (*posteriora Dei*), which are only made known in the cross. The theses allude to Exodus 33: 23, which refers to Moses only being allowed to catch a glimpse of God from the rear, as God disappears into the distance. See also 1.18, 1.27, 3.38.

19 The person who looks on the invisible things of God, as they are seen in visible things, does not deserve to be called a theologian.
20 But the person who looks on the visible rearward parts of God [*visibilia et posteriora Dei*] as seen in suffering and the cross does deserve to be called a theologian.

Comment

For Luther, the cross is the center of the Christian faith. The image of the crucified Christ is the crucible in which all responsible Christian thinking about God is forged. Luther expresses the centrality of the cross in a series of terse statements, such as "the cross alone is our theology" (*crux sola nostra theologia*) and "the cross puts everything to the test" (*crux probat omnia*). Luther draws a now-famous distinction between the "theologian of glory," who seeks God apart from Jesus Christ, and the "theologian of the cross," who knows that God is revealed in and through the cross of Christ.

The two biblical texts which govern Luther's thinking in this matter are Exodus 33: 23, and 1 Corinthians 2: 2: "I decided to know nothing among you except Jesus Christ and him crucified." This latter text, for Luther, establishes the centrality of the cross. The former, however, establishes the notion of a "hidden revelation" of God. The text, set in its context (Exodus 33: 21–23), reads as follows: "And the Lord said, 'Behold, there is a place by me where you shall stand upon the rock; and while my glory passes by I will put you in a cleft of the rock, and I will cover you with my hand until I have passed by; then I will take away my hand, and you shall see my back; but my face shall not be seen.' " The words are addressed to Moses and suggest, for Luther, that the best that human beings can hope for is to get a glimpse of the back of God as God passes by, rather than be permitted to gaze on the face of God. This theme is clearly stated in the second of the two theses set out for study above.

Questions for Study

1 Try to set out clearly Luther's distinction between a "theologian of glory" and a "theologian of the cross."
2 Luther makes reference to "visible rearward parts of God [*visibilia et posteriora Dei*] as seen in suffering and the cross." What does he mean by this? And how does this relate to Luther's idea that the cross is the supreme locus and focus of the revelation of God?
3 On the basis of these theses, what attitude would you expect Luther to adopt to the idea of a "natural theology" – that is, that God can be known through the natural order?

1.13

John Calvin on the Nature of Faith

In an important analysis of the nature of faith, provided in the 1559 edition of the *Institutes of the Christian Religion*, the Genevan reformer John Calvin (1509–64) establishes a direct relation between faith and the merciful promises of God. Note the emphasis placed upon the role of the Holy Spirit in revealing and sealing this knowledge. Calvin also deals with the question of whether the certainty of faith necessarily implies that doubt is excluded from the Christian life. For Calvin, doubt is a normal part of the Christian life and is not inconsistent with his emphasis upon the trustworthiness of God's promises. See also 6.33, 6.37.

Now we shall have a right definition of faith if we say that it is a steady and certain knowledge of the divine benevolence towards us [*divinae erga nos benevolentiae firmam certamque cognitionem*], which is founded upon the truth of the gracious promise of God in Christ, and is both revealed to our minds and sealed in our hearts [*revelatur mentibus nostris et cordibus obsignatur*] by the Holy Spirit. [. . .] When we stress that faith ought to be certain and secure, we do not have in mind a certainty without doubt, or a security without any anxiety. Rather, we affirm that believers have a perpetual struggle with their own lack of faith, and are far from possessing a peaceful conscience, never interrupted by any disturbance. On the other hand, we want to deny that they may fall out of, or depart from, their confidence [*fiducia*] in the divine mercy, no matter how much they may be troubled.

Comment

This important definition of faith firmly links the notion to the promises of God. Faith is not about believing that God exists; it is about trusting the promises of a benevolent God. Calvin does not draw the conclusion that faith exists without doubt, but stresses that a trust in the reliability of the divine promises may coexist with a human failure to trust in those promises.

Calvin's concept of faith is closely linked with the person of Christ, who is seen as a confirmation of the promises of God.

Questions for Study

1 Calvin's definition of faith is trinitarian, in that quite definite roles are assigned to different persons of the Trinity. Set out, in your own words, the respective involvements of the three persons of the Trinity in this account of faith.
2 Faith "is founded upon the truth of the gracious promise of God in Christ." What considerations might lie behind Calvin's wording at this point? You might find it helpful to ask why Calvin does *not* offer the following definition: "Faith is founded on God's promise." What insights are safeguarded by Calvin's specific form of words?
3 "Believers have a perpetual struggle with their own lack of faith." What does Calvin mean by this? Does he imply that a lack of faith means that God is one who cannot be trusted? If not, how does Calvin account for this weakness in faith?

1.14

The Heidelberg Catechism on Images of God

This Protestant catechism of faith, written in German in 1563, was intended to set out the main features of the Reformed faith for a German audience. In this section, the catechism develops the idea that images of God are neither necessary nor helpful for Christian believers. There is an interesting parallel with Islam here, in that both Islam and Reformed theology are concerned to avoid images of God becoming objects of worship in themselves, instead of being aids to the worship of God. See also 3.39, 4.20.

Question 96. What does God require in the next commandment?
Answer: That we should not portray God in any way, nor worship him in any other manner than he has commanded in his Word.
Question 97. So should we not make any use of images?
Answer: God cannot and should not be depicted in any way. As for creatures, although they may indeed be depicted, God forbids making use of or having any likeness of them, in order to worship them or to use them to serve him.
Question 98. But should we allow pictures instead of books in churches, for the benefit of the unlearned?
Answer: No. For we should not presume to be wiser than God, who does not want Christendom to be taught by means of dumb idols, but through the living preaching of his Word.

Comment

Note the question-and-answer format of the catechism. The same format can be seen in other catechisms of the period, including Luther's Lesser Catechism of 1529. The work was designed to be learned by rote, offering short answers which could easily be remembered.

The text shows the traditional Reformed emphasis which gives priority to word over image. Note especially the importance which is attached to preaching as a means of consolidating the Christian faith. The target of the criticism implied in these questions is both the eastern Orthodox use of icons, and the Roman Catholic use of devotional images – such as a crucifix, or an altar painting showing Christ on the cross. Lutherans, however, saw no difficulty in continuing to use such devotional aids.

Questions for Study

1 The text of the second commandment reads as follows: "You shall not make for yourself a graven image, or any likeness of anything that is in heaven above, or that is in the earth beneath, or that is in the water under the earth" (Exodus 20: 4). In what way do the responses to the three questions under consideration reflect the concerns of this biblical passage?
2 What specific objection is offered to the devotional use of any kind of images?
3 How do the ideas set out in this extract help us gain an understanding of early Reformed approaches to religious art?

1.15

John Locke on the Formation of the Concept of God

In this passage from his *Essay Concerning Human Understanding*, which was published in December 1689, the English empiricist philosopher John Locke (1632–1704) argues that the notion of God is derived from experience, and is not already embedded within the human mind as an "innate idea." The human mind constructs the idea of God by extrapolating ideas already present in the world to infinity, thus leading to the idea of God as a supreme being. The idea of God thus results from reflection on experience, rather than being deduced from pure reason. See also 1.21.

For if we examine the idea we have of the incomprehensible supreme Being, we shall find that we come by it the same way; and that the complex ideas we have both of God, and separate Spirits, are made up of the simple ideas we receive from Reflection; v.g., having from what we experiment in our selves, got the ideas of existence and duration; of knowledge and power; of pleasure and happiness; and of several other qualities and powers which it is better to have, than to be without; when we would frame an idea the most suitable we can to the supreme Being, we enlarge every one of these with our idea of Infinity; and so putting them together, make our complex idea of God. For that the mind has such a power of enlarging some of its ideas, received from sensation, has been already shewed.

If I find that I know some few things, and some of them, or all, perhaps imperfectly, I can frame an idea of knowing twice as many; which I can double again, as often as I can add to Number, and thus enlarge my idea of Knowledge, by extending its Comprehension to all things existing, or possible. The same I can also do of knowing them more perfectly; i.e., all their Qualities, Powers, Causes, Consequences, and Relations, etc., till all be perfectly known, that is in them, or can any way relate to them, and thus frame the idea of infinite or boundless knowledge. The same may also be done of Power, till we come to that we call infinite; and also of the Duration of Existence, without beginning or end; and so frame the idea of an eternal Being; the Degrees of Extent, wherein we ascribe Existence, Power, Wisdom, and all other Perfection (which we can have any ideas of) to that Sovereign Being, which we call God, being all boundless and infinite, we frame the best idea of him our Minds are capable of; all which is done, I say, by enlarging those simple ideas, we have taken from the Operations of our own Minds, by Reflection; or by our Senses, from exterior things, to that vastness, to which Infinity can extend them.

For it is Infinity, which, joined to our ideas of Existence, Power, Knowledge, etc., makes that complex idea, whereby we represent to our selves the best we can, the supreme Being.

Comment

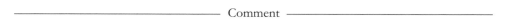

Locke is an empiricist philosopher, who places considerable emphasis on gaining knowledge through an analysis of experience. Note how his argument is that experience allows us to form an idea of certain core qualities, which we then "enlarge" to form the idea of God.

Locke's *Essay* is often thought to lay the intellectual foundations of Deism. Locke argued later in the *Essay* that "reason leads us to the knowledge of this certain and evident truth, that there is an *eternal, most powerful and most knowing Being.*" The attributes of this being are those which human reason recognizes as appropriate for God. Having considered which moral and rational qualities are suited to the deity, Locke argues that "we enlarge every one of these with our idea of infinity, and so, putting them together, make our complex *idea of God.*" In other words, the idea of God is made up of human rational and moral qualities, projected to infinity. Note also the language that Locke uses to refer to God, such as "the supreme Being."

Note that the English text has not been modernized, and that there are a few points which might cause difficulty for modern readers. Two points in particular should be noted: the word "shew" is the older form of "show;" "v.g." is best rendered as "e.g."

Questions for Study

1 Does Locke assign any place to the Bible in forming the idea of God?
2 On the basis of Locke's analysis, what are the most reliable grounds for asserting the existence of a "supreme Being"?
3 Locke speaks of making "our complex idea of God." Locate this passage in the text. Is Locke suggesting that God is the free construction of the human mind?

1.16

René Descartes on the Existence of God

René Descartes's argument for the existence of God, dating from 1642, bears obvious resemblances to that set out in the eleventh century by Anselm (see 1.7). According to Descartes (1596–1650), God is a "supremely perfect being." As existence is a perfection, it follows that God must have the perfection of existence, as he would otherwise not be perfect. Descartes supplements this argument with two examples (triangles and mountains). To think of God is to think of his existence, in just the same way as to think of a triangle is to think of its three angles being equal to two right angles, or thinking of a mountain is to think of a valley. See also 1.7, 1.8, 1.15, 1.17, 1.19, 1.26.

Having given the matter careful attention, I am convinced that existence can no more be taken away from the divine essence than the magnitude of its three angles taken together being equal to two right angles can be taken away from the essence of a triangle, or than the idea of a valley can be taken away from the idea of a mountain. So it is no less absurd to think [*cogitare*] of God (that is, a supremely perfect being) lacking existence (that is, lacking a certain perfection), than to think of a mountain without a valley. [...] I am not free to think of God apart from existence (that is, of a supremely perfect being apart from supreme perfection) in the way that I am free to imagine a horse either with wings or without wings. [...] Whenever I choose to think of the First and Supreme Being, and as it were bring this idea out of the treasury of my mind, it is necessary that I ascribe all perfections to him. [...] This necessity clearly ensures that, when I subsequently point out that existence is a perfection, I am correct in concluding that the First and Supreme Being exists.

Comment

Descartes's emphasis upon the notion of divine perfection is of considerable importance, and allows him to make an appeal to geometrical analogies in his discussion of the existence of God.

Descartes's basic concern was to establish the existence of God on grounds that would not be vulnerable to criticism. His appeal to reason initially proved very attractive, and can be seen as allowing a new form of rational apologetics to develop within French Catholicism. However, this excessive reliance upon reason proved to be a liability in the longer term, in that the rise of the Enlightenment worldview seriously eroded the rational foundations on which Descartes had constructed his defense of God's existence.

Questions for Study

1 Why does Descartes's emphasis on the perfection of God make the issue of suffering and evil in the world a more serious problem for faith than it need be?
2 "The God in whom the nineteenth century ceased to believe was invented in the seventeenth century" (Alasdair MacIntyre). How helpful is this comment in understanding the role of Descartes's ideas?
3 "This necessity clearly ensures that, when I subsequently point out that existence is a perfection, I am correct in concluding that the First and Supreme Being exists." Locate this sentence in the passage for discussion. What is the point that Descartes is making? How convinced are you by his assertion? And how does his approach relate to that adopted by Anselm of Canterbury (see 1.7)?

1.17

Blaise Pascal on Proofs for the Existence of God

Blaise Pascal's *Pensées* ("Thoughts"), originally written in French during the period 1658–62, represent a collection of jottings and musings which were assembled after his death. In this selection, Pascal (1623–62) stresses the role of the heart, rather than reason, in our knowledge of God, as well as the limitations of reason. He also makes the point that "knowledge of God" is of little use to anyone unless it is accompanied by an awareness of human misery and of the possibility of redemption in Christ. See also 1.7, 1.8, 1.15, 1.19, 1.26.

110. We know the truth, not only through our reason [*raison*], but also through our heart [*cœur*]. It is through this latter that we know first principles; and reason, which has nothing to do with this, vainly tries to refute them. The skeptics have no intention other than this; and they fail to achieve it. We know that we are not dreaming. Yet however unable we may be to prove this by reason, this inability demonstrates nothing but the weakness of our reason, and not the uncertainty of all our knowledge, as they assert. [...] Our inability must therefore do nothing except humble reason – which would like to be the judge of everything – while not confuting our certainty. As if reason could be the only way in which we can learn! [...]

188. The final step which reason can take is to recognize that there are an infinite number of things which are beyond it. It is merely impotent if it cannot get as far as to realize this. And if natural things are beyond it, what are we to say about supernatural things? [...]

190. The metaphysical proofs for the existence of God [*les preuves de Dieu métaphysiques*] are so remote from human reasoning, and so complex, that they have little impact. Even if they were of help to some people, this would only be for the moment during which they observed the demonstration, because an hour later, they would be afraid that they had deceived themselves. [...]

449. [...] It is equally as dangerous for someone to know God without knowing their misery as it is for someone to know their misery without knowing the Redeemer who can heal them. Only one of these insights [*connaissances*] leads to the pride of the philosophers, who have known God but not their misery, the other to the despair of the atheists, who know their misery without a Redeemer. [...] Even if someone were to be convinced that the relations between numbers are immaterial and eternal truths, which depend upon a first truth, called God, in which they subsist, I would not think that he or she had made much progress towards being saved.

Comment

The format of Pascal's *Pensées* makes them difficult to study, in that they take the form of individual isolated passages. There is thus a certain "bittiness" to them which makes them difficult to study as a whole. The four which are noted here are best studied as individual statements in their own right, rather than as a collected whole, or a coherent argument.

Pascal may be regarded as an important critic of the growing trend towards rationalist defenses of the Christian faith. While in no way decrying human reason, Pascal is nevertheless concerned to point out its weaknesses. One such concern is that the human mind is exalted over the human heart; another is that the metaphysical "proofs" of God's existence are virtually unintelligible.

Note that the numeration of the *Pensées* used follows that of the edition of Louis Lafuma, rather than that of the older Braunschweig edition.

Questions for Study

1 "We know the truth, not only through our reason, but also through our heart." Why does Pascal demand that increased attention be given to the heart? What respective roles does he allocate to "reason" and "heart"? And what are the implications of this approach for the debate over the existence of God?
2 "It is equally as dangerous for someone to know God without knowing their misery as it is for someone to know their misery without knowing the Redeemer who can heal them." Locate this passage. What point is Pascal making? And what are its implications for human self-awareness?
3 Pascal suggests that a faith which is based on arguments for God's existence is a vulnerable faith, in that there will always be a question concerning the reliability of the argument which brought about faith in the first place. What are the consequences of this insight for the nature and grounds of faith? And how does it relate to Pascal's insistence that both reason and heart are involved in this matter?

1.18

Blaise Pascal on the Hiddenness of God

In a series of brief passages known as *Pensées*, written over the period 1658–62, Pascal argues that it is both proper and necessary for God to be at least partly concealed. If this is not the case, humanity would become arrogant, trusting in its own ability to discover the full truth. The "obscurity" of God in the world forces humanity to recognize its own limitations, and thus to pay attention to God's self-revelation in Christ. See also 1.12.

232. We can understand nothing of the works of God unless we accept as a matter of principle that he wished to blind some and enlighten others. [. . .]

242. As God is hidden, any religion that does not say that God is hidden is not true, and any religion which does not explain why this is does not educate. [. . .]

446. If there was no obscurity, humanity would not be aware of its own corruption. If there was no light, humanity could not hope for a cure. Thus it is not only right for us that God should be partly concealed and partly revealed; it is also useful, in that it is equally dangerous for humanity to know God without knowing its own misery or to know its own misery without knowing God. [. . .]

449. What can be seen on earth points to neither the total absence nor the obvious presence of divinity, but to the presence of a hidden God. Everything bears this mark.

Comment

In these comments, Pascal develops some of the points made concerning the limitations placed upon human reason. For this reason, you are advised to read 1.17 to gain an idea of the general approach adopted by Pascal, before exploring this specific aspect of his thought.

Pascal's basic point is that the existence of God is *not* obvious to human reason. This means that humanity is obliged to seek assistance – specifically, in the form of divine revelation – if God is to be found and known. God's hiddenness can thus be seen as part of a divine strategy to impress upon humanity the limitations placed upon human reason, and the need for humility in matters of faith.

Note that the numeration of the *Pensées* used follows that of the edition of Louis Lafuma, rather than that of the older Braunschweig edition.

Questions for Study

1 What reasons, according to Pascal, may be given for God's desire to be hidden from us? How does this relate to his views on proofs of God's existence (1.17)?

2 In what way does Pascal's approach to the "hiddenness of God" differ from that adopted by Martin Luther (see 1.12)? Are there any similarities between them, either in terms of their specific ideas, or the insights which they draw from them?

3 "If there was no obscurity, humanity would not be aware of its own corruption. If there was no light, humanity could not hope for a cure." Locate this passage. What does Pascal mean by these words? What light do they cast on his understanding of human nature? And of the Christian faith?

1.19

Immanuel Kant on Anselm's Ontological Argument

The noted German philosopher Immanuel Kant (1724–1804) was unimpressed by the arguments of either Anselm (1.7) or Descartes (1.16) for the existence of God. Kant, who appears to be have been the first person to refer to this approach as the "ontological argument," insists that "being is not a predicate." As a result, conceiving the idea of God cannot in any way be thought to necessarily lead to conceiving the idea "God exists." His analogy of the "hundred dollars" makes more or less the same point made earlier by Gaunilo (see 1.8) – namely, that having an idea does not imply that its object exists. See also 1.7, 1.8, 1.15, 1.16, 1.17.

Now "Being" is clearly not a genuine predicate; that is, it is not a concept of something which could be added to the concept of a thing. It is merely the positing of a thing, or of certain determinations, as existing in themselves. Logically, it is merely the copula of a judgement. The proposition "God is omnipotent" contains two concepts, each of which has its object – God and omnipotence. The little word "is" adds no new predicate, but only serves to posit the predicate *in its relation* to the subject. Now if we take the subject (God) with all its predicates (among which is omnipotence), and say "God exists" or "There is a God," we do not attach any new predicate to the concept of God; we merely posit the subject in itself with all its predicates. In fact, we posit it as being an object that stands in relation to the concept. The content of both must be one and the same. Nothing can have been added to the concept, which expresses merely what is possible, by my thinking its object (through the expression "it is") as given absolutely. Otherwise stated, the real contains no more than the merely possible. A hundred real dollars would not be worth more than a hundred possible dollars. For as the latter signify the concept, and the former the object and the positing of the object, my concept would not, in that case, express the whole object, and would not therefore be an adequate concept of it. My financial position is, however, affected in a very different manner by a hundred real dollars than it is by the mere concept of a hundred dollars (that is, the concept of their possibility). For the object, as it actually exists, is not analytically contained in my concept, but is added to my concept (which is a determination of my state) synthetically; and yet the conceived hundred dollars are not themselves in the least increased through thus acquiring existence outside my concept.

Comment

The most fundamental point stressed by Kant is that existence is not a predicate. There is no connection between the idea of God and the reality of God. It is possible to clarify the relation of terms in statements such as "God is omnipotent." Yet statements about God cannot become proofs that there is a God.

Kant distinguishes *in intellectu* ("in the mind") from *in re* ("in fact"). *In intellectu* is associated with such notions as being "well-formed," "not self-contradictory," and so forth; *in re* concerns a definite proposition which is based on empirical evidence and is capable of being actually true. Questions of existence are always to be decided *a posteriori* by evidence, and cannot ever be settled *a priori*, by an appeal to ideas.

In the original German, Kant uses the German word *Thaler* as a unit of currency; I have translated this as "dollar" to give a more contemporary feel to the passage, taking advantage of the fact that the word "dollar" derives directly from this original German term.

Questions for Study

1. What are the implications of Kant's analysis for the arguments for God's existence put forward by (a) Anselm of Canterbury (1.7); (b) René Descartes (1.16)?
2. In what ways does Kant's criticism of the ontological argument differ from that offered by Gaunilo (1.8)?
3. "A hundred real dollars would not be worth more than a hundred possible dollars." Locate this statement. What does Kant mean by it?

1.20

Søren Kierkegaard on the Subjectivity of Truth

The Danish philosopher Søren Kierkegaard (1813–55) gave much thought to the relation of faith and truth. Where many earlier writers had explored the objective truth of the Christian faith through reasoned argument or an appeal to evidence from nature, Kierkegaard emphasized the inner nature of truth. In particular, Kierkegaard distinguished between speculative philosophy as a mode of reasoning which seeks objective truth, and religious faith as a mode of being which seeks subjective truth. In this extract from his *Unscientific Postscript*, written in Danish in 1846, Kierkegaard stresses the inwardness of faith, especially the need for an inward appropriation of the truth. See also 1.7, 1.9, 1.16, 1.21, 1.22, 1.26.

When subjectivity is the truth, the conceptual determination of the truth must include an expression for the antithesis to objectivity, a memento of the fork in the road where the way swings off; this expression will at the same time serve as an indication of the tension of the subjective inwardness. Here is such a definition of truth:

An objective uncertainty held fast in an appropriation-process of the most passionate inwardness is the truth, the highest truth attainable for an *existing* individual. At the point where the way swings off (and where this is cannot be specified objectively, since it is a matter of subjectivity), there objective knowledge is placed in abeyance. Thus the subject merely has, objectively, the uncertainty; but it is this which precisely increases the tension of that infinite passion which constitutes his inwardness. The truth is precisely the venture which chooses an objective uncertainty with the passion of the infinite. I contemplate the order of nature in the hope of finding God, and I see omnipotence and wisdom; but I also see much else that disturbs my mind and excites anxiety. The sum of all this is an objective uncertainty. But it is for this very reason that the inwardness becomes as intense as it is, for it embraces this objective uncertainty with the entire passion of the infinite. In the case of a mathematical proposition the objectivity is given, but for this reason the truth of such a proposition is also an indifferent truth.

But the above definition of truth is an equivalent expression for faith. Without risk there is no faith. Faith is precisely the contradiction between the infinite passion of the individual's inwardness and the objective uncertainty. If I am capable of grasping God objectively, I do not believe, but precisely because I cannot do this I must believe. If I wish to preserve myself in faith I must constantly be intent upon holding fast the objective uncertainty, so as to remain out upon the deep, over seventy thousand fathoms of water, still preserving my faith.

In the principle that subjectivity, inwardness, is the truth, there is comprehended the Socratic wisdom, whose everlasting merit it was to have become aware of the essential significance of existence, of the fact that the knower is an existing individual. For this reason Socrates was in the truth by virtue of his ignorance, in the highest sense in which this was possible within paganism. To attain to an understanding of this, to comprehend that the misfortune of speculative philosophy is again and again to have forgotten that the knower is an existing individual, is in our objective age difficult enough. But to have made an advance upon Socrates without even having understood what he understood, is at any rate not "Socratic."

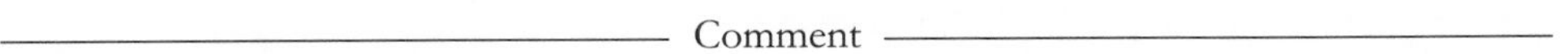

Comment

Kierkegaard is often regarded as one of the founders of an "existentialist" approach to life, placing particular emphasis upon the inward, subjective aspects of human existence. Truth is not mere assent to external facts, but represents an "appropriation-process of the most passionate inwardness." As Kierkegaard wrote in his journal, "I must find a truth that is true for me [. . .] the idea for which I can live or die." So how does this relate to the idea of faith? Kierkegaard stressed the ambiguity and absurdity of the human situation, which made simplistic, rationalist accounts of existence unsustainable. The only appropriate response to this situation must be to live a totally committed life, and to be prepared to defy the norms of society for the sake of the higher authority of a personally valid way of life. Kierkegaard ultimately advocated a "leap of faith" into a Christian way of life, which, although ultimately incomprehensible and full of risk, he believed to be the only commitment that could save the individual from despair.

Questions for Study

1 What is the significance of Kierkegaard's distinction between "objective" and "subjective" truth?
2 "Faith is precisely the contradiction between the infinite passion of the individual's inwardness and the objective uncertainty." What does Kierkegaard mean by this? How is it related to his idea of subjective truth?
3 On the basis of this passage, how do you think Kierkegaard would respond to attempts to argue for the existence of God?

1.21

The First Vatican Council on Faith and Reason

The First Vatican Council (1869–70) was convened in Rome by Pope Pius IX, partly in response to the new situation in Europe as a result of the French Revolution and Napoleonic wars, which had caused serious difficulties for the Roman Catholic Church in southern Europe, and also in response to various intellectual trends which seemed to call into question the authority of the church and the truth of many traditional Christian teachings. In its third session, the Council set out its views on the relation of faith and reason in the Dogmatic Constitution "Dei Filius" ("The Son of God"). This important document sets out the fundamental themes of the Catholic faith, indicating that limits had to be set to the free use of human reason, especially in relation to matters of faith. See also 1.7, 1.9, 1.11, 1.16, 1.20, 1.24.

The consensus of the catholic church has maintained and maintains that there is a twofold order of knowledge, distinct not only in relation to its source, but also in relation to its object. In relation to the source, we have knowledge at one level by natural reason, and at another level by divine faith. In relation to the object, in addition to those things to which natural reason can attain, we have knowledge of mysteries which are hidden in God which, unless they are divinely revealed, are incapable of being known. Wherefore, when the Apostle, who affirms that God was known to the gentiles through the created order (Romans 1: 20), comes to deal with the grace and truth which came by Jesus Christ (John 1: 17), he declares: "We speak of a secret and hidden wisdom of God, which God decreed before the ages for our glorification. None of the rulers of this age understood this. God has revealed it to us through the Spirit. For the Spirit searches everything, even the depths of God" (1 Corinthians 2: 7, 8, 10). And the Only-begotten himself, in his confession to the Father, acknowledges that the Father has hidden these things from the wise and prudent and revealed them to the little ones (Matthew 11: 25). [...] Reason is never able to penetrate the mysteries in the way in which it penetrates those truths which form its proper object. For the divine mysteries, by their very nature, so far surpass the created understanding that, even when a revelation has been given and accepted by faith, they remain covered by the veil of that same faith and wrapped, as it were, in a certain obscurity, as long as in this mortal life we are away from the Lord, for we walk by faith, and not by sight (2 Corinthians 5: 6–7).

While it is true that faith is above reason, there can never be any real disagreement between faith and reason, since it is the same God who both reveals mysteries and infuses faith, and who has endowed the human mind with the light of reason. God cannot deny himself, nor can truth ever be opposed to truth. The appearance of this kind of inane contradiction is chiefly due to the fact that either the dogmas of faith are not understood and explained in accordance with the mind of the church, or that mere opinions are mistaken for the conclusions of reason. Therefore we assert "that every assertion contrary to the truth of enlightened faith is totally false" (Lateran V).

Furthermore the church which, with its apostolic mandate of teaching, has received the charge of preserving the deposit of faith, has also the sacred right and duty of condemning what "wrongly passes for knowledge" (1 Timothy 6: 20), in case anyone should be "led astray by philosophy and empty deceit" (Colossians 2: 8). Hence all faithful Christians are forbidden to defend such opinions which are known to be contrary to the doctrine of faith as if they were the legitimate conclusions of science, particularly if they have been condemned by the church. Furthermore, they are absolutely bound to hold them to be errors which have the appearance of truth.

Not only can faith and reason never be in tension with each other; they mutually support each other. On the one hand right reason, established upon the foundations of the faith and illuminated by its light, develops the science of divine things; on the other hand, faith delivers reason from errors, protects it, and provides it with knowledge of many kinds. For this reason, the church does not hinder the development of human arts and studies; in fact she assists and promotes them in many ways. She is neither ignorant nor contemptuous of the advantages which derive from this source for human life, but acknowledges that these things derive from God, the lord of all sciences (1 Kings 2: 3), and, if they are properly used, may lead to God by the help of his grace. Nor does the church forbid these studies to make use of its own proper principles and method within its own specific area of study; but while she grants this legitimate freedom, she takes particular care that they do not become infected with errors by conflicting with divine teaching, or by going beyond their proper limits, and thus intruding upon what belongs to faith and thus give rise to confusion.

For the doctrine of the faith, which God has revealed, is handed down, not as some philosophical discovery capable of being perfected by human intelligence, but as a divine deposit committed to the spouse of Christ to be faithfully protected and infallibly declared. The meaning of these sacred dogmas which has once been stated by holy mother church must be maintained, and there must never be any abandonment of this sense under the pretext or in the name of a more profound understanding. "May understanding, knowledge and wisdom increase as the ages and centuries pass, and greatly and vigorously flourish, in each and all, in the individual and the whole church: but this only in its own proper kind, that is to say, in the same doctrine, the same sense, and the same understanding."

Comment

It is important to appreciate that the First Vatican Council (often referred to simply as "Vatican I") met against the backdrop of increasing hostility to traditional approaches to authority, especially within the church. There was a need for re-affirmation and defense of traditional teachings. The new intellectual climate which was emerging in Europe at the time made it essential to clarify the way in which members of the Roman Catholic Church were to relate to these developments. Vatican I developed an approach which affirmed the right of Roman Catholics to become involved in these disciplines (Vatican I uses the Latin term *scientia*, which can be translated as "science" or "discipline"), while realizing that each discipline made use of its own distinctive methods which could not necessarily be applied to matters of faith. The long closing quote is taken from the fifth-century Gallic theologian Vincent of Lérins.

Questions for Study

1 How does Vatican I understand the relation between faith and reason? Is there a tension between revealed truths and other kinds of truth?
2 In what way does Vatican I suggest that faith and reason may be mutually supportive?
3 The language of the "deposit of faith" is especially important. What does Vatican I mean by this expression?

1.22

John Henry Newman on the Grounds of Faith

In his important *Essay in Aid of a Grammar of Assent* (1870), the English theologian and philosopher John Henry Newman (1801–90) argues that the grounds of assurance of faith rest on a deep-seated intuitive or instinctive knowledge of God, which is not necessarily enhanced by rational arguments or demonstrations. The full logical structures of faith can thus never be fully understood, as religion ultimately depends upon an immediate and spontaneous "feeling" or "revelation," which cannot be adequately grasped or expounded on the basis of reason. There are important parallels here, probably unknown to Newman, with Pascal's emphasis upon the role of the heart in religious knowledge and experience. See also 1.7, 1.8, 1.14, 1.17, 1.20, 1.26.

We know from experience that beliefs may endure without the presence of the inferential acts upon which they were originally elicited. It is plain that, as life goes on, we are not only inwardly formed and changed by the accession of habits, but we are also enriched by a great multitude of beliefs and opinions, and that on a variety of subjects. These, held, as some of them are, almost as first principles, constitute as it were the furniture and clothing of the mind. Sometimes we are fully conscious of them; sometimes they are implicit, or only now and then come directly before our reflective faculty. Still they are beliefs, and when we first admitted them we had some kind of reason, slight or strong, recognized or not, for doing so. However, whatever those reasons were, even if we ever realized them, we have long since forgotten them. Whether it was the authority of others, or our own observation, or our reading, or our reflections which became the warrant of our belief, anyhow we received the matters in question into our minds, and gave them a place there. We believed them and we still believe, though we have forgotten what the warrant was. At present they are self-sustained in our minds, and have been so for long years. They are in no sense "conclusions," and imply no process of reasoning. Here, then, is the case where belief stands out as distinct from inference.

Comment

In this essay Newman concerned himself with the question of the rationality of religious belief. What reasons may be given for believing? What are the warrants of faith? The question had occupied Newman for some time; some years earlier, he had written a tract with the title "On the Introduction of Rationalistic Principles into Religion." Newman's basic concern is to uphold the reasonableness of the Christian faith, without making it depend upon rationalist presuppositions. In effect, Newman wishes to distance himself from the kind of approach offered by Descartes and his followers.

The basic argument is that there is no knock-down argument for God's existence, but rather a series of cumulative considerations which, taken together, persuade the individual of the truth of the gospel. In particular, Newman develops the "illative" sense of moral judgment – which can be argued to parallel a similar approach found in the writings of Aristotle, known as *phronesis* – by which the human mind reaches conclusions on grounds which, though rational, lie outside the limits of strict logic.

Questions for Study

1 Newman opens this section of the work by considering how faith, originally based upon one given consideration, can exist apart from that original factor, or can come to rest on another. What is the practical importance of this concern?

2 Writing of the factors which shape our beliefs, Newman observes that "Sometimes we are fully conscious of them; sometimes they are implicit, or only now and then come directly before our reflective faculty." What does he mean by this? And how does this relate to Pascal's insistence that the human heart, as well as human reason, is important in such matters (1.17)?
3 "Here, then, is the case where belief stands out as distinct from inference." What does Newman mean by this? And what are the implications of the conclusions that he draws?

1.23

Adolf von Harnack on the Origins of Dogma

In a series of important works, especially his mammoth *History of Dogma* (1886–9), the German Protestant theologian and "historian of dogma" Adolf von Harnack (1851–1930) set out his understanding of how "dogma" arose within the church. Harnack's basic conviction was that many of the dogmas of the early church – such as that of the incarnation – resulted from an unhappy and quite inappropriate marriage between the Christian gospel and Hellenistic philosophy. In this extract, taken from the briefer work *The Outlines of the History of Dogma*, Harnack sets out his understanding of how dogma had its origins, and subsequently came to develop within the church. See also 1.34, 2.38.

3. The most thorough-going attempt at solution hitherto is that which the Catholic Church made, and which the churches of the Reformation (with more or less restrictions) have continued to make, viz., Accepting a collection of Christian and Pre-Christian writings and oral traditions as of Divine origin, to deduce from them a system of doctrine, arranged in scientific form for apologetic purposes, which should have as its content the knowledge of God and of the world and of the means of salvation; then to proclaim this complex system (*of dogma*) as the *compendium* of Christianity, to demand of every mature member of the Church a faithful acceptance of it, and at the same time to maintain that the same is a necessary preparation for the blessedness promised by the religion. With this augmentation the Christian brotherhood, whose character as the Catholic Church is essentially indicated under this conception of Christianity, took a definite and, as was supposed, incontestable attitude toward the science of nature and of history, expressed its religious faith in God and

Christ, and yet gave (inasmuch as it required of all its members an acceptance of these articles of faith) to the thinking part of the community a system which is capable of a wider and indeed boundless development. *Thus arose dogmatic Christianity.*

4. The aim of the *history of dogma*: (1) To explain the *origin* of this dogmatic Christianity, and, (2) To describe its *development*.

5. The *history of the rise* of dogmatic Christianity would seem to close when a well-formulated system of belief had been established by scientific means, and had been made the *articulus constitutivus ecclesiae*, and as such had been imposed upon the entire Church. This took place in the transition from the first to the fourth century when the Logos-Christology was established. The *development* of dogma is *in abstracto* without limit, but *in concreto* it has come to an end. For,

(a) the *Greek* Church maintains that its system of dogma has been complete since the end of the "Image Controversy";

(b) the *Roman Catholic* Church leaves the possibility of the formulating of new dogmas open, but in the Tridentine Council and still more in the Vatican it has in fact on political grounds rounded out its dogma as a legal system which above all demands obedience and only secondarily conscious faith; the Roman Catholic Church has consequently abandoned the original motive of dogmatic Christianity and has placed a wholly new motive in its stead, retaining the mere semblance of the old;

(c) the *Evangelical* churches have, on the one hand, accepted a greater part of the formulated doctrines of dogmatic Christianity and seek to ground them, like the Catholic Church, in the Holy Scriptures. But, on the other hand, they took a different view of the authority of the Holy Scriptures, they put aside tradition as a source in matters of belief, they questioned the significance of the empirical Church as regards the dogma, and above all they tried to put forward a formulation of the Christian religion, which goes directly back to the "*true understanding of the Word of God.*" Thus in principle the ancient dogmatic conception of Christianity was set aside, while however in certain matters no fixed attitude was taken toward the same, and reactions began at once and still continue. Therefore is it announced that the history of Protestant doctrine will be excluded from the history of dogma, and within the former will be indicated only the position of the Reformers and of the churches of the Reformation, out of which the later complicated development grew. Hence the history of dogma can be treated as relatively a completed discipline.

6. The claim of the Church that the dogmas are not simply the exposition of the Christian revelation, because deduced from the Holy Scriptures, is not confirmed by historical investigation. On the contrary, it becomes clear that dogmatic Christianity (the dogmas) in its conception and in its construction was *the work of the Hellenic spirit upon the Gospel soil.* The intellectual medium by which in early times men sought to make the Gospel comprehensible and to establish it securely, became inseparably blended with the content of the same. Thus arose the dogma, in whose formation, to be sure, other factors (the words of Sacred Scripture, requirements of the cult, and of the organization, political and social environment, the impulse to push things to their logical consequences, blind custom, etc.) played a part, yet so that the desire and effort

to formulate the main principles of the Christian redemption, and to explain and develop them, secured the upper hand, at least in the earlier times.

7. Just as the formulating of the dogma proved to be an illusion, so far as the same was to be the *pure* exposition of the Gospel, so also does historical investigation destroy the other illusion of the Church, viz., that the dogma, always having been the same therein, has simply been explained, and that ecclesiastical theology has never had any other aim than to explain the unchanging dogma and to refute the heretical teaching pressing in from without. The formulating of the dogma indicates rather that theology constructed the dogma, but that the Church must ever conceal the labor of the theologians, which thus places them in an unfortunate plight. In each favorable case the result of their labor has been declared to be a *reproduction* and they themselves have been robbed of their best service; as a rule in the progress of history they fell under the condemnation of the dogmatic scheme, whose foundation they themselves had laid, and so entire generations of theologians, as well as the chief leaders thereof, have, in the further development of dogma, been afterwards marked and declared to be heretics or held in suspicion. Dogma has ever in the progress of history devoured its own progenitors.

8. Although dogmatic Christianity has never, in the process of its development, lost its original style and character as a work of the spirit of perishing antiquity upon Gospel soil (*style of the Greek apologists and of Origen*), yet it experienced first through Augustine and later through Luther a deeper and more thorough transformation. Both of these men, the latter more than the former, championed a new and more *evangelical* conception of Christianity, guided chiefly by Paulinism; Augustine however hardly attempted a revision of the traditional dogma, rather did he co-ordinate the old and the new; Luther, indeed, attempted it, but did not carry it through. The Christian quality of the dogma gained through the influence of each, and the old traditional system of dogma was relaxed somewhat – this was so much the case in Protestantism that one does well, as remarked above, no longer to consider the symbolical teaching of the Protestant churches as wholly a recasting of the old dogma.

9. An understanding of the dogmatico-historic process cannot be secured by isolating the special doctrines and considering them separately (Special History of Dogma) after the epochs have been previously characterized (General History of Dogma). It is much better to consider the "general" and the "special" in each period and to treat the periods separately, and as much as possible to prove the special doctrines to be the outcome of the fundamental ideas and motives. It is not possible, however, to make more than four principal divisions, viz.:

I The Origin of Dogma.

II. a. The Development of Dogma in accordance with the principles of its original conception (Oriental Development from Arianism to the Image Controversy).

II. b. The Occidental Development of Dogma under the influence of Augustine's Christianity and the Roman papal politics.

II. c. The Threefold Issuing of Dogma (in the churches of the Reformation – in Tridentine Catholicism – and in the criticism of the rationalistic age, i.e., of Socinianism).

Comment

It is important to appreciate that Harnack is a critic of dogma, who believes that uncovering its history is the first stage in effecting its removal.

The term "evangelical" is best understood as "Protestant" throughout this passage. The German term *evangelisch* is at times difficult to translate into English, and there is no doubt that Harnack intends the term to refer to the Protestant churches.

The "Image Controversy" to which Harnack refers is better known as the "Iconoclastic controversy," which took place within the eastern Orthodox church, and primarily concerned the question of whether the use of icons was appropriate in worship or personal devotion.

Questions for Study

1 Does Harnack consider the Roman Catholic, Eastern Orthodox, and Protestant churches to have equal commitments to the notion of "dogma"? How would you account for any differences between them?
2 "Dogmatic Christianity . . . was the work of the Hellenic spirit upon the Gospel soil." Locate this citation within the text. What does Harnack mean by this? And what are the implications of this assertion, if true?
3 Read paragraph 7, which deals with the development of dogma, and asserts that dogma has, as a matter of observable historical fact, not been the same throughout Christian history. How does this contrast with the language of the First Vatican Council concerning the permanence of the "deposit of faith" (1.21)?

1.24

Karl Barth on the Nature and Task of Theology

Over the period April 10–12, 1934, Karl Barth (1886–1968) delivered three lectures on theology to the Free Protestant Theological Faculty at Paris. The lectures were given alongside three seminars on the theology of Calvin, and dealt with the general topics of "Revelation," "Church," and "Theology." This extract from the third of Barth's three lectures, which dealt with the topic of "Theology," sets out a vision of the inspirational nature of the subject, and mounts a vigorous protest against any temptation to professionalize the subject. Theology is a matter for the church, not for some professional elite. See also 1.4, 1.28, 2.38, 3.32, 5.31.

Of all the sciences which stir the head and heart, theology is the fairest. It is closest to human reality, and gives us the clearest view of the truth after which all science quests. It best illustrates the time-honored and profound word: "Fakultät". It is a landscape, like the landscape of Umbria or Tuscany, in which distant perspectives are always clear. Theology is a masterpiece, as well-planned and yet as bizarre as the cathedrals of Cologne and Milan. What a miserable lot of theologians – and what miserable periods there have been in the history of theology – when they have not realized this! [. . .]

The task which is laid upon theology, and which it should and can fulfil, is its service in the Church, to the Lord of the Church. It has its definite function in the Church's liturgy, that is, in the various phases of the Church's expression; in every reverend proclamation of the gospel, or in every proclaiming reverence, in which the Church listens and attends to God. Theology does not exist in a vacuum, nor in any arbitrarily selected field, but in that province between baptism and confirmation, in the realm between the Scriptures and their exposition and proclamation. Theology is, like all other functions of the Church, uniquely based upon the fact that God has spoken to humanity and that humanity may hear his Word through grace. Theology is an act of repentant humility, which is presented to humanity through this fact. This act exists in the fact that in theology the Church seeks again and again to examine itself critically as it asks itself what it means and implies to be a Church among humanity. [. . .]

The task of theology consists in again and again reminding the people in the Church, both preachers and congregations, that the life and work of the Church are under the authority of the gospel and the law, that God should be heard. [. . .] It has to be a watchman so as to carefully observe that constant threatening and invasive error to which the life of the Church is in danger, because it is composed of fallible, erring, sinful people. [. . .]

Theology is not a private subject for theologians only. Nor is it a private subject for professors. Fortunately, there have always been pastors who have understood more about theology than most professors. Nor is theology a private subject of study for pastors. Fortunately, there have repeatedly been congregation members, and often whole congregations, who have pursued theology energetically while their pastors were theological infants or barbarians. Theology is a matter for the Church.

Comment

This lecture was given in 1934, at a time when Hitler had come to power in Germany, and a serious threat to the well-being of the German churches and the integrity of German Christianity had arisen. Although given in Paris, the lectures show an awareness of the importance of theology for maintaining the true identity of the Christian church, in the face of pressure to conform to the social norms of Nazi Germany. These points were developed further in the Barmen Declaration, which also dates from around this time (7.24).

The lecture offers a vision of theology which liberates the discipline from the stuffiness of the academic world, and insists upon its relevance to the life and mission of the church. There are obvious parallels with the Reformation doctrine of the "priesthood of all believers," which asserts that all believers have a priestly ministry; for Barth, all Christians are, whether they realize it or not, potentially theologians.

Although by this stage Barth had established a reputation as a vigorous critic of liberal theology, and a forthright defender of the priority of divine revelation, these concerns are not as apparent from this lecture as might be expected; the earlier Paris lecture on "Revelation" is perhaps most clearly influenced by these concerns. The present passage is marked above all by its vision of theology as an exciting intellectual discipline with a real integrity and relevance, which can be grasped by ordinary believers as much as by academics.

Questions for Study

1 What purpose is served by the analogy of the Tuscan or Umbrian landscapes? What point does Barth hope to make from it?
2 Etienne Gilson, a famous French historian of medieval philosophy, suggested that scholastic theology was a "cathedral of the mind." Barth hints at some such idea when he compares theology to the cathedrals of Cologne or Milan. What is the point of this comparison?
3 "It has to be a watchman so as to carefully observe that constant threatening and invasive error to which the life of the Church is in danger, because it is composed of fallible, erring, sinful people." Locate this passage. What specific relevance might this have for the situation faced by the German churches, as a result of the Nazification of Germany at this time?
4 "Theology is a matter for the Church." What does Barth mean by this? What viewpoint might he be critiquing in making this assertion?

1.25

Ludwig Wittgenstein on Analogy

In this passage from his *Philosophical Investigations*, originally published in German with an accompanying English translation in 1953, two years after the author's death, the Austrian philosopher Ludwig Wittgenstein (1889–1951) argues that the meaning of words is established by their use in real life. The use of terms in this way allows their "family resemblances" to be established. Wittgenstein's insistence upon the actual usage of words is an important corrective to more ontological approaches to analogy. See also 1.10, 1.15.

Consider for example the proceedings that we call "games". I mean board-games, card-games, ball-games, Olympic games, and so on. What is common to them all? Don't say: "There must be something common, or they would not be called 'games' " – but *look and see* whether there is anything common to them all. – For if you look at them you will not see something that is common to *all*, but similarities, relationships, and a whole series of them at that. To repeat: don't think, but look! – Look for example at board-games with their multifarious relationships. Now pass to card-games; here you find many correspondences with the first group, but many common features drop out, and others appear. When we pass next to ball-games, much that is common is retained, but much is lost. – Are they all "amusing"? Compare chess with noughts and crosses. Or is there always winning and losing, or competition between players? Think of patience. In ball games there is winning and losing; but when a child throws his ball at the wall and catches it again, this feature has disappeared. Look at the parts played by skill and luck; and at the difference between skill in chess and skill in tennis. Think now of games like ring-a-ring-a-roses; here is the element of amusement, but how many other characteristic features have disappeared! And we can go through the many, many other groups of games in the same way; can see how similarities crop up and disappear.

And the result of this examination is: we see a complicated network of similarities overlapping and criss-crossing: sometimes overall similarities, sometimes similarities of detail.

I can think of no better expression to characterize these similarities than "family resemblances"; for the various resemblances between members of a family: build, features, colour of eyes, gait, temperament, etc. etc. overlap and criss-cross in the same way. – And I shall say: "games" form a family.

Comment

One of Wittgenstein's most familiar concerns is to examine the ways in which words are *used*. For Wittgenstein, the *Lebensform* ("form of living") within which a word was used was of decisive importance in establishing the meaning of that word. The Christian *Lebensform* is thus of controlling importance in understanding what the Christian concept of salvation implies, presupposes, and expresses.

This has important implications for how we use words. As Wittgenstein himself pointed out, the same word can be used in a large number of senses. One way of dealing with this might be to invent a totally new vocabulary, in which the meaning of each word was tightly and unequivocally defined. But this is not a real option. Languages, like religions, are living entities, and cannot be forced to behave in such an artificial way. A perfectly acceptable approach, according to Wittgenstein, is to take trouble to define the particular sense in which a word should be understood, in order to avoid confusion with its many other senses. This involves a careful study of its associations and its use in the "form of living" (*Lebensform*) to which it relates.

On the basis of this, Wittgenstein suggests the image of "family resemblance" to explore the way in which words relate to each other. They are not identical; yet they are related.

Questions for Study

1 How does Wittgenstein propose that we set about establishing the meanings of words?
2 How might this approach be applied to the vocabulary of the Christian faith? For example, what would Wittgenstein urge us to do if we were to ask what was meant by the term "redemption"?
3 How does Wittgenstein's approach relate to that set out by Thomas Aquinas (1.10)?
4 How is Wittgenstein's general approach helpful in identifying the specifically Christian associations of words which are used to mean other things in different contexts? For example, St Paul uses the term "justification" to refer to a new relationship established between God and humanity through faith (see, e.g., Romans 5: 1–2). But in everyday English, "justification" means such things as "aligning lines of printed text so that they form a straight line at the margins." How does Wittgenstein help the theologian retain and clarify the vocabulary of the Christian faith?

1.26

Ludwig Wittgenstein on Proofs for the Existence of God

In this passage from the work *Culture and Value*, originally written in German and published after his death, the important twentieth-century philosopher Ludwig Wittgenstein demonstrates the limitations of logical deductions of the existence of God, and stresses the importance of experience and life in bringing about belief in God. See also 1.7, 1.8, 1.16, 1.17, 1.18, 1.19, 1.20.

God's essence is supposed to guarantee his existence – what this really means is that what is at issue here is not the existence of something. Couldn't one actually say equally well that the essence of colour guarantees its existence? As opposed, say, to white elephants. Because all that really means is: I cannot explain what "colour" is, what the word "colour" means, except with the help of a colour sample. So in this case there is no such thing as explaining "what it *would* be like if colours were to exist". [...] And now we might say: "There can be a description of what it would be like if there were gods on Olympus" – but not "what it would be like if there were such a thing as God." And to say this is to determine the concept "God" more precisely. [...] How are we taught the word "God" (its use, that is)? I cannot give a full grammatical description of it. But I can, as it were, make some contributions to such a description; I can say a good deal about it and perhaps in time assemble a sort of collection of examples. [...]

A proof of God's existence ought really to be something by means of which one could convince oneself that God exists. But I think that what *believers* who have furnished such proofs have wanted to do is to give their "belief" an intellectual analysis and foundation, although they themselves would never have come to believe as a result of such proofs. [...] Life can educate one to a belief in God. And *experiences* too are what bring this about: but I don't mean visions and other forms of sense experience which show us the "existence of this being," but, e.g., sufferings of various sorts. These neither show us God in the way a sense impression shows us an object, nor do they give rise to *conjectures* about him. Experiences, thoughts – life can force this concept on us.

Comment

In this interesting passage, Wittgenstein makes a number of fundamental criticisms of traditional metaphysical approaches to the question of whether there is indeed a God. Notice in particular his insistence that believers themselves do not base their faith upon such arguments.

As we noted earlier (1.25), Wittgenstein places considerable emphasis upon the way in which words are used in real life in determining their meaning. The role of life-experiences in relation to faith is clearly indicated in this passage, especially in relation to suffering.

Questions for Study

1 "I think that what believers who have furnished such proofs have wanted to do is to give their 'belief' an intellectual analysis and foundation, although they themselves would never have come to believe as a result of such proofs." How valid is this comment? How might it apply to Anselm of Canterbury (1.7) and Thomas Aquinas (1.9)? Did they come to faith as a result of their "proofs," or were those "proofs" the consequence and expression of their faith?
2 "I cannot explain what "colour" is, what the word "colour" means, except with the help of a colour sample." What does Wittgenstein mean by this? And what is its relevance to the notion of God?
3 What does Wittgenstein mean when he suggests that life can "force" the concept of God upon us?

1.27

Vladimir Lossky on Apophatic Approaches to Theology

Vladimir Lossky (1904–58) was one of Russian Orthodoxy's most significant theologians of the twentieth century. Following the Russian Revolution, he settled in Paris, where he wrote several works, of which the greatest is his *Mystical Theology of the Eastern Church*, which sets out the leading themes of Orthodox theology, including its distinctively apophatic (see Glossary) approach to theology. Lossky begins by tracing the roots of such an approach to Dionysius the pseudo-Areopagite, who is widely regarded as its intellectual fountainhead. See also 1.12, 1.14, 1.18, 1.28.

Dionysius begins his treatise with an invocation of the Holy Trinity, whom he prays to guide him "to the supreme height of mystical writings, which is beyond what is known, where the mysteries of theology, simple, unconditional, invariable, are laid bare in a darkness of silence beyond the light". He invites Timothy, to whom the treatise is dedicated, to "mystical comtemplation" (*mystica theamata*). It is necessary to renounce both sense and all the workings of reason, everything which may be known by the senses or the understanding, both that which is and all that is not, in order to be able to attain in perfect ignorance to union with Him who transcends all being and all knowledge. It is already evident that this is not simply a question of a process of dialectic but of something else: a purification, a *katharsis*, is necessary. One must abandon all that is impure and even all that is pure. One must then scale the most sublime heights of sanctity leaving behind one all the divine luminaries, all the heavenly sounds and words. It is only thus that one may penetrate to the darkness wherein He who is beyond all created things makes his dwelling.

This way of ascent, in the course of which we are gradually delivered from the hold of all that can be known, is compared by Dionysius to Moses' ascent of Mount Sinai to meet with God. Moses begins by purifying himself. Then he separates himself from all that is unclean. It is then that he hears "the many notes of the trumpets", he sees the many lights which flash forth many pure rays; then he is separated from the many, and with the chosen priests he reaches the height of the divine ascents. Even here he does not associate with God, he does not contemplate God (for He is unseen), but the place where He is. I think this means that the highest and most divine of the things which are seen and understood are a kind of hypothetical account of what is subject to Him who is over all.

Through them is revealed the presence of Him who is above all thought, a presence which occupies the intelligible heights of His holy places. It is then that Moses is freed from the things that see and are seen: he passes into the truly mystical darkness of ignorance, where he shuts his eyes to all scientific apprehensions, and reaches what is entirely untouched and unseen, belonging not to himself and not to another, but wholly to Him who is above all. He is united to the best of his powers with the unknowing quiescence of all knowledge, and by that very unknowing he knows what surpasses understanding.

It is now clear that the apophatic way, or mystical theology – or such is the title of the treatise devoted to the way of negations – has for its object God, in so far as He is absolutely incomprehensible. It would even be inaccurate to say that it has God for its object. The latter part of the passage which we have just quoted shows that once arrived at the extreme height of the knowable one must be freed from that which perceives as much as from that which can be perceived: that is to say, from the subject as well as from the object of perception. God no longer presents Himself as object, for it is no more a question of knowledge but of union. Negative theology is thus a way towards mystical union with God, whose nature remains incomprehensible to us.

Comment

Lossky's exposition of the apophatic approach to theology highlights the mystery of God, and the limitations placed upon any human attempt to represent or describe the divine nature. For Lossky, it is axiomatic that God is unknowable in his essence and transcends his revelation. The passage stresses the incomprehensibility of God – not in the sense of God being irrational, but rather in the sense that the human mind is incapable of fully grasping the reality of God.

Questions for Study

1 Having read this passage, how would you characterize Lossky's teaching on how God is known? What role does he ascribe to contemplation? How do you think that differs from the emphasis on rational reflection, so characteristic of much western theology?
2 What point does Lossky make through the analogy of Moses ascending Mount Sinai?
3 On the basis of this passage, do you think that Lossky is saying that nothing can be known of God?

1.28

Dietrich Bonhoeffer on God in a Secular World

In this letter from Tegel prison, the German theologian and pastor Dietrich Bonhoeffer (1906–45) speaks of the new challenge to Christianity in a world in which the existence of God is not taken for granted. He identifies a central theme of Christianity, which distinguishes it from all other religions, in its focus in the sufferings of God in Christ. Bonhoeffer is one of the most vigorous critics of the idea that human "religiosity" is a point of contact for the gospel. The theme of a suffering God is of major importance to Bonhoeffer, as this passage makes clear. See also 1.20, 1.24, 1.27, 3.33, 3.38.

Now for a few more thoughts on our theme. I'm only gradually working my way to the non-religious interpretation of biblical concepts; the job is too big for me to finish just yet.

On the historical side: There is one great development that leads to the world's autonomy. In theology one sees it first in Lord Herbert of Cherbury, who maintains that reason is sufficient for religious knowledge. In ethics it appears in Montaigne and Bodin with their substitution of rules of life for the commandments. In politics Machiavelli detaches politics from morality in general and founds the doctrine of "reasons of state." Later, and very differently from Machiavelli, but tending like him towards the autonomy of human society, comes Grotius, setting up his natural law as international law, which is valid *etsi deus non daretur*, "even if there were no God." The philosophers provide the finishing touches: on the one hand we have the deism of Descartes, who holds that the world is a mechanism, running by itself with no interference from God; and on the other hand the pantheism of Spinoza, who says that God is nature. In the last resort, Kant is a deist, and Fichte and Hegel are pantheists. Everywhere the thinking is directed towards the autonomy of man and the world.

(It seems that in the natural sciences the process begins with Nicolas of Cusa and Giordano Bruno and the "heretical" doctrine of the infinity of the universe. The classical *cosmos* was finite, like the created world of the Middle Ages. An infinite universe, however it may be conceived, is self-subsisting, *etsi deus non daretur*. It is true that modern physics is not as sure as it was about the infinity of the universe, but it has not gone back to the earlier conceptions of its finitude.)

God as a working hypothesis in morals, politics, or science, has been surmounted and abolished; and the same thing has happened in philosophy and religion (Feuerbach!). For the sake of intellectual honesty, that working hypothesis should be dropped, or as far as possible eliminated. A scientist or physician who sets out to edify is a hybrid.

Anxious souls will ask what room there is left for God now; and as they know of no answer to the question, they condemn the whole development that has brought them to such straits. I wrote to you before about the various emergency exits that have been contrived; and we ought to add to them the *salto mortale* [death-leap] back into the Middle Ages. But the principle of the Middle Ages is heteronomy in the form of clericalism; a return to that can be a counsel of despair, and it would be at the cost of intellectual honesty. It's a dream that reminds one of the song *O wusst'ich doch den Weg zurück, den weiten Weg ins Kinderland*. There is no such way – at any rate not if it means deliberately abandoning our mental integrity; the only way is that of Matthew 18: 3, i.e., through repentance, through *ultimate* honesty.

And we cannot be honest unless we recognize that we have to live in the world *etsi deus non daretur*. And this is just what we do recognize – before God! God himself compels us to recognize it. So our coming of age leads us to a true recognition of our situation before God. God would have us know that we must live as men who manage our lives without him. The God who is with us is the God who forsakes us (Mark 15: 34). The God who lets us live in the world without the working hypothesis of God is the God before whom we stand continually. Before God and with God we live without God. God lets himself be pushed out of the world on to the cross. He is weak and powerless in the world, and that is precisely the way, the only way, in which he is with us and helps us. Matthew 8: 17 makes it quite clear that Christ helps us, not by virtue of his omnipotence, but by virtue of his weakness and suffering.

Here is the decisive difference between Christianity and all religions. Man's religiosity makes him look in his distress to the power of God in the world: God is the *deus ex machina*. The Bible directs man to God's powerlessness and suffering; only the suffering God can help. To that extent we may say that the development towards the world's coming of age outlined above, which has done away with a false conception of God, opens up a way of seeing the God of the Bible, who wins power and space in the world by his weakness. This will probably be the starting-point for our secular interpretation.

Comment

Bonhoeffer wrote this letter from prison shortly before his execution. The letter deals with the vulnerability of approaches to religion and theology which proceed on the assumption that humanity is intrinsically religious. For Bonhoeffer, the Nazi experience has called that presupposition into question.

The letter deals extensively with the issue of the autonomy of the world, and the apparent powerlessness of God, which Bonhoeffer regards as exhibited on the cross. Bonhoeffer's brief account of intellectual history since the Middle Ages is concerned to bring out how the world has come of age, and lives as if there were no God.

Note that the German song title referred to in the text is to be translated as "If only I knew the way back, the long way to the land of childhood." The Latin slogan *etsi Deus non daretur* is used by the Dutch writer Hugo Grotius (1583–1645), and is widely seen as marking a recognition of the growing importance of secular trends in the west.

Questions for Study

1. What is the distinction between living "as if there were no God" and atheism?
2. How does Bonhoeffer account for the world's "coming of age"? What factors does he see as leading to its development? Although Bonhoeffer does not directly address this issue in the passage, in what way does the Nazi period illustrate this point?
3. "Before God and with God we live without God. God lets himself be pushed out of the world on to the cross. He is weak and powerless in the world, and that is precisely the way, the only way, in which he is with us and helps us." Locate this passage within the text. What does Bonhoeffer mean by these words?

1.29

Paul Tillich on the Method of Correlation

Paul Tillich (1886–1965) was a German émigré who settled in the United States and became one of the most significant American theologians of the twentieth century. One of his primary concerns was apologetic. To ensure the continuing credibility of Christianity, he argued, it was necessary to correlate the gospel proclamation with the questions which secular culture raised, especially in North America. For Tillich, culture raised what he termed "ultimate questions," to which theology was obliged to respond. In this important passage, Tillich explores the general principles of correlating the Christian message with secular culture.

The passage in question is lengthy, and has been cited to allow more extended engagement with a text than is normal in this collection of readings. See also 1.1, 1.2, 1.4, 1.10, 1.30, 1.33.

The principle of methodological rationality implies that, like all scientific approaches to reality, systematic theology follows a method. A method is a tool, literally a way around, which must be adequate to its subject matter. Whether or not a method is adequate cannot be decided *a priori*; it is continually being decided in the cognitive process itself. Method and system determine each other. Therefore, no method can claim to be adequate for every subject. Methodological imperialism is as dangerous as political imperialism; like the latter, it breaks down when the independent elements of reality revolt against it. A method is not an "indifferent net" in which reality is caught, but the method is an element of the reality itself. In at least one respect the description of a method is a description of a decisive aspect of the object to which it is applied. The cognitive relation itself, quite apart from any special act of cognition, reveals something about the object, as well as about the subject, in the relation. The cognitive relation in physics reveals the mathematical character of objects in space (and time). The cognitive relation in biology reveals the structure [*Gestalt*] and spontaneous character of objects in space and time. The cognitive relation in historiography reveals the individual and value-related character of objects in time (and space). The cognitive relation in theology reveals the existential and transcending character of the ground of objects in time and space. Therefore, no method can be developed without a prior knowledge of the object to which it is applied. For systematic theology this means that its method is derived from a prior knowledge of the system which is to be built by the method.

Systematic theology uses the method of correlation. It has always done so, sometimes more, sometimes less, consciously, and must do so consciously and outspokenly, especially if the apologetic point of view is to prevail. The method of correlation explains the contents of the Christian faith through existential questions and theological answers in mutual interdependence.

The term "correlation" may be used in three ways. It can designate the correspondence of different series of data, as in statistical charts; it can designate the logical interdependence of concepts, as in polar relations; and it can designate the real interdependence of things or events in structural wholes. If the term is used in theology all three meanings have important applications. There is a correlation in the sense of correspondence between religious symbols and that which is symbolized by them. There is a correlation in the logical sense between concepts denoting the human and those denoting the divine. There is a correlation in the factual sense between man's ultimate concern and that about which he is ultimately concerned. The first meaning of correlation refers to the central problem of religious knowledge. [. . .]

The second meaning of correlation determines the statements about God and the world; for example, the correlation of the infinite and the finite. [. . .] The third meaning of correlation qualifies the divine–human relationship within religious experience. The third use of correlative thinking in theology has evoked the protest of theologians such as Karl Barth, who are afraid that any kind of divine–human correlation makes God partly dependent on man. But although God in his abysmal nature is in no way dependent on man, God in his self-manifestation to man is dependent on the way man receives his manifestation. This is true even if the doctrine of predestination, namely, that this way is foreordained by God and entirely independent of human freedom, is maintained. The divine–human relation, and therefore God as well as man within this relation, changes with the stages of the history of revelation and with the stages of every personal development. There is a mutual interdependence between "God for us" and "we for God." God's wrath and God's grace are not contrasts in the "heart" of God (Luther), in the depth of his being; but they are contrasts in the divine–human relationship. The divine–human relation is a correlation. The "divine–human encounter" (Emil Brunner) means something real for both sides. It is an actual correlation, in the third sense of the term.

The divine–human relationship is a correlation also in its cognitive side. Symbolically speaking, God answers man's questions, and under the impact of God's answers man asks them. Theology formulates the questions implied in human existence, and theology formulates the answers in divine self-manifestation under the guidance of the questions implied in human existence. This is a circle which drives man to a point where question and answer are not separated. This point, however, is not a moment in time. It belongs to man's essential being, to the unity of his finitude with the infinity in which he was created, and from which he is separated. [. . .] A symptom of both the essential unity and the existential separation of finite man from his infinity is his ability to ask about the infinite to which he belongs: the fact that he must ask about it indicates that he is separated from it.

The answers implied in the event of revelation are meaningful only in so far as they are in correlation with questions concerning the whole of our existence, with existential questions. Only those who have experienced the shock of transitoriness, the anxiety in which they are aware of their finitude, the threat of nonbeing, can understand what the notion of God means. Only those who have experienced the tragic ambiguities of our historical existence and have totally questioned the meaning of existence can understand what the symbol of the Kingdom of God means. Revelation answers questions which have been asked and always will be asked because they are "we ourselves." Man is the question he asks about himself, before any question has been formulated. It is, therefore, not surprising that the basic questions were formulated very early in the history of mankind. Every analysis of the mythological material shows this. Nor is it surprising that the same questions appear in early childhood, as every observation of children shows. Being human means asking the questions of one's own being and living under the impact of the answers given to this question. And, conversely, being human means receiving answers to the questions of one's own being and asking questions under the impact of the answers.

In using the method of correlation, systematic theology proceeds in the following way: it makes an analysis of the human situation out of which the existential questions arise, and it demonstrates that the symbols used in the Christian message are the answers to these questions. The analysis of the human situation is done in terms which today are called "existential." Such analyses are much older than existentialism; they are, indeed, as old as man's thinking about himself, and they have been expressed in various kinds of conceptualization since the beginning of philosophy. Whenever man has looked at his world, he has found himself in it as a part of it. But he also has realized that he is a stranger in the world of objects, unable to penetrate it beyond a certain level of scientific analysis. And then he has become aware of the fact that he himself is the door to the deeper levels of reality, that in his own existence he has the only possible approach to existence itself. This does not mean that man is more approachable than other objects as material for scientific research. The opposite is the case! It does mean that the immediate experience of one's own existing reveals something of the nature of existence generally. Whoever has penetrated into the nature of his own finitude can find the traces of finitude in everything that exists. And he can ask the question implied in his finitude as the question implied in finitude universally. In doing so, he does not formulate a doctrine of man; he expresses a doctrine of existence as experienced in him as man. When Calvin in the opening sentences of the *Institutes* correlates our knowledge of God with our knowledge of man, he does not speak of the doctrine of man as such and of the doctrine of God as such. He speaks of man's misery, which gives the existential basis for his understanding of God's glory, and of God's glory, which gives the essential basis for man's understanding of his misery. Man as existing, representing existence generally and asking the question implied in his existence, is one side of the cognitive correlation to which Calvin points, the other side being the divine majesty. In the initial sentences of his theological system Calvin expresses the essence of the method of correlation.

The analysis of the human situation employs materials made available by man's creative self-interpretation in all realms of culture. Philosophy contributes, but so do poetry, drama, the novel, therapeutic psychology, and sociology. The theologian organizes these materials in relation to the answer given by the Christian message. In the light of this message he may make an analysis of existence which is more penetrating than that of most philosophers. Nevertheless, it remains a philosophical analysis. The analysis of existence, including the development of the questions implicit in existence, is a philosophical task, even if it is performed by a theologian, and even if the theologian is a reformer like Calvin. The difference between the philosopher who is not a theologian and the theologian who works as a philosopher in analyzing human existence is only that the former tries to give an analysis which will be part of a broader philosophical world, while the latter tries to correlate the material of his analysis with the theological concepts he derives from the Christian faith. This does not make the philosophical work of the theologian heteronomous. As a theologian he does not tell himself what is philosophically true. As a philosopher he does not tell himself what is theologically true. But he cannot help seeing human existence and existence generally in such a way that the Christian symbols appear meaningful and understandable to him. His eyes are partially focused by his ultimate concern, which is true of every philosopher. Nevertheless, his act of seeing is autonomous, for it is determined only by the object as it is given in his experience. If he sees something he did not expect to see in the light of his theological answer, he holds fast to what he has seen and reformulates the theological answer. He is certain that nothing he sees can change the substance of his answer, because this substance is the *logos* of being, manifest in Jesus as the Christ. If this were not his presupposition, he would have to sacrifice either his philosophical honesty or his theological concern.

The Christian message provides the answers to the questions implied in human existence. These answers are contained in the revelatory events on which Christianity is based and are taken by systematic theology *from* the sources, *through* the medium, *under* the norm. Their content cannot be derived from the questions, that is, from an analysis of human existence. They are "spoken" to human existence from beyond it. Otherwise they would not be answers, for the question is human existence itself. But the relation is more involved than this, since it is correlation. There is a mutual dependence between question and answer. In respect to content the Christian answers are dependent on the revelatory events in which they appear; in respect to form they are dependent on the structure of the questions which they answer. God is the answer to the question implied in human finitude. This answer cannot be derived from the analysis of existence. However, if the notion of God appears in systematic theology in correlation with the threat of nonbeing which is implied in existence, God must be called the infinite power of being which resists the threat of nonbeing. In classical theology this is being-itself. If anxiety is defined as the awareness of being finite, God must be called the infinite ground of courage. In classical theology this is universal providence. If the notion of the Kingdom of God appears in correlation with the riddle of our historical existence, it must be called the meaning, fulfilment, and unity of history. In this way an interpretation of the traditional symbols of Christianity is achieved which preserves the power of these symbols and which opens them to the questions elaborated by our present analysis of human existence.

Comment

From the outset, Tillich regarded one of the most important tasks of theology to be the relation of theological thought to nonreligious situations. In this sense, his theology may be seen as apologetic, rather than dogmatic, primarily concerned with making Christianity both attractive and intelligible to twentieth-century secular culture. His "method of correlation" between the situation and the Christian message reflects this concern to make the Christian proclamation relevant to a world come of age.

Tillich clearly sees existentialism as offering important insights and resources to Christian theology as it seeks to engage with this new situation. The key to this task was existentialism in the form associated with Martin Heidegger. For a short period in 1924–5 Tillich and Heidegger were colleagues at Marburg, and it is evident, both from Tillich's own personal reflections, as well as the substance of his ontology, that he was greatly influenced by the Marburg existentialist.

Tillich sees the task of theology as the identification of the "ultimate questions" being asked by the culture, and offering answers which meet the real existential concerns which lie behind these questions. In this sense, Tillich could be said to develop an apologetics as much as a theology.

Tillich's theological program can be summarized in the term "correlation." By the "method of correlation" Tillich understands the task of modern theology to be to establish a conversation between human culture and Christian faith. Tillich reacted with alarm to the theological program set out by Karl Barth, seeing this as a misguided attempt to drive a wedge between theology and culture. For Tillich, existential questions – or "ultimate questions," as he often terms them – are thrown up and revealed by human culture. Modern philosophy, writing, and the creative arts point to questions which concern humans. Theology then formulates answers to these questions, and by doing so it correlates the gospel to modern culture. The gospel must speak to culture, and it can do so only if the actual questions raised by that culture are heard.

Questions for Study

1 What does Tillich understand by "correlation"? What is being related to what? And how is this to be done? You might like to explore each of the three aspects of correlation which Tillich identifies in this passage.
2 Tillich is critical of Barth in this passage. Why? He also interacts with Emil Brunner and with John Calvin. How would you assess his evaluation of these two Protestant writers?
3 "The Christian message provides the answers to the questions implied in human existence." Locate this sentence within the passage. What does Tillich mean by this?
4 Tillich sets out an understanding of the relation of philosophy and theology in this passage. How would you summarize this? What is specific to philosophy? And to theology? Are they autonomous disciplines, in Tillich's view?

1.30

Sallie McFague on Metaphor in Theology

In several of her writings, including *Metaphorical Theology* (1987), the noted American theologian Sallie McFague (born 1933) develops the idea that Christian ways of speaking about God are primarily metaphorical in character, drawing attention to thedifferences between God and humanity as well as the similarities. After making the point that theology needs images or models to stimulate and inform its reflection, she considers the particular role of metaphors, focusing on the metaphor "God as mother." See also 1.10, 1.25, 3.41, 3.42.

The first thing to say is that theology, as constructive and metaphorical, does not "demythologize" but "remythologizes." To envision theology as metaphorical means, at the outset, to refuse the attempt to denude religious language of its concrete, poetic, imagistic and hence inevitably anthropomorphic, character, in the search for presumably more enlightened (and usually more abstract) terminology. It is to accept as one of theology's primary tasks remythologizing for our time: identifying and elucidating primary metaphors and models from contemporary experience which will express Christian faith for our day in powerful, illuminating ways. Theologians are not poets, but neither are they philosophers (as, in the Christian tradition, they have often become). Their place, as understood by metaphorical theology, is an anomalous one that partakes of both poetry and philosophy: they are poets insofar as they must be sensitive to the metaphors and models that are at once consonant with the Christian faith and appropriate for expressing that faith in their own time, and they are philosophers insofar as they must elucidate in a coherent, comprehensive, and systematic way the implications of these metaphors and models. [...]

A second and more complex issue in regard to theology, as constructive and metaphorical, concerns metaphor and model. What are they, and why call theology metaphorical? A metaphor is a word or phrase used inappropriately. It belongs properly in one context but is being used in another: the arm of the chair, war as a chess game, God the father. From Aristotle until recently, metaphor has been seen mainly as a poetic device to embellish or decorate. The idea was that in metaphor one used a word or phrase inappropriately but one need not have: whatever was being expressed could be said directly without the metaphor. Increasingly, however, the idea of metaphor as unsubstitutable is winning acceptance: what a metaphor expresses cannot be said directly or apart from it, for if it could be, one would have said it directly. Here, metaphor is a strategy of desperation, not decoration; it is an attempt to say something about the unfamiliar in terms of the familiar, an attempt to speak about what we do not know in terms of what we do know. Not all metaphors fit this definition, for many are so enmeshed in conventional language (the arm of the chair) that we do not notice them and some have become so familiar that we do not recognize them as attempting to express the unfamiliar (God the father). But a fresh metaphor, such as in the remark that "war is a chess game," immediately sparks our imaginations to think of war, a very complex phenomenon, as viewed through a concrete grid or screen, the game of chess. Needless to say, war is not a chess game; hence, a description of war in terms of chess is a partial, relative, inadequate account that, in illuminating certain aspects of war (such as strategizing), filters out other aspects (such as violence and death).

Metaphor always has the character of "is" and "is not": an assertion is made but as a likely account rather than a definition. That is, to say, "God is mother," is not to define God as mother, not to assert identity between the terms "God" and "mother," but to suggest that we consider what we do not know how to talk about – relating to God – through the metaphor of mother. The assumption here is that all talk of God is indirect: no words or phrases refer directly to God, for God-language can refer only through the detour of a description that properly belongs elsewhere. To speak of God as mother is to invite us to consider some qualities associated with mothering as one partial but perhaps illuminating way of speaking of certain aspects of God's relationship to us. It also assumes, however, that many other metaphors may qualify as partial but illuminating grids or screens for this purpose.

Comment

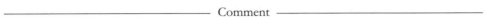

One of the tasks which Sallie McFague undertakes in her work *Metaphorical Theology* is to reclaim the use of the metaphor in theology. Inevitably, this involves clarifying what is meant by the word "metaphor," and especially clarifying its relation to the word "analogy." In the course of this section, it becomes clear that McFague sees the metaphor as possessing the virtue of flexibility: it is nonrigid and allows a variety of interpretations to be placed upon it.

Note how McFague stresses that a metaphor is about both "being like" and "not being like." To suggest, for example, that "God is a wolf" – and that this is to be taken metaphorically – encourages those hearing this statement to look for points of similarity and dissimilarity between God and a wolf. It cannot be assumed that the use of this image is purely analogical; the metaphor may stress distinction, rather than similitude.

McFague is opposed to the elimination of the metaphorical from theology, partly because she believes that it would be impoverished linguistically and iconically as a result. To reject metaphor is to reject imagery – often very powerful and moving imagery.

Questions for Study

1 The word "metaphor" means different things to different people. What does McFague mean by the term? And how does this affect her evaluation of its theological potential?
2 McFague makes it clear that she intends to resist any attempt "to denude religious language of its concrete, poetic, imagistic" character. What reasons does she give for doing so?
3 McFague offers a number of religious metaphors in this passage, including "God as mother." What insights does this metaphor convey?
4 McFague notes that "many other metaphors may qualify as partial but illuminating grids." This suggests that she sees metaphors as possessing a cumulative force, so that a range of metaphors is necessary to gain an increasing understanding of God. How might a variety of metaphors be used, in order to gain such a better understanding? How would one work out which aspects of the metaphors were to be used, and which not?

1.31

Gustavo Gutiérrez on Theology as Critical Reflection

The Peruvian theologian Gustavo Gutiérrez (born 1928) is one of the most important representatives of Latin American liberation theology, noted particularly for its emphasis on practice rather than theory. This emphasis, whose origins may be traced back to Karl Marx's distinction between *theory* and *praxis*, shows itself particularly in the liberationist emphasis on the need for practical social involvement and political commitment, and the implicit criticism of western understandings of theology as a disinterested and detached academic discipline. In this extract from his *Theology of Liberation*, Gutiérrez explores the significance of this point for a critical understanding of the nature of Christian theology. See also 3.35, 7.28, 9.3.

Theology must be critical reflection on humankind, on basic human principles. Only with this approach will theology be a serious discourse, aware of itself, in full possession of its conceptual elements. But we are not referring exclusively to this epistemological aspect when we talk about theology as critical reflection. We also refer to a clear and critical attitude regarding economic and socio-cultural issues in the life and reflection of the Christian community. To disregard these is to deceive both oneself and others. But above all, we intend this term to express the theory of a definite practice. Theological reflection would then necessarily be a criticism of society and the Church, insofar as they are called and addressed by the Word of God; it would be a critical theory, worked out in the light of the Word accepted in faith and inspired by a practical purpose – and therefore indissolubly linked to historical praxis.

By preaching the Gospel message, by its sacraments, and by the charity of its members, the Church proclaims and shelters the gift of the Kingdom of God in the heart of human history. The Christian community professes a faith which works through charity. It is – at least ought to be – real charity, action, and commitment to the service of others. Theology is reflection, a critical attitude. *Theology follows*; it is the second step. What Hegel used to say about philosophy can likewise be applied to theology: it rises only at sundown. The pastoral activity of the Church does not flow as a conclusion from theological premises. Theology does not produce pastoral activity; rather it reflects upon it. Theology must be able to find in pastoral activity the presence of the Spirit inspiring the action of the Christian community. A privileged *locus theologicus* for understanding the faith will be the life, preaching, and historical commitment of the Church.

To reflect upon the presence and action of the Christian in the world means, moreover, to go beyond the visible boundaries of the Church. This is of prime importance. It implies openness to the world, gathering the questions it poses, being attentive to its historical transformations. In the words of Yves Congar, "If the Church wishes to deal with the real questions of the modern world and to attempt to respond to them, . . . it must open as it were a new chapter of theologicopastoral epistemology. Instead of using only revelation and tradition as starting points, as classical theology has generally done, it must start with facts and questions derived from the world and from history." It is precisely this opening to the totality of human history that allows theology to fulfill its critical function *vis-à-vis* ecclesial praxis without narrowness.

This critical task is indispensable. Reflection in the light of faith must constantly accompany the pastoral action of the Church. By keeping historical events in their proper perspective, theology helps safeguard society and the Church from regarding as permanent what is only temporary. Critical reflection thus always plays the inverse role of an ideology which rationalizes and justifies a given social and ecclesial order. On the other hand, theology, by pointing to the sources of revelation, helps to orient pastoral activity; it puts it in a wider context and so helps it to avoid activism and immediatism. Theology as critical reflection thus fulfills a liberating function for humankind and the Christian community, preserving them from fetishism and idolatry, as well as from a pernicious and belittling narcissism. Understood in this way theology has a necessary and permanent role in liberation from every form of religious alienation – which is often fostered by the ecclesiastical institution itself when it impedes an authentic approach to the Word of the Lord.

As critical reflection on society and the Church, theology is an understanding which both grows and, in a certain sense, changes. If the commitment of the Christian community in fact takes different forms throughout history, the understanding which accompanies the vicissitudes of this commitment will be constantly renewed and will take untrodden paths. A theology which has as its points of reference only "truths" which have been established once and for all – and not the Truth which is also the Way – can be only static and, in the long run, sterile. In this sense the often-quoted and misinterpreted words of Bouillard take on new validity: "A theology which is not up-to-date is a false theology."

Finally, theology thus understood, that is to say as linked to praxis, fulfills a prophetic function insofar as it interprets historical events with the intention of revealing and proclaiming their profound meaning. According to Oscar Cullmann, this is the meaning of the prophetic role: "The prophet does not limit himself as does the fortune-teller to isolated revelations, but his prophecy becomes preaching, proclamation. He explains to the people the true meaning of all events; he informs them of the plan and will of God at the particular moment." But if theology is based on this observation of historical events and contributes to the discovery of their meaning, it is with the purpose of making Christians' commitment within them more radical and clear. Only with the exercise of the prophetic function understood in this way, will the theologian be – to borrow an expression from Antonio Gramsci – a new kind of "organic intellectual." Theologians will be personally and vitally engaged in historical realities with specific times and places. They will be engaged where nations, social classes, and peoples struggle to free themselves from domination and oppression by other nations, classes, and peoples. In the last analysis, the true interpretation of the meaning revealed by theology is achieved only in historical praxis – "The hermeneutics of the Kingdom of God," observed Schillebeeckx, "consists especially in making the world a better place. Only in this way will I be able to discover what the Kingdom of God means." We have here a political hermeneutics of the Gospel.

Theology as a critical reflection on Christian praxis in the light of the Word does not replace the other functions of theology, such as wisdom and rational knowledge; rather it presupposes and needs them. But this is not all. We are not concerned here with a mere juxtaposition. The critical function of theology necessarily leads to redefinition of these other two tasks. Henceforth, wisdom and rational knowledge will more explicitly have ecclesial praxis as their point of departure and their context. It is in reference to this praxis that an understanding of spiritual growth based on Scripture should be developed, and it is through this same praxis that faith encounters the problems posed by human reason. Given the theme of the present work, we will be especially aware of this critical function of theology with the ramifications suggested above. This approach will lead us to pay special attention to the life of the Church and to commitments which Christians, impelled by the Spirit and in communion with others, undertake in history. We will give special consideration to participation in the process of liberation, an outstanding phenomenon of our times, which takes on special meaning in the so-called Third World countries.

This kind of theology, arising from concern with a particular set of issues, will perhaps give us the solid and permanent albeit modest foundation for the *theology in a Latin American perspective* which is both desired and needed. This Latin American focus would not be due to a frivolous desire for originality, but rather to a fundamental sense of historical efficacy and also – why hide it? – to the desire to contribute to the life and reflection of the universal Christian community. But in order to make our contribution, this desire for universality – as well as input from the Christian community as a whole – must be present from the beginning. To concretize this desire would be to overcome particularistic tendencies – provincial and chauvinistic – and produce something *unique*, both particular and universal, and therefore fruitful.

"The only future that theology has, one might say, is to become the theology of the future," Harvey Cox has said. But this theology of the future must necessarily be a critical appraisal of historical praxis, of the historical task in the sense we have attempted to sketch. Jürgen Moltmann says that theological concepts "do not limp after reality. . . . They illuminate reality by displaying its future." In our approach, to reflect critically on the praxis of liberation is to "limp after" reality. The present in the praxis of liberation, in its deepest dimension, is pregnant with the future; hope must be an inherent part of our present commitment in history. Theology does not initiate this future which exists in the present. It does not create the vital attitude of hope out of nothing. Its role is more modest. It interprets and explains these as the true underpinnings of history. To reflect upon a forward directed action is not to concentrate on the past. It does not mean being the caboose of the present. Rather it is to penetrate the present reality, the movement of history, that which is driving history toward the future. To reflect on the basis of the historical praxis of liberation is to reflect in the light of the future which is believed in and hoped for. It is to reflect with a view to action which transforms the present. But it does not mean doing this from an armchair;

rather it means sinking roots where the pulse of history is beating at this moment and illuminating history with the Word of the Lord of history, who irreversibly committed himself to the present moment of humankind to carry it to its fulfillment.

It is for all these reasons that the theology of liberation offers us not so much a new theme for reflection as a *new way* to do theology. Theology as critical reflection on historical praxis is a liberating theology, a theology of the liberating transformation of the history of humankind and also therefore that part of humankind – gathered into *ecclesia* – which openly confesses Christ. This is a theology which does not stop with reflecting on the world, but rather tries to be part of the process through which the world is transformed. It is a theology which is open – in the protest against trampled human dignity, in the struggle against the plunder of the vast majority of humankind, in liberating love, and in the building of a new, just, and comradely society – to the gift of the Kingdom of God.

Comment

Gustavo Gutiérrez represents the tradition of Latin American liberation theology, which has had a profound impact on western theological thinking since about 1968. It had its origins in the Latin American situation in the 1960s and 1970s. In 1968, the Catholic bishops of Latin America gathered for a congress at Medellín, Colombia. This meeting – often known as CELAM II – acknowledged that the church had often sided with oppressive governments in the region, and declared that in future it would be on the side of the poor.

This pastoral and political stance was soon complemented by a solid theological foundation. In his *Theology of Liberation* (1971), Gutiérrez introduced the characteristic themes that would become definitive of the movement, and which we shall explore from the reading above. Other writers of note include the Brazilian Leonardo Boff, the Uruguayan Juan Luis Segundo, and the Argentinian José Miguel Bonino. This last is unusual in one respect, in that he is a Protestant (more precisely, a Methodist) voice in a conversation dominated by Catholic writers.

The basic themes of Latin American liberation theology may be summarized as follows. First, liberation theology is orientated towards the poor and oppressed. In the Latin American situation, the church is on the side of the poor. The fact that God is on the side of the poor leads to a further insight: the poor occupy a position of especial importance in the interpretation of the Christian faith. All Christian theology and mission must begin with the "view from below," with the sufferings and distress of the poor. Second, liberation theology involves critical reflection on practice. As Gutiérrez himself puts it, theology is a "critical reflection on Christian praxis in the light of the word of God." Theology is not, and should not be, detached from social involvement or political action. Whereas classical western theology regarded action as the result of reflection, liberation theology inverts the order: action comes first, followed by critical reflection. "Theology has to stop explaining the world, and start transforming it" (Bonino). True knowledge of God can never be disinterested or detached, but comes in and through commitment to the cause of the poor. There is a fundamental rejection of the Enlightenment view that commitment is a barrier to knowledge.

Questions for Study

1. Theology is "critical reflection on historical praxis." According to this passage, why must priority be given to praxis? What criticisms may be directed against the traditional western emphasis upon theory preceding action?
2. Why is the Latin American situation seen as being so significant for theology?
3. Theology is seen as being orientated towards the future. Why is this so? What factors help us to understand this emphasis on relating to the future?
4. Gutiérrez declares that one of the tasks of theology is to equip the church to fulfill its mission. Yet it is clear that he sees this "equipping" as being both positive and critical. Give some examples of ways in which theology supports the mission of the church, and of ways in which theology critiques the church for undertaking inappropriate actions or aligning itself with inappropriate allies in the course of its history.

1.32

Brian A. Gerrish on Accommodation in Calvin's Theology

For John Calvin, divine revelation takes place in a form which is "accommodated" or "adjusted" to human capacities and abilities. In this helpful analysis, Brian A. Gerrish (born 1931) sets out the basic features of Calvin's approach, which has had a considerable influence on Reformed theology in particular. See also 1.10, 1.13, 1.29.

According to Calvin, the forms of revelation are adapted in various ways to the nature of man as the recipient. His general term for the several types of adaptation is "accommodation." It is axiomatic for Calvin that God cannot be comprehended by the human mind. What is known of God is known by revelation; and God reveals himself, not as he is in himself, but in forms adapted to man's capacity. Hence in preaching he communicates himself through a man speaking to men, and in the sacraments he adds a mode of communication adapted to man's physical nature. Now in speaking of the Bible, Calvin extends the idea of accommodation beyond the mode to the actual content of revelation, and argues that the very diction of biblical language is often adapted to the finitude of man's mind. God does not merely condescend to human frailty by revealing himself in the prophetic and apostolic word and by causing the Word to be written down in sacred books: he also makes his witnesses employ accommodated expressions. For example, God is represented anthropomorphically as raising his hand, changing his mind, deliberating, being angry, and so on. Calvin admits that this accommodated language has a certain impropriety about it. It bears the same relation to divine truth as does the baby talk of a nurse or mother to the world of adult realities.

Comment

The basic issue is how divine revelation is "adapted" to the abilities and cultural situation of its addressees. Gerrish explores the way in which Calvin understands this process, and identifies some of its implications.

The issue is not simply of historical importance, but is of continuing relevance in relation to biblical interpretation and theological construction.

Questions for Study

1 According to Gerrish, what are the implications of the concept of "accommodation" to the biblical anthropomorphisms? In other words, how does Calvin's approach help us to make sense of biblical passages which speak of God in human and physical terms – such as those referring to the "arm of the Lord"?
2 How does the analogy of a nurse or mother speaking to a baby illuminate the points at issue?

1.33

George Lindbeck on Postliberal Approaches to Doctrine

George Lindbeck's *Nature of Doctrine* (1984) is widely regarded as a manifesto of postliberalism, a theological position sometimes also known as the "Yale school." In this work, Lindbeck (born 1923) sets out a "cultural-linguistic" approach to Christian doctrine, which argues that doctrine regulates the language of the Christian tradition. After considering approaches to doctrine which treat it as making cognitive truth claims or expressing human experience, Lindbeck turns to set out his own position, as follows. See also 1.1, 1.2, 1.4, 1.10, 1.29, 1.30.

The description of the cultural-linguistic alternative that I shall now sketch is shaped by the ultimately theological concerns of the present inquiry, but it is consonant, I believe, with the anthropological, sociological, and philosophical studies by which it has been for the most part inspired. In the account that I shall give, religions are seen as comprehensive interpretive schemes, usually embodied in myths or narratives and heavily ritualized, which structure human experience and understanding of self and world. Not every telling of one of these cosmic stories is religious, however. It must be told with a particular purpose or interest. It must be used, to adopt a suggestion of William Christian, with a view to identifying and describing what is taken to be "more important than everything else in the universe," and to organizing all of life, including both behavior and beliefs, in relation to this. If the interpretive scheme is used or the story is told without this interest in the maximally important, it ceases to function religiously. To be sure, it may continue to shape in various ways the attitudes, sentiments, and conduct of individuals and of groups. A religion, in other words, may continue to exercise immense influence on the way people experience themselves and their world even when it is no longer explicitly adhered to.

Stated more technically, a religion can be viewed as a kind of cultural and/or linguistic framework or medium that shapes the entirety of life and thought. It functions somewhat like a Kantian *a priori* although in this case the *a priori* is a set of acquired skills that could be different. It is not primarily an array of beliefs about the true and the good (though it may involve these), or a symbolism expressive of basic attitudes, feelings, or sentiments (though these will be generated). Rather, it is similar to an idiom that makes possible the description of realities, the formulation of beliefs, and the experiencing of inner attitudes, feelings, and sentiments. Like a culture or language, it is a communal phenomenon that shapes the subjectivities of individuals rather than being primarily a manifestation of those subjectivities. It comprises a vocabulary of discursive and nondiscursive symbols together with a distinctive logic or grammar in terms of which this vocabulary can be meaningfully deployed. Lastly, just as a language (or "language game," to use Wittgenstein's phrase) is correlated with a form of life, and just as a culture has both cognitive and behavioral dimensions, so it is also in the case of a religious tradition. Its doctrines, cosmic stories or myths, and ethical directives are integrally related to the rituals it practices, the sentiments or experiences it evokes, the actions it recommends, and the institutional forms it develops. All this is involved in comparing a religion to a cultural-linguistic system. [. . .]

Thus the linguistic-cultural model is part of an outlook that stresses the degree to which human experience is shaped, molded, and in a sense constituted by cultural and linguistic forms. There are numberless thoughts we cannot think, sentiments we cannot have, and realities we cannot perceive unless we learn to use the appropriate symbol systems. It seems, as the cases of Helen Keller and of supposed wolf children vividly illustrate, that unless we acquire language of some kind, we cannot actualize our specifically human capacities for thought, action, and feeling. Similarly, so the argument goes, to become religious involves becoming skilled in the language, the symbol system of a given religion. To become a Christian involves learning the story of Israel and of Jesus well enough to interpret and experience oneself and one's world in its terms. A religion is above all an external word, a *verbum externum*, that molds and shapes the self and its world, rather than an expression or thematization of a preexisting self or of preconceptual experience. The *verbum internum* (traditionally equated by Christians with the action of the Holy Spirit) is also crucially important, but it would be understood in a theological use of the model as a capacity for hearing and accepting the true religion, the true external word, rather than (as experiential-expressivism would have it) as a common experience diversely articulated in different religions. [. . .]

In thus inverting the relation of the internal and external dimensions of religion, linguistic and cultural approaches resemble cognitivist theories for which external (i.e., propositionally statable) beliefs are primary, but without the intellectualism of the latter. A comprehensive scheme or story used to structure all dimensions of existence is not primarily a set of propositions to be believed, but is rather the medium in which one moves, a set of skills that one employs in living one's life. Its vocabulary of symbols and its syntax may be used for many purposes, only one of which is the formulation of statements about reality. Thus while a religion's truth claims are often of the utmost importance to it (as in the case of Christianity), it is, nevertheless, the conceptual vocabulary and the syntax or inner logic which determine the kinds of truth claims the religion can make. The cognitive aspect, while often important, is not primary.

This stress on the code, rather than the (e.g., propositionally) encoded, enables a cultural-linguistic approach to accommodate the experiential-expressive concern for the unreflective dimensions of human existence far better than is possible on a cognitivist outlook. Religion cannot be pictured in the cognitivist (and voluntarist) manner as primarily a matter of deliberate choosing to believe or follow explicitly known propositions or directives. Rather, to become religious – no less than to become culturally or linguistically competent – is to interiorize a set of skills by practice and training. One learns how to feel, act, and think in conformity with a religious tradition that is, in its inner structure, far richer and more subtle than can be explicitly articulated. The primary knowledge is not about the religion, nor that the religion teaches such and such, but rather how to be religious in such and such ways. Sometimes explicitly formulated statements of the beliefs or behavioral norms of a religion may be helpful in the learning process, but by no means always. Ritual, prayer, and example are normally much more important. Thus – insofar as the experiential-expressive contrast between experience and knowledge is comparable to that between "knowing how" and "knowing that" – cultural-linguistic models, no less than expressive ones, emphasize the experiential or existential side of religion, though in a different way.

Comment

The emergence of postliberalism is widely regarded as one of the most important aspects of western theology since 1980. The movement had its origins in the United States, and was initially associated with Yale Divinity School, and particularly with theologians such as Hans Frei, Paul Holmer, David Kelsey, and George Lindbeck. While it is not strictly correct to speak of a "Yale school" of theology, there are nevertheless clear "family resemblances" between a number of the approaches to theology to emerge from Yale during the late 1970s and early 1980s. Since then, postliberal trends have become well established within North American and British academic theology. Its central foundations are narrative approaches to theology, such as those developed by Hans Frei, and the schools of social interpretation which stress the importance of culture and language in the generation and interpretation of experience and thought.

Lindbeck's *Nature of Doctrine* is widely seen as the most important work to set out the position of the "postliberal" camp. The "cultural-linguistic" approach set out by Lindbeck denies that there is some universal unmediated human experience which exists apart from human language and culture. Rather, it stresses that the heart of religion lies in living within a specific historical religious tradition, and interiorizing its ideas and values. This tradition rests upon a historically mediated set of ideas, for which the narrative is an especially suitable means of transmission.

Questions for Study

1 In what way can doctrine be seen as the grammar of the Christian language? What are the strengths and weaknesses of this approach?
2 "Thus the linguistic-cultural model is part of an outlook that stresses the degree to which human experience is shaped, molded, and in a sense constituted by cultural and linguistic forms." Locate this citation within the text. What does Lindbeck mean by this? And how does this illustrate the importance of tradition and social structures for Lindbeck's approach?
3 The use of the word "postliberal" suggests that Lindbeck and his colleagues regard liberalism as being superseded. On the basis of the passage, what reasons may be given for this belief?

1.34

Dumitru Staniloae on the Nature of Dogma

The Romanian theologian Dumitru Staniloae (1903–93) is recognized as one of the most significant voices in the Orthodox tradition. His writings show a particular concern to emphasize the inner coherence of dogmatic truth, and the significance of each dogma for the personal life of the Christian. For Staniloae, it is the theologian's task to explore and develop the link between dogma and personal spirituality. His particular approach to dogma is evident in this extract from his *Orthodox Dogmatic Theology*, which was begun in 1946, and was finally published in Romanian in 1978. See also 1.23, 1.27, 2.39.

Dogmas are definitions or strict "delimitations" (horoi). Yet, dogmas delimit God's infinity over against what is finite and they delimit man's infinite capacity for advancement, that is to say, the infinity of God and finite man's capacity for the infinite, a capacity which exists in solidarity with the infinity of God and draws endlessly closer to it.

To renounce the delimitation of either of these realities or to renounce their common delimitation – for neither the one nor the other lacks the principle of movement – would transform the fathomless depths of their combined existence into a meaningless slough where anything was possible, but nothing was truly new and profound. Dogmas are rather general formulae; they do not enter into details, yet this is precisely how they assure the breadth of the infinite content they contain. Their general character does not mean, however, that all precision is lacking. The fundamental structures of salvation are well specified within their general contours.

The paradoxical character of the dogmatic formulae has already been mentioned. God is one in essence and threefold in persons. He is unchangeable but alive, active and new in his providential action of saving the world. Christ is God and man; man remains a created being, and yet is deified. The paradox is to be found everywhere, but it belongs particularly to the person in general because person is not subject to a law that makes everything uniform and because person can embrace all. The person is a unity but one of endless richness; person remains the same and yet is endlessly different and new in its manifestations and states. Relations between persons show this same paradoxical character even more strongly. Man is autonomous and yet he cannot live or realize his own being except in communion with others. Any forced reduction of one of the aspects of human existence to another produces suffering within that aspect because such reduction is contrary to its existence. Even in relations with the world, the person shows this inner paradoxical character: person embraces the world in all its variety and brings it into a unity, yet person itself remains distinct and one, and preserves the world in its variety. How much more inevitable this paradox becomes in the domain of the infinite God's relations with the limited and created world: the one God, who has life in a manner beyond all understanding, exists within an interpersonal love.

The dogmatic formulae are paradoxical because they comprise essentially contradictory aspects of a living and inexhaustibly rich reality. In themselves, therefore, dogmas express all: the infinite and the finite united – without loss of their own being in all their dimensions.

Theology has an object of unending reflection in the all-comprehensive and infinite content of the dogmatic formulae, for these delimit and strictly secure this infinite reality in the unconfused richness of its own dimensions of inexhaustible depth and complexity.

But theology, in its turn, has to remain within the framework of the general and yet precise formulae of the dogmas precisely so as to maintain them as objects of unending reflection and deepening. The divine nature and the human nature – especially as these have been united in a climactic but unconfused manner in the divine person of Christ – comprise and offer to reflexion an infinite content. We can never exhaust the explanation of the divine and human natures in their richness of life and, simultaneously, in their unalterable character, just as there can be no end to depicting the depth and complexity of their union in one person, who is himself an inexhaustible mystery, always new and yet unchangeable.

Every theology which – within the framework of the precise formulae of the dogmas – makes explicit their infinite content is a broadened expression of those dogmas. There has often been talk of a distinction between dogmas and *theologoumena*. In this view dogmas would be the formulae established by the church while *theologoumena* would refer to various theological explanations which have not yet received an official ecclesiastical formulation, but which arise from the dogmas. This implies, however, alongside the distinction between dogmas and *theologoumena* a further distinction between those explanations which are taken as *theologoumena* and other kinds of explanations, these latter depending organically on the dogmas. In such a case, however, why would the *theologoumena* not also depend organically on the dogmas if they arose from them?

In fact, all the explanations of dogmas, so long as they remain within the framework of the dogmatic formulae, depend organically on the dogmas. Moreover, if they do not remain within the framework of those formulae, they cannot be considered as *theologoumena* either, nor can they hope to be invested with the character of dogmatic formulae at some undetermined point in the future. They are explanations which the Church does not make her own in the explanation of her dogmas and so in time they become obsolete.

However, although any true theology constructed within the framework of the Church makes the content of her dogmas more explicit, the Church does not invest any and every such explanation with the authority of her teaching. Alternatively, these explanations have authority by the very fact that they are implied in dogmas which have been formulated. The Church unceasingly multiplies her dogmatic explanations, but she concentrates – in a strictly dogmatic formula – the deeper explicitation of an older formula only when this deep explicitation is confronted by non-organic interpretations of the older formulae or when these kinds of interpretations are beginning to produce confusion and schisms within the Church.

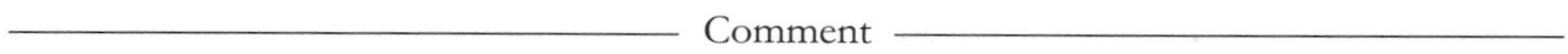

Comment

Staniloae here presents theology as wrestling with a mystery, recognizing that this process of engagement must be ongoing. Theology is "unending reflection" on the "inexhaustible depths and complexity" of the central truths of the Christian faith. Staniloae notes a distinction between dogmas (fundamental truths accepted by the church) and *theologoumena* (theological explanations or theories advanced by individuals). While recognizing the value of the distinction, Staniloae is ultimately skeptical concerning its utility. All theological statements, he argues, ultimately depend upon those dogmas.

Questions for Study

1 Orthodox theology is often characterized as an attempt to "preserve the mystery" of faith. Do you find this theme in Staniloae's discussion in this passage?

2 In what way does Staniloae find the church's reflection on the "inexhaustible mystery" of Christ a model for Christian theology?
3 The opening section of this passage speaks of dogma as something that "delimits." What does Staniloae mean by this? How does he illustrate it?

For Further Reading

Carl E. Braaten, "Prolegomena to Christian Dogmatics," in C. E. Braaten and R. W. Jenson (eds), *Christian Dogmatics*, 2 vols (Philadelphia: Fortress Press, 1984), vol. 1, pp. 5–78.

David K. Clark, *To Know and Love God : Method for Theology* (Wheaton, IL: Crossway Books, 2003).

Stephen T. Davis, *God, Reason and Theistic Proofs: How Do We Prove the Existence of God?* (*Reason and Religion* series) (Grand Rapids, MI: Eerdmans, 1997).

C. Stephen Evans, *Philosophy of Religion: Thinking about Faith* (Downers Grove, IL: Inter-Varsity Press, 1982).

Paul D. Janz, *God, the Mind's Desire: Reference, Reason and Christian Thinking* (Cambridge, UK: Cambridge University Press, 2004).

Basil Mitchell, *The Justification of Religious Belief* (Oxford: Oxford University Press, 1981).

Wolfhart Pannenberg, *Theology and the Philosophy of Science* (London: Darton, Longman and Todd, 1976), pp. 3–22.

Richard G. Swinburne, *Faith and Reason* (Oxford: Clarendon Press, 1981).

Nicholas Wolterstorff, *Reason within the Bounds of Religion*, 2nd edn (Grand Rapids, MI: Eerdmans, 1984).

Nicholas Wolterstorff, *Divine Discourse: Philosophical Reflections on the Claim That God Speaks* (Cambridge: Cambridge University Press, 1995).

2

The Sources of Theology

Introduction

What are the sources of Christian theology? There is widespread agreement within the Christian tradition that the most fundamental source is the collection of texts usually known as "the Bible." One of the most fundamental questions in Christian theology therefore relates to the authority and interpretation of Scripture. (Note that many theological writings tend to use the term "Scripture" or "Holy Scripture" in preference to "the Bible," even though these terms refer to exactly the same collection of writings.) A substantial number of the readings assembled in this chapter deal directly with this issue.

However, from the earliest of times, it was realized that Scripture was open to a series of interpretations which were not even remotely Christian. This insight is especially associated with the Gnostic controversies of the second century, during which Gnostic writers put forward some intensely speculative interpretations of Scripture. In response to this, writers such as Irenaeus emphasized the need to interpret Scripture within the parameters of the living tradition of the church. This led to growing interest in the way in which tradition was to be understood as a source for theology.

Many other questions of importance are touched on in this chapter. For example, what is revelation – the imparting of knowledge, or the establishment of a personal relationship? The different positions associated with Karl Barth, Emil Brunner, and James I. Packer will indicate the importance of this question, as well as allowing readers to sample the answers given. Finally, another debate of interest may be noted. To what extent may God be known from nature? This issue is of perennial importance, in relation to the classical debate over how theology relates to philosophy, and more recently, to the debate over how Christianity relates to other religions. A selection of readings explores this important issue. Each reading is prefaced with an introduction and followed by study questions designed to encourage readers to engage with the text.

Five general themes are of especial interest; the appropriate associated readings are indicated below.

The Authority of Scripture	
2.7	Cyril of Jerusalem on the Role of Creeds
2.9	Jerome on the Role of Scripture
2.16	Martin Luther on Revelation in Christ
2.18	John Calvin on the Relation between Old and New Covenants
2.19	The Council of Trent on Scripture and Tradition
2.20	The Gallic Confession on the Canon of Scripture
2.23	The Formula of Concord on Scripture and the Theologians
2.29	Philip Jakob Spener on Scripture and the Christian Life
2.35	Archibald Alexander Hodge on the Inspiration of Scripture
2.44	Karl Rahner on the Authority of Scripture
2.48	James I. Packer on the Nature of Revelation
2.50	The *Catechism of the Catholic Church* on Scripture and Tradition

The Interpretation of Scripture	
2.3	Hippolytus on Typological Interpretation of Scripture
2.4	Clement of Alexandria on the Fourfold Interpretation of Scripture
2.6	Origen on the Three Ways of Reading Scripture
2.8	Augustine on the Literal and Allegorical Senses of Scripture
2.11	Bernard of Clairvaux on the Allegorical Sense of Scripture
2.12	Stephen Langton on the Moral Sense of Scripture
2.13	Ludolf of Saxony on Reading Scripture Imaginatively
2.14	Jacques Lefèvre d'Etaples on the Senses of Scripture
2.15	Martin Luther on the Fourfold Sense of Scripture
2.22	Melchior Cano on the Church as Interpreter of Scripture
2.36	Benjamin Jowett on the Interpretation of Scripture
2.38	Charles Gore on the Relation of Dogma to the New Testament
2.43	Rudolf Bultmann on Demythologization and Biblical Interpretation
2.45	Phyllis Trible on Feminist Biblical Interpretation
2.46	Donald G. Bloesch on Christological Approaches to Biblical Hermeneutics

The Theological Role of Tradition

2.2 Irenaeus on the Role of Tradition
2.5 Tertullian on Tradition and Apostolic Succession
2.7 Cyril of Jerusalem on the Role of Creeds
2.10 Vincent of Lérins on the Role of Tradition
2.19 The Council of Trent on Scripture and Tradition
2.22 Melchior Cano on the Church as Interpreter of Scripture
2.28 Francis White on Scripture and Tradition
2.33 Johann Adam Möhler on Living Tradition
2.34 John Henry Newman on the Role of Tradition
2.44 Karl Rahner on the Authority of Scripture
2.47 John Meyendorff on Living Tradition
2.50 The *Catechism of the Catholic Church* on Scripture and Tradition

The Nature of Revelation

2.16 Martin Luther on Revelation in Christ
2.39 James Orr on the Centrality of Revelation for Christianity
2.40 Wilhelm Herrmann on the Nature of Revelation
2.41 Karl Barth on Revelation as God's Self-Disclosure
2.42 Emil Brunner on the Personal Nature of Revelation
2.48 James I. Packer on the Nature of Revelation

Revelation in Nature

2.16 Martin Luther on Revelation in Christ
2.17 John Calvin on the Natural Knowledge of God
2.21 The Belgic Confession on the Book of Nature
2.27 Sir Thomas Browne on the Two Books of Revelation
2.31 Jonathan Edwards on the Beauty of Creation
2.32 William Paley on the Wisdom of the Creation
2.37 Gerald Manley Hopkins on God's Grandeur in Nature
2.49 Thomas F. Torrance on Karl Barth's Criticism of Natural Theology

2.1

The Muratorian Fragment on the New Testament Canon

This writing, discovered by L. A. Muratori in 1740, represents the oldest known listing of the books of the New Testament. Written in appalling Latin, the fragment lists all of the New Testament books, except for Hebrews and James. Although Matthew and Mark are also omitted, this is simply because the opening lines of the work are missing. Internal evidence suggests that the work was composed around 190. See also 2.2, 2.5, 2.10.

The third book of the gospel is according to Luke. This Luke was a physician who Paul had taken after the ascension of Christ to be a legal expert. Yet he had not seen the Lord in the flesh. So, as far as he could, he begins his story with the birth of John. The fourth of the gospels was written by John from the Decapolis, one of the disciples. When urged to do so by his fellow disciples, he said "Fast with me for three days, and we will tell each other of whatever is revealed to any of us." That same night, it was revealed to Andrew, one of the apostles, that John would write everything under his own name, and that they would certify it. And although there are various ideas taught in the main books of the gospel, it makes no difference to the faith of believers, since all things are set out in each of them, by the one Spirit, concerning the birth, passion, resurrection, the conversation with the disciples, and his two comings, one in humility and the other, to be in the future, in royal power. It is therefore a wonder that John so clearly sets out each statement in his letters as well, saying in relation to himself "What we have seen with our eyes and heard with our ears and have touched with our hands, these things we have written to you." He thus declares that he is not just an eyewitness and hearer, but also a writer of all the wonders of the Lord, which are set out in order.

The Acts of all the apostles are written in one book. Luke, writing to the excellent Theophilus, includes events which took place in his own presence. He shows this clearly by leaving out the passion of Peter, and also the departure of Paul from the city as he journeyed to Spain. The letters of Paul themselves make clear to those who wish to understand them which letters were written by him, where they were written from, and why they were written. He wrote at some length first of all to the Corinthians, forbidding the schism of heresy. Next he wrote to the Galatians about circumcision, then to the Romans about the rule of the Scriptures, whose first principle is Christ, and writing at greater length about other things which it is not necessary for us to discuss.

The blessed apostle Paul, following the order of his predecessor John, writes by name only to seven churches in the following order: the first to the Corinthians, the second to the Ephesians, the third to the Philippians, the fourth to the Colossians, the fifth to the Galatians, the sixth to the Thessalonians, and the seventh to the Romans. It is true, however, that he followed this up, for the sake of correction [with second letters to] the Corinthians and Thessalonians. One church, however, is recognized as being dispersed throughout the world. For John in the Apocalypse also writes to seven churches, while speaking to all. It is true that one [letter] to Philemon, one to Titus and two to Timothy were written out of personal inclination and affection; however, they are to be held in honour throughout the catholic church for the ordering of church discipline. Letters under the name of Paul to the Laodiceans and Alexandrians were also written promoting the heresy of Marcion and others, which cannot be accepted in the catholic church, as it is not fitting that honey should be mixed with gall.

The letter of Jude and the two under the name of John are accepted as sound in the catholic church, as is the wisdom written by the friends of Solomon in his honour. We also accept the Apocalypse of John and [the letters] of Peter, which some of our friends do not wish to be read in our churches. But "the Shepherd" was written by Hermas in our times in the city of Rome, while his brother Pius was sitting in the chair of the church of the city of Rome. Therefore it ought to be read, but should not be read in public to the people of the church, since it is not among the complete number of the prophets nor apostles to the end of time.

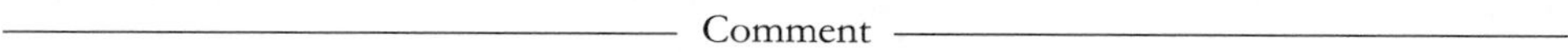

This is an extremely important early witness to the way in which the New Testament was used by the early church. Although there are a number of difficulties in interpreting the text, it is clear that it is a significant account of the understanding of the place of the New Testament documents. Note especially the reasons given for the second letters of Paul to the churches at Corinth and Thessalonia, and the references to two missing letters of Paul. Note that the "conversation with the disciples" (*conuersatio cum decipulis suis*) is almost certainly a reference to the incident on the road to Emmaus. Marcion was a heretic who declared that the Old Testament was an irrelevance to Christians, in that it related to a different God than the New Testament. The reference to "sitting in the chair of the church of the city of Rome" (*sedente cathedra urbis romae aeclesiae*) is a technical term referring to Pius being bishop of the city.

Questions for Study

1 Four present books of the New Testament are *not* mentioned in this fragment. Which are they?

2 The fragment makes reference to "The Shepherd of Hermas." What value does it attach to this work? And why does it not rank among canonical works of the New Testament?

2.2

Irenaeus on the Role of Tradition

In his writings "Against Heresies," originally written in Greek towards the end of the second century, but now known mainly through a Latin translation, Irenaeus of Lyons (c.130–c.200) insisted that the living Christian community possessed a tradition of interpreting Scripture which was denied to heretics. By their historical succession from the apostles, the bishops ensure that their congregations remain faithful to their teachings and interpretations. See also 2.5, 2.7, 2.10, 2.19, 2.26, 2.33, 2.34, 2.47.

When [the heretics] are refuted out of the Scriptures, they turn to accusing the Scriptures themselves, as if they were not right or did not possess authority, because the Scriptures contain a variety of statements, and because it is not possible for those who do not know the tradition to find the truth in them. For this has not been handed down by means of writings, but by the "living voice." [...] And each one of them claims that this wisdom is something that he has come across by himself, which is clearly a fiction. [...] Yet when we appeal once more to that tradition which is from the apostles, safeguarded in the churches by successions of presbyters, we provoke them into becoming the enemies of traditions, claiming to be wiser than those presbyters, and even the apostles themselves, and to have discovered the undefiled truth. [...] Thus they end up agreeing with neither the Scriptures nor with tradition. [...] Everyone who wishes to perceive the truth should consider the apostolic tradition, which has been made known in every church in the entire world. We are able to number those who are bishops appointed by the apostles, and their successors in the churches to the present day, who taught and knew nothing of such things as these people imagine. For if the apostles had known secret mysteries [*recondita mysteria*] which they taught privately and secretly to the perfect, they would have passed them down to those to whom they entrusted the churches. For they would have wanted those who they left as their successors, and to whom they handed over their own office of authority [*locum magisterii*], to be perfect and blameless. [...] We point to the greatest, most ancient and most glorious of churches, the church known to everyone, which was founded and established at Rome by the two most glorious apostles, Peter and Paul, through which the apostolic tradition and the faith which is preached to humanity has come down to us through the successions of bishops. [...] For every church ought to agree with this church, on account of its powerful position, for in this church the apostolic tradition has always been preserved by the faithful. [...]

Therefore, as there are so many demonstrations of this fact, there is no need to look anywhere else for the truth which we can easily obtain from the church. The apostles have, as it were, deposited this truth in all its fullness in this depository, so that whoever wants to may draw from this water of life. This is the gate of life; all others are thieves and robbers.

Comment

Irenaeus is noted especially for his vigorous defense of Christian orthodoxy in the face of a challenge from Gnosticism. His most significant work, "Against Heresies" (*adversus haereses*) represents a major defense of the Christian understanding of salvation, and especially of the role of tradition in remaining faithful to the apostolic witness in the face of non-Christian interpretations. It is important to realize that Irenaeus sees tradition as offering both stability to the teaching of the church, and a defense against the Gnostic positions.

Questions for Study

1 Why does Irenaeus see the idea of a "living voice" as a threat to his position? And how does he meet this threat?
2 What especial value does Irenaeus ascribe to the historical nature of the apostolic succession?
3 Why is it important to Irenaeus that the teaching of the church should be publicly accessible, and not hidden away, or secretly entrusted to Christian leaders?

2.3

Hippolytus on Typological Interpretation of Scripture

Typological exegesis involved the forging of links between persons, events, or objects mentioned in the Old Testament and corresponding persons, events, or doctrines in the New. In this passage, Hippolytus (c.170–c.236) takes the typological interpretation of Scripture to what might seem to be ridiculous lengths. During the course of commenting on Isaiah 18: 2, which mentions ships, Hippolytus expands on the typological significance of virtually every aspect of a ship's structure. See also 2.6, 2.8, 2.9, 2.11, 2.12, 2.15.

The oars of the ship are the churches. The sea is the universe [*kosmos*], in which the church, like a boat on the open sea, is shaken but does not sink, because she has Christ on board as an experienced navigator. At the center she has the prize of the passion of Christ, carrying with her his cross. Her prow points towards the east, and her stern to the west. The two steering oars are the two Testaments. The sheets are tight, like the love of Christ which sustains the church. She carries water on board, like the washing of regeneration. Her white sail receives the breath of the Spirit, by which believers are sealed. The sailors stand to port and to starboard, just like our holy guardian angels.

Comment

This is clearly a somewhat idiosyncratic reading of Isaiah 18: 2. The text reads as follows: "Ah, land of whirring wings which is beyond the rivers of Ethiopia; which sends ambassadors by the Nile, in vessels of papyrus upon the waters! Go, you swift messengers, to a nation, tall and smooth, to a people feared near and far, a nation mighty and conquering, whose land the rivers divide." The interpretation which Hippolytus imposes on this text (for he can hardly be said to have read it out of the text) shows how early biblical interpretation often departed extensively from the plain sense of the text itself.

Questions for Study

1 Why does Hippolytus treat this text in this way?
2 Hippolytus is concerned to identify and interpret every possible element of the ship's construction, and find in it some hidden theological significance. How do you respond to this approach?

2.4

Clement of Alexandria on the Fourfold Interpretation of Scripture

The eight books of Clement's *Stromata* (the word literally means "carpets") deal with a variety of questions, including the way in which Scripture is to be interpreted. In this extract from the *Stromata*, originally written in Greek in the early third century, Clement (c.150–c.215) succinctly sets out the fundamental principle that there are four senses (or meanings) of Scripture: a literal sense, and three additional spiritual senses. This would later be formalized in what came to be known as the *Quadriga*, which recognized literal, allegorical, moral or tropological, and anagogical senses of Scripture. See also 2.3, 2.6, 2.8, 2.9, 2.11, 2.12, 2.15.

The meaning of the law is to be understood by us in three ways [in addition to its literal sense]: as displaying a sign, as establishing a command for right conduct, or as making known a prophecy.

Comment

This is a very brief text, yet it is of some considerable importance. It appears to suggest that there are, in addition to the literal sense of the text, three nonliteral or "spiritual" senses. We can see in this an anticipation of the fourfold medieval scheme – the *Quadriga* – which took the following form:

1 The literal sense.
2 The allegorical sense, which conveys something to be believed.
3 The moral (or tropological) sense, which conveys something which is to be done.
4 The anagogical sense, which conveys something which is to be hoped for.

Questions for Study

1 Clement identifies three aspects of the text, in addition to its literal sense. In what way, and to what extent, can we see anticipations of the *Quadriga*?
2 How would you relate the medieval scheme of allegorical, moral, and anagogical senses to the "displaying a sign, establishing a command for right conduct, or making known a prophecy" noted by Clement?

2.5

Tertullian on Tradition and Apostolic Succession

In this early second-century analysis of the sources of theology, Tertullian (c.160–c.225) lays considerable emphasis upon the role of tradition and apostolic succession in the defining of Christian theology. Orthodoxy depends upon remaining historically continuous with and theologically dependent upon the apostles. The heretics, in contrast, cannot demonstrate any such continuity. See also 2.2, 2.7, 2.10, 2.19, 2.34.

The apostles first bore witness to faith in Jesus Christ throughout Judea, and established churches there, after which they went out into the world and proclaimed the same doctrine of the same faith to the nations. And they likewise established churches in every city, from which the other churches subsequently derived the origins of faith and the seeds of doctrine, and are still deriving them in order that they may become churches. It is through this that these churches are counted as "apostolic," in that they are the offspring of apostolic churches. It is necessary that every kind of thing is to be classified according to its origins. For this reason, the churches, however many and significant they are, are really the one first [church] which derives from the apostles, from which all have their origins. So all are first [*prima*] and all are apostolic, while all are one. And this unity is demonstrated by their sharing of peace, by their title of "brotherhood," and by their obligation of hospitality. For these laws have no basis other than the one tradition of the same revelation.

It is therefore for this reason that we lay down this ruling [*praescriptio*]: if the Lord Jesus Christ sent out the apostles to preach, no preachers other than those which are appointed by Christ are to be received, since "no one knows the Father except the Son and those to whom the Son has revealed him," and the Son appears to have revealed him to no one except the apostles who he sent to preach what he had revealed to them. What they preached – that is, what Christ revealed to them – ought, by this ruling, to be established only by those churches which those apostles founded by their preaching and, as they say, by the living voice, and subsequently through their letters. If this is true, all doctrine which is in agreement with those apostolic churches, the sources and originals of the faith, must be accounted as the truth, since it indubitably preserves what the churches received from the apostles, the apostles from Christ, and Christ from God. [. . .]

If any of these [heresies] dare to trace their origins back to the apostolic era, so that it might appear that they had been handed down by the apostles because they existed under the apostles, we are able to say: let them therefore show the origins of their churches; let them unfold the order of their bishops, showing that there is a succession from the beginning, so that their first bishop had as his precursor [*auctor*] and predecessor an apostle or some apostolic man who was associated with the apostles.

Comment

Tertullian, like Irenaeus, was faced with the threat of heretical teaching. As we noted earlier (1.3), he saw this threat as originating partly through the intrusion of pagan philosophy into theology. Realizing the importance of this threat, Tertullian sought to lay down guidelines for identifying heresy and dealing with the threat which it posed. As a lawyer, Tertullian was clearly aware of the need to be alert to the practical aspects of the discernment and refutation of heresy, and in this passage, practical advice is offered to his readers.

Questions for Study

1 What guidance does Tertullian offer his readers to help them deal with the threat of heresy?
2 What critically important role does Tertullian ascribe to the apostles? And how does this help in dealing with heresy?
3 Why does Tertullian demand that the heretics establish their historical credentials?

2.6

Origen on the Three Ways of Reading Scripture

The Alexandrian theologian Origen (c.185–c.254), who wrote extensively in the first half of the third century, is widely regarded as one of the early church's most influential and creative interpreters of Scripture. Origen here uses the imagery of "body, soul, and spirit" to distinguish three different ways in which Scripture may be read, according to the maturity of the reader in question. The distinction between different levels of maturity and advancement on the part of Christians is characteristic of both Clement of Alexandria and Origen. See also 2.3, 2.8, 2.9, 2.11, 2.12, 2.15.

There are three ways in which the meaning of the Holy Scriptures should be inscribed on the soul of every Christian. First, the simpler sort are edified by what may be called the "body" of Scripture. This is the name I give to the immediate acceptance. Secondly, those who have made some progress are edified by, as it were, the "soul." Thirdly, the perfect [...] are edified by the "spiritual" Law, which contains the shadow of the good things to come. Thus just as a human being consists of body, soul, and spirit, so also does the Scripture which is the gift of God designed for human salvation. [...]

Some parts of Scripture have no "body." In these parts, we must look only for the "soul" and "spirit." Perhaps this is the point of the description in John's gospel of the water-pots "for the purifying of the Jews, holding two or three measures" (John 2: 6). The Word implies by this that the apostle calls the Jews in secret, so that they may be purified through the word of the Scripture which sometimes holds two measures, that is what one may call the "soul" and "spirit"; sometimes three, that is, the "body" as well. [...] The usefulness of the "body" is testified by the multitude of simple believers and is quite obvious. Paul gives us many examples of the "soul." [...] The spiritual interpretation belongs to people who are able to explain the way in which the worship of the "Jews after the flesh" (1 Corinthians 10: 18) yields images and "shadows of heavenly things" (Hebrews 8: 5) and how the "Law had the shadow of good things to come."

Comment

Origen draws a distinction, which was not universally recognized, between uneducated Christians and their more sophisticated counterparts, among which latter group he clearly numbered himself. The basic distinction being made is between "fleshly" and "spiritual" ways of reading Scripture, which Origen illustrates with reference to various ways of interpreting certain biblical verses.

Questions for Study

1 What do you make of Origen's distinction between the "simpler sort" of Christians and those who are "perfect"?
2 What difference does this distinction make to the way in which the Bible is read, according to Origen?
3 How does Origen's reading of John 2: 6 help illustrate his point?

2.7

Cyril of Jerusalem on the Role of Creeds

In a series of 24 lectures given around the year 350 to those who were about to be baptized, Cyril of Jerusalem (c.315–86) explains the various aspects of the Christian faith and its practices. In the section which follows, he explains the origins and role of creeds, noting their importance as summaries of Scripture. See also 2.2, 2.5, 2.10, 2.19.

This synthesis of faith was not made to be agreeable to human opinions, but to present the one teaching of the faith in its totality, in which what is of greatest importance is gathered together from all the Scriptures. And just as a mustard seed contains a great number of branches in its tiny grain, so also this summary of faith brings together in a few words the entire knowledge of the true religion which is contained in the Old and New [Testaments].

Comment

This is a very brief passage, but it illustrates an important point. By Cyril's time, creeds were becoming increasingly important as public statements of the Christian faith. So the question could not be avoided: are these creeds to be seen as alternatives to the Bible? And if not, what is their status? Cyril's response to this issue reflects a wide consensus on this matter within Christendom at this time.

Questions for Study

1 In what way can a creed be thought of as a "gathering together" of biblical insights?
2 Explain precisely what Cyril means by the analogy of the mustard seed. You might like to read Mark 4: 31–2 to see where this image comes from.
3 How might the approach advocated by Cyril in this passage be applied to the Apostles' Creed (1.6)?

2.8

Augustine on the Literal and Allegorical Senses of Scripture

One of Augustine's earliest and most important controversies related to the Manichaeans, a sect which dismissed the Old Testament as an irrelevance, on the basis of an excessively literal approach to its meaning. In this passage, originally written in Latin during the 390s, Augustine (354–430) draws a distinction between the literal sense of the Old Testament and its allegorical or spiritual sense. He argues that the spiritual sense has always been present in the Old Testament; however, it is only seen properly in the light of the New Testament. He compares the reading of the Old Testament in the light of the New to the lifting of the veil which had hitherto covered the true sense of the Old Testament. See also 2.3, 2.6, 2.9, 2.11, 2.12, 2.15.

Now while [the Manichaeans] maliciously try to make the Law into an irrelevance, at the same time they force us to approve of these same Scriptures. They pay attention where it is said that those who are under the Law are in bondage, and brandish this decisive passage above all others: "You who are justified by the Law are banished from Christ. You have fallen from grace" (Galatians 5: 4). Now we admit that all this is true. We do not say the Law is necessary except for those for whom bondage is a good thing. It was laid down with good reason because human beings, who could not be won from their sins by reason, had to be coerced by threats and terrors of penalties which even fools can understand. When the grace of Christ sets people free from such threats and penalties it does not condemn the Law but invites us now to submit to His love and not to be slaves to fear. Grace is a benefaction conferred by God, which those who wish to continue under the bondage of the Law do not understand. Paul rightly calls such people unbelievers, by way of reproach, who do not believe that they are now set free by our Lord Jesus from a bondage to which they had been subjected by the just judgment of God. This is the form of words used by the Apostle: "The Law was our *paedagogus* to Christ" (Galatians 3: 24). God thus gave humanity a pedagogue whom they might fear, and later gave them a master whom they might love. But in these precepts and commands of the Law which Christians may not now lawfully obey, such as the Sabbath, circumcision, sacrifices, and the like, there are contained such mysteries that every religious person may understand there is nothing more dangerous than to take whatever is there literally, and nothing more wholesome than to let the truth be revealed by the Spirit. For this reason: "The letter kills but the Spirit brings life" (2 Corinthians 3: 6). And again: "The same veil remains in the reading of the Old Testament and there is no revelation, for in Christ the veil is removed" (2 Corinthians 3: 14). It is not the Old Testament that is abolished in Christ but the concealing veil, so that it may be understood through Christ.

That which without Christ is obscure and hidden is, as it were, opened up. [. . .] [Paul] does not say: "The Law or the Old Testament is abolished." It is not the case, therefore, that by the grace of the Lord that which was covered has been abolished as useless; rather, the covering which concealed useful truth has been removed. This is what happens to those who earnestly and piously, not proudly and wickedly, seek the sense of the Scriptures. To them is carefully demonstrated the order of events, the reasons for deeds and words, and the agreement of the Old Testament with the New, so that not a single point remains where there is not complete harmony. The secret truths are conveyed in figures that are to be brought to light by interpretation.

Comment

This is an important passage, as it sets out an approach to the relation of the Old and New Testaments which would become widely accepted within Christianity. Note especially the way in which Augustine uses the image of a "veil," which he finds in Paul's second letter to the Corinthians. There is, he argues, no tension between the Old and New Testaments; it is simply that we are unable to see their proper connection and relationship until the veil which obscures our view is removed. The development of a proper hermeneutical scheme is therefore an integral element of theological reflection.

Questions for Study

1 According to Augustine, are the Law and grace in tension with each other, or to be set against each other?
2 What does Augustine mean when he declares that "It is not the Old Testament that is abolished in Christ but the concealing veil, so that it may be understood through Christ"?
3 What role did the Law play before the coming of the gospel, according to Augustine?
4 How does the approach to the Old Testament Law advocated by Augustine compare with that adopted by Clement of Alexandria (1.2)?

2.9

Jerome on the Role of Scripture

Jerome (c.342–420), along with Origen, was the early church's leading expositor and interpreter of Scripture, with a particular concern for biblical translation. Underlying this was a profound conviction of the fundamental importance of Scripture to the life and thought of the church and the individual believer, which is clearly expressed in this letter. See also 2.2, 2.6, 2.7, 2.19, 2.23.

[Paul] speaks of a "wisdom of God hidden in a mystery, which God ordained before the world" (1 Corinthians 2: 7). God's wisdom is Christ, for Christ, we are told, is "the power of God and the wisdom of God" (1 Corinthians 1: 30). This wisdom remains hidden in a mystery. It is to this that the title of Psalm 9: 1, "for the hidden things of the Son," refers. In him are hidden all the treasures of wisdom and knowledge. The one who was hidden in mystery is the same who was predestined before the world, and was foreordained and prefigured in the Law and the Prophets. That is why the prophets were called seers: they saw him whom others did not see. Abraham also saw his day, and was glad (John 8: 56). The heavens which were sealed to a rebellious people were opened to Ezekiel (Ezekiel 1: 1). "Open my eyes," says David, "so that I may behold the wondrous things of your law" (Psalm 118: 18). For the law is spiritual, and in order to understand it we need the veil to be removed and the glory of God to be seen with an uncovered face (2 Corinthians 3: 14–18). [...]

In the Acts of the Apostles, the holy eunuch [...] was reading Isaiah, when he was asked by Philip: "Do you understand what you are reading?" "How can I," he replied, "unless someone teaches me?" (Acts 8: 30–31). I am no more holy nor more learned than this eunuch, who was from Ethiopia, that is from the ends of the world. He left a royal court and went as far as the temple; and such was his love for divine knowledge that he was reading the Holy Scriptures while in his chariot. Yet even though he was holding a book in his hand and was reflecting on the words of the Lord, even sounding them with his tongue and pronouncing them with his lips [*lingua volveret, labiis personaret*)], he did not know who he was worshiping in this book. Then Philip came, and showed him Jesus hidden in the letter [*qui clausus latebat in littera*]. What a marvelous teacher! In the same hour the eunuch believed and was baptized. He became one of the faithful and a saint. From being a pupil he became a master. He found more in the desert spring of the church than he had done in the gilded temple of the synagogue. [...]

This matter I have dealt with only briefly – I could not manage any more within the limits of a letter – so that you will understand that you cannot advance in the Holy Scriptures unless you have an experienced guide to show you the way. [...]

I beg you, my dearest brother, to live among these [sacred books], to meditate on them, to know nothing else, to seek nothing else. Does not this seem to you to be a little bit of heaven here on earth [*in terris regni caelestis habitaculum*]? Do not take offence on account of the simplicity of Holy Scripture or the unsophistication of its words [*quasi vilitate verborum*], for these are due either to translation faults or have some deeper purpose. For Scripture offers itself in such a way that an uneducated congregation can more easily learn from it, some benefit there, and both the learned and the unlearned can discover different meanings in the same sentence. I am not so arrogant nor so forward as to claim that I know this, which would be like wanting to pick on earth the fruits of trees whose roots are in heaven. However, I confess that I would like to do so. [...] The Lord has said: "ask, and it shall be given; knock, and it shall be opened; seek, and you will find" (Matthew 7: 7). So let us study here on earth that knowledge which will continue with us in heaven.

Comment

Jerome was concerned to encourage Christians to read the Bible, and devoted much of his efforts to making this possible, through translations. Yet he was also aware of some of the difficulties of reading and studying the Bible, as this passage makes clear.

Questions for Study

1 Why does Jerome suggest that the reader of Scripture may require assistance, perhaps in the form of a skilled guide? And how does he defend this, on the basis of Scripture?
2 The image of "seeing" plays an important role in this text, especially in its first paragraph. How does Jerome develop the metaphor of sight in his engagement with Scripture?
3 Jerome is sensitive to the charge (which is known to have been a favorite among Greek critics of Christianity) that the Bible is an unsophisticated work of literature. How does he begin to meet this charge?

2.10

Vincent of Lérins on the Role of Tradition

Writing in the year 434, in the aftermath of the Pelagian controversy, Vincent (who died at an unknown date before 450) expressed his belief that the controversies of that time had given rise to theological innovations. It is clear that he regarded Augustine's doctrine of double predestination as a case in point. But how could such doctrinal innovations be identified? In response to this question, he argues for a triple criterion by which authentic Christian teaching may be established: *ecumenicity* (being believed everywhere), *antiquity* (being believed always), and *consent* (being believed by all people). See also 2.2, 2.5, 2.7, 2.19, 2.28, 2.33, 2.34, 2.47, 2.50.

Therefore I have devoted considerable study and much attention to enquiring, from men of outstanding holiness and doctrinal correctness, in what way it might be possible for me to establish a kind of fixed and, as it were, general and guiding principle for distinguishing the truth of the catholic faith from the depraved falsehoods of the heretics. And the answer I receive from all can be put like this: if I or anyone else wish to detect the deceits of the heretics or avoid their traps, and to remain healthy and intact in a sound faith, we ought, with the help of the Lord, to strengthen our faith in two ways; first, by the authority of the divine law, and then by the tradition of the catholic church.

Here someone may ask: since the canon of the scriptures is complete, and is in itself adequate, why is there any need to join to its authority the understanding of the church? Because Holy Scripture, on account of its depth, is not accepted in a universal sense. The same statements are interpreted in one way by one person, in another by someone else, with the result that there seem to be as many opinions as there are people. [...] Therefore, on account of the number and variety of errors, there is a need for someone to lay down a rule for the interpretation of the prophets and the apostles in such a way that is directed by the rule of the catholic church.

Now in the catholic church itself the greatest care is taken that we hold that which has been believed everywhere, always, and by all people [*quod ubique, quod semper, quod ab omnibus creditum est*]. This is what is truly and properly catholic. This is clear from the force of the word and reason, which understands everything universally. We shall follow "universality" in this way, if we acknowledge this one faith to be true, which the entire church confesses throughout the world. We affirm "antiquity" if we in no way depart from those understandings which it is clear that the greater saints and our fathers proclaimed. And we follow "consensus" if in this antiquity we follow all (or certainly nearly all) the definitions of the bishops and masters.

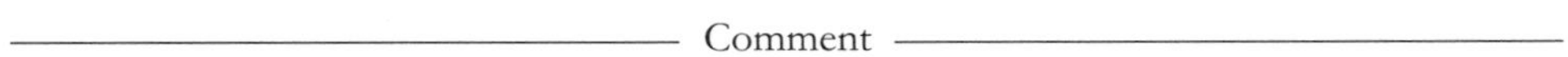

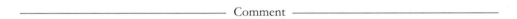

Vincent was concerned for the stability of the Christian theological tradition, and was anxious that certain doctrinal innovations were being introduced without adequate reason. Vincent was especially troubled by some of Augustine's views on predestination, which he regarded as unwise and hasty improvisations. There was a need to have public standards by which such doctrines could be judged. So what standard was available, by which the church could be safeguarded from such errors? For Vincent, the answer was clear – tradition. The phrase "that which has been believed everywhere, always, and by all people" (*quod ubique, quod semper, quod ab omnibus creditum est*) has come to be known as the "Vincentian Canon."

Questions for Study

1. How does Vincent arrive at the need for a publicly agreed standard of Christian orthodoxy?
2. "Christian orthodoxy is just repeating what the Bible says." How would Vincent respond to such a suggestion?
3. What does Vincent mean by "that which has been believed everywhere, always, and by all people"? Is this a workable definition of orthodoxy?

2.11

Bernard of Clairvaux on the Allegorical Sense of Scripture

In the course of his exposition of the Song of Songs, written in Latin in the first half of the twelfth century, Bernard (1090–1153) provides an allegorical interpretation of verse 1.17 "the beams of our houses are of cedar, and our panels are of cypress." This extract is an excellent illustration of the way in which doctrinal or spiritual meaning was "read into" otherwise unpromising passages at this time. See also 2.3, 2.6, 2.8, 2.9, 2.12, 2.15.

By "houses" we are to understand the great mass of the Christian people, who are bound together with those who possess power and dignity, rulers of the church and the state, as "beams." These hold them together by wise and firm laws; otherwise, if each of them were to operate in any way that they pleased, the walls would bend and collapse, and the whole house would fall in ruins. By the "panels" [*laqueria*], which are firmly attached to the beams and which adorn the house in a royal manner, we are to understand the kindly and ordered lives of a properly instructed clergy, and the proper administration of the rites of the church. Yet how can the clergy carry out their work, or the church discharge her duties, unless the princes, like strong and solid beams, sustain them through their goodwill and munificence, and protect them through their power?

Comment

This text illustrates well the allegorical interpretations of Scripture favored by some medieval spiritual writers. Given that the literal or historical reading of the text seems, at least on a first reading, to be somewhat unpromising in terms of spiritual enlightenment, Bernard uses an allegorical approach to its interpretation which correlates its ideas with already known theological concepts. The text is thus read in a way that reinforces existing ideas, using allegory as a means of establishing the connection between the text itself and these spiritual notions.

Questions for Study

1 What justification does Bernard offer for his interpretation of the various parts of the building?
2 How does the approach offered by Bernard compare with that offered earlier by Hippolytus (2.3)?
3 Bernard concludes this passage by making an application to the ecclesiastical life of his time. How convincing is the application, given the foundations on which it rests?

2.12

Stephen Langton on the Moral Sense of Scripture

In this twelfth-century commentary on an incident involving the priest Amaziah (here: Amasius) and king Jeroboam, partly related in Amos 7: 10–13, the great medieval biblical commentator and preacher Stephen Langton (died 1228) develops the "moral" or "tropological" sense of the passage. This technique involves the extraction of a moral from a biblical passage. Just as Amasius, the high priest of Bethel, denounced the prophet Amos to Jeroboam in biblical times, so modern priests show just the same weakness. The style adopted is that of "glossing" – in other words, adding extensive interpretive comments to the words of Scripture. In what follows, the text of the biblical passage is printed in italics, with Langton's comments in normal type. See also 2.3, 2.6, 2.8, 2.9, 2.11, 2.15.

Amasius is to be understood as a type [*typus*] of a bad priest, a bad and evil prelate, who is set in his evil ways and has no interest in good. He is a stranger to the fire of charity. He would be happy to travel two miles or more on a winter's night to visit a prostitute or for financial gain. But he would not even leave his table for a few minutes to hear a dying man's confession. [...] When he comes across someone who is correctly preaching the way of truth, which he fears will put an end to his own evil ways, he does not mention this anxiety (even though it is his chief concern) and instead denounces the preacher to his king or prince. He pretends to be worried about the disrespect being shown to the king, and so tries to incite him to take vengeance. But note how Jeroboam dismisses the accusation as groundless. This shows that prelates are far more evil than secular princes. Yet although the prince dismisses the false accusation of this evil priest, he does not stop doing evil. *And Amasius said to Amos: you seer.* You prophet and learned doctor who threatens us so terribly through your preaching *go, run away to the land of Judah.* Leave my bishopric or my parish, and go back to your studies at Paris. *Eat bread there and prophesy there.* Restrict your teaching and preaching to Paris! *In Bethel*, that is, in my bishopric, *do not prophesy any more*, that is, stop preaching here. Your remarks are offensive to the king, and as this place belongs to him, he can hire and fire any person of the church as he likes.

Comment

Stephen Langton probably had a personal interest in the kind of situation envisaged in this passage, not least on account of his stormy relations with the King of England as Archbishop of Canterbury. The passage illustrates well the medieval practice of "glossing" the text. This could take two forms: a gloss inserted above a word or phrase, and a longer marginal gloss, which was more of a commentary on the text than a brief explanation of the meaning of a word or phrase.

Questions for Study

1 How convincing is the interpretation of the passage offered in this text?
2 The University of Paris was a center of theological excellence at this time, and Langton himself taught there for a while. How does Langton make use of Paris in this passage?

2.13

Ludolf of Saxony on Reading Scripture Imaginatively

Ludolf of Saxony (c.1300–78) is a somewhat enigmatic figure, of whom relatively little is known. He is known to have entered the Order of Preachers and gained a qualification in theology before joining the Carthusians at Strasbourg in 1340. In 1343 he moved to the Carthusian house at Coblenz, becoming its Prior. However, he does not appear to have been particularly enthusiastic for the responsibilities of this office, and in 1348 he resumed his life as an ordinary monk. The remainder of his life was spent in the cities of Mainz and Strasbourg. It should be noted that this writer is also known as Ludolf the Carthusian, and that the German name "Ludolf" is often spelled in its Latinized forms as "Ludolphus" or "Ludolph."

Ludolf's *Vita Christi* takes the form of an extended meditation on the life of Christ, interspersed with prayers and citations from earlier writers. Such compilations of earlier sayings or anecdotes were popular in the late Middle Ages, and were widely used both for personal devotion and as source-books for preaching. In this work, Ludolf sets out his intention to "recount things according to certain imaginative representations" so that his readers may "make themselves present for those things which Jesus did or said." See also 2.3, 2.6, 2.8, 2.9, 2.11, 2.12, 2.15.

Draw close with a devout heart to the one who comes down from the bosom of the Father to the Virgin's womb. In pure faith be there with the angel, like another witness, at the moment of the holy conception, and rejoice with the Virgin Mother now with child for you. Be present at his birth and circumcision, like a faithful guardian, with St Joseph. Go with the Wise Men to Bethlehem and adore the little king. Help his parents carry the child and present him in the Temple. Alongside the apostles, accompany the Good Shepherd as he performs his miracles. With his blessed mother and St John, be there at his death, to have compassion on him and to grieve with him. Touch his body with a kind of devout curiosity, handling one by one the wounds of your Savior who has died for you. With Mary Magdalene seek the risen Christ until you are found worthy to find him. Look with wonder at his ascent into heaven as though you were standing among his disciples on the Mount of Olives. Take your place with the apostles as they gather together; hide yourself away from other things so that you may be found worthy to be clothed from on high with the power of the Holy Spirit. If you want to draw fruit from these mysteries, you must offer yourself as present to what was said and done through our Lord Jesus Christ with the whole affective power of your mind, with loving care, with lingering delight, thus laying aside all other worries and care. Hear and see these things being narrated, as though you were hearing with your own ears and seeing with your own eyes, for these things are most sweet to him who thinks on them with desire, and even more so to him who tastes them. And although many of these are narrated as past events, you must meditate them all as though they were happening in the present moment, because in this way you will certainly taste a greater sweetness. Read then of what has been done as though they were happening now. Bring before your eyes past actions as though they were present. Then you will feel how full of wisdom and delight they are.

Comment

Ludolf offers an excellent summary of the general approach he wishes to commend: "If you want to draw fruit from these mysteries, you must offer yourself as present to what was said and done through our Lord Jesus Christ with the whole affective power of your mind, with loving care, with lingering delight, thus laying aside all other worries and care." Ignatius Loyola read Ludolf's *Vita Christi* while recovering from wounds acquired in battle, and developed a similar approach to reading Scripture in his *Spiritual Exercises*.

Questions for Study

1 Note the way in which Ludolf is concerned to draw his readers into the life of Christ. In what ways does he do this?

2 Ludolf identifies a number of episodes in the life of Christ which he regards as being of particular importance, and links these specifically with certain individuals who were present on those occasions. Make a list of the occasions and the witnesses; for example, the circumcision is witnessed by Joseph, and so forth. You will also find it helpful to identify the biblical passages to which he alludes.

3 Now note the way in which Ludolf draws us into the narrative. He does not simply recount what happened; he asks us to do things which draw us into the narrative. In each of the episodes which Ludolf describes, identify what it is he asks you to do. For example, he asks you to help Mary and Joseph carry the baby Jesus to the Temple. Notice how Ludolf portrays you, the reader, as an active participant in the events which are being described. You are to project *yourself* into the action.

2.14

Jacques Lefèvre d'Etaples on the Senses of Scripture

In the preface to his 1508 edition of the Hebrew text of five selected psalms, the French humanist biblical scholar Jacques Lefèvre d'Etaples (also known as Stapulensis, c.1455–1536) sets out his understanding of the way in which the Old Testament is to be interpreted. A distinction is drawn between the "literal-historical" sense of Scripture, which understands the Old Testament as a historical narrative, and the "literal-prophetic" sense ("a literal sense which coincides with the Spirit"), which understands it as a prophecy of the coming of Jesus Christ. He thus argues that there are two "literal" senses of Scripture. Note that the context of this passage requires that the Latin term *litera* should often be translated as "literal sense" rather than simply as "letter." See also 2.3, 2.6, 2.8, 2.9, 2.11, 2.12, 2.15.

Then I began to realize that perhaps this had not really been the true literal sense at all; rather, just like bad pharmacists and their herbs, one thing is substituted for the other – a false sense for the true literal sense. Therefore I went immediately for advice to our first leaders – to the apostles (I mean, Paul) and the prophets, who first entrusted this seed to the furrows of our souls and opened the door of understanding of the letter of Holy Scripture. I then seemed to see another sense of Scripture – the *intention* of the prophet and of the Holy Spirit speaking in him. This I call the "literal" sense – but a literal sense which coincides with the Spirit. The Spirit has conveyed no other literal sense to the prophets or to those who have open eyes, although I do not want to deny the other senses, the allegorical, tropological, and anagogical, especially where the content of the text requires it. To those who do not have open eyes but still think that they have, another literal sense takes its place, which, as the Apostle [Paul] says, kills and opposes the Spirit.

This literal sense is pursued today by the Jews, in whom even now this prophecy is being fulfilled. Their eyes are darkened so that they cannot see, and their whole outlook is seriously distorted. This kind of sense they call "literal," yet not the literal sense of their prophets, but rather of certain of their rabbis. These interpret the divine hymns of David for the most part as applying to David himself, such as his difficulties during his persecution by Saul and the other wars he fought. They do not regard him in these psalms as a prophet; rather, they regard him as a narrator of what he has seen and done, as if he were writing his own history. But David himself says regarding himself, "The Spirit of the Lord spoke through me, his word is upon my tongue." And Holy Scripture calls him the man in all of Israel to whom it was given to sing about the Christ of the God of Jacob and the true Messiah. And where else does he sing of the Christ of the God of Jacob and the true Messiah other than in the Psalms?

And so I came to believe that there is a twofold literal sense. One is the distorted sense of those who do not have open eyes and who interpret divine things according to the flesh and in human terms. The proper literal sense is grasped by those who can see and receive insight. The former is the invention of human understanding, the latter is a gift of God's Spirit, which the false sense represses, and the other exalts. Hence there seems to be good reason for the complaint of monks [*religiosi*] that when they attended a "literal" exposition, they came away from it gloomy and miserable. All their religious devotion had suddenly collapsed and disappeared, just as if icy water had been thrown on a burning fire. For just as the healthy body is aware of what is harmful to it, so also the mind is also aware of what mortifies it. Therefore I have good reason to feel that this should be avoided. We should aspire to that sense which is given life by the Spirit, just as colors are given life by light. With this goal in mind, I have tried to write a short exposition of the Psalms with the assistance of Christ, who is the key to the understanding of David. He is the one about whom David spoke, commissioned by the Holy Spirit, in the Book of Psalms.

In order that it might be clear how great the difference is between the proper and improper sense, let us consider a few examples which demonstrate this. Psalm 2: "Why do the nations conspire and the peoples plot in vain? The kings of the earth set themselves up and the rulers take counsel together against the Lord and his Christ, and so on." For the Jews, the literal sense of this passage is that the people of Palestine rose up against David, the Messiah of the Lord. But the true literal sense, according to Paul and the other Apostles, refers to Christ the Lord, the true Messiah and true Son of God (which is both true and appropriate). Now take Psalm 18. For the Jews, the literal sense here is that David expresses thanks to God for being liberated from the hands of Saul and his other enemies. Yet Paul takes the literal sense to mean Christ the Lord. The Jews understand Psalm 19 to deal with the first giving of the law. Paul takes it to be not the first but the second giving of the law when it was declared to all nations through the blessed apostles and their successors.

Comment

This is a very important passage, not least because some scholars have argued that its basic insights underlie the approach to the interpretation of the Bible adopted by the young Luther (see 2.15). Lefèvre sets out both his misgivings concerning traditional ways of reading Scripture literally, and also an alternative approach, which he regards as considerably more satisfactory.

Questions for Study

1 What does Lefèvre mean by "a twofold literal sense" of Scripture? How does he distinguish these two senses?
2 How does the use made by Lefèvre of Psalm 2 illuminate his approach?
3 What does Lefèvre mean when he declares that Christ "is the key to the understanding of David"?

2.15

Martin Luther on the Fourfold Sense of Scripture

This passage, written around 1516, sets up a contrast between the "spirit" and "flesh" which Luther (1483–1546) regards as two different ways of living, each with their associated ways of understanding the meaning of the Old Testament. Clearly dependent on the works of Jacques Lefèvre d'Etaples (see 2.14), Luther here retains the traditional fourfold scheme for interpreting Scripture (usually referred to as the *Quadriga*), while insisting that each of these four senses may be understood purely historically (relating to the history of Israel) or prophetically (relating to the coming of Jesus Christ). Thus there are two literal senses of the Old Testament, the "literal-historic" and the "literal-prophetic." The passage dates from Luther's earliest period, before his "Reformation breakthrough," and is important witness to the merging of scholastic and humanist approaches to biblical interpretation in the second decade of the sixteenth century. The eightfold interpretation of "Mount Zion" is here presented in a tabular form, to bring out Luther's meaning more clearly. See also 2.3, 2.6, 2.8, 2.9, 2.11, 2.12, 2.14.

"I will sing with the spirit, and I will also sing with the mind" (1 Corinthians 14: 15). To "sing with the spirit" is to sing with spiritual devotion and feeling, which contrasts with those who sing only with the flesh. [. . .] Those who have a purely fleshly understanding of the Psalter, such as the Jews, always apply this text to ancient history apart from Christ. But Christ has opened the mind of his people, so that they might understand the Scripture. [. . .]

Mount Zion [. . .]

according to the letter which kills	*according to the spirit which gives life*
Historically, the land of Canaan	Historically, the people living in Zion
Allegorically, the synagogue, or some person of importance in it	Allegorically, the church, or some doctor, bishop, or person of importance
Tropologically, Pharisaic and legal righteousness	Tropologically, the righteousness of faith or something else excellent
Anagogically, the future glory of the flesh	Anagogically, the eternal glory in the heavens

[. . .] In Scripture, therefore, no allegory or tropology or anagogy is valid, unless the same truth is explicitly stated in an historical manner somewhere else. Otherwise, Scripture would become ludicrous.

Comment

As we noted earlier, the fourfold medieval scheme for the interpretation of the Bible – the *Quadriga* – took the following form:

1 The literal sense.
2 The allegorical sense, which conveys something to be believed.
3 The moral (or tropological) sense, which conveys something which is to be done.
4 The anagogical sense, which conveys something which is to be hoped for.

Luther supplements this traditional reading of Scripture with the distinction introduced by Jacques Lefèvre d'Etaples, which recognized a "double literal sense" of Scripture (2.14).

Questions for Study

1 In what way does Luther's scheme represent a development of the approach offered by Jacques Lefèvre d'Etaples (2.14)?
2 How does Luther try to avoid the suggestion that he is reading into Scripture arbitrary or whimsical ideas? What limits his freedom in using the various spiritual senses of Scripture?

2.16

Martin Luther on Revelation in Christ

In the course of his major Galatians commentary of 1535, Luther turns to deal with the question of how God may be known. While affirming that God may be known through nature, Luther insists that this is a limited and inadequate knowledge of God which must be supplemented and corrected in the light of Scripture. Note the strongly Christocentric understanding of the knowledge of God which Luther develops in this passage. See also 2.39, 2.41, 2.46.

According to John 1: 18, God does not want to be known except through Christ; nor can he be known in any other way. Christ is the offspring promised to Abraham; on him God has grounded all his promises. Therefore

Christ alone is the means, the life, and the mirror through which we see God and know his will.

Through Christ God declares his favor and mercy to us. In Christ we see that God is not an angry master and judge but a gracious and kind father, who blesses us, that is, who delivers us from the law, sin, death, and every evil, and gives us righteousness and eternal life through Christ. This is a certain and true knowledge of God and divine persuasion, which does not fail, but depicts [*depingit*] God himself in a specific form, apart from which there is no God. [. . .]

Everyone naturally has a general idea that there is a God. This can be seen from Romans 1: 19–20: "To the extent that God can be known, he is known to them. For his invisible nature, etc." In any case, the various cults and the religions, past and present, among all nations are abundant evidence that at some time all people have had a general knowledge of God. Whether this was on the basis of nature or from the tradition of their parents, I do not propose to discuss now.

But someone may object: "If all people know God, why does Paul say that before the proclamation of the gospel the Galatians did not know God?" I reply that there is a twofold knowledge of God [*duplex est cognitio Dei*], general and particular. All people have the general knowledge, namely, that God exists, that he has created heaven and earth, that he is righteous, that he punishes the wicked, etc. But people do not know what God proposes concerning us, what he wants to give and to do, so that he might deliver us from sin and death, and to save us – which is the proper and the true knowledge of God [*propria et vera est cognitio Dei*]. Thus it can happen that someone's face may be familiar to me but I do not really know him, because I do not know his intentions. So it is that people know naturally that there is a God, but they do not know what he wants and what he does not want. For it is written (Romans 3: 11): "No one understands God"; and elsewhere (John 1: 18): "No one has ever seen God," that is, no one knows what the will of God is. Now what good does it do you if you know that God exists, but do not know what his will is for you? Now here others imagine things differently. The Jews imagine that it is the will of God that they should worship God according to the commandment of the Law of Moses; the Turks, that they should observe the Koran; the monk, that he should do what he has been told to do. But all of them are deceived and, as Paul says in Romans 1: 21, "become futile in their thinking." Being ignorant of what is pleasing to God and what is displeasing to him, they worship the imaginations of their own heart as though these were true God by nature, when by nature these are nothing at all.

Paul indicates this when he says: "When you did not know God," that is, when you did not know what the will of God is, "you were in bondage to beings that by nature are no gods"; that is, you were in bondage to the dreams and imaginations of your own hearts, by which you invented the idea that God is to be worshiped with this or that work or ritual." Now, because people accept this as a major premise, "There is a God," all kinds of human idolatry came into being, which would have been unknown in the world without the knowledge of divinity. But because people had this natural knowledge about God, they conceived empty and evil thoughts about God apart from and contrary to his Word; they embraced these as the very truth, and on the basis of them they imagined God otherwise than he is by his own nature. Thus a monk imagines a God who forgives sins and grants grace and eternal life on account of observance of his Rule of Life. This God does not exist anywhere; therefore [the monk] neither serves nor worships the true God; in fact, he serves and worships one who by nature is no God, namely, a figment and idol of his own heart, his own false and empty notion about God, which he supposes to be certain truth. But even reason itself is obliged to admit that human opinion is not God. Therefore whoever wants to worship God or serve him without the Word is serving, not the true God but, as Paul says, "one who by nature is no god."

Comment

This passage can be seen as an important development of Luther's "theology of the cross" (1.12), which retains his emphasis on God's self-revelation in Christ. It offers a clear distinction between a general knowledge of God, accessible to humanity as a whole, and a more specific knowledge which exists within the Christian community alone.

Questions for Study

1 What conclusions does Luther draw from his insistence that "God does not want to be known except through Christ; nor can he be known in any other way"?
2 Does Luther's insistence that revelation takes place through Christ call into question his emphasis upon the importance of Scripture as a means of revelation?
3 What role does Luther ascribe to a natural knowledge of God?

2.17

John Calvin on the Natural Knowledge of God

John Calvin (1509–64) opens the 1559 edition of his *Institutes* with a discussion of how we know anything about God. According to Calvin, a true and full knowledge of God is only available through Scripture. However, Calvin insists that a natural knowledge of God is possible, which prepares the way for the full knowledge of God, and eliminates any human excuse for being ignorant of God's existence or nature. Note especially Calvin's argument for an implanted sense of divinity within human beings. See also 2.21, 2.32, 2.49.

There is within the human mind, and that by natural instinct, a sense of divinity [*divinitatis sensus*]. This we take to be beyond controversy. So that no one might take refuge in the pretext of ignorance, God frequently renews and sometimes increases this awareness, so that all people, recognizing that there is a God and that he is their creator, are condemned by their own testimony because they have failed to worship him and to give their lives to his service. If ignorance of God is to be looked for anywhere, surely one is most likely to find an example of it amongst the more backward peoples and those who are really remote from civilization [*ab humanitatis cultu remotiores*]. Yet, in fact (as a pagan has said) there is no nation so barbarous, no people so savage, that they do not have a pervasive belief that there is a God. [...] There has been no region since the beginning of the world, no city, no home, that could exist without religion; this fact in itself points to a sense of divinity inscribed in the hearts of all people. [...]

There are innumerable witnesses in heaven and on earth that declare the wonders of his wisdom. Not only those more arcane matters for the closer observation of which astronomy, medicine, and all of natural science [*tota physica scientia*] are intended, but also those which force themselves upon the sight of even the most unlearned and ignorant peoples, so that they cannot even open their eyes without being forced to see them.

Comment

Calvin is often presented as an opponent of natural theology. However, it is important to read Calvin and let him speak his own mind on the matter of a natural knowledge of God. Many twentieth-century theologians base their understanding of Calvin on the historical sections of Karl Barth's *Church Dogmatics*, which portray Calvin as being uniformly hostile to natural theology. In fact, this is quite misleading. Nevertheless, this misunderstanding of Calvin has gained a considerable following, and it is thus important to study Calvin's own statements on the matter.

Questions for Study

1 Calvin draws a distinction between a natural knowledge of God which has been implanted within the human mind, and a natural knowledge of God which can be acquired from inspection of the natural world. What is the point of this distinction?

2 What purpose, according to Calvin, does a natural knowledge of God serve?

3 Note how Calvin especially commends the work of "astronomy, medicine, and all natural science." Given Calvin's considerable authority, might this have any bearing on the development of the natural sciences around this time, especially in areas of Europe influenced by Calvin's writings?

2.18

John Calvin on the Relation between Old and New Covenants

Martin Luther argued for a sharp distinction between "law" and "gospel." While conceding that the Old Testament contained "gospel" and the New Testament contained "law," Luther's general line of argument is that the Old Testament belongs to a different category from the New. In contrast, Calvin insists on the continuity between the Old and New Testaments. They are identical in terms of their substance; their difference relates to their administration. Calvin sets out three such points of difference. See also 2.3, 2.4, 2.6, 2.8, 2.9, 2.11, 2.12, 2.13, 2.14, 2.24.

Now from what has been said above, we can see clearly that all people who have been adopted by God into the company of his people since the beginning of the world were covenanted [*foederatos*] to him by the same law and by the bond of the same doctrine as remains in force among us. [. . .] The covenant made with all the patriarchs is so similar to ours, both in substance and in fact, that the two are really one and the same; what differences there are relate to their administration. [. . .] First, we hold that it was not material prosperity and happiness which was the goal set before the Jews, and to which they were to aspire, but the hope of immortality. Faith in this adoption was made certain to them by oracles, by the law, and by the prophets. Second, the covenant [*foedus*] by which they were bound to the Lord did not rest upon their own merits, but solely upon the mercy of the God who called them. Thirdly, they both possessed and knew Christ as mediator, through whom they were joined to God and were to benefit from his promises.

Comment

The basic approach set out by Calvin can be seen as an extension of that offered by Augustine (see 2.8), and avoids the conclusion that the Old and New Testaments are basically unrelated works, while allowing their distinct – and different – characters to be appreciated.

Questions for Study

1 According to Calvin, what are the fundamental points of difference between the Old and New Testaments?
2 In what ways does Calvin safeguard the continuity between the Testaments, while still respecting their distinctive natures?

2.19

The Council of Trent on Scripture and Tradition

The Council of Trent was the definitive Roman Catholic response to the Reformation. As part of its agenda, the Council dealt with the question of the relation of tradition and Scripture. The Council of Trent reacted forcefully to what it regarded as Protestant irresponsibility in relation to the questions of the authority and interpretation of Scripture. The Fourth Session of the Council, which concluded its deliberation on April 8, 1546, laid down the following challenges to the Protestant position.

1 Scripture could not be regarded as the only source of revelation; tradition was a vital supplement, which Protestants irresponsibly denied.
2 Trent ruled that Protestant lists of canonical books were deficient, and published a full list of works which it accepted as authoritative. This included all the apocryphal books, the canonicity of which Protestant writers had rejected.
3 The Vulgate edition of Scripture was affirmed to be reliable and authoritative.
4 The authority of the church to interpret Scripture was defended, against what the Council of Trent clearly regarded as the rampant individualism of Protestant interpreters.

Our extract is taken from the Council's statement on the relation of Scripture and tradition – the first of the four points noted above – which clearly affirms the importance of both as sources of revelation. See also 2.2, 2.10, 2.33, 2.34, 2.47, 2.50.

This truth and discipline are contained in the written books and the unwritten traditions [*in libris scriptis et sine scripto traditionibus*] which, received by the apostles from the mouth of Christ himself, or from the apostles themselves, the Holy Spirit dictating, have come down to us, transmitted as it were from hand to hand; following the examples of the orthodox Fathers, [the church] receives and venerates with an equal affection of piety, and reverence, all the books both of the Old and of the New Testament – seeing that the one God is the author of both – as also the said traditions, whether these relate to faith or to morals, as having been dictated, either by Christ's own word of mouth, or by the Holy Spirit, and preserved in the Catholic Church by a continuous succession.

Comment

The position adopted by the Council of Trent remains important for Roman Catholics, as the recent *Catechism of the Catholic Church* makes clear (2.50). This statement must therefore be seen as an important theological landmark, and its significance fully appreciated.

Questions for Study

1 Why does Trent emphasize the importance of a "continuous succession" in setting out its position on the relation of Scripture and tradition? How would this have helped it in its critique of Protestantism?
2 How does Trent distinguish between Scripture and tradition? Some interpreters of Trent have suggested that Scripture can be thought of as "the written tradition" and tradition as "the unwritten tradition." How helpful is this?
3 What does Trent mean when it states that the church "receives and venerates with an equal affection of piety" both Scripture and tradition?

2.20

The Gallic Confession on the Canon of Scripture

This Confession of Faith, published in French in 1559, sets out clearly the characteristic Protestant understanding of the canon of Scripture. Note how each book is specified by name, with variants of the name being noted (for example, in the case of Proverbs and Revelation). Note also that the letter to the Hebrews is not ascribed to St Paul, but is treated as an independent writing. This is followed by an affirmation of the authority of Scripture, in which the authority in question is clearly stated to be inherent to the Bible, rather than something which is imposed by the church. See also 2.1, 2.5, 2.7, 2.9, 2.17, 2.28.

3. All of this Holy Scripture is contained in the canonical books of the Old and New Testaments, as follows: the five books of Moses, namely Genesis, Exodus, Leviticus, Numbers, Deuteronomy; then Joshua, Judges, Ruth, the first and second books of Samuel, the first and second books of the Kings, the first and second books of the Chronicles, otherwise called Paralipomenon, the first book of Ezra; then Nehemiah, the book of Esther, Job, the Psalms of David, the Proverbs or Maxims of Solomon; the book of Ecclesiastes, called the Preacher, the Song of Solomon; then the books of Isaiah, Jeremiah, Lamentations of Jeremiah, Ezekiel, Daniel, Hosea, Joel,

Amos, Obadiah, Jonah, Micah, Nahum, Habakkuk, Zephaniah, Haggai, Zechariah, Malachi; then the holy Gospel according to St Matthew, according to St Mark, according to St Luke, and according to St John; then the second book of St Luke, otherwise called the Acts of the Apostles; then the letters of St Paul: one to the Romans, two to the Corinthians, one to the Galatians, one to the Ephesians, one to the Philippians, one to the Colossians, two to the Thessalonians, two to Timothy, one to Titus, one to Philemon; then the letter to the Hebrews, the letter of St James, the first and second letters of St Peter, the first, second, and third letters of St John, the letter of St Jude; and then the Apocalypse, or Revelation of St John.

4. We know these books to be canonical, and the sure rule of our faith, not so much by the common accord and consent of the Church, as by the testimony and inward persuasion of the Holy Spirit [*par les tesmoignage et interieure persuasion du sainct esprit*], which enables us to distinguish them from other ecclesiastical books which, however useful, can never become the basis for any articles of faith.

5. We believe that the Word contained in these books has proceeded from God, and receives its authority from him alone, and not from human beings. And in that it is the rule of all truth, containing all that is necessary for the service of God and for our salvation, it is not lawful for anyone, even for angels, to add to it, to take away from it, or to change it. It therefore follows that no authority, whether of antiquity, or custom, or numbers, or human wisdom, or judgments, or proclamations, or edicts, or decrees, or councils, or visions, or miracles, should be opposed to these Holy Scriptures, but, on the contrary, all things should be examined, regulated, and reformed according to them. And therefore we confess the three creeds as follows: the Apostles', the Nicene, and the Athanasian, because they are in accordance with the Word of God.

Comment

The important point to appreciate here is the specificity of the pronouncements. The Gallic Confession, like most Protestant works of this type, provides a detailed list of biblical works whose canonicity is not in question, for the guidance of its readers. The Confession also insists upon the supreme authority of Scripture in matters of life and thought, and states that this authority is intrinsic, not derivative – that is, that Scripture is not authoritative because some ecclesiastical authority has permitted it to possess such authority, but because this authority is already present by virtue of its inspired character.

Questions for Study

1 For what reasons does the Gallic Confession hold these books to be canonical? What alternative position exists, and how does the Confession respond to this?
2 What role does the Confession ascribe to the creeds? And in what way are these understood to relate to Scripture?

2.21

The Belgic Confession on the Book of Nature

Calvin's strong affirmation of a natural knowledge of God (see 2.17) gave a significant stimulus to the development of the concept of natural theology within the confessional element of the Reformed tradition. Thus the Gallic Confession (1559) stated that God's revelation to humanity takes two forms. First, through God's works, both in their creation and their preservation and control. Second, and more clearly, in God's Word, which was revealed through oracles in the beginning, and which was subsequently committed to writing in the books which we call the Holy Scriptures.

A related idea was set out in the Belgic Confession (1561), which expanded the brief statement on natural theology found in the Gallic Confession. Once more, knowledge of God is affirmed to come about by two means: nature and Scripture. The two themes which emerge clearly from these confessional statements can be summarized as follows:

1 There are two modes of knowing God, one through the natural order, and the second through Scripture.
2 The second mode is clearer and fuller than the first.

In what follows, we shall examine the teaching on this issue set out in the second article of the Belgic Confession – or, to use its full title, "The Confession of Faith of the Reformed Walloon and Flemish Churches" – which was drawn up by Guido des Brès in 1561. The document is clearly dependent upon the earlier Gallic Confession (1559) at points, and can be seen as an expansion of its ideas at certain places. See also 2.17, 2.25.

We know [God] in two manners. First, by the creation, preservation, and government of the universe, which is before our eyes as a most beautiful book, in which all creatures, great and small, are like so many characters leading us to contemplate the invisible things of God, namely, his eternal power and Godhead, as the Apostle Paul declares (Romans 1: 20). All of these things are sufficient to convince humanity, and leave them without excuse. Second, he makes himself known more clearly and fully to us by his holy and divine Word; that is to say, as far as is necessary for us to know in this life, to his glory and our salvation.

Comment

This brief statement proved to be of considerable importance to the development of both the biological and physical sciences in the Lowlands. The development of the microscope can be seen as an attempt to inspect the "little book" of nature in more detail, and hence to appreciate to a greater extent the wisdom of God in creation.

Questions for Study

1 How does this Confession distinguish between the two books? What are their similarities and dissimilarities?
2 How important is Romans 1: 20 as a proof text for the approach adopted by the Confession at this point?
3 According to this Confession, does the study of nature render the study of Scripture superfluous?

2.22

Melchior Cano on the Church as Interpreter of Scripture

The sixteenth century witnessed considerable disagreement over the role of the institution of the church in interpreting the Bible. In response to the rise of Protestantism, the Spanish Dominican theologian Melchior Cano (1525–60) set out eight rules for the interpretation of Scripture, in which the role of the church is particularly emphasized. This discussion extends over many pages; what follows is an abbreviated account of his eight basic points, using his own words. After stressing the obscurity of Scripture, Cano turns to consider the implications of this observation for its interpretation. See also 2.2, 2.5, 2.10, 2.19, 2.25, 2.44, 2.50.

1. If the meaning of Scripture is obscure, then the true meaning of Scripture is the meaning determined by the church [. . .]

2. The term [*nomen*] "church" is to be understood as referring not only to the assembly of all the faithful, but also to the pastors and teachers of the church, particularly when meeting together as a Council. [. . .]

3. If the Apostolic See defines the meaning of Scripture, then that is to be considered as a catholic truth [. . .]

4. An understanding of Scripture which is commonly accepted and is accepted by all the saints is a catholic truth. [. . .]

5. If it is the common custom of the church to accept a particular interpretation of Scripture from the tradition of the apostles, then that must be held as a truth of the faith [. . .]

6. If something has been held to be a dogma of faith, either by the church or by a Council which is approved by the authority of the Pope himself, or has been constantly and consistently held to be certain by all the saints, then we must accept that this is a catholic truth, and its opposite to be heretical, even if it is not stated, either clearly or obscurely, in Holy Scripture [. . .]

7. If either the church, or a Council, or the Apostolic See, or even the saints, speaking with one mind and with the same voice, derive a theological conclusion, and prescribe this to the faithful, then this must be considered to be a catholic truth just as if it had been directly revealed by Christ; just as anyone who rejects it is to be considered as much a heretic as if he had opposed the Holy Scripture, or the apostolic traditions [. . .]

8. If all the scholastic theologians have established the same firm and fixed conclusion with one voice, and if they have constantly and continually taught it as a certain theological truth to be accepted by the faithful, then it should certainly be accepted as a catholic truth.

Comment

Cano's analysis of the role of the church reflects the growing awareness of the importance of clarifying the relationship of various authorities in the interpretation of Scripture, in the light of the controversies which emerged as a result of the Protestant Reformation. Notice how Cano distinguishes the authority of the Pope, Councils, scholastic theologians, and the "saints." The context suggests that Cano uses the word "saints" to refer to patristic writers. His eight principles of biblical interpretation give the institution of the church a decisive role in biblical interpretation, while leaving certain issues unresolved – most notably, what happens when the patristic testimony is ambivalent or contradictory.

Questions for Study

1 What do you think makes Cano give such emphasis to the role of the church as the interpreter of Scripture?

2 Cano's approach reflects his core conviction that the church, considered as an assembly of believers, is older than Scripture. For at least a period of its history, the church therefore existed without a Bible. What might the theological implications of this be?

3 On the basis of Cano's criteria, should the idea of the immaculate conception of Mary (see 6.28) have been considered a theological truth at this time?

2.23

The Formula of Concord on Scripture and the Theologians

The Lutheran Formula of Concord (1577) arose through a series of 10 major internal controversies within Lutheranism during the period 1537–77. One of the points which emerged as significant was the individual theological authority of Luther and certain of his followers, such as Philip Melanchthon. Determined to ensure that Lutheranism was based on Scripture, rather than on individual theologians, the Formula asserted that the opinions of all theologians, no matter how venerable, had to be judged in the light of Scripture. See also 1.5, 1.6, 2.2, 2.5, 2.7, 2.10, 2.19, 2.21.

We believe, teach, and confess that there is only one rule and norm according to which all teachings [*dogmata*] and teachers are to be appraised and judged, which is none other than the prophetic and apostolic writings of the Old and New Testaments. [. . .] Other writings, whether of the fathers or more recent theologians, no matter what their names may be, cannot be regarded as possessing equal status to Holy Scripture. All must be considered to be subordinate to it, and to witness to the way in which the teaching of the prophets and apostles was preserved in postapostolic times and in different parts of the world. [. . .] Holy Scripture remains the only judge, rule, and norm according to which all doctrines are to be understood and judged, as to which are good or evil, and which are true or truly false. Certain other creeds [*symbola*] and writings [. . .] do not themselves possess the authority of judges, as in the case of Holy Scripture, but are witnesses of our religion as to how [the Holy Scriptures] were explained and presented.

Comment

One of the debates which raged within Lutheranism at this time was whether the teachings of Martin Luther – in many ways, the founder of Lutheranism – had supreme authority. The answer given in this document is that Scripture alone has supreme authority, even though there are many excellent and helpful things stated in the writings of others, including some more recent writers. This approach prevented Lutheranism from being simply a wooden repetition of the ideas of Luther, and encouraged its theologians to continue a direct engagement with Scripture. Luther was, in effect, being allocated a ministerial rather than a magisterial role in Lutheran theology. It is important to note that Luther is not mentioned by name; this was a sensitive subject, and the matter was treated with considerable tact and diplomacy.

Questions for Study

1 In what ways does this document affirm the supreme authority of Scripture?
2 "Other writings, whether of the fathers or more recent theologians, no matter what their names may be, cannot be regarded as possessing equal status to Holy Scripture." How would you read between these particular lines?

2.24

King James I on the Relation of Old and New Testaments

A curious work entitled *Basilikon Doron* ("the kingly gift") is one of the few works of theology ever to have been written by a British monarch. James VI of Scotland (1566–1625) succeeded Elizabeth I on her death in 1603, and became James I of England. One of his most important contributions to English-language theology was the commissioning of a new English translation of the Bible in 1604; this eventually appeared in 1611, and is widely known as the "King James Version." James was, however, himself a keen student of theology, especially the variant of Calvin's thinking which was gaining the ascendancy in Scotland in the late sixteenth century under the influence of writers such as John Knox. While still king of Scotland, James wrote the *Basilikon Doron*, basically as a primer in the art of kingship for the benefit of his son, Prince Henry. The first section of the book deals with the importance of the Christian faith for monarchs; in the course of his discussion, James sets out his understanding of the place of the Bible in general, and the relation of the Old and New Testaments in particular. Note that the English text has been modernized for the purposes of this translation. See also 2.18.

The whole Scripture is dited by God's Spirit, thereby (as by his lively word) to instruct and rule the whole Church militant, till the end of the world. It is composed of two parts, the Old and New Testament. The ground of the former is the Law, which shows our sin and contains justice. The ground of the other is Christ, who pardoning sin, contains Grace. The sum of the Law is the ten Commands, more largely dilated in the Law, interpreted by the Prophets: and by the histories are the examples shown of obedience or disobedience thereto, and what *praemium* or *poena* was accordingly given by God. But because no man was able to keep the Law, nor any part thereof, it pleased God of his infinite wisdom and goodness, to incarnate his only Son in our nature, for satisfaction of his justice in his suffering for us: that since we could not be saved by doing, we might (at least) be saved by believing. The ground therefore of the Law of Grace, is contained in the four histories of the birth, life, death, and resurrection of Christ.

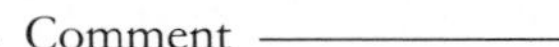

Comment

This work had little historical significance. Only half a dozen copies were produced initially, and Prince Henry died before he could do anything with the advice offered by his father. The work provides a lucid explanation of the role of the Old and New Testaments within the overall economy of salvation, viewed from a generally Reformed perspective. Note the meanings of the two Latin terms: *praemium* ("reward") and *poena* ("penalty" or "punishment"). The word "dited" is best translated into modern English as "spoken."

Questions for Study

1 How does James distinguish the Old and New Testaments?
2 What does James see as being the theological justification of the incarnation of Christ?

2.25

Roberto Bellarmine on Protestant Biblical Interpretation

The Protestant Reformation raised the question of who had the right to interpret Scripture. Roberto Bellarmine (1542–1621), one of the most articulate critics of the Reformation, argued that the Protestant response to this question ended up making the interpretation of the Bible a matter for the private judgment of the individual. Scripture, he argued, was often obscure, and needed the church as its faithful interpreter. See also 2.2, 2.5, 2.10, 2.19, 2.22, 2.44, 2.50.

Since Scripture is obscure and requires interpretation, another question emerges – namely, whether this interpretation of Scripture is to be sought in one visible, common judge, or is to be left to the judgment of each individual. This is surely a most serious question, and all controversies depend upon it [. . .]

Our [Protestant] opponents agree with us that the Scriptures ought to be interpreted in the Spirit in which they were written – that is, the Holy Spirit. The apostle Peter teaches this in 2 Peter 1, when he says, "understand this first, that no prophecies are due to individual interpretation. For the prophecies do not result from human effort. Rather, God's saints spoke as inspired by the Holy Spirit." By this, Peter shows that the Scriptures ought not to be interpreted by individual minds, but by the Holy Spirit, because they were written by the inspiration of this Holy Spirit, not the human mind.

So the whole question concerns this: where is that Spirit to be found? We maintain that this Spirit, though often absent from individual people, is most certainly to be found in the church – that is, in a Council of bishops established by the supreme pastor of the whole church, or in the supreme pastor within a Council of the other pastors. [...] We assert, in general, that the judge of the true meaning of Scripture, and of all related controversies, is the church – that is, the pontiff with a Council, on which all catholics agree, as set out explicitly in the fourth session of the Council of Trent.

But the heretics of today teach that the Holy Spirit, which interprets Scripture, is not found within a group of bishops, or any other people. Therefore each individual ought to be the judge, either by following his own spirit if he has the gift of interpretation, or by placing himself under someone who be believes to have this gift. In his preface to *Assertio omnium Articulorum*, Martin Luther clearly refers us to the spirit possessed by each person when they read Scripture [...] In his *Institutes*, John Calvin urges a precise interpretation of the definitions of Scripture, and particularly of the Holy Councils. However, he then goes on to make individual people the judges in matters of faith [*proinde privates homines iudices facit in caussa fidei*], not only in relation to the Fathers, but also the Councils. He leaves almost nothing to the common judgment of the church.

Comment

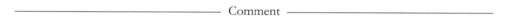

Bellarmine was one of the most successful and celebrated of the apologists for the Catholic church in the late sixteenth and early seventeenth century. This passage is extracted from his *Disputations*, which focused on debates arising from the Reformation. The extract concerns how Scripture is to be interpreted. Bellarmine's fundamental argument is that Protestantism ends up making the individual believer the judge of the meaning of the Bible, and has no real place for the corporate judgment of the church. The reference to Martin Luther concerns a defense of his early teachings, published in a work entitled "I assert all of the articles," published in 1520. The passages of the 1559 edition of Calvin's *Institutes* that Bellarmine has in mind are IV.ix.8, 12–13. Note that the phrases "supreme pastor" and "pontiff" are terms used to refer to the Pope.

Questions for Study

1 Bellarmine's approach echoes that of Melchior Cano (2.22). Why does he place such an emphasis on the role of the church?
2 In what way can Bellarmine's argument be seen as an extension of the teaching of the Council of Trent (2.19)?
3 Bellarmine's most fundamental criticism is that Protestantism lacks a legitimate corporate means for determining the meaning of the Bible, which is often obscure. How would you evaluate this argument?

2.26

The King James Translators on Biblical Translation

In 1604, King James I of England – himself a keen amateur theologian (see 2.24) – authorized the production of a new English translation of the entire Bible. The task of translation was complex, and involved six groups of translators working at Westminster, Oxford, and Cambridge over a period of several years. Each group was assigned a specific section of the Bible, including the Apocrypha, to translate. The final translation was published in 1611, and became the most influential English translation of the Bible, having exercised an immense influence over English-language literature, devotion, and worship. See also 2.6, 2.8, 2.16, 2.24

The first editions of the King James Version included a dedication "to the most high and mighty King James" and a lengthy preface entitled "The Translators to the Reader." The latter was written by Miles Smith on behalf of the entire company of 47 translators, and is generally omitted from modern editions of the work. While this is understandable, given both the length and the verbosity of the piece, this omission deprives readers of a fascinating defense of the principle of translation of the Bible into the vernacular, and the specific features of the King James Version. In what follows, we consider the defense offered by the King James Translators for providing a translation of the Bible into modern English. The text is presented in its original form, and has not been modernized.

The Scriptures then being acknowledged to be so full and so perfect, how can we excuse ourselves of negligence, if we do not study them, of curiosity, if we be not content with them? Men talk much of an olive bow wrapped about with wood, whereupon did hang figs, and bread, honey in a pot, and oil, how many sweet and goodly things it had hanging on it; of the Philosopher's stone, that it turned copper into gold; of Cornucopia, that it had all things necessary for food in it, of Panaces the herb, that it was good for diseases, of Catholicon the drug, that it is instead of all purges; of Vulcan's armor, that it was an armor of proof against all thrusts, and all blows, etc. Well, that which they falsely or vainly attributed to these things for bodily good, we may justly and with full measure ascribe unto the Scripture, for spiritual. It is not only an armor, but also a whole armory of weapons, both offensive and defensive; whereby we may save ourselves and put the enemy to flight. It is not an herb, but a tree, or rather a whole paradise of trees of life, which bring forth fruit every month, and the fruit thereof is for meat, and the leaves for medicine. It is not a pot of Manna, or a cruse of oil, which were for memory only, or for a meal's meat or two, but as it were a shower of heavenly bread sufficient for a whole host, be it never so great; and as it were a whole cellar full of oil vessels; whereby all our necessities may be provided for, and our debts discharged. In a word, it is a Panary of wholesome food, against fenowed traditions; a Physician's shop (Saint Basil called it) of preservatives against poisoned heresies; a Pandect of profitable laws, against rebellious spirits; a treasury of most costly jewels, against beggarly rudiments; finally a fountain of most pure water springing up unto everlasting life. And what marvel? The original thereof being from heaven, not from earth; the author being God, not man; the inditer, the holy spirit, not the wit of the Apostles or Prophets; the Penmen such as were sanctified from the womb, and endued with a principal portion of God's spirit; the matter, verity, piety, purity, uprightness; the form, God's word, God's testimony, God's oracles, the word of truth, the word of salvation, etc.; the effects, light of understanding, stableness of persuasion, repentance from dead works, newness of life, holiness, peace, joy in the holy Ghost; lastly, the end and reward of the study thereof, fellowship with the Saints, participation of the heavenly nature, fruition of an inheritance immortal, undefiled, and that never shall fade away: Happy is the man that delighted in the Scripture, and thrice happy that meditateth in it day and night.

But how shall men meditate in that, which they cannot understand? How shall they understand that which is kept close in an unknown tongue? As it is written, "Except I know the power of the voice, I shall be to him that speaketh, a Barbarian, and he that speaketh, shall be a Barbarian to me" (1 Corinthians 14). The Apostle excepteth no tongue; not Hebrew the ancientest, not Greek the most copious, not Latin the finest. Nature taught a natural man to confess, that all of us in those tongues which we do not understand, are plainly deaf; we may turn the deaf ear unto them. The Scythian counted the Athenian, whom he did not understand, barbarous; so the Roman did the Syrian, and the Jew (even S. Jerome himself called the Hebrew tongue barbarous, belike because it was strange to so many) so the Emperor of Constantinople calleth the Latin tongue, barbarous, though Pope Nicolas do storm at it: so the Jews long before Christ called all other nations, Lognazim, which is little better than barbarous. Therefore as one complaineth, that always in the Senate of Rome, there was one or other that called for an interpreter: so lest the Church be driven to the like exigent, it is necessary to have translations in a readiness. Translation it is that openeth the window, to let in the light; that breaketh the shell, that we may eat the kernel; that putteth aside the curtain, that we may look into the most Holy place; that removeth the cover of the well, that we may come by the water, even as Jacob rolled away the stone from the mouth of the well, by which means the flocks of Laban were watered (Genesis 29: 10). Indeed without translation into the vulgar tongue, the unlearned are but like children at Jacob's well (which is deep) (John 4: 11) without a bucket or something to draw with; or as that person mentioned by Isaiah, to whom when a sealed book was delivered, with this motion, "Read this, I pray thee", he was fain to make this answer, "I cannot, for it is sealed" (Isaiah 29: 11).

Comment

This long preface explains the reasons for producing a new English translation of the Bible. In doing so, it offers a rationale for the translation process in general, in addition to the specific translation which was now being undertaken. The work is learned and elegant, although to more modern readers it is likely to seem rather pretentious. The section chosen for study deals specifically with the spiritual benefits of biblical translation. "Fenowed" means "corrupted, decayed, or moldy."

Questions for Study

1 Note the images used in explaining the importance of translation. What did Miles Smith want his readers to understand from them? In particular, note the use of the image of the "well."
2 What spiritual benefits does Smith believe result from the reading and study of the Bible in English?

2.27

Sir Thomas Browne on the Two Books of Revelation

Sir Thomas Browne (1605–82) was educated at Winchester and Oxford, and trained for the practice of medicine. After traveling throughout continental Europe, he finally settled down as a physician in Norwich, and enjoyed a distinguished professional reputation as a scholar and antiquary. Browne's most important work is his *Religio Medici*, which seems to have been written about 1635, without actually being intended for publication. In 1642, however, two unauthorized editions appeared, and he was induced by the inaccuracies of these to issue an authorized edition in 1643. The section singled out for particular discussion is taken from Book II of the work, which deals with the question of whether the natural world can act as a window into the purposes and character of God. See also 2.17, 2.21.

Thus there are two Books from whence I collect my Divinity; besides that written one of God, another of His servant Nature, that universal and publick Manuscript, that lies expans'd unto the Eyes of all: those that never saw Him in the one, have discovered Him in the other. This was the Scripture and Theology of the Heathens: the natural motion of the Sun made them more admire Him than its supernatural station did the Children of Israel; the ordinary effects of Nature wrought more admiration in them than in the other all His Miracles. Surely the Heathens knew better how to joyn and read these mystical Letters than we Christians, who cast a more careless Eye on these common Hieroglyphicks, and disdain to suck Divinity from the flowers of Nature. Nor do I so forget God as to adore the name of Nature; which I define not, with the Schools, to be the principle of motion and rest, but that straight and regular line, that settled and constant course the Wisdom of God hath ordained the actions of His creatures, according to their several kinds. To make a revolution every day is the Nature of the Sun, because of that necessary course which God hath ordained it, from which it cannot swerve but by a faculty from that voice which first did give it motion. Now this course of Nature God seldom alters or perverts, but, like an excellent Artist, hath so contrived His work, that with the self same instrument, without a new creation, He may effect His obscurest designs. Thus He sweetneth the Water with a Wood, preserveth the Creatures in the Ark, which the blast of His mouth might have as easily created; for God is like a skilful Geometrician, who, when more easily and with one stroak of his Compass he might describe or divide a right line, had yet rather do this in a circle or longer way, according to the constituted and forelaid principles of his Art. Yet this rule of His He doth sometimes pervert, to acquaint the World with His Prerogative, lest the arrogancy of our reason should question His power, and conclude He could not. And thus I call the effects of Nature the works of God, Whose hand and instrument she only is; and therefore to ascribe His actions unto her, is to devolve the honour of the principal agent upon the instrument; which if with reason we may do, then let our hammers rise up and boast they have built our houses, and our pens receive the honour of our writings. I hold there is a general beauty in the works of God, and therefore no deformity in any kind or species of creature whatsoever. I cannot tell by what Logick we call a Toad, a Bear, or an Elephant ugly; they being created in those outward shapes and figures which best express the actions of their inward forms, and having past that general Visitation of God, Who saw that all that He had made was good, that is, conformable to His Will, which abhors deformity, and is the rule of order and beauty. There is no deformity but in Monstrosity; wherein, notwithstanding, there is a kind of Beauty; Nature so ingeniously contriving the irregular parts, as they become sometimes more remarkable than the principal Fabrick. To speak yet more narrowly, there was never any thing ugly or mis-shapen, but the Chaos; wherein, notwithstanding, (to speak strictly,) there was no deformity, because no form; nor was it yet impregnant by the voice of God. Now Nature is not at variance with Art, nor Art with Nature, they being both servants of His Providence. Art is the perfection of Nature. Were the World now as it was the sixth day, there were yet a Chaos. Nature hath made one World, and Art another. In brief, all things are artificial; for Nature is the Art of God.

Comment

The work is of particular importance on account of its full statement of the "two books" of God – that is, the "book of nature" and the "book of Scripture." Browne here builds on the ideas we noted earlier in the case of John Calvin (2.17) and the Belgic Confession (2.21). The original English orthography has been retained, partly to allow readers to gain an impression of the way in which the English language has changed over the centuries.

Questions for Study

1 How does Browne understand the "two books" to be related?
2 Browne's particular interest lies in the "book of nature." Why? And how does this interest show itself?
3 "All things are artificial; for Nature is the Art of God." The word "artificial" has changed its meaning since Browne's time; its sense here is probably best conveyed by the phrase "a work of art" or "crafted." What point does Browne make in this statement?

2.28

Francis White on Scripture and Tradition

Francis White (1564–1638), a leading representative of early seventeenth-century Anglican theology, was Bishop of Ely at the time of writing this piece. It represents a classic statement of the "Reformed Catholicism" of the Church of England at this time, combining the Reformation's insistence upon the theological priority of Scripture with a Catholic understanding of the institutional mediation of Scripture through the church. See also 2.2, 2.5, 2.10, 2.19, 2.22, 2.25, 2.44, 2.50.

The Church of England in her public and authorised doctrine and religion proceedeth in manner following. It buildeth her faith and religion upon the sacred and canonical Scriptures of the Holy Prophets and Apostles, as upon her main and prime foundation. Next unto Holy Scripture, it relieth upon the consentient testimony and authority of the Bishops and pastors of the true and ancient Catholic church; and it preferreth the sentence thereof before all other curious or profane novelties. The Holy Scripture is the fountain and lively spring, containing in all sufficiency and abundance the pure Water of Life, and whatsoever is necessary to make God's people wise unto salvation. The consentient and unanimous testimony of the true Church of Christ, in the Primitive Ages thereof, is *canalis*, a conduit pipe, to derive and convey to succeeding generations the celestial water contained in Holy Scripture. The first of these, namely the Scripture, is the sovereign authority and for itself worthy of all acceptation. The latter, namely the voice and testimony of the Primitive Church, is a ministerial and subordinate rule and guide, to preserve us and direct us in the right understanding of the Scriptures.

Comment

An issue which became significant in the theological debates between Puritans and Anglicans during this period was whether the Bible could be interpreted directly, without the need of intermediaries, or whether it was to be interpreted in the light of the teaching of the church. In this extract, White takes the latter position, arguing that the faithful need to be guided in the right interpretation of the Bible by the "consentient and unanimous testimony" of the "Primitive" (here meaning "early") church. For White, the recognition of this "ministerial and subordinate" role of tradition does not in any way compromise the basic Reformation principle of the supreme authority of the Bible; it simply enables us to interpret it more reliably.

Questions for Study

1 Read the passage carefully, noting White's vocabulary. How would you characterize his understanding of the relation of the Bible and tradition?
2 White refers to the church as a "conduit pipe." What do you think he means by this? What does this image suggest of the historical role of the church in the transmission of revelation?
3 White is clearly concerned about the emergence of "curious or profane novelties." What do you think he has in mind?

2.29

Philip Jakob Spener on Scripture and the Christian Life

A major Pietist belief was that the reading of Scripture was of central importance to the shaping of the Christian life. In his *Pia Desideria* ("Pious Longings") of 1675, Spener (1635–1705) set out a program for the revitalization of the Christian appreciation of Scripture. This program involved giving Scripture a higher priority than it had hitherto been given, along with the setting up of "church meetings" for the study of the Bible. These are generally regarded as the ancestors of the Bible study groups which are a widespread feature of many modern churches. See also 2.9.

Thought should be given to the more extensive use of the Word of God among us. We know that by nature we have no good in us. If there is to be any good in us, it must be brought about by God. To this end the Word of God is the powerful means, since faith must be enkindled through the gospel, and the law provides the rules for good works and many wonderful impulses to attain them. The more at home the Word of God is among us, the more we shall bring about faith and its fruits.

It may appear that the Word of God has sufficiently free course among us inasmuch as at various places (as in this city [Frankfurt am Main]) there is daily or frequent preaching from the pulpit. When we reflect further on the matter, however, we shall find that with respect to this first proposal, more is needed. I do not at all disapprove of the preaching of sermons in which a Christian congregation is instructed by the reading and exposition of a certain text, for I myself do this. But I find that this is not enough. In the first place, we know that "all Scripture is inspired by God and profitable for teaching, for reproof, for correction, and for training in righteousness" (2 Timothy 3: 16). Accordingly all Scripture, without exception, should be known by the congregation if we are all to receive the necessary benefit. If we put together all the passages of the Bible which in the course of many years are read to a congregation in one place, they will comprise only a very small part of the Scriptures which have been given to us. The remainder is not heard by the congregation at all, or is heard only insofar as one or another verse is quoted or alluded to in sermons, without, however, offering any understanding of the entire context, which is nevertheless of the greatest importance. In the second place, the people have little opportunity to grasp the meaning of the Scriptures except on the basis of those passages which may have been expounded to them, and even less do they have opportunity to become as practiced in them as edification requires. Meanwhile, although solitary reading of the Bible at home is in itself a splendid and praiseworthy thing, it does not accomplish enough for most people.

It should therefore be considered whether the church would not be well advised to introduce the people to Scripture in still other ways than through the customary sermons on the appointed lessons. This might be done, first of all, by diligent reading of the Holy Scriptures, especially of the New Testament. It would not be difficult for every housefather to keep a Bible, or at least a New Testament, handy and read from it every day or, if he cannot read, to have somebody else read. [. . .]

Then a second thing would be desirable in order to encourage people to read privately, namely, that where the practice can be introduced the books of the Bible be read one after another, at specified times in the public service, without further comment (unless one wished to add brief summaries). This would be intended for the edification of all, but especially of those who cannot read at all, or cannot read easily or well, or of those who do not own a copy of the Bible.

For a third thing it would perhaps not be inexpedient (and I set this down for further and more mature reflection) to reintroduce the ancient and apostolic kind of church meetings. In addition to our customary services with preaching, other assemblies would also be held in the manner in which Paul describes them in 1 Corinthians 14: 26–40. One person would not rise to preach (although this practice would be continued at other times), but others who have been blessed with gifts and knowledge would also speak and present their pious opinions on the proposed subject to the judgment of the rest, doing all this in such a way as to avoid disorder and strife.

Comment

Spener's concern in this passage is to ensure both that the Bible is read and known, and that its message should be applied to the lives of individual believers. It can be regarded as a protest against a purely formal belief, or an approach to the reading of the Bible which cultivates a detached or "academic" approach.

Questions for Study

1 What is the specific proposal that Spener is advocating in this passage? And why does he believe it to be important for both the church and for individual believers?
2 Why does Spener object to the selectivity on the part of the Lutheran preachers of his day in relation to the biblical passages which they expound? And what is his solution to this problem?
3 "The Word of God is the powerful means, since faith must be enkindled through the gospel, and the law provides the rules for good works and many wonderful impulses to attain them." Find this passage in the text. What understanding of the nature of the Bible is reflected in these words?

2.30

Nikolaus Ludwig von Zinzendorf on Reason and Experience

Pietism reacted strongly against the rationalist insistence that God could be known adequately through reason alone, believing that this failed to do justice to the experiential and relational side of the Christian life. In this passage, the noted Pietist writer Nikolaus Ludwig von Zinzendorf (1700–60) stresses the importance of the experiential aspects of faith. The experiences of faith cannot be contradicted by reason. See also 1.1, 1.2, 1.3, 1.4, 1.12, 1.16, 1.19.

1. Religion can be grasped without the conclusions of reason; otherwise no one could have religion except a person of intelligence. As a result the best theologians would be those who have the greatest reason. This cannot be believed and is contradicted by experience.

2. Religion must be a matter which is able to be grasped through experience alone without any concepts. If this were not so, someone born deaf or blind, or a

mentally deficient person [*ein wachsinniger Mensch*], or a child, could not have the religion necessary for salvation. The first could not hear the truth, the second would lack the mental ability to think about and understand matters, and the third would lack the ability to grasp concepts to put them together and to test them.

3. There is less at stake in the truth of concepts than in the truth of experience; errors in doctrine are not as bad as errors in methods and an ignorant person is not as bad as a fool.

4. Understanding which arises out of concepts changes with age, education, and other circumstances. Understanding arrived at through experience is not subject to these changes; such understanding becomes better with time and circumstances.

5. If the divinity did not give itself in a recognizable form to a person, it could not desire that this person should recognize it.

6. Revelation is indispensably necessary in human experience; however, it is not so much necessary as useful that revelation should be reduced to comprehensible concepts. [...]

11. Religion cannot be grasped by reason, so long as reason sets itself against experience.

12. The experience of something cannot be dismissed on the basis of any conclusion of reason.

Comment

Zinzendorf is here reacting against the growing trend of his day, which reached a crescendo later in the eighteenth century, to see reason as a fundamental arbiter in matters of faith and theology. While Zinzendorf is not commending an antirational or irrational approach to faith, he nevertheless raises questions about the scope of reason in faith. In particular, Zinzendorf wishes to stress the importance of personal religious experience, which he believes to lie beyond the scope of rational inquiry.

Questions for Study

1 In paragraphs (1) and (2) Zinzendorf sets out some reasons why reason must have a limited role in matters of faith. Summarize these in your own words.

2 In paragraphs (11) and (12) Zinzendorf develops his criticism of the role of reason in matters of religion. What points does he make here? Are these the same points as in (1) and (2), or are they developments of them?

3 The point made in paragraph (6) is central to Pietist thinking. Revelation is grasped in human experience; it is helpful, but not necessary, to be able to express this revelation conceptually. What attitude would you expect Zinzendorf to adopt to the teaching of systematic theology on the basis of this belief? And how does this relate to the central Pietist theme of "a living faith"?

2.31

Jonathan Edwards on the Beauty of Creation

The text which follows was never intended for publication. It is basically a collection of the notes and jottings of leading American theologian Jonathan Edwards (1703–58), now on deposit at Yale University Library. In it, Edwards develops the idea that God can be known, to a limited extent, through the created order. Like Calvin, Edwards regards nature as echoing what may be found in Scripture, while maintaining the greater clarity and authority of the latter. See also 2.17, 2.21, 2.32, 2.37.

57. It is very fit and becoming of God who is infinitely wise, so to order things that there should be a voice of His in His works, instructing those that behold him and painting forth and shewing divine mysteries and things more immediately appertaining to Himself and His spiritual kingdom. The works of God are but a kind of voice or language of God to instruct intelligent beings in things pertaining to Himself. And why should we not think that he would teach and instruct by His works in this way as well as in others, viz., by representing divine things by His works and so painting them forth, especially since we know that God hath so much delighted in this way of instruction. [...]

70. If we look on these shadows of divine things as the voice of God purposely by them teaching us these and those spiritual and divine things, to show of what excellent advantage it will be, how agreeably and clearly it will tend to convey instruction to our minds, and to impress things on the mind and to affect the mind, by that we may, as it were, have God speaking to us. Wherever we are, and whatever we are about, we may see divine things excellently represented and held forth. And it will abundantly tend to confirm the Scriptures, for there is an excellent agreement between these things and the holy Scripture. [...]

156. The book of Scripture is the interpreter of the book of nature in two ways, viz., by declaring to us those spiritual mysteries that are indeed signified and typified in the constitution of the natural world; and secondly, in actually making application of the signs and types in the book of nature as representations of those spiritual mysteries in many instances. [...]

211. The immense magnificence of the visible world in inconceivable vastness, the incomprehensible height of the heavens, etc., is but a type of the infinite magnificence, height and glory of God's world in the spiritual world: the most incomprehensible expression of His power, wisdom, holiness and love in what is wrought and brought to pass in the world, and the exceeding greatness of the moral and natural good, the light,

knowledge, holiness and happiness which shall be communicated to it, and therefore to that magnificence of the world, height of heaven. These things are often compared in such expressions: Thy mercy is great above the heavens, thy truth reacheth; thou hast for thy glory above the heavens, etc.

Comment

In many ways, the approach adopted by Edwards in these fragments parallels that of John Calvin; however, it is clear that the issue is of considerably greater importance, both theologically and spiritually, to Edwards, not least on account of the growing challenge to Christian theology posed by the rationalism of the Enlightenment. By stressing the congruence between the "book of nature" and the "book of Scripture" (see 2.21, 2.27), Edwards was attempting to show how a "religion of nature" could only find its fulfillment in the Christian gospel.

Questions for Study

1 What is the point being made in paragraph (57)? What implications does this have for natural theology, and especially the study of nature through the natural sciences?
2 What are the consequences of referring to various aspects of the created order as "shadows of divine things"?
3 In what ways, according to Edwards, does the "book of Scripture" interpret the "book of nature"?

2.32

William Paley on the Wisdom of the Creation

The English theologian and natural philosopher William Paley (1743–1805) is widely credited with having brought about a new interest and confidence in natural theology. His *Natural Theology; or Evidences of the Existence and Attributes of the Deity, Collected from the Appearances of Nature* (1802) had a profound influence on popular English religious thought in the first half of the nineteenth century, and is known to have been read by Charles Darwin. The passage for consideration is taken from the opening chapter of *Natural Theology*, which opens with the famous analogy of a watch found on a lonely heath. What, Paley asks, does this suggest to its finder? See also 2.31.

In crossing a heath, suppose I pitched my foot against a *stone*, and were asked how the stone came to be there: I might possibly answer, that, for any thing I knew to the contrary, it had lain there for ever; nor would it perhaps be very easy to show the absurdity of this answer. But suppose I had found a *watch* upon the ground, and it should be inquired how the watch happened to be in that place; I should hardly think of the answer which I had before given, – that, for any thing I knew, the watch might have always been there. Yet why should not this answer serve for the watch as well as for the stone? why is it not as admissible in the second case, as in the first? For this reason, and for no other, viz. that, when we come to inspect the watch, we perceive (what we could not discover in the stone) that its several parts are framed and put together for a purpose, e.g. that they are so formed and adjusted as to produce motion, and that motion so regulated as to point out the hour of the day; that, if the different parts had been differently shaped from what they are, of a different size from what they are, or placed after any other manner, or in any other order, than that in which they are placed, either no motion at all would have been carried on in the machine, or none which would have answered the use that is now served by it. To reckon up a few of the plainest of these parts, and of their offices, all tending to one result: We see a cylindrical box containing a coiled elastic spring, which by its endeavour to relax itself, turns round the box. We next observe a flexible chain (artificially wrought for the sake of flexure) communicating the action of the spring from the box to the fusee. We then find a series of wheels, the teeth of which catch in, and apply to, each other, conducting the motion from the fusee to the balance, and from the balance to the pointer: and at the same time, by the size and shape of those wheels, so regulating that motion, as to terminate in causing an index, by an equable and measured progression, to pass over a given space in a given time. We take notice that the wheels are made of brass in order to keep them from rust; the springs of steel, no other metal being so elastic; that over the face of the watch there is placed a glass, a material employed in no other part of the work, but in the room of which, if there had been any other than a transparent substance, the hour could not be seen without opening the case. This mechanism being observed (it requires indeed an examination of the instrument, and perhaps some previous knowledge of the subject, to perceive and understand it; but being once, as we have said, observed and understood), the inference we think is inevitable, that the watch must have had a maker: that there must have existed, at some time, and at some place or other, an artificer or artificers who formed it for the purpose which we find it actually to answer: who comprehended its construction, and designed its use.

1. Nor would it, I apprehend, weaken the conclusion, that we had never seen a watch made; that we had never known an artist capable of making one; that we were altogether incapable of executing such a piece of workmanship ourselves, or of understanding in what manner it was performed; all this being no more than what is true of some exquisite remains of ancient art, of some lost arts, and, to the generality of mankind, of the more curious productions of modern manufacture. Does one man in a million know how oval frames are turned? Ignorance of this kind exalts our opinion of the unseen and unknown artist's skill, if he be unseen and unknown, but raises no doubt in our minds of the existence and agency of such an artist, at some former time,

and in some place or other. Nor can I perceive that it varies at all the inference, whether the question arise concerning a human agent, or concerning an agent of a different species, or an agent possessing, in some respects, a different nature.

2. Neither, secondly, would it invalidate our conclusion, that the watch sometimes went wrong, or that it seldom went exactly right. The purpose of the machinery, the design, and the designer, might be evident, and in the case supposed would be evident, in whatever way we accounted for the irregularity of the movement, or whether we could account for it or not. It is not necessary that a machine be perfect, in order to shew with what design it was made: still less necessary, where the only question is, whether it were made with any design at all.

3. Nor, thirdly, would it bring any uncertainty into the argument, if there were a few parts of the watch, concerning which we could not discover, or had not yet discovered, in what manner they conduced to the general effect; or even some parts, concerning which we could not ascertain, whether they conduced to that effect in any manner whatever. For, as to the first branch of the case; if by the loss, or disorder, or decay, of the parts in question, the movement of the watch were found in fact to be stopped, or disturbed, or retarded, no doubt would remain in our minds as to the utility or intention of these parts, although we should be unable to investigate the manner according to which, or the connection by which, the ultimate effect depended upon their action or assistance; and the more complex is the machine, the more likely is this obscurity to arise. Then, as to the second thing supposed, namely, that there were parts which might be spared, without prejudice to the movement of the watch, and that we had proved this by experiment, these superfluous parts, even if we were completely assured that they were such, would not vacate the reasoning which we had instituted concerning other parts. The indication of contrivance remained, with respect to them, nearly as it was before.

4. Nor, fourthly, would any man in his senses think the existence of the watch, with its various machinery, accounted for, by being told that it was one out of possible combinations of material forms; that whatever he had found in the place where he found the watch, must have contained some internal configuration or other; and that this configuration might be the structure now exhibited, viz. of the works of a watch, as well as a different structure.

5. Nor, fifthly, would it yield his inquiry more satisfaction, to be answered, that there existed in things a principle of order, which had disposed the parts of the watch into their present form and situation. He never knew a watch made by the principle of order; nor can he even form to himself an idea of what is meant by a principle of order, distinct from the intelligence of the watchmaker.

6. Sixthly, he would be surprised to hear that the mechanism of the watch was no proof of contrivance, only a motive to induce the mind to think so.

7. And not less surprised to be informed, that the watch in his hand was nothing more than the result of the laws of *metallic* nature. It is a perversion of language to assign any law, as the efficient, operative cause of any thing. A law presupposes an agent; for it is only the mode, according to which an agent proceeds: it implies a power;

for it is the order according to which that power acts. Without this agent, without this power, which are both distinct from itself, the law does nothing, is nothing. The expression "the law of metallic nature" may sound strange and harsh to a philosophic ear; but it seems quite as justifiable as some others which are more familiar to him, such as "the law of vegetable nature", or indeed "the law of nature" in general, when assigned as the cause of phenomena, in exclusion of agency and power; or when it is substituted into the place of these.

8. Neither, lastly, would our observer be driven out of his conclusion, or from his confidence in its truth, by being told that he knew nothing at all about the matter. He knows enough for the argument: he knows the utility of the end; he knows the subserviency and adaptation of the means to the end. These points being known, his ignorance of other points, his doubts concerning other points, affect not the certainty of his reasoning, The consciousness of knowing little need not beget a distrust of that which he does know.

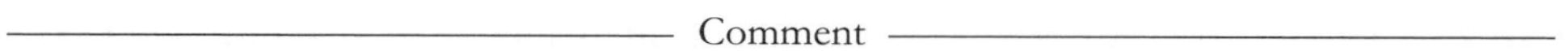

Comment

Paley was deeply impressed by Newton's discovery of the regularity of nature, especially in relation to the area usually known as "celestial mechanics." It was clear that the entire universe could be thought of as a complex mechanism, operating according to regular and understandable principles.

For Paley, the Newtonian image of the world as a mechanism immediately suggested the metaphor of a clock or watch, raising the question of who constructed the intricate mechanism which was so evidently displayed in the functioning of the world. One of Paley's most significant arguments is that mechanism implies "contrivance" – that is, design and construction for a specific purpose. Writing against the backdrop of the emerging Industrial Revolution, Paley sought to exploit the apologetic potential of the growing interest in machinery – he elsewhere singled out "watches, telescopes, stocking-mills, steam-engines" – within England's literate classes.

The general lines of Paley's approach are well known. At the time, England was experiencing the Industrial Revolution, in which machinery was coming to play an increasingly important role in industry. Paley argues that only someone who is mad would suggest that such complex mechanical technology came into being by purposeless chance. Mechanism presupposes contrivance – that is to say, a sense of purpose and an ability to design and fabricate. Both the human body in particular, and the world in general, could be seen as mechanisms which had been designed and constructed in such a manner as to achieve harmony of both means and ends. It must be stressed that Paley is not suggesting that there exists an analogy between human mechanical devices and nature. The force of his argument rests on an identity: nature *is* a mechanism, and hence was intelligently designed.

A "fusee," by the way, is a watch wheel which counterbalances the tension of the watch spring.

Questions for Study

1 Summarize the use that Paley makes of the analogy of the watch. In what way does the finding of a watch differ from the finding of a stone?
2 How much is Paley's argument shaped by the new interest in mechanical things resulting from the Industrial Revolution?
3 Paley sets out a series of eight additional reflections, relating to his analogy of the watch. Summarize the points being made in each of these eight sections.

2.33

Johann Adam Möhler on Living Tradition

In this passage, published in 1832, Johann Adam Möhler (sometimes encountered as "Moehler" in English-language works, 1796–1848), one of the founders of the influential Catholic Tübingen school, sets out an understanding of tradition as a living voice within the church, by which the Christian community's interpretation of Scripture is safeguarded from error. Möhler argues that it is of little value to have an infallible Bible, if this is constantly misunderstood or misrepresented by fallible human beings. The church is thus a divinely appointed means by which the correct interpretation of Scripture is ensured. Note in particular the declaration that "tradition is the living Word, perpetuated in the hearts of believers." The translation has been modified at points from the original English translation to take account of inaccuracies. See also 2.2, 2.5, 2.7, 2.10, 2.34, 2.47, 2.50.

The main question we must now address is this: how do we come to have possession of the true doctrine of Christ? Or, to express this in a more general and accurate manner, how do we come to a clear knowledge of the foundation of salvation, which is offered to us in Christ Jesus? The Protestant replies: "by searching Holy Scripture, which is infallible." The Catholic, on the other hand, replies: "by the Church, in which alone we arrive at a true understanding of Holy Scripture." To give a more detailed exposition of his or her views, the Catholic continues: "doubtless the Sacred Scriptures contain divine communications, and, consequently, the pure truth: whether they contain *all* the truths, which from a religious and ecclesiastical point of view are necessary, or at least very useful to be known, is a question which does not yet come under consideration." Thus, Scripture is God's unerring Word: but however the predicate of inerrability may belong to it, we ourselves are not exempt from error; indeed, we only become so when we have unerringly received the Word, which is in itself inerrable. In this reception of the Word, human activity, which is fallible, necessarily has a part.

But, in order that, in this transfer of the divine contents of the Holy Scriptures into possession of the human intellect, no gross illusion or general misrepresentation may occur, it is taught, that the Holy Spirit, to which are entrusted the guidance and vivification of the Church, becomes, in its union with the human spirit in the Church, a peculiarly Christian sense, a deep and sure feeling, which, as it abides in truth, leads also into all truth. By a confiding attachment to the perpetuated apostleship, by education in the Church, by hearing, learning, and living within her realm, by the reception of the higher principle, which renders her eternally fruitful, a deep interior sense is formed that alone is fitted for the perception and acceptance of the written word, because it entirely coincides with the sense in which the Holy Scriptures themselves were composed. If, with such a sense acquired in the Church, the sacred volume be perused, then its general essential import is conveyed unaltered to the reader's mind. Indeed, when instruction through the apostleship, and the ecclesiastical education in the way described, takes place in the individual, the Holy Scriptures are not even necessary for our acquisition of their general contents.

This is the ordinary and regular course. But errors and misunderstandings, more or less culpable, will never fail to occur; and, as in the times of the apostles, the Word of God was combated out of the Word of God, so this combat has been renewed at all times. What, under such circumstances, is the course to be pursued? How is the Divine Word to be secured against the erroneous conceptions that have arisen? The general sense decides against particular opinion – the judgment of the Church against that of the individual: the Church interprets the Holy Scriptures. The Church is the body of the Lord: it is, in its universality, his visible form – his permanent, ever-renewed, humanity – his eternal revelation. He dwells in the community; all his promises, all his gifts are bequeathed to the community – but to no individuals, as such, since the time of the apostles. This general sense, this ecclesiastical consciousness is tradition, in the subjective sense of the word. What then is tradition? The peculiar Christian sense existing in the Church, and transmitted by ecclesiastical education; yet this sense is not to be conceived as detached from its subject-matter; indeed, it is formed in and by this matter, so it may be called a full sense. Tradition is the living Word, perpetuated in the hearts of believers. To this sense, as the general sense, the interpretation of Holy Writ is entrusted. The declaration, which it pronounces on any controverted subject, is the judgment of the Church; and, therefore, the Church is judge in matters of faith. Tradition, in the objective sense, is the general faith of the Church through all ages, manifested by outward historical testimonies; in this sense, tradition is usually termed the norm, the standard of Scriptural interpretation – the rule of faith.

Comment

This important passage merits careful study, not least because Möhler shows himself aware of weaknesses in both the traditional Protestant and Roman Catholic positions. The weakness with the traditional Protestant position is set out as follows: "Thus, Scripture is God's unerring Word: but however the predicate of inerrability may belong to it, we ourselves are not exempt from error; indeed, we only become so when we have unerringly received the Word, which is in itself inerrable. In this reception of the Word, human activity, which is fallible, necessarily has a part." In other words, it is difficult to speak of an "inerrant Bible" when the meaning of that text is determined by errant interpreters. Möhler thus points to the importance of the *magisterium* in interpreting Scripture. However, Möhler is also critical of the notion of tradition as a received body of material from the past, which must be defended at all costs. In the place of this approach, he speaks of tradition as the "living Word," possessing both subjective and objective senses. Möhler's emphasis on the subjective side of tradition is of especial interest.

Questions for Study

1 Summarize Möhler's misgivings concerning existing approaches to tradition, whether Roman Catholic or Protestant.
2 What does Möhler mean when he states: "Tradition is the living Word, perpetuated in the hearts of believers"?
3 This passage incorporates some interesting reflections on the interaction of individual and corporate interpretation of the Bible, and reflection on Christian doctrines. What are Möhler's views on the limitations of the role of individuals in this matter? And how are they corrected, if at all, through the community of faith?

2.34

John Henry Newman on the Role of Tradition

One of Newman's earliest works dates from 1837, during his period as vicar of the University Church, Oxford. The *Lectures on the Prophetical Office of the Church* sets out an understanding of the place of the Church of England on an ecclesiological map. For Newman (1801–90), the Church of England is to be seen as a *via media* ("middle way") between Protestantism and Roman Catholicism. In the course of this discussion, Newman offers an analysis of the role of tradition in Christian theology, contrasting the approaches offered by Protestants and Roman Catholics, and suggesting a more acceptable synthesis of these two theological resources than he found in these two approaches. In essence, Newman sets the authority of Scripture and the patristic writers against what he sees as a Protestant emphasis upon Scripture alone, and a Roman Catholic emphasis upon the magisterium, the teaching office of the church. See also 2.2, 2.10, 2.19, 2.33, 2.47, 2.50.

Protestant denominations, I have said, however they may differ from each other in important points, so far agree, that one and all profess to appeal to Scripture, whether they be called Independents, or Baptists, or Unitarians, or Presbyterians, or Wesleyans, or by any other title. But the case is different as regards Romanists: they do not appeal to Scripture unconditionally; they are not willing to stand or fall by mere arguments from Scripture; and therefore, if we take Scripture as our ground of proof in our controversies with them, we have not yet joined issue with them. Not that they reject Scripture, it would be very unjust to say so; they would shrink from doing so, or being thought to do so; and perhaps they adhere to Scripture as closely as some of those Protestant bodies who profess to be guided by nothing else; but, though they admit Scripture to be the word of God, they conceive that it is not the whole word of God, they openly avow that they regulate their faith by something else beside Scripture, by the existing traditions of the Church. They maintain that the system of doctrine which they hold came to them from the apostles as truly and certainly as their inspired writings; so that, even if those writings had been lost, the world would still have had the blessings of a revelation. Now, they must be clearly understood if they are to be soundly refuted. We hear it said that they go by tradition, and we fancy in consequence that there are a certain definite number of statements ready framed and compiled, which they profess to have received from the apostles. One may hear the question sometimes asked, for instance, *where* their professed traditions are to be found, whether there is any *collection* of them, and whether they are printed and published.

Now though they would allow that the traditions of the Church are in fact contained in the writings of her doctors, still this question proceeds on somewhat of a misconception of their real theory, which seems to be as follows. By tradition they mean the whole system of faith and ordinances which they have received from the generation before them, and that generation again from the generation before itself. And in this sense undoubtedly we all go by tradition in matters of this world. Where is the corporation, society, or fraternity of any kind, but has certain received rules and understood practices which are nowhere put down in writing? How often do we hear it said that this or that person has "acted unusually", that so and so "was never done before", that it is "against rule", and the like; and then perhaps, to avoid the inconvenience of such irregularity in future, what was before a tacit engagement is turned into a formal and explicit order or principle. The want of a regulation must be discovered before it is supplied; and the virtual transgression of it goes before its adoption. At this very time great part of the law of the land is administered under the sanction of such a tradition; it is not contained in any formal or authoritative code, it depends on custom and precedent. There is no explicit written law, for instance, simply declaring murder to be a capital offence; unless indeed we have recourse to the divine command in the ninth chapter of the book of Genesis (Genesis 9: 6). Murderers are hanged by *custom*. Such as this is the tradition of the Church; tradition is uniform custom. When the Romanists say they adhere to tradition, they mean that they believe and act as Christians have always believed and acted; they go by the custom, as judges and juries do. And then they go on to allege that there is this important difference between their custom and all other customs in the world; that the tradition of the law, at least in its details, though it has lasted for centuries upon centuries, anyhow had a beginning in human appointments; whereas theirs, though it has a beginning too, yet, when traced back, has none short of the apostles of Christ, and is in consequence of divine not of human authority – is true and intrinsically binding as well as expedient.

If we ask why it is that these professed traditions were not reduced to writing, it is answered that the Christian doctrine, as it has proceeded from the mouth of the apostles, is too varied and too minute in its details to allow of it. No one you fall in with on the highway can tell you all his mind at once; much less could the apostles, possessed as they were of great and supernatural truths, and busied in the propagation of the Church, digest in one epistle or treatise a systematic view of the revelation made to them. And so much at all events we may grant, that they did not do so; there being confessedly little of system or completeness in any portion of the New Testament.

If again it be objected that this notion of an unwritten transmission of the truth being supposed, there is nothing to show that the faith of today was the faith of yesterday, nothing to connect this age and the apostolic, Romanists maintain, on the contrary, that over and above the corroborative though indirect testimony of ecclesiastical writers, no error could have arisen in the Church without its being protested against and put down on its first appearance; that from all parts of the Church a cry would have been raised against the novelty, and a declaration put forth, as we know was the practice of the early Church, denouncing it. And thus they would account for the indeterminateness on the one hand, yet on the other the accuracy and availableness of their existing tradition or unwritten creed. It is latent, but it lives. It is silent, like the rapids of a river, before the rocks intercept it. It is the Church's unconscious habit of opinion and feeling; which she reflects upon, masters, and expresses, according to the emergency. We see then the mistake of asking for a complete collection of the Roman traditions; as well might we ask for a collection of a man's tastes and opinions on a given subject. Tradition in its fulness is necessarily unwritten; it is the mode in which a society has felt or acted during a given period, and it cannot be circumscribed any more than a man's countenance and manner can be conveyed to strangers in any set of propositions.

Such are the traditions to which the Romanists appeal, whether viewed as latent in the Church's teaching, or as passing into writing and being fixed in the decrees of the councils or amid the works of the ancient Fathers.

Comment

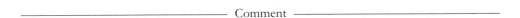

John Henry Newman is an exceptionally interesting English theologian, who began his career as an ordained minister of the Church of England, and eventually felt he had to leave that church and become a Roman Catholic. His many writings include some significant reflections on the nature of the church, and especially the role of the church and its traditions in relation to the formulation of Christian doctrine. One of Newman's more important later works specifically engages with the question of whether Christian doctrine may be said to "develop" – and, if so, what principles may be discerned as governing that development, and allowing judgments to be made as to whether certain developments in doctrine are appropriate or not.

The passage selected for study deals with the more general question of the role of the past in the interpretation of Scripture, and especially the manner in which the theological judgments of the past have relevance today, the manner in which they are transmitted, and the extent to which they should be appropriated within the Church of England in particular. Although in one sense reflecting the specifics of the debates within early Victorian Anglicanism, the points that Newman makes have much wider validity.

Questions for Study

1 Why does Newman regard the questions under discussion to be important? Why is there any need to engage with the theological debates and consensus of the past?
2 What difficulties does Newman see with a Protestant appeal to Scripture alone in the formulation of doctrine?
3 "By tradition they mean the whole system of faith and ordinances which they have received from the generation before them, and that generation again from the generation before itself." Newman adopts a slightly ambivalent attitude to the notion of "unwritten tradition," especially as he finds this idea in the writings of some Roman Catholic apologists of his day. What difficulties does he identify? And what strengths?
4 "It is latent, but it lives. It is silent, like the rapids of a river, before the rocks intercept it. It is the Church's unconscious habit of opinion and feeling; which she reflects upon, masters, and expresses, according to the emergency." Locate this passage within the text. To what does this refer? And how does Newman respond to this?

2.35

Archibald Alexander Hodge on the Inspiration of Scripture

The leading Princeton theologian Charles Hodge (1797–1878) set out a view of the authority and inspiration of the Bible which had enormous influence in nineteenth-century America. In this passage, his son Archibald Alexander Hodge (1823–86) sets out the main features of the "Old Princeton Theology" (as it is generally known) on biblical authority and inspiration in a particularly clear and direct way. Note especially how biblical authority is specifically linked with correct biblical interpretation. See also 2.9, 2.18, 2.22, 2.46.

In what Sense and to what Extent has the Church Universally Held the Bible to be Inspired?

That the sacred writers were so influenced by the Holy Spirit that their writings are as a whole and in every part God's Word to us – an authoritative revelation to us from God, indorsed by him, and sent to us as a rule of faith and practice, the original autographs of which are absolutely infallible when interpreted in the sense intended, and hence are clothed with absolute divine authority.

What is Meant by "Plenary Inspiration"?

A divine influence full and sufficient to secure its end. The end in this case secured is the perfect infallibility of the Scriptures in every part, as a record of fact and doctrine both in thought and verbal expression. So that although they come to us through the instrumentality of the minds, hearts, imaginations, consciences, and wills of men, they are nevertheless in the strictest sense the word of God.

What is Meant by the Phrase "Verbal Inspiration," and how Can it be Proved that the Words of the Bible were Inspired?

It is meant that the divine influence, of whatever kind it may have been, which accompanied the sacred writers in what they wrote, extends to their expression of their thoughts in language, as well as to the thoughts themselves. The effect being that in the original autograph copies the language expresses the thought God intended to convey with infallible accuracy, so that the words as well as the thoughts are God's revelation to us.

That this influence did extend to the words appears – first, from the very design of inspiration, which is, not to secure the infallible correctness of the opinions of the inspired men themselves [. . .] but to secure an infallible record of the truth. But a record consists of language. Second, men think in words, and the more definitely they think the more are their thoughts immediately associated with an exactly appropriate verbal expression. Infallibility of thought can not be secured or preserved independently of all infallible verbal rendering. Third, the Scriptures affirm this fact (1 Corinthians 2: 13; 1 Thessalonians 2: 13). Fourth, the New Testament writers, while quoting from the Old Testament for purposes of argument, often base their argument upon the very words used, thus ascribing authority to the word as well as the thought. [. . .]

By what Means does the Church Hold that God has Effected the Result Above Defined?

The Church doctrine recognizes the fact that every part of Scripture is at once a product of God's and of man's agency. The human writers have produced each his part in the free and natural exercise of his personal faculties under his historical conditions. God has also so acted concurrently in and through them that the whole organism of Scripture and every part thereof is his word to us, infallibly true in the sense intended and absolutely authoritative.

God's agency includes the three following elements:

1. His PROVIDENTIAL agency in producing the Scriptures. The whole course of redemption, of which revelation and inspiration are special functions, was a special providence directing the evolution of a specially providential history. Here the natural and the supernatural continually interpenetrate. But, as is of necessity the case, the natural was always the rule and the supernatural the exception; yet as little subject to accident, and as much the subject of rational design as the natural itself. Thus God providentially produced the very man for the precise occasion, with the faultless qualities, education, and gracious experience needed for the production of the intended writing. Moses, David, Isaiah, Paul, or John, genius and character, nature and grace, peasant, philosopher, or prince, the man, and with him each subtile personal accident, was providentially prepared at the proper moment as the necessary instrumental precondition of the work to be done.
2. REVELATION of truth not otherwise attainable. Whenever the writer was not possessed, or could not naturally become possessed, of the knowledge God intended to communicate, it was supernaturally revealed to him by vision or language. This revelation was supernatural, objective to the recipient, and assured to him to be truth of divine origin by appropriate evidence. This direct revelation applies to a large element of the sacred Scriptures, such as prophecies of future events, the peculiar doctrines of Christianity, the promises and threatenings of God's word, etc., but it applies by no means to all the contents of Scripture.
3. INSPIRATION. The writers were the subjects of a plenary divine influence, called inspiration, which acted upon and through their natural faculties in all they wrote, directing them in the choice of subject and the whole course of thought and verbal expression, so as while not interfering with the natural exercise of their faculties, they freely and spontaneously produce the very writing which God designed, and which thus possesses the attributes of infallibility and authority as above defined.

This inspiration differs, therefore, from revelation, first, in that it was a constant experience of the sacred writers in all they wrote, and it affects the equal infallibility of all the elements of the writings they produced. While, as before said, revelation was supernaturally vouchsafed only when it was needed. Second, in that revelation communicated objectively to the mind of the writer truth otherwise unknown. While inspiration was a divine influence flowing into the sacred writer subjectively, communicating nothing, but guiding their faculties in their natural exercise to the producing an infallible record of the matters of history, doctrine, prophecy, etc., which God designed to send through them to his Church.

Comment

A. A. Hodge can be regarded as a leading exponent of the classic Protestant position on the inspiration of Scripture, although other advocates must also be noted – such as Charles Hodge and Benjamin B. Warfield. All these theologians were professors of theology at Princeton Theological Seminary, which gained a reputation throughout the nineteenth century as a stronghold of traditional Protestant teaching on this matter. The phrase "the Old Princeton School" is often used to refer to the general view of writers such as Hodge on the authority and inspiration of Scripture.

Questions for Study

1 What does Hodge mean by the "inspiration of Scripture"? Does the word refer, according to Hodge, to the general content of the Bible, or to the specific words that it uses to convey this content?
2 How does Hodge understand the Holy Spirit and the human writers to relate in the process of inspiration? Does inspiration override the "natural exercise of their faculties"?
3 Hodge offers some "proofs" of the inspiration of the Bible. Set these out in your own words. In what sense are these "proofs"?

2.36

Benjamin Jowett on the Interpretation of Scripture

The publication of a collection of articles on aspects of Christian belief, entitled *Essays and Reviews* (1860), caused something of a scandal in conservative religious circles in England. One of the most important essays in the work was penned by classicist Benjamin Jowett (1817–93). Jowett was Master of Balliol College, Oxford, and one of England's best-known academics. In his "Essay on the Interpretation of Scripture," Jowett argued that the Bible should be interpreted in the same way as other books, such as the classics of Greek literature. The primary aim of biblical interpretation ought therefore to be to recover the authors' original meaning within their own specific historical context, rather than develop additional layers of interpretation. In the section reprinted below, Jowett summarizes his position. See also 2.3, 2.4, 2.8, 2.14, 2.15, 2.46.

[It is evident] that Scripture, like other books, has one meaning, which is to be gathered from itself without reference to the adaptations of Fathers and Divines; and without regard to *a priori* notions about its nature and origins. It is to be interpreted like other books with attention to the character of its authors, and the prevailing state of civilization and knowledge, with allowance for peculiarities of style and language, and modes of thought and figures of speech. Yet not without a sense that as we read there grows upon us the witness of God in the world, anticipating in a rude and primitive age the truth that was to be, shining more and more unto the perfect day in the life of Jesus Christ, which again is reflected from different points of view in the teaching of His Apostles.

Comment

The seven authors who contributed to *Essays and Reviews* belonged to the Broad Church party within the Church of England, a loose affiliation of generally liberal thinkers who wanted changes in doctrine and reforms in institutions based on advances in new fields of knowledge, including modern biblical hermeneutics. Jowett's essay is notable for its insistence that the insights of radical German New Testament criticism were to be welcomed, along with its insistence that later ecclesiastical interpretations of the Bible (which Jowett refers to as "the adaptations of Fathers and Divines") were to be discarded in favour of historical scholarship.

Questions for Study

1 Jowett insists that biblical passages possess only one meaning. How do you think he deals with the New Testament interpretation of Old Testament passages, which often apply ideas originally associated with Israel to Jesus Christ?
2 Do you think that Jowett's insistence on only one meaning for the biblical text, to be determined by historical scholarship, can be made to work?
3 Read the following passage from John William Burgon (1818–88), whose writings on biblical authority were greatly revered at this time: "The Bible is none other than the Voice of Him that sitteth upon the Throne – Every book of it – every chapter of it – every verse of it – every word of it – every syllable of it – (where are we to stop?) every letter of it – is the direct utterance of the Most High! The Bible is none other than the word of God – not some part of it more, some part of it less." How does Jowett's position relate to this?

2.37

Gerard Manley Hopkins on God's Grandeur in Nature

The English Jesuit writer Gerard Manley Hopkins (1844–89) was strongly influenced by the aesthetic theory of John Ruskin, and by the poetry of Anglicans such as George Herbert and Christina Rossetti. Hopkins' religious views underwent significant development during his time at Oxford, when he came under the influence of John Henry Newman, who had converted from Anglicanism to Roman Catholicism in 1845; this clearly provided Hopkins with a convenient role model. In 1866, he followed Newman into the Catholic Church. Virtually none of his poetry was published in his own lifetime. His friend Robert Bridges (1844–1930), whom he met at Oxford and who became Poet Laureate in 1913, agreed to serve as his literary executor. The recognition of Hopkins' greatness came late in the day, and it was not until the 1930s that he came to be appreciated as one of the greatest Victorian poets.

Although many consider Hopkins' greatest poem to be "The Wreck of the Deutschland," others have argued that his genius is best to be seen in his shorter poems, especially those which reflect the themes of natural theology. Perhaps the finest of his poems to address the reflection of God in the creation is "God's Grandeur." This sonnet explores the theologically important notion that God's glory flames forth from creation, like the light reflected from foil that is being shaken. See also 2.17, 2.21, 2.27, 2.31, 2.32, 2.49.

The world is charged with the grandeur of God.
It will flame out, like shining from shook foil;
It gathers to a greatness, like the ooze of oil
Crushed. Why do men then now not reck his rod?
Generations have trod, have trod, have trod;
And all is seared with trade; Bleared, smeared with toil;
And wears man's smudge and shares man's smell: the soil
Is bare now, nor can foot feel, being shod.

And for all this, nature is never spent;
There lives the dearest freshness deep down things;
And though the last lights off the black West went
Oh, morning, at the brown brink eastward, springs –
Because the Holy Ghost over the bent
World broods with warm breast and with ah! bright wings.

Comment

This celebrated poem is best understood as a statement of nature's silence in the face of its human observers. Some tread it underfoot, missing its transcendent significance. Yet the human failure to discern its capacity to point to its divine origins, and bear witness to God's glory – Hopkins here prefers to speak of "grandeur" – does not eliminate nature's God-given capacity to proclaim its maker's greatness. For Hopkins, the Holy Spirit can illuminate otherwise uncomprehending human minds, allowing them to discern the true significance of nature.

Questions for Study

1 What is the fundamental concern that Hopkins expresses in the first stanza? Is this a response to the Industrial Revolution's impact on the British landscape? Or is there something deeper at stake?
2 The sestet develops the theme of the renewal of the creation by its creator. What points does Hopkins make in this section of the poem?
3 The poem ends with a reference to the Holy Spirit. What does Hopkins mean by these lines? How does this relate to the human destruction, degradation, and disregard for nature that he highlights earlier in the poem?

2.38

Charles Gore on the Relation of Dogma to the New Testament

Charles Gore (1853–1932) is widely regarded as one of the most important English theologians of the late nineteenth and early twentieth centuries. His Bampton Lectures of 1891, entitled "The Incarnation of the Son of God," were regarded with great interest by his contemporaries. The lectures are of importance in several respects, including the obvious sympathy which they demonstrated for a "kenotic" approach to the incarnation (see "kenoticism" in Glossary). Our concern in this extract, however, has to do with the transition from the statements of the New Testament to the more advanced credal and metaphysical statements concerning Jesus Christ. Adolf von Harnack and others had suggested that this was an improper transition, resulting from the influence of Greek metaphysics on Christian theologizing (1.23). Gore, however, offers a different approach, defending such dogmatic formulas as essential if the insights of the New Testament were to be defended. See also 1.23, 1.34.

Now these decisions do, it is contended, simply express in a new form, without substantial addition, the apostolic teaching as it is represented in the New Testament. They express it in a new form for protective purposes, as a legal enactment protects a moral principle. They are developments only in the sense that they represent the apostolic teaching worked out into formulas by the aid of a terminology which was supplied by Greek dialectics.

In justifying this position, it is obvious to admit, first of all, that the earliest language of the apostolic teachers has not the explicitness of the later language of the Church. But there is a development inside the New Testament, and the reason of this gradual unfolding of teaching, in part at least intentional, is sufficiently plain. The apostles themselves had been led gradually on in correspondence with their consciences to explicit belief in Jesus Christ. They led their first disciples by a similar process. To have preached "Jesus Christ is God", nakedly and simply, would have shocked every right-minded Jew, who would have seen in the assertion the proclamation of a second God, and would have been welcomed by every pagan, only too easily, because he believed in "Gods many". Thus, according to the account given in the Acts of the Apostles, the early preaching of St Paul to the heathen goes to lay a basis of belief in the one true God as a background for Christianity, and the early preaching to Jews, or those under Jewish influence, goes to make good that Jesus was the Christ. Both Jews and Greeks are to be brought to their belief in Christ's true nature, through acceptance, along different lines of argument, of His moral authority and divine mission. They are to obey and trust Him first of all, that is, to believe in Him practically; and so afterwards to know the true doctrine about Him. Thus if you take St Paul's early epistles, those of the first two groups, or the first epistle of St Peter, or the epistle of St James, *you* find the Godhead of Jesus Christ more often implied than asserted; but when you advance a step further, *you* find it dwelt upon, and made explicit and unmistakable, though in language still carefully calculated to guard the unity of God and the truth that in the Father only is the fount of Godhead – as in the great dogmatic passages of St Paul's epistles to the Philippians and to the Colossians, or in the epistle to the Hebrews, or in St John's epistles and his Gospel.

The language of these writings is such that I say, not only that there is nothing in the decrees of the councils that is not adequately, if untechnically, represented there; but that also, whereas the decrees of the council are of the nature of safeguards, and are rather repudiations of error than sources of positive teaching, the apostolic language is a mine from which, first taught and guided by the creed of the Church, we can draw a continual and inexhaustible wealth of positive teaching. The decrees are but the hedge, the New Testament is the pasture-ground.

Comment

Charles Gore here suggests that, in order to defend the conceptual content of the New Testament, it is necessary to go beyond the vocabulary – and perhaps also the conceptuality – of the New Testament itself. Gore does not see this suggestion as in any way compromising the adequacy of the New Testament as a source of revelation; rather, he argues that the New Testament is like a "mine" from which various truths and insights can be quarried – and that certain definite principles are necessary in order to ensure that error does not arise in the process of "quarrying." It is interesting to note that both Gore and Adolf von Harnack are agreed that it is necessary to go beyond Scripture in formulating dogma; Gore, however, sees this as a perfectly proper matter, whereas Harnack believes that it inevitably involves distortion through outside influences, such as Hellenistic philosophy.

Questions for Study

1 "The decrees are but the hedge, the New Testament is the pasture-ground." What does Gore mean by this? Do you think that he is right?
2 The decrees of various councils or credal statements "simply express in a new form, without substantial addition, the apostolic teaching as it is represented in the New Testament." Locate this passage. According to Gore, why was this process necessary? And why does Gore believe that he can affirm identity of substance, yet difference of form, between dogma and the New Testament?
3 The theme of "protection" is important for Gore, and reflects his belief that dogma arose in order to protect Christian teachings against heretical viewpoints. How do you evaluate this position?

2.39

James Orr on the Centrality of Revelation for Christianity

James Orr (1834–1913) was one of the most noted Scottish theologians of the late nineteenth and early twentieth centuries. During his long period as professor at the Free Church of Scotland theological college in Glasgow, Orr produced many works relating to dogmatic theology. The present extract is taken from a series of lectures which sought to establish the centrality of the doctrine of the incarnation to Christian life and thought – a common theme at this point in British theological reflection. Orr's particular concern at this juncture is to demonstrate that the concept of revelation is central to Christianity. If this concept is denied, or its content deformed, Christian thought and life would be robbed of their distinctive nature. See also 2.40, 2.41.

In entering on the task of unfolding the Christian view of the world under its positive aspects, and of considering its relations to modern thought, I begin where religion itself begins, with the existence of God. Christianity is a theistic system; this is the first postulate – the personal, ethical, self-revealing God.

Volkmar has remarked that of monotheistic religions there are only three in the world – the Israelitish, the Christian, and the Mohammedan; and the last-named is derived from the other two. "So," he adds, "is the 'Israel of God' the one truly religious, the religiously-elect, people of antiquity; and ancient Israel remains for each worshipper of the one, therefore of the true God, who alone is worthy of the name, the classical people.... Christianity is the blossom and fruit of the true worship of God in Israel, which has become such for all mankind." This limitation of Monotheism in religion to the peoples who have benefited by the Biblical teaching on this subject, suggests its origin from a higher than human source; and refutes the contention of those who would persuade us that the monotheistic idea is the result of a long process of development through which the race necessarily passes, beginning with Fetishism, or perhaps Ghost-worship, mounting to Polytheism, and ultimately subsuming the multitude of Divine powers under one all-controlling will. It will be time enough to accept this theory when, outside the line of the Biblical development, a single nation can be pointed to which has gone through these stages, and reached this goal.

I should like further at the outset to direct attention to the fact that, in affirming the existence of God as Theism apprehends Him, we have already taken a great step into the supernatural, a step which should make many others easy. Many speak glibly of the denial of the supernatural, who never realise how much of the supernatural they have already admitted in affirming the existence of a personal, wise, holy, and beneficent Author of the universe. They may deny supernatural actions in the sense of miracles, but they have affirmed supernatural Being on a scale and in a degree which casts supernatural action quite into the shade. If God is a reality, the whole universe rests on a supernatural basis. A supernatural presence pervades it; a supernatural power sustains it; a supernatural will operates in its forces; a supernatural wisdom appoints its ends. The whole visible order of things rests on another, an unseen, spiritual, supernatural order, – and is the symbol, the manifestation, the revelation of it. It is therefore only to be expected that the feeling should grow increasingly in the minds of thoughtful men, that if this supernatural basis of the universe is to be acknowledged, a great deal more must be admitted besides. On the other hand, if the opposition to the supernatural is to be carried out to its logical issue, it must not stop with the denial of miracle, but must extend to the whole theistic conception. This is the secret of the intimate connection which I showed in the last Lecture to exist between the idea of God and the idea of Revelation. A genuine Theism can never long remain a bare Theism. At the height to which Christianity has raised our thoughts of God, it is becoming constantly more difficult for minds that reflect seriously to believe in a God who does not manifest Himself in word and deed. This is well brought out in a memorable conversation which Mr Froude had with Mr Carlyle in the last days of his life. "I once said to him," says Mr Froude, "not long before his death, that I could only believe in a God which did something. With a cry of pain, which I shall never forget, he said, 'He does nothing.' " This simply means that if we are to retain the idea of a living God, we must be in earnest with it. We must believe in a God who expresses Himself in living deeds in the history of mankind, who has a word and message for mankind, who, having the power and the will to bless mankind, does it. Theism, as I contended before, needs Revelation to complete it.

Here, accordingly, it is that the Christian view of God has its strength against any conception of God based on mere grounds of natural theology. It binds together, in the closest reciprocal relations, the two ideas of God and Revelation. The Christian doctrine, while including all that the word Theism ordinarily covers, is much more than a doctrine of simple Theism. God, in the Christian view, is a Being who enters into the history of the world in the most living way. He is not only actively present in the material universe, – ordering, guiding, controlling it, – but He enters also in the most direct way into the course of human history, working in it in His general and special providence, and by a gradual and progressive Revelation, which is, at the same time, practical discipline and education, giving to man that knowledge of Himself by which he is enabled to attain the highest ends of his own existence, and to co-operate freely in the carrying out of Divine ends; above all, discovering Himself as the God of Redemption, who, full of long-suffering and mercy, executes in loving deeds, and at infinite sacrifice, His gracious purpose for the salvation of mankind. The Christian view of God is thus bound up with all the remaining elements of the Christian system, – with the idea of Revelation in Christ, with a kingdom of God to be realised through Christ, with Redemption from sin in Christ, – and it is inseparable from them. It is through these elements – not in its abstract character as Theism – that it takes the hold it does on the living convictions of men, and is felt by them to be something real. If I undertake to defend Theism, it is not Theism in dissociation from Revelation, but Theism as completed in the entire Christian view.

Comment

In the course of this passage, Orr deals with a number of nineteenth-century writers who have now been forgotten, such as Herntrich Volkmar. This inevitably makes it more difficult to interact with the text, in that a certain knowledge of at least something of what such writers argued is needed to make sense of Orr's analysis. However, the basic points that Orr wishes to make can still be identified without difficulty, despite this interaction with the writers of his own day. The fundamental theme is whether revelation is necessary for the Christian faith. Orr affirms that this is so, and offers some specific reasons for his assertion.

Questions for Study

1 How does Orr respond to the suggestion that natural theology is perfectly adequate on its own as a source for knowledge of God or religious beliefs?

2 Give an explanation of Orr's understanding of the relationship of Christianity to "Theism." Are they the same thing? And if not, in what do the differences lie?

3 "We must believe in a God who expresses Himself in living deeds in the history of mankind, who has a word and message for mankind, who, having the power and the will to bless mankind, does it." Locate this text within the passage. What does Orr mean by this? And how does this text relate to his general concern to defend the necessity of revelation?

2.40

Wilhelm Herrmann on the Nature of Revelation

Wilhelm Herrmann (1846–1922) is widely regarded as the most important German liberal Protestant theologian of the era immediately preceding World War I, standing in direct succession to F. D. E. Schleiermacher and A. B. Ritschl. Herrmann's long period as professor of systematic theology at the University of Marburg from 1879 gave him a dominant influence over a rising generation of theologians, including the young Karl Barth. One of Herrmann's most important writings is *The Communion of the Christian with God* (1886), which sets out many of his most distinctive ideas, including his emphasis on the importance of the historical figure of Jesus of Nazareth as the basis for the Christian's knowledge and experience of God. See also 2.41, 2.42.

1 Revelation as Communicated Knowledge

We may speak of having communion with God only when we are certain that God speaks clearly to us, and also hears and considers our speech in his operations.

In order to commune with us, God makes himself known to us. The God of whose communion with men the Sacred Scripture tells, does not, for his own holiness' sake, suffer men to reach him through any efforts of their own. He will vouchsafe this in one way alone, and that way he opens to us himself. Now, further, if it is impossible for a man to rise unaided above all fightings and doubts into the realm of real communion with God, it is equally certain that no mere information of any kind concerning God could thus raise a man, even although that information should claim to be a divine revelation. We might indeed form a conception of God on the ground of such information. We might consent to acknowledge the reality of that revelation, and we might therefore believe our conception of God to be correct. But in that case we should still have to win for ourselves the impression that the God thus revealed did actually commune with us. If we had received only information concerning God, it would still be left to us to obtain the certainty of a real communion of God with ourselves. And no such endeavour of ours could ever conquer doubt, for it is just amid such endeavours that doubt does always rise. *Information concerning God*, therefore, although it may claim to be of divine revelation, can only bring that troubled piety which lives by no delivering act of God, but by men's own exertions. God has left us in no such miserable condition, and Protestants, at least, may know this, if they will only refuse to be led aside from the one thing needful by common cries like the following: "you must believe that God made the world; that men sprang from a single pair; that God's Son became a man; that God's demand for the punishment of the guilty has been satisfied by the death of his Son; and finally that all this happened for your sake." He who determines so to believe, can only cause distress to his soul. For in such doctrines, however true they may be in themselves, we are not brought face to face with that reality which gives faith its certainty; they simply tell us something, and we are then expected by our own efforts to hold that information to be true.

2 Revelation as Inward Experience

But we leave all these fruitless endeavours at religious self-help behind, when we entirely reject the idea that we are to believe doctrines. Untroubled by these suggestions we must put ourselves the one question: "Whereby shall we know that a living God is communing with us?" Then, when we come to see and understand the reality which makes us certain of this fact, we see also that the painful effort which had been demanded of us is taken away by God's own act. For when the Christian has once experienced the fact that God is striving to make himself known to him, and when he sees how God so strives, then he begins to see also what is true in those aforesaid doctrines.

God makes himself known to us, so that we may recognise him, through *a fact, on the strength of which we are able to believe on him*. No doctrine of any kind can do more than tell us how we ought to represent God to ourselves. No doctrine can bring it about that there shall arise in our hearts the full certainty that God actually exists for us; only a fact can inspire such confidence within us. Now we Christians hold that we know only one fact in the whole world which can overcome every doubt of the reality of God, namely, the appearance of Jesus in history, the story of which has been preserved for us in the New Testament. Our certainty of God may be kindled by many other experiences, but has ultimately its firmest basis in the fact that within the realm of history to which we ourselves belong, we encounter the man Jesus as an undoubted reality.

Of course, we may have heard about Jesus for a long time without his becoming manifest to us in his power. We can hardly put it that it is only in the vision of the Person of Jesus that our eyes are first opened to the invisible. Probably for all of us that revelation comes from those in our immediate circle, and we ought in our turn to do a like service to others. But such men, in whose earnestness and brotherly love we can trace a hidden life with God, are fragments of God's revelation. The whole revelation that God has ordained for us in our historical situation is ours only when we can see that the Person of Jesus surpasses all else that is great and noble in humanity, and that behind those whose influence upon us is strongest, he is visible as their life-giver and their Lord. The revelation of God that we get from those of our most immediate circle is not pushed aside or emptied of its value, but only deepened and perfected as we become acquainted with Jesus himself.

The true Christian confession is that Jesus is the Christ. Rightly understood, however, it means nothing else than this: that through the man Jesus we are first lifted into a true fellowship with God. If it be asked what we are to understand by that, the reply is that for those who truly seek God it should be wonderfully simple. But it is often made difficult by those thieves amid Christendom (John 10. 1), who pretend to come into fellowship with God by some other way than through the man Jesus. The by-path most frequented is that of doctrines concerning Jesus which give him the highest praise, and so form the most convenient means of avoiding his Person. By this means the only way of salvation is closed to persons without number. The divinely simple fact that the man Jesus is the Christ is made distasteful to them by the idea instilled into them that they may come into possession of much higher things, namely, a number of wonderful doctrines, the *fides quae creditur*, by simply believing them. The result is that even among us Protestants it has become very difficult for the majority to regard the finding of God as the highest good, or even to look upon it as a wonderful gift from him at all. Most men think it of small importance that Jesus alone makes us certain of a living God, for they imagine that of all the doctrines in which they "believe" the doctrine of the existence of God is the most elementary.

Comment

Wilhelm Herrmann may be regarded as continuing and developing the Ritschlian approach to the religious life in general, and to Christology in particular. Like Schleiermacher and Ritschl before him, he insists upon the close relationship of Christology and soteriology: who Christ is becomes known through his effect upon us. The religious importance of Jesus resides in his religious personality, specifically his "inner being," and the impact which this makes upon the heart of the believer.

It is possible to arrive at a certainty of faith, not on the basis of critical-historical research, but upon the subjective impression which the Jesus of the Gospels makes upon the sensitive reader. As Hermann argued elsewhere in this same work, "If we understand by God a power which so affects us that we, through this experience, gain strength to overcome the world, it is self-evident that we can know this God only in so far as he reveals himself to us by this work in us." This also points to a central theme of Herrmann's thought – the notion of revelation, which at points appears to become synonymous with "the work of God within us." It must, however, be stressed that Herrmann does not understand revelation to mean a generally valid knowledge; rather, he takes it to mean a human experience, in which one becomes aware of a divine, life-giving power. This point comes out clearly in the passage under consideration.

Questions for Study

1 What does Herrmann understand by the word "revelation"?
2 In what way does Herrmann involve human experience in the theme of revelation? Does revelation take place within the realm of religious experience, or in the form of concepts of divinity?
3 "Our certainty of God may be kindled by many other experiences, but has ultimately its firmest basis in the fact that within the realm of history to which we ourselves belong, we encounter the man Jesus as an undoubted reality." Locate this text within the passage. What does Herrmann mean by this? And how does this relate to his conception of revelation?

2.41

Karl Barth on Revelation as God's Self-Disclosure

In this important passage from the first half-volume of the *Church Dogmatics*, written in German in 1932, Barth (1886–1968) sets out his understanding of the relationship between "revelation," "the Word of God," and Jesus Christ. It is a complex and nuanced account, which places emphasis on the necessity of divine revelation if human beings are to know anything of God. The German word *Mensch*, here translated as "man," is actually common gender, and should be translated as "a human person." See also 2.39, 2.40, 2.46, 2.48.

Primarily and originally the Word of God is undoubtedly the Word that God speaks by and to himself in eternal concealment. We shall have to return to this great and inalienable truth when we develop the concept of revelation in the context of the doctrine of the Trinity. But undoubtedly, too, it is the Word that is spoken to men in revelation, Scripture and preaching. Hence we cannot speak or think of it at all without remembering at once the man who hears and knows it. The Word of God, Jesus Christ, as the being of the Church, sets us ineluctably before the realization that it was and will be men who are intended and addressed and therefore characterized as recipients but as also themselves bearers of this Word. The Word of God thus sets us before the so-to-speak anthropological problem. How then can men be this? Before the "so-to-speak" anthropological problem, I said, and I indicated thereby that it can be called this only with some reserve. Or is this not so? Shall we say unreservedly that the question of the possibility of the knowledge of God's Word is a question of anthropology? Shall we ask what man generally and as such, in addition to all else he can do, can or cannot do in this regard? Is there a general truth about man which can be made generally perceptible and which includes within it man's ability to know the Word of God? We must put this question because an almost invincible development in the history of Protestant theology since the Reformation has led to an impressive affirmative answer to this question in the whole wing of the Church that we have called Modernist. [. . .]

The question is whether this event ranks with the other events that might enter man's reality in such a way that to be able to enter it actually requires on man's part a potentiality which is bought by man as such, which consists in a disposition native to him as man, in an organ, in a positive or even a negative property that can be reached and discovered by self-reflection, by anthropological analysis of his existence, in short, in what philosophy of the Kantian type calls a faculty.

It might also be that this event did not so much presuppose the corresponding possibility on man's part as bring it with it and confer it on man by being event, so that it is man's possibility without ceasing (as such) to be wholly and utterly the possibility proper to the Word of God and to it alone. We might also be dealing with a possibility of knowledge which can be made intelligible as a possibility of man, but, in contrast to all others, only in terms of the object of knowledge or the reality of knowledge and not at all in terms of the subject of knowledge, i.e., man as such. In the light of the nature of God's Word, and especially of what we said above about its purposiveness or pertinence, its being aimed at man, its character as an address to man, we must decide against the first view and in favour of the second. From this standpoint, the same that concerns us here, we had to understand the Word of God as the act of God's free love and not as if the addressed and hearing man were in any way essential to the concept of the Word of God. That man is the recipient of God's Word is, to the extent that it is true, a fact, and it cannot be deduced from anything we might previously know about God's nature. Even less, of course, can it be deduced from anything we previously knew about the nature of man. God's Word is no longer grace, and grace itself is no longer grace, if we ascribe to man a predisposition towards this Word, a possibility of knowledge regarding it that is intrinsically and independently native to him. But the same results from what was said in the same passage about the content of the Word of God addressed to man.

We then made the assertion that this content, whatever it might be *in concretissimo* for this man or that man, will always be an authentic and definitive encounter with the Lord of man, a revelation which man cannot achieve himself, the revelation of something new which can only be told him. It will also be the limitation of his existence by the absolute "out there" of his Creator, a limitation on the basis of which he can understand himself only as created out of nothing and upheld over nothing. It will also be a radical renewal and therewith an obviously radical criticism of the whole of his present existence, a renewal and a criticism on the basis of which he can understand himself only as created out of nothing and upheld over nothing. It will also be a radical renewal and therewith an obviously radical criticism of the whole of his present existence, a renewal and a criticism on the basis of which he can understand himself only as a sinner living by grace and therefore as a lost sinner closed up against God on his side. Finally it will be the presence of God as the One who comes, the Future One in the strict sense, the Eternal Lord and Redeemer of man, a presence on the basis of which he can understand himself only as hastening towards this future of the Lord and expecting him. To be sure, it is not these formulae which describe the real content of the Word of God, but the content of the Word which God himself speaks and which he does so always as these formulae indicate, the real content of the real Word of God, that tells man also that there can be no question of any ability to hear or understand or know on his part, of any capability that he the creature, the sinner, the one who waits, has to bring to this Word, but that the possibility of knowledge corresponding to the real Word of God that it represents an inconceivable *novum* compared to all his ability and capability, and that it is to be understood as a pure fact, in exactly the same way as the real Word of God itself.

Comment

This is an important passage, which sets out the basic themes of Barth's theology of revelation and forges a connection between the actuality of revelation and the doctrine of the Trinity. One of the most interesting aspects of Barth's theology is the vigorous theological link which he establishes between the fact that revelation has taken place and the doctrine of the triunity of God. Historically, there is little doubt that the very considerable revival of interest in the doctrine of the Trinity in the second half of the twentieth century owes much to Barth's stimulus. Barth uses two Latin terms that might need comment: *in concretissimo* is best translated as "in actuality," and *novum* as "new thing."

Questions for Study

1 Why is Barth so anxious that discussion of the "Word of God" might become a question of anthropology? What is the general issue that troubles him at this point? Why does he not like the idea of speaking about a "predisposition towards this Word" within human nature?
2 On the basis of this passage, what does Barth understand by the phrase "the Word of God"?
3 "The Word of God, Jesus Christ, as the being of the Church, sets us ineluctably before the realization that it was and will be men who are intended and addressed and therefore characterized as recipients but as also themselves bearers of this Word." Locate this text within the passage as a whole. What does Barth mean by this? And what point does he make by identifying the dual aspect of humanity as recipients and bearers of the Word?

2.42

Emil Brunner on the Personal Nature of Revelation

During the 1930s, a growing alienation developed between Emil Brunner and Karl Barth. Although both writers were initially regarded as "dialectical theologians," stressing the "otherness" of God over and against humanity, Brunner came increasingly to place emphasis upon the personal disclosure of God to humanity, with this latter being the "conversation-partner of God." In this passage, Brunner (1889–1966) stresses the personal nature of divine revelation, which is an integral aspect of his notion of this divine–human dialogue. See also 2.41.

The self-revelation of God is no object, but wholly the doing and self-giving of a subject – or, better expressed, a Person. A Person who is revealing himself, a Person who demands and offers Lordship and fellowship with himself, is the most radical antithesis to everything that could be called object or objective. Likewise, the personal act of trust is something quite other than subjectivity – that subjectivity which can become actual only when it is over against an object, that subjectivity which appropriates what is foreign to it. If we were to speak of appropriation in this context, it could be only of such a kind as when man gives himself to God to be owned by him. But if we know as believers, we recognize what is meant here, that that which happens in revelation and faith cannot be pushed into the framework of truth and knowledge of truth without its becoming in that way something quite different. Yet in the Bible what we have been talking about is just what is called truth. [. . .] This Biblical "truth" is as different from what otherwise is called truth as this personal encounter and the double-sided self-giving and its resulting fellowship are different from the comprehension of facts by means of reasoning. This is not to say that there do not also exist between both this Biblical and the general rational conception of truth positive relations outside of these differences. [. . .] The concern of the Bible is personal correspondence as it is realized in the correlation between the Word of God and faith; and, contrariwise, such an understanding of the concept of the Word of God and faith as is yielded by reflection about the fundamental Biblical category of personal correspondence. Through it the Biblical conception of truth is determined and differentiated from every other understanding of truth.

Comment

It is clear that Brunner's thinking has been influenced by the "personalist" philosophy of the Jewish writer Martin Buber at this point. In his major work *I and You* (1927) (*Ich und Du*; often translated as "I and Thou"), Buber drew a fundamental distinction between two categories of relations: *I–You* relations, which are "personal," and *I–It* relations, which are impersonal. Buber argues that an "I–You" relation exists between two active subjects, between two *persons*. It is something which is *mutual* and *reciprocal*. "The I of the primary word I–You makes its appearance as a person, and becomes conscious of itself." In other words, Buber is suggesting that human personal relationships exemplify the essential features of an I–You relation. It is the relationship itself, that intangible and invisible bond which links two persons, which is the heart of Buber's idea of an I–You relation.

Brunner applies this idea of an "I–You" relationship to the doctrine of revelation. Revelation, Brunner argues, cannot simply be the communication of information, for this implies that God is an "It." If God is indeed a "You," revelation must take the form of a personal disclosure.

Questions for Study

1 Explain why Brunner places so much emphasis on the concept of a "Person" in the opening section of this passage.

2 For Brunner, the biblical notion of truth implies a personal relationship, or "personal correspondence." Why does he think this? And what concepts of revelation does he appear to critique in setting out this position?
3 "A Person who is revealing himself, a Person who demands and offers Lordship and fellowship with himself, is the most radical antithesis to everything that could be called object or objective." What does Brunner mean by this?

2.43

Rudolf Bultmann on Demythologization and Biblical Interpretation

On June 4, 1941, Rudolf Bultmann (1884–1976) delivered a lecture which introduced the phrase "the demythologization of the New Testament." The basic contention of this controversial lecture was that the New Testament proclamation or *kerygma* concerning Christ is stated and understood in mythological terms (which Bultmann attempted to derive from existing Jewish apocalyptic and Gnostic redemption myths, borrowing ideas deriving from the "history of religions school") which, although perfectly legitimate and intelligible in the first century, cannot be taken seriously today. It is therefore the task of New Testament interpretation to eliminate this mythological cosmology, and extract the existential truths which lie beneath it. See also 2.3, 2.4, 2.6, 2.8, 2.9, 2.11, 2.12, 2.13, 2.14, 10.19.

The cosmology of the New Testament is essentially mythical in character. The world is viewed as a three-storied structure with the earth in the center, the heaven above, and the underworld beneath. [...] History does not follow a smooth unbroken course; it is set in motion and controlled by supernatural forces. This aeon is held in bondage by Satan, sin and death [...] and hastens towards its end. That end will come very soon, and will take the form of a cosmic catastrophe. It will be inaugurated by the "woes" of the last time. Then the Judge will come from heaven, the dead will rise, the last judgement will take place, and people will enter into eternal salvation or damnation. This, then, is the mythical view of the world which the New Testament presupposes when it presents the event of redemption which is the subject of its preaching. [...]

Can Christian preaching expect modern people to accept the mythical view of the world as true? To do so would be both senseless and impossible. It would be senseless, because there is nothing specifically Christian in the mythical view of the world as such. It is simply the cosmology of a pre-scientific age. Again, it would be impossible, because nobody can adopt a view of the world as a matter of choice; it has already been determined by our place in history. [...] It is impossible to use electric light and the wireless and to avail ourselves of modern medical and surgical discoveries, and at the same time to believe in the New Testament world of spirits and miracles. [...]

The real purpose of myth is not to present an objective picture of the world as it is, but to express human understandings of themselves in the world in which they live. Myth should be interpreted not cosmologically, but anthropologically, or better still, existentially. [...] Hence the importance of New Testament mythology lies not in its imagery but in the understanding of existence which it enshrines. The real question is whether this understanding of existence is true. Faith claims that it is, and faith ought not to be tied down to the imagery of New Testament mythology. [...] Our task is to produce an existentialist interpretation of the dualistic mythology of the New Testament. [...] We have to discover whether the New Testament offers us an understanding of ourselves which will challenge us to a genuine existential decision.

Comment

Bultmann follows Wilhelm Herrmann in emphasizing that theological statements cannot, in principle, be made about God as he is in himself, but rather as he relates to us (see 2.40). Therefore, according to Bultmann, they must consist in statements concerning the human existential situation. For Bultmann, the New Testament makes statements about God, which are to be interpreted in terms of human existence. Bultmann therefore argues that it is both possible and necessary to interpret the New Testament myths in existentialist terms. It must be emphasized that the term "myth," as used by Bultmann, does not in any way imply that the "religious story" in question is in any sense untrue. Indeed, Bultmann defines myth as a form of thought which seeks to represent a transcendent reality in this-worldly terms. Bultmann declares that these stories possess an underlying existential meaning, which can be perceived and appropriated by a suitable process of interpretation.

Bultmann's theology may be regarded as an ellipse constructed around two foci: first, the program of demythologization, or existential interpretation, of the New Testament; second, the idea of the *kerygma*, the proclamation of a divine word addressed to us, occasioning an existential crisis and demanding an existential decision on our part. Beneath the strange language of the New Testament lies the proclamation of a way of life which is a present possibility for us and which we may appropriate as our own. The "husk" of the myth contains the "kernel" of the *kerygma*: by translating the mythological "husk" into contemporary existential terms, the heart of the Christian proclamation may be recovered and made intelligible to modern humanity.

Questions for Study

1 What reasons does Bultmann give for abandoning what he terms a "pre-scientific" worldview? Bultmann argues that to abandon such a worldview is simply to eliminate archaic ways of thinking from the Christian gospel. What reasons does he give for this assertion? How do you respond?

2 "The real purpose of myth is not to present an objective picture of the world as it is, but to express human understandings of themselves in the world in which they live." Locate this passage within the text. What understanding of "myth" does it embody?
3 What does Bultmann understand by "demythologization"? How would he respond to the criticism that he is, in fact, remythologizing, in that he is casting the gospel in terms of twentieth-century "human understandings of themselves in the world in which they live" – existentialism – which is, by Bultmann's own criteria, a "myth," in the technical sense of the term?
4 How does Bultmann's approach to myth relate to that of C. S. Lewis (see 9.5)?

2.44

Karl Rahner on the Authority of Scripture

Karl Rahner (1904–84), one of the most influential Catholic theologians of the twentieth century, here explores the issue of biblical authority from a Catholic perspective. Note in particular the constant emphasis on the mutually interrelated character of church and Scripture. Rahner also explores two other issues of considerable importance to the theme of the authority of Scripture: the manner in which Scripture relates to Jesus Christ, and the hermeneutical issues associated with the interpretation of Scripture. See also 2.2, 2.5, 2.7, 2.10, 2.19, 2.22, 2.50.

We regard [Holy Scripture] as the church's book, the book in which the church of the beginning always remains tangible as a norm for us in the concrete. Indeed it is a norm which is already distinguished from those things which are found in the original church but which cannot have a normative character for our faith and for the life of the later church. If the church in every age remains bound to its origins in its faith and in its life; if the church as the community of faith in the crucified and risen Jesus is itself to be in its faith and in its life the eschatological and irreversible sign of God's definitive turning to the world in Jesus Christ, a sign without which Jesus Christ himself would not signify God's irreversible coming into the world and would not be the absolute savior; and if this church of the beginning objectifies itself in scriptural documents at least in fact, and also does so necessarily given the historical and cultural presuppositions in which the church came to be, then in all of this together we have a point of departure for understanding the essence of scripture.

It is also a point of departure from whose perspective we can arrive at an adequate and at the same time a critical understanding of what is really meant by the inspiration of scripture and by a binding canon of scripture. Since scripture is something derivative, it must be understood from the essential nature of the church, which is the eschatological and irreversible permanence of Jesus Christ in history. It is to be understood from this perspective as something normative in the church. [...]

During the apostolic age the real theological essence of the church is constituted in a historical process in which the church comes to the fullness of this essence and to the possession of this essence in faith. This self-constitution of the essence of the church until it reaches its full historical existence (and it is not until then that it can fully be the norm for the future church) implies written objectifications. Therefore this process is *also*, but not exclusively, the process of the formation of the canon: the church objectifies its faith and its life in written documents, and it recognizes these objectifications as so pure and so successful that they are able to hand on the apostolic church as a norm for future ages. From this perspective there is no insuperable difficulty with the fact that the formation of these writings and the knowledge that they are representative as objectifications of the apostolic church do not simply coincide in time, and that the formation of the canon was not finished until the post-apostolic age. In this understanding the canonicity of scripture is established by God insofar as he constitutes the church through the cross and the resurrection as an irreversible event of salvation, and the pure objectifications of its beginning are constitutive for this church. [...]

From this perspective, or so it seems to us, we can also clarify what is called "inspiration" in the church's doctrine on scripture. In the documents of the church it is said again and again that God is the *auctor* (author) of the Old and New Testaments as scripture. The school theology, which is at work in the encyclicals of Leo XIII and up to those of Pius XII, tried time and time again to clarify by means of psychological theories how God himself is the literary author or the writer of Holy Scripture. And it tried to formulate and to clarify the doctrine of inspiration in such a way that it becomes clear that God is the literary author of scripture. This, however, did not deny (and the Second Vatican Council affirmed it explicitly) that this understanding of God's authorship and of inspiration may not reduce the human authors of these writings merely to God's secretaries, but rather it grants them the character of a genuine literary authorship of their own.

This interpretation of the inspired nature of scripture which we have done no more than sketch can of course be understood in such a way that even today one does not necessarily have to accuse it of being mythological. We would have to recall in this connection what we said [...] about the unity between transcendental revelation and its historical objectification in word and in writing, and about the knowledge of the success of these objectifications. In any case it cannot be denied in the Catholic church that God is the author of the Old and New Testaments. But he does not therefore have to be understood as the literary author of these writings. He can be understood in a variety of other ways as the author of scripture, and indeed in such a way that in union with grace and the light of faith scripture can truly be called the word of God. This is true especially because, as we said elsewhere, even if a word about God is caused by

God, it would not by this very fact be a word of God in which God offers himself. It would not be such a word of God if this word did not take place as an objectification of God's self-expression which is effected by God and is borne by grace, and which comes to us without being reduced to our level because the process of hearing it is borne by God's Spirit.

If the church was founded by God himself through his Spirit and in Jesus Christ, if the *original* church as the norm for the future church is the object of God's activity in a qualitatively unique way which is different from his preservation of the church in the course of history, and if scripture is a constitutive element of this original church as the norm for future ages, then this already means quite adequately and in both a positive and an exclusive sense that God is the author of scripture and that he inspired it. Nor at *this* point can some special psychological theory of inspiration be appealed to for help. Rather we can simply take cognizance of the actual origins of scripture which follow for the impartial observer from the very different characteristics of the individual books of scripture. The human authors of Holy Scripture work exactly like other human authors, nor do they have to know anything about their being inspired in reflexive knowledge. If God wills the original church as an indefectible sign of salvation for all ages, and wills it with an absolute, formally pre-defining and eschatological will within salvation history, and hence if he wills with this quite definite will everything which is constitutive for this church, and this includes in certain circumstances scripture in a preeminent way, then he is the inspirer and the author of scripture, although the inspiration of scripture is "only" a moment within God's primordial authorship of the church.

From the doctrine that Holy Scripture is inspired theology and the official doctrine of the church derive the thesis that scripture is inerrant. We can certainly say with the Second Vatican Council (*Dei Verbum*, art. 11): "Therefore, since everything asserted by the inspired authors or sacred writers must be considered to be asserted by the Holy Spirit, we must profess of the books of scripture that they teach with certainty, with fidelity and without error the truth which God wanted recorded in the sacred writings for the sake of our salvation." But if because of the very nature of scripture as the message of salvation we acknowledge the inerrancy of scripture first of all in this global sense, we are still far from having solved all of the problems and settled all of the difficulties about the meaning and the limits of this statement which can be raised because of the actual state of the scriptural texts. The inerrancy of scripture was certainly understood earlier in too narrow a sense, especially when inspiration was interpreted in the sense of verbal inspiration, and the sacred writers were only regarded as God's secretaries and not as independent and also historically conditioned literary authors. That difficulties still exist here in the understanding and in the exact interpretation of the church's doctrine on the inerrancy of scripture is shown even by the history of the conciliar text just cited. It follows from this history that the Council evidently wanted to leave open the question whether the phrase about the truth which God wanted to have recorded for the sake of our salvation is supposed to restrict or to explicate the meaning of the sentence. [. . .]

We only want to say here very briefly: scripture in its unity and totality is the objectification of God's irreversible and victorious offer of salvation to the world in

Jesus Christ, and therefore in its unity and totality it cannot lead one away from God's truth in some binding way. We must read every individual text within the context of this single whole in order to understand its true meaning correctly. Only then can it be understood in its real meaning, and only then can it really be grasped as "true." The very different literary genre of the individual books must be seen more clearly than before and be evaluated in establishing the real meaning of individual statements. [. . .] Scriptural statements were expressed within historically and culturally conditioned conceptual horizons, and this must be taken into account if the question of what is "really" being said in a particular text is to be answered correctly. In certain circumstances it can be completely legitimate to distinguish between the "correctness" and the "truth" of a statement. Nor may we overlook the question whether the really binding meaning of a scriptural statement does not change if a particular book has its origins outside the canon as the work of some individual, and then is taken into the totality of the canonical scriptures.

Just as by the very nature of the case there is an analogy of faith which is a hermeneutical principle for the correct interpretation of individual statements in the official teaching of the church, so that the individual statement can only be understood correctly within the unity of the church's total consciousness of the faith, so too and in an analogous sense, or as a particular instance of this principle, there is also an *analogia scripturae* or an analogy of scripture which is a hermeneutical principle for interpreting individual texts of scripture. If there is a "hierarchy of truths", that is, if a particular statement does not always have the same objective and existential weight which another statement has, then this has to be taken into account in interpreting individual scriptural statements. This does not mean that the statement which is "less important" in relation to another statement has to be qualified as incorrect or as false.

If we grant the validity of and apply these similar principles, which follow from the very nature of the case and from the nature of human speech and are not the principles of a cheap "arrangement" or a cowardly attempt to cover up difficulties, then we certainly do not inevitably have to get into the difficulty of having to hold that particular statements of scripture are "true" in the meaning which is really intended and is intended in a binding way, although a sober and honest exegesis might declare that they are incorrect and erroneous in the sense of a negation of the "truth".

Comment

This is a very important statement from one of the leading Roman Catholic theologians of the twentieth century, and it merits very close attention. The passage sets out a full account of the interaction of Scripture, revelation, Christ, and the church, which Rahner clearly considers to reflect the concerns of the Second Vatican Council.

Questions for Study

1 What does Rahner understand by "inspiration"? In what ways does Rahner's account of this process differ from the classic Protestant position, set out by A. A. Hodge (2.35)?

2 How does Rahner relate the formation of the canon of Scripture to the question of the authority of Scripture, and the authority of the church?
3 "Scripture in its unity and totality is the objectification of God's irreversible and victorious offer of salvation to the world in Jesus Christ, and therefore in its unity and totality it cannot lead one away from God's truth in some binding way." Locate this passage within the text. What does Rahner mean by this statement? And how does it affect his understanding of how Scripture is to be interpreted?

2.45

Phyllis Trible on Feminist Biblical Interpretation

Phyllis Trible (born 1948), one of North America's most respected feminist biblical scholars, here provides an excellent example of the way in which a feminist theological agenda leads to the rereading of Scripture, in order to gain insights which have been overlooked or suppressed by previous generations of (mainly male) interpreters. The passage represents a classic illustration of modern feminist biblical interpretation. See also 3.41, 3.42, 6.55, 6.56.

Born and bred in a land of patriarchy, the Bible abounds in male imagery and language. For centuries interpreters have explored and exploited this male language to articulate theology: to shape the contours and content of the Church, synagogue and academy; and to instruct human beings – female and male – in who they are, what rules they should play, and how they should behave. So harmonious has seemed this association of Scripture with sexism, of faith with culture, that only a few have even questioned it.

Within the past decade, however, challenges have come in the name of feminism, and they refuse to go away. As a critique of culture in light of misogyny, feminism is a prophetic movement, examining the status quo, pronouncing judgment and calling for repentance. In various ways this hermeneutical pursuit interacts with the Bible in its remoteness, complexity, diversity and contemporaneity to yield new understandings of both text and interpreter. Accordingly, I shall survey three approaches to the study of women in Scripture. Though these perspectives may also apply to "intertestamental" and New Testament literature, my focus is the Hebrew Scriptures.

When feminists first examined the Bible, emphasis fell upon documenting the case against women. Commentators observed the plight of the female in Israel. Less desirable in the eyes of her parents than a male child, a girl stayed close to her mother, but her father controlled her life until he relinquished her to another man for marriage. If either of these male authorities permitted her to be mistreated, even abused, she had to submit without recourse. Thus, Lot offered his daughters to the men of Sodom to protect a male guest (Genesis 19: 8); Jephthah sacrificed his daughter to remain faithful to a foolish vow (Judges 11: 29–40); Amnon raped his half-sister Tamar (2 Samuel 13); and the Levite from the hill country of Ephraim participated with other males to bring about the betrayal, rape, murder and dismemberment of his own concubine (Judges 19). Although not every story involving female and male is so terrifying, the narrative literature nevertheless makes clear that from birth to death the Hebrew woman belonged to men.

What such narratives show, the legal corpus amplifies. Defined as the property of men (Exodus 20: 17; Deuteronomy 5: 21), women did not control their own bodies. A man expected to marry a virgin, though his own virginity need not be intact. A wife guilty of earlier fornication violated the honor and power of both her father and husband. Death by stoning was the penalty (Deuteronomy 22: 13–21). Moreover, a woman had no right to divorce (Deuteronomy 24: 1–4) and most often, no right to own property. Excluded from the priesthood, she was considered far more unclean than the male (Leviticus 15). Even her monetary value was less (Leviticus 27: 1–7).

Clearly, this feminist perspective has uncovered abundant evidence for the inferiority, subordination and abuse of women in Scripture. Yet the approach has led to different conclusions. Some people denounce biblical faith as hopelessly misogynous, although this judgment usually fails to evaluate the evidence in terms of Israelite culture. Some reprehensibly use these data to support anti-Semitic sentiments. Some read the Bible as a historical document devoid of any continuing authority and hence worthy of dismissal. The "Who cares?" question often comes at this point.

Others succumb to despair about the ever-present male power that the Bible and its commentators hold over women. And still others, unwilling to let the case against women be the determining word, insist that text and interpreters provide more excellent ways.

The second approach, then, grows out of the first while modifying it. Discerning within Scripture a critique of patriarchy, certain feminists concentrate upon discovering and recovering traditions that challenge the culture. This task involves highlighting neglected texts and reinterpreting familiar ones.

Prominent among neglected passages are portrayals of deity as female. A psalmist declares that God is midwife (Psalm 22: 9–10): "Yet thou art the one who took me from the womb; thou didst keep me safe upon my mother's breast." In turn, God becomes mother, the one upon whom the child is cast from birth: "Upon thee was I cast from my birth, and since my mother bore me thou hast been my God." Although this poem stops short of an exact equation, in it female imagery mirrors divine activity. What the psalmist suggests, Deuteronomy 32: 18 makes explicit: "You were unmindful of the Rock that begot you and you forgot the God who gave you birth."

Though the Revised Standard Version translates accurately "The God who gave you birth," the rendering is tame. We need to accent the striking portrayal of God as a woman in labor pains, for the Hebrew verb has exclusively this meaning. (How scandalous, then, is the totally incorrect translation in the Jerusalem Bible, "You forgot the God who fathered you.") Yet another instance of female imagery is the metaphor of the womb as given in the Hebrew radicals *rhm*. In its singular form the word denotes the physical organ unique to the female. In the plural, it connotes the compassion of both human beings and God. God the merciful (*rahum*) is God the mother. (See, for example, Jeremiah 31: 15–22.) Over centuries, however, translators and commentators have ignored such female imagery, with disastrous results for God, man and woman. To reclaim the image of God female is to become aware of the male idolatry that has long infested faith.

If traditional interpretations have neglected female imagery for God, they have also neglected females, especially women who counter patriarchal culture. By contrast, feminist hermeneutics accents these figures. A collage of women in Exodus illustrates the emphasis. So eager have scholars been to get Moses born that they pass quickly over the stories that lead to his advent (Exodus 1: 8–2: 10). Two female slaves are the first to oppose the Pharaoh; they refuse to kill newborn sons. Acting alone, without advice or assistance from males, they thwart the will of the oppressor. Tellingly, memory has preserved the names of these women, Shiprah and Puah, while obliterating the identity of the king so successfully that he has become the burden of innumerable doctoral dissertations. What these two females begin, other Hebrew women continue:

> A woman conceived and bore a son and when she saw that he was a goodly child she hid him three months. And when she could hide him no longer, she took for him a basket made of bulrushes ... and she put the child in it and placed it among the reeds at the river's bank. And his sister stood at a distance to know what would be done to him.
>
> (Exodus 2: 2–4)

In quiet and secret ways the defiance resumes as a mother and daughter scheme to save their baby son and brother, and this action enlarges when the daughter of Pharaoh appears at the riverbank. Instructing her maid to fetch the basket, the princess opens it, sees a crying baby, and takes him to her heart even as she recognizes his Hebrew identity. The daughter of Pharaoh aligns herself with the daughters of Israel. Filial allegiance is broken; class lines crossed; racial and political difference transcended. The sister, seeing it all from a distance, dares to suggest the perfect arrangement: a Hebrew nurse for the baby boy; in reality, the child's own mother. From the human side, then, Exodus faith originates as a feminist act. The women who are ignored by theologians are the first to challenge oppressive structures.

Not only does this second approach recover neglected women but also it reinterprets familiar ones beginning with the primal woman in the creation story of Genesis 2–3. Contrary to tradition, she is not created the assistant or subordinate of the man. In fact, most often the Hebrew word *'ezer* ("helper") connotes superiority [...] thereby posing a rather different problem about this woman. Yet the accompanying phrase "fit for" or "corresponding to" ("a helper corresponding to") tempers the connotation of superiority to specify the mutuality of woman and man.

Further, when the serpent talks with the woman (Genesis 3: 1–5), he uses plural verb forms, making her the spokesperson for the human couple – hardly the pattern of a patriarchal culture. She discusses theology intelligently, stating the case for obedience even more strongly than did God: "From the fruit of the tree that is in the midst of the garden, God said: 'You shall not eat from it, and you shall not touch it, lest you die.'" If the tree is not touched, then its fruit cannot be eaten. Here the woman builds "a fence around the Torah," a procedure that her rabbinical successors developed fully to protect divine law and ensure obedience.

Speaking with clarity and authority, the first woman is theologian, ethicist, hermeneut and rabbi. Defying the stereotypes of patriarchy, she reverses what the Church, synagogue and academy have preached about women. By the same token, the man "who was with her" (many translations omit this crucial phrase) throughout the temptation is not morally superior but rather belly-oriented. Clearly this story presents a couple alien to traditional interpretations. In reclaiming the woman, feminist hermeneutics gives new life to the image of God female. These and other exciting discoveries of a counter-literature that pertains to women do not, however, eliminate the male bias of Scripture. In other words, this second perspective neither disavows nor neglects the evidence of the first. Instead, it functions as a remnant theology.

The third approach retells biblical stories of terror *in memoriam*, offering sympathetic readings of abused women. If the first perspective documents misogyny historically and sociologically, this one appropriates such evidence poetically and theologically. At the same time, it continues to look for the remnant in unlikely places.

The betrayal, rape, murder and dismemberment of the concubine in Judges 19 is a striking example. When wicked men of the tribe of Benjamin demand to "know" her master, he instead throws the concubine to them. All night they ravish her; in the morning she returns to her master. Showing no pity, he orders her to get up and go. She does not answer, and the reader is left to wonder if she is dead or alive. At any rate, the master puts her body on a donkey and continues the journey. When the couple arrive home, the master cuts the concubine in pieces, sending them to the tribes of Israel as a call to war against the wrong done to him by the men of Benjamin.

At the conclusion of this story, Israel is instructed to "consider, take counsel and speak" (Judges 19: 30). Indeed, Israel does reply – with unrestrained violence. Mass slaughter follows; the rape, murder and dismemberment of one woman condones similar crimes against hundreds and hundreds of women. The narrator (or editor) responds differently, however, suggesting the political solution of kingship instead of the anarchy of the judges (Judges 12: 25) [sic: Judges 21: 25 is clearly intended. Editor]. This solution fails. In the days of David there is a king in Israel, and yet Amnon rapes Tamar. How, then, do we today hear this ancient tale of terror as the imperatives "consider, take counsel and speak" address us? A feminist approach, with attention to reader response, interprets the story on behalf of the concubine as it calls to remembrance her suffering and death.

Similarly, the sacrifice of the daughter of Jephthah documents the powerlessness and abuse of a child in the days of the judges (Judges 11). No interpretation can save her from the holocaust or mitigate the foolish vow of her father. But we can move through the indictment of the father to claim sisterhood with the daughter. Retelling her story, we emphasize the daughters of Israel to whom she reaches out in the last days of her life (Judges 11: 37). Thus, we underscore the postscript, discovering in the process an alternative translation.

Traditionally, the ending has read, "she [the daughter] had never known man. And it became a custom in Israel that the daughters of Israel went year by year to lament the daughter of Jephthah the Gileadite four days in the year" (11: 40). Since the verb *become*, however, is a feminine form (Hebrew has no neuter), another reading is likely: "Although she had never known a man, nevertheless she became a tradition [custom] in Israel. From year to year the daughters of Israel went to mourn the daughter of Jephthah the Gileadite, four days in the year." By virtue of this translation, we can understand the ancient story in a new way. The unnamed virgin child becomes a tradition in Israel because the women with whom she chooses to spend her last days do not let her pass into oblivion; they establish a living memorial. Interpreting such stories of terror on behalf of women is surely, then, another way of challenging the patriarchy of Scripture.

I have surveyed three feminist approaches to the study of women in Scripture. The first explores the inferiority, subordination and abuse of women in ancient Israel. Within this context, the second pursues the counter-literature that is itself a critique of patriarchy. Utilizing both of these approaches, the third retells sympathetically the stories of terror about women. Though intertwined, these perspectives are distinguishable. The one stressed depends on the occasion and the talents and interests of the interpreter. Moreover, in its work, feminist hermeneutics embraces a variety of methodologies and disciplines. Archaeology, linguistics, anthropology and literary and historical criticism all have contributions to make. Thereby understanding of the past increases and deepens as it informs the present.

Finally, there are more perspectives on the subject of women in Scripture than are dreamt of in the hermeneutics of this essay. For instance I have barely mentioned the problem of sexist translations which, in fact, is receiving thoughtful attention from many scholars, male and female. But perhaps I have said enough to show that in various and sundry ways feminist hermeneutics is challenging interpretations old and new. In time, perhaps, it will yield a biblical theology of womanhood (not to be subsumed under the label humanity) with roots in the goodness of creation female and male. Meanwhile, the faith of Sarah and Hagar, Naomi and Ruth, the two Tamars and a cloud of other witnesses empowers and sobers the endeavor.

Comment

Feminist critiques of traditional Christian doctrines have become an accepted aspect of mainstream theology since about 1980. Those critiques have often dealt with the perceived difficulty of the "maleness" of God – as in the images of God as "father" or "shepherd" – or of Jesus Christ. In this article, Phyllis Trible looks at a number of women role models in the Old Testament, and attempts to explore both the role of women in Old Testament narratives, and how the patriarchal context of the Old Testament militates against allowing women to have the prominent roles that modern western society has come to expect of them and for them.

Questions for Study

1 What are the main roles allocated to women by the Old Testament, according to Trible in this article?
2 How does Trible set about "reclaiming the image of God female" in this situation?
3 Set out and critique the three main feminist approaches to the study of women in the Old Testament that Trible identifies in this article.

2.46

Donald G. Bloesch on Christological Approaches to Biblical Hermeneutics

In this passage Donald Bloesch (born 1928), one of North America's leading evangelical theologians, sets out a series of options for biblical interpretation, indicating his anxieties concerning each. The passage provides both a summary of available options, along with a critique from an evangelical perspective. Later in the article, in a section not reprinted here, Bloesch sets out his own proposal in much greater detail, based on a strongly Christological approach to the issues, avoiding some of the difficulties he here identifies. See also 2.3, 2.4, 2.6, 2.8, 2.9, 2.11, 2.12, 2.13, 2.14, 2.38, 2.48.

The discipline of biblical hermeneutics, which deals with the principles governing the interpretation of Scripture, is presently in crisis. For some time it has been obvious in the academic world that the scriptural texts cannot simply be taken at face value but presuppose a thought world that is alien to our own. In an attempt to bring some degree of coherence to the interpretation of Scripture, scholars have appealed to current philosophies or sociologies of knowledge. Their aim has been to come to an understanding of what is essential and what is peripheral in the Bible, but too often in the process they have lost contact with the biblical message. It is fashionable among both theologians and biblical scholars today to contend that there is no one biblical view or message but instead a plurality of viewpoints that stand at considerable variance with one another as well as with the modern worldview.

There are a number of academically viable options today concerning biblical interpretation, some of which I shall consider in this essay. These options represent competing theologies embracing the whole of the theological spectrum.

First, there is the hermeneutic of Protestant scholastic orthodoxy, which allows for grammatical–historical exegesis, the kind that deals with the linguistic history of the text but is loathe to give due recognition to the cultural or historical conditioning of the perspective of the author of the text. Scripture is said to have one primary author, the Holy Spirit, with the prophets and Apostles as the secondary authors. For this reason Scripture is believed to contain an underlying theological and philosophical unity. It is therefore proper to speak of a uniquely biblical life- and world-view. Every text, it is supposed, can be harmonized not only with the whole of Scripture but also with the findings of secular history and natural science. The meaning of most texts is thought to be obvious even to an unbeliever. The end result of such a treatment of Scripture is a coherent, systematic theological system, presumably reflecting the very mind of God. This approach has been represented in Reformed circles by the so-called Princeton School of Theology associated with Charles Hodge, Archibald Alexander Hodge, and Benjamin Warfield.

In this perspective, hermeneutics is considered a scientific discipline abiding by the rules that govern other disciplines of knowledge. Scripture, it is said, yields its meaning to a systematic, inductive analysis and does not necessarily presuppose a faith commitment to be understood. Some proponents of the old orthodoxy (such as Gordon Clark and Carl Henry) favor a metaphysical–deductive over an empirical–inductive approach, seeking to deduce the concrete meanings of Scripture from first principles given in Scripture.

A second basic approach to biblical studies is historicism in which Scripture is treated in the same way as any worthy literature of a given cultural tradition. The tools of higher criticism are applied to Scripture to find out what the author intended to say in that particular historical cultural context. Higher criticism includes an analysis of the literary genre of the text, its historical background, the history of the oral tradition behind the text, and the cultural and psychological factors at work on the author and editor (or editors) of the text. With its appeal to the so-called historical–critical method for gaining an insight into the meaning of the text, this approach is to be associated with the liberal theology stemming from the Enlightenment.

Historicism is based on the view that the historicity of a phenomenon affords the means of comprehending its essence and reality (H. Martin Rumscheidt). It is assumed that meaning is to be found only in the historical web of things. The aim is the historical reconstruction of the text, in other words, seeing the text in its historical and cultural context (*Sitz im Leben*). Historical research, it is supposed, can procure for us the meaning of the Word of God.

Ernst Troeltsch articulated the basic principles of historicism, but this general approach has been conspicuous in J. S. Semler, David Friedrich Strauss, Ferdinand Christian Baur, Adolf von Harnack, and, in our day, Will Marxsen and Krister Stendahl. A historicist bent was apparent in Rudolf Bultmann and Gerhard Ebeling, especially in their earlier years, though other quite different influences were also at work on them.

It was out of this perspective that the quest for the historical Jesus emerged, since it was believed that only by ascertaining by historical science what Jesus really believed in terms of his own culture and historical period can we find a sure foundation for faith. Albert Schweitzer broke with historicism when he discovered that the historical Jesus indisputably subscribed to an apocalyptic vision of the kingdom of God. Finding this incredible to the modern mind, he sought a new anchor for faith in the mystical Christ.

A third option in hermeneutics is the existentialist one, popularized by Rudolf Bultmann, Ernst Fuchs, Gerhard Ebeling, and Fritz Buri, among others. This approach does not deny the role of historical research but considers it incapable of giving us the significance of the salvific events for human existence. It can tell us much about the thought-world and language of the authors, but it cannot communicate to us the interiority of their faith. Demonstrating an affinity with the Romanticist tradition of Schleiermacher and Dilthey, these men seek to uncover the seminal experience or creative insight of the authors of the texts in question, the experience that was objectified in words. Only by sharing this same kind of experience or entering into the same type of vision do we rightly understand the meaning of the text. Drawing upon both Hegel and Heidegger, these scholars affirm that real knowledge is self-knowledge and that the role of the text is to aid us in self-understanding.

In existentialist hermeneutics history is dissolved into the historicity of existence. The Word becomes formative power rather than informative statement. The message of faith becomes the breakthrough into freedom. Jesus is seen as a witness to faith or the historical occasion for faith rather than the object of faith. It is contended that we should come to Scripture with the presuppositions of existentialist anthropology so that the creative questions of our time can be answered.

In contradistinction to the above approaches I propose a christological hermeneutic by which we seek to move beyond historical criticism to the christological, as opposed to the existential, significance of the text. The text's christological meaning can in fact be shown to carry tremendous import for human existence. I believe that I am here being true to the intent of the scriptural authors themselves and even more to the Spirit who guided them, since they frequently made an effort to relate their revelatory insights to the future acts of cosmic deliverance wrought by the God of Israel (in the case of the Old Testament) or to God's self-revelation in Jesus Christ (in the case of the New Testament). This approach, which is associated with Karl Barth, Jacques Ellul, and Wilhelm Vischer, among others, and which also has certain affinities with the confessional stances of Gerhard von Rad and Brevard Childs, seeks to supplement the historical–critical method by theological exegesis in which the innermost intentions of the author are related to the center and culmination of sacred history mirrored in the Bible, namely, the advent of Jesus Christ. It is believed that the fragmentary insights of both Old and New Testament writers are fulfilled in God's dramatic incursion into human history which we see in the incarnation and atoning sacrifice of Jesus Christ, in his life, death, and resurrection.

Here the aim is to come to Scripture without any overt presuppositions or at least holding these presuppositions in abeyance so that we can hear God's Word anew speaking to us in and through the written text. According to this view, the Word of God is not procured by historical–grammatical examination of the text, nor by historical–critical research, nor by existential analysis, but is instead received in a commitment of faith.

This position has much in common with historical orthodoxy, but one major difference is that it welcomes a historical investigation of the text. Such investigation, however, can only throw light on the cultural and literary background of the text; it does not give us its divinely intended meaning. Another difference is that we seek to understand the text not simply in relation to other texts but in relation to the Christ revelation. Some of the theologians of the older orthodoxy would agree, but others would say that what the Bible tells us about creation, for example, can be adequately understood on its own apart from a reference to the incarnation. With the theology of the Reformation and Protestant orthodoxy, I hold that we should begin by ascertaining the literal sense of the text – what was in the mind of the author – and we can do this only by seeing the passage in question in its immediate context. But then we should press on to discern its christological significance – how it relates to the message of the cross of Jesus Christ.

In opposition to liberalism, I believe that the text should be seen not simply against its immediate historical environment but also against the background of Eternity. To do this, we need to go beyond authorial motivation to theological relation. Moreover, it is neither the faith of Jesus (as in Ebeling) nor the Christ of faith (as in Bultmann and Tillich) but the Jesus Christ of sacred history that is our ultimate norm in faith and conduct.

According to this approach, God reveals himself fully and definitively only in one time and place, viz., in the life history of Jesus Christ. The Bible is the primary witness to this event or series of events. This revelation was anticipated in the Old Testament and remembered and proclaimed in the New Testament. [. . .]

The christological hermeneutic that I propose is in accord with the deepest insights of both Luther and Calvin. Both Reformers saw Christ as the ground and center of Scripture. Both sought to relate the Old Testament, as well as the New, to the person and work of Christ. Their position, which was basically reaffirmed by Barth and Vischer, was that the hidden Christ is in the Old Testament and the manifest Christ in the New Testament.

Luther likened Christ to the "star and kernel" of Scripture, describing him as "the center part of the circle" about which everything else revolves. On one occasion he compared certain texts to "hard nuts" which resisted cracking and confessed that he had to throw these texts against the rock (Christ) so that they would yield their "delicious kernel."

Comment

Donald Bloesch's article is of interest not only for his own views, but also for his exploration of the varieties of approaches to be found in twentieth-century theology. The passage can be read as a review of and commentary on the twentieth-century discussion of this issue, and it is possible that many readers will find this a very helpful overview of a complex field.

Questions for Study

1 In this article, Bloesch identifies a number of "schools" of biblical interpretation. What are they? Who are their leading representatives? And what are their distinctive features?
2 Give a critical account of the specific proposal put forward by Bloesch himself. How does it relate to alternative approaches?
3 According to Bloesch, "God reveals himself fully and definitively only in one time and place, viz., in the life history of Jesus Christ." Locate this passage within the text. What are the implications of this idea? Does Bloesch follow them through consistently?

2.47

John Meyendorff on Living Tradition

John Meyendorff (1926–92) was one of the most distinguished representatives of the Orthodox tradition in Christian theology. He graduated from the Orthodox Theological Seminary of Saint Sergius in Paris in 1949, theological education having ceased within the former Russian territories as a result of the Russian Revolution. Meyendorff established himself as a leading historian and contemporary exponent of the Orthodox theological tradition, especially in his works *Byzantine Theology* (1974) and *Christ in Eastern Christian Thought* (1969). From 1959 until his death, Meyendorff served as professor of theology at St Vladimir's Theological Seminary in New York State. Meyendorff's Orthodox roots are perhaps best seen in his exposition of the importance of the "living tradition" for the life of the church, a theme which he explored in one of his later books, simply entitled *Living Tradition* (1978). See also 2.2, 2.10, 2.33, 2.34, 2.50.

How is the Orthodox Christian to maintain and witness to his faith in the complicated and changing world of the twentieth century? There can be no answer to this challenge of our age without *living tradition.*

Of necessity, any Orthodox theology and any Orthodox witness is *traditional*, in the sense that it is consistent not only with Scripture but also with the experience of the Fathers and the saints, as well as with the continuous celebration of Christ's death and resurrection in the liturgy of the Church. However the term "traditional theology" can also denote a dead theology, if it means identifying traditionalism with simple repetition. Such a theology may prove incapable of recognizing the issues of its own age, while it presents yesterday's arguments to confront new heresies.

In fact, dead traditionalism cannot be truly traditional. It is an essential characteristic of patristic theology that it was able to face the challenges of its own time while remaining consistent with the original apostolic Orthodox faith. Thus simply to *repeat* what the Fathers said is to be unfaithful to their spirit and to the intention embodied in their theology.

The great Cappadocian Fathers of the fourth century – St Basil the Great, St Gregory of Nazianzus, and St Gregory of Nyssa – are true pillars of Orthodox Christianity because they succeeded in preserving the faith in the face of two great dangers. The first was the Arian heresy, which denied the divinity of Christ, and the second was the influential challenge of ancient Greek philosophy. The latter had ruled the minds of educated people for centuries; and precisely because it appeared as so attractive, so traditional, and so prestigious, it prevented many educated Greeks from adopting the new biblical faith of Jesus' disciples. The Fathers faced both of these problems clearly and dealt with them specifically. They did not simply anathematize the Arians but also provided a positive and contemporary terminology to explain the mystery of the Holy Trinity: the terminology enshrined in the Church's creed. They did not simply deny the validity of Greek philosophy but demonstrated as well that its best intuitions could successfully be used in Christian theology, provided one accepted the Gospel of Christ as the ultimate criterion of truth.

Thus for us to be "traditional" implies an imitation of the Fathers in their creative work of discernment. Like them we must be dedicated to the task of saving human beings from error, and not just maintaining abstract propositional truths. We must imitate their constant effort to understand their contemporaries and to use words and concepts which could truly reach the minds of the listeners. True tradition is always a *living* tradition. It changes while remaining always the same. It changes because it faces different situations, not because its essential content is modified. This content is not an abstract proposition; it is the living Christ Himself, who said, "I am the Truth."

Comment

John Meyendorff here offers an interpretation of the Orthodox notion of tradition, which he believes contrasts with both the Protestant and Roman Catholic approach to this issue. It is important to note how he regards certain eastern Orthodox writers as having normative importance in his presentation. He writes: "Thus for us to be 'traditional' implies an imitation of the Fathers in their creative work of discernment." Of particular interest is Meyendorff's insistence that the content of tradition is not abstract propositions, but "the living Christ."

Questions for Study

1 What exactly is "tradition," according to Meyendorff?
2 "True tradition is always a *living* tradition." What does Meyendorff mean by this? And what do you think Meyendorff regards as a "dead tradition"?
3 "True tradition is always a *living* tradition. It changes while remaining always the same." How does Meyendorff understand this dynamic concept of tradition?

2.48

James I. Packer on the Nature of Revelation

In this passage, first published in 1964, the noted evangelical writer James I. Packer (born 1926) responds to the idea of revelation as God's self-disclosure. This approach was particularly associated with Emil Brunner (see 2.42), but was popularized in England by writers such as William Temple (1881–1944), who wrote of revelation simply in terms of "divine presence." Packer here argues for the impossibility of such a personal self-disclosure without an accompanying informational or verbal element. See also 2.16, 2.39, 2.41, 2.42.

What is revelation? From one standpoint it is God's act, from another His gift. From both standpoints it is correlative to man's knowledge of God, as on the one hand an experience and on the other a possession. As God's act, revelation is the personal self-disclosure whereby He brings us actively and experimentally to know Him as our own God and Saviour. As God's gift, revelation is the knowledge about Himself which He gives us as a means to this end. Revelation as God's act takes place through the bestowing of revelation as God's gift; the first sense of the word thus comprehends the second. Accordingly, revelation in the narrower sense ought always to be studied in the setting of revelation in the broader sense.

How does God reveal what has to be revealed in order that we may know Him? By verbal communication from Himself. Without this, revelation in the full and saving sense cannot take place at all. For no public historical happening, as such (an exodus, a conquest, a captivity, a crucifixion, an empty tomb), can reveal God apart from an accompanying word from God to explain it, or a prior promise which it is seen to confirm or fulfil. Revelation in its basic form is thus of necessity propositional; God reveals Himself by telling us about Himself, and what He is doing in His world. The statement in Hebrews 1: 1, that in Old Testament days God spoke "in divers manners", reminds us of the remarkable variety of means whereby, according to the record, God's communications were on occasion given: theophanies, angelic announcements, an audible voice from heaven (Exodus 19: 9; Matthew 3: 17, 2 Peter 1: 17), visions, dreams, signs [. . .] as well as the more organic type of inspiration, whereby the Spirit of God so controlled the reflective operations of men's minds as to lead them to a right judgment in all things. But in every case the disclosures introduced, or conveyed, or confirmed, by these means were propositional in substance and verbal in form.

Why does God reveal Himself to us? Because, as we saw, He who made us rational beings wants, in His love, to have us as His friends; and He addresses His words to us – statements, commands, promises – as a means of sharing His thoughts with us, and so of making that personal self-disclosure which friendship presupposes, and without which it cannot exist.

What is the content of God's revelation? This is determined primarily by our present plight as sinners. Though we have lapsed into ignorance of God and a godless way of life, God has not abandoned His purpose to have us as His friends; instead, He has resolved in His love to rescue us from sin and restore us to Himself. His plan for doing this was to make Himself known to us as our Redeemer and Recreator, through the incarnation, death, resurrection and reign of His Son. The working out of this plan required a long series of preparatory events, starting with the promise to the woman's seed (Genesis 3: 15) and spanning the whole of Old Testament history. Also, it required a mass of concurrent verbal instruction, predicting each item in the series before it came and applying its lessons in retrospect, so that at each stage men might understand the unfolding history of salvation, hope in the promise of its full accomplishment, and learn what manner of persons they, as objects of grace, ought to be. Thus the history of salvation (the acts of God) took place in the context of the history of revelation (the oracles of God).

Comment

The background to this passage is the kind of approach to revelation associated with Emil Brunner, in which revelation is discussed more in terms of a "personal presence" than a body of information (see 2.42). Ideas similar to Brunner's were developed by a number of English writers around the same time, and became influential in English-language theology in the 1960s. Packer's argument involves challenging the assumption that the concept of "personal presence" constitutes an adequate conception of revelation.

Questions for Study

1 Packer considers revelation both in terms of divine acts and divine words. How does he hold these two concepts together?
2 What does Packer have to say about the motivation for divine revelation, and the content of that revelation? Are these two matters related to each other?
3 "As God's act, revelation is the personal self-disclosure whereby He brings us actively and experimentally to know Him as our own God and Saviour. As God's gift, revelation is the knowledge about Himself which He gives us as a means to this end." Locate this passage within the text. What does Packer mean by this? And how are the "act" and "gift" of revelation correlated?

2.49

Thomas F. Torrance on Karl Barth's Criticism of Natural Theology

Thomas F. Torrance (born 1913), widely regarded as the most important British theologian of the twentieth century, was noted both as an interpreter and translator of Karl Barth. In this important passage, which formed part of the Page-Barbour and James W. Richard Lectures at the University of Virginia, Torrance sets out clearly Karl Barth's fundamental objections to natural theology. See also 2.17, 2.21, 2.41.

How are we, in the light of all this, to understand Karl Barth's objections to natural theology? They certainly have nothing at all to do with some kind of deistic dualism between God and the world implying no active relation between God and the world, or with some form of Marcionite dualism between redemption and creation implying a depreciation of the creature, as so many of Barth's critics have averred;

nor have they to do with a skepticism coupled with a false fideism, such as was condemned by the First Vatican Council. On the contrary, Barth's position rests upon an immense stress on the concrete activity of God in space and time, in creation as in redemption, and upon his refusal to accept that God's power is limited by the weakness of human capacity or that the so-called natural reason can set any limits to God's self-revelation to mankind. The failure to understand Barth at this point is highly revealing, for it indicates that his critics themselves still think within the dualist modes of thought that Barth had himself long left behind, in his restoration of an interactionist understanding of the relation between God and the world in which he operated with an ontological and cognitive bridge between the world and God, which God himself has already established. Thus Barth's objections to traditional natural theology are on grounds precisely the opposite of those attributed to him!

Barth's thought, it must be understood, moves within the orbit of the Reformation's restored emphasis on the creation of the world out of nothing and thus upon its utter contingence, in which the natural is once again allowed to be natural, for nature is set free from the hidden divinization imposed upon it when it was considered to be impregnated with final causes – the notion of *deus sive natura*. That is the way nature is treated if God is actually thought of as deistically detached from it, so that nature can in some measure substitute for God by providing out of itself a bridge to the divine. Hence Barth attacked the kind of Augustinian metaphysics advocated by Erich Przywara, in which the Aristotelian notion of a divine entelechy embedded in nature was reinforced with a neoplatonic notion of infused grace and enlightenment. Thus it could be claimed that all being is intrinsically analogical to the divine and that man endowed with grace is inherently capable of participating in God. Barth understood the immanentism latent in this theology to be the other side of the deism he found so unacceptable, and in contrast he emphasized all the more the Godness of God and the humanity of man, substituting for an illicit divinity inherent in man – which could easily be made the ground for a synthesis between God and the world – the Judeo-Christian understanding of God's creative, revelatory, and redemptive activity in space and time, as it had come to formulated expression in the theology of the early church, when Christians thought out the interrelation between the incarnation and the creation.

Barth's particularly sharp opposition to Przywara's thought was due to his conviction that this was, from the Roman Catholic side, a new version of the immanentist philosophy that lay behind German romantic idealist thought, within the thought-forms of which Protestant theology in Germany had been so imprisoned that it had lost the ground for any effective opposition to the demonic natural theology of the Nazis. This was also the reason for his no-less-sharp rejection of Emil Brunner's attempt to provide a basis for a Protestant natural theology on the double ground of nature and grace, without coming to grips with the fundamental issues at stake. Apart from these polemics, however, Barth's real objection to traditional natural theology rested on theological and scientific grounds. It is the actual content of our knowledge of God, together with the scientific method that inheres in it, that excludes any movement of thought that arises on some other, independent ground as ultimately irrelevant and as an inevitable source of confusion when it is adduced as a second or co-ordinate basis for positive theology.

So far as theological content is concerned, Barth's argument runs like this. If the God whom we have actually come to know through Jesus Christ really is Father, Son, and Holy Spirit in his own eternal and undivided Being, then what are we to make of an independent natural theology that terminates, not upon the Being of the triune God – i.e., upon God as he really is in himself – but upon some Being of God in general? Natural theology by its very operation abstracts the existence of God from his act, so that if it does not begin with deism, it imposes deism upon theology. If really to know God through his saving activity in our world is to know him as triune, then the doctrine of the Trinity belongs to the very groundwork of knowledge of God from the very start, which calls in question any doctrine of God as the one God gained apart from his trinitarian activity – but that is the kind of knowledge of God that is yielded in natural theology of the traditional kind.

So far as scientific method is concerned, Barth demands a rigorous mode of inquiry in which form and content, method and subject-matter are inseparably joined together, and he rejects any notion that we can establish how we know apart from our actual knowledge and its material content. Thus Barth stands squarely on the same grounds as rigorous science when he insists on the freedom to develop a scientific method appropriate to the field of theological inquiry and to elaborate epistemological structures under the compulsion of the nature of the object as it becomes disclosed in the progress of the inquiry, quite untrammelled by *a priori* assumptions of any kind or by any preconceptions deriving from some other field of investigation. As an *a posteriori* science, theology involves the questioning of all presuppositions and all structures of thought independent of or antecedent to its own operations. This is why Barth makes so much of the epistemological implications of justification by grace alone, for it forces upon us relentless questioning of all we thought we knew beforehand, or of all prejudgments and external authorities, philosophical or ecclesiastical, in such a way that in the last resort theology is thrown back wholly upon the nature and activity of God for the justification or verification of our concepts and statements about him. It is here in the doctrine of justification that we can see clearly how form and content, method and subject-matter, in theological inquiry coincide.

Epistemologically, then, what Barth objects to in traditional natural theology is not any invalidity in its argumentation, nor even its rational structure, as such, but its *independent* character – i.e., the autonomous rational structure that natural theology develops on the ground of "nature alone," in abstraction from the active self-disclosure of the living and Triune God – for that can only split the knowledge of God into two parts, natural knowledge of the One God and revealed knowledge of the triune God, which is scientifically as well as theologically intolerable. This is not to reject the place of a proper rational structure in knowledge of God, such as natural theology strives for, but to insist that unless that rational structure is intrinsically bound up with the actual content of knowledge of God, it is a distorting abstraction. That is why Barth claims that, properly understood, natural theology is included within revealed theology, where we have to do with actual knowledge of God as it is grounded in the intelligible relations in God himself, for it is there under the compulsion of God's self-disclosure in Being and Act that the rational structure appropriate to him arises in our understanding of him. But in the nature of the case it is not a rational structure that can be abstracted from the actual knowledge of God with which it is integrated, and made to stand on its own as an independent or autonomous system of thought, for then it would be meaningless, like something that is complete and consistent in itself but without any ontological reference beyond itself: it becomes merely a game to be enjoyed like chess – which Barth is as ready to enjoy as much as anyone else, although he cannot take it seriously.

Comment

Torrance here offers a sympathetic account of Karl Barth's difficulties over natural theology, which locates the fundamental Barthian objection to natural theology in the concept of human autonomy. For Barth, natural theology involves human self-assertion – the idea that humanity can determine the conditions of revelation, and deal with the question of the "knowledge of God" apart from the actual revelation of God in Christ. This point is made especially in the concluding section of the passage, in which Torrance states: "Epistemologically, then, what Barth objects to in traditional natural theology is not any invalidity in its argumentation, nor even its rational structure, as such, but its *independent* character – i.e., the autonomous rational structure that natural theology develops on the ground of 'nature alone,' in abstraction from the active self-disclosure of the living and Triune God."

Questions for Study

1 "All being is intrinsically analogical to the divine." Locate this text within the passage. What, according to Torrance, was the basis of Barth's hostility to the doctrine of analogy found in the writings of Erich Przywara?
2 "Barth's position rests upon an immense stress on the concrete activity of God in space and time, in creation as in redemption, and upon his refusal to accept that God's power is limited by the weakness of human capacity or that the so-called natural reason can set any limits to God's self-revelation to mankind." Locate this text within the passage. What does Torrance mean by this assertion?
3 What does Torrance mean when he declares that "Barth claims that, properly understood, natural theology is included within revealed theology"? Do you think Torrance is right in this matter?

2.50

The *Catechism of the Catholic Church* on Scripture and Tradition

In 1985 an extraordinary Synod of Bishops gathered in Rome to celebrate the twentieth anniversary of the Second Vatican Council and find ways to develop its work. There was considerable pressure for the production of a new vernacular catechism, reflecting the needs of the church in the late twentieth century. The synod noted that:

There were many who expressed the wish that a catechism or a compendium of all Catholic doctrine regarding both faith and morals be prepared so that it could serve as a kind of point of reference for catechisms or compendia prepared in different regions. The presentation of doctrine should be biblical and liturgical. It is to embody a sound doctrine applied to the present life of Christians.

The *Catechism of the Catholic* Church was the direct result of this wish. The work was published in 1992, and soon established itself as a major teaching resource. The process by which the Catechism was produced was lengthy, reflecting the many issues which its compilers had to face. John Paul II appointed an ad hoc commission to undertake the work on November 15, 1986. It was not until February 14, 1992 that it concluded its work. The resulting Catechism was accepted by the Pope on June 25 of the same year. The work was published in Latin and many translations. The first English translation appeared in 1992, and a series of revisions to the translation were introduced in September 1997. The text reprinted here includes the 1997 changes, although it should be noted that none of the alterations then introduced affects this specific section. See also 2.2, 2.10, 2.19, 2.33, 2.34, 2.47.

I The Apostolic Tradition

75. "Christ the Lord, in whom the entire Revelation of the most high God is summed up, commanded the apostles to preach the Gospel, which had been promised beforehand by the prophets, and which he fulfilled in his own person and promulgated with his own lips. In preaching the Gospel, they were to communicate the gifts of God to all men. This Gospel was to be the source of all saving truth and moral discipline."[1]

In the apostolic preaching [. . .]

76. In keeping with the Lord's command, the Gospel was handed on in two ways:

- *orally* "by the apostles who handed on, by the spoken word of their preaching, by the example they gave, by the institutions they established, what they themselves had received – whether from the lips of Christ, from his way of life and his works, or whether they had learned it at the prompting of the Holy Spirit";[2]
- *in writing* "by those apostles and other men associated with the apostles who, under the inspiration of the same Holy Spirit, committed the message of salvation to writing."[3]

[. . .] continued in apostolic succession.

77. "In order that the full and living Gospel might always be preserved in the Church the apostles left bishops as their successors. They gave them their own position of teaching authority."[4] Indeed, "the apostolic preaching, which is expressed in a special way in the inspired books, was to be preserved in a continuous line of succession until the end of time."[5]

78. This living transmission, accomplished in the Holy Spirit, is called Tradition, since it is distinct from Sacred Scripture, though closely connected to it. Through Tradition, "the Church, in her doctrine, life and worship, perpetuates and transmits to every generation all that she herself is, all that she believes."[6] "The sayings of the holy Fathers are a witness to the life-giving presence of this Tradition, showing how its riches are poured out in the practice and life of the Church, in her belief and her prayer."[7]

79. The Father's self-communication made through his Word in the Holy Spirit, remains present and active in the Church: "God, who spoke in the past, continues to converse with the Spouse of his beloved Son. And the Holy Spirit, through whom the living voice of the Gospel rings out in the Church – and through her in the world – leads believers to the full truth, and makes the Word of Christ dwell in them in all its richness."[8]

II. The Relationship between Tradition and Sacred Scripture

One common source [. . .]

80. "Sacred Tradition and Sacred Scripture, then, are bound closely together, and communicate one with the other. For both of them, flowing out from the same divine well-spring, come together in some fashion to form one thing, and move towards the same goal."[9] "Each of them makes present and fruitful in the Church the mystery of Christ, who promised to remain with his own 'always, to the close of the age.' "[10]

. . . two distinct modes of transmission.

81. "*Sacred Scripture* is the speech of God as it is put down in writing under the breath of the Holy Spirit."[11] "And [Holy] *Tradition* transmits in its entirety the Word of God which has been entrusted to the apostles by Christ the Lord and the Holy Spirit. It transmits it to the successors of the apostles so that, enlightened by the Spirit of truth, they may faithfully preserve, expound and spread it abroad by their preaching."[12]

82. As a result the Church, to whom the transmission and interpretation of Revelation is entrusted, "does not derive her certainty about all revealed truths from the holy Scriptures alone. Both Scripture and Tradition must be accepted and honored with equal sentiments of devotion and reverence."[13]

Notes

[Editor's note: the abbreviation DV refers to *Dei Verbum*]

1 DV 7; cf. Matthew 28: 19–20; Mark 16: 15.
2 DV 7.
3 DV 7.
4 DV 7 # 2; St Irenaeus, *Adv. haeres*. 3, 3, 1: PG 7/1, 848.
5 DV 8 # 1.
6 DV 8 # 1.
7 DV 8 # 3.
8 DV 8 # 3; cf. Colossians 3: 16.
9 DV 9.
10 Matthew 28: 20.
11 DV 9.
12 DV 9.
13 DV 9.

Comment

The extract deals with the relation of Scripture and tradition, and draws heavily on the earlier writing *Dei Verbum*, also known as the "Constitution on Divine Revelation," which was produced by the Second Vatican Council. The *Catechism* argues that Scripture and tradition are to be regarded as sharing a common source, while differing in the mode of transmission. It is instructive to compare this passage with the statements of the Council of Trent on the same issue (2.19).

Questions for Study

1 How does the *Catechism* understand the relation between Scripture and tradition? Are they the two sides of the same coin? How does this relate to the position set out in 1546 by the Council of Trent (see 2.19)?
2 The *Catechism* states that the teachings of Christ were passed on in two different manners or modes. What are they? And how are they related?

3 What role does the *Catechism* ascribe to the teaching office of the church in defending and interpreting divine revelation?

For Further Reading

R. J. Coggins and J. L. Houlden, *A Dictionary of Biblical Interpretation* (London: SCM Press, 1990).

Avery Dulles, *Models of Revelation* (Dublin: Gill & Macmillan, 1983).

Edward Farley and Peter Hodgson, "Scripture and Tradition," in P. Hodgson and R. King (eds), *Christian Theology* (Philadelphia: Fortress Press, 1982), pp. 35–61.

George Lindbeck, *The Nature of Doctrine* (Philadelphia: Fortress Press, 1984).

Henri de Lubac, *Scripture in the Tradition* (New York: Crossroad Publishing, 2000).

I. Howard Marshall, Kevin J. Vanhoozer, and Stanley E. Porter, *Beyond the Bible: Moving From Scripture to Theology* (Grand Rapids, MI: Baker Academic, 2004).

Bruce M. Metzger, *The New Testament Canon* (Oxford: Oxford University Press, 1987).

Robert Morgan, *Biblical Interpretation* (Oxford: Oxford University Press, 1988).

Jaroslav Pelikan, *Credo: Historical and Theological Guide to Creeds and Confessions of Faith in the Christian Tradition* (New Haven, CT: Yale University Press, 2005).

Manlio Simonetti, Anders Bergquist, and Markus N. A. Bockmuehl, *Biblical Interpretation in the Early Church: An Historical Introduction to Patristic Exegesis* (Edinburgh: T&T Clark, 2001).

Anthony C. Thiselton, *New Horizons in Hermeneutics* (Grand Rapids, MI: Zondervan, 1992).

K. R. Tremblath, *Evangelical Theories of Biblical Inspiration* (Oxford: Oxford University Press, 1988).

Kevin J. Vanhoozer, *The Drama of Doctrine: A Canonical-Linguistic Approach To Christian Theology* (Louisville, KY: Westminster John Knox Press, 2005).

Allan Verhey, *Remembering Jesus: Christian Community, Scripture, and the Moral Life* (Grand Rapids, MI: Eerdmans, 2005).

David M. Williams, *Receiving the Bible in Faith: Historical and Theological Exegesis* (Washington, DC: Catholic University of America Press, 2004).

Frances M. Young, *Biblical Exegesis and the Formation of Christian Culture* (Peabody, MA: Hendrickson Publishers, 2002).

3

The Doctrine of God

Introduction

The term "theology" literally means "talk about God." Although the modern understanding of the word now goes beyond this, meaning something like "the study of the distinctive ideas of a religion," this point reminds us of the centrality of God to Christian theology. The collection of readings assembled in this chapter surveys a range of issues concerning the doctrine of God, such as the doctrine of the Trinity, the concept of God as creator, and issues concerning the attributes of God.

A major issue in recent theological discussion has been whether God can be said to suffer. This question has become of particular importance since World War I, partly in response to a perceived need to relate God to the suffering of the human situation. As the texts will indicate, there was discussion of the relation of God and human suffering within the Christian tradition long before World War I focused attention on this issue.

Does God Suffer?

3.7 Origen on the Suffering of God
3.8 Origen on the Changelessness of God
3.21 Anselm of Canterbury on the Compassion of God
3.22 Richard of St Victor on Love within the Trinity
3.23 Alexander of Hales on the Suffering of God in Christ
3.30 Benedict Spinoza on the Impassibility of God
3.33 Jürgen Moltmann on the Suffering of God
3.37 Hans Küng on the Immutability of God
3.38 Eberhard Jüngel on the Crucified God
4.24 Martin Luther's Critique of Nestorianism

One of the most important themes to note here is that of the Trinity – the distinctively Christian understanding of the nature of God. The readings noted here focus on this theme, dealing with the reasons for conceiving of God in this way, and with ways of making sense of what is generally conceded to be a difficult doctrine to understand.

The Doctrine of the Trinity

3.3	Irenaeus on the Trinity
3.9	Gregory of Nyssa on Human Analogies of the Trinity
3.11	Gregory of Nazianzus on the Gradual Revelation of the Trinity
3.12	Hilary of Poitiers on the Trinity
3.13	Augustine on the Trinity
3.16	Epiphanius of Constantia on Sabellianism
3.20	The Eleventh Council of Toledo on the Trinity
3.22	Richard of St Victor on Love within the Trinity
3.28	Thomas à Kempis on the Limits of Trinitarian Speculation
3.31	F. D. E. Schleiermacher on the Trinity
3.33	Jürgen Moltmann on the Suffering of God
3.35	Leonardo Boff on the Trinity as Good News for the Poor
3.36	Robert Jenson on the Trinity
3.40	Walter Kasper on the Rationality of the Trinity
3.41	Paul Jewett on Noninclusive Language and the Trinity
3.43	Sarah Coakley on Social Models of the Trinity

However, the theme of the Trinity by no means exhausts any Christian discussion of the nature of God. Several classic debates are touched on in this collection of readings, including the way in which God can be considered to have created the world, what it means to speak of God as all-powerful, and the distinctive character of the Holy Spirit.

An issue which is constantly debated within the Christian tradition is the relation of a good God and the evil that is observed within the world, and experienced within human nature. Are these incompatible? Or can they be reconciled? A number of answers can be given, and are represented among the readings.

God and Evil

3.2	Irenaeus on the Origin of Evil
3.6	Origen on the Relation of God and Evil
3.14	Augustine on the Relation of God and Evil
3.25	Bonaventure on the Origin of Evil

One other theme dealt with in this collection has emerged as particularly important in more recent times. An increased awareness of the past tendency of male theologians to treat women as invisible has led to increased interest in whether God is to be thought of as male. This debate is reflected both in the discussion of God, and also discussions concerning the identity and significance of Jesus Christ.

A Male God and Savior?

3.26	Julian of Norwich on God as our Mother
3.41	Paul Jewett on Noninclusive Language and the Trinity
3.42	Anne Carr on Feminism and the Maleness of God
4.38	Rosemary Radford Ruether on the Maleness of Christ
4.39	Daphne Hampson on the Possibility of a Feminist Christology
6.56	Mary Hayter on Human Sexuality and the Image of God

3.1

Athenagoras of Athens on the Christian God

In this defense of the Christian faith against pagan criticisms, written in Greek around 177 and addressed to the Roman emperors Marcus Aurelius Antonius and Lucius Aurelius Commodus, the second-century writer Athenagoras of Athens sets out the main features of the gospel in a lucid and reasoned manner. The early Christians were accused of atheism on account of their refusal to worship the emperor. In this extract, in which Athenagoras explains what Christians believe about God, important anticipations of later thinking on the Trinity can be detected. The work is known by various names, including *Apologia*, *Legatio* (as in this edition), and *Supplicatio pro Christianis*. See also 1.1, 1.2, 1.3, 1.4.

So we are not atheists, in that we acknowledge one God, who is uncreated, eternal, invisible, impassible, incomprehensible, and without limit. He is apprehended only by the intellect and the mind, and is surrounded by light, beauty, spirit, and indescribable power. The universe was created and ordered, and is presently sustained, through his Logos. [. . .] For we acknowledge also a "son of God." Nobody should think it ridiculous that God should have a son. Although the pagan poets, in their fictions, represent the gods as being no better than human beings, we do not think in the same way as they do concerning either God the Father or God the Son. For the Son of God is the Logos of the Father, both in thought and in reality. It was through his action, and after his pattern, that all things were made, in that the Father and Son are one. [. . . The Son] is the first creation of the Father – not meaning that he was brought into existence, in that, from the beginning, God, who is the eternal mind [*nous*], had the Logos within himself, being eternally of the character of the Logos [*logikos*]. Rather, it is meant that he came forth to be the pattern and motivating power of all physical things. [. . .] We affirm that the Holy Spirit, who was active in the prophets, is an effluence of God, who flows from him and returns to him, like a beam of the sun.

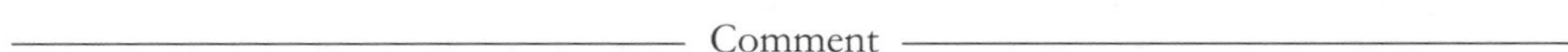

Comment

Early Christian writers were often branded as atheists by their critics within the secular imperial establishment, in that they denied either the divinity of the classic Roman pantheon, or refused to conform to the imperial cult which had become particularly well established in the eastern regions of the Roman Empire. Part of the task of the first Christian apologists was to rebut the charge of atheism; this was often combined with an explanation of the nature of Christian belief. It must be remembered that

Christianity was still being oppressed at this time, so that most Christian meetings took place in secret. There was little way that the public could gain an informed understanding of what Christians believed, other than through the writings of Christians who were prepared to take seriously the concerns of secular culture, such as Athenagoras.

Questions for Study

1 Notice the terms that Athenagoras uses to refer to Jesus Christ. How does this help us understand the way in which Christ was understood within Christian circles at this time?
2 What are the characteristics of Athenagoras's teaching about the nature of God? How would this help him refute the charge of atheism?
3 Notice how Athenagoras makes an appeal to the pagan poets. What reasons might lie behind this? And how does he make use of this appeal?

3.2

Irenaeus on the Origin of Evil

In his *Demonstration of the Apostolic Preaching*, originally written in Greek but now known only in an Armenian translation, the second-century theologian Irenaeus of Lyons (c.130–c.200) sets out the view that the origin of evil lies in human frailty. God did not create humanity in perfection, but with the capacity for this perfection through a process of growth. The initial vulnerability of humanity thus led directly to its seduction. See also 3.6, 3.14, 3.25, 6.1.

God made humanity to be master of the earth and of all which was there. [. . .] Yet this could only take place when humanity had attained its adult stage. [. . .] Yet humanity was little, being but a child. It had to grow and reach full maturity. [. . .] God prepared a place for humanity which was better than this world [. . .] a paradise of such beauty and goodness that the Word of God constantly walked in it, and talked with humanity; prefiguring that future time when he would live with human beings and talk with them, associating with human beings and teaching them righteousness. But humanity was a child; and its mind was not yet fully mature; and thus humanity was easily led astray by the deceiver.

Comment

In marked contrast to the ideas later associated with Augustine, Irenaeus argues that humanity was created weak and powerless, and was thus easily led astray. Where

Augustine spoke of a "Fall," Irenaeus tends to think more in terms of a deflection or loss of direction for humanity.

Questions for Study

1. What place does Irenaeus assign to humanity within creation?
2. Does the fact that humanity was created in weakness call into question either the goodness or the power of God?
3. What is Irenaeus's explanation of the origins of evil?

3.3

Irenaeus on the Trinity

This important statement of the basic elements of the doctrine of the Trinity is set out in a credal form, presumably to allow its readers to relate the passage to any of the creeds then in circulation. The importance of the passage lies in the way in which it clearly assigns distinct functions to each person of the Trinity, and links the three persons together as a "rule of faith," which expresses the distinctively Christian understanding of the nature of God. See also 2.7, 3.9, 3.10, 3.11, 3.12, 3.15, 3.16, 3.20.

This is the rule of our faith, the foundation of the building, and what gives support to our behaviour.

God the Father uncreated, who is uncontained, invisible, one God, creator of the universe; this is the first article of our faith. And the second is:

The *Word of God*, the Son of God, our Lord Jesus Christ, who appeared to the prophets according to their way of prophesying, and according to the dispensation of the Father. Through him all things were created. Furthermore, in the fullness of time, in order to gather all things to himself, he became a human being amongst human beings, capable of being seen and touched, to destroy death, bring life, and restore fellowship between God and humanity. And the third article is:

The *Holy Spirit*, through whom the prophets prophesied, and our forebears learned of God and the righteous were led in the paths of justice, and who, in the fullness of time, was poured out in a new way on our human nature in order to renew humanity throughout the entire world in the sight of God.

Comment

We can see here an early trinitarian credal formulation, in which the basic ideas of the Christian understanding of God are set out clearly, especially in order to refute Gnostic claims. The reference to the "rule of faith" is especially important, as it points to the growing trend to crystallize central defining Christian insights into short formulas for pedagogic and defensive purposes.

Questions for Study

1 What general roles does Irenaeus assign to Christian beliefs concerning the Father, Son, and Spirit?
2 Notice the specific affirmations made concerning the Son. What insights do these allow concerning Irenaeus's understanding of revelation and redemption?
3 Note the specific affirmations made about the Holy Spirit. What does this suggest concerning Irenaeus's understanding of the role of the Spirit?

3.4

Tertullian on Creation from Pre-existent Matter

In this controversial work, written to refute the views of his opponent Hermogenes, Tertullian (c.160–c.225) deals with Hermogenes' idea that God created the world out of pre-existing matter. How can God be Lord, he asked, unless there has always been something – such as pre-existent matter – to rule? Tertullian argues that a distinction may be drawn between the terms "God" and "Lord." God has always been "God," he only became "Lord" when there was something to be Lord over – in other words, once the creation had been brought into being. Tertullian's views should be compared with those of Origen (3.5) at this point.

[Hermogenes] argues that God made everything either out of himself, or out of nothing, or out of something. His intention here is to refute the first two of these possibilities, and to establish the third, namely, that God created out of something, and that the "something" was matter [*materia*]. He argues that God could not have created anything out of himself, because whatever he created would then have been part of himself. But God cannot be reduced to parts in this way, in that he is indivisible and unchangeable, and always the same, in that he is Lord. Further, anything made of himself would have been something of himself. His creation and his creating would then have to be accounted as being imperfect, so that they are only a partial creation and a partial creating. Or if God completely made a complete creation, then God must have been at one and the same time complete and incomplete;

complete, that he might make himself, and incomplete, that he might be made of himself. There is a further serious difficulty; if he existed he could not be created, if he did not exist, he could not create. Again he who always exists cannot become, but is for everlasting. Therefore he did not create out of himself; that would be inconsistent with his nature. Similarly, he argues that he could not have created out of nothing. He defines God as good, totally good, and therefore wishing to make all things good, just as totally good as he is himself [. . .] but evil is found in his creation, and this is certainly not according to his will [. . .] therefore we must assume it came into being as a result of a fault in something, and that something is undoubtedly matter.

He adds another argument; God has always been God, and always Lord. Now he could not be regarded as always Lord, as he is always God, if there had not been something already existing over which he could be accounted Lord. Therefore matter always existed for God to be always Lord over it. [. . .] We maintain that he always has the title of God, but not always that of Lord; for the nature of these two titles is different. God is the title of the substance, the divine nature: Lord the title of power. [. . .] He became Lord and acquired that name from the time when things come into being over which the power of the Lord was exercised: the position and the title come through the accession of power. God is father and judge: but it does not follow that he is father and judge eternally because he is always God. He could not be father before he had a son; nor a judge before sin was committed.

Comment

This is an example of a specifically polemical work, in which Tertullian engages with ideas which he regards as mistaken and pose a threat to the integrity of the Christian faith. The specific issue is whether God created the world out of pre-existing matter – a Platonic idea, which enjoyed some popularity with several early Christian writers – or whether everything required to be created. Tertullian argues for the latter position, which would eventually become the norm within Christian thinking.

Questions for Study

1 Summarize the position of Hermogenes on the questions being discussed in this passage.
2 Set out, in your own words, how Tertullian responds to each of these arguments. How convincing do you find his replies?
3 "God is father and judge: but it does not follow that he is father and judge eternally because he is always God. He could not be father before he had a son; nor a judge before sin was committed." Locate this passage within the text. What does Tertullian mean by this? How is this argument important in meeting Hermogenes' assertions at this point?

3.5

Origen on Creation from Pre-existent Matter

In this work, written in the first half of the third century, the Alexandrian theologian Origen (c.185–c.254) argues that God created the world from pre-existing matter. This matter is understood to be formless, so that the act of creation consists in fashioning this material into its proper form. Origen's views on this matter should be compared with those of Tertullian (3.4).

For this material is so considerable and of such a nature that it is enough for the creation of all the bodies of the world, to whom God wishes to give existence, and can serve the creator in any way which he wishes in making all the forms and species, and in providing them with the qualities which he wished to impose upon them. I do not understand how so many distinguished people have thought that it was uncreated, that is to say, that it was not made by God, the creator of the world; or how they thought that its nature and action were the result of chance. I am astonished that these people blame those who deny that God is the creator and sustainer of the world, accusing them of impious thoughts, because they hold that the work [*opus*] of the world endures without a creator or someone to tend it, when they themselves are just as guilty of impiety when they say that matter is uncreated [*ingenitus*] and co-eternal with the uncreated God. According to this line of thought, God would have had nothing to do, not having any matter with which he could have begun his work; for they allege that he could not make anything out of nothing, and that matter was present by chance rather than by God's design. They thus believe that something which came into being by chance could be good enough for the mighty work of creation. [. . .] This seems to me to be absurd, the result of people who ignore the power and the intelligence of the uncreated nature. But, in order to be able to consider the arguments at stake here, let us suppose provisionally that matter did not exist, and that God, at a point at which nothing existed, gave existence to whatever he wished. What follows? That this material which God was obliged to create, and to bring into existence through his power and wisdom, could have been better or superior to, or something very different from, what these people call "uncreated"? Or, on the contrary, that it could have been inferior or worse, or even similar or identical? I think that it is clear that neither a better material, nor a worse material, could have taken on the forms and species which are in the world; it would have had to be the kind of matter which, in fact, actually did assume them. Therefore it must be considered impious to call something "uncreated" which, if it is believed to have been created by God, would undoubtedly be found to be of the same type as that which is called "uncreated."

Comment

This passage represents a continuation of the early Christian debate over the manner in which the credal assertion that God is "creator of the world" is to be understood. Origen was one of the group of early Christian writers who believed that God fashioned the world from pre-existent matter. The process of creation is thus to be conceived more in terms of the imposition of ordering upon the world. Origen was very sympathetic to Platonist ideas, and this can be seen clearly in his positive evaluation of the Platonic concept of creation.

Questions for Study

1 What arguments does Origen recognize against his own position? How does he respond to them?
2 What, in your judgment, is the driving force behind Origen's doctrine of creation through divine ordering of formless matter?
3 "This seems to me to be absurd, the result of people who ignore the power and the intelligence of the uncreated nature." Locate this passage within the text. What seems to be absurd to Origen? And what reasons does he offer for this evaluation of this position?

3.6

Origen on the Relation of God and Evil

This passage develops the idea of "necessary evil" which, within God's providence, can lead to the fulfillment of God's purposes. It is not God's intention or will that evil should exist in the world. However, given that it does exist, God is able to direct it in such a way that good comes out of it. Origen illustrates this by pointing out how the treachery of Judas led to the redemption of the world through the death of Christ. See also 3.2, 3.14, 3.25.

God does not create evil; still, he does not prevent it when it is shown by others, although he could do so. But he uses both evil and those who show it for necessary purposes. For through those in whom there is evil, he brings distinction and testing to those who strive for the glory of virtue. Virtue, if unopposed, would not shine out nor become more glorious by being tested. Virtue is not virtue if it be untested and unexamined. [...] If you remove the wickedness of Judas and cancel his treachery you take away likewise the cross of Christ and his passion: and if there were no cross then principalities and powers have not been stripped nor triumphed over by the wood of the cross. Had there been no death of Christ, there would certainly have been no resurrection and there would have been no "firstborn from the dead" (Colossians 1: 18) and then there would have been no hope of resurrection for us. Similarly concerning the devil himself, if we suppose, for the sake of argument, that he had been forcibly prevented from sinning, or that the will to do evil had been taken away from him after his sin; then at the same time there would have been taken from us the struggle against the wiles of the devil, and there would be no crown of victory in store for those who struggled.

Comment

The question of how evil was to be accounted for troubled many early Christian writers, including Origen. For some, the existence of evil called into question either – or both – the goodness and the power of God. In this passage, Origen is concerned to point how how some things which we might, at first sight, assume to be intrinsically evil, can actually be argued to bring about good in the longer term.

Questions for Study

1 What benefit can evil bring, according to Origen?
2 Set out, in your own words, how the betrayal of Christ by Judas Iscariot illustrates this point. How do you evaluate Origen's argument at this point?
3 According to Origen, what would be the result if there was no devil?

3.7

Origen on the Suffering of God

This remarkable third-century passage suggests that God was understood to experience suffering, on account of the incarnation. This runs counter to the prevailing consensus of the early patristic period, which insisted that Christ suffered only in his human nature, leaving his divinity immune from such suffering. Although originally written in Greek, this text survives only in the Latin translation of Rufinus of Aquilea. It is possible that the translation process from Greek to Latin may have led to a slight distortion in Origen's meaning. See also 3.21, 3.30, 3.33, 3.37, 3.38.

The savior descended to earth to grieve for the human race, and took our sufferings on himself before he endured the cross and deigned to assume our flesh. If he had not suffered, he would not have come to share in human life. What is this suffering which he suffered for us beforehand? It is the suffering of love. For the Father himself, the God of the universe, who is "long-suffering and full of mercy" (cf. Psalm 102: 8) and merciful, does he not suffer in some way [*nonne quodammodo patitur*]? Or do you now know that, when he deals with humanity, he suffers human suffering [*passionem patitur humanam*]? "For the Lord your God has taken your ways upon him as a man bears his son" (cf. Deuteronomy 1: 31). Therefore God has taken our ways upon himself, just as the Son of God bore our sufferings. The Father himself is not impassible [*Ipse Pater non est impassibilis*].

Comment

Conventional theological wisdom has it that most early Christian writers took the view that God was not "passible," so that God was not in any way affected by the pain and suffering of the creation. It has been argued that this is especially the case with writers who were influenced by Platonism. This extract from Origen's commentary on the Book of Ezekiel indicates that the situation is not quite as straightforward as the theology textbooks would have us believe! It is instructive to compare this with 3.8, in which Origen seems to take a different view.

Questions for Study

1 How important is the link that Origen establishes between divine suffering and the incarnation?
2 How is Origen's thinking affected by the two biblical passages which he cites or alludes to during his discussion?
3 "If [the savior] had not suffered, he would not have come to share in human life." Locate this passage within the text. What does Origen mean by this?

3.8

Origen on the Changelessness of God

In this passage Origen argues that the Word of God is not changed in any temporal way by the incarnation. The Word therefore does not suffer human pain, whether physical or mental. This suggests that Origen upholds the traditional view of the apatheia of God – that is, that God does not experience suffering or change. Compare this passage with the different view expressed in 3.7. See also 3.37.

It seems to Celsus that the assumption by the immortal divine Word of a mortal body and a human soul means a temporal change and alteration. He ought to learn that the Word remains the Word in his essential being and does not suffer what the body or soul suffers; that he comes down at a certain time to be with him who cannot behold the splendor and brightness of his godhead, and as it were becomes flesh, or to use physical terms, until he who has received him in this shape, being gradually raised to a higher level by the Word, may be able to gaze upon what I may call his primary form.

Comment

It is important to note that this statement is to be found within a polemical work, which deals with criticisms made against Christianity by Celsus, a well-informed pagan writer. Celsus's argument is that the incarnation is a contradiction, in that it implies that God undergoes change – which, at least to Celsus, implies a fatal inconsistency. Origen attempts to refute this with a series of clarifications and distinctions.

Questions for Study

1 How does Origen resist the charge that God undergoes change in the incarnation?
2 How does the approach that Origen adopts lead him to deny that God undergoes or experiences human suffering?
3 Is there an inconsistency in what Origen asserts in this passage? And how would you reconcile his approach here with that which he adopts in 3.7?

3.9

Gregory of Nyssa on Human Analogies of the Trinity

Surely the doctrine of the Trinity implies that there are three gods? This objection was frequently raised against the emerging Christian consensus on the nature of the godhead. One of the most important responses to this takes the form of a short doctrinal treatise written by Gregory of Nyssa (c.330–c.395), in response to a question raised by Ablabius. Three men might indeed share a common human nature – but they remain three individuals, nonetheless. Surely the same is true of the Trinity? The three persons may share in a common godhead – but are not all gods? And do not Christians therefore really believe in three Gods? What follows is Gregory's response. See also 3.11, 3.12, 3.13, 3.16, 3.20, 3.43.

The question that you have raised before us is no small matter, nor is it such that only a little harm will arise if it is not answered properly. At first sight, your question forces us to accept one of two incorrect opinions, and either to say that "there are three Gods," which is blasphemous, or not to acknowledge the Godhead of the Son and the Holy Spirit, which is impious and absurd.

The argument that you present runs something like this. Peter, James, and John, are called "three men," despite the fact that they share a common human nature. Now there is nothing absurd about describing those who are united in their nature using a plural form, if there is more than one of them. So if, as in this case, custom admits this, and no one forbids us to speak of those who are two as two, or those who are more than two as three, how is it that in the case of our statements about the mysteries of the faith, which acknowledge three persons without any difference of nature between them, we are in some way undermining our belief that there is one godhead of the Father and of the Son and of the Holy Spirit, and yet forbid people to say that "there are three Gods"? The question is, as I said, very difficult to deal with [...]

To begin with, we may say that the practice of calling those who do not differ in their nature by the actual name of that shared nature in the plural (by saying they are "many men") is a customary misuse of language. We could equally say that they are "many human natures." We can see the truth of this from the following example. When we address someone, we do not call him by the name of his nature. Otherwise, confusion would result with everyone who shared this name. Every one of those who heard it might think that he himself was the person being addressed, in that this address would not be made using the proper name of any specific individual, but by the common name of their nature. In order to distinguish that specific person from the group as a whole, we must use that name which properly belongs to him as his own, signifying him as its specific subject. Thus there are many who share the same nature – for example, there are many disciples, apostles, or martyrs – but the human nature within them all is the same. As we have said, the term "man" does not belong to any particular individual as such, but the common nature that men share. Thus Luke is a man, and Stephen is a man – but it does not follow that if any one is a man, he is therefore Luke or Stephen for that reason. [...] So it would be much better if we were to correct our erroneous habit, so that we no longer extend the name of a common nature to a group, so that this force of habit no longer caused us to transfer this mistake to our statements about God.

But the correction of this habit is probably impracticable. How could you persuade people not to speak of those who share the same nature as "many men"? Habit is a thing hard to change! In any case, we are not seriously misled when we follow this habit for the lower nature, which does not give rise to serious error. But in the case of our statements about the divine nature, this way of speaking is no longer free from danger. It is no longer a trivial matter. Therefore we must confess one God, according to the testimony of Scripture, "Hear, O Israel, the Lord your God is one Lord," even though the name of Godhead extends throughout the Holy Trinity. [...]

Our argument has been that the word "Godhead" does not signify a specific nature but an operation. Given this, we can perhaps understand why, in the human case, men who share common interests are enumerated and spoken of using the plural, while on the other hand the deity is spoken of in the singular as one God and one Godhead, even though the three persons are not separated from what is signified by the term "Godhead." Indeed, men, even if several of them are engaged in the same occupation, work separately each by himself at the task he has undertaken, and not sharing his individual actions with others who are nevertheless engaged in the same occupation. For instance, orators share the same occupation, and thus have the same name in each case – yet each of them works by himself as an orator, this one arguing in his own distinctive way, and another in his own way. Thus, since at the human level, the action of each individual sharing the same occupation can be distinguished, they are properly called "many," since each of them is separated from the others within his own environment, according to the special character of his operation.

But in the case of the divine nature, we do not believe that the Father does anything by himself in which the Son is not also involved. Again, we do not believe that the Son acts on his own apart from the Holy Spirit. Rather, every operation of God upon his creation is named according to our conceptions of it, and takes its origin from the Father, proceeds through the Son, and is perfected in the Holy Spirit. For this reason the name derived from the operation is not divided with regard to the number of those who carry it out, because the action of each concerning anything is not separate and individual, but whatever takes place, in relation either to the acts of God's providence towards us, or to the government and constitution of the universe, takes place by the action of the Three – yet what takes place is not three things. We may grasp the meaning of this from an example. We say that we who have shared in grace received our life from the one who is the chief source of gifts. When we ask where this good gift came from, we find by the guidance of the Scriptures that it came from the Father, Son, and Holy Spirit. Yet although we set forth Three Persons and three names, we do not consider that we have had bestowed upon us three lives, one from each person separately. Rather, the same life is wrought within us by the Father and prepared by the Son, and depends on the will of the Holy Spirit. Since then the Holy Trinity fulfills every operation in a manner similar to that of which I have spoken, not by separate action according to the number of the persons, but so that there is one motion and disposition of the good will which is communicated from the Father through the Son to the Spirit [...] so neither can we call those who exercise this divine governing power and operation towards ourselves and all creation, conjointly and inseparably, by their mutual action, three Gods. [...]

In the same way, savior of all people, especially of those who believe, is spoken of by the Apostle as "one" (1 Timothy 4: 10). But nobody argues that this phrase means either that the Son does not save those who believe, or that salvation is given to those who receive it without the intervention of the Spirit. The meaning is that God, who is over all, is the Savior of all, while the Son works salvation by means of the grace of the Spirit. Yet this does not mean that Scripture speaks of three saviors (although salvation is acknowledged to proceed from the Holy Trinity).

Comment

Gregory's argument is as complex as it is important. The easiest way to grasp his point is his insistence that "the word 'Godhead' does not signify a specific nature but an operation." We might think of individual shoemakers, farmers, or orators: each may share a common profession, but they are *defined* individually in that they operate *individually*. In the case of the Trinity, however, we are dealing with single operations in which all persons are involved cooperatively. To anticipate a later slogan, *opera Trinitatis ad extra indivisa sunt* ("external actions of the Trinity are indivisible"). Therefore the Trinity cannot be thought of as three gods.

Questions for Study

1 Set out the problem, as Ablabius appears to have stated it, on the basis of Gregory's response.
2 What is the point that Gregory wishes to make by his analogy of calling people by their individual names, rather than their generic humanity? What role does this play in his argument.
3 The critical point is best appreciated by looking at Gregory's argument based on 1 Timothy 4: 10: "we have our hope set on the living God, who is the Savior of all people, especially of those who believe." Gregory notes that there is only one Savior – but that this does not mean that Father, Son, and Spirit do not play definite individual roles within the work of salvation as a whole. Set out clearly, in your own words, the argument that Gregory develops, and the conclusion he reaches.

3.10

Basil of Caesarea on the Work of the Holy Spirit

After reflecting on the biblical terms used for the Holy Spirit, Basil of Caesarea (c.330–79) turns to deal with the particular roles of the Spirit. After an initial discussion of the role of the Spirit in sanctification, Basil notes the work of the Spirit in relation to "being made like God" and "being made God." The close connection between the Spirit and deification is a distinctive feature of much eastern Greek thought of this period. See also 3.3, 3.11, 3.15, 3.16, 3.17.

He is called "spirit of God" (Matthew 12: 28), "spirit of truth which proceeds from the Father" (John 15: 26), "right Spirit" (Psalm 51: 12), and "Lord Spirit" (Psalm 50: 14). His proper and peculiar title is "Holy Spirit," which is a name specially appropriate to all that is not physical, purely immaterial and indivisible. That is why the Lord, when teaching the woman who thought God was an object of local worship that what is not physical cannot be limited, said, "God is Spirit" (John 4: 24). So it is not possible when one hears this name of Spirit to conceive of a limited nature, which is subject to change and variation, or at all like any creature. On the contrary, we must raise our thought to the highest level and think of a substance endowed with intelligence, of infinite power, of a greatness which knows no limit, which cannot be measured in times or ages, and which lavishes its good gifts.

All who are in need of sanctification turn to the Spirit; all those seek him who live by virtue, for his breath refreshes them and comes to their aid in the pursuit of their natural and proper end. Capable of perfecting others, the Spirit himself lacks nothing. He is not a being who needs to restore his strength, but himself supplies life; he does not grow by additions, but possesses abundant fullness; he abides in himself, but is also present everywhere. The source of sanctification, a light perceptible to the mind, he supplies through himself illumination to every force of reason searching for the truth. By nature inaccessible, he can be understood by reason of his goodness; filling all things with his power, he communicates himself only to those who are worthy of him, not by sharing himself according to a unique measure but by distributing his energy in proportion to faith. Simple in essence, varied in his miracles, he is wholly present to everyone and wholly everywhere at the same time. He is shared without being affected; he remains whole and yet gives himself in the sharing, like a sunbeam whose warming light shines on the one who enjoys it as though it shone for him alone, yet it also lights the land and the sea, and mingles with the air.

Similarly, the Spirit is present to all who are capable of receiving him as though given to them alone, and yet he sends forth full and sufficient grace for all humanity, and is enjoyed by all who share in him, according to the capacity, not of his power but of their nature. Souls in which the Spirit dwells, illuminated by the Spirit, themselves become spiritual and send forth their grace to others. From here comes foreknowledge of the future, understanding of mysteries, apprehension of what is hidden, the sharing of the gifts of grace, heavenly citizenship, a place in the chorus of angels, joy without end, abiding in God, being made like God and – the greatest of them all – being made a god.

Comment

The argument set forth in this passage is of considerable importance in the patristic discussion concerning the divinity of the Holy Spirit. The basic argument is that the Holy Spirit *does* something that only God can do. Didymus the Blind (d. 398) was one of many writers to point out that the Spirit was responsible for the creating, renewing, and sanctification of God's creatures. Yet how could one creature renew or sanctify another creature? Only if the Spirit was divine could sense be made of these functions. If the Holy Spirit performed functions which were specific to God, it must follow that the Holy Spirit shares in the divine nature. The ontological affirmation that the Holy Spirit is divine is thus grounded in the functional affirmation that the Holy Spirit carries out divine roles.

Questions for Study

1 Set out the main line of argument in this passage. How does Basil establish a link between the task of sanctification and the nature of the Holy Spirit?
2 What analogies does Basil deploy in setting out his case? How do these illuminate his arguments?
3 "On the contrary, we must raise our thought to the highest level and think of a substance endowed with intelligence, of infinite power, of a greatness which knows no limit, which cannot be measured in times or ages, and which lavishes its good gifts." Locate this passage within the text. What does Basil mean by this? What conclusions does he draw from this general line of argument?

3.11

Gregory of Nazianzus on the Gradual Revelation of the Trinity

In this work, written around 380, Gregory of Nazianzus (329–89) sets out the main features of the Christian faith. In this section he explains why the doctrine of the Trinity is not explicitly stated in Scripture. Note especially his understanding of the gradual revelation of the doctrine, through the guidance of the Holy Spirit within the church. Note also that the "theological orations" are generally distinguished from the "orations" as a whole, of which they are part. "Theological Oration 1" is "Oration 27," "Theological Oration 5" is "Oration 31," and so forth. See also 3.3, 3.9, 3.12, 3.13, 3.15, 3.16, 3.19.

The Old Testament preached the Father openly and the Son more obscurely. The New Testament revealed the Son, and hinted at the divinity of the Holy Spirit. Now the Spirit dwells in us, and is revealed more clearly to us. It was not proper to preach the Son openly, while the divinity of the Father had not yet been admitted. Nor was it proper to accept the Holy Spirit before [the divinity of] the Son had been acknowledged. [. . .] Instead, by gradual advances and [. . .] partial ascents, we should move forward and increase in clarity, so that the light of the Trinity [*Trias*] should shine.

Comment

An analysis of the development of patristic thinking about the nature of the Godhead indicates that there are three stages in the evolution of the doctrine of the Trinity.

Stage 1: the recognition of the full divinity of Jesus Christ.
Stage 2: the recognition of the full divinity of the Spirit.
Stage 3: the definitive formulation of the doctrine of the Trinity, embedding and clarifying these central insights, and determining their mutual relationship.

This sequential development is acknowledged in this passage by Gregory, who argues for a gradual progress in clarification and understanding of the mystery of God's revelation in the course of time. It was, he argued, impossible to deal with the question of the divinity of the Spirit until the issue of the divinity of Christ had been settled. The mind of the church thus developed gradually, in that the full exploration of the depths of the self-revelation of God requires many generations to undertake. The recognition of the dogma of the Trinity is thus the climax of the long and cautious process of reflection and analysis. Gregory is concerned to stress that the dogma of the Trinity is not a human imposition upon divine revelation, but a human discernment of the realities which are disclosed by that process of divine revelation.

Questions for Study

1 Why does Gregory regard this question as being important?
2 What stages within the discernment of the dogma of the Trinity does Gregory identify?
3 Would you style Gregory's argument as "historical" or "theological" in nature?

3.12

Hilary of Poitiers on the Trinity

In this important witness to the role of the trinitarian formula in baptism, and more specifically the relation of the Spirit to the Father and Son, Hilary of Poitiers (c.315–67) emphasizes that the Christian faith rests upon revelation, rather than reason. The most important section of the passage sets out an understanding of the relation of the Spirit to the Father and the Son: the Spirit is "from the Father" and "through the Son." See also 3.3, 3.10, 3.11, 3.13, 3.15, 3.19.

For as long as I enjoy the life which you have given me by your Spirit, O Holy Father, Almighty God, I shall proclaim you as the eternal God and also as the eternal Father. Nor shall I ever show such folly and impiety as to make myself judge of your omnipotence and mysteries, and put the feeble understanding of my weakness above a true understanding of your infinity and faith in your eternity. I shall never declare that you could have existed without your wisdom, your virtue, your word: the only-begotten God, my Lord Jesus Christ. [...]

Preserve, I ask of you, this piety of my faith without any contamination, and to the end of my life give me this awareness of my knowledge, that I always may hold fast to what I possess, that is, what I professed in the creed of my regeneration when I was baptized in the name of the Father, and of the Son, and of the Holy Spirit. Grant that I may adore you, our Father, and your Son together with you, and that I may be worthy of the Holy Spirit who is from you through your only-begotten [*sanctum Spiritum tuum qui ex te per unigenitum tuum est*]. He bears witness to my faith who says, "Father, all things that are mine are yours, and yours are mine" – my Lord Jesus Christ, who for ever abides as God in you, from you and with you, who is blessed for ever and ever. Amen.

Comment

Note that this theological reflection takes the form of meditation and prayer, rather than logical theological analysis. Hilary is setting out his insights in a doxological context, in which prayer and adoration serve an important theological role. The most interesting section of this passage deals with the relation of the Father, Son, and Holy Spirit, in that Hilary clearly regards the Spirit as deriving from the Father through the Son – an important early statement of the classic western position on the Holy Spirit, summarized in the *filioque* clause, which would cause such difficulties for the eastern church in years to come (see Glossary).

Questions for Study

1 Some scholars have suggested that liturgical or credal material is incorporated into this passage. Without necessarily agreeing with this suggestion, can you identify any sections of the passage which might fall into this category of material?
2 "I shall proclaim you as the eternal God and also as the eternal Father." Locate this passage within the text. What might the implications of Hilary's distinction between "God" and "Father" be?
3 What role does this passage assign to the Holy Spirit?

3.13

Augustine on the Trinity

In this important discussion, originally written over the period 400–16, Augustine of Hippo (354–430) sets out a distinctive approach to the Trinity which would have a major impact on western trinitarian thought. The passage is notable on account of its detailed analysis of the concept of "love," in which it is argued that this concept necessarily implies a lover, a beloved, and their mutual love. On the basis of this psychological analogy, Augustine argues for a threefold understanding of the Godhead, in terms of Father, Son, and Holy Spirit. See also 3.3, 3.9, 3.10, 3.11, 3.12, 3.15, 3.19.

We believe that Father, Son, and Holy Spirit are one God, maker and ruler of every creature, and that "Father" is not "son," nor "Holy Spirit" "Father" or "son"; but a Trinity of mutually related persons, and a unity of equal essence. So let us attempt to understand this truth, praying that he who we wish to understand would help us in doing so, so that we can set out whatever we thus understand with such careful reverence that nothing unworthy is said (even if we sometimes say one thing instead of another). In this way, if we say something about the Father which is not properly appropriate to him, it may be appropriate to the Son or to the Holy Spirit, or to the whole Trinity; or if we say something about the Son which does not properly apply to the Son, it may at least apply to the Father, or to the Holy Spirit, or to the whole Trinity; or if we say something about the Holy Spirit which is not proper in his case, then it may not be incorrect in the case of the Father or the Son, or the one God which is the Trinity itself. Now we want to see whether that most excellent gift of charity is properly the Holy Spirit. If this is not the case, then either the Father is charity, or the Son is, or the whole Trinity is (since we may not oppose the certainty of faith and most valid authority of the Scripture which says "God is love" (1 John 4: 8, 16). But we must never allow any error to lead us astray in such a way that we say something about the Trinity which relates to the *creature* rather than the *Creator*, or results from wild speculation.

In view of all this let us consider those three things which we wish to discover more about. We are not yet talking about things in heaven, nor about God, Father, Son, and Holy Spirit; but about this flawed image (but an image none the less), that is, humanity, which is so much more familiar and less difficult for the weakness of our mind to study.

Now when I, who am asking about this, love anything, there are three things present: I myself, what I love, and love itself. For I cannot love love unless I love a lover [*non enim amo amorem nisi amantem*]; for there is no love where nothing is loved. So there are three things: the lover, the loved, and love [*amans et quod amatur et amor*]. Yet if the object of my love is myself, then the three become two – the object of love, and love. For when the lover loves himself, subject and object are the same; just as loving and being loved are in the love of self the same thing. So there would be no difference between saying "he loves himself," and "he is loved by himself." In that case, "to love" and "to be loved" are not two things, any more than the lover and the loved are two persons. But still the love and what is loved remain two. For the one who loves himself can be identical with love only if love itself is what is loved. It is one thing to love oneself and another to love one's love, since love which is loved must love something, because when nothing is loved, there is no love. So there are two things present when someone loves themselves, love and what is loved (the lover and the loved being one). From this it seems that three things are not understood to be present wherever there is love.

Let us remove from this discussion all the other things of which human nature is composed, so that we may find what we are looking for in as clear a form as possible. So let us take the mind alone. In the love of the mind for itself, two things are shown – mind and love. Now what is love of oneself other than the will to be at one's own disposal for self-enjoyment? If the mind wills itself to be what it is, then "will" corresponds to "mind" and "love" to "lover." If love is some kind of substance, it is not body but spirit, just as the mind is not body but spirit. Yet the mind and its love are not two spirits, but one spirit, not two essences but one. In other words, the two are as one, "lover" and "love," or (as you might say) "love" and "that which is loved." And these two are mutually related terms; "lover" being related to "love" and "love" to "lover"; for the lover loves in virtue of a particular love and love is the activity of a particular lover. Mind and spirit, on the other hand, are not relative terms but refer to essence in itself. It is not the fact that mind and spirit belong to a particular human being that determines that they are mind and spirit. Remove whatever it is that, when it is added, constitutes a human being (that is, the body), and mind and spirit will still remain. But remove the lover and there will be no love; remove the love and there will be no lover. Thus these two terms are mutually related: in themselves, each is spirit, and both together are one spirit; each is mind, and both together are one mind. Where then is there a trinity? Let us consider this as best we are able, asking the everlasting Light to lighten our darkness, that we may see in ourselves *the image of God.*

The mind cannot love itself unless it also knows itself. How can it love something it does not know? The suggestion that the mind forms either a general or a specific knowledge [*notitia*] from its experience of other minds, and believes itself to belong to the same class of being and on that basis loves itself, is to be regarded as absurd. How can a mind know any other mind, if it does not know itself? [. . .] We may say then that the mind acquires knowledge of physical things by the bodily senses, and of things that are not physical through the fact that it is not physical. It must know itself by itself: if it does not know itself, it cannot love itself.

Now just as there are two things (the mind and its love) present when it loves itself, so there are also two things present, the mind and its knowledge, when it knows itself. So there are three things – the mind, its love, and its knowledge [*mens et amor et notitia eius*] – which are one, and when perfect they are equal. If it loves itself less than the word implies – as, for example, if the human mind, which is greater than the human body, loves itself only with the love due to the human body – then it sins, and its love is not perfect. Again, if it loves itself more than it should – as, for example, if the human mind loves itself with the love due to God, to whom it is incomparably inferior – then it also sins greatly, and its love is not perfect. It sins in a particularly perverse and iniquitous manner when it loves the body to the extent that God is to be loved. Similarly a knowledge which falls short of its object, where full knowledge is possible, is not perfect. A knowledge which is greater than its object implies a superiority in the nature of the knower to that of the known: the knowledge of a body is greater than the body which is the object of the knowledge. For knowledge is a mode of life in the knowing mind, whereas the body is not life; and any life is greater, not in extent but in power, than any body. But when the mind knows itself, the knowledge does not exceed the self, for the self is both subject and object of the knowledge. If it knows the whole of itself, without anything else being added from outside, the knowing corresponds to the mind; for it is no less apparent that in this knowledge of itself the knowing is not dependent on any other source. And when this knowledge takes in the whole self and nothing more, it is neither less nor greater than the self. Thus it is true to say that when each member of these three is perfect, it follows that all three are equal.

Now we are challenged to see how these [three things] are present in the soul. [. . .] The mind knows not only itself but many other things as well. Therefore love and knowledge [*cognitio*] are not present in the mind simply as aspects of their subject: their existence is as substantive as that of the mind itself. They are to be understood as mutually related things, each of which are distinctive substances. As mutually related things they cannot be compared to "color" and "that which is colored" [*color et coloratum*], in that the color possesses no substance proper to itself: the substance is the colored body; the color is in the substance. It is like two friends, who are both men and are therefore substances. While "men" is not a relative term, "friends" is.

"Lover" and "knower," "knowledge" and "love" are all substances. But while "lover" and "love," "knower" and "knowledge" are – like "friends" – relative terms, "mind" and "spirit" – like "men" – are not. Now men who are friends can exist apart from each other. Yet this is not the case with "lover" and "love," "knower" and "knowledge." It may seem that friends can be separated in body only and not in soul. But it is possible for a friend to begin to hate his friend and thereby cease to be his friend, though the other may not know it and may continue to love him. On the other hand, if the love with which the mind loves itself ceases to exist, the mind will also cease to be a lover. Similarly, if the knowledge with which the mind knows itself ceases to exist, the mind will cease to know itself. [. . .]

If any bodies exist which cannot be severed or divided in any way, they must still consist of their parts or they would not be bodies. "Part" and "whole" are related terms, since every part belongs to some whole, and the whole is whole on account of its totality of parts. But since the body is both "part" and "whole," these exist not only as mutually related terms but as substances. It may thus be said that the mind is a whole, and that the love with which it loves itself and the knowledge with which it knows itself are like two parts composing the whole; or that they and the mind itself are equal parts making up the one whole. [. . .] Wine, water, and honey make a single drink, in which each of these will extend throughout the whole, and yet they remain three. There would be no part of the drink which does not contain all three – not side by side as in the case of oil and water, but completely mixed. All are substances, and the whole fluid is one definite substance made out of the three. Can we suppose that the three things – mind, love, and knowledge – exist together in the same sort of way? Yet water, wine, and honey do not derive from a single substance, though one single substance of drink results from that mixture. But I do not see how these three are not the same essence, since the mind loves itself and knows itself, without being loved or known by anything else. The three must then necessarily have one and the same essence, so that if they were to be intermingled in such a way as to be confused, they would not be three things nor could they be said to be in a mutual relation. It would be like three similar rings made out of the same gold, which are mutually related on the basis of their similarity, since everything that is similar is similar to something else, and there would be a trinity of rings [*trinitas anulorum*] and one gold. However, if they were mixed together to form a single lump, this trinity would be destroyed. We could still speak of "one gold" as in these three rings, but no longer of three golden objects.

In the case of the three things by which the mind knows and loves itself, the trinity of mind, love, and knowledge remains [*manet trinitas, mens, amor, notitia*]. There is no intermingling or loss of identity. [. . .] The mind is distinct in itself, and is itself called "mind," even though it is termed "knowing," "known," or "knowable" in relation to its knowledge, and "loving," "loved," or "lovable" in relation to the love with which it loves itself. Knowledge is indeed related to the mind which knows or is known, but it is still properly termed "known" and "knowing" in itself, for the knowledge by which the mind knows itself is not unknown to the knowledge itself. Similarly love, though related to the loving mind to which it belongs, still remains distinct by itself and in itself; for love is loved, and that can only be by the love itself. This shows that each of the three is distinct in itself. Again, they are alternately in one another: the loving mind is in the love, love is in the lover's knowledge, and knowledge in the knowing mind. [. . .] In a wonderful way, the three are inseparable from one another, and yet each one of them is a distinct substance, and all together are one substance or essence, even though they are said to be mutually related to each another.

Comment

This is a highly important passage, which would have an immense influence on western Christian thinking about the Trinity. One of the most distinctive features of Augustine's approach to the Trinity is his development of "psychological analogies." Augustine argues that in creating the world, God has left a characteristic imprint (*vestigium*) upon that creation. As humanity is the height of God's creation, Augustine argues, we should look to humanity in our search for the image of God. On the basis of his neo-Platonic worldview, Augustine asserts that the human mind is to be regarded as the apex of humanity. It is therefore to the individual human mind that the theologian should turn, in looking for "traces of the Trinity" (*vestigia Trinitatis*) in creation. The radical individualism of this approach, coupled with its obvious intellectualism, means that Augustine chooses to find the Trinity in the inner mental world of individuals, rather than – for example – in personal relationships (an approach favored by medieval writers, such as Richard of St Victor: see 3.22).

Augustine discerns a triadic structure to human thought and argues that this structure of thought is grounded in the being of God. He himself argues that the most important such triad is that of mind, knowledge, and love (*mens, notitia*, and *amor*), although the related triad of memory, understanding, and will (*memoria, intelligentia*, and *voluntas*) is also given considerable prominence. The human mind is an image – inadequate, to be sure, but still an image – of God himself. So just as there are three such faculties in the human mind, which are not ultimately totally separate and independent entities, so there can be three "persons" in God.

Questions for Study

1 Set out, in your own words, Augustine's analysis of the concept of love. How many aspects of his trinitarianism can be grounded on this analysis? In particular, consider the role which Augustine allocates to three entities: the lover, that which is loved, and love itself.

2 Set out, in your own words, the way in which Augustine uses an analysis of the inner workings of the human mind to illuminate his understanding of the Trinity. How convincing do you find this?
3 "Wine, water, and honey make a single drink, in which each of these will extend throughout the whole, and yet they remain three." Locate this passage within the text. What does Augustine mean by this analogy? How does he develop it? And what is its trinitarian application?

3.14

Augustine on the Relation of God and Evil

In his early period, Augustine was attracted to Manicheism, partly because it provided a simple explanation of the origin of evil. According to this movement, evil had its origins in an evil or defective deity, who was opposed to the true and righteous God. On becoming a Christian, Augustine rejected this dualism, and was therefore obliged to give an alternative explanation of the origins of evil. In this passage, written in Latin during the period 388–95, he argues that evil represents a free turning away from God, rather than a positive entity in its own right. However, he is unable to provide a convincing explanation of why someone should wish to turn away from God in this manner. See also 3.2, 3.4, 3.5, 3.25.

If there is a movement, that is a turning away [*aversio*] of the human will from the Lord God, which without doubt is sin, can we then say that God is the author of sin? God, then, will not be the cause of that movement. But what will its cause be? If you ask this question, I will have to answer that I do not know. While this will sadden you, it is nevertheless a true answer. For that which is nothing cannot be known. But hold to your pious opinion that no good thing can happen to you, to your senses or to your intelligence or to your way of thinking which does not come from God. Nothing of any kind can happen which is not of God. [. . .] For all good is from God. Hence there is no nature which is not from God. The movement of turning away, which we admit is sin, is a defective movement; and all defect comes from nothing. Once you have understood where it belongs, you will have no doubt that it does not belong to God. Because that defective movement is voluntary, it is placed within our power. If you fear it, all you have to do is simply not to will it. If you do not will it, it will not exist. What can be safer than to live a life where nothing can happen to you which you do not will? But since we cannot rise by our own free will as we once fell by our own free will spontaneously, let us hold with steadfast faith the right hand of

God stretched out to us from above, even our Lord Jesus Christ, and look forward to receiving the certain hope and love which we greatly long for.

Comment

On the basis of his Christian belief Augustine is denied a simple dualist answer to the problem of evil. The Manicheans could argue that there was a good god and an evil god, and that the latter causes all the problems in the world. Yet this road is closed off to Augustine, on account of his emphatic insistence that there is only one God, who alone created the world. Augustine therefore develops an approach which he believes preserves God's integrity, even though Augustine is conscious of not having answered the question to everyone's satisfaction.

Questions for Study

1 What are the implications of declaring that evil is fundamentally a defect?
2 Augustine implies that humanity itself is the cause of evil. Locate the section of the passage which appears to imply this. What would be the implications of a human causality for sin?
3 "Since we cannot rise by our own free will as we once fell by our own free will spontaneously, let us hold with steadfast faith the right hand of God stretched out to us from above." Augustine is clear that humanity needs God's grace in order to achieve its God-given goal. What does this need for grace imply about the ability of human nature? And about the origins of evil?

3.15

Augustine on the Holy Spirit

This text deals with the distinctive role and identity of the Holy Spirit within the Trinity, and especially the manner in which the Holy Spirit can be thought of as "love." In this discussion, originally written in Latin over the period 400–16, Augustine develops an argument for it being especially appropriate to think of the Holy Spirit in terms of "love," while at the same time recognizing the involvement of the entire Trinity in the process. The major difficulty which Augustine has to face is that there is no biblical text which explicitly affirms that the "Holy Spirit is love." For this reason, Augustine is obliged to enter into a complex – and, to some of his critics, somewhat unconvincing – argument to show that this is implied by the texts in question. See also 3.3, 3.9, 3.10, 3.11, 3.12, 3.13, 3.16, 3.22.

We have now said enough concerning the Father and the Son as we have found possible to discern by means of this dark mirror (1 Corinthians 13: 12) of the human mind. Now we must consider, with such insight as God's gift may grant us, the Holy Spirit. Scripture teaches us that he is the Spirit neither of the Father alone nor of the Son alone, but of both; and this suggests to us the mutual love [*caritas*] by which the Father and the Son love one another. [. . .] Yet Scripture does not say: "the Holy Spirit *is* love." If it had, much of our inquiry would have been rendered unnecessary. Scripture does indeed say: "God is charity" (1 John 4: 8, 16); and so left us to ask whether it is God the Father, or God the Son, or God the Holy Spirit, or God the Trinity itself, who is love. Now it is no use to say that love is called "God" because it is a gift of God and that therefore it is not a substantive reality worthy to be named God. There are, it is true, passages in Scripture where God is addressed in such terms as "you are my patience" (Psalm 71: 5), and there the meaning is not that our patience is the substance of God, but that it comes to us from him, as indeed we read elsewhere: "from him is my patience" (Psalm 62: 5). But in the case of love any such interpretation is at once refuted by the actual language of the Scriptures. "You are my patience" is like "You, Lord, are my hope" (Psalm 91: 9), and "My God is my compassion" (Psalm 59: 17) and many expressions of the kind; but we do not read: "the Lord is my love," or "You are my love," or "God is my love." Instead, we read: "God is love" – just as "God is spirit" (John 4: 24). Anyone who cannot see the difference should ask for understanding from the Lord, rather than explanation from us; for words cannot make this point clearer.

God, then, is love. The question is whether this refers to Father, or Son, or Holy Spirit, or the Trinity itself (which is not three gods, but one God). I have argued earlier in the present book that the divine Trinity must not be so conceived, from the likeness or the three members [that is, memory, understanding, love] displayed in our mental trinity, as to make the Father "memory" or all three, the Son "understanding" or all three, and the Holy Spirit "love" or all three. It is not as if the Father neither understood nor loved for himself, but the Son understood for him and the Holy Spirit loved for him, while he himself did nothing but "remember," both for himself and for them. Nor is it as if the Son neither remembered nor loved for himself, but the Father remembered for him and the Holy Spirit loved for him, while he himself did nothing but understand both for himself and for them. Nor is it as if the Holy Spirit neither remembered nor understood for himself, but the Father remembered for him and the Son understood for him, while he himself loved both for himself and for them. Rather must we think that all and each of them possess all three powers in their proper nature; and that in them, the three are not separate (whereas in ourselves, memory is one thing, understanding another, and love another). Rather, there is one single power whose capacity is sufficient for all, such as wisdom itself, which is so to be found in the nature of each individual person that he who possesses it is that which he possesses, in that he is a changeless and incomposite substance. If this be understood and its truth is clear, so far as we may be allowed to see or to conjecture in these great matters, I see no reason why, just as Father, Son and Holy Spirit are each called "wisdom," and all together are not three wisdoms but one, so Father, Son and Holy Spirit may not each be called "love," and all together one charity. In the same way the Father is God, the Son is God, and the Holy Spirit God; and all together are one God.

Yet there is good reason why in this Trinity we speak of the Son alone as Word of God, of the Holy Spirit alone as Gift of God, and of God the Father alone as the one of whom the Word is begotten and from whom the Holy Spirit principally proceeds [*nec de quo genitum est verbum et de quo quo procedit principaliter spiritus sanctus nisi Deus pater*]. I add the word "principally," because we learn that the Holy Spirit proceeds also from the Son. But this is again something given by the Father to the Son – not that he ever existed without it, for all that the Father gives to his only-begotten Word he gives in the act of begetting him. He is begotten in such a manner that the common gift proceeds from him as well, and the Holy Spirit is Spirit of both. And this distinction within the indivisible Trinity is not of minor importance, but to be noted carefully. For it is especially appropriate that the Word of God is also called the "wisdom of God," though both Father and Holy Spirit are wisdom. Now if it is especially appropriate that one of the three is to be called "love," this name is most appropriately given to the Holy Spirit. And this means that in the indivisible and supreme being of God, substance is not to be distinguished from love, but substance is itself love, and love itself is substance, whether in the Father or in the Son or in the Holy Spirit, and yet it is especially appropriate that the Holy Spirit is named "love." [. . .]

We may say, then, that just as it is especially appropriate for us to give the name of "wisdom" to the one Word of God, though in general both the Holy Spirit and the Father himself are wisdom, so it is especially appropriate that the Spirit be called "love," though both Father and Son are love in general. The Word of God, God's only-begotten Son, is explicitly named as the "wisdom of God" in the apostle's own phrase, "Christ the power of God and the wisdom of God" (1 Corinthians 1: 24). But we can also find authority for calling the Holy Spirit "love," by a careful examination of the apostle John's language (1 John 4: 7, 19). After saying "Beloved, let us love one another, for love is of God," he goes on to add, "and everyone who loves is born of God; he who does not love has not known God, for God is love." This makes it plain that the love which he calls "God" is the same love which he has said to be "*of* God." Love, then, is God of (or from) God [*Deus ergo ex deo est dilectio*]. But since the Son is begotten from God the Father and the Spirit proceeds from God the Father, we must ask to which of them we should apply this saying that God is love. Only the Father is God without being "of God"; so that the love which is God and "of God" must be either the Son or the Holy Spirit. Now in what follows the writer refers to the love of God – not that by which we love him, but that by which "he loved us, and sent his Son as expiator for our sins" (1 John 4: 10); and on this he bases his exhortation to us to love one another, that so God may dwell in us, since God (as he has said) is love. And there follows at once, designed to express the matter more plainly, the saying: "hereby we know that we dwell in him, and he in us, because he has given us of his Spirit." Thus it is the Holy Spirit, of whom he has given us, who makes us dwell in God, and God in us. But that is the effect of love. The Holy Spirit himself therefore is the God who is love. A little further on, after repeating his statement that "God is love," John adds immediately, "he who abides in love abides in God, and God abides in him," which corresponds to the earlier saying, "hereby we know that we abide in him and he in us, because he has given us of his Spirit." It is the Spirit therefore who is signified in the text "God is love." God the Holy Spirit who proceeds from God is the one who, when given to us, set us on fire with the love of God and of our neighbor, and is himself love. For we have no means of loving God, unless it comes of God: that is why John says a little later on "let us love because he first loved us." It is the same in the apostle Paul: "the love of God is shed abroad in our hearts through the Holy Spirit which is given to us" (Romans 5: 5).

There is no more excellent gift of God than this. It alone distinguishes between the sons of the eternal kingdom and the sons of eternal damnation. Other favors also are given through the Spirit, but without love they are of no use. Unless the Holy Spirit is bestowed on us to such an extent that we are made to be lovers of God and of our neighbor, we cannot pass from the left hand to the right. The name of Gift belongs specially to the Spirit, only on account of love. [...] Thus the love which is of God and is God is especially the Holy Spirit, through whom is spread abroad in our hearts the love of God by which the whole Trinity will make its habitation within us. And therefore the Holy Spirit, God though he is, is most rightly called also the "gift of God." What gift is more proper than love, which brings us to God, and without which no other gift of God, whatever it may be, can bring us to God?

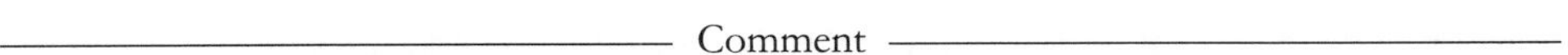

In this important passage, Augustine offers his reflections on the divinity of the Holy Spirit, and above all its relation to "love." The argument is complex, and at times quite difficult to follow. However, the basic issue can be stated as follows: Scripture declares "God is love" (1 John 4: 8, 16) and so leaves us to ask whether it is God the Father, or God the Son, or God the Holy Spirit, or God the Trinity itself, who is love. Augustine's argument is that "the love which is of God and is God is especially the Holy Spirit." Note that Augustine makes two assertions in this statement: (1) love comes from God; (2) love is God. A series of arguments leads Augustine to the conclusion that it is the Holy Spirit which is best thought of as being this love, which God bestows upon us.

Questions for Study

1. Set out in your own words the arguments that lead Augustine to the conclusion that the Holy Spirit is love.
2. Why is it "especially appropriate" that the Holy Spirit is named "love"? And which person of the Trinity does Augustine argue is most appropriately named "wisdom"? For what reasons?
3. "What gift is more proper than love, which brings us to God, and without which no other gift of God, whatever it may be, can bring us to God?" Locate this passage in the text. What does Augustine mean by this?

3.16

Epiphanius of Constantia on Sabellianism

In his *Panarion*, written in Greek in the late fourth century, Epiphanius of Constantia (c.315–403) provided a vigorous defense of Christian orthodoxy against every heresy which had emerged by this stage. In the course of this survey and exposition, he deals with the origins and nature of Sabellianism. See also 3.3, 3.9, 3.10, 3.11, 3.12, 3.13, 3.15.

A certain Sabellius arose not long ago (in fact, quite recently); it is from him that the Sabellians take their name. His opinions, with a few unimportant exceptions, are the same as those of the Noetians. Most of his followers are to be found in Mesopotamia and the region of Rome. [. . .]

Their doctrine is that Father, Son, and Holy Spirit are one and the same being, in the sense that three names are attached to one substance [*hypostasis*]. It is just like the body, soul, and spirit in a human being. The body is as it were the Father; the soul is the Son; while the Spirit is to the Godhead as his spirit is to a human being. Or it is like the sun, being one substance [*hypostasis*], but having three manifestations [*energia*]: light, heat, and the orb itself. The heat [. . .] is analogous to the Spirit; the light to the Son; while the Father himself is represented by the essence of each substance. The Son was at one time emitted, like a ray of light; he accomplished in the world all that related to the dispensation of the gospel and the salvation of humanity, and was then taken back into heaven, as a ray is emitted by the sun and then withdrawn again into the sun. The Holy Spirit is still being sent forth into the world and into those individuals who are worthy to receive it.

Comment

This is an important historical comment on the nature of Sabellianism. Sabellius was concerned to safeguard the unity of the Godhead, fearing a lapse into some form of tritheism as a result of the doctrine of the Trinity. This vigorous defense of the absolute unity of God led him to insist that the self-revelation of the one and only God took place in different ways at different times. The divinity of Christ and the Holy Spirit is to be explained in terms of three different ways or modes of divine self-revelation (hence the term "modalism" to refer to Sabellianism). The following trinitarian sequence is thus proposed:

1 The one God is revealed in the manner of creator and lawgiver. This aspect of God is referred to as "the Father."
2 The same God is then revealed in the manner of savior, in the person of Jesus Christ. This aspect of God is referred to as "the Son."
3 The same God is then revealed in the manner of the one who sanctifies and gives eternal life. This aspect of God is referred to as "the Spirit."

There is thus no difference, save that of appearance and chronological location, between the three entities in question.

Questions for Study

1 Sabellius uses the analogy of the sun to explain his modalist approach to the Trinity. Set out, in your own words, how this analogy is interpreted.
2 On the basis of the passage, explain how Sabellius understood the role of each person of the Trinity.
3 "Father, Son and Holy Spirit are one and the same being, in the sense that three names are attached to one substance." Locate this important statement within the text. What did this doctrine mean to the Sabellians?

3.17

Cyril of Alexandria on the Role of the Holy Spirit

In his commentary on John's gospel, an early fifth-century work written in Greek, Cyril of Alexandria (died 444) focuses on the role of the Spirit as the bringer of unity within the church. Note especially how the unifying role of the Spirit within the church is explicitly linked to a comparable role for the flesh in the incarnation of Christ; just as the humanity of Christ unites him with believers, so the Spirit bonds believers together. See also 3.10, 3.11, 3.15.

All of us who have received the one and the same Spirit, that is, the Holy Spirit, are in a sense merged together with one another and with God. For if Christ, together with the Spirit of the Father and himself, comes to dwell in each one of us, even though there are many of us, then it follows that the Spirit is still one and undivided. He binds together the spirit of each and every one of us [. . .] and makes us all appear as one in him. For just as the power of the holy flesh of Christ united those in whom it dwells into one body, I think that, in much the same way, the one and undivided Spirit of God, who dwells in us all, leads us all into spiritual unity.

Comment

This brief passage suggests that Cyril, like Augustine, saw the Holy Spirit as playing an important role in uniting believers together. However, they offer very different reasons for allocating this role to the Spirit.

Questions for Study

1 Set out, in your own words, the role which Cyril allocates to the Spirit in this passage.
2 "For just as the power of the holy flesh of Christ united those in whom it dwells into one body, I think that, in much the same way, the one and undivided Spirit of God, who dwells in us all, leads us all into spiritual unity." What does Cyril mean by this? And how does it illuminate the distinctive yet complementary roles of Son and Spirit?

3.18

Fulgentius of Ruspe on the Holy Spirit and Eucharist

In his critique of Fabianus, which dates from the early sixth century, Fulgentius of Ruspe (c.462–527) develops the idea that receiving the Holy Spirit is equivalent to receiving the gift of God's love. The text refers to the moment in the eucharist when the Holy Spirit is invoked (usually referred to as the *epiklesis*). See also 3.10, 3.15.

Since Christ died for us out of love, when we celebrate the memorial of his death, at the moment of sacrifice we ask that love may be granted to us by the coming of the Holy Spirit. We humbly pray that, in the strength of this love, by which Christ willed to die for us, we may be able to regard the world as being crucified to us, and ourselves as being crucified to the world, by receiving the gift of the Holy Spirit. [. . .] Having received this gift of love, let us die to sin and live to God.

Comment

This brief passage requires little in the way of comment, other than to note the important theological link which has been established between the Spirit and love.

Questions for Study

1 What function does the gift of love play for believers, according to this passage?

3.19

John of Damascus on the Holy Spirit

The patristic period saw intense debate over the status of the Holy Spirit. Some earlier writers of this era, noting that the Bible did not explicitly ascribe divinity to the Spirit, preferred to avoid speaking about the Spirit in terms that implied its divinity. During the fourth century, however, the arguments in favor of the Spirit's divinity began to gain the upper hand. By the time John of Damascus (c.675–c.749) wrote his classic work *de fide orthodoxa* ("on the orthodox faith"), the divinity of the Spirit was fully conceded, as is clear from this extract. See also 3.10, 3.11, 3.15, 3.17, 3.18.

In the same way, we believe in the Holy Spirit, the Lord and Giver of life, who proceeds from the Father and dwells in the Son; who is adored and glorified together with the Father and the Son as consubstantial and co-eternal with them; who is the true and authoritative Spirit of God and the source of wisdom and life and sanctification; who is God together with the Father and the Son and is proclaimed as such; who is uncreated, complete, creative, almighty, all-working, infinite in power; who dominates all creation but is not dominated; who deifies but is not deified; who fills but is not filled; who is shared in but does not share; who sanctifies but is not sanctified; who, as receiving the intercessions of all, is the Intercessor; who is like the Father and the Son in all things; who proceeds from the Father and is communicated through the Son and is participated in by all creation; who through Himself creates and gives substance to all things and sanctifies and preserves them; who is distinctly subsistent and exists in His own Person indivisible and inseparable from the Father and the Son; who has all things whatsoever the Father and the Son have except being unbegotten and being begotten. For the Father is uncaused and unbegotten, because he is not from anything, but has his being from himself and does not have from any other anything whatsoever that he has. Rather, he himself is the principle and cause by which all things naturally exist as they do. And the Son is begotten of the Father, while the Holy Spirit is himself also of the Father – although not by begetting, but by procession. Now, we have learned that there is a difference between begetting and procession, but what the manner of this difference is we have not learned at all. However, the begetting of the Son and the procession of the Holy Spirit from the Father are simultaneous.

Comment

John of Damascus – often referred to as "the Damascene" – here sets out a comprehensive assertion of the divinity of the Spirit, emphazing both the Spirit's divine *identity* and the Spirit's divine *function*. While insisting on the unity of Father, Son, and Spirit, he simultaneously affirms their distinctive roles within the economy of salvation.

Questions for Study

1 Read the passage carefully, and try to group the Damascene's statements about the Spirit under three categories: (1) what is done to the Spirit; (2) what the Spirit is; (3) what the Spirit does. What overall understanding of the Spirit emerges from this?
2 We learn that the Spirit "deifies but is not deified." Why is this so important to the Damascene?
3 What distinctive roles does the Spirit play, according to the Damascene? How does this compare with Augustine's understanding of the Trinity, which links the work of the Spirit more closely to the work of the Son?

3.20

The Eleventh Council of Toledo on the Trinity

Perhaps the clearest statement of the doctrine of the Trinity to be found in the patristic period is that set out by the Eleventh Council of Toledo (675). This Council, which met in the Spanish city of Toledo and was attended by a mere 11 bishops, is widely credited with setting out the western view of the Trinity with an enviable clarity, and is regularly cited in later medieval discussions of this doctrine. In what follows, the Council explains the relation of the words "Trinity" and "God," and stresses the importance of the relationalities within the Godhead, focusing especially on the relation of the Holy Spirit to the Son and Father. See also 3.3, 3.11, 3.12, 3.22.

We believe that the Holy Spirit, the third person in the Trinity, is God, one and equal with God the Father and God the Son, of one substance and of one nature; not, however, begotten or created, but proceeding from both, and that He is the Spirit of both. We also believe that the Holy Spirit is neither unbegotten nor begotten, for if we called Him "unbegotten" we would assert two Fathers, or if we called him "begotten," we would appear to preach two Sons. Yet He is called the Spirit not of the Father alone, nor of the Son alone, but of both Father and Son. For He does not proceed from the Father to the Son, nor from the Son to sanctify creatures, but He is shown to have proceeded from both at once, because He is known as the love or the holiness of both. Hence we believe that the Holy Spirit is sent by both, as the Son is sent by the Father. But He is not less than the Father and the Son.

This is the way of speaking about the Holy Trinity as it has been handed down: it must not be spoken of or believed to be "threefold" [*triplex*], but to be "Trinity." Nor can it properly be said that in the one God there is the Trinity; rather, the one God is the Trinity. In the relative names of the persons, the Father is related to the Son, the Son to the Father, and the Holy Spirit to both. While they are called three persons in view of their relations, we believe in one nature or substance. Although we profess three persons, we do not profess three substances, but one substance and three persons. For the Father is Father not with respect to Himself but to the Son, and the Son is Son not to Himself but in relation to the Father; and likewise the Holy Spirit is not referred to Himself but is related to the Father and the Son, inasmuch as He is called the Spirit of the Father and the Son. So when we use the word "God," this does not express a relationship to another, as of the Father to the Son or of the Son to the Father or of the Holy Spirit to the Father and the Son, but "God" refers to Himself only [*sed ad se specialiter dicitur*].

Comment

This important text sets out some of the basic features of the emerging western understanding of the Trinity. It is of particular importance in several respects. The text stresses the importance of relationalities within the Godhead, and also clarifies the relation of the terms "God" and "Trinity." The text also explicitly avoids a serious misunderstanding which could arise from the western view that the Holy Spirit proceeds from the Father and the Son – namely, that there are *two* divine sources of the Spirit. The text makes it clear that there is only one source of the Spirit.

Questions for Study

1 According to this text, when – and in what kind of contexts – should the words "God" and "Trinity" be used?
2 "Yet He is called the Spirit not of the Father alone, nor of the Son alone, but of both Father and Son." Locate this passage within the text. What does it mean? How is it to be justified? And what is its importance in clarifying the origins of the Spirit?

3.21

Anselm of Canterbury on the Compassion of God

The eleventh-century writer Anselm of Canterbury (c.1033–1109) here argues that God may be said to be compassionate in terms of his behavior towards us, but not in terms of his own experience. God responds positively towards suffering, without himself experiencing suffering. It is clear that Anselm regards it as axiomatic that God cannot be affected in any way by human suffering. See also 3.7, 3.8, 3.23, 3.30, 3.33, 3.38.

But how are you merciful, yet at the same time impassible [*impassibilis*]? For if you are impassible, you do not feel sympathy. And if you do not feel sympathy, your heart is not miserable on account of its sympathy for the miserable. Yet this is what compassion is. Yet if you are not compassionate, where does such great comfort for the miserable come from?

So how, O Lord, are you both compassionate and not compassionate, unless it is because you are compassionate in terms of our experience, and not in terms of your own being [*secundum te*]. You are truly compassionate in terms of our experience. Yet you are not so in terms of your own. For when you see us in our misery, we experience the effect of compassion; you, however, do not experience this feeling [*non sentis affectum*]. Therefore you are compassionate, in that you save the miserable and spare those who sin against you; and you are not compassionate, in that you are not affected by any sympathy for misery.

Comment

Anselm clearly wishes to affirm that God knows that humanity suffers, and that God has compassion on humanity in its plight. Yet Anselm does not feel he can move on to affirm that God suffers with us, or that God in some sense "experiences" suffering. It is clear that Anselm believes that any suggestion that God "suffers," as we suffer, is undignified, and brings God down to the human level. Note that God's mercy and graciousness towards suffering humanity is never called into question. The issue concerns how that compassion is expressed.

Questions for Study

1 Anselm, in effect, argues that God "knows about" suffering, but does not "know" suffering. Do you think that there is a contradiction in Anselm's position?
2 How does Anselm conceive God's compassion?
3 Why do you think that Anselm is reluctant to allow that God suffers?

3.22

Richard of St Victor on Love within the Trinity

In this analysis of the nature of love within the Godhead, dating from the second half of the twelfth century, Richard of St Victor (d. 1173) argues that the idea of the "sharing of love" can only be sustained if there are three persons within the Godhead. See also 3.3, 3.10, 3.11, 3.12, 3.13, 3.20.

If we concede that there exists in the true divinity some one person of such great benevolence that he wishes to have no riches or delights that he does not wish to share with others, and if he is of such great power that nothing is impossible for him, and of such great happiness that nothing is difficult for him, then it is necessary to acknowledge that a Trinity of divine persons must exist. In order that the reasons for this may be clear, let us draw together all our arguments at this point.

If there were only one person in the divinity, that one person would certainly not have anyone with whom he could share the riches of his greatness. But on the other hand, the abundance of delights and sweetness, which would have been able to increase for him on account of intimate love, would lack any eternal dimension. But the fullness of goodness does not permit the supremely good One to keep those riches for himself, nor does his fullness of blessedness allow him to be without a full abundance of delights and sweetness. And on account of the greatness of his honor, he rejoices at sharing his riches as much as he glories over enjoying the abundance of delights and sweetness.

On the basis of these considerations, it is clearly impossible that any one person in the divinity could lack the fellowship of association. If he were to have only one partner, he would not be without anyone with whom he could share the riches of his greatness. However, he would not have anyone with whom he could share the delights of love. There is nothing which gives more pleasure or which delights the soul more than the sweetness of loving. Only someone who has a partner and a loved one in that love that has been shown to him possesses the sweetness of such delights.

So it follows that such a sharing of love cannot exist except among less than three persons. As we said earlier, there is nothing more glorious and nothing more magnificent than sharing in common whatever is useful and pleasant. This fact can hardly be unknown to the supreme wisdom, not can it fail to please the supreme benevolence. And as the happiness of the supremely powerful One cannot be lacking in what pleases him, so in the divinity it is impossible for two persons not to be united to a third.

Comment

Richard of St Victor is one of the most important trinitarian thinkers of the Middle Ages. His understanding of the Trinity, set out above, makes much of the idea of social relationships within the Trinity – notice in particular the emphasis upon "sharing" and the language of "partnership." This contrasts sharply with the more individualist approach to the Trinity adopted by Augustine (see especially 3.15, but also 3.13). This is an important example of the "social Trinity" model, which sees a model for the Trinity in human relationships – where Augustine chose to use the inner workings of the individual human mind as a resource for trinitarian analysis. Yet both base their analyses, at least in part, on an examination of the concept of "love," which they explore in different manners.

Questions for Study

1 Set out, in your own words, the arguments and considerations which lead Richard to "acknowledge that a Trinity of divine persons must exist." Identify the core considerations, and evaluate how convincing you find his approach.
2 Read Augustine's analysis of the "trace" (vestigium) of the Trinity in the human mind as a consequence of its creation by God (3.13). What are the main differences between the approaches? Are they complementary or divergent? Which do you prefer?
3 "There is nothing which gives more pleasure or which delights the soul more than the sweetness of loving." Locate this passage within the text. What does Richard mean by this? And what function does this conclusion play in his argument?

3.23

Alexander of Hales on the Suffering of God in Christ

In this important early work, the thirteenth-century English Franciscan theologian Alexander of Hales (c.1186–1245) argues that God, who was not obliged to suffer, chose to suffer in Christ. The work carefully avoids an explicit statement to the effect that God experienced suffering in his own person. Note that the passage in question may not be due to Alexander himself, but may have been compiled by William of Melitona, who completed the work after Alexander's death in 1245. See also 3.7, 3.8, 3.21, 3.30, 3.33, 3.37, 3.38.

In our case, the possibility [of suffering] is linked to the necessity of suffering, and the will not to suffer (which, however, cannot prevent suffering from taking place). In the case of Adam, there was the possibility of being in the state of innocence without any necessity or disposition towards suffering, and the will to suffer or not to suffer, as he wished. In the case of the Lord, however, this possibility (which was not merely remote, as in the case of Adam) is not linked with the necessity of suffering, as in our case. Rather, it is linked with an inclination to suffer, and a will which would have had the power to prevent that suffering.

Comment

This text again illustrates the issue which we noted in relation to Anselm of Canterbury's discussion of the divine compassion (3.21) – namely, the desire to affirm that God is compassionate and merciful, while avoiding the suggestion that God suffers. Alexander here deals with the following question. Did not Christ suffer? And, as a result, does not the "dual nature" of Christ as divine and human mean that God therefore experienced suffering in Christ? At first sight, the answer would appear to be that God did indeed suffer in Christ, and that it is therefore appropriate to speak of God suffering. However, Alexander introduces a distinction which allows him to avoid this assertion.

Why was Alexander (and before him, Anselm) so anxious to avoid the suggestion that God suffered? Part of the answer lies in the fact that this position was regarded as theologically suspect. The doctrine known as "theopaschitism," which arose during the sixth century, had long been dismissed as heretical. The basic slogan associated with the movement was "one of the Trinity was crucified." The formula can be interpreted in a perfectly orthodox sense and was defended as such by writers such as John Maxentius and Leontius of Byzantium. However, it was regarded as potentially misleading and confusing by more cautious writers, including Pope Hormisdas (d.523), and the formula gradually fell into disuse. An awareness of the dubious associations of the term may well have led many medieval writers to avoid the idea of a "suffering God" altogether.

Questions for Study

1 Alexander introduces a comparison between Adam and Christ in this passage. What purpose does this comparison serve? And what conclusion does Alexander draw from it?
2 Alexander draws a distinction between the "possibility" and the "necessity" of suffering. What does he do with this distinction?

3.24

Thomas Aquinas on Divine Omnipotence

The great scholastic theologian Thomas Aquinas (c.1225–74) provided a particularly influential account of the nature of divine omnipotence, which includes an important discussion of the question "Can God sin?" At first sight, it might seem that the suggestion that "God cannot sin" amounts to a denial of God's omnipotence. However, Aquinas argues that sin is a defect, and is therefore inconsistent with the idea of God as a perfect being. God cannot sin, because it is not in God's nature to be deficient. The *Summa Theologiae* ("The Totality of Theology"), which Aquinas began to write in Latin in 1265 and left unfinished at the time of his death, is widely regarded as the greatest work of medieval theology. See also 3.25, 3.27.

It is commonly said that God is almighty. Yet it seems difficult to understand the reason for this, on account of the doubt about what is meant when it is said that "God can do 'everything.'" [...] If it is said that God is omnipotent because he can do everything possible to his power, the understanding of omnipotence is circular, doing nothing more than saying that God is omnipotent because he can do everything that he can do. [...] To sin is to fall short of a perfect action. Hence to be able to sin is to be able to be deficient in relation to an action, which cannot be reconciled with omnipotence. It is because God is omnipotent that he cannot sin. [...] Anything that implies a contradiction does not relate to the omnipotence of God. For the past not to have existed implies a contradiction. Thus to say Socrates is, and is not, seated is contradictory, and so also to say that he had, and had not, been seated. To affirm that he had been seated is to affirm a past event; to affirm that he had not been seated is thus to affirm what was not the case.

Comment

In this passage Aquinas explores a number of issues relating to the omnipotence of God. One of these is the rule of noncontradiction, often stated in forms of the question: "Can God create a square triangle?" Such things cannot be done due to a logical contradiction within the proposal. Aquinas explores this issue with reference to someone being both seated, and not seated, at the same time. More importantly, Aquinas addresses the following question: "Can God sin?" At first sight, this question must be answered in the affirmative; to do otherwise would be to suggest that there is something which God cannot do. On closer inspection, however, this turns out to be an inappropriate answer. Aquinas offers his readers an explanation of this point in this passage.

Questions for Study

1 Outline, in your own words, why Aquinas believes that God cannot sin.
2 What aspect of the nature of sin forces Aquinas to this conclusion?
3 On the basis of the issues explored in this passage, try responding to this question: "Can God create a weight which is so heavy that God cannot lift it?"

3.25

Bonaventure on the Origin of Evil

The question of the nature and origin of sin and evil has played a major role in Christian theology. One of the classic answers to the problem of evil can be traced back to Augustine of Hippo. According to this view, evil is not a positive reality, existing in its own right. Rather, it is to be seen as an absence of goodness – a privation, or deprivation, of the good. This view is set out with particular clarity in the writings of Bonaventure of Bagnoregio (1221–74), the leading Franciscan theologian of the thirteenth century. Our extract is taken from his *Breviloquium*, written in Latin around the year 1257. Bonaventure described this work as "a brief summary of true theology." It consists of a preface and seven chapters, the third of which deals with "the corruption of sin". See also 3.6, 3.14, 3.24.

Having already established certain truths about the divine Trinity and the creation of the world, we now briefly touch on the corruption of sin. On this subject we must hold that sin is not any kind of essence but a defect and corruption [*non est essentia aliqua sed defectus et corruptela*] by which the mode, species and order of the created will are corrupted. Hence the corruption of sin is opposed to good itself. It has no existence except in the good. It has no source other than the good which is the free choice of the will, and the will is neither completely evil (since it can wish good) nor completely good (since it can fall into evil).

This is to be explained as follows. Since the first principle is a being from itself and not from another [*sum sit ens a se ipso non ab alio*], it is necessary that it is a being because of itself and hence completely good, having no defect. Therefore there is not anything, nor can there be anything, which is the first and complete evil because the first principle implies the greatest perfection, and the greatest evil implies the very greatest defect. Since the first principle as the greatest and most perfect being cannot be deficient, either in essence or in operation, the greatest evil cannot exist, nor does something evil exist, nor can evil in any way reign. Because the first principle is omnipotent, it is able to bring good from nonexistence into existence without the need for any matter. The first principle did this when it shaped the creature to whom it gave existence, life, intelligence, and choice. It is appropriate that the creature since it has an existence according to this triple cause, should have in its substance and will a mode, species, and order. The creature was born to perform its works from God, according to God, and because of God, and to do this according to the mode, species, and order implanted within it.

Because the creature originates from nothing and is defective, it can withdraw from acting because of God, so that it may do something because of itself, and not because of God. It may thus do something which is not from God, according to God, or because of God. This is sin, which is the corruption of mode, species, and order. Because sin is a defect, it cannot be said to have an efficient cause; rather, it has a deficient cause – namely, the defection of the created will [*defectum voluntatis creatae*].

Comment

Bonaventure locates the origin of sin in the human creature's tendency to focus on itself, rather than on God, its creator and sustainer. Since evil is an absence of goodness, evil itself cannot really be said to have a nature. Nor can there be a "greatest evil" that exists as a principle in its own right, because this "greatest evil" would not be able to exist. There is thus no question of there being an evil equivalent of "the first principle." Evil is not a reality in its own right, but a deprivation of the good. It is like a hole in a piece of paper – something that is noted by its absence, not its presence. Note that thoughout the *Breviloquium,* Bonaventure uses the term "the first principle" to refer to God.

Questions for Study

1. If God is good, how does Bonaventure account for the existence of evil within God's creation?
2. If Bonaventure is right, does Satan exist? What understanding of Satan would be consistent with his approach?
3. Bonaventure speaks of a "triple cause" of creation, according to mode, species, and order. What do you think he means by each of these ideas?

3.26

Julian of Norwich on God as our Mother

The *Revelation of Divine Love* is an account of 16 visions which appeared to the English recluse Julian of Norwich (c.1342–c.1415) in May 1373. The visions are notable for their constant emphasis upon the love and kindness of God, even to the most frail of sinners. The sections which follow, all of which are drawn from the 14th revelation, show Julian's distinctive tendency to refer to both God and Jesus Christ in strongly maternal terms, paralleling her regular use of "mother" to refer to the church. See also 1.30, 3.42.

In this way, I saw that God rejoices to be our Father, and also that he rejoices to be our Mother; and yet again, that he rejoices to be our true Husband, with our soul as his beloved bride. And Christ rejoices to be both our Brother and our Saviour. [. . .]

[God's] love never allows us to lag behind. All this is due to God's innate goodness, and comes to us by the operation of his grace. God is kind because it is his nature. Goodness-by-nature implies God. He is the foundation, substance and the thing itself, what it is by nature. He is the true Father and Mother of what things are by nature. Every kind of "nature" that he has caused to flow out of himself to fulfil his purpose will be brought back and restored to him when we are saved by the work of grace. [. . .]

We need have no fear of this, unless it is the kind of fear that urges us on. But we make our humble complaint to our beloved Mother, and he sprinkles us with his precious blood, and makes our soul pliable and tender, and restores us to our full beauty in the course of time. [. . .] Thus in Jesus, our true Mother, has our life been grounded, through his own uncreated foresight, and the Father's almighty power, and the exalted and sovereign goodness of the Holy Spirit. [. . .] Beautiful and sweet is our heavenly Mother in the sight of our souls; and, in the sight of our heavenly Mother, dear and lovely are the gracious children; gentle and humble, with all the lovely natural qualities of children. The natural child does not despair of its mother's love. [. . .] There is no higher state in this life than that of childhood, because of our inadequate and feeble capacity and intellect, until such time as our gracious Mother shall bring us up to our Father's bliss.

Comment

Julian is an important medieval spiritual writer, and incorporates much theological reflection in her spirituality. The passage to be studied is striking on account of her explicit use of male and female language to refer to God. At points, the Bible uses strongly maternal language to refer to the love of God for Israel and the church. Two examples will make the point in question.

1 "As one whom his mother comforts, so I will comfort you" (Isaiah 66: 13).
2 "Can a woman forget her sucking child, that she should have no compassion on the son of her womb? Even these may forget, yet I will not forget you" (Isaiah 49: 15).

The second is especially striking, as it compares the love of God for Israel to the natural love of a mother for her child. In her reflections on the nature of God, Julian uses both paternal and maternal language and imagery to refer to God.

Questions for Study

1 Read through the passage and identify the imagery that Julian uses for God. What use does she make of this?

2 There is a strong emphasis on the concept of the "goodness of God" throughout this work. Why? And what points does Julian make through this emphasis?
3 "The natural child does not despair of its mother's love." Locate this passage within the text. What does Julian mean by this? How does it relate to the two biblical passages mentioned in the "Comment" section above? And what does Julian do with this idea?

3.27

William of Ockham on the Two Powers of God

In this dense yet highly important passage, William of Ockham (c.1285–1347) draws a distinction between two modes of divine action. God must originally have been able to act in any manner, provided it did not involve contradiction. Ockham designates this as the "absolute power of God." Ockham notes that God has now chosen to act in a specified and reliable way, by which he has limited his freedom to act. This is referred to as his "ordained power." See also 3.24.

Concerning the first point, it must be said that God is able to do some things by his ordained power [*de potentia ordinata*] and others by his absolute power [*de potentia absoluta*]. This distinction should not be understood to mean that there are actually in God two powers, one of which is "ordained" and the other of which is "absolute," because there is only one power of God directed towards the external world, the exercise of which is in all respects God himself. Nor should this be understood to mean that God can do some things by his ordained power, and others by his absolute, not his ordained, power, in that God does nothing without having first ordained it. But it should be understood in this way: God can do something in a manner which is established by laws which were ordained and established by God. In this respect, God acts according to his ordained power.

Comment

In his discussion of the opening line of the Apostles' creed – "I believe in God the Father almighty" – Ockham asks precisely what is meant by the word "almighty" (*omnipotens*). It cannot, he argues, mean that God is *presently* able to do everything; rather, it means that God was *once* free to act in this way. God has now established an order of things which reflects the divine will and that order, once established, will remain until the end of time. Ockham uses two important terms to refer to these different options. The "absolute power of God" (*potentia absoluta*) refers to the options which existed before God had decided upon any course of action or world ordering. The "ordained power of God" (*potentia ordinata*) refers to the way things now are, which reflects the order established by God their creator. Ockham's point is this: by choosing to actualize some options, God has to choose not to actualize others. Choosing to do something means choosing to reject something else. Once God has chosen to create the world, the option of *not* creating the world is set to one side. This means that there are certain things which God could do *once* which can *no longer* be done. Although God could have decided not to create the world, God has now deliberately rejected that possibility. And that rejection means that this possibility is no longer open. This leads to what seems, at first sight, to be a paradoxical situation. On account of the divine omnipotence, God is not now able to do everything. By exercising the divine power, God has limited options. For Ockham, God *cannot* now do everything. God has deliberately limited the possibilities. God chose to limit the options which are now open. Is that a contradiction? No. If God is really capable of doing anything, then God must be able to become committed to a course of action – and stay committed to it. God, in exercising the divine omnipotence, chose to restrict the range of options available.

Questions for Study

1 What does Ockham mean by "the two powers of God"? Try to avoid using Ockham's own words; paraphrase him.
2 Can you construct an example which would illuminate his meaning at this point?
3 "God chose not to do certain things." Does this mean that God cannot do those things? And how does your answer to this question relate to the question of whether God is omnipotent?

3.28

Thomas à Kempis on the Limits of Trinitarian Speculation

The noted late medieval spiritual writer Thomas à Kempis (c.1380–1471) here sets out a strongly antispeculative approach to the Christian faith, which rests firmly on the need to obey Christ rather than indulge in flights of intellectual fancy. Speculation concerning the Trinity is singled out as a case of such a pointless activity, which he urges his readers to avoid. See also 3.3, 3.10, 3.11, 3.12, 3.13, 3.16, 3.20.

What good does it do you if you dispute loftily about the Trinity, but lack humility and therefore displease the Trinity? It is not lofty words that make you righteous or holy or dear to God, but a virtuous life. I would much rather experience contrition [*compunctio*] than be able to give a definition of it. If you knew the whole of the Bible by heart, along with all the definitions of the philosophers, what good would this be without grace and love? "Vanity of vanities, and all is vanity" (Ecclesiastes 1: 2) – except, that is, loving God and serving God alone. For this is supreme wisdom: to draw nearer to the heavenly kingdom through contempt for the world. [. . .]

Naturally, everyone wants knowledge. But what use is that knowledge without the fear of God? A humble peasant who serves God is much more pleasing to him than an arrogant academic [*superbus philosophus*] who neglects his own soul to consider the course of the stars. [. . .] If I were to possess all the knowledge in the world, and yet lacked love, what good would this be in the sight of God, who will judge me by what I have done? So restrain an extravagant longing for knowledge, which leads to considerable anxiety and deception. Learned people always want their wisdom to be noticed and recognized. But there are many things, knowledge of which leads to little or no benefit to the soul. In fact, people are foolish if they concern themselves with anything other than those things which lead to their salvation.

Comment

Thomas was more than a little irritated by what he saw as the pointlessness of much theological speculation. Fooling around with logical riddles seemed to have taken the place of deepening a personal love and knowledge of God. Erasmus of Rotterdam experienced a similar feeling when he spent some time studying at the University of Paris in the 1490s; the big theological issues of the day seemed to be whether God could have become incarnate as a cucumber, or whether God could make prostitutes into virgins. Serious theological issues were no doubt involved; but the debates seemed rather pointless and unreal. Thomas à Kempis here argues for a more devotional approach to theology, avoiding the flights of intellectual fancy which he especially associates with theological debates about the Trinity.

Questions for Study

1 "I would much rather experience contrition than be able to give a definition of it." Locate this passage within the text. What does Thomas mean by this? What fundamental concerns lie behind this statement?
2 What is Thomas's fundamental difficulty with the concept of human knowledge, as expressed in this passage? Is knowledge a bad thing in itself? Or is he arguing that it is too easily abused?
3 According to Thomas, what should true knowledge do for us? And how would this show itself?

3.29

John Owen on the Sovereignty of God

During the course of his exposition of Psalm 130: 5–6, which was first published in 1668, the leading English Puritan theologian John Owen (1616–83) set out the characteristic Reformed emphasis on the total sovereignty of God as creator, by which every aspect of the creation has been ordered by God. Despite the disruptive effects of the Fall, Owen insists that every aspect of the creation remains under God's sovereign authority, by which God is able to determine what happens to all of his creatures. For Owen, and the Reformed tradition in general, the doctrine of the sovereignty of God finds a special application in the area of election; whether an individual is saved or not depends solely upon the will and good pleasure of God. Here, Owen explores related insights, focusing on the creation in general. See also 3.24, 3.27.

God made all this world of nothing, and could have made another, more, or all things, quite otherwise than they are. It would not subsist one moment without his omnipotent supportment. Nothing would be continued in its place, course, use, without his effectual influence and countenance. If any thing can be, live, or act a moment without him, we may take free leave to dispute its disposal with him, and to haste unto the accomplishment of our desires. But from the angels in heaven to the worms of the earth and the grass of the field, all depend on him and his power continually. Why was this part of the creation an angel, that a worm; this a man, that a brute beast? Is it from their own choice, designing or contrivance, or brought about by their own wisdom? or is it merely from the sovereign pleasure and will of God? And what a madness it is to repine against what he doth, seeing all things are as he makes them and disposeth them, nor can be otherwise! Even the repiner himself hath his being and subsistence upon his mere pleasure. [. . .] All is one; whatever God doth, and towards whomsoever, be they many or few, a whole nation, or city, or one single person, be they high or low, rich or poor, good or bad, all are the works of his hands, and he may deal with them as seems good unto him.

Comment

This passage sets out the classic Puritan view of the divine sovereignty, inherited from the Reformed tradition. Indeed, many would argue that the English Puritanism of the seventeenth century represents a development and pastoral application of the intellectual heritage of Calvin and his immediate intellectual successors, such as Theodore Beza. Note that Owen is concerned to apply, not just explain, the concept of divine sovereignty.

Questions for Study

1 What does Owen mean by the sovereignty of God? Illustrate your answer using some of the examples given within the passage.
2 According to Owen, does God's sovereignty depend upon its recognition by humans before it can operate?
3 "[God] made all this world of nothing, and could have made another, more, or all things, quite otherwise than they are." What point is Owen making here? How does this relate to the point made by William of Ockham concerning the "two powers of God" (3.27)?

3.30

Benedict Spinoza on the Impassibility of God

The Jewish philosopher Benedict (or Baruch) Spinoza (1632–77) made an important contribution to the question of the rational foundations of both philosophy and theology. Philosophy, he argued, was like geometry. For Spinoza, it was possible to lay down a few fundamental axioms and then proceed to develop an entire philosophical, ethical, or theological system on their basis. Our concern in this important passage has to do with Spinoza's question concerning whether God may be said to "suffer," or to "love." The answers given had an important influence on the discussion of these issues during the period of the Enlightenment. See 3.7, 3.21, 3.33.

Proposition 17. God is without passions, nor is he affected with any experience of joy [*laetitia*] or sadness [*tristitia*].

Demonstration. All ideas, in so far as they have reference to God, are true, that is, they are adequate: and therefore God is without passions [*Deus expers est passionum*]. Again, God cannot pass to a higher or a lower perfection: and therefore he is affected with no emotion of joy or sadness. Q.E.D.

Corollary: God, strictly speaking, loves no one nor hates any one. For God is affected with no emotion of joy or sadness, and consequently loves no one [*neminem etiam amat*] nor hates any one.

In this important philosophical argument, which had some considerable influence on Christian theology in the eighteenth century, Spinoza reasons that any passion on the part of God involves a change in his being. Either he moves to a greater perfection, or to a lesser. In either case, the perfection of God is compromised, in that God either becomes more perfect (in which case he was not perfect to start with), or less perfect (in which case, suffering leads to him ceasing to be perfect). As a result, Spinoza argues, it is not possible to speak of God loving anyone, as this proves to be inconsistent with the idea of a perfect God. Note that Spinoza's original text is littered with cross-references to earlier sections of the work, making it somewhat difficult to follow the argument. These have been omitted here, to allow for easier reading. The sense of the argument is not altered or distorted by these omissions.

"Q.E.D." is a standard abbreviation, often used in geometrical puzzles, for the Latin phrase *quod erat desmonstrandum*, which basically means: "which is what was required to be proved."

Questions for Study

1 According to Spinoza, is God able to love or hate anyone? What reasons are given for this answer?

2 "God cannot pass to a higher or a lower perfection." Locate this statement. What does Spinoza mean by this? Why does he place such an emphasis upon the "perfection" of God? And what specific concept of "perfection" does he use?

3.31

F. D. E. Schleiermacher on the Trinity

F. D. E. Schleiermacher (1768–1834) is widely regarded as having introduced the ideas which came to dominate German liberal Protestant theology during the nineteenth century. Schleiermacher's discussion of the doctrine of the Trinity comes right at the end of his *Christian Faith*, and represents the "last word" of theology on the doctrine of God. In this passage, Schleiermacher sets out his understanding of the distinctive place and function of the doctrine as the "coping-stone" of Christian theology. See also 3.3, 3.10, 3.11, 3.12, 3.15, 3.19, 3.20.

An essential element of our exposition [. . .] has been the doctrine of the union of the Divine Essence with human nature, both in the personality of Christ and in the common Spirit of the Church; therewith the whole view of Christianity set forth in our

Church teaching stands and falls. For unless the being of God in Christ is assumed, the idea of redemption could not be thus concentrated in His Person. And unless there were such a union also in the common Spirit of the Church, the Church could not thus be the Bearer and Perpetuator of the redemption through Christ. Now these exactly are the essential elements in the doctrine of the Trinity, which, it is clear, only established itself in defence of the position that in Christ there was present nothing less than the Divine Essence, which also indwells the Christian Church as its common Spirit, and that we take these expressions in no reduced or sheerly artificial sense, and know nothing of any special higher essences, subordinate deities (as it were) present in Christ and the Holy Spirit. The doctrine of the Trinity has no origin but this; and at first it had no other aim than to equate as definitely as possible the Divine Essence considered as thus united to human nature with the Divine Essence in itself. This is the less doubtful that those Christian sects which interpret the doctrine of redemption differently are also necessarily without the doctrine of the Trinity – they have no point of belief to which it could be attached – which could not possibly be the case if even in Catholic doctrine there existed at least some other points than this to which the attachment could be made. It is equally clear from this why those divergent sects which are chiefly distinguishable by their denial of the Trinity are not thereby forced into still other divergences in the doctrine of God and the divine attributes, as must have been the case if the doctrine of the Trinity were rooted in a special view of the nature of the Supreme Being as such. But on the other hand, they are forced to set up a different theory of the person of Christ, and hence also of the human need for redemption and of the value of redemption. In virtue of this connexion, we rightly regard the doctrine of the Trinity, in so far as it is a deposit of these elements, as the coping-stone of Christian doctrine [*als den Schlußstein der christlichen Lehre*], and this equating with each other of the divine in each of these two unions, as also of both with the Divine Essence in itself, as what is essential in the doctrine of the Trinity.

Comment

Karl Barth's highly critical engagement with the liberal Protestant tradition often focuses directly on Schleiermacher, who he regarded as the founder and chief representative of this tradition. Given Barth's emphasis on the importance of the Trinity, and the close linkage which he establishes between the doctrine of the Trinity and the actuality of revelation (see 2.41), it is no cause for surprise that Barth should be severely critical of Schleiermacher's treatment of the doctrine. For Barth, Schleiermacher relegated the doctrine to an appendix, where it ought to have been affirmed and proclaimed at the very beginning of a Christian dogmatics.

Questions for Study

1 What does Schleiermacher mean when he refers to the doctrine of the Trinity as the "coping-stone (*Schlußstein*) of Christian doctrine"? How does this affect Barth's criticism of Schleiermacher, noted above?
2 How does Schleiermacher account for the origins of the doctrine of the Trinity?
3 How does Schleiermacher relate the doctrine of the Trinity to the person of Christ?

3.32

Karl Barth on the "Otherness" of God

Karl Barth's Romans commentary, which first appeared in German in 1919, caused a sensation on account of its vision of a dialectic between God and humanity. There is a total gulf between God and the world, which can never be bridged from our side. The fact that we know anything about God is itself the result of God's self-revelation, not human activity or insight. God is totally distinct from human thought and civilization. This relentless emphasis on the "total qualitative distinction" between God and humanity established Barth (1886–1968) as a radical voice in the theology of the period immediately after World War I. See also 9.4.

Paul appeals only to the authority of God. This is the ground of his authority. There is no other.

Paul is authorized to deliver – *the Gospel of God*. He is commissioned to hand over to humanity something quite new and unprecedented, joyful and good – the truth of God. Yes, precisely – *of God!* The Gospel is not a religious message to inform humanity of their divinity, or to tell them how they may become divine. The Gospel proclaims a God utterly distinct from humanity. Salvation comes to them from him, and because they are, as human beings, incapable of knowing him, they have no right to claim anything from him. The Gospel is not one thing in the midst of other things, to be directly apprehended and comprehended. The Gospel is the Word of the Primal Origin of all things, the Word which, since it is ever new, must ever be received with renewed fear and trembling. [. . .]

Jesus Christ our Lord. This is the Gospel and the meaning of history. In this name two worlds meet and go apart, two planes intersect, the one known and the other unknown. The known plane is God's creation, fallen out of its union with him, and therefore the world of the "flesh" needing redemption. The world of human beings, and of time, and of things – our world. This known plane is intersected by another plane that is unknown – the world of the Father, of the Primal Creation, and of the final Redemption. The relation between us and God, between this world and his world, presses for recognition, but the line of intersection is not self-evident. The point on the line of intersection at which the relation becomes observable and observed is Jesus, Jesus of Nazareth, the historical Jesus.

Comment

This extract is taken from the work which first brought Barth to attention: the Romans commentary. The origins of the great turning point in modern theology are generally agreed to lie in this commentary on Romans. Perhaps the work may be regarded as a midwife to a new theological trend rather than its cause; there is considerable evidence for the accumulation of considerable dissatisfaction with liberal theology in the period 1914–19, and Barth's work may simply have triggered off a looming antiliberal reaction. The Romans commentary, first published in 1919, is often regarded as a work of prophecy rather than theology. Although its main impact appears to date from the publication of its heavily rewritten second edition (1922), even the first edition caused a mild sensation. It was through this work that the full power of Søren Kierkegaard's critique of the presuppositions of liberal Protestantism was first channeled into the German theological consciousness. Time and time again in this work, Barth turns to stress Kierkegaard's idea of an "infinite qualitative distinction" (*unendliche qualitative Unterschied*) between God and human beings.

God "stands over and against humanity and everything human in an infinite qualitative distinction, and is never, ever identical with anything which we name, experience, conceive or worship as God," as Barth says elsewhere in his commentary on Romans. God cannot and must not be constructed or conceived in human terms, as if he were some kind of projection of human culture, reason, or emotion. Time and time again Barth emphasizes the vastness of the gulf fixed between God and humanity, and the impossibility of bridging this gulf from our side. Barth substitutes for Lessing's "ugly great ditch" of history (see 4.26) the "glacial crevasse" of time and eternity. God is *totaliter aliter*, wholly and absolutely different from us. Such themes dominate the Romans commentary, and are set out clearly in the brief extract from this work.

Questions for Study

1 How does Barth describe the gospel? And how does he understand this to relate to the natural religious tendencies of human beings?
2 How does Barth estimate the capacity of humanity to discern and receive divine revelation?
3 "The point on the line of intersection at which the relation becomes observable and observed is Jesus." Locate this passage within the text. What does Barth mean by this? What is the "intersection" of which he speaks? And how is this related to Jesus?

3.33

Jürgen Moltmann on the Suffering of God

Jürgen Moltmann (born 1926) is widely regarded as one of the most important contemporary exponents of a "theology of the cross." This is especially evident in his major work *The Crucified God*, which sets out an understanding of the doctrine of God which takes the cross of Christ as foundational to an authentically Christian understanding of

God. The present extract from a published article by Moltmann provides a lucid overview and condensation of the themes of this work. Note especially the radical emphasis upon the cross, and the criticism of philosophical ideas of God, such as those found in the patristic period. Note also the way in which Moltmann distinguishes his approach from Patripassianism and Theopaschitism, and the manner in which he uses this approach to lay the foundations for a doctrine of the Trinity. See also 1.12, 3.7, 3.21, 3.23, 3.30, 3.38.

The Council of Nicaea rightly declared, in opposition to Arius, that: God was not so changeable as his creature. This is not an absolute statement about God, but a comparative statement. God is not subject to compulsion by what is not divine. This does not mean, however, that God is not free to change himself or to be changed by something else. We cannot deduce from the relative statement of Nicaea that God is unchangeable – that he is absolutely unchangeable.

The early Fathers insisted on God's inability to suffer in opposition to the Syrian Monophysite heresy. An essential inability to suffer was the only contrast to passive suffering recognized in the early Church. There is, however, a third form of suffering – active suffering, the suffering of love, a voluntary openness to the possibility of being affected by outside influences. If God were really incapable of suffering, he would also be as incapable of loving as the God of Aristotle, who was loved by all, but could not love. Whoever is capable of love is also capable of suffering, because he is open to the suffering that love brings with it, although he is always able to surmount that suffering because of love. God does not suffer, like his creature, because his being is incomplete. He loves from the fullness of his being and suffers because of his full and free love.

The distinctions that have been made in theology between God's and man's being are externally important, but they tell us nothing about the inner relationship between God the Father and God the Son and therefore cannot be applied to the event of the cross which took place between God and God. Christian humanists also find this a profound *aporia*. In regarding Jesus as God's perfect man, and in taking his exemplary sinlessness as proof of his "permanently powerful consciousness of God," they interpret Jesus' death as the fulfillment of his obedience or faith, not as his being abandoned by God. God's incapacity, because of his divine nature, to suffer (*apatheia*) is replaced by the unshakeable steadfastness (*ataraxia*) of Jesus' consciousness of God. The ancient teaching that God is unchangeable is thus transferred to Jesus' "inner life," but the *aporia* is not overcome. Finally, atheistic humanists who are interested in Jesus but do not accept the existence of God find it impossible to think of Jesus as dying abandoned by God and therefore regard his cry to God from the cross as superfluous.

All Christian theologians of every period and inclination try to answer the question of Jesus' cry from the cross and to say, consciously or unconsciously, why God abandoned him. Atheists also attempt to answer this question in such a way that, by depriving it of its foundation, they can easily dismiss it. But Jesus' cry from the cross is greater than even the most convincing Christian answer. Theologians can only point to the coming of God, who is the only answer to this question.

Christians have to speak about God in the presence of Jesus' abandonment by God on the cross, which can provide the only complete justification of their theology. The cross is either the Christian end of all theology or it is the beginning of a specifically Christian theology. When theologians speak about God on the cross of Christ, this inevitably becomes a trinitarian debate about the "story of God" which is quite distinct from all monotheism, polytheism or pantheism. The central position occupied by the crucified Christ is the specifically Christian element in the history of the world and the doctrine of the Trinity is the specifically Christian element in the doctrine of God. Both are very closely connected. It is not the bare trinitarian formulas in the New Testament, but the constant testimony of the cross which provides the basis for Christian faith in the Trinity. The most concise expression of the Trinity is God's action on the cross, in which God allowed the Son to sacrifice himself through the Spirit (B. Steffen).

It is informative to examine Paul's statements about Jesus' abandonment on the cross in this context. The Greek word for "abandon" (*paradidōmi*) has a decidedly negative connotation in the gospel stories of the passion, meaning betray, deliver, give up and even kill. In Paul (Romans 1: 18–21), this negative meaning of *paredōken* is apparent in his presentation of God's abandonment of ungodly men. Guilt and punishment are closely connected and men who abandon God are abandoned by him and "given" up to the way they have chosen for themselves – Jews to their law, Gentiles to the worship of their idols and both to death.

Paul introduced a new meaning into the term *paredōken* when he presented Jesus' abandonment by God not in the historical context of his life, but in the eschatological context of faith. God "did not spare his own Son, but gave him up for us all; will he not also give us all things with him?" (Romans 8: 32). In the historical abandonment of the crucified Christ by the Father, Paul perceived the eschatological abandonment or "giving up" of the Son by the Father for the sake of "ungodly" men who had abandoned and been abandoned by God. In stressing that God had given up "his own Son," Paul extended the abandonment of the Son to the Father, although not in the same way, as the Patripassian heretics had done, insisting that the Son's sufferings could be predicated of the Father. In the Pauline view, Jesus suffered death abandoned by God. The Father, on the other hand, suffered the death of his Son in the pain of his love. The Son was "given up" by the Father and the Father suffered his abandonment from the Son. Kazoh Kitamori has called this "the pain of God."

The death of the Son is different from this "pain of God" the Father, and for this reason it is not possible to speak, as the Theopaschites did, of the "death of God." If we are to understand the story of Jesus' death abandoned by God as an event taking place between the Father and the Son, we must speak in terms of the Trinity and leave the universal concept of God aside, at least to begin with. In Galatians 2: 20, the word *paradontos* appears with Christ as the subject: "... the Son of God, who loved me and gave himself for me." According to this statement, then, it is not only the Father who gives the Son up, but the Son who gives himself up. This indicates that Jesus' will and that of the Father were the same at the point where Jesus was abandoned on the cross and they were completely separated. Paul himself interpreted Christ's being abandoned by God as love, and the same interpretation is found in John (John 3: 16). The author of 1 John regarded this event of love on the cross as the very existence of God himself; "God is love" (1 John 4: 16). This is why it was possible at a later period to speak, with reference to the cross, of *homoousia*, the

Son and the Father being of one substance. In the cross, Jesus and his God are in the deepest sense separated by the Son's abandonment by the Father, yet at the same time they are in the most intimate sense united in this abandonment or "giving up." This is because this "giving up" proceeds from the event of the cross that takes place between the Father who abandons and the Son who is abandoned, and this "giving up" is none other than the Holy Spirit.

Any attempt to interpret the event of Jesus' crucifixion according to the doctrine of the two natures would result in a paradox, because of the concept of the one God and the one nature of God. On the cross, God calls to God and dies to God. Only in this place is God "dead" and yet not dead. If all we have is the concept of one God, we are inevitably inclined to apply it to the Father and to relate the death exclusively to the human person of Jesus, so that the cross is "emptied" of its divinity. If, on the other hand, this concept of God is left aside, we have at once to speak of persons in the special relationship of this particular event, the Father as the one who abandons and "gives up" the Son, and the Son who is abandoned by the Father and who gives himself up. What proceeds from this event is the Spirit of abandonment and self-giving love who raises up abandoned men.

My interpretation of the death of Christ, then, is not as an event between God and man, but primarily as an event within the Trinity between Jesus and his Father, an event from which the Spirit proceeds. This interpretation opens up a number of perspectives. In the first place, it is possible to understand the crucifixion of Christ non-theistically. Secondly, the old dichotomy between the universal nature of God and the inner triune nature of God is overcome and, thirdly, the distinction between the immanent and the "economic" Trinity becomes superfluous. It makes it necessary to speak about the Trinity in the context of the cross, and re-establishes it as a traditional doctrine. Seen in this light, this doctrine no longer has to be regarded as a divine mystery which is better venerated with silent respect than investigated too closely. It can be seen as the tersest way of expressing the story of Christ's passion. It preserves faith from monotheism and from atheism, because it keeps it close to the crucified Christ. It reveals the cross in God's being and God's being in the cross. The material principle of the trinitarian doctrine is the cross; the formal principle of the theology of the cross is the trinitarian doctrine. The unity of the Father, the Son and the Holy Spirit can be designated as "God." If we are to speak as Christians about God, then, we have to tell the story of Jesus as the story of God and to proclaim it as the historical event which took place between the Father, the Son and the Holy Spirit and which revealed who and what God is, not only for man, but in his very existence. This also means that God's being is historical and that he exists in history. The "story of God" then is the story of the history of man.

Comment

The ideas which are set out in this passage, and more fully in *The Crucified God*, have been highly influential. In particular, it may be noted that Moltmann was able to argue for the idea of a suffering God without committing himself to either of two discredited theological positions – Patripassianism or Theopaschitism. According to Moltmann, both the Father and the Son suffer – but they experience that suffering in different manners. The Son suffers the pain and death of the cross; the Father gives up and suffers the loss of the Son. Although both Father and Son are involved in the cross, their involvement is not *identical* (the Patripassian position), but *distinct*. As Moltmann states this in *The Crucified God*: "In the passion of the Son, the Father himself suffers the pains of abandonment. In the death of the Son, death comes upon God himself, and the Father suffers the death of his Son in his love for forsaken man."

The emphasis upon "love" is also of importance. Central to Moltmann's argument is that the notion of love implies suffering. Can God be said to "love" without being said to "suffer"? For Moltmann, the answer is emphatically negative, as the passage reprinted above makes abundantly clear.

Questions for Study

1. Why does Moltmann agree with Nicaea's critique of Arius, while not agreeing with the conclusions which many patristic writers drew from that critique? Is his position tenable?
2. "Whoever is capable of love is also capable of suffering." Locate this passage within the text. What does Moltmann mean by this? And how does it relate to his argument?
3. Moltmann, Augustine, and Richard of St Victor all appeal to the notion of "love" in developing their trinitarian theology. Compare this passage with 3.15 and 3.22. How do each analyze the notion of "love"? And how do you account for the different outcomes of this engagement in each case?

3.34

Richard Swinburne on God as Creator

The concept of "creation" is of considerable interest to both Christian theologians and philosophers of religion. One of the most interesting late twentieth-century philosophers of religion is Richard Swinburne (born 1934), whose *Coherence of Theism* evoked admiration and critical comment in about equal amounts. The following passage, taken from this important work, explores what it means to speak of "creation." See also 6.25.

Theists claim that God is the creator of all things. (In the Nicene Creed he is said to be "Maker of Heaven and Earth, and of all things, visible and invisible".) But initial restrictions must be put on this loose claim. Firstly, the theist does not normally claim that God is the creator of himself. That something should create itself is a difficult idea of which to attempt to make sense – to say the least; and the theist normally sees no need to make the attempt. [...] The claim that there is an individual who is the creator of all things, is to be understood with the qualification "apart from himself" or, more precisely, "apart from anything the existence of which is entailed by his own existence". Secondly, the theist is presumably not claiming that God is the creator of prime numbers, concepts, or logical relations. There are certain things which exist as a matter of logical necessity; that is, the statement that they exist is a logically necessary truth. It is a logically necessary truth that there exists a prime number between 16 and 18, or that there exists a relation of entailment between "John is over 5 foot tall" and "John is over 4 foot tall". Such things which exist as a matter of logical necessity do not, we feel, exist in the hard real way in which tables, chairs, and people do. To say that they exist is not to give us any real information about how things are. That they exist cannot be due to the act of any creator; for they exist just because they are, because the propositions which assert their existence say what they do. For these reasons I suggest that the claim that there exists an omnipresent spirit who is the creator of all things is to be understood as the claim that there exists an omnipresent spirit who is the creator of all things which exist, the existence of which is neither a logically necessary truth nor entailed by his own existence. This we may phrase more briefly as the claim that there exists an omnipresent spirit who is the creator of all logically contingent things apart from himself.

How next is "create" to be understood? We could understand it as "bring about the existence of". But if we understand it in that simple way, there is an obvious difficulty for the theist who claims that God creates all logically contingent things apart from himself. This is that, superficially, agents other than God bring about a lot of things. Men, not God, bring about the existence of tables and chairs. Sun and rain, not God, bring about the existence of healthy plants. One could say that really men, sun, and rain do not do these things – they only appear to, really it is God alone who does them. But most theists have not wished to deny that men, sun, and rain bring about things.

The claim that God is the creator of all has been understood more subtly. By it the theist has wanted to make one main claim and sometimes also one subsidiary claim. The main claim is that God either himself brings about or makes or permits some other being to bring about (or permits to exist uncaused) the existence of all things that exist (with the qualifications on this latter expression, stated above, being understood); that those things exist only because of God's action or permission. Other beings, that is, often bring about the existence of things, but when they do, they do so only because (in the case of beings without free will) God makes them do so, or because (in the case of beings with free will) God permits them to do so. Agents other than God act only because he makes or permits them to act.

The subsidiary claim which has often been made, e.g. by scholastic theologians, is that God alone brings about the existence of certain things, such as matter and human souls. I shall not consider this subsidiary claim further. It would need very careful and lengthy articulation to bring out what is meant by "matter" and "human soul" and the doctrine does not seem to be very central to theism. It would hardly seem to matter for theism if God on occasion permitted some other being to create matter. He would hardly be less worthy of worship if he did. I shall therefore understand the doctrine that God is the creator of all things as the doctrine that God himself either brings about or makes or permits some other being to bring about the existence of all logically contingent things that exist (i.e. have existed, exist, or will exist), apart from himself.

I could have set out the doctrine of God as creator as the doctrine that God brings about (or makes or permits others to bring about) the *beginnings* of the existence of all things which exist. But the theist believes that God's action (or permission) is needed not merely for things to begin to exist but also for them to continue in existence. We could phrase this point by describing God as the creator *and sustainer* of all things, but it is simpler and in conformity with the usage of medieval theology (though not perhaps of much modern writing) to make both points by the use of the one word "create," and this I shall do. Aquinas held that natural reason was unable to prove either that the universe (in either the wider or narrower senses to be delineated below) was eternal or that it had a beginning of existence. Revelation alone (the Bible and the Church, that is) showed us that it had a beginning of existence. Nevertheless, natural reason could prove that it had a creator. Theists both before and after Aquinas have usually held that the universe (at any rate in the narrower sense to be delineated below) had a beginning, but for them, as for Aquinas, this doctrine can hardly have the importance in their thought possessed by the doctrine that God is responsible for the existence of the universe at each moment of its existence. In the old legend Atlas holding up the earth is responsible for it being in place – whether he has been holding it for a few years or for ever. So on the theist's view God keeps the universe in being, whether he has been doing so for ever or only for a finite time.

The theist claims that God is the creator of the world or the universe. What is meant by "the world" or "the universe?" Different men may well mean different things by these phrases. For some "the universe" or "the world" may mean simply all that there is. But the theist cannot give these phrases this meaning – for the reasons given above. He may mean by them "all logically contingent things apart from God." Or he may mean something narrower. He may mean the system of all the physical things which are spatially related to the earth. By physical things I mean roughly material objects, such as stars and planets and the tables, houses, and (embodied) persons on them and things similar thereto (such as packets of energy, which, like material objects, have mass and charge and can be converted into or obtained from matter). By "spatially related" I mean "in some direction at some distance" (e.g. a million miles along such-and-such a line). Planets, stars, and galaxies and the physical things between them and on them, however distant in whatever direction, form the universe. This definition, however, allows for the logical possibility of the existence of universes or worlds other than ours. For maybe there are planets and stars other than those which lie in some direction along some line from ourselves. The theist who claims that God is the creator of the universe, will, if he uses the expression "the universe" in this narrower sense, also claim that God is the creator of anything else logically contingent which exists. He claims, that is, that God is creator of the universe both in the narrower sense of "all physical things spatially related to ourselves" and in the wider sense of "all logically contingent things apart from God". The latter class of things includes the movements of physical things, the way they behave. The theist claims that not merely does God bring about (or makes or permits others to bring about or permits to exist uncaused) the existence of tables and chairs, (embodied) persons and stars, but that he brings about (or makes or permits others to bring about) their moving and interacting in the way in which they do; and that their motion or interaction would not occur but for his action or permission. God's action (or permission) is needed, for example, not merely for the existence of the wind, but for it to blow this way rather than that. Theists may hold that the universe in the wider sense includes many other things beside physical things more naturally called "things" than the movements and interactions of bodies. They may hold that as well as physical things spatially related to ourselves, there are angels and devils, disembodied spirits and other worlds – or they may not hold this. The doctrine that there is an omnipresent spirit who is the creator of the universe is therefore to be understood, in view of the tradition of theism, as follows. There is an omnipresent spirit who either himself brings about or makes or permits other beings to bring about (or permits to exist uncaused) the existence of all logically contingent things that exist (i.e. have existed, exist, or will exist), apart from anything, the existence of which is entailed by his own existence.

Comment

Philosophy has been described as an attempt to clarify questions before offering answers. In his passage, Swinburne aims to achieve a clarification of terms. What does the word "create" actually mean? Swinburne's analysis is so clear that little is needed in the way of comment, other than noting the importance of definition of terms – something that theologians are not always good at.

Questions for Study

1 According to Swinburne, what does the word "create" mean?
2 "There is an omnipresent spirit who either himself brings about or makes or permits other beings to bring about (or permits to exist uncaused) the existence of all logically contingent things that exist (i.e. have existed, exist, or will exist), apart from anything, the existence of which is entailed by his own existence." Locate this long quotation in the text. Why are there so many qualifications and subsidiary clauses in this statement? Why not just say: "to create something" means "to bring about the existence of something"? From the text, make sure that you can explain each of the qualifications that Swinburne introduces.
3 Swinburne introduces the figure of Atlas to make a point. What is the point which is illustrated in this manner? And how does it affect the meaning of the word "create"?

3.35

Leonardo Boff on the Trinity as Good News for the Poor

The Brazilian writer Leonardo Boff (born 1938), one of the most noted exponents of Latin American liberation theology, here provides an exploration of the manner in which the Trinity itself can provide a model for social living, arguing that the mutual relationship of Father, Son, and Holy Spirit acts as a basis for Christian social theory and practice. See also 1.31, 3.23, 3.30, 3.33, 3.37, 3.38, 7.28.

In what sense can the Trinity be called "gospel," good news, to people, especially to the poor and oppressed? For many Christians it is simply a mystery in logic: how can the one God exist in three Persons? How can a Trinity of Persons form the unity of the one God? Any Christian coming into contact with debates on the Trinity for the first time might well form this impression: the Christian faith developed intellectually in the Hellenic world; Christians had to translate their doxology into a theology appropriate to that world in order to assert the truth of their faith. So they used expressions accessible to the critical reasoning of that time, such as substance, person, relation, perichoresis, procession. This was a most difficult path to follow [...]; it has left its mark even today, even though the mystery defies all human categories and calls for new approaches, springing from an encounter between biblical revelation and dominant cultures. We should never forget that the New Testament never uses the expressions "trinity of persons" and "unity of nature." To say that God is Father, Son and Holy Spirit is revelation; to say that God is "one substance and three Persons" is theology, a human endeavor to fit the revelation of God within the limitations of reason.

The same thing happens when Christians read the pronouncements of the *magisterium*. These are statements of great pithiness and logical coherence, designed to curb the speculative exuberance of theologians. Dogmatic progress virtually came to an end with the Council of Florence (1439–45); from then to the present (with some noted exceptions, as we have seen) theological works have generally confined themselves to commenting on the terms defined and investigating historical questions of detail of the system already constructed.

It is not easy to explain to Christians caught up in the "logical mystery" of the Trinity that the number "three" in the Trinity (*Trias* and *Trinitas*, words established by Theophilus of Antioch and Tertullian at the end of the second century) does not signify anything that can be counted and has nothing to do with arithmetical processes of addition and subtraction. The scriptures count nothing in God; they know only one divine number – the number "one": one God, one Lord, one Spirit. This "one" is not a number, nor the number "one" in the sense of first in a series; it is rather the negation of all numbers, simply "the only." The Father is "an only," as are the Son and the Holy Spirit; these "onlies" cannot be added together. [. . .] it is the eternal communion between these Onlies that forms the divine oneness in the power of life and love (the divine nature). Nevertheless, by reason of the communion and relationship revealed to us between the Father, Son and Holy Spirit, there is an order to the divine names. Though each Person is co-eternal with the others and, therefore, none can exist before the others, we must, nevertheless, affirm that the Father who begets is logically "before" the Son who is begotten, as is the Son "before" the Spirit, breathed out by the Father with and through the Son. This is the explanation for the order of the divine names, and from this comes the human convention of speaking of three "Persons." But theology has never been satisfied with the expression "three Persons," as the continuous debates have shown.

We need to go beyond the understanding of Trinity as logical mystery and see it as saving mystery. The Trinity has to do with the lives of each of us, our daily experiences, our struggles to follow our conscience, our love and joy, our bearing the sufferings of the world and the tragedies of human existence; it also has to do with the struggle against social injustice, with efforts at building a more human form of society, with the sacrifices and martyrdoms that these endeavors so often bring. If we fail to include the Trinity in our personal and social odyssey, we shall have failed to show the saving mystery, failed in evangelization. If oppressed believers come to appreciate the fact that their struggles for life and liberty are also those of the Father, Son and Holy Spirit, working for the Kingdom of glory and eternal life, then they will have further motives for struggling and resisting; the meaning of their efforts will break out of the restricting framework of history and be inscribed in eternity, in the heart of the absolute Mystery itself. We are not condemned to live alone, cut off from one another; we are called to live together and to enter into the communion of the Trinity. Society is not ultimately set in its unjust and unequal relationships, but summoned to transform itself in the light of the open and egalitarian relationships that obtain in the communion of the Trinity, the goal of social and historical progress. If the Trinity is good news, then it is so particularly for the oppressed and those condemned to solitude.

Comment

Leonardo Boff is one of the most theologically alert representatives of liberation theology. It is helpful to regard Boff as an essentially quite conservative Roman Catholic theologian whose radical reputation rests primarily upon the way in which he applies the traditional teachings of the church. This is especially clear from his exploration of the doctrine of the Trinity in his *Trinity and Society*, in which he offers a fairly traditional account of the biblical basis and historical development of the doctrine, before moving on to apply the doctrine to the social situation of his day.

Questions for Study

1 What, according to Boff, are the social implications of the doctrine of the Trinity? You should try to write these down in your own words.
2 Richard of St Victor (3.22) used social relations to illustrate the trinitarian relations; Boff inverts this order of proceeding. What are the implications of this change?
3 "We need to go beyond the understanding of Trinity as logical mystery and see it as saving mystery." Locate this passage within the text. What does Boff mean by this? How does it illuminate his goals and concerns?

3.36

Robert Jenson on the Trinity

The American Lutheran writer Robert Jenson (born 1930) here argues that the Trinity is the distinctively Christian means of identifying or naming God. The Trinity can be thought of in terms of the proper name of the Christian God, which establishes the identity of God on the basis of an affirmation and identification of God's redemptive acts in history. See also 3.3, 3.10, 3.11, 3.12, 3.13, 3.15, 3.19, 3.20.

Meditating on the foundation of biblical faith, the exodus, Israel's first theologians made Moses' decisive question be: "If I come to the people of Israel and say to them, 'The God of your fathers has sent me to you': and they ask me, 'What is his name?' what shall I say to them?" If Israel was to risk the future of this God, to leave secure nonexistence in Egypt and venture on God's promises, Israel had first and fundamentally to know which future this was. The God answered, "Say this to the people of Israel, [Yahweh], the God of your fathers, the God of Abraham, the God of Isaac, and the God of Jacob, has sent me to you, this is my name for ever, and thus I am to be remembered throughout all generations" (Exodus 3: 13–15)!

The answer provides a proper name, "Yahweh." It also provides what logicians now call an identifying description, a descriptive phrase or clause, or set of them, that fits just the one individual thing to be identified. Here the description is "the God whom Abraham and Isaac and Jacob worshipped." The more usual description is that found in a parallel account a few chapters later: God said to Moses, "Say . . . to the people of Israel, 'I am [Yahweh], and I will bring you out from under the burdens of the Egyptians . . . ; and you shall know that I am [Yahweh] your God, *who* has brought you out. . . . I am [Yahweh]' " (Exodus 6: 2–7; emphasis added).

In general, proper names work only if such identifying descriptions are at hand. We may say, "Mary is coming to dinner" and be answered with, "Who is Mary?" Then we must be able to say, "Mary is the one who lives in apartment 2C, and is always so cheerful, and . . . ," continuing until the questioner says, "Oh, *that* one!" We may say, "Yahweh always forgives:" and be answered with, "Do you mean the Inner Self?" Then we must be able to say, "No. We mean the one who rescued Israel from Egypt, and. . . . "

[. . .] Trinitarian discourse is Christianity's effort to identify the God who has claimed us. The doctrine of the Trinity comprises both a proper name, "Father, Son, and Holy Spirit," in several grammatical variants, and an elaborate development and analysis of corresponding identifying descriptions [. . .]

The gospel of the New Testament is the provision of a new identifying description for this same God [as that of Israel]. The coming-to-apply of this new description is the event, the witness to which is the whole point of the New Testament. God, in the gospel, is "whoever raised Jesus from the dead." Identification of God by the resurrection did not replace identification by the exodus; it is essential to the God who raised Jesus that he is the same one who freed Israel. But the new thing that is the content of the gospel is that God has now identified himself also as "him that raised from the dead Jesus our Lord" (Romans 4: 24). In the New Testament such phrases become the standard way of referring to God.

To go with this new identifying description there are not so much new names as new kinds of naming. "Yahweh" does not reappear as a name in use. The habit of saying "Lord" instead has buried it too deeply under the appellative. But in the church's missionary situation, actual use of a proper name in speaking of God is again necessary in a variety of contexts. It is the naming of Jesus that occurs for all such functions. Exorcism, healing, and indeed good works generally are accomplished "in Jesus' name" (e.g., Mark 9: 37ff.). Church discipline and quasi-discipline are carried out by sentences pronounced in Jesus' name (e.g., 1 Corinthians 1: 10), and forgiveness is pronounced in the same way (e.g., 1 John 2: 12). Baptism is described as into Jesus' name (e.g., Acts 2: 38), whether or not it was ever actually performed with this formula. Undergoing such baptism is equated with that calling on the name "Yahweh" by which, according to Joel 3: 5, Israel is to be saved (Acts 2: 21, 38). Above all, perhaps, prayer is "in Jesus' name" (e.g., John 14: 13–14), in consequence of which the name can be posited as the very object of faith (e.g., John 1: 12). Believers are those "who call on the name of our Lord Jesus Christ" (e.g., Acts 9: 14).

So dominant was the use of the name "Jesus" in the religious life of the apostolic church that the whole mission can be described as proclamation "in his name" (Luke 24: 47), "preaching good news about the kingdom of God and the name of Jesus Christ" (Acts 8: 12), indeed, as "carrying" Jesus' name to the people (e.g., Acts 9: 15). The gatherings of the congregations can be described as "giving thanks . . . in the name of our Lord Jesus Christ" (Ephesians 5: 20), indeed, simply as meetings in his name (Matthew 18: 20). Where faith must be confessed over against the hostility of society, this is "confession of the name" (e.g., Mark 13: 13). The theological conclusion was drawn in such praises as the hymn preserved in Philippians in which God's own eschatological triumph is evoked as cosmic obeisance to the name "Jesus" (Philippians 1: 10), or in such formulas as that in Acts which makes Jesus' name the agent of salvation (Acts 4: 12). However various groups in the primal church may have conceived Jesus' relation to God, "Jesus" was the way they all invoked God.

One other new naming appears in the New Testament, the triune name: "Father, Son, and Holy Spirit." Its appearance is undoubtedly dependent on naming God by naming Jesus, as just discussed, but the causal connections are no longer recoverable. It is of course toward this name that we have been steering. That the biblical God must have a proper name, we have seen in the Hebrew Scriptures. In the life of the primal church, God is named by uses that involve the name of Jesus. "Father, Son, and Spirit" is the naming of this sort that historically triumphed.

That "Father, Son, and Holy Spirit" in fact occupies in the church the place occupied in Israel by "Yahweh" or, later, "Lord" even hasty observation of the church's life must discover [. . .] Our services begin and are punctuated with "In the name of the Father, Son, and Holy Spirit." Our prayers conclude, "In his name who with you and the Holy Spirit is. . . . " Above all, the act by which people are brought both into the fellowship of believers and into their fellowship with God is an initiation "into the name 'Father, Son, and Holy Spirit.' "

The habit of trinitarian naming is universal through the life of the church. How far back it goes, we cannot tell. It certainly goes further back than even the faintest traces of trinitarian reflection, and it appears to have been an immediate expression of believers' experience of God. It is in liturgy, when we talk not *about* God but to and for him, that we need and use God's name, and that is where the trinitarian formulas appear, both initially and to this day. In the immediately postapostolic literature there is no use of a trinitarian formula as a piece of theology or in such fashion as to depend on antecedent development in theology, yet the formula is there. Its home is in the liturgy, in baptism and the eucharist. There its use was regularly seen as the heart of the matter.

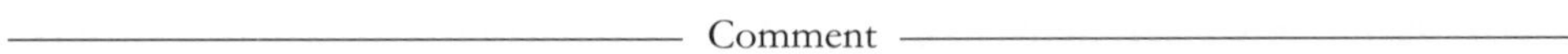

Comment

Jenson argues that the phrase "Father, Son, and Holy Spirit" is the proper name for the God whom Christians know in and through Jesus Christ. It is imperative, he argues, that God should have a proper name. Trinitarian discourse is Christianity's effort to identify its God. The doctrine of the Trinity thus comprises both a proper name – "Father, Son, and Holy Spirit" – and an elaborate development and analysis of corresponding identifying descriptions. Jenson points out that ancient Israel existed and thought within a polytheistic context, in which the term "god" conveyed relatively little information. It was necessary to *name and identify* the god in question. A similar situation was confronted by the writers of the New Testament, who were obliged to identify the god at the heart of their faith, and distinguish this god from the many other gods worshiped and acknowledged in the region, especially in Asia Minor. The doctrine of the Trinity thus *identifies* and *names* the Christian God – but identifies and names this God in a manner consistent with the biblical witness. It is not a name which we have chosen; it is a name which has been chosen for us, and which we are authorized to use. In this way, Jenson defends the priority of God's self-revelation against human constructions of concepts of divinity.

Questions for Study

1 "Trinitarian discourse is Christianity's effort to identify the God who has claimed us." Locate this statement within the text. Why, according to Jenson, do we need to "name" God? Isn't the word "God" good enough to convey our meaning?
2 The Old Testament writers knew the importance of naming God, according to Jenson. However, they did not use the name "Father, Son, and Holy Spirit," which is a distinctively New Testament way of referring to God. How does Jenson respond to this observation?
3 Notice how Jenson makes an appeal to the liturgical or doxological tradition of the church in clinching his argument. How important is this principle of correlating theology with doxology? Can you think of any other theological debates in which it has been an issue?

3.37

Hans Küng on the Immutability of God

The question of whether God can suffer is linked, both historically and philosophically, with the issue of the immutability of God. In an important study of the implications of the philosophy of G. W. H. Hegel for the doctrine of the incarnation, the Roman Catholic theologian Hans Küng (born 1928) offered an important series of reflections on the question of whether God can be said to "change" or "suffer". In the extract which follows, Küng sets out some of the issues of relevance to this debate. See also 3.8, 3.30.

Mediaeval theology, like that of the early Church, as a result of its dependence on classical Greek philosophy, was inclined much more to a metaphysic of being than to a metaphysic of becoming. And, as the notion of God's immutability, taken over from Greek metaphysics, served the apologists and the later Fathers (especially Origen and Augustine) well in the struggle against Stoic pantheism and Gnostic and Manichaean dualism and for stressing the eternity and constancy of God, in the middle ages it was an important aid in resisting any kind of pantheism – as, for instance, in the statement of the Fourth Lateran Council about the *Deus incommutabilis* and in modern times in the definition of the First Vatican Council referring to God as a *simplex omnino et incommutabilis substantia spiritualis*. But [. . .] the idea created a variety of difficulties for the apologists and the later Fathers in their Christology and it was the same with the scholastics when they came to reflect on the christological question. It was not least for this reason that the Johannine "becoming man" and the Pauline "self-emptying" (both understood ontologically from the earliest times) manifestly slipped well into the background in the course of centuries in favour of other interpretations of the Christ-event, particularly the idea of an "assumption" of the human nature.

The term "assumption," however, can easily be understood as putting on humanity like an article of clothing which remains purely external and does not affect the person inwardly; the Logos would not need to become man or to empty himself. But this was the way in which the "assumption" of the human nature was understood and repeatedly applied in a number of variations in the early Church by some who upheld a disjunction Christology. In the middle ages also the term was used similarly, especially by defenders of the *habitus* theory, widespread in early scholasticism and later condemned, by going back to Abelard who had treated the christological statement "God is man" as a figurative or metaphorical expression. The *assumptus* theory, maintained until well into the period of high scholasticism, envisaged man's becoming God more than God's becoming man. These difficulties arose out of a particular metaphysical interpretation of God's immutability.

Aquinas not only rejected the *habitus* theory, but was the first to condemn outright the *assumptus* theory and even to describe it as Nestorian. In his doctrine of creation he tackled successfully the difficult task of qualifying the one-sided transcendence of the Aristotelian "unmoved Mover" in the light of Aristotelian principles. In Christology he was faced with more serious difficulties. After seeking in the light of Aristotelian metaphysics to understand the Christ-event as becoming man, the question arose as to how this unmoving transcendent God of Greek metaphysics could *become* man. Aquinas, here too basing himself on Augustine, produced the ingenious solution which he had prepared in working out his theory of creation, making use of the concept of *relatio rationis*. This means that the divine Logos remains unchanged in the incarnation; what is changed is the human nature, which is taken up into the divine person. The human nature has a real relationship – a *relatio realis* – to the Logos. On the other hand, the Logos has only a conceptual relationship – a *relatio rationis* – to the human nature. Aquinas gives the example of someone at first sitting on my left, then changing his place to sit on my right, with the result that I am now sitting on his left; but I have not changed my position, it is the other person who made the move. I have not acquired any new reality, only a new conceptual relationship. Hence, according to Aquinas, in the incarnation the human nature (not of course pre-existing in time) is changed by being completely assumed into the divine nature. But the divine Logos remains completely unchanged in the incarnation.

This theory of the *relatio rationis* was not meant to raise doubts about the Logos *becoming* man, but to avoid the danger of reducing God to a process of becoming. It has the important consequence of bringing out clearly the fact that God in becoming man neither loses anything (becoming man means no loss to God) nor gains anything (becoming man means no gain to God), and anyway that becoming man is something different from the coming to be of man and the world. In God there is no movement in Aristotle's sense: no completion of what was hitherto incomplete, of what was *in potentia*, no actualization as transference from pure possibility to reality. Is it permissible to lose sight of this consequence? It is scarcely possible to probe more deeply into the problems by questioning God's fullness of perfection either before or after his becoming man.

Would God be really God if in him there were imperfection needing to be perfected, a potency calling for actualization? But, from the standpoint also of the Aristotelian-scholastic theory of God, the question might perhaps be raised in the opposite way. If according to this theory God is *actus purus*, purest reality, active *energeia*, whose being is operation, whose essence is action, must he not be understood as life at its most vital? But could not this divine life be understood, not in the light of potentiality, but in the light of supreme actuality, as becoming in an analogous sense? And then would not a real becoming man on the part of the divine Logos be conceivable? For classical Christology has always firmly maintained that the divine Logos *himself* became man. And at this decisive point the theory of the *relatio rationis* would not be adequate: a theory of a Logos remaining unmoved which was scarcely ever preached at all and certainly not at Christmas. For although this theory is able to explain that the Word of God in becoming man remained completely what it was – that is, God – it cannot show convincingly that the Word *itself* became man. For it is not flesh that became the Logos, but the Logos that became flesh. It is a question of the self-emptying of the Logos: not of an apotheosis of flesh, but of an *ensarkōsis* of the Logos. Even though (according to this scholastic understanding) only the human nature is unchangeable in itself. Nevertheless this changeable human nature is the Logos' own nature. Its history is the history of the Logos, its time his time, its dying his dying. According to scholastic theory the Logos himself assumed it and in this way emptied himself into it. If the Word had not himself become flesh and if this becoming did not affect the Word himself, the Word himself would not have become anything. He would then not have become man. How could the theory of an immutable Logos be compatible with the statements of the New Testament that the Logos himself is involved in becoming flesh (John 1: 14), that he emptied himself and humbled himself (Philippians 2: 7–8), that he gave himself (Galatians 1: 4; 1 Timothy 2: 6), that he delivered himself up (Galatians 2: 20; Ephesians 5: 2), that he offered himself (Hebrews 7: 27; 9: 14), that he, the Son of God, became obedient (Philippians 2: 8; Hebrews 5: 8)?

The dilemma cannot be overlooked, nor can it be simply dismissed as a "mystery". The mystery is to be sought in the fact that God, to whom the metaphysicians out of fear of imperfection have denied life and becoming, in fact lives, acts and becomes in perfection and from perfection. To accept this would however involve a revision of the static, Parmenidean understanding of God. It does not imply a simple decision for a philosophy of becoming as opposed to a philosophy of being. It means taking seriously the God who is wholly other, in whom being and becoming, remaining in himself and going out from himself, transcendence and descendence, are not mutually exclusive.

Comment

Küng here traces the continuing impact of some themes of classical philosophy upon the Christian discussion of God, and the way in which God relates to the world, especially humanity in its suffering. The doctrine of the incarnation is seen as being of especial importance to the clarification of such issues. If God cannot change, how can God become incarnate? How can God be said to "assume" human nature without being mutable? In this extract, Küng tries to clarify the confusions which have muddled this discussion, while offering guidance as to future reflection on such matters.

Questions for Study

1 According to Küng, how important have explicitly philosophical considerations been to Christian theological reflection on the nature of God?
2 Küng makes much of the distinction between *relatio rationis* ("a relation of reason") and *relatio realis* ("a real relation"). Explain the point which he makes in this way, and assess its importance to the discussion.
3 "The mystery is to be sought in the fact that God, to whom the metaphysicians out of fear of imperfection have denied life and becoming, in fact lives, acts, and becomes in perfection and from perfection." Locate this passage within the text. What does Küng mean by this? And how does this line of thought relate to the issues set out by Spinoza (3.30)?

3.38

Eberhard Jüngel on the Crucified God

The German theologian Eberhard Jüngel (born 1934) has attracted considerable attention on account of his attempt to demonstrate the extent to which Christian theology has become imprisoned or distorted by metaphysical assumptions concerning the nature of God. Jüngel is especially concerned to point out the often unrecognized influence of Cartesian ideas – that is, ideas which derive from René Descartes – on the doctrine of God, especially in relation to the concept of "perfection." In his important and difficult work *God as the Mystery of the World*, Jüngel stresses the importance of attending to God as God has been revealed, rather than relying upon philosophically derived concepts of God. See also 1.12, 1.16, 1.17, 1.26, 3.30, 3.37.

Since Christian theology understands God himself, for the sake of Jesus, in this sense as the one who speaks, as the word, it ascribes to the word "God" a function of announcing God himself, but solely on the basis of the word of God. The traditional language of Christianity [*die christliche Sprachüberlieferung*] insists, therefore, on the fact that we *must have said to us* what the word "God" should be thought to mean. The presupposition is that ultimately only the speaking God himself can say what the word "God" should provide us to think about. Theology comprehends this whole subject with the category of revelation.

We have understood that God is one who speaks and as such one who expresses himself as an assertion which is inseparably tied to faith in Jesus. Hebrews, like Romans 1: 2, relates Old Testament talk about God (as God speaking through prophets) to Jesus. This expresses the fact that in the person Jesus is revealed what God as the one who speaks is all about. The humanity of this person is extremely relevant to the meaning of the word "God", according to the New Testament view. This is true not just of the life but especially of the death of this person. Therefore, when we attempt to think of God as the one who communicates and expresses himself in the person Jesus, it must be remembered that, in fact, this man was *crucified*, that he was killed in the name of God's law. For responsible Christian usage of the word "God," the Crucified One is virtually the real definition of what is meant with the word "God". Christianity is thus fundamentally the "theology of the Crucified One" [*Theologie der Gekreuzigten*].

Comment

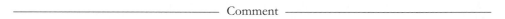

Eberhard Jüngel is widely regarded as one of the most articulate contemporary representatives of a "theology of the cross" – that is, a theology which argues that the Christian knowledge of God is uniquely grounded in and is decisively shaped by the cross of Christ. This approach can be traced back to Martin Luther, especially the ideas which he developed in the Heidelberg Disputation of 1519 (see 1.12). Jüngel argues that the theology of the Enlightenment has been deeply shaped by Cartesian assumptions, and that a return to a "theology of the cross" provides the means of liberation from this Cartesian framework. In this brief extract, Jüngel stresses the need to be told what God is like, and that the cross of Christ provides both a locus and focus for this process of "being told." Note that the German original of the phrase "we *must have said to us* what the word 'God' should be thought to mean" would more naturally be translated as "we *need to be told* what the word 'God' should be understood to mean."

Questions for Study

1 How does Jüngel think we should approach the word "God"?
2 To what extent might the ideas set out by Spinoza (3.30) illustrate the concerns which Jüngel expresses concerning philosophical influences on the Christian doctrine of God?
3 "For responsible Christian usage of the word 'God,' the Crucified One is virtually the real definition of what is meant with the word 'God.' " What does Jüngel mean by this? How does this relate to the approach set out by Martin Luther in the Heidelberg Disputation (1.12)?

3.39

Jacques Ellul on the Theology of Icons

In this critique of the use of icons, based on an interaction with Paul Evdokimov's *L'Art de l'icône; théologie de la beauté* (Paris: Desclée, 1970), the French Protestant theologian and sociologist Jacques Ellul (1912–94) argues for the need for an understanding of the divine nature which is based primarily upon the word of God, rather than images. The critique offers some characteristic Reformed perspectives on the nature and origins of the knowledge of God, and especially the type of knowledge of God available through Christ. See also 1.14, 2.16, 4.20.

The icon, of course, is not worshiped for itself; in itself, it has no value. It is not a work of art. [. . .] The object is not venerated; Beauty is by means of the resemblance mysteriously conveyed by the icon. It irradiates "the ineffable reflections of divine Beauty." The image is clearly superior to the word: "the image shows what the word says." [. . .] The word is not sufficient. The icon is a symbol, but must be surpassed; though nothing in itself, it is indispensable in mystical contemplation. As a kind of sacrament that makes transcendent communion possible, in itself it is transcendent. The icon *alone* enables a person to participate in the indescribable. [. . .]

All of this is closely linked to a theology of the Incarnation understood as "sanctification of matter and transfiguration of the flesh." The Incarnation enables us to *see* both spiritual bodies and nature as transformed by Christ. In other words, the Incarnation of Jesus has transformed the entire human species and all of nature; it is a completely finished work, and this transformed nature enables us to contemplate the divine through "indirect thought." Human beings are (already) deified.

This symbolic knowledge needs a material vehicle. But, starting from the symbol, by means of the contemplation and true imagination with its evocative power, such knowledge grasps the figurative presence as an epiphany of the transcendent. This presence is symbolized, but *very real*. The icon guides our *gaze* towards the Highest – toward the Most High, toward the only necessity. [. . .]

The icon of Christ, of course, is certainly not Christ. It is only an image, not a prototype. But it bears witness to a well-defined presence, and permits prayerful communion (which is not eucharistic communion, because it permits spiritual communion with the *Person* of Christ). "The presence of the icon is a circle whose center is found in the icon, but whose circumference is nowhere. As a material point in the world, the icon opens a breach through which the Transcendent bursts." [. . .] Coming back to the Incarnation, Evdokimov concludes: "A hypostasis in two natures signifies an image in two modes: visible and invisible. The divine is invisible, but it is reflected by the visible human object. The icon of Christ is possible, *true and real*, because his image in the human mode is identical to the invisible image in the divine mode."

Fundamentally, the theology of icons involves first a switch from signs to symbols, because the icon is essentially symbolic. Then, the icon is inserted into an entire liturgy. It implies a theology of the concrete presence of the spiritual realm, and of divine light, which can be symbolically retranscribed and which is the image of glory itself. [...]

[This theology of icons] rests on a certain conception of the Incarnation that utterly fails to take into account its unfulfilled aspect: the waiting and the hope. "Having *reestablished* the tarnished image in its former dignity, the Word unites it with divine Beauty." Everything is already accomplished.

Furthermore, this theology rests on a conception of the image of God in the creation that makes of it a concrete resemblance: "the image of God" *is* the materiality of visible humanity. This concept tries to place humanity permanently on Tabor, the mount of Transfiguration. [...] That corresponds exactly to the error of the disciples who accompanied Jesus and who wanted to set up tents in order to remain permanently in the Transfiguration.

We must not try to find humanity's deification in God's humanization, as if God became human so that humanity might become God. Humanity goes from being a microcosm to being a micro-theos in this case. This is applied very concretely: to material, corporeal, visual humanity. The human being in himself, as we see him, is the face of God. One wonders then why the Gospels find it necessary to say of Jesus: "Behold the man." He is the *only*, the *unique*, case of a human being as the image of God. But he is God's image precisely in the visible image of the condemned, scourged, individual. [...]

One more matter before we leave the controversy over iconoclasm in Orthodox belief. The iconoclasts, whose beliefs were judged in the seventh council, refused to admit the symbolic character of the icon. Consequently, they did not believe in "a mysterious presence of the Model in the image." "They could not seem to understand that besides the visible representation of a visible reality (the portrait) there is a completely different art in which the image presents what is visible of the invisible." In reality, this was not a problem of "understanding"; the iconoclasts simply did not believe this doctrine! They were accused of being docetics, of having a purely realistic view of art, since they refused to ascribe a sacred character to the icon. They denied that a representation of Christ or the Virgin Mary could be anything other than a representation. They denied that even symbolically the icon could have any sacramental value at all.

But the argument against the iconoclasts is utterly fallacious: it is denied that one can have an idolatrous attitude towards an icon, since an idol is the expression of something that does not exist – a fiction, a semblance, a nothing. [...] This argument is false because, in many of the religions condemned in the Bible, the idol was a visible representation of an invisible religious reality, to which it referred. [...] As for the argument that the iconoclasts were docetics who denied the reality of the Incarnation, this rests on a cosmic conception of a realized Incarnation. This concept eliminates both the period of promise and history itself, since Jesus as crucified is considered already to be fully the glorious Christ. This "heresy" is the exact counterpart of the real docetic heresy (of which the iconoclasts were falsely accused), but it is no better.

Comment

Jacques Ellul is widely regarded as one of the most important French Reformed theologians and social commentators of the twentieth century. The Reformed tradition has always been hostile to the use of any form of images in worship or personal devotion – see, for example, the comments of the Heidelberg Catechism on this matter (1.14). In this passage, Ellul sets out a series of concerns he has about the use of icons, in particular his suspicion that the emphasis upon "image" over "word" leads to a diminution of the theological integrity of the Christian faith. It should be noted that Orthodox critics of Ellul argue that he has misunderstood Evdokimov at points, and failed to appreciate that he is arguing for icons as "windows into the divine," rather than as something which is divine in itself.

Questions for Study

1 What are the precise objections against the use of images of any kind in worship, according to the Reformed tradition? You should study the teaching of the Heidelberg Catechism on this question (1.14), and write them down in your own words. How does Ellul's position reflect these views?
2 "In many of the religions condemned in the Bible, the idol was a visible representation of an invisible religious reality, to which it referred." Locate this passage within the text. What is the point that Ellul is making? Do you think he is fair to Evdokimov here?
3 "The word is not sufficient." Locate this statement within the text. In what way does it summarize Ellul's concerns about trends in Protestant theology in general? And how does it relate specifically to the question of icons?

3.40

Walter Kasper on the Rationality of the Trinity

The question of whether the doctrine of the Trinity is "rational" has been the subject of much debate. While there is not total unanimity on the matter, the general consensus within Christian theology is that the doctrine cannot be demonstrated or established on the basis of pure reason, even though the doctrine can be shown to be reasonable, once it has been established by reflection on revelation. In this extract, Walter Kasper (born 1933), one of the most important Catholic writers of the late twentieth century, presents a lucid summary of this traditional position. See also 1.21, 3.9, 3.11, 3.38.

Although theologians have a good deal to learn from modern philosophy and in particular from Hegel, at the decisive point they must say a resolute No. Reason cannot prove the necessity of the Trinity either from the concept of absolute spirit or from the concept of love. The Trinity is a mystery in the strict sense of the term. What is said in the scriptures applies here: 'No one knows the Son except the Father, and no one knows the Father except the Son and any one to whom the Son chooses to reveal him' (Matthew 11.27; cf. John 1.18). No one knows God except the Spirit of God (1 Corinthians 2.11). The thesis regarding the Trinity as a strict mystery is directed primarily against rationalism which seeks to prove the doctrine of the Trinity by reason, whether it does this by way of the history of religions from the so-called extra-biblical parallels, or speculatively from the essence of divinity or the essence of human consciousness. The thesis is also directed against semi-rationalism, as it is called, which admits that prior to the revelation of them we cannot deduce the mysteries of faith, but then goes on to assert that once they have been revealed we are able to understand them. It is a fact, of course, that the theological tradition offers rational arguments for faith in the Trinity. But the analogies from the life of the human spirit which Augustine in particular introduced into the discussion serve only to illustrate and never to demonstrate the truth of the Trinity. Admittedly, some medieval Scholastics (especially Richard of St Victor and Anselm of Canterbury) did try to produce *rationes necessariae* (demonstrative reasons) for faith in the Trinity. The question is, however, whether their cogent rational arguments were not in fact simply arguments of suitability and did not in fact presuppose the trinitarian faith and argue in the light of it. It was only with Albert the Great and Thomas Aquinas that a clear distinction was made between faith and knowledge; not until the modern age were the two separated. Therefore in the medieval theologians I have been discussing there may have been an exaggerated intellectual optimism, but we can hardly speak of them as rationalists in the modern sense of the word.

The positive reason for the basic incomprehensibility of the Trinity even after it has been revealed is that even in the economy of salvation God is revealed to us only in the medium of history and in the medium of human words and deeds, or, in other words, in finite forms. What Paul says holds at this point too: we see in a mirror and not face to face (1 Corinthians 13.12). Or, to use the language of Thomas Aquinas: even in the economy of salvation we know God only indirectly through his effects. These effects are clearer and less ambiguous in the history of salvation than they are in creation; nonetheless, they enable us to know only that God is and that he is triune, but do not permit us to understand his essence (*quid est*) from within. We are therefore united to God as to one unknown (*quasi ignoto*). Nowadays we would say rather that we know the triune God only through his words and actions in history; these are the real symbols of his love that freely communicates itself to us. God's freedom-in-love in the form of a gratuitous self-communication would in fact be annulled if it could be shown to be rationally necessary. The revelation given in the history of salvation does not therefore explain the mystery of God to us but rather leads us deeper into this mystery; in this history the mystery of God is revealed to us as mystery.

There are three points in particular that remain incomprehensible and impenetrable to our minds: 1. the absolute unity of God despite the distinction of persons; 2. the absolute equality of the persons despite the dependence of the second on the first and of the third on the first and second; 3. the eternity of God as Father, Son and Spirit despite the fact that they are established as such by the activities of generation and spiration. But then, do we even grasp the absolute simplicity of God despite the multiplicity and differentiation of his attributes, or his absolute immutability and eternity despite the multiplicity of his activities and of his involvements in history? No, God is unknowable in every aspect of his being and not just in his internal personal relations. Neither the That of the triune God nor his What (his inner nature) nor his How are accessible to our finite knowledge.

Comment

The passage begins by asking whether the doctrine of the Trinity can be proved by reason, and offers a negative answer. Kasper then notes that certain medieval writers appear to have given a more positive answer, but points out that their arguments are not strictly proofs of the doctrine. Rather, they assume the doctrine, and then demonstrate its consistency or "suitability." Kasper affirms the ultimate mystery of God, not in the sense that God is "irrational," but in the deeper sense that the human mind cannot completely grasp and represent the divine reality.

Questions for Study

1 "If you can understand it, it's not God" (Augustine of Hippo). Would Kasper agree?
2 Find 1 Corinthians 13: 12 in the Bible. What does Paul seem to be saying here? And how does Kasper apply this to the doctrine of the Trinity?
3 Summarize in your own words the three fundamental aspects of the doctrine of the Trinity that Kasper regards as lying beyond rational proof.

3.41

Paul Jewett on Noninclusive Language and the Trinity

In recent years the issue of whether God must necessarily be referred to using male language has become significant. The question has particular relevance in connection with the doctrine of the Trinity, where the traditional language of "Father, Son, and Holy Spirit" includes reference to two apparently male entities. So what options are available here? How can Christian integrity be maintained alongside a concern to recognize and respond to the proper sensitivities of women? In this reading, the American evangelical theologian Paul Jewett (1919–91) explores some options.

We have already addressed the question of the analogical character of theological language, including the language used in the trinitarian name: Father, Son, and Holy Spirit. Now that we have finished our treatment of the nature of God and are about to turn to the question of the divine attributes, it is fitting that we make a few added comments on our speech about God, as that speech in its traditional form reflects a use of language that many regard as sexist. We say it is fitting because, at this juncture, we shall turn not only from the subject of the divine nature to the divine attributes, but also from the traditional male use of language about God to the use of female language. In speaking of the attributes, God will be likened not to a father (Psalms 103: 13) but to a mother (Isaiah 66: 13).

Analogical language, to be meaningful, must of course rest upon some univocal element between the human reality from which it is taken and the divine reality to which it refers. In our exposition of the doctrine of the Trinity, so far as God's name – Father, Son, and Spirit – is concerned, we have identified the univocal element in the concept of origins. The second and third persons in the Godhead originate, as persons, with the first person, who is therefore called "Father." The Father "begets" the Son and "breathes" ("spirates") the Spirit. But obviously in using such terms as "begetting" and "breathing" to describe how the second and third persons of the Godhead have their origin in the first, we speak analogically, not univocally. And since this is so, feminine figures could as well be used without altering the substance of our thought about God. If the woman, like the man, is created in the image of God (Genesis 1: 27) and is therefore as much like God as the man, then female imagery is just as capable as is male imagery of bearing the truth that God is a trinitarian fellowship of holy love. After all, women have as much to do with origins, at the human level, as men – unless one subscribes to the discredited biological theory that our essential humanity is carried from generation to generation by the sperm lodged in the womb.

If we describe the relationship between the first and second persons of the Godhead analogically as a "begetting" and a "being begotten," may we not as well, still speaking analogically, describe it as a "bearing" and a "being born"? Since God is like a woman as well as a man, may God not be likened to a mother who eternally bears a daughter as well as to a father who eternally begets a son? And may not a mother also breathe the Spirit as well as a father? Do not women have breath as well as men? Are they not alive? We are, it is granted, speaking in a purely hypothetical way, since, as a matter of fact, in the Incarnation God assumed male humanity. But there is nothing either in the concept of God, or in the concept of Incarnation, that leads by logical entailment to masculinity. Given the patriarchal society of Israel, the revelation of God naturally takes a patriarchal form. (We say "naturally" rather than "necessarily" because even in patriarchal cultures female gods were known and worshipped.) It is not surprising, then, that God reveals himself to Israel as the "Father" of "his" people. Being disclosed as the Father of Israel, it is likewise natural that God should send one called a "son" who naturally assumes male humanity. Here an element of necessity does come into the picture; but it is a necessity of a secondary sort. It is due not to the essential, masculine nature of God but to the sexual polarity in which the Creator has given us our humanity. As a result of the way in which we are given our individual humanity, we describe ourselves, not analogically but literally, as male or female. This is why God, in becoming one with us, must of necessity become a man or a woman. Neither the gospels, however, nor the Chalcedonian Christology of the church, lays any emphasis on the maleness of Jesus. In the Incarnation he who is *vere Dei* becomes *vere homo*, not *vere masculus*. Of course, once "the matchless deed's achieved, determined, dared, and done" (Smart), there is a kind of finality, though not ultimacy, in the form of God's self-disclosure that is normative for the church. Christ Jesus is the one mediator between God and humankind (1 Timothy 2: 5), and this Christ Jesus is the *man* Christ Jesus.

Nonetheless, to speak of God as a mother who discloses herself to us in a daughter, though it is a hypothetical way of speaking, is not a heretical way of speaking. Given the realities of salvation history, we grant that it is a way of speaking with no prospects of being other than hypothetical. God the Creator, as we have observed, has given us our humanity in a sexual polarity and God the Savior has assumed that humanity as a male rather than a female. Yet the need to speak in this hypothetical way comes from the fact that women are justified in their complaint that the traditional understanding of our traditional language about God has made them second-class citizens both as members of the human race and as members of the family of God.

Comment

Jewett is an evangelical theologian, based for many years at Fuller Theological Seminary in Pasadena, California. The passage is of interest in that it shows how, in the final decade of the twentieth century, an awareness of gender-specific language concerning God ceased to be a specific distinctive of feminist theology, and became a question for mainstream Christian theology. As the passage from Anne Carr (3.42) makes clear, of course, the issue continues to be especially significant for feminist theology.

Questions for Study

1 Jewett makes use of an appeal to the "analogical" nature of theological language in this discussion. What purpose does this serve for him? What points does it allow him to make? How successful is he?
2 "If the woman, like the man, is created in the image of God (Genesis 1: 27) and is therefore as much like God as the man, then female imagery is just as capable as is male imagery of bearing the truth that God is a trinitarian fellowship of holy love." Locate this passage within the text. What point is being made here? How important is the text from Genesis?
3 "Given the patriarchal society of Israel, the revelation of God naturally takes a patriarchal form." Locate this statement within the text. What understanding of the mode of divine revelation does Jewett seem to presuppose? How does the Calvinian idea of "accommodation" – which Jewett does not, incidentally, mention here – help in this respect? You will find it helpful to read 1.32 in answering this question.

3.42

Anne Carr on Feminism and the Maleness of God

The use of predominantly male language to refer to God within the Christian tradition has been the subject of attention by many feminist writers. In this lucid survey of some responses to this situation, Anne Carr (born 1934) focuses on the contributions of Sallie McFague, Rosemary Radford Ruether, and Judith Plaskow. In particular, she notes the importance of "metaphorical" approaches (see 1.30) to male imagery for God, and the development of metaphors such as "God as friend." See also 1.30, 3.41, 4.38, 4.39.

The fundamental feminist question about the maleness of God in the imagery, symbolism and concepts of traditional Christian thought and prayer leads to new reflection on the doctrine of God. In spite of theological denials of sexuality (or any materiality) in God, the persistent use of masculine pronouns for God and the reaction of many Christians against reference to God as "she" would appear to affirm the "maleness" attributed to God. Yet it is also logical that "she" is not only as appropriate as "he," but is perhaps necessary to reorient Christian imagination from the idolatrous implications of exclusively masculine God-language and the dominant effects of the father image in the churches and Christian practice. A new theory of the thoroughly metaphorical character of religious language has emerged in the light of feminist discussion of the doctrine of God. This theory argues that traditional analogical understanding has tended to stress the similarity between human concepts and God's own selfhood while a metaphorical theology should focus rather on the God–human relationship and on the unlikeness of all religious language in reference to God even as it affirms some similarity (McFague, 1982).

There have been proposals for referring to God as "parent" or as "father and mother" or for the balancing use of feminine language for the Spirit since the Hebrew word for Spirit is grammatically feminine. On the other hand some feminist scholars have urged the move away from parental images entirely since these are suggestive of childish rather than adult religious dependence. While parental images express compassion, acceptance, guidance and discipline, they do not express the mutuality, maturity, cooperation, responsibility and reciprocity required by contemporary personal and political experience. One feminist theologian argues that there is no adequate name for God at present, given the overwhelming bias of traditional Christian thought about God and suggests the designation "God/ess" for the matrix and source of all life (Radford Ruether, 1983).

Some feminist theologians call for the use of multiple metaphors and models for God and for the divine–human relationship, since none alone is adequate. The Bible itself uses many different human and cosmic designations, while in fact one metaphor (father) has become the dominant model in Christian thought and practice. One suggestion is the metaphor of God as "friend" (McFague, 1982, 1987). There is a biblical basis for this in Jesus' saying about laying down one's life for one's friends (John 15: 13) and his reference to the Son of Man as friend of tax collectors and sinners (Matthew 11: 19); Jesus *is* the parable of God's friendship with people. This friendship is shown in his parables of the lost sheep, the prodigal son, the good Samaritan, and the "enacted parable" of Jesus' inclusive table fellowship. The Gospels describe Jesus as critical of views of familial ties that failed to recognize the inclusive significance of his new community. They depict his presence as transforming the lives of his friends. Friendship to the stranger, both as individual and as nation or culture, is a model "on our increasingly small and beleaguered planet where, if people do not become friends, they will not survive" (McFague, 1982).

The metaphor of God as friend corresponds to the feminist ideal of "communal personhood," an ideal that entails non-competitive relationships among persons and groups that are characterized by mutuality and reciprocity rather than dualism and hierarchy. It responds to feminist concerns for expressions of divine–human relation that overcome the images of religious self-denial that have shaped women's experience in patterns of low self-esteem, passivity and irresponsibility. It suggests the ideas of mutuality, self-creation in community, and the creation of ever wider communities with other persons and the world (Plaskow, 1980). The theme of God's friendship is intensified in the life and death of Jesus, who reveals a God who suffers for, with, and in people and invites them into a community of suffering with God and for others (Moltmann, [1980] 1981). The theme unites theology with feminist spirituality in its emphasis on women's friendship and interdependence as these are related to the reciprocal interdependence of the whole of creation. There are limitations to the metaphor of God as friend, as there are to any metaphor, and these limitations point to the importance of the use of many different metaphors to suggest the unfathomable character of the divine–human relationship.

References

McFague, Sallie 1982. *Metaphorical Theology: Models of God in religious language*. Philadelphia: Fortress Press.

McFague, Sallie 1987. *Models of God: Theology for an ecological, nuclear age*. Philadelphia: Fortress Press.

Moltman, Jürgen [1980] 1981. *The Trinity and the Kingdom*, trans. Margaret Kohl. San Francisco: Harper & Row.

Plastow, Judith 1980. *Sex, sin and grace: women's experience and the theologies of Reinhold Niebuhr and Paul Tillich*. Washington, DC: University Press of America.

Radford Ruether, Rosemary 1983. *Sexism and God-talk. Toward a feminist theology*. Boston: Beacon Press.

Comment

Anne Carr, based at the University of Chicago Divinity School, here offers an overview of contemporary feminist responses to the issues posed by the "maleness" of God. The article from which this extract has been taken is essentially a review of the question, rather than a proposal for its solution. As a result, Carr adopts a balanced and judicious perspective in setting out the various aspects of the question, and introduces and assesses some seminal contributions to its discussion. The main feminist writers to which Carr refers are Judith Plaskow and Rosemary Radford Ruether. Sallie McFague is also noted on account of her contribution to exploring the uses of metaphor in theology, including the metaphor of "God as father."

Questions for Study

1 How might Sallie McFague's discussion of the metaphor "God as father" be relevant to this discussion? You will find it helpful to read 1.30 before answering this question. How does McFague's metaphor of "God as friend" illuminate matters?
2 According to Carr, what responses have been offered to the traditional Christian anxiety about the use of the female pronoun to refer to God?
3 Is there any way of referring to God which avoids gender-specific language or imagery?

3.43

Sarah Coakley on Social Models of the Trinity

In a 2002 essay on social approaches to the doctrine of the Trinity, Sarah Coakley (born 1951) explores how the trinitarian theology of Gregory of Nyssa illuminates and informs contemporary approaches to the Trinity, particularly "social" models of the doctrine. The opening section of the paper surveys criticially some trends in contemporary trinitarian theology. See also 3.9, 3.11, 3.20, 3.36.

Let me begin this essay by sketching out some intriguing features of the context in which the current trinitarian debate is taking place. In the remarkable recent outpouring of writing on the doctrine of the Trinity we may detect, I suggest, an interesting double paradox. On the one hand, sophisticated logicians amongst the analytic philosophers of religion have devoted much energy to defending the so-called 'Social' (or 'Plurality') doctrine of the Trinity, whilst decrying the coherence of a 'Latin' (or 'Unity') model. In so doing, however, they have – with only one or two important exceptions, to be examined below – paid relatively little attention to the *type* of entity that they are calling 'person' when they count 'three' of them in the Godhead. Indeed, when we probe a little with the tools of the hermeneutics of suspicion, we may detect distinct whiffs of influence from 'modern' perceptions of 'person' (or 'individual') smuggled into the debate, and read back into the patristic texts which are being claimed as authoritative.

On the other hand, and simultaneously, systematic theologians have been at work debunking precisely those 'modern' notions of individualism that they perceive to have distorted Christian anthropology since the Enlightenment and to have undermined trinitarian conceptuality altogether. For them, construing 'persons' as 'relations' (whatever this means exactly) has become a theological watchword. Unhappily, these two camps of scholarship, despite their shared commitment to the reinstatement of trinitarian theology, show little mutual regard for each other's work.

This paradox of intention and starting point recapitulates itself, in a rather curious way, in intra-feminist debates on the Trinity – a fact so far rarely commented upon; but this is why I speak of a 'double paradox'. On the one hand, we have the radical feminist spoof of trinitarianism (in Mary Daly's work) as the so-called 'Men's Association', a barely concealed symbolic endorsement, in Daly's view, of the all-male club, which on rare occasions admits a stereotypical "feminine" principle into its magic circle as a token presence ('You're included under the Holy Spirit. He's feminine'). Clearly what underlies Daly's deliberately "absurd" accusation here is a deep – and not altogether unfounded – suspicion that modern patriarchal thinking has here found its projective trinitarian manifestation as an association of like-minded males. In contrast to Daly's dismissive rejection of trinitarianism, the patiently irenic work of Elizabeth Johnson on the Trinity attempts to reclaim its significance for feminism by concentrating on its celebration of 'mutuality' and 'relationship'. So the divergence between analytic philosophers of religion and theologians on the Trinity is in some form recapitulated in the feminist camp: whilst Daly assumes a threefold 'individualism' in the doctrine (and rejects it), Johnson prefers to construe 'persons' in terms of 'relationships'.

It will be the central thesis of this paper that neither side in either of these somewhat curiously parallel disjunctions has fully grasped the complexity and subtlety of late fourth-century trinitarianism at its best. Moreover, it will be suggested by the end that the modern contestants' predetermined commitments to (divergent) perceptions of 'personhood' may lead, in the end, to insoluble difficulties. In arguing thus I shall take Gregory of Nyssa as my focus and example, a figure whose trinitarian contribution is often too easily conflated with that of the other 'Cappadocians', but whose profoundly apophatic sensibilities make the assessment of the intended status of his trinitarian language a particularly subtle matter for reflection. One of the more surprising conclusions to which my argument will lead is that Gregory's approach to the Trinity is not 'social' in the sense often ascribed to that term today; it does not 'start' with three and proceed to the one. Nor does it attempt to 'nail' the meaning of divine hypostasis by particular reference to the analogy of three individual men: the analytic discussions here have been misled by an over-concentration on Gregory's *Ad Ablabium*, as well as by an insufficiently nuanced reading of that text. If we take a wider view of Gregory's corpus (and especially if we look at the rich range of imagery on the Trinity that he uses in contexts not restricted to the polemical or apologetic), a rather different perception of his trinitarian theology emerges, one which is in no doubt about the unity of the divine will in action, but which is highly diffident about probing the details of the nature of God in Godself beyond a certain, cautiously delimited point. Such diffidence may appear intrinsically unsatisfactory to the analytic school of philosophy of religion; but it raises questions about apophaticism that are, at the very least – or so I shall argue – worthy of greater analytic attention, and have implications for our understanding of the linguistic status of trinitarian claims.

If the gender interests of the feminist debates seem somewhat irrelevant to the analytic discussion as currently pursued, Gregory's example should also give pause for thought. The perplexing fluidity of gender reference which characterizes Gregory's trinitarian discussions as a whole gives the lie to attempts to sanitize the matter from any such taint; as we shall attempt to show, Gregory's approach demonstrates how unwise it is to dislocate trinitarian debates from the matrix of human transformation that is that Trinity's very point of intersection with our lives. If Gregory is right, moreover, such transformation is unthinkable without profound, even alarming, shifts in our gender perceptions, shifts which have bearing as much on our thinking about God as on our understanding of ourselves.

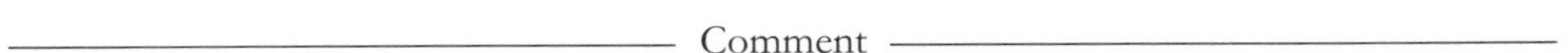

Comment

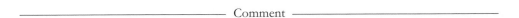

In this scene-setting piece, Sarah Coakley explores trends in recent Christian reflection on the doctrine of the Trinity, noting particularly the critique of individualist approaches to the doctrine, inspired by the Enlightenment (Coakley has the work of Colin Gunton and others in mind here). Alongside this, she notes feminist engagements with the traditional doctrine, including Mary Daly's highly critical *Gyn/Ecology* (Boston: Beacon Press, 1978) and Elizabeth Johnson's more constructive *She Who Is* (New York: Crossroads, 1992). Having noted these modern debates, Coakley moves on to suggest that a properly nuanced reading of Gregory of Nyssa has an important role to play in illuminating and advancing them.

Questions for Study

1 Why should the rise of individualism have any effect on trinitarian theology?
2 Identify the differences between the approaches of Mary Daly and Elizabeth Johnson, as expounded by Coakley.
3 Read Gregory of Nyssa's treatise to Ablabius, extracted earlier in this collection (3.9). How do the themes of this work relate to the issues that Coakley raises?

For Further Reading

Lewis Ayres, *Nicea and its Legacy: An Approach to Fourth-Century Trinitarian Theology* (Oxford: Oxford University Press, 2005).

Vincent Brümmer, *Speaking of a Personal God: An Essay in Philosophical Theology* (Cambridge, UK: Cambridge University Press, 1992).

Martin Buber, *I and Thou* (New York: Scribners, 1970).

Stephen T. Davis, Daniel Kendall, and Gerald O'Collins (eds), *The Trinity: An Interdisciplinary Symposium on the Trinity* (Oxford: Oxford University Press, 2002).

Langdon Gilkey, "God," in P. Hodgson and R. King (eds), *Christian Theology* (Philadelphia: Fortress Press, 1982), pp. 62–87.

Stanley M. Grenz, *Rediscovering the Triune God: The Trinity in Contemporary Theology* (Minneapolis: Augsburg Fortress Press, 2004).

Colin E. Gunton, *The Promise of Trinitarian Theology* (Edinburgh: T&T Clark, 1991).

Joshua Hoffman and Gary S. Rosenkrantz, *The Divine Attributes* (Oxford: Blackwell, 2002).

Veli-Matti Kärkkäinen, *The Doctrine of God: A Global Introduction* (Grand Rapids, MI: Baker Academic, 2004).

Gerhard May, *Creatio Ex Nihilo: The Doctrine of "Creation out of Nothing" in Early Christian Thought* (Edinburgh: T&T Clark, 1995).

Sallie McFague, *Models of God* (Philadelphia: Fortress Press, 1987), pp. 91–180.

Ronald H. Nash, *The Concept of God* (Grand Rapids, MI: Zondervan, 1983).

Anthony B. Pinn, *Why, Lord? Suffering and Evil in Black Theology* (New York: Continuum, 1995).

Samuel M. Powell, *Participating in God: Creation and Trinity* (Minneapolis: Augsburg Fortress Press, 2003).

Kathleen Mullen Sands, *Escape from Paradise: Evil and Tragedy in Feminist Theology* (Minneapolis: Fortress Press, 1994).

Robert Sherman, *The Shift To Modernity: Christ and the Doctrine of Creation in the Theologies of Schleiermacher and Barth* (London: T&T Clark, 2005).

Thomas F. Torrance, *The Christian Doctrine of God: One Being, Three Persons* (Edinburgh: T&T Clark, 1996).

A. W. Wainwright, *The Trinity in the New Testament* (London: SPCK, 1969).

4

The Person of Christ

Introduction

Christology – that is, the section of Christian theology which focuses on the identity of Jesus Christ – has long been recognized as being of central importance. Who is Jesus Christ? What is his relevance to our thinking about God? Or to human nature and destiny? From the outset, Christian theology has appreciated the urgency of the need to clarify how Jesus of Nazareth is to be placed on a conceptual map. Where is he to be located in relation to the coordinates of divinity and humanity? Time and eternity? The present chapter brings together a series of texts relating to these themes.

This collection includes readings relating directly to the classic debates of patristic Christology, such as Docetism, Gnosticism, Arianism, Apollinarianism, Nestorianism, Patripassianism, and the Monophysite controversy. This allows readers to gain a good understanding of the issues which shaped this formative period in the development of Christian understandings of the identity of Christ, and the most appropriate ways of expressing these ideas.

The Patristic Christological Debates

4.1	Ignatius of Antioch on Docetism
4.2	Irenaeus on Gnosticism in Christology
4.3	Tertullian on Patripassianism
4.4	Tertullian on the Incarnation
4.5	Novatian on the Divinity of Christ
4.6	Origen on the Two Natures of Christ
4.7	Arius on the Status of Christ
4.8	Athanasius on the Two Natures of Christ
4.9	Apollinarius of Laodicea on the Person of Christ
4.10	Gregory of Nazianzus on Apollinarianism
4.11	Theodore of Mopsuestia on the "Union of Good Pleasure"
4.12	Nestorius on the Term "Theotokos"
4.13	Cyril of Alexandria on Nestorius's Christology
4.14	Cyril of Alexandria on the Incarnation
4.15	Cyril of Alexandria on Mary as the Mother of God
4.16	Leo the Great on the Two Natures of Christ
4.17	The Chalcedonian Definition of the Christian Faith (451)

4.18	The Emperor Zeno on the Natures of Christ
4.19	The Monophysites on the Natures of Christ
4.20	John of Damascus on the Incarnation and Icons

However, Christological debate did not end with the closing of the patristic period. Although Christology was not of fundamental importance to the debates of the Reformation, it became of major importance once more at the dawn of the Enlightenment. One of the most important debates in modern Christology focuses on the historical aspects of the question, in particular the issue of "faith and history." Was there, as some suggested, a gulf fixed between the historical figure of Jesus of Nazareth, and the interpretations placed upon him by the church? The debate probably generated as much heat as light, but it served to emphasize the historical rootedness of the Christian faith, and the central place of Jesus for the church.

Faith and History	
4.26	Gotthold Ephraim Lessing on the Ditch of History
4.29	Martin Kähler on the Historical Jesus
4.30	George Tyrrell on the Christ of Liberal Protestantism
4.31	Albert Schweitzer on the Failure of the "Quest of the Historical Jesus"
4.33	Ernst Troeltsch on Faith and History
4.35	Paul Tillich on the Dispensability of the Historical Jesus
4.36	Wolfhart Pannenberg on the Indispensability of the Historical Jesus
4.41	N. T. Wright on History and Christology

Other issues have subsequently emerged as important, perhaps most significantly the question of whether the maleness of Jesus compromises his significance for women. Two diverging approaches to this question from leading feminist writers will allow the reader to gain an appreciation of the direction in which this debate is heading.

4.1

Ignatius of Antioch on Docetism

Ignatius of Antioch (c.35–c.107) is an important witness to a formative period in the development of Christian doctrine, and the controversies attending it. This text, written several years before Ignatius's martyrdom around 107, deals with an early form of the Docetist heresy, which declared that Christ did not suffer in reality, but suffered only in appearance, and was thus not truly human. See also 4.2, 4.12.

So do not pay attention when anyone speaks to you apart from [*chōris*] Jesus Christ, who was of the family of David, the child of Mary, who was truly born, who ate and drank, who was truly persecuted under Pontius Pilate, was truly crucified, and truly died, in full view of heaven, earth and hell, and who was truly raised from the dead. It was his Father who raised him again, and it is him [i.e., the Father] who will likewise raise us in Jesus Christ, we who believe in him, apart from whom we have no true life. But if, as some godless people [*atheoi*], that is, unbelievers, say, he suffered in mere appearance [*to dokein peponthenai*] – being themselves mere appearances – why am I in bonds? [. . .]

[Jesus Christ] submitted to all of this for our sakes, so that we might have salvation. And he did suffer, really and truly, just as he really and truly rose again. His passion was no imaginary illusion, as some skeptics assert, themselves subject to illusion. The fate of those miserable people will one day match their beliefs, when they will themselves become such phantoms without any real substance. As far as I am concerned, I know and believe that he existed in real human flesh, even after the resurrection. When he appeared to Peter and his companions, he said to them: "Take hold of me, touch me, and see that I am no incorporeal phantom." And they touched him there and then, and believed, for they had contact with his physical reality.

Comment

Docetism arose at a very early stage, although its full development can be argued to have taken place later in the second century. In this extract we have a statement of something which is clearly recognizable as Docetism itself, or an early variant of the heresy. The term "Docetism" was derived from the Greek verb *dokein*, meaning "to appear" or "to seem," referring to the Docetist belief that Christ was not really human, and so only "seemed" to suffer.

Questions for Study

1 Note how Ignatius stresses the humanity and real historical existence of Jesus. Why? What purpose might this serve at this juncture?

2 What is the specific belief which Ignatius sets out to counter in this passage?
3 What link does Ignatius establish between the suffering of Christ and the salvation of humanity? How significant do you think this is?

4.2

Irenaeus on Gnosticism in Christology

In this account of the impact of Gnosticism, dating from the second half of the second century, Irenaeus of Lyons (c.130–c.200) sets out a list of various Christological heresies which are due to Gnostic influence. Of particular importance is his reference to the Docetic view that Christ was a human being in appearance only. See also 4.1, 4.3.

Among these, Saturninus came from Antioch [. . .] like Menander, he taught that there is one unknown Father [*unum patrem incognitum*], who made angels, archangels, virtues, powers; and that the world, and everything in it, was made by seven angels. Humanity was also created by these angels. [. . .]

He also declared that the Savior was unborn, incorporeal and without form, asserting that he was seen as a human being in appearance only [*putative autem visum hominem*]. The God of the Jews, he declares, was one of the angels; and because the Father wished to destroy all the rulers [*principes*], Christ came to destroy the God of the Jews, and to save all who believed in him, and these are they who have a spark of life [*scintillam vitae eius*]. He was the first to say that two kinds of human beings were fashioned by the angels, one bad and the other good. And because the demons assist the worst, the Savior came to destroy evil human beings and the demons and to save the good. But marriage and procreation, they declare, is of Satan. The majority of his disciples abstain from meat, and by this false temperance have led many people astray. As far as prophecies go, they say that some were made by the angels who created the world, and others by Satan. This last, according to Saturninus, is himself an angel, but an angel who is opposed to the creators of the world and, above all, to the God of the Jews.

Comment

In his important work *adversus haereses* ("against heresies"), Irenaeus offers his readers both information concerning what the Gnostic opponents of Christianity taught, and responses to these teachings. The present passage focuses on the views of Saturninus, which reflect Docetic ideas at several points. A number of strongly dualist ideas can also be discerned, including the good and evil angels who are respectively responsible for good and evil in the world.

Questions for Study

1 Set out the main views of Saturninus, as they are presented by Irenaeus.
2 It is important to understand why these Gnostic ideas could have been attractive. Consider Augustine's explanation of the origin of evil (3.14), which avoids dualist presuppositions. Which is the simpler to understand, the position of Saturninus or that of Augustine?
3 The Gnostics generally argued that the New Testament and Old Testaments referred to different gods. The god of the Old Testament was a creator god, and that of the New Testament a redeemer god. Can you discern this doctrine in this passage?

4.3

Tertullian on Patripassianism

Patripassianism was a theological heresy which arose during the third century, associated with writers such as Noetus, Praxeas, and Sabellius, focusing on the belief that the Father suffered as the Son. In other words, the suffering of Christ on the cross is to be regarded as the suffering of the Father. In this attack on his opponent Praxeas, Tertullian (c.160–c. 225) identifies the main features of this teaching. See also 3.16.

The devil is opposed to the truth in many ways. He has sometimes even attempted to destroy it by defending it. He declares that there is only one God, the omnipotent creator of the world, only to make a heresy out of that uniqueness. He says that the Father himself descended into the virgin, was himself born of her, himself suffered; in fact that he himself was Jesus Christ. [. . .] It was [Praxeas], a restless foreigner, who first brought this kind of perversity from Asia to Rome [. . .] he put the Holy Spirit to flight and crucified the Father.

Comment

Patripassianism centered on the belief that the Father suffered as the Son. According to these writers, the only distinction within the Godhead was a succession of modes or operations. In other words, Father, Son, and Spirit were just different modes of being, or expressions, of the same basic divine entity. This form of modalism, often known as Sabellianism, can be explored further in relation to the doctrine of the Trinity (see 3.16).

Questions for Study

1. In what way can the belief in only one God become heretical, according to Tertullian? You may find it helpful to read the following passage (4.4), in which the improper use of the divine "monarchia" is discussed further, before answering this question.
2. What does Tertullian mean when he declares that Praxeas "crucified the Father"?

4.4

Tertullian on the Incarnation

In this polemical passage, directed against the teachings of Praxeas, Tertullian insists upon the unity of the person of Christ, while distinguishing the proper functions of the humanity and divinity of Christ. Note especially Tertullian's rejection of the incarnational model of an "amalgam," in which two metals are fused together in such a way as to lose their distinctive characteristics. "Electrum," to which he refers in this context, is a naturally occurring amalgam of gold and silver. See also 4.8, 4.10, 4.14, 4.16, 4.20.

Others attempt to distinguish two beings in one person, the Father and the Son, saying that the Son is the flesh, that is, the human being that is Jesus; while the Father is the spirit, that is, God that is Christ. Thus those who are trying to demonstrate the identity of the Father and Son seem to end up dividing them, rather than uniting them. [. . .] Maybe they heard about this kind of "monarchy" [*talem monarchiam*], which distinguishes Jesus from Christ, from Valentinus. But [. . .] their "Father" is described as Word *of* God, Spirit *of* God. [. . .] Who was the God born in flesh? The Word, and the Spirit, who was born with the Word in accordance with the Father's will. Therefore the Word was in flesh; but we must ask *how* the Word "was made flesh," whether by transformation into flesh or by being clothed with that flesh. The latter is surely the case. We must believe that God's eternal nature precludes change or transformation. Transformation involves the destruction of what originally existed: what is transformed ceases to be what it was and begins to be something else. But God does not cease to be, nor can he be other than what he is: and the Word is God, and "the Word of the Lord remains for ever," that is, it continues in the same form. [. . .] It follows that his incarnation means that he comes to be in flesh and through flesh is revealed, seen, and touched. Other things also support this interpretation. For if he was incarnate by transformation and change of substance, Jesus would then be one substance made of two, of flesh and spirit, a kind of mixture, as electrum is an amalgam of gold and silver. Thus he would come to be neither gold (i.e., spirit) nor silver (i.e., flesh), since the one element is changed by the other and a third thing is produced. Then

Jesus will not be God, since he ceases to be the Word, which was made flesh; nor will he be flesh, that is, a human being; for that which was the Word is not flesh in the true sense. Thus out of the two a thing is produced which is neither one nor the other, but a third something, very different from either. [. . .] We see a twofold mode of being, not confused but conjoined in one person, Jesus, who is God and human. [. . .] And the proper quality of each substance remains so intact that the spirit carried out in him his own activities; the powers and works and signs: while the flesh underwent the experiences proper to it; hunger, when it met the devil; thirst, when with the Samaritan woman; weeping, for Lazarus; troubled even unto death; and, at the last, the flesh died.

Comment

One of the most important achievements of the patristic period was the clarification of the nature of the incarnation. In what way did the human and divine natures of Jesus relate to one another? The patristic discussion of this question involved the examination of a number of possible models for the divine–human unity within Christ, which preserved both the unity and the distinctiveness of both natures. This passage is of interest because it sets forth one specific model for analysis. Tertullian rejects it as inadequate – not surprising, given its origins, and the agenda which lay behind it. However, the principles which Tertullian uses in reaching this judgment are themselves of considerable interest.

Questions for Study

1. What are Tertullian's objections to the "electrum" model of the incarnation?
2. What activities of Jesus Christ does Tertullian attribute to his divinity? What activities of Jesus Christ does he attribute to his humanity?
3. "Therefore the Word was in flesh; but we must ask how the Word 'was made flesh,' whether by transformation into flesh or by being clothed with that flesh. The latter is surely the case." Locate this passage within the text. What does Tertullian mean by this? And what conclusions does he draw from this?

4.5

Novatian on the Divinity of Christ

Novatian's treatise on the Trinity, written about 235, sets out some of the basic considerations underlying the doctrine of the Trinity, and how it is to be understood. In laying the ground for the doctrine, he turns to consider the divinity of Christ. If Christ is God, then we are forced to reconsider our thinking about God. In the course of his argument, Novatian sets out some of the arguments that seem to him to point towards the divinity of Christ, drawing particularly on John's Gospel. See also 4.4, 4.8, 4.10, 4.14, 4.16.

If Christ was only a human being, why did he lay down for us a rule of faith in which he said, "And this is life eternal, that they should know you, the only and true God, and Jesus Christ, who you have sent?" (John 17: 3). If Christ did not wish us to believe that he also should be understood to be God, why did he add, "And Jesus Christ, who you have sent," unless it was because he wished to be received as God also? Because if he had not wished to be understood to be God, he would have added, "And the human being Jesus Christ, who you have sent," but, in fact, he neither added this, nor did Christ deliver himself to us as a human being only, but associated himself with God, as he wished to be understood by this conjunction to be God also, as he actually is. We must therefore believe, according to the rule prescribed, on the Lord, the one true God, and consequently on him whom he has sent, Jesus Christ, who by no means, as we have said, would have linked himself to the Father had he not wished to be understood to be God also. For he would have separated himself from him had he not wished to be understood to be God.

Comment

Novatian's argument finds its parallels in many writers of this period. The basic argument is that John's Gospel contains a number of highly significant passage which point to an identity of action, or even an identity of being, between the Father and Son. Whereas Arius would later argue that such passages were to be understood honorifically or nonliterally, Novatian insists that they are to be taken at face value, and their Christological implications accepted.

Questions for Study

1 Find the passage cited by Novatian from John's Gospel, and consider its possible meaning. Are there any other passages in John's Gospel that seem to make similar claims?
2 Summarize Novatian's argument. How persuasive do you find it?
3 Why does Novatian place so much weight on Jesus having been sent by the Father?

4.6

Origen on the Two Natures of Christ

Origen (c.185–c.254) here sets out the case for the necessity of a mediator between God and humanity, noting the respective importance of both Christ's divine and human natures in relation to his work. Note that althought Origen originally wrote in Greek, many of his works only survive in Latin translation, as in this case. See also 4.4, 4.8, 4.16.

Therefore with this soul acting as a mediator between God and flesh – for it was not possible for the nature of God to be mingled with flesh without a mediator – there was born the God-man [*deus-homo*], that "substance" [*substantia*] being the connecting link which could assume a body without denying its own nature. [. . .] The Son of God by whom all things were created is called Jesus Christ, the Son of man. For the Son of God is said to have died in respect of that nature which was certainly capable of death; and he is called the Son of man who is proclaimed about to come "in the glory of God the Father with the holy angels." And for this reason through the whole of Scripture the divine nature is spoken of in human terms, and at the same time the human nature is accorded the distinctive epithets proper to the divine. In this case more than any other, one could say, as it is written, "The two shall be in one flesh, and they are now not two but one flesh" (Matthew 19: 6).

Comment

Origen made a number of significant contributions to the development of Christology. Some of them have been regarded with suspicion, not least on account of what many regard as an excessive reliance upon Platonic ideas at critical junctures. The present passage deals with the question of what qualities or abilities a mediator must possess if the task of mediation between God and humanity is to proceed satisfactorily. It is clear that Origen's discussion has been shaped at this point by a biblical passage: "For there is one God, and there is one mediator between God and men, the man Christ Jesus, who gave himself as a ransom for all" (1 Timothy 2: 5–6).

Questions for Study

1 Set out, in your own words, the way in which Origen develops the "mediator" concept. What conclusions does he draw?
2 Notice how Origen sets the biblical Christological titles "Son of God and "Son of man" in parallel. What do you think he gains by doing this?
3 How do you respond to Origen's use of Matthew 19: 6 to refer to the incarnation? Do you think that this is an appropriate use of this text?

4.7

Arius on the Status of Christ

This letter, written in Greek around 321, is one of the few documents relating to Arius's Christological views known to have been written by Arius (c.250–c.336) himself. His views tend to be found primarily in the writings of his opponents, such as Athanasius. Arius's characteristic emphasis is upon the Son having a beginning. Note the connection between this axiom and Arius's firm insistence upon the unchangeability of God. For Arius, the fact that God cannot change is itself a powerful argument against the incarnation. See also 1.5, 4.4, 4.6, 4.8, 4.16, 4.17, 4.32.

Since my father Ammonius is coming to Nicomedia, I thought it right to send you my greetings by him, and at the same time to tell you [...] how desperately the bishop attacks, persecutes, and pursues us, so that he drives us from the city as if we were atheists because we do not agree with him when he publicly preaches: "God always, the Son always; at the same time the Father, at the same time the Son; the Son co-exists with God, unbegotten; he is ever-begotten, he is not born-by-begetting; neither by thought nor by any moment of time does God precede the Son; God always, Son always, the Son exists from God himself." And Eusebius, your brother, Bishop of Caesarea, Theodotus, Paulinus, Athanasius, Gregory, Aetius, and all the other bishops of the East, have been condemned for saying that God existed, without beginning, before the Son; except Philogonius, Hellanicus, and Macarius, men who are heretics and unlearned in the faith; some of whom say that the Son is an effluence, others a projection, others that he is co-unbegotten. We cannot even listen to these faithless things, even though the heretics threaten us with a thousand deaths. But what we say and think we both have taught and continue to teach; that the Son is not unbegotten, nor part of the unbegotten in any way, nor is he derived from any substance; but that by his own will and counsel he existed before times and ages fully God, only-begotten, unchangeable. And before he was begotten or created or appointed or established, he did not exist; for he was not unbegotten. We are persecuted because we say: "the Son has a beginning, but God is without beginning." For that reason we are persecuted, and because we say that he is from what is not. And this we say because he is neither part of God nor derived from any substance. For this we are persecuted; the rest you know.

Comment

Most of Arius's views are known through the writings of his opponents. There is thus at least some risk that these views have been distorted in the polemical process, or that highly selective citations from these works, perhaps out of context, have led to misunderstandings of what Arius actually said. The text here reprinted is therefore of especial interest, in that it represents Arius's own words concerning his views on the identity of Jesus Christ.

The most fundamental Arian belief was that Jesus Christ was not divine in any meaningful sense of the term. He was "first among the creatures" – that is, pre-eminent in rank, yet unquestionably a creature rather than divine. The Father is regarded as existing before the Son. "There was a time when he was not." This statement places Father and Son on different levels, and is consistent with Arius's rigorous insistence that the Son is a creature. Only the Father is "unbegotten"; the Son, like all other creatures, derives from this one source of being. However, as we have noted, Arius is careful to emphasize that the Son is not like every other creature. There is a distinction of rank between the Son and other creatures, including human beings.

Arius has some difficulty in identifying the precise nature of this distinction. The Son, he argued elsewhere in this letter, is "a perfect creature, yet not as one among other creatures; a begotten being, yet not as one among other begotten beings." The implication seems to be that the Son outranks other creatures, while sharing their essentially created and begotten nature. The consequences of this viewpoint were critiqued by many at the time, especially Athanasius (see 4.8).

Questions for Study

1. "The Son is not unbegotten, nor part of the unbegotten in any way." Locate this statement in the text. What does Arius mean by this?
2. "Before he was begotten or created or appointed or established, he did not exist." Locate this statement in the text. What does Arius mean by this?
3. "The Son has a beginning, but God is without beginning." Locate this statement in the text. What does Arius mean by this?

4.8

Athanasius on the Two Natures of Christ

In this letter, written in Greek around 350, Athanasius of Alexandria (c.296–373) argues for the divinity of Christ on soteriological grounds, while affirming the full humanity of Christ. See also 1.5, 4.4, 4.5, 4.13, 4.16, 4.17, 5.4, 5.5, 5.32.

Being God, he became a human being: and then as God he raised the dead, healed all by a word, and also changed water into wine. These were not the acts of a human being. But as a human being, he felt thirst and tiredness, and he suffered pain. These experiences are not appropriate to deity. As God he said, "I am in the Father, the Father is in me"; as a human being, he criticized the Jews, thus: "Why do you seek to kill me, when I am a man who has told you the truth, which I heard from my Father?" And yet these are not events occurring without any connection, distinguished according to their quality, so that one class may be ascribed to the body, apart from the divinity, and the other to the divinity, apart from the body. They all occurred in such a way that they were joined together; and the Lord, who marvellously performed those acts by his grace, was one. He spat in human fashion; but his spittle had divine power, for by it he restored sight to the eyes of the man blind from birth. When he willed to make himself known as God, he used his human tongue to signify this, when he said, "I and the Father are one." He cured by his mere will. Yet it was by extending his human hand that he raised Peter's mother-in-law when she had a fever, and raised from the dead the daughter of the ruler of the synagogue, when she had already died.

Comment

Athanasius here offers an implicit critique of the Arian understanding of the identity of Christ, focusing especially on Arius's denial of the divinity of Christ. What, asks Athanasius, follows if this denial is correct? What are the soteriological implications of this ontological affirmation? Athanasius makes the point that it is only God who can save. God, and God alone, can break the power of sin and bring us to eternal life. An essential feature of being a creature is that one requires to be redeemed. No creature can save another creature. Only the creator can redeem the creation. Having emphasized that it is God alone who can save, Athanasius then makes the logical move which the Arians found difficult to counter. The New Testament and the Christian liturgical tradition alike regard Jesus Christ as Savior. Yet, as Athanasius emphasized, only God can save. So how are we to make sense of this? The only possible solution, Athanasius argues, is to accept that Jesus is God incarnate. This kind of logic lies behind the passage for study, even if the issues are not expressed quite as clearly as set out above.

Questions for Study

1 Athanasius is a vigorous defender of the humanity and divinity of Christ. What respective roles does he allocate to the humanity and divinity of Christ?
2 If Arius's approach to the identity of Jesus was correct, which aspects of Athanasius's understanding of the work of Christ would be compromised?
3 "Being God, he became a human being: and then as God he raised the dead." Locate this passage in the text. Why is this affirmation so important to Athanasius?

4.9

Apollinarius of Laodicea on the Person of Christ

This passage, taken from a letter written to the bishops at Diocaesarea, sets out the leading features of the Christology of Apollinarius of Laodicea (c.310–c.390). The most important is the unequivocal assertion that the Word did not assume a "changeable" human mind in the incarnation, which would have led to the Word being trapped in human sin. Rather, it assumed "an immutable and heavenly divine mind." As a result, Christ cannot be said to be totally human. See also 4.1, 4.4, 4.5, 4.10, 4.13, 4.16, 4.17.

We confess that the Word of God has not descended upon a holy man, which was what happened in the case of the prophets. Rather, the Word himself has become flesh without having assumed a human mind – that is, a changeable mind, which is enslaved to filthy thoughts – but which exists as an immutable and heavenly divine mind.

Comment

Apollinarius of Laodicea had anxieties about the increasingly widespread belief that the Logos assumed human nature in its entirety. It seemed to him that this implied that the Logos was contaminated by the weaknesses of human nature. The sinlessness of Christ would be compromised, in Apollinarius's view, if he were to possess a purely human mind; was not the human mind the source of sin and rebellion against God? Only if the human mind were to be replaced by a purely divine motivating and directing force could the sinlessness of Christ be maintained. For this reason, Apollinarius argued that, in Christ, a purely human mind and soul were replaced by a divine mind and soul. This view was severely criticized by Gregory of Nazianzus, to which the reader is referred (4.10). Note that this writer is also known as "Apollinaris of Laodicea"; both variants of his name will be encountered in the literature.

Questions for Study

1 What concerns do you think lay behind the ideas which Apollinarius expresses in this passage?
2 "The Word himself has become flesh without having assumed a human mind." What does Apollinarius mean by this? What might its implications be?

4.10

Gregory of Nazianzus on Apollinarianism

In this letter, written in Greek at some point in 380 or 381, Gregory of Nazianzus (329–89) mounts a frontal assault on the central thesis of Apollinarianism: that Christ was not fully human, in that he possessed "an immutable and heavenly divine mind," rather than a human mind. For Gregory, this amounts to a denial of the possibility of redemption. Only what is assumed by the Word in the incarnation can be redeemed. If Christ did not possess a human mind, humanity is not redeemed. Note the use of the term "Theotokos" or "God-bearer" as a term for Mary. See also 4.9, 4.12, 4.11, 4.12, 4.13, 4.14, 4.15, 4.16, 4.17.

Do not let people deceive themselves and others by saying that the "Man of the Lord," which is the title they give to him who is rather "Our Lord and God," is without a human mind. We do not separate the humanity from the divinity; in fact, we assert the dogma of the unity and identity of the Person, who aforetime was not just human but God, the only Son before all ages, who in these last days has assumed human nature also for our salvation; in his flesh passible, in his Deity impassible; in the body subject to limitation, yet unlimited in the Spirit; at one and the same time earthly and heavenly, tangible and intangible, comprehensible and incomprehensible; that by one and the same person, a perfect human being and perfect God, the whole humanity, fallen through sin, might be recreated.

If any one does not believe that holy Mary is *Theotokos*, they will be cut off from the Deity. [. . .] If anyone asserts that humanity was created and only afterwards endued with divinity, they also are to be condemned. [. . .] If anyone brings in the idea of two sons, one of God the Father, the other of the mother, may they lose their share in the adoption. [. . .] For the Godhead and the humanity are two natures, as are soul and body, but there are not two Sons or two Gods. [. . .] For both natures are one by the combination, the Godhead made man or the manhood deified, or whatever be the right expression. [. . .]

If anyone has put their trust in him as a human being lacking a human mind, they are themselves mindless and not worthy of salvation. For what has not been assumed has not been healed; it is what is united to his divinity that is saved. [. . .] Let them not grudge us our total salvation, or endue the Savior only with the bones and nerves and mere appearance [*zōgraphia*] of humanity.

Comment

Gregory here expresses his fundamental misgivings concerning Apollinarius's approach. The basic soteriological principle is that Christ had to take fallen human nature upon himself in order to heal, renew, and redeem it. If Christ assumed an incomplete human nature, then human nature was not redeemed. It is this consideration which lies behind the important statement: "what has not been assumed has not been healed; it is what is united to his divinity that is saved."

Questions for Study

1 Does Gregory believe that God can suffer? And how does this compare to other patristic writers on this theme?

2 "By one and the same person, a perfect human being and perfect God, the whole humanity, fallen through sin, might be recreated." What does Gregory understand by this statement? How does this relate to his famous statement: "what has not been assumed has not been healed; it is what is united to his divinity that is saved"?

3 Why does Gregory place so much emphasis on the idea of the "Theotokos" – that is, that Mary is the "bearer of God"? What reasons might be given for this? You will find it interesting to compare Gregory's views on this matter with those of Nestorius, to which we shall turn presently (4.12).

4.11

Theodore of Mopsuestia on the "Union of Good Pleasure"

During the years 1932–3, the patristic scholar Alphonse Mingana published two newly discovered Syriac versions of the lost *Catechetical Orations* on the Creed, the Lord's Prayer, and the Mysteries of Theodore of Mopsuestia (c.350–428). These texts cast much light on Theodore's understanding of the incarnation, suggesting that he tended to think of a "conjunction" between the human and divine natures, rather than a "union" in the stricter sense of the term. This passage, taken from Theodore's eighth Catechetical Oration, deals with the relationship of these natures in the incarnation, and casts light on fourth century debates on the nature of the incarnation. See also 4.4, 4.5, 4.8, 4.9, 4.10, 4.14, 4.16.

The distinction between the natures does not annul the exact conjunction, nor does the exact conjunction destroy the distinction between the natures, but the natures remain in their respective existence while separated, and the conjunction remains intact because the one who was assumed is united in honour and glory with the one who assumed, according to the will of the one who assumed him [. . .] The fact that a husband and wife are "one flesh" does not impede them from being two. Indeed, they will remain two because they are two, but they are one because they are also one and not two. In this same way here [i.e., in the incarnation] they are two by nature and one by conjunction; two by nature, because there is a great difference between the natures, and one by conjunction because the adoration offered to the one who has been assumed is not divided from that offered to the one who assumed him, since he [i.e., the one that is assumed] is the temple, from which it is not possible for the one who dwells in it to depart.

Comment

In this passage, Theodore defends the growing consensus within the church concerning the identity of Christ. However, he formulates it in a way that caused concern to writers such as Cyril of Alexandria. The union between humanity and divinity in Christ is not described as a "union by nature," but as a conjunction according to the will of the parties involved. This idea of a "union according to good pleasure" (*henōsis kat' eudokian*) was conceived more as a contractual arrangement, comparable to a human marriage, than as a genuine union of natures. This point becomes especially clear through Theodore's use of the marriage analogy to stress the common honor and dignity shared by the couple, rather than their physical union.

Questions for Study

1 Identify the analogies used by Theodore in this passage. What kind of union do they model?
2 Theodore suggests that the incarnation is like a human marriage, in which the humanity and divinity of Christ "are two by nature and one by conjunction." What does he mean by this? What concept of the incarnation does it imply?
3 Consider the following comment made by Cyril of Alexandria in response to similar ideas found in the writings of Nestorius: "Equality of honor does not unite the natures." What point is Cyril making? And is he justified in seeing a problem with Theodore's position at this point? See further 4.13.

4.12

Nestorius on the Term "Theotokos"

Relatively few of the writings of Nestorius (died c.451), sometime Patriarch of Constantinople, have been passed down to us. What follows is an extract from a history of the church compiled by Socrates, also known as "Scholasticus." While there is probably a degree of bias in the reporting of Nestorius's actions and words, what is found in this passage corresponds well with what is known of the situation at this time. Notice how the controversy focuses on whether Mary, the mother of Jesus Christ, may properly be referred to as "Theotokos" (God-bearer). Nestorius is here depicted as confused about whether to use the term or not, hesitant as to what its use affirmed, yet fearful as to what its denial might imply. See also 4.8, 4.10, 4.11, 4.13, 4.14, 4.15, 4.16, 4.25.

Now [Nestorius] had as a colleague the presbyter Anastasius, who he had brought from Antioch. He had high regard for him, and consulted him over many matters. Anastasius was preaching one day in church, and said, "Let no one call Mary the Mother of God [*Theotokos*]: for Mary was only a human being, and it is impossible that God should be born of a human being." This caused a great scandal, and caused distress to both the clergy and the laity, as they had been taught up to this point to acknowledge Christ as God, and not to separate his humanity from his divinity on account of the economy [of salvation]. [. . .] While great offence was taken in the church at what was proclaimed in this way, Nestorius, who was eager to establish Anastasius' proposition – for he did not wish to have someone who he so highly esteemed found guilty of blasphemy – continually kept on giving instruction in church on this subject. He adopted a controversial attitude, and totally rejected the term *Theotokos*. The controversy on the matter was taken one way by some and another way by others, with the result that the ensuing discussion divided the church, and began to look like people fighting in the dark, with everyone coming out with the most confused and contradictory assertions. Nestorius acquired the popular reputation of asserting that the Lord was nothing more than a human being, and attempting to impose the teaching of Paul of Samosata and Photinus on the church. This led to such a great outcry that it was thought necessary to convene a general council to rule on the matter in dispute. Having myself studied the writings of Nestorius, I have found him to be an unlearned man and shall express quite frankly my own views about him [. . .] I cannot concede that he was a follower of either Paul of Samosata or of Photinus, or that he ever said that the Lord was nothing more than a human being. However, he seemed scared of the term *Theotokos*, as though it were some terrible phantom. The fact is, the groundless alarm he showed on this subject just showed up his extreme ignorance: for being a man of natural ability as a speaker, he was considered well educated, but in reality he was disgracefully illiterate. In fact he had no time for the hard work which an accurate examination of the ancient expositors would have involved and, made arrogant on account of his readiness of expression, he did not give his attention to the ancients, but thought himself above them.

Comment

By the time of Nestorius, the use of the title *Theotokos* (literally, "bearer of God") to refer to Mary had become widely accepted within both popular piety and academic theology. We have already seen an example of its use in Gregory of Nazianzus's response to Apollinarius (4.10). Nestorius was, however, alarmed at the implications of using this term. It seemed to deny the humanity of Christ. Why not call Mary *anthrōpotokos* ("bearer of humanity") or even *Christotokos* ("bearer of the Christ")? His suggestions were met with outrage and indignation, on account of the enormous theological investment which had come to be associated with the term *theotokos*.

Questions for Study

1 Socrates suggests that Nestorius was partly motivated in his criticisms of the term *theotokos* by a high personal regard for Anastasius of Antioch. Does this seem a plausible explanation of events?
2 "Nestorius acquired the popular reputation of asserting that the Lord was nothing more than a human being." Locate this statement within the passage. What does Socrates mean by this? And is he suggesting that Nestorius's real views on this matter might be somewhat different from those which the public associated with him?

4.13

Cyril of Alexandria on Nestorius's Christology

In an important section of a letter to Nestorius, written around 430, Cyril of Alexandria (died 444) condemns 12 propositions associated with the Antiochene school of Christology. Although Cyril regards these views as heretical, there are points at which it seems that his primary concern is to establish the supremacy of the Alexandrian over the Antiochene position. Of the 12 propositions, the following are particularly significant theologically. See also 4.8, 4.9, 4.10, 4.11, 4.12, 4.14, 4.15, 4.17, 4.24.

1. If any one does not acknowledge that Emmanuel is truly God, and that the holy Virgin is, in consequence, "Theotokos," for she gave birth in the flesh to the Word of God who has become flesh, let them be condemned.
2. If any one does not acknowledge that the Word of God the Father was substantially (*kath' hypostasin*) united with flesh, and with his own flesh is one Christ, that is, one and the same God and human being together, let them be condemned.
3. If any one divides the persons in the one Christ after their union, joining them together in a mere conjunction in accordance with their rank, or a conjunction effected by authority or power, instead of a combination according to a union of natures, let them be condemned.
4. If any one distributes between two characters or persons the expressions used about Christ in the gospels, and apostolic writings [...] applying some to the human being, conceived of separately, apart from the Word, [...] and others exclusively to the Word, let them be condemned.
5. If any one dares to call Christ a "God-bearing human being" (*theophoros anthrōpos*) [...] let them be anathema.
6. If any one says that the Word of God the Father is the god or master of Christ, instead of confessing that this Christ is both God and a human being [...] let them be condemned.
7. If anyone says that Jesus as a human being was controlled by God the Word, and that the "glory of the only-begotten" was attached to him, as something existing apart from himself, let them be condemned.
8. If anyone dares to say that "the human being who was assumed is to be worshipped together with the Divine Word" [...] let them be condemned.

9. If anyone says that the one Lord Jesus Christ was glorified by the Spirit, as if Christ used a power alien to himself which came to him through the Spirit [. . .] let them be condemned. [. . .]

12. If anyone does not confess that the Word of God suffered in the flesh, and was crucified in the flesh, and tasted death in the flesh [. . .] let them be condemned.

Comment

In this letter, Cyril set out a series of propositions which he regarded as essential to an orthodox Christology. The ideas are important and merit close study. Underlying this debate, some scholars have seen an important play for power – namely, with Cyril trying to establish his own reputation, and that of the see of Alexandria, as a bastion of Christian orthodoxy. By implication, Nestorius and Constantinople had lost their way and needed help to recover their former eminence.

Questions for Study

1 Why is Cyril so hostile to the suggestion that Christ could be understood as a "God-bearing human being"?
2 Note that one of the first points made by Cyril concerns the use of the term "Theotokos." Why is this so important for Cyril? What issues might be at stake if the use of this title were to be challenged? You will find it useful to read 4.15 for a fuller view of this matter.
3 Cyril condemns anyone who does not confess that "the Word of God suffered in the flesh." Does this mean that he believes that God suffered in Christ? If not, just what does he mean by this important statement?

4.14

Cyril of Alexandria on the Incarnation

In this letter, written in February 430, Cyril of Alexandria sets out his understanding of the mechanics of the incarnation. Note the emphasis upon the totality of the union between the divinity and humanity of Christ, without in any way allowing that a change occurred in the divinity as a result. Note also Cyril's rejection of the idea of a "union of good pleasure," an approach especially associated with Antiochene theologians such as Theodore of Mopsuestia, who argued that the divinity and humanity were not really united, but merely agreed to coexist in a specific manner. For Cyril, a real union took place. See also 4.8, 4.9, 4.10, 4.11, 4.12, 4.13, 4.15.

In declaring that the Word was made to "be incarnate" and "made human", we do not assert that there was any change in the nature of the Word when it became flesh, or that it was transformed into an entire human being, consisting of soul and body; but we say that the Word, in an indescribable and inconceivable manner, united personally to himself flesh endowed with a rational soul, and thus became a human being and was called the Son of man. And this was not by a mere act of will or favour, nor simply adopting a role or taking to himself a person. The natures which were brought together to form a true unity were different; but out of both is one Christ and one Son. We do not mean that the difference of the natures is annihilated by reason of this union; but rather that the divinity and humanity, by their inexpressible and inexplicable concurrence into unity, have produced for us the one Lord and Son Jesus Christ. It is in this sense that he is said to have been born also of a woman after the flesh, though he existed and was begotten from the Father before all ages. [...] It was not that an ordinary human being was first born of the holy Virgin, and that afterwards the Word descended upon him. He was united with the flesh in the womb itself, and thus is said to have undergone a birth after the flesh, inasmuch as he made his own the birth of his own flesh.

In the same way we say that he "suffered and rose again." We do not mean that God the Word suffered blows or the piercing of nails or other wounds in his own nature, in that the divine is impassible because it is not physical. But the body which had become his own body suffered these things, and therefore he himself is said to have suffered them for us. The impassible was in the body which suffered.

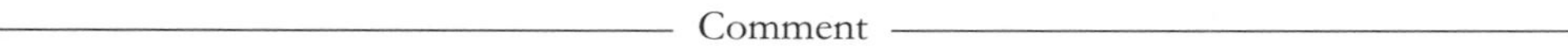

Comment

Nestorius had taught that Christ is one, by *synapheia*, conjunction, combination, connection. This term disturbed many theologians who used the stronger term *henōsis* ("union" or "unification"). In a period when it was becoming common to speak of Christ as one because his human and divine natures are the natures of the one *hypostasis* of the person, Nestorius spoke of a union *kat' eudokian*, a union "according to good pleasure" (an idea that we also find in Theodore of Mopsuestia – see 4.11). Many interpreted Nestorius to teach that Jesus is two persons, the Divine Logos and the human son of Mary, held in a merely "moral" unity by union of will, action, and choice. This view is opposed strongly by Cyril.

The patristic period saw the development of two rather different modes of understanding the nature of the union between humanity and divinity in the incarnation. One was associated with the school of Antioch, the other with Alexandria. As political considerations became increasingly important in the fourth century, the purely theological aspects of the question began to become mixed up with ecclesiastical political bickering over the role of the see of Alexandria. Alexandria was committed to the model of *henōsis kata physin* ("a union of natures"), with a real interpenetration of the two natures. Antioch preferred the model of *henōsis kat' eudokian* ("union according to good pleasure"), in which the two natures coexisted amicably, but without any interaction or interpenetration. In effect, this latter model posited two insulated compartments within Christ, both of which were genuinely present, but did not interact with each other. Cyril is highly critical of this model, for reasons which become clear in this passage.

Questions for Study

1 How does Cyril deal with the suggestion that Christ became the Son of God after his birth – a position sometimes known as "adoptionism"?
2 "And this was not by a mere act of will or favour." Locate this statement within this passage. To what is Cyril referring? And why does he reject this position?
3 "We do not mean that God the Word suffered blows or the piercing of nails or other wounds in his own nature, in that the divine is impassible because it is not physical. But the body which had become his own body suffered these things, and therefore he himself is said to have suffered them for us. The impassible was in the body which suffered." Locate this passage. What are its implications for the idea that "God suffered in Christ"? Why is Cyril so concerned to avoid any such statement?

4.15

Cyril of Alexandria on Mary as the Mother of God

At the Council of Ephesus (431), the term "Theotokos" (literally, "bearer of God") was formally endorsed as an appropriate title for Mary, as mother of Jesus Christ. Cyril's homily celebrates the dignity of Mary as a result of her bearing Jesus Christ. The homily is known by various titles; in this edition, it is referred to as "Homily 4." See also 4.8, 4.9, 4.10, 4.11, 4.12, 4.13, 4.14, 4.17.

I see here a joyful assembly of holy bishops who, at the invitation of the blessed Mother of God (*Theotokos*) – Mary, forever a virgin – have gathered enthusiastically. And although I am sad, the presence of these holy fathers fills me with joy. Among us are fulfilled the sweet words of the psalmist David: "Behold how good and sweet it is, brethren, to dwell together in unity."

So we hail you, mysterious holy Trinity, who have brought us all together in this church of holy Mary, Mother of God. We hail you, Mary, Mother of God, sacred treasure of all the universe, star who never sets, crown of virginity, scepter of the orthodox law, indestructible temple, dwelling-place of the incommensurable, Mother and Virgin, for the sake of the one who is called "blessed" in the holy Gospels, the one who "comes in the name of the Lord." We hail you, who held in your virginal womb him whom the heavens cannot contain, through whom the Trinity is glorified and worshiped throughout the world; through whom the heavens exult; through whom the angels and archangels rejoice; through whom the demons are put to flight; through whom the tempter fell from heaven; through whom the fallen creation is raised to the heavens; through whom the whole world, held captive by idolatry, has come to know the truth; through whom holy baptism is given to those who believe, with "the oil of gladness"; through whom churches have been founded throughout the world; through whom pagan nations have been led to conversion.

What more shall I say? It is through you that the light of the only-begotten Son of God has shone "for those who dwelt in darkness and in the shadow of death"; it is through you that the prophets proclaimed the future, that the apostles preach salvation to the nations, that the dead are raised and that kings reign, in the name of the holy Trinity. Is there a single person who can worthily celebrate the praises of Mary? She is both mother and virgin. What a marvelous thing! It is a marvel which overwhelms me! Has anyone ever heard it said that the builder was prevented from dwelling in the temple which he himself built? Has anyone the right to speak ill of the one who gave his own servant the title of mother? Thus everyone rejoices! [. . .]

May it be given us to worship and adore the unity, to worship and honor the indivisible Trinity, by singing the praises of Mary ever virgin, that is the holy church, and those of her Son and immaculate Spouse, to whom be glory for ever and ever, Amen.

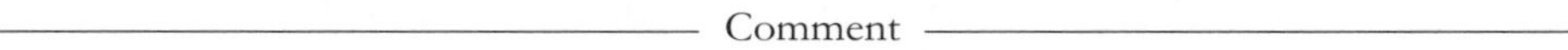

This passage illuminates the reasons why so many patristic writers of the eastern church saw it as essential to maintain that Mary was indeed "the bearer of God" (*Theotokos*). Cyril clearly regards this teaching as safeguarding a series of important theological and spiritual insights which could be lost if this title were to be abandoned or declared to be incorrect. Cyril's remarks about "sadness" in the opening section of this address reflect his regret that there was any need to convene the Council of Ephesus in the first place, due to the rise of division and error within the church, largely on account of Nestorius.

Questions for Study

1 List the titles which Cyril uses to refer to Mary. What are their theological implications?

2 At two points in this sermon, Cyril explicitly links together Mary with the holy Trinity. Is there any reason for this linkage? What points might he wish to make in this way?

3 "Has anyone ever heard it said that the builder was prevented from dwelling in the temple which he himself built?" Locate this rhetorical question within the passage. What point does Cyril make through it? What is the "building" to which he refers?

4.16

Leo the Great on the Two Natures of Christ

This letter, written in Latin by Pope Leo I (died 461) to Flavian, Patriarch of Constantinople on June 13, 449, is usually referred to as the "Tome of Leo." Leo here sets out the prevailing Christological consensus within the Latin church. The letter was later elevated to a position of authority by the Council of Chalcedon (451), which recognized it as a classic statement of Christological orthodoxy. The letter is primarily a critique of the views of Eutyches, especially his rejection of the true humanity of Christ. For Leo, the formula *totus in suis, totus in nostris* sums up the correct position on this matter. See also 4.4, 4.5, 4.8, 4.9, 4.10, 4.11, 4.12, 4.13, 4.15, 4.17.

[Eutyches] did not realize what he ought to believe concerning the incarnation of the Word of God, and did not want to seek out the light of understanding by careful study throughout Holy Scripture in all its breadth. But he might at least have received with careful attention that common and universal confession, in which the whole body of the faithful confess their faith in "God the Father Almighty, and in Jesus Christ his only Son, our Lord, who was born of the Holy Spirit and the Virgin Mary." For by these three statements the strategies of almost all the heretics are overthrown. God is believed to be both Almighty and Father; as a result, the Son is seen to be co-eternal with God, differing in no respect from the Father. For Christ was born God of God, Almighty of Almighty, co-eternal of eternal; not later in time, not inferior in power, not different in glory, not divided in essence. The same only-begotten, eternal Son of the eternal Father was born of the Holy Spirit and the Virgin Mary. But this birth in time has taken nothing from, and added nothing to, that divine eternal nativity, but has bestowed itself wholly on the restoration of humanity, which had been deceived: that it might overcome death and by its own virtue overthrow the devil who had the power of death. For we could not overcome the author of sin and death, unless he had taken our nature and made it his own, whom sin could not defile nor death retain, since he was conceived of the Holy Spirit, in the womb of his Virgin Mother, whose virginity remained entire in his birth as in his conception.

[...] That birth, uniquely marvelous and marvelously unique, ought not to be understood in such a way as to preclude the distinctive properties of the kind [i.e. of humanity] through the new mode of creation. For it is true that the Holy Spirit gave fruitfulness to the Virgin, but the reality of his body was received from her body. [...]

Thus the properties of each nature and substance were preserved in their totality, and came together to form one person. Humility was assumed by majesty, weakness by strength, mortality by eternity; and to pay the debt that we had incurred, an inviolable nature was united to a nature that can suffer. And so, to fulfill the conditions of our healing, the human being Jesus Christ, one and the same mediator between God and humanity, was able to die in respect of the one, yet unable to die in respect of the other. Thus there was born true God in the entire and perfect nature of true humanity, complete in his own properties, complete in ours [*totus in suis, totus in nostris*]. By "ours" we mean those things which the Creator formed in us at the beginning, which he assumed in order to restore; for in the Savior there was no trace of the properties which the deceiver brought in, and which humanity, being deceived, allowed to enter. Christ did not become partaker of our sins because he entered into fellowship with human infirmities. He assumed the form of a servant without the stain of sin, making the human properties greater, but not detracting from the divine. For that "emptying of himself," by which the invisible God chose to become visible, and the Creator and Lord of all willed to be a mortal, was an inclination of compassion, not a failure of power [*inclinatio fuit miserationis, non defectio potestatis*].

Accordingly, the one who created humanity, while remaining in the form of God, was made a human being in the form of a servant. Each nature preserves its own characteristics without diminution, so that the form of a servant does not detract from the form of God. Now the devil boasted that humanity, deceived by his guile, had been deprived of the divine gifts and, stripped of the power of immortality, had incurred the stern sentence of death; that he himself had found some consolation in his plight from having a companion in sin. He boasted too that God, because justice required it, had changed his purpose in respect of humanity, which God had created in such honor. Therefore there was need for a dispensation by which God might carry out God's own hidden plan, that the unchangeable God, whose will cannot be deprived of its own mercy, might accomplish the first design of God's affection towards us by a more secret mystery; and that humanity, driven into sin by the devil's wicked craftiness, should not perish contrary to the purpose of God.

The Son of God therefore came down from his throne in heaven without withdrawing from his Father's glory, and entered this world, born after a new order, by a new mode of birth. After a new order, inasmuch as he is invisible in his own nature, and he became visible in ours. [. . .] From his mother the Lord took nature, not sin. Jesus Christ was born from a virgin's womb, by a miraculous birth. And yet his nature is not on that account unlike to ours, for he that is true God is also truly human. There is no unreality in this unity since the humility of the manhood and the majesty of the deity exist in reciprocity. For just as the divinity is not changed by his compassion, so the humanity is not swallowed up by the dignity. Each nature performs its proper functions in communion with the other; the Word performs what pertains to the Word, the flesh what pertains to the flesh. The one is resplendent with miracles, the other submits to insults. The Word withdraws not from his equality with the Father's glory; the flesh does not desert the nature of our kind.

Comment

Unlike the eastern church, the church in the west never became embroiled in complex and subtle Christological debates. The great debates in the west concerned the nature of the church and grace, rather than the person of Christ. The "Tome of Leo" is of importance on account of its conciliatory approach, and its clear intention to ascertain what was absolutely *essential* to the orthodox Christological positions, and what was open to negotiation or discussion. The document was well received, and is often seen as a landmark of positive theological synthesis at a time dominated by polemical works and considerations.

Questions for Study

1 What reasons does Leo give for the incarnation? Why did God become a human being?
2 "The properties of each nature and substance were preserved in their totality." Locate this statement within the text. What does Leo mean by this? And why is it so important for him to make this statement?
3 "Christ did not become partaker of our sins because he entered into fellowship with human infirmities." Locate this statement within the text. Why does Leo need to make this point clear? What would be the implications if it were not so? And what use does Leo make of this statement in what follows?

4.17

The Chalcedonian Definition of the Christian Faith (451)

The Council of Chalcedon (451) laid down an understanding of the relation of the humanity and divinity of Jesus Christ which became normative for the Christian churches, both east and west. Notice how the Council is adamant that Christ must be accepted to be truly divine and truly human, without specifying precisely how this is to be understood. In other words, a number of Christological models are affirmed to be legitimate, provided they uphold this essential Christological affirmation. See also 1.5, 2.38, 4.8, 4.9, 4.10, 4.11, 4.12, 4.13, 4.14, 4.20.

Following the holy Fathers, we all with one voice confess our Lord Jesus Christ to be one and the same Son, perfect in divinity and humanity, truly God and truly human, consisting of a rational soul and a body, being of one substance with the Father in relation to his divinity, and being of one substance with us in relation to his humanity, and is like us in all things apart from sin (Hebrews 4: 15). He was begotten of the Father before time in relation to his divinity, and in these recent days, was born from the Virgin Mary, the *Theotokos*, for us and for our salvation. In relation to the humanity, he is one and the same Christ, the Son, the Lord, the only-begotten, who is to be acknowledged in two natures, without confusion, without change, without division, and without separation. This distinction of natures is in no way abolished on account of this union, but rather the characteristic property of each nature is preserved, and concurring into one Person and one subsistence, not as if Christ were parted or divided into two persons, but remains one and the same Son and only-begotten God, Word, Lord, Jesus Christ; even as the Prophets from the beginning spoke concerning him, and our Lord Jesus Christ instructed us, and the Creed of the Fathers was handed down to us.

Comment

It is important to appreciate that the councils which took such important theological decisions were often influenced by all kinds of political factors. This is especially clear in relation to the convening of the Council of Constantinople in 451. After Ephesus had condemned Nestorius, a writer known as Eutyches mounted a vigorous attack on Nestorius's teaching in Constantinople. Eutyches made generous use of some phrases used earlier by Cyril of Alexandria. Unfortunately, Eutyches expressed his ideas in a rather muddled way, and gave the impression that he was denying that Christ is truly human. Opposition to his ideas grew. In November 448 Eusebius of Dorylaeum, a leading figure in the campaign against Nestorianism, charged Eutyches with heresy. Having been summoned before the Standing Synod by Flavian, Bishop of Constantinople, Eutyches was excommunicated; he appealed to Pope Leo I.

Dioscoros, the Pope of Alexandria, became interested in the affair, and a retrial of Eutyches was eventually ordered. A second Council thus convened at Ephesus in 449. Leo's legates arrived at Ephesus carrying his *Tome* (see 4.16), in the form of a letter to Flavian, but had little chance of a hearing. The proceedings were dominated by Pope Dioscoros, imperial troops, and aggressive Egyptian monks armed with staves. This Council, which Pope Leo was to name the *Latrocinium*, the "Robber Council" of Ephesus, restored and exonerated Eutyches and deposed Flavian, who was so violently treated that he eventually died of his injuries.

This was not the end of the matter. In 451 the Emperor Marcian convened another Council at Chalcedon which anathematized both Nestorius and Eutyches. The Council also deposed and excommunicated Dioscoros, who was exiled to Gangra, where he died in 454. It seemed to some that Chalcedon had condemned not only Eutyches, but also Cyril of Alexandria, despite its warm references to him. Many loyal to the theology of Cyril repudiated Chalcedon as a result. Despite repeated endeavors to heal the breach, from Chalcedon onwards there have existed in eastern Christianity two orthodoxies, one accepting the Council as of ecumenical authority, the other rejecting it. The second tradition, that of the Oriental Orthodox, is often described as *Monophysite*. We shall consider its teachings presently (4.19).

Questions for Study

1 List the theological titles used by the Council. What are their implications? In particular, you should note the use of the term *Theotokos*.
2 Find sections of this text which, in your view, represent criticisms of (a) Arius; (b) Apollinarius of Laodicea; (c) Nestorius.
3 "This distinction of natures is in no way abolished on account of this union." Locate this statement within the text. What does it mean? Who is being criticized here?

4.18

The Emperor Zeno on the Natures of Christ

This important document, which dates from 482, represents an attempt by the emperor Zeno (c.450–91) to resolve the differences which were opening up within the church over the "Monophysite" controversy. Unfortunately, the document – generally known as the "Henotikon" – served to make division even worse, leading to growing division between eastern and western Christians. Although Zeno may have assuaged Monophysite anxieties, the Henotikon caused considerable offence to orthodox Christians. The document's affirmations concerning the divinity and humanity of Christ are an important witness to the tensions in Christology at this period. See also 4.15, 4.16, 4.17.

We confess that our Lord Jesus Christ, the only begotten Son of God, the same God who himself truly assumed human nature, is consubstantial [*homoousios*] with the Father in respect of the Godhead, and consubstantial with us in respect of his humanity. He descended [from heaven] and became incarnate of the Holy Spirit and Mary, the Virgin and *Theotokos*. He is one, not two, for we affirm that both his miracles and the sufferings which he voluntarily endured in his flesh are those of a single person. In no way do we agree with those who make a division on confusion, or introduce a phantom. For his truly sinless incarnation from the *Theotokos* did not produce an additional son, because the Trinity

[*Trias*] contained a Trinity even when one member of the Trinity (that is, God the Word) became incarnate.

Comment

As we noted in our comments on the Council of Chalcedon (4.17), there was unease over the way in which the Council appeared to criticize the views of Cyril of Jerusalem. As a result, some groups refused to accept the authority of the Council. The uncritical use of the single term "Monophysite" (Greek: "only one nature") to refer to such groups is dangerous: a variety of different Monophysite positions exist, to some of which the fathers of the eastern Orthodox tradition were sternly opposed. Julian, Bishop of Halicarnassus, for example, taught that the flesh of Christ was incorruptible from the moment of the incarnation. This view was condemned by Severus of Antioch, one of the most important anti-Chalcedonian theologians, as a form of Docetism; he labeled Julian and his followers "phantasiasts," although it should be noted that they are more commonly known in the technical literature as "Aphthartodocetists." Some of Severus's followers were known as *aktistoi* ("uncreated ones"), since they denied that Christ's body had ever been created.

Severus himself represents a tradition which aimed to remain loyal to Cyril's doctrine, and was sternly opposed to anything which could conceivably be regarded as Nestorianism, including the rulings of the Council of Chalcedon, which they held to be Nestorian in substance, even if not in intention. However, it is clear that Severus accepted that Christ is *homoousios* with the rest of humanity and *homoousios* with the Father and the Holy Spirit, so that, at least at this crucial point, he was in agreement with the eastern Orthodox and with western Christians who accept the authority of Chalcedon. This point becomes especially important in the document drawn up by the emperor Zeno, who wanted to restore peace within his empire over this matter.

The recognition that a substantial measure of agreement was possible between Chalcedonians and moderate Monophysites underlay several imperially sponsored attempts to generate a compromise doctrinal formula. The attempts ended in failure, not because no such formula could be constructed, but because the divisions between the parties were not merely theological. As we have stressed, political factors were deeply implicated in the ecclesiastical debates of this period. We here consider one such effort, due to the emperor Zeno.

Questions for Study

1 Are there any indications within the text that it represents an attempt to broker a deal between disputing parties?
2 Set out, in your own words, the basic points that the text aims to make. Notice how the term *Theotokos* is used.
3 How might Severus have reacted to this text?

4.19

The Monophysites on the Natures of Christ

In an importand theological petition of 532, the Monophysites rejected the Chalcedonian definition of "two natures" in Christ, and vigorously reaffirmed their view that there is only one nature in Christ. The document asserts the orthodoxy of this position, and is particularly critical of the views of Apollinarius. See also 4.16, 4.17.

We confess a holy Trinity, worthy of adoration, of one nature, power and honor, which is made known in three persons. We worship the Father and his only Son, the Word, who was begotten of him eternally before all ages, and who is of the nature of the Father and of the Son. We declare that one of the persons of this holy Trinity, that is, God the Word, by the will of the Father and for the salvation of humanity took flesh of the Holy Spirit and of the holy Virgin and *Theotokos* Mary, in a body which was endowed with a rational and intellectual soul, passible like our natures, and became a human being without being changed from what he was. And so we confess that while in the Godhead he was of the nature of the Father, he was also of our nature in his state of humanity. So he who is the perfect Word, the unchangeable Son of God, became a perfect human being, and left nothing wanting for us in respect of our salvation. This is what the foolish Apollinarius said, when he declared that God the Word did not become human in a perfect manner, and deprives us of things that are of major importance in relation to our salvation. For, if our intellect was not united with him, as Apollinarius maintained, then we are not saved, and in the matter of salvation we have fallen short of what was of the greatest importance for us. However, he is wrong: the perfect God became a perfect human being without change for our sake, and in this becoming human, God the Word did not omit anything. Nor was it a phantom, as the impious Mani and the erring Eutyches suggested.

Now Christ is truth, and, because he is God, does not know how to lie or to deceive, it may be said that God the Word truly became incarnate, in truth and not merely in appearance, with natural and innocent feelings. [. . .] And just as God the Word left nothing missing, and did not become a phantom in his incarnation and becoming human, so he did not divide it into two persons and two natures, according to the teaching introduced by Nestorius. [. . .]

If, as according to our holy Fathers (which your Serenity also acknowledges) God the Word, who was previously simple and not composite, became incarnate of the Virgin and *Theotokos* Mary, and united an intellectual flesh, possessing a soul, to himself personally, and made it his own and was joined together with it in the incarnation, it is clear that [. . .] we ought to confess one nature of God the Word, who took flesh and perfectly became a human being. For this reason, God the Word, who was previously simple, cannot be considered to have become composite in a body, if division results after this union through his having two natures. But just as an ordinary human being, who is made up of various natures (such as soul, body and so on) is not divided into two natures on account of a soul being joined by composition with a body to make up the one nature and person of a human being, so also God the Word, who was personally united to and joined by composition with a flesh which possesses a soul cannot be "in two natures" on account of his union or composition with a body. [...]

For this reason, we do not accept either the Tome [of Leo] or the definition of Chalcedon, because we maintain the canon and law of our fathers who gathered together at Ephesus, and condemned and deprived Nestorius and excommunicated any who were bold enough to lay down any other definition of faith apart from that of Nicea, which was correctly and faithfully laid down by the Holy Spirit.

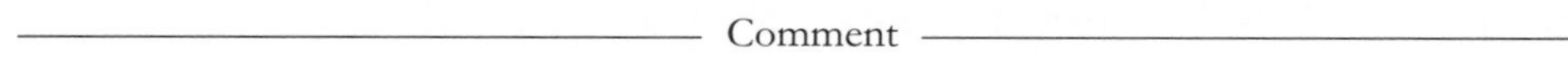

Comment

For the origins of the Monophysite movement, and some of the issues involved in defining its theology, see the comments to 4.18. This letter can be seen as expressing many of those concerns, and is an important landmark in the church's reception of the Council of Nicea.

Questions for Study

1 According to this document, why did the Monophysites reject the Tome of Leo and the Council of Chalcedon?
2 Set out, in your own words, the criticisms which the document makes of the following: (a) Eutyches; (b) Apollinarius; (c) Nestorius.
3 "God the Word, who was personally united to and joined by composition with a flesh which possesses a soul cannot be 'in two natures' on account of his union or composition with a body." Locate this statement within the text. How does the document reach this conclusion (which, incidentally, is an excellent summary statement of the Monophysite position)?

4.20

John of Damascus on the Incarnation and Icons

In this, the first of three treatises aimed against those who reject the use of icons, originally written in Greek in the first half of the eighth century, John of Damascus (c.675–c.749) argues that the theological fact of the incarnation of Christ provides a solid foundation for the use of icons in devotion. An "icon" (*eikōn*) is a religious painting or picture, which is understood to act as a window through which the worshiper may catch a closer glimpse of the divine than would otherwise be possible. John uses a strongly incarnational approach to defend the use of physical items – such as icons – in worship and adoration. See also 1.14, 3.39, 4.8, 4.9, 4.10, 4.11, 4.12, 4.13, 4.14, 4.15, 4.16.

Previously there was absolutely no way in which God, who has neither a body nor a face, could be represented by any image. But now that he has made himself visible in the flesh and has lived with people, I can make an image of what I have seen of God. I do not worship matter; I worship the Creator of matter, who became matter for my sake, and who worked out my salvation through matter. I will never cease to honor the matter which brought about my salvation – but while I honor it, it is not as God. How could God be said to be born out of things which have no independent existence? God's body is divine because it is joined to his person by a union that shall never pass away. The divine nature remains the same; the flesh, created in time, is given life by a rational soul. For this reason, I honor all remaining matter, because God has filled it with his grace and power, and because salvation has come to me through it. Was not the triply blessed wood of the cross matter? Was not the holy and elevated hill of Calvary matter? Was not the life-bearing rock, the holy and life-giving tomb, the source of our resurrection, also matter? Is not the ink in the most holy Gospel book matter? Is not the life-giving altar, from which we receive the bread of life, constructed from matter? Are not gold and silver matter? Yet from them, we make crosses, patens, and chalices. And more importantly than any of these things, are not the body and blood of our Lord matter? Either dispense with the honor and veneration that these things deserve, or accept the tradition of the church and the veneration of images.

Comment

The use of icons was controversial within early Christianity, and led to the famous "Iconoclastic" (Greek: "breaking of the images") controversy in the eastern church. The iconoclasts accused those who used icons of idolatry, and claimed the making and worship of images was forbidden in the Bible. Their opponents rejected such charges, pointing out that, in the Old Testament, God commanded the making of certain images (such as the Cherubim on the cover of the Ark, Exodus 25: 19). The ending of that controversy, however, did not stall debate on the proper subjects of icons. The Synod of Trullo (692) prohibited the depiction of Christ as a lamb, despite this having been a common image in the past, and insisted he be represented in his full humanity. The reason for this is that the image is to lead us to remember "his life in the flesh, his sufferings, his saving death, and the deliverance which he accomplished for the world." The Council of Moscow (1667) prohibited representations of God the Father as a human being; it was the Son, it was argued, who took on humanity, not the Father, and representations of the Father in human form would have been deeply misleading.

The present passage is important in several respects. First, it sets out the case for using icons, against those opposed to their use. Second, and perhaps more important, the incarnation of God is offered as a theological justification for the practice of using icons and other material objects as devotional aids.

Questions for Study

1 According to John of Damascus, why could images not be used for devotional purposes prior to the incarnation? What new principle does the incarnation introduce into the use of material objects in devotion?

2 "No human being can withstand the full glory of the Lord." How does John develop the theology of icons to deal with this common Christian insight?

3 "Now that [God] has made himself visible in the flesh and has lived with people, I can make an image of what I have seen of God." What does John mean by this?

4.21

Honorius of Autun on the Cause of the Incarnation

Little is known about the twelfth-century theologian Honorius of Autun, who was active during the period 1106–35. While most Christian theologians have seen the incarnation as a consequence of the Fall, Honorius suggests that Christ would have become incarnate irrespective of the sin of humanity. The extract is taken from his "Book of Eight Questions on Angels and Humanity," which takes the form of a dialogue between a student and a master. See also 4.22, 5.16.

The Student: Would Christ have become incarnate, if humanity had remained in paradise? For all of Scripture declares that Christ became incarnate in order to redeem humanity. Therefore he would not have become incarnate if humanity had not sinned and needed redeeming. So, from this, it would seem that the sin of humanity was the cause of Christ's incarnation. And if this is so, then sin did not lead to evil, but to a greater good, in that it led to God becoming human, and consequently to humanity becoming God.

The Master: Human sin is not good, but is the greatest of evils, as the whole world declares on account of its miseries. And why does death, along with all the destruction it brings, reign in the world, if it is not through human sin? Therefore the first human sin was not the cause of Christ's incarnation; rather, it was the cause of death and damnation. The cause of Christ's incarnation was the predestination of human deification [*causa autem Christi incarnationis fuit praedestinatio humanae deificationis*]. It was indeed predestined by God from all eternity that humanity would be deified, for the Lord said, "Father, you have loved them before the creation of the world," (John 17: 24) – those, that is, who are made divine through me [...] It was necessary, therefore, for him to become incarnate, so that humanity could be deified, and thus it does not follow that sin was the cause of the incarnation, but it follows all the more logically that sin could not alter God's plan for making humanity divine, since in fact both the authority of Holy Scripture and clear reason declare that God would have assumed humanity even if humanity had never sinned.

Comment

Most Christian writers thought it pointless to speculate about what might have happened if Adam had never sinned. Thomas Aquinas, for example, held that the coming of Christ was the result of the Fall, and declared that there was little to be gained by considering alternatives (see 4.22). Honorius of Autun and his contemporary Rupert of Deutz (5.16) represent a significant minority view, which held that the incarnation was the climax of God's creation, leading to the deification of humanity as God's ultimate goal – an idea also found in the Greek tradition, such as Maximus the Confessor. Note that there seems to be an error in the text's citation of John 17: 24 as "Father, you have loved them before the creation of the world." The correct reading is "me" rather than "them."

Questions for Study

1 Set out the argument of the Master. What, in his view, is the cause of the incarnation? And how does this relate to the salvation of humanity?
2 What role does sin play in the economy of salvation, according to Honorius?
3 Compare this with the views of Thomas Aquinas (4.22). Which writer do you think has the better of the argument?

4.22

Thomas Aquinas on the Necessity of the Incarnation

As is clear from the previous extract (4.21), medieval theologians explored a number of ways of making sense of the incarnation. Thomas Aquinas (c.1225–74) offered an analysis of the question that can be thought of as establishing a general consensus on the matter. There are, he suggests, several reasons for the incarnation, and there is little to be gained from speculating about what would have happened if there had been no Fall. The Fall did happen, and the incarnation happened in consequence. And to go further than this is somewhat pointless. See also 4.21, 5.16, 5.17.

It would seem that if humanity had not sinned, God would still have become incarnate. For if the cause remains, so does the effect. As Augustine says, "there are many other things to be considered in the incarnation of Christ than absolution from sin," as discussed above (article 2). Therefore if humanity had not sinned, God would still have become incarnate. [...] But on the contrary, Augustine, in expounding Luke 19: 10, "For the Son of Man came to seek and save the lost," comments that "if humanity had not sinned, the Son of Man would not have come." [...]

I answer that there are different opinions on this question. Some say that the Son of God would have become incarnate, even if humanity had not sinned. Others assert the opposite, and it would seem that our assent ought to be given to this opinion. For those things that originate from God's will, lying beyond what is due to the creature, can only be made known to us through being revealed in Holy Scripture, in which the divine will is made known to us. Therefore, since the sin of the first human being is described as the cause of the incarnation throughout Holy Scripture, it is more in accordance with this to say that the work of the incarnation was ordained as a remedy for sin, so that, if sin had not existed, the incarnation would never have taken place. Yet the power of God is not limited in this way. Even if sin had not existed, God could still have become incarnate.

Comment

Following his normal practice, Aquinas begins by noting a variety of opinions within the theological literature, before offering his own resolution of the question. In this case, he points out what seems to be a tension within Augustine's writings, which requires to be resolved. The resolution in question is perhaps more diplomatic than theological, in that Aquinas does not actually rule out rival viewpoints, but merely suggests that his own position is "more in accordance" with the evidence.

Questions for Study

1 Read Honorius of Autun's discussion of this same question (4.21). How does Aquinas evaluate this position?
2 Summarize the position that Aquinas adopts in his response to this question. How confident is he about it?
3 What seem to be the major factors that move Aquinas to this conclusion?

4.23

Gregory Palamas on the Divine Condescension in the Incarnation

In the course of commenting on Matthew 16: 28, "there are some here who will not taste death before they have seen the kingdom of God coming with power," the noted Byzantine theologian Gregory Palamas (c.1296–1359) deals with the manner in which God descends to his people in Christ. The text, written in Greek around 1335, stresses the importance of the divine descent (*katabasis*) to humanity, and the resulting ascent (*anabasis*) of humanity to God. See also 4.8, 5.5, 5.28.

The king of all is everywhere, and his kingdom is everywhere. This means that the coming of the kingdom cannot mean that it is transferred from this place here to that place there, but that it is revealed in the power of the divine Spirit. This is why [Christ] said "coming with power." And this power does not come upon everyone, but upon "those who have stood with the Lord," that is, those who are firmly grounded in the faith, such as Peter, James, and John, who were first brought by the Word to this high mountain, in order to symbolize those who are thus able to rise above their humble natures. For this reason, Scripture shows us God descending from his supreme dwelling place and raising us up from our humble condition on a mountain, so that the one who is infinite may be surely but within limits encompassed by created nature.

Comment

One of the most fundamental insights of eastern Christian writers is that God descended to humanity in order that humanity might ascend to God. The central theme is that of the incarnation. God assuming human flesh is viewed as both divine descent and human ascent. God descends to where we are, in order to raise us to where God is. The incarnation is the means by which God confers this extraordinary transformation upon human nature. It is thus clear that the incarnation is of central importance to eastern Christian thinking on both the means and nature of salvation. For such writers, salvation is primarily to be thought of in terms of *theōsis* ("becoming divine") or *theopoiēsis* ("being made divine").

Questions for Study

1 "Scripture shows us God descending from his supreme dwelling place and raising us up from our humble condition on a mountain." Locate this statement within the text. How is the image of the mountain used to illuminate the incarnation?
2 In what way are believers enabled to "rise above their humble natures"?

4.24

Martin Luther's Critique of Nestorianism

Although Christology was not an issue of major controversy at the time of the Reformation, its leading representatives dealt with this aspect of theology in some depth. In this important section of his reforming treatise of 1539, Martin Luther (1483–1546) digresses from his analysis of the history and authority of Councils to focus on the Christology of Nestorius. Luther develops his characteristic position concerning the relation of the distinctive attributes (or *idiomata*, to use the technical term which recurs throughout the passage) of God and humanity in Christ. For Luther, the incarnation means that everything that can be said about God is also true of humanity in the specific case of Christ. This leads to his startling assertion that, since Jesus was crucified, suffered, and died, it must follow that God was crucified, suffered, and died. See also 4.8, 4.9, 4.10, 4.11, 4.12, 4.13, 4.14, 4.15.

So Nestorius's error was not that he thought that Christ was simply a human being, or that he made him into two persons. On the contrary, he confesses that there are two natures, God and humanity, in one person. He does not, however, concede the *communicatio idiomatum*, something which I cannot put into a single word. "Idioma" means something which is inherent in a nature, or is its attribute, such as dying, suffering, crying, speaking, laughing, eating, drinking, sleeping, being sad, being happy, being born [...Luther provides a long list here] and other things like these, which are called *idiomata naturae humanae*, that is, qualities which belong to human nature, which humanity can and must do or have done to it. [...] Again, an *idioma deitatis* – that is, an attribute of the divine nature – is that it is immortal, all-powerful, and infinite; it is not born, it does not eat, drink, sleep, stand, walk, become sad, or cry. So what more can be said? To be God is clearly something completely different to being human. So the *idiomata* of both these two natures cannot coincide. And this is the opinion of Nestorius.

Now suppose I were to preach like this: "Jesus the carpenter of Nazareth (for that is what the Gospels call him) is walking down the street over there, fetching a jug of water and a pennyworth of bread for his mother, so that he could eat and drink with her. And this same Jesus the carpenter is the true son of God in one person." Now Nestorius would agree with this, and say that it is true. But now suppose that I say: "There is God going down the street, fetching some water and bread so that he could eat and drink with his mother." Nestorius would not agree with this, but would say: "Fetching water, buying bread, having a mother, and eating and drinking with her, are *idiomata* of a human, not a divine, nature." So if I were to say: "Jesus the carpenter was crucified by the Jews. And this same Jesus is really God," Nestorius would say to me that this is true. But if I were to say: "God was crucified by the Jews," he would say: "No! For to suffer the cross and to die are not divine, but human, *idiomata* or attributes." [. . .]

So we Christians must allow the *idiomata* of the two natures of Christ, the persons, equally and totally. As a result, Christ is God and a human being in one person because whatever is said about him as a human being must also be said of him as God, namely, "Christ has died," and, as Christ is God, it follows that "God has died" – not God in isolation [*der abgesonderte Gott*], but God united with humanity. For neither of the statements "Christ is God' and "God has died" are true in the case of God in isolation; both are false, for then God is not a human being. If it seems strange to Nestorius that God should die, he should find it just as strange that God becomes a human being; for by doing so, the immortal God becomes that which must die and suffer, and have all the human *idiomata*. If this was not the case, what kind of human being would God have become united to, if it did not have truly human *idiomata*? It would be a phantom [*gespenst*], as the Manicheans taught earlier. On the other hand, whatever is said of God must also be attributed to the human being. Thus "God created the world and is almighty," and the human being Christ is God; therefore, the human being Christ created the world and is almighty. The reason for this is that since God and the human being have become one person, this person bears the *idiomata* of both natures in consequence.

Comment

This passage shows Luther writing as a popular theologian in everyday German, with an easy turn of phrase which made the ideas easy to follow to his lay audience. The passage is of especial importance in that it offers a theological justification for Luther's "theology of the cross" (1.12); namely, that God can be said to have suffered upon the cross. The term "the crucified God" was developed by Luther around 1519, and remains one of his most powerful phrases. It does not involve any new theological principles; the idea of the "communication of attributes" was well known. What is radical is the extent to which Luther presses this principle, not its use in the first place. Luther had no hesitation in arguing along the following lines:

> Jesus Christ was crucified.
> Jesus Christ is God.
> Therefore God was crucified.

Or, again:

> Jesus Christ suffered and died.
> Jesus Christ is God.
> Therefore God suffered and died.

Luther's distinctive "theology of the cross" may thus be regarded as a radical application of the "communication of attributes," abandoning certain limits which had been respected up to this point.

Questions for Study

1 Set out, in your own words, Luther's understanding of the "communication of attributes." What attributes does he regard as characteristic of God? And what of human nature?
2 How does Luther represent Nestorius's position?
3 "If it seems strange to Nestorius that God should die, he should find it just as strange that God becomes a human being." Locate this statement within the text. What does Luther mean by this? And how would he use this to justify his radical application of the communication of attributes?

4.25

François Turrettini on the Threefold Office of Christ

The writings of John Calvin, especially his *Institutes of the Christian Religion* (1559), established a pattern which would become widespread within Reformed Christology. The significance of Christ was explored using the model of the "threefold office," which depicted him as prophet, priest, and king. As a prophet, Christ declared the will of God; as a priest, he made atonement for sins; and as king, he rules over his people. The seventeenth-century Genevan theologian François Turrettini (1623–87), a noted exponent of the Reformed tradition, here sets out this understanding more fully, in a text originally published in Latin in 1679. See also 5.17, 5.19.

The office of Christ is nothing other than a mediation between God and humanity, which he was sent into the world by the Father and anointed by the Holy Spirit to carry out. It embraces all that Christ was required to achieve during his mission and calling in relation to an offended God and offending humanity [*erga Deus offensum et homines offendentes*], reconciling and uniting them to each other. [. . .] This mediatorial office of Christ is distributed among three functions, which are individual parts of it: the prophetic, priestly, and kingly. Christ sustained these together rather than separately, something which he alone was able to do. For what would, in the case of other people, be divided on account of their weakness (as no mortal could discharge them alone, so great are their dignity and responsibility) are united in Christ on account of his supreme perfection. There could indeed be people who were both kings and priests (such as Melchizedek) or kings and prophets (such as David), or priests and prophets (as in the case of some high priests) – but there is no other who perfectly fulfilled all three. This was reserved for Christ alone, in that he was able to uphold the truth which is embodied in these types. [. . .] The threefold misery of humanity resulting from sin (that is, ignorance, guilt, and the oppression and bondage of sin) required this threefold office. Ignorance is healed through the prophetic office, guilt through the priestly, and the oppression and bondage of sin through the kingly. The prophetic light scatters the darkness of error; the merit of the priest removes guilt and obtains reconciliation for us; the power of the king takes away the bondage of sin and death. The prophet shows God to us; the priest leads us to God; and the king joins us together with God, and glorifies us with him. The prophet illuminates the mind by the spirit of enlightenment; the priest soothes the heart and conscience by the spirit of consolation; the king subdues rebellious inclinations by the spirit of sanctification.

Comment

The origins of the "threefold office" of Christ can be traced back to the patristic period; it was during the Reformation era that this began to be developed more fully, not least because it was a convenient way of explaining the significance of Jesus to a lay audience in sermons. The threefold framework allowed the multiple nature of sin and redemption to be explained, and also enabled some basic misunderstandings concerning the person of Christ to be addressed – especially those which resulted from reductionist approaches which omitted important aspects of his identity.

Questions for Study

1 Explain precisely what Turrettini means by referring to Christ as prophet, priest, and king.
2 How does Turrettini use his threefold Christological framework to explore (a) the nature of sin, and (b) the human predicament?
3 Why, according to Turrettini, is Christ able to combine all three offices in his own person?

4.26

Gotthold Ephraim Lessing on the Ditch of History

In this important discussion, published in German in 1777, G. E. Lessing (1729–81) argued that there was no connection between the "accidental truths of history" and the "necessary truths of reason." As a result, the total history of Jesus of Nazareth – including his resurrection – can have no metaphysical significance. Even if this history could be known with total accuracy and certainty (which Lessing doubts in any case), it could not serve as the basis of a philosophical or theological system. The title of the work, "On the Proof of Spirit and Power," refers to a phrase in the writings of Origen, with which Lessing takes issue. See also 4.28, 4.29, 4.30, 4.31, 4.33, 4.36, 4.31.

Origen was quite right when he declared that the Christian religion, on account of its spirit and power, was able to provide a demonstration which was far more divine than anything that Greek dialectic had to offer. For in his period, there was still a continuing power to do miracles among those who lived by Christ's precepts. [...] But I am no longer in the same situation as Origen. I live in the eighteenth century, in which no more miracles happen. [...] The problem is that this demonstration of the "spirit and power" no longer possesses any spirit or power, but has degenerated to human reports of spirit and power. [...]

If no historical truth can be demonstrated, then nothing can be demonstrated by means of historical truths. That is: the accidental truths of history can never become the proof of necessary truths of reason. [...] If I have no objection, on historical grounds, to the statement "Christ raised a dead man to life," must I therefore accept as true "God has a Son who is of the same essence as himself"? What is the connection between not having any objection to the former, and being obliged to believe something against which my reason revolts? [...] I gladly and heartily believe that Christ (against whose resurrection I can raise no significant historical objection) declared himself to be the Son of God, and that his disciples believed him in this matter. For these truths, which are truths of one and the same class, follow naturally on from each other. But to move on from that historical truth to a totally different class of truth, and to ask me to formulate all my metaphysical and moral ideas on its basis, or to expect me to change all my basic ideas about God because I cannot raise any credible argument against the resurrection of Christ – well, if that is not a *metabasis eis allo genos*, then I don't know what Aristotle meant by the phrase.

That, then, is the ugly great ditch [*der garstige breite Graben*] which I cannot cross, however often and however earnestly I have tried to make this leap. If anyone can help me to cross it, I implore him to do so. And so I repeat what I said earlier. I do not for one moment deny that Christ performed miracles. But since the truth of these miracles has completely ceased to be demonstrable by miracles happening in the present, they are no more than reports of miracles. [. . .] I deny that they could and should bind me to have even the smallest faith in the other teachings of Jesus.

So what does bind me? Nothing but the teachings themselves. Eighteen hundred years ago, they were so new, so strange, and so foreign to the entire mass of truth recognized in that period, that nothing less than miracles and fulfilled prophecies would have been needed if people were to take them seriously. [. . .] But what does it matter to me whether this story [*Sage*] is false or true? Its fruits are excellent.

Comment

In this passage, Lessing raises the general problem which is usually known as "faith and history." There are a number of aspects to this issue, and Lessing touches on them in the course of this extract. To begin with, the Gospel accounts of Jesus Christ place him firmly in the past. We are unable to verify those accounts, but are obliged to rely upon the eyewitness reports which underlie the Gospels for our knowledge of Jesus. But, Lessing asked, how reliable are those accounts? Why should we trust reports from the past, when they cannot be verified in the present? However, Lessing argues that the problem goes deeper than this. Even if we could be certain about the past, a new difficulty would arise: what conceivable value has historical knowledge? How can an historical event give rise to ideas? How can anyone make the move from history (which Lessing regards as a collection of accidental and contingent truths) to reason (which is concerned with necessary and universal truths)? Lessing thus argued there was a gap – an "ugly great ditch," to be more precise – between historical and rational truth which could not be bridged. Finally, Lessing poses a series of questions which are existential in their orientation. What, he asks, can the relevance of such an outdated and archaic message be for the modern world?

Questions for Study

1 Outline, in your own words, the difficulties which Lessing sees arising from the traditional Christian insistence upon the person of Jesus being, in some sense, the foundation of the Christian faith.

2 "The accidental truths of history can never become the proof of necessary truths of reason." Locate this statement in the passage. What does Lessing mean by this? How conditioned do you think he is by his Enlightenment beliefs at this point? And what are the implications of this statement for the metaphysical status of history?

3 "That, then, is the ugly great ditch which I cannot cross, however often and however earnestly I have tried to make this leap." Locate this statement within the text. What is this "ditch"? How does it arise? And what are the implications for the question of "faith and history"?

4 What does Lessing mean by his concluding comments about the "fruit" of the story of Jesus?

4.27

F. D. E. Schleiermacher on the "Natural Heresies" of Christianity

The German liberal Protestant theologian Friedrich Schleiermacher (1768–1834) here argues that the "four natural heresies of Christianity" – which he identifies as Docetism and Ebionitism on the Christological side, and Pelagianism and Manicheism on the soteriological – arise from inadequate understandings of the person and work of Christ. In the section reprinted here, Schleiermacher demonstrates the importance of maintaining a critical degree of commonality between Christ and believers, while at the same time acknowledging a fundamental distinction between them. Although the precise historical forms taken by these two kinds of heresy differ from Schleiermacher's presentation, the basic thrust of his argument has found wide acceptance. See also 4.1, 4.7, 4.12, 4.24.

Now, if the distinctive essence of Christianity consists in the fact that in it all religious emotions are related to the redemption wrought by Jesus of Nazareth, there will be two ways in which heresy can arise. That is to say: this fundamental formula will be retained in general (for otherwise the contradiction would be manifest and complete, so that participation in Christian communion could not even be desired), but *either* human nature will be so defined that a redemption in the strict sense cannot be accomplished, *or* the Redeemer will be defined in such a way that He cannot accomplish redemption.

But each of these two cases, again, can appear in two different ways. As regards the former: if people are to be redeemed, they must both be in need of redemption and be capable of receiving it. Now, if one of these conditions is openly stated, but the other implicitly denied, the contradiction at the same time touches the fundamental formula itself, only this is not directly apparent. If, then, in the first place, the need of redemption in human nature, i.e., its inability to bring the feeling of absolute dependence into all human states of consciousness, is stated in such an absolute way that the ability to receive redeeming influences is made actually to disappear, so that human nature is not simultaneously in need of redemption and capable of receiving it, but only becomes capable of receiving it after a complete transformation, this is equivalent to an annulling of our fundamental formula. Now this is the unfailing consequence, if we suppose an Evil-in-itself as being original and opposed to God, and think of human nature as suffering from that inability by reason of a dominion which this original Evil exercises over it; and therefore we call this deviation the Manichean.

But, on the other hand, suppose the ability to receive redemption is assumed so absolutely, and consequently any hindrance to the entry of the God-consciousness becomes so utterly infinitesimal, that at each particular moment in each individual it can be satisfactorily counterbalanced by an infinitesimal overweight. Then the need of redemption is reduced to zero, at least in the sense that it is no longer the need of one single Redeemer, but merely, for each person in one of their weak moments, the need of some other individual who, if only for the moment, is stronger as regards the eliciting of the God-consciousness. Thus redemption would not need to be the work of one particular person, but would be a common work of all for all, in which at most, some would only have a greater share than others; and this aberration we may with good reason call, as above, the Pelagian.

Turn now to the other kind of heresy. If Christ is to be the Redeemer, i.e., the real origin of constant living unhindered evocation of the God-consciousness, so that the participation of all others in it is mediated through Him alone, it is, on the one hand, necessary that He should enjoy an exclusive and peculiar superiority over all others, and, on the other hand, there must also be an essential likeness between Him and all people, because otherwise what He has to impart could not be the same as what they need. Therefore on this side also the general formula can be contradicted in two different ways, because each of these two requisites may be conceived so unlimitedly that the other no longer remains co-posited, but disappears. If the difference between Christ and those who are in need of redemption is made so unlimited that an essential likeness is incompatible with it, then His participation in human nature vanishes into a mere appearance; and consequently our God-consciousness, being something essentially different, cannot be derived from His, and redemption also is only an appearance. Now though the Docetics, properly so called, directly denied only the reality of the body of Christ, yet this likewise excludes the reality of human nature in His person generally, since we never find body and soul given in separation from each other; and therefore we may fitly call this aberration the Docetic. Finally, if on the other hand the likeness of the Redeemer to those who are to be redeemed is made so unlimited that no room is left for a distinctive superiority as a constituent of His being, which must then be conceived under the same form as that of all other people, then there must ultimately be posited in Him also a need of redemption, however absolutely small, and the fundamental relationship is likewise essentially annulled. This aberration we call by the name given to those who are supposed first to have regarded Jesus entirely as an ordinary human being, the Nazarean or Ebionitic.

Comment

Schleiermacher here argues that heresy was that which preserved the *appearance* of Christianity, yet contradicted its *essence*. If, as Schleiermacher suggests, the distinctive essence of Christianity consists in the fact that God has redeemed us through Jesus Christ, and through no one else and in no other way, it must follow that the Christian understanding of God, Jesus Christ, and human nature should be consistent with this understanding of redemption. Thus the Christian understanding of God must be such that God can effect the redemption of humanity through Christ; the Christian understanding of Christ must be such that God may effect our redemption through him; the Christian understanding of humanity must be such that redemption is both possible and genuine. In other words, it is essential that the Christian understanding of God, Christ, humanity is *consistent* with the principle of redemption through Christ alone.

According to Schleiermacher, the rejection or denial of the principle that God has redeemed us through Jesus Christ is nothing less than the rejection of Christianity itself. In other words, to deny that God has redeemed us through Jesus Christ is to deny the most fundamental truth claim which the Christian makes. The distinction between what is *Christian* and what is *not* Christian lies in whether this principle is accepted. The distinction between what is *orthodox* and what is *heretical*, however, lies in how this principle, once conceded and accepted, is understood. In other words, heresy is not a form of unbelief; it is something that arises within the context of faith itself. For Schleiermacher, heresy is fundamentally an *inadequate or inauthentic form of Christian faith*.

Heresy thus arises through accepting the basic principles of the Christian faith, but interpreting its terms in such a way that internal inconsistency results. In other words, the principle is granted, but it is inadequately understood. The principle may be accepted, and yet be interpreted in such a way that:

1 either Christ cannot effect the redemption of humanity; or
2 humanity, which is the object of Christ's work of redemption, cannot be redeemed, in the proper sense of that word.

In the passage under consideration, these points are developed and illustrated with reference to the four "natural" heresies of the Christian faith.

Questions for Study

1 Set out, in your own words, Schleiermacher's understanding of the nature of heresy. Notice how heresy is distinguished from unbelief.
2 What, specifically, does Schleiermacher understand to be the failing of the Ebionite heresy?
3 "If the difference between Christ and those who are in need of redemption is made so unlimited that an essential likeness is incompatible with it, then His participation in human nature vanishes into a mere appearance." Locate this passage within the text. What is the point that Schleiermacher is making? Which of the "four natural heresies" is he describing at this point?

4.28

A. B. Ritschl on the Uniqueness of Jesus Christ

It is generally agreed that the successor to F. D. E. Schleiermacher within German liberal Protestantism was Albrecht Benjamin Ritschl (1822–89). Ritschl's most important work was entitled *The Christian Doctrine of Justification and Reconciliation*, which appeared in three volumes over the period 1870–4. The first volume explored the history of these doctrines; the second, their biblical foundations; and the third set out Ritschl's own views on these matters. This extract is taken from this third volume, and sets out Ritschl's understanding of the uniqueness of Jesus Christ, seen from a liberal Protestant perspective. See also 4.26, 4.27, 4.29, 5.25.

The nature of Christianity as a universal religion is such that *in the Christian view of the world a definite place is assigned to its historical founder*. In the two ethnic religions which come nearest to Christianity (though in different degrees), and which have preserved some recollection of their historical founders, namely in the Persian religion and in the religion of Israel, Zoroaster and Moses are indeed acknowledged as the founders and lawgivers of the faith; but there is no need of a personal confession either of the one or of the other, because for the religions which they founded the religious community is the nation, and the nation is the community. In the universal religions, on the other hand, it is through express recognition of the founder of the religion that membership in the religious community is described and attained. At the same time, in these religions a certain gradation presents itself in the worth and significance of personal adherence to the founder. In Islam it is enough to name the Prophet alongside of God, because for this religion of law he is merely the lawgiver. Nearer to the religious estimate of Jesus Christ in the Christian religion comes the significance which in Buddhism is attached to Sakyamuni Buddha as an incarnation of Deity. But in this case there is the difference that, whereas what Buddha aimed at was not by any means what his followers believe themselves to have received from him, Jesus, on the other hand, had in view for his own Person essentially that significance which is claimed for it in his religious community. In other words, Buddha had no intention of founding a religion; he did not so much as set forth any conception of God, or any explanation of the world in its relation to God; he did not explain how man is to reach a definite attitude towards the world or a definite position in the world: he merely indicated the direction along which man is to achieve his own redemption from the misery of actual existence, namely, by the ascetic annihilation of personal life. A philosophy or ethic such as this, which addresses itself to human freedom, may be the basis of a school, but not of religious fellowship; therefore, the significance it secures for its author is that of the founder of a school. That it was afterwards associated with the Indian idea of God, and that the corresponding idea of Divine incarnation was applied to Buddha and to his successors, was a result utterly foreign to the view of the antagonist of Brahmanism. It is true that within the Christian community there are those who hold exactly the same view with regard to the purpose of Jesus, and the fate which has befallen the doctrine of his Person in the Christian Church. According to their reading of the Gospels, Jesus taught a lofty morality, but in the exercise of this vocation never transgressed the limits of a purely human estimate of himself; only through influences that are wholly external have his followers been led to regard him as an incarnation of the Deity. But this view is historically inaccurate. For beyond all doubt Jesus was conscious of a new and hitherto unknown relation to God, and said so to his disciples; and his aim was to bring his disciples into the same attitude toward the world as his own, and to the same estimate of themselves, that under these conditions he might enlist them in the world-wide mission of the Kingdom of God, which he knew to be not only his own business, but theirs. But this involves the assumption that he himself means more for his disciples than the passing occasion of their religion or a lawgiver for their conduct, who would be of no more account when once the law which he proclaimed was thoroughly learned. In the case of Buddhism, on the other hand, the system as a system does not secure for its founder any abiding significance. For if Buddha himself has attained to that personal annihilation to which he showed his followers the way, he can be remembered by them only as a pattern of past days, because each one becomes himself a Buddha, an enlightened one, that is, he too recognises the worthlessness of existence, and acts accordingly, with a view to his own annihilation.

In Christianity the case is otherwise. The aim of the Christian is conceived as the attainment of eternal life. This means the consistent realisation of the personal self-end, of which the test is that the whole world does not compare in worth with the personal life, and that by the acquisition of spiritual lordship over the world, this, the true worth of life, is vindicated. Now this religious vocation of the members of the Christian community is prefigured in the person of its Founder, and rests upon his person as its abiding source of strength for all imitation of him, because he himself made God's supreme purpose of the union of men in the Kingdom of God the aim of his own personal life; and thereby realised in his own experience that independence toward the world which through him has become the experience of the members of his community. This ideal, the true development of the spiritual personality, cannot be rightly or fully conceived apart from contemplation of him who is the prototype of man's vocation. Thus what in the historically complete figure of Christ we recognise to be the real worth of his existence, gains for ourselves, through the uniqueness of the phenomenon and its normative bearing upon our own religious and ethical destiny, the worth of an abiding rule, since we at the same time discover that only through the impulse and direction we receive from him, is it possible for us to enter into his relation to God and to the world. On the other hand, this specific estimate of their founders, even when known, is quite alien to the ethnic religions, because in these there is not posited as ideal aim the independent development of the personal character to the worth of a whole, as against the natural and particular impulses of life. The genius of an ethnic religion is satisfied if there be participation in the fixed tradition and custom of the nation; and such participation, when regarded as the supreme standard of human fellowship, imposes on personal independence impassable limits. Because this ideal of self-realisation has not come within the horizon of any of the ethnic religions, therefore in none of these has the founder received a place which can be compared with the significance of Christ. Even in the case of Zoroaster and of Moses, the ideal interests of their religions are so bound up with the natural consciousness of belonging to a particular nation, that the decision of the Parsees for Zoroaster, and of the Israelites for Moses, was the inevitable result of hostility toward the Hindus in the one case, and toward the Egyptians in the other.

There is yet another reason why the Person of Christ maintains its place in the Christian view of the world. Christ founds his religion with the claim that he brings the perfect revelation of God, so that beyond what he brings no further revelation is conceivable or is to be looked for. Whoever, therefore, has a part in the religion of Christ in the way Christ himself intended, cannot do other than regard Christ as the Bearer of the final revelation of God. At the same time, this point of view is conclusive only in connection with what has already been set forth. For Islam also claims to be the perfect religion, and yet is content with a superficial recognition of its prophet, to whom, under this title, there is actually no place assigned in the Mohammedan view of the world. Thus the claim Christ makes to the perfect revelation of God in himself is only defined as against the rival claim of Mohammed, by the fact that on the ground of his peculiar relation to God, Christ lived a life of mastery over the world, such as makes possible the community in which each Christian is to attain the similar destiny of the life eternal. Because this goal is not the reward of fulfilling a statutory law, Christ does not count, like Mohammed, merely as a lawgiver. On the contrary, since the aim of the Christian is to be attained under the form of personal freedom, therefore the twofold significance we are compelled to ascribe to Christ as being at once the perfect revealer of God and the manifest [*offenbar*] type of spiritual lordship over the world, finds expression in the single predicate of his Godhead.

Comment

Ritschl's argument is not especially easy to follow, and it is hoped that the following comments may be helpful. For Ritschl, Jesus of Nazareth brings something new to the human situation, something which reason had hitherto neglected. "Jesus was conscious of a *new and hitherto unknown relation to God*." Where the rationalists of the Enlightenment believed in a universal rational religion, of which individual religions were at best shadows, Ritschl argues that Christianity possesses certain definite theological and cultural characteristics as a historical religion, which are partly due to the influence of Jesus of Nazareth. Christ occupies a unique position towards all those within the community of faith, expressed in a religious judgment concerning his status. Those who "believe in Christ" (in Ritschl's sense of the phrase) participate in the kingdom of God, and are therefore reconciled to God, sharing in the same kind of relationship with God and the world as the founder of their religion.

Questions for Study

1 What points does Ritschl establish through his comparison of Jesus and Mohammed?
2 "The aim of the Christian is conceived as the attainment of eternal life." Locate this passage within the text. What does Ritschl mean by this statement? How does he relate this goal to Jesus? And how does he use this to explore the status and identity of Jesus?
3 In what sense is Jesus "unique," according to Ritschl?

4.29

Martin Kähler on the Historical Jesus

Martin Kähler's important work *Der sogenannte historische Jesus und der geschichtliche, biblische Christus* ("The So-Called Historical Jesus and the Historic, Biblical Christ") appeared in 1892. A mere 45 pages in length, it represents the expanded form of a lecture originally given in 1892. Kähler (1835–1912) here argues that it is the "Christ who is preached" rather than the "historical Jesus" which is of decisive importance to Christian faith. In doing so, he unleashed a theological critique of the "life of Jesus movement" which had a profound influence on writers such as Barth and Bultmann. See also 4.26, 4.28, 4.30, 4.33, 4.36, 4.41.

"Christ is Lord." Neither flesh nor blood can attain, sustain, or impart this certainty. Jesus himself said this to Peter after his confession (Matthew 16: 17), and he said it also as he reproached the unbelieving Jews (John 6: 43–44); it was confirmed by Peter's denial in the outer court of the High Priest; later, it was said by Paul to his congregations in full expectation of their assent (1 Corinthians 12: 3). Yet, wherever this certainty has arisen and exercised influence, it has clearly been linked to another conviction – that Jesus is the crucified, risen, and living Lord. And when we ask at what point in their discussions the historians deal with this certainty, we find that they do not begin with the much disputed and disconnected final narratives of the evangelists, but with the experience of Paul. They determine the constant faith of the early church, to the extent that they can, on the basis of the testimonies and traces left by those early witnesses. The risen Lord is not the historical Jesus behind the Gospels, but the Christ of the apostolic preaching, of the entire New Testament. And if this Lord is called "Christ" (Messiah), it is to confess his historical mission, or as we say today, his vocation, or as our forebears said, meaning the same thing, his "threefold office," that is to say: to confess his unique, supra-historical significance for the whole of humanity [*das Bekenntnis zu seiner einzigarten, übergeschichtlichen Bedeuting für die ganze Menschheit*]. Christians became certain that Jesus was the Messiah, the Christ, in total opposition to public opinion, not just in relation to the idea of the Messiah (that is, the way the Messiah was understood and what one expected of him), but also with regard to the person of this Jesus of Nazareth. This was as true then as it is today. When Christians tried to make the Messiahship of Jesus credible in their sermons and then in the letters and Gospels, they always made use of two kinds of evidence: personal testimony to his resurrection, based on experience, and the witness of the Scriptures. As the living Lord, he was for them the Messiah of the Old Covenant.

And so we speak of the historic Christ of the Bible [*von dem geschichtlichen Christus der Bibel*]. The historical Jesus [*historische Jesus*], as we see him in his earthly ministry, certainly did not win from his disciples a faith capable of witnessing to him, but only a very shaky loyalty, easily prone to panic and betrayal. It is clear that they were all born again, like Peter, into a living hope only through the resurrection of Jesus from the dead (1 Peter 1: 3) and that they needed the gift of the Spirit to "bring to remembrance" what Jesus had said, before they were able to understand what he had already given them and to grasp what they had been unable to bear (John 14: 26; 16: 12, 13). It is clear that they did not subsequently go out into the world to make Jesus the head of a "school" by propagating his teachings, but to witness to his person and his eternal significance for every person, in the same way that it is certain that his first followers could understand his person and mission, his deeds and his word as the offer of God's grace and faithfulness only after he appeared to them in his state of fulfillment – in which he was himself the fruit and the eternal bearer of his own work of universal and lasting significance, a work (to be exact) whose most difficult and decisive part was the *end* of the historical Jesus. Even though we once knew the Messiah according to the flesh, now we no longer see him in this way (2 Corinthians 5: 16).

This is the first characteristic of his influence, that he won faith from his disciples. And the second characteristic is, and continues to be, that this faith was confessed. His promise depends upon this (Romans 10: 9–10), as does our own decision [*Entscheidung*] of faith and the history of Christianity. The real Christ, that is, the influential Christ, with whom millions in history have had fellowship in a childlike faith, along with the great witnesses of faith as they struggled, gained, triumphed, and proclaimed for this relationship – the real Christ is the preached Christ [*Der wirkliche Christus ist der gepredigte Christus*]. The preached Christ, however, is precisely the one who is believed in. He is the Jesus whom the eyes of faith see in every step he takes and through every syllable he utters – the Jesus whose image we impress upon our minds because we both would and do have fellowship with him, as the ascended and living one. From the features of that portrait, which has deeply impressed itself upon the memory of his own people, the person of our living Savior, the person of the Word incarnate, of God revealed [*die Person unseres lebendigen Heilandes an, die Person des fleischgewordenen Wortes, des offenbaren Gottes*], gazes upon us.

Comment

Kähler states his two objectives in this work as follows: first, to criticize and reject the errors of the "life of Jesus" movement; and second, to establish the validity of an alternative approach, this latter being by far the more important. The work may be regarded as an attempt to establish a secure basis for faith in the midst of the crisis which he perceived to be developing in the final decade of the nineteenth century, based partly on the kind of issues raised by G. E. Lessing's famous essay on faith and history (4.26). Kähler rightly saw that the provisional Jesus of the academic historian cannot become the object of faith. Yet how can Jesus Christ be the authentic basis and content of Christian faith, when historical science can never establish certain knowledge concerning the historical Jesus? How can faith be based upon an historical event without being vulnerable to the charge of historical relativism? It was precisely these questions which Kähler addressed in this famous work.

Kähler makes an important and influential distinction between two senses of "historical," which cannot be easily explained in English. The German term *historisch* is used to refer to Jesus as the object of critical-historical investigation, whereas the German term *geschichtlich* is used to refer to Jesus as the object of faith. Of the various suggested English equivalents for the word-pair *historisch–geschichtlich*, two may be noted:

1 *Historisch* may be translated as "objective-historical," and *geschichtlich* as "existential-historical." This brings out the distinction between the objective empirical facts of history and their perceived significance for the individual.
2 Alternatively, *historisch* may be translated as "historical," and *geschichtlich* as "historic." This translation emphasizes the distinction between an event which is located in history and an event which makes history.

Questions for Study

1 According to Kähler, can faith be based upon the historical figure of Jesus? You may need to explore various possible meanings of the word "historical" in answering this question.
2 "The risen Lord is not the historical Jesus behind the Gospels, but the Christ of the apostolic preaching, of the entire New Testament." Locate this passage within the text. What does Kähler mean by this? In what sense is the "preached Christ" the real Christ?
3 What does Kähler mean when he speaks of the "end" of the historical Jesus?

4.30

George Tyrrell on the Christ of Liberal Protestantism

The Roman Catholic modernist writer George Tyrrell (1861–1909) here argues for the futility of the liberal Protestant approach to the "historical Jesus," pointing out that it simply involves projecting the views and values of modern scholars onto the distant historical figure of Jesus. His comment about Adolf von Harnack and the "deep well" is particularly well known. See also 2.38, 4.26, 4.28, 4.29, 4.31, 4.33, 4.36.

The Jesus of the school of critics, represented today by Harnack and Bousset, was a Divine Man because He was full of the Spirit of God; full of Righteousness. He came (it is assumed rather than proved) at a time when the Jews were full of apocalyptic expectations as to the coming of the Messiah, who was to avenge them of their enemies and establish a more or less miraculous and material Kingdom of God upon earth. He Himself seems to have shared this view in a spiritual form, translating it from material to ethical terms. As destined by a Divine vocation to inaugurate a reign of Righteousness, a Kingship of God over men's hearts and consciences, He felt Himself to be the true, because the spiritual, Messiah. With difficulty He trained a few of His followers to this conception of the Kingdom and the Christ. He went about doing good (even working cures which He supposed to be miraculous) and teaching goodness. The essence of His Gospel was the Fatherhood of God and the Brotherhood of man; or else the two great Commandments of the law – the love of God and of one's neighbour; or else the Kingdom of God that is within us. True, these were platitudes of contemporary Jewish piety, and even of pagan philosophy. But Jesus drove them home to the heart by the force of personal example and greatness of character – above all, by dying for His friends and for these ethical principles. Of course He was, to some extent, of His time. He believed in miracles, in diabolic possession; above all, He believed in the immediate end of the world; and a great deal of His ethics, coloured by that belief, was the ethics of a crisis. But these were but accidents of His central idea and interest, in regard to which we may say He was essentially modern, so far as our rediscovery of the equation Religion = Righteousness is modern, not to say Western and Teutonic.

For this almost miraculous modernity the first century was not prepared. No sooner was the Light of the World kindled than it was put under a bushel. The Pearl of Great Price fell into the dustheap of Catholicism, not without the wise permission of Providence, desirous to preserve it till the day when Germany should rediscover it and separate it from its useful but deplorable accretions. Thus between Christ and early Catholicism there is not a bridge but a chasm. Christianity did not cross the bridge; it fell into the chasm and remained there, stunned, for nineteen centuries. The explanation of this sudden fall – more sudden because they have pushed Catholicism back to the threshold of the Apostolic age – is the crux of Liberal Protestant critics. [. . .]

It was to the credit of their hearts, if to the prejudice of their scientific indifference, that these critics were more or less avowedly actuated by apologetic interests. They desired to strip Jesus of His medieval regalia, and to make Him acceptable to a generation that had lost faith in the miraculous and any conception of another life that was not merely a complement, sanction and justification of this life. They wanted to bring Jesus into the nineteenth century as the Incarnation of its ideal of Divine Righteousness, i.e. of all the highest principles and aspirations that ensure the healthy progress of civilization. They wanted to acquit Him of that exclusive and earthscorning otherworldliness, which had led men to look on His religion as the foe of progress and energy, and which came from confusing the accidental form with the essential substance of His Gospel. With eyes thus preoccupied they could only find the German in the Jew; a moralist in a visionary; a professor in a prophet; the nineteenth century in the first; the natural in the supernatural. Christ was the ideal man; the Kingdom of Heaven, the ideal humanity. As the rationalistic presupposition had strained out, as spurious, the miraculous elements of the Gospel, so the moralistic presupposition strained out everything but modern morality. That alone was the substance, the essence, of Christianity – *das Wesen des Christentums*. If God remained, it was only the God of moralism and rationalism – the correlative of the Brotherhood of man; not the God of Moses, of Abraham, Isaac and Jacob; of David and the prophets.

[. . . Yet] here the Liberal Protestant critics failed no less than the positively anti-Christian critics. Their hypothesis was an article of faith, not an instrument of inquiry. If they have been beaten off the field we need not, perhaps, set it down to the severer detachment of their conquerors, but to the stricter application of that critical method which they invoked.

It is by that method that Johannes Weiss and his followers have been forced back, very unwillingly in most cases, to the eschatological and apocalyptic interpretation of the Gospel. Very unwillingly, because it destroys the hope of smoothing away the friction between Christianity and the present age; because, in closing the chasm between the Gospel and early Catholicism, it makes the Christianity of Christ, in all essentials, as unacceptable as that of Catholicism.

Of this state of things Loisy was not slow to take advantage in *L'évangile et l'église*, directed against the Liberal Protestantism of Harnack's *Wesen des Christentums*. The Christ that Harnack sees, looking back through nineteen centuries of Catholic darkness, is only the reflection of a Liberal Protestant face, seen at the bottom of a deep well.

Comment

This important comment on the development of the "Quest of the Historical Jesus" exposes some of the more worrying assumptions that underlay the movement, most notably its concept of the early corruption of a "primitive gospel" at the hands of the early church. Adolf von Harnack had argued that the simple gospel of Jesus had become complicated and muddled through the Hellenistic assumptions of the early church; Tyrrell argues that Harnack introduces just as many distortions and confusions through his own attempt to reconstruct the "historical Jesus."

Questions for Study

1 What is Tyrrell's most fundamental criticism of the liberal Protestant quest for the historical Jesus?
2 "The Pearl of Great Price fell into the dustheap of Catholicism, not without the wise permission of Providence, desirous to preserve it till the day when Germany should rediscover it and separate it from its useful but deplorable accretions." Locate this statement within the text. What is the point being made here? Who does Tyrrell have in mind in making this stinging criticism?
3 "The Christ that Harnack sees, looking back through nineteen centuries of Catholic darkness, is only the reflection of a Liberal Protestant face, seen at the bottom of a deep well." Locate this famous statement within the text. What does Tyrrell mean by this? How does he build up to this conclusion?

4.31

Albert Schweitzer on the Failure of the "Quest of the Historical Jesus"

In his work *The Quest of the Historical Jesus*, Albert Schweitzer (1875–1965) argues that the "Jesus of history" movement has failed. According to Schweitzer, Jesus remains a partly unknown, distant, and strange figure, whose basic features cannot be reconstructed on the basis of the methods and approaches offered by the nineteenth century. See also 4.26, 4.29, 4.30, 4.33, 4.36.

Anyone who wants to talk about negative theology will not find it difficult to do so here. For there is nothing more negative than the result of the "Life of Jesus movement" [*Leben-Jesu-Forschung*]. The Jesus of Nazareth who came forward as the Messiah, who preached the ethic of the Kingdom of God, who founded the Kingdom of Heaven upon earth, and died to give his work its dignity, never existed. He is a figure who was thrown up by rationalism, brought to life by liberalism, and clothed by modern theology using the historical method.

This portrait [*Bild*] has not been destroyed from the outside. It has fallen to pieces internally, having been shattered, disintegrated through the actual historical problems which came to the surface one after another. Despite all the ingenuity, skill, inspiration and force which was applied to them, they refused to conform to fit the pattern on the basis of which the Jesus of the theology of the last hundred and thirty years had been constructed. As soon had they been laid to rest, they appeared again in a new form. Thoroughgoing skepticism and the thoroughgoing eschatology [*Der konsequente Skeptizismus und die konzequente Eschatologie*] have just brought this work of destruction to completion by connecting the problems together so that they form a system and so making an end of the "divide and rule" of modern theology, which undertook to solve each of them separately, that is, in a less difficult form. Henceforth it is no longer acceptable to take one problem out of the series and dispose of it by itself, since the weight of the whole hangs upon each.

Whatever the definitive solution of this may be, this can be said: the historical Jesus [*historische Jesus*], who future criticism, which takes as its starting-point the problems which have been recognized and conceded, can never render modern theology the services which it claimed from its own half-historical, half-modern, Jesus. He will be a Jesus, who was Messiah, and lived as such, either on the basis of a literary fiction of the earliest Evangelist, or on the basis of a purely eschatological-messianic conception.

In both cases, he will not be a Jesus Christ to whom the religious present can relate in any recognizable manner, in terms of its customs, thoughts, and ideas, as it did with the Jesus of its own making. He is also no figure which can be created by a historical treatment so sympathetic and universally intelligible to people in general. The historical Jesus will be a stranger and a riddle to our time.

The "Life of Jesus Movement" has a remarkable history. It set out to find the historical Jesus, believing that when it had found him, it could bring him straight into our time as a teacher and Savior. It loosed the bands by which he had been fettered for centuries to the rock of ecclesiastical doctrine, and was delighted to see life and movement returned to his figure again, and the historical Jesus coming to meet it. But he did not remain there, but passed by our time and returned to his own. What startled and dismayed the theology of the last forty years was that, despite all of its forced and arbitrary interpretations, it could not keep him in our time, but had to let him go. He returned to his own time, not through any historical ingenuity, but by the same inevitable necessity by which a pendulum, once let go, returns to its original position.

The historical foundation of Christianity as set out by rationalism, liberalism, and modern theology, no longer exists. But this does not mean that Christianity has lost its historical foundation. The work which historical theology felt itself obliged to carry out, and which fell to pieces just as it was nearing completion, was only the facade of the real and unshakeable historical foundation which is independent of any historical confirmation or justification.

Jesus means something to our world because a powerful spiritual force [*gewaltige geistige Strömung*] derives from him and flows through our time also. This fact can neither be disproved nor confirmed by any historical discovery. It is the solid foundation [*Realgrund*] of Christianity.

Only some thought that Jesus could come to mean more to our time if he were to enter it, living as a human being just like ourselves [*als ein Mensch unser Menscheit*]. That is not possible. In the first place, because this Jesus never existed. But also, although historical knowledge can no doubt bring greater clarity to a spiritual existence which is already present, it cannot create such a spiritual life in the first place. History [*Geschichte*] can destroy the present, or reconcile the present to the past. It can even, at least to a certain extent, allow the present to project itself into the past. But it cannot construct the present. [. . .]

We are experiencing what Paul experienced. In the very moment when we were coming so close to the historical Jesus – closer than ever before – and were already stretching out our hands to draw him into our own time, we have been obliged to give up the attempt and acknowledge our failure in that paradoxical saying: "If we have known Christ after the flesh yet henceforth we know him no more." And further we must be prepared to find that the historical knowledge of the personality and life of Jesus will not be helpful to, but perhaps even a nuisance to religion.

But it is not the historically known [*historisch erkannte*] Jesus, but Jesus as one who is spiritually resurrected within humanity, who can mean something for our time and be of use to it. It is not the historical Jesus, but the spirit which goes forth from him and which strives for new influence and rule in the spirits of people, which overcomes the world.

It is not given to history to distinguish what is of lasting and eternal importance in the being of Jesus from the historical forms in which it worked itself out, and to introduce this as a living influence into our world. It has labored in vain at this undertaking. Just as a water-plant flowers beautifully so long as it is growing in the water, but once torn from its roots, withers and becomes unrecognizable, so it is with the historical Jesus when he is torn from the soil of eschatology, and the attempt is made to conceive him "historically" as someone who belongs nowhere in time. What is of lasting and eternal importance in Jesus is absolutely independent of historical knowledge and can only be understood by contact with his spirit, which is still at work in the world. We possess true knowledge of Jesus only to the extent that we possess the spirit of Jesus.

Jesus as a total historical personality remains a stranger to our time. However, his spirit, which lies hidden in his words, is known simply and directly. Every saying contains in its own way the whole Jesus. The very strangeness and absoluteness in which he stands before us makes it easier for individuals to find their own personal standpoint in relation to him.

It was feared that admitting the claims of eschatology would abolish the significance of his words for our time, so there was a hectic enthusiasm to discover in them any elements that could be considered as not eschatologically conditioned. So there was great rejoicing when any sayings were found, the wording of which did not absolutely imply an eschatological connection. Something of value in them had been saved from future destruction. [. . .]

The modern "lives of Jesus" are too general in their scope. They aim to give the total impression of the life of Jesus on an entire community. But the historical Jesus, as he is depicted in the Gospels, influenced individuals by the individual word. They understood him so far as it was necessary for them to understand, without forming any conception of his life as a whole, since this in its ultimate aims remained a mystery even for the disciples. [. . .]

It is a good thing that the historical Jesus should overthrow the modern Jesus, and that it should revolt against the modern spirit and send upon earth, not peace, but a sword. He was not a teacher or a disputer, but someone who commands and rules [*Gebieter und Herrscher*]. It was because he was so in his inner being that he could think of himself as the "son of Man." That was only the temporally conditioned expression [*zeitlich bedingte Ausdruck*] of the fact that he was someone who commands and rules. The names in which men expressed their recognition of him as such – "Messiah," "Son of Man," "Son of God" – have become for us historical parables. We can find no way of expressing what he means for us.

He comes to us as someone who is unknown and nameless, just as he came to those by the lakeside, who did not know who he was. He speaks to us the same word: "Follow me!" and directs us to the tasks which he has to fulfill for our time. He commands. And to those who obey Him, whether they are wise or simple, he will reveal himself in whatever they must do, struggle, and suffer in his fellowship. And they shall experience who he is as an inexpressible mystery. [. . .]

Comment

Schweitzer's *Geschichte der Leben-Jesu-Forschung* ("Quest of the Historical Jesus") succeeded in highlighting the deficiencies of the "Life of Jesus" movement in a manner which was more thoroughgoing than anything that had been seen before. Schweitzer, by bringing together the results of the critical study of the life of Jesus, erected a monument to the "Life of Jesus" movement which actually turned out to be its gravestone, precisely because the full coherence of the case against the movement was now obvious. Schweitzer did not, in fact, add to the history which he so carefully documented; rather, he brought it to an end by demonstrating its inner tensions and contradictions. Schweitzer did not need to employ extensive dogmatic arguments (such as those of Martin Kähler, noted at 4.29) in reaching his conclusions: the case was established simply on the basis of the history of the *Leben-Jesu-Forschung* itself, which was shown to have reconstructed the "historical Jesus" on the basis of the assumptions of its authors. Every portrait of Jesus produced by a New Testament scholar seemed to look remarkably like a self-portrait.

Questions for Study

1 Schweitzer is strongly skeptical about the possibility of reconstructing the historical figure of Jesus. At what points in the passage does this skepticism become especially obvious?
2 One of the themes which Schweitzer develops is that Jesus would seem a strange figure to the modern world. Give some examples of sections of this text which illustrate this. What point does Schweitzer make in this way?
3 "He comes to us as someone who is unknown and nameless." Locate this statement within the text. What does Schweitzer mean by this? How does this conclusion follow from the kinds of argument developed within the text?

4.32

Peter Taylor Forsyth on the Person of Christ

The Christology of liberal Protestantism placed an emphasis upon the humanity of Jesus, which was occasionally expressed in terms of sharing the faith of Jesus, rather than having faith in Christ. In this critique of such trends, P. T. Forsyth (1848–1921) argues that this approach is without historical foundation or justification. See also 4.29, 4.36, 4.41.

There is nothing we are told more often by those who would discard an evangelical faith than this – that we must now do what scholarship has only just enabled us to do, and return to the religion of Jesus. We are bidden to go back to practise Jesus' own personal religion, as distinct from the Gospel of Christ, from a gospel which calls him its faith's object, and not its subject, founder or classic only. We must learn to believe not *in* Christ, but *with* Christ, we are told. [...]

Let us observe what is the effect of the most recent views about the origin of Christianity upon this point, upon the plea that the first form of Christianity was the so-called religion of Jesus. I refer to the new religious–historical school of Germany. [...] There is one great service which this religious–historical school has rendered. It has destroyed the fiction of the nineteenth century that there was ever a time in the earliest history of the Church when it cultivated the religion of Jesus as distinct from the Gospel of Christ. The school, of course, may believe itself able to insulate that religion of Jesus and cultivate it, to disengage it from the gospels by a critical process, and preach it to a world pining for a simple creed rescued from the Apostles. That is another matter which I do not here discuss. But it is a great thing to have it settled that, as far as the face value of our record goes, and apart from elaborate critical constructions of them, such imitation of the faith of Jesus never existed in the very first Church; but that, as far back as we can go, we find only the belief and worship of a risen, redeeming, and glorified Christ, whom they could wholly trust but only very poorly imitate; and in his relation to God could not imitate at all.

Comment

Forsyth was a British theologian with a particular interest in German-language theology, who believed that the ideas developed by Martin Kähler needed to be taken very seriously. In this passage, we find a significant criticism of the assumptions of the "Quest of the Historical Jesus," linked with some pithy comments concerning the identity of Jesus. Forsyth is especially critical of those wishing to reclaim the "religion of Jesus," meaning the personal faith of Jesus in God, rather than the religion about Jesus, otherwise known as Christianity.

Questions for Study

1 What comments does Forsyth offer concerning those who believe it is possible and necessary to rediscover and reclaim the "religion of Jesus"?
2 Forsyth makes an appeal to history in his assertion that "we find only the belief and worship of a risen, redeeming, and glorified Christ" in early Christian history. Locate this statement within the text. Why does Forsyth appeal to history in this way? And what point does he hope to make by doing so?
3 Speaking of Christ, Forsyth comments that: "in his relation to God, [humanity] could not imitate [him] at all." Locate this text. What does Forsyth mean by this? And why is it so important for his understanding of the nature of Christian faith, and the person of Jesus himself?

4.33

Ernst Troeltsch on Faith and History

In this essay, which was first published in German in 1910, Ernst Troeltsch (1865–1923) sets out the new questions dealing with "faith and history" which Christian theology needed to address. The issues explored here have been of considerable importance in relation to understanding the way in which the historical event of Jesus Christ has been, and continues to be, of central importance to Christian life and thought. See also 4.26, 4.29, 4.30, 4.36, 4.41.

A. The Historical Connections of Christian Faith

A particularly difficult problem for current religious thought is posed by the connection of faith with historical matters. Religion is understood and experienced as a *present* religion, as a certainty about God and the eternal world which is apprehended now through inner experience. It is felt to be a difficulty that this experience of God is supposed to depend on the mediation of historical personages and forces, and to include a religious appreciation of historical matters. When the problem is posed in this manner, the first question that arises is what historical connections are actually asserted and how these connections relate to the essential aspects of the Christian faith. From the standpoint of the psychology of religion the following points come to mind:

(a) Faith is always faith in a concrete thought-content. This thought-content never originates solely from the individual subject. On the contrary, the richer and stronger it is, the more it is the communal work of great epochs of intellectual history and of whole generations, or of outstanding personalities that have profited from these communal achievements. Faith feels a need to gather up this whole world of ideas in its starting point and to embody it in an archetype, in order always to be able to rectify and to revitalize itself. This archetype is naturally the personality of the founding prophet or revealer. On the higher levels of religion, moreover, faith becomes increasingly the appropriation of outstanding personages. As its requirements increase, its need for support from personalities that supply direction and impetus increases also. Faith therefore depends upon history, but not only for sustenance and information; its own self-understanding depends upon history, and within history upon the embodiment of revelation to which it looks. Without a conscious relationship to Christ the Christian faith is unthinkable, even though one's faith in God may be regarded as resting upon its own inner evidence and power. The Christian faith originated in the historical disclosure of the life of God, and for the sake of clarity and power it must be constantly referred back to this foundation, which is vitally present to the imagination. Even though some individuals may be able to forego this historical referral because they are carried along by the power of the community, the community as a whole cannot forego it if the community is to retain its vital force.

(b) Christian faith is a redemption through faith in the God who reveals himself in Christ. Through the powers of faith communicated to us by Christ, the Christian faith raises men to a higher level of intellectual, moral, and religious strength, where confidence of victory prevails and where worldly sorrow and the consciousness of guilt are overcome. This means the individual experiences something that elevates and liberates him, something that is not merely a product of his own efforts but that approaches him from the outside with a superior power. Of course, only his own living, actual faith in God himself redeems the individual, but he does not puzzle his way to this faith on his own. He receives it as a liberating and uplifting force through religious impressions that impinge upon him and that essentially have Christ as their starting point and authentication. Even in its redemptive aspect, faith must cling to the historical connection with the sources from which it derives this liberating impulse, the power to provide certainty – in short, the whole wealth of these ideas.

(c) The Christian faith has its goal in the creation of a great community of humanity which strengthened and elevated through faith, is at the same time united in a common recognition of the divine will to which it owes its existence and by which it is directed to mutual works of love. Such an ethical community requires means of solidarity and demarcation. These means can lie only in the realization and common recognition of the historical powers that have brought it into being. At any rate, such means are necessary so long as this community has to broaden itself through conflict. The situation might be different if this community were a victorious power naturally present in all and carrying all before it. Such a state of affairs, however, is unthinkable on earth. Even the ethical community of faith necessitates a conscious historical connection with the foundation that keeps the community together.

(d) Christian faith at the same time maintains, for its propagation and consolidation, a Christian cultus. This is unavoidable if religion is to stay alive. As a means of illustration and edification, and as a classical archetype, this cultus is bound, in the first instance, to cultivate the memory of the origin and personality of the founder, the revealer, the hero. However else the cultus may utilize forces of the present day, it always remains bound to the historical foundations and their realization.

(e) The faith of Christianity regards itself as the completion of revelation and redemption, and hence must take a stand regarding the faith of other circles of religious belief, which, on their higher levels, likewise depend on revelatory personalities and a content of redemptive faith. The doctrine of the church has taken such a stand by regarding the Christian revelation and redemption as the supernatural restoration of the perfect beginning of history; and by designating the non-Christian religions, insofar as they contain elements of truth, as postulates and products of vestigial reason, and insofar as they contain elements of untruth, as products of sinful human nature left to its own devices. Even when this Christian philosophy of history is abandoned, some sort of philosophy of history must be taken into account; it remains necessary to relate the Christian faith in revelation and redemption to the non-Christian religions in such a way that Christianity can maintain the conviction of its supreme validity.

All these arguments entail the essential and inseparable connection of faith with history and the necessity of a religious view of history. From time to time it may well be necessary to relax these historical connections and to make room for one's own religious creativity. But, basically, innovations will hardly be more than new positions regarding history and new fruitful applications of what was already given. To abandon history would be tantamount to faith's abandoning itself and settling for the fleeting and trivial religious stirrings produced by a subjectivity left to its own resources. The earliest Christian era established these historical connections by setting off Jesus, the church, and the Bible from the natural course of ordinary history; and secured the permanence of the connection by making these historical elements divine. The connection with history, then, was forced by psychological requirements immanent in faith itself.

B. Objections to Such Historical Relationships

Until modern times, the Christian faith was content to bear these historical connections. While interpretations differed, faith always found its strongest support in them. Even when the content of faith was transformed into a pure religion of the "now" (*Gegenwartsreligion*), the historical connections were not abolished. The modern world first raised fundamental objections. They are the following:

(a) In every area the modern world is the world of individual autonomy. In every field, and hence in religion, compelling personal insight into the universal validity of judgements is the means by which the modern world attains certainty. Religious autonomy can lead to universal judgements and unanimous conviction only when religious truth is contained in the nature of reason itself, and hence shares the universal validity of the latter; that is, if it can be derived from reason as such. This attitude implies a departure from the historical authority: faith is put on its own. It further implies that the content of faith is a universally valid conceptual necessity that follows from the general nature of reason. If autonomous assent to that content is to be possible, faith must be a present self-apprehension of the religious content of reason. Otherwise faith would be formally an unworthy belief in authority and materially a mere attachment to accidental historical occurrences whose spheres of influence we have simply been born into. The age of autonomy and science emancipates itself from mere positive authority and from the historical accident of birth.

(b) The analysis supplied by the psychology of religion, which tries to view faith from a scientific, psychological viewpoint, shows us that in reality faith can be connected only with what is present and eternal, and never with what is merely past and transitory. Whenever faith adheres to historical facts, it alters these into non-historical realities, into miracles that proclaim the eternal purposes of God or into human incarnations of the divine, into transfigurations or resurrections of the historical in which the historical is only the veiling or revealing of the eternal. In addition to establishing historical connections, dogma pertaining to Christ, the church, and the

Bible constitutes above all an abrogation of the historicity of these entities and their transformation into timeless metaphysical potencies. This procedure can be continued, however, only so long as the ostensible historical bases do not become the object of real historical research, which would show them to be, like all historical data, relative and conditioned. As soon as historical research is thus employed, the historical and the present separate. Only the latter can be a direct object of faith.

(c) A truly historical consideration of historical matters, such as was unknown to the ancient church and to the Middle Ages, not only shows that such data are relative and conditioned but even makes them objects of criticism. We do not possess the facts themselves but only the traditions concerning the facts. The task is critically to reconstruct from these traditions what probably happened in reality. But the picture of what happened becomes uncertain and shifting as a result of this critical treatment. The upshot can be an utterly unrecognizable opinion or a denial of the alleged facts themselves. A decision can be reached only through scholarly examination, which by its nature is accessible to few, and whose results are by no means assured, since it depends on religious traditions passed on from uncritical ages and social classes. Faith, however, cannot tolerate any uncertainty or dependence on erudition. Faith, therefore, retreats to positions that are not subject to historical criticism.

(d) Furthermore, modern Christianity with its various intermingled denominations is itself historically segmented. The Catholic doctrine of the sole truth of Catholicism and the Old Protestant doctrine of the sole truth of its Bible-Christianity no longer have a place in the general consciousness. They have been replaced by the demand for toleration and, consequently, by a certain relativization of all the historical forms of Christianity. In this toleration and the relativism connected with it, there is implicit a standpoint above all these particular historical forms. This standpoint lies above these particular forms only because it does not itself lie in history, but in present conviction on the basis of which relative values can be assessed and tolerated. Modern tolerance and relativism may also be due to a complete absence of conviction, which give full play to the different historical forms because there is no fixed standard by which they might be measured. At any rate, there is a tendency toward emancipation from history in the modern idea of tolerance.

(e) Difficulties arise not merely from the relation of Christianity to its own historical elements, but also from its relation to the other historical religions. Christianity appears more and more as one religion among many. This results either in complete skeptical relativism or in the attainment of a general concept of religious truth by which the different historical manifestations are measured. Such a concept derives its validity not from any historical foundation or authority, but from its own inner necessity and correctness. Here again there is a liberation of religion from history.

(f) All these difficulties, which grow out of religious thought itself, coincide with a general frame of mind that is sensitive to the oppressiveness of history and historical erudition. This historical erudition will not allow us direct, ingenuous, and living creativity; instead, it stifles every such innovation with historical comparisons and relations. As a result, the desire for freedom from history characterizes the temper of the times, in reaction to an excess of historical thought and scholarship. Add to this the effects of the temporal and spatial expansion of the historical horizon, which knows a stay of humanity on earth for more than a hundred thousand years and the prospect of a future stay of indefinite length, presumably lasting till the earth becomes uninhabitable. Christianity now appears as only another wave in the ebb and flow of the largely unknown history of mankind. Religious conviction cannot permanently attach itself to a particular historical phenomenon of this sort.

For all these reasons the problem of history is almost more difficult for faith than the problem of modern metaphysics and the modern natural sciences. History presents modern life with a truly serious and grave problem that, like both the others, works for a manifold transformation of our religious thought. The old attitude toward history can no longer be maintained. That the history of humanity reaches through immeasurable stretches of time, that all historical occurrences are alike conditioned and temporal, and that the principles of historical criticism are universally dominant – all these points must be admitted. Amid such concessions the question comes very much to the fore how the historical connections of faith are to stand their ground.

Comment

Ernst Troeltsch argued strongly for the need to study Christianity as a historical phenomenon, which was subject to the same principles of historical inquiry as any other discipline. This means that Christianity is seen as one religion among many, with a founder who was a human being, analogous to others. In this essay, Troeltsch draws out some of the implications of this approach.

Questions for Study

1 Why does Troeltsch insist on approaching Christianity in this historical manner?
2 What specific issues does Troeltsch envisage as arising from this approach?
3 'We do not possess the facts themselves but only the traditions concerning the facts.'' Locate this text within the passage. What does Troeltsch mean by this? And what are its implications?

4.34

Dorothy L. Sayers on Christology and Dogma

In this analysis of the relation of the divinity and humanity of Christ, originally delivered as a lecture in England in 1940, Dorothy L. Sayers (1893–1957) argued for their mutual importance in relation to our knowledge of God. Using the rise of Nazism in Germany under Adolf Hitler as an example, she argues that claims to moral or cultural authority must be grounded in something intrinsic to the person of Christ. Otherwise, Christ is judged by moral and cultural principles, instead of acting as their basis. See also 1.5, 4.8, 4.14, 5.26.

That you cannot have Christian principles without Christ is becoming increasingly clear, because their validity as principles depends on Christ's authority; and as we have seen, the Totalitarian States, having ceased to believe in Christ's authority, are logically quite justified in repudiating Christian principles. If "the average man" is required to "believe in Christ" and accept His authority for "Christian principles", it is surely relevant to inquire who or what Christ is, and why His authority should be accepted. But the question, "What think ye of Christ?" lands the average man at once in the very knottiest kind of dogmatic riddle. It is quite useless to say that it doesn't matter particularly who or what Christ was or by what authority He did those things, and that even if He was only a man, He was a very nice man and we ought to live by His principles: for that is merely Humanism, and if the "average man" in Germany chooses to think that Hitler is a nicer sort of man with still more attractive principles, the Christian Humanist has no answer to make.

It is not true at all that dogma is "hopelessly irrelevant" to the life and thought of the average man. What is true is that ministers of the Christian religion often assert that it is, present it for consideration as though it were, and, in fact, by their faulty exposition of it make it so. The central dogma of the Incarnation is that by which relevance stands or falls. If Christ was only man, then He is entirely irrelevant to any thought about God; if He is only God, then He is entirely irrelevant to any experience of human life. It is, in the strictest sense, necessary to the salvation of relevance that a man should believe rightly the Incarnation of Our Lord Jesus Christ. Unless he believes rightly, there is not the faintest reason why he should believe at all. And in that case, it is wholly irrelevant to chatter about "Christian principles."

[...] If the "average man" is going to be interested in Christ at all, it is the dogma that will provide the interest. The trouble is that, in nine cases out of ten, he has never been offered the dogma. What he has been offered is a set of technical theological terms which nobody has taken the trouble to translate into language relevant to ordinary life. [...] Teachers and preachers never, I think, make it sufficiently clear that dogmas are not a set of arbitrary regulations invented *a priori* by a committee of theologians enjoying a bout of all-in dialectical wrestling. Most of them were hammered out under pressure of urgent practical necessity to provide an answer to heresy.

Comment

Dorothy L. Sayers is perhaps best known for her crime novels, which introduced Lord Peter Wimsey as an amateur aristocratic sleuth. However, she also developed a considerable interest in Christian theology, as this lecture makes clear. The lecture was given during World War II, so the reference to "totalitarianism" would have resonated strongly with her audience. The basic theme is that it is not good enough to agree that Jesus had some useful ideas, unless we have good reasons for asserting that there is something distinctive about Jesus which requires us to take those ideas with compelling seriousness. Hence, Sayers argues, the great questions of Christology are inevitable, and must be addressed.

Questions for Study

1 What point does Sayers make in the first paragraph? What is her fundamental criticism of "Christian Humanism"?
2 What justification does Sayers offer for traditional Christological affirmations?
3 "If Christ was only man, then He is entirely irrelevant to any thought about God; if He is only God, then He is entirely irrelevant to any experience of human life." Locate this statement within the text. How does Sayers arrive at this conclusion? And how does she further develop the ideas contained in it?

4.35

Paul Tillich on the Dispensability of the Historical Jesus

Paul Tillich (1886–1965) is noted for his existential approach to theology, which often leads him to treat the specifically historical aspects of the Christian faith as being of less than critical importance. Christianity is about universal existential possibilities, an idea which Tillich discussed with particular reference to the idea of "New Being." But how does this "New Being" relate to Jesus Christ? In this extract, Tillich indicates that he believes that the historical existence of Jesus is not of decisive importance. See also 4.26, 4.29, 4.30, 4.36, 4.41.

The preceding evaluation of the historical approach to the biblical records led to a negative and a positive assertion. The negative assertion is that historical research can neither give nor take away the foundation of the Christian faith. The positive assertion is that historical research has influenced and must influence Christian theology, first, by giving an analysis of the three different semantic levels of biblical literature (and, analogously, of Christian preaching in all periods); second, by showing in several steps the development of the christological symbols (as well as the other systematically important symbols); and, finally, by providing a precise philological and historical understanding of the biblical literature by means of the best methods developed in all historical work.

But it is necessary systematically to raise once more a question which is continuously being asked with considerable religious anxiety. Does not the acceptance of the historical method for dealing with the source documents of the Christian faith introduce a dangerous insecurity into the thought and life of the church and of every individual Christian? Could not historical research lead to a complete skepticism about the biblical records? Is it not imaginable that historical criticism could come to the judgment that the man Jesus of Nazareth never lived? Did not some scholars, though only a few and not very important ones, make just this statement? And even if such a statement can never be made with certainty, is it not destructive for the Christian faith if the non-existence of Jesus can somehow be made probable, no matter how low the degree of probability? In reply, let us first reject some insufficient and misleading answers. It is inadequate to point out that historical research has not yet given any evidence to support such skepticism. Certainly, it has not yet! But the anxious question remains of whether it could not do so sometime in the future! Faith cannot rest on such unsure ground. The answer, taken from the "not-yet" of skeptical evidence, is insufficient. There is another possible answer, which, though not false, is misleading. This is to say that the historical foundation of Christianity is an essential element of the Christian faith itself and that this faith, through its own power, can overrule skeptical possibilities within historical criticism. It can, it is maintained, guarantee the existence of Jesus of Nazareth and at least the essentials in the biblical picture. But we must analyze this answer carefully, for it is ambiguous. The problem is: Exactly what can faith guarantee? And the inevitable answer is that faith can guarantee only its own foundation, namely, the appearance of that reality which has created the faith. This reality is the New Being, who conquers existential estrangement and thereby makes faith possible. This alone faith is able to guarantee – and that because its own existence is identical with the presence of the New Being. Faith itself is the immediate (not mediated by conclusions) evidence of the New Being within and under the conditions of existence. Precisely that is guaranteed by the very nature of the Christian faith. No historical criticism can question the immediate awareness of those who find themselves transformed into the state of faith. One is reminded of the Augustinian–Cartesian refutation of radical skepticism. That tradition pointed to the immediacy of a self-consciousness which guaranteed itself by its participation in being. By analogy, one must say that participation, not historical argument, guarantees the reality of the event upon which Christianity is based. It guarantees a personal life in which the New Being has conquered the old being. But it does not guarantee his name to be Jesus of Nazareth. Historical doubt concerning the existence and the life of someone with this name cannot be overruled. He might have had another name. (This is a historically absurd, but logically necessary, consequence of the historical method.) Whatever his name, the New Being was and is actual in this man.

Comment

Tillich's theology is often described as "existentialist," meaning that it addresses or engages with fundamental questions of human existence. Tillich argues that Christianity proclaims and enables a new form of human existence to come into being. But how is this new possibility related to Jesus of Nazareth? For Tillich, the event upon which Christianity is based has two aspects: the historical fact which is called "Jesus of Nazareth," and the reception of this fact by those who received him as the Christ. The factual, or objective–historical, Jesus is not the foundation of faith apart from his reception as the Christ; here, the influence of Martin Kähler may easily be discerned (see 4.29). Tillich has no real interest in the historical figure of Jesus of Nazareth: all that he is prepared to affirm about him (insofar as it relates to the foundation of faith) is that it was a "personal life," analogous to the biblical picture, who might well have had another name other than "Jesus." "Whatever his name, the New Being was and is active in this man." If historical criticism were ever to demonstrate that the man Jesus of Nazareth never actually existed, Tillich declares that his theology would not be affected by this result.

Questions for Study

1 What purpose does history serve for Tillich? He is often accused of "retreating from history." Does this passage support this complaint?
2 Notice how the concept of "skepticism" plays a very important role in this passage. What points does Tillich make concerning the causes and effects of skepticism? And how does this relate to his attitude to history?
3 "It guarantees a personal life in which the New Being has conquered the old being. But it does not guarantee his name to be Jesus of Nazareth." Locate this passage within the text. What does Tillich mean by this? How does he arrive at this conclusion? What are the implications of this statement?

4.36

Wolfhart Pannenberg on the Indispensability of the Historical Jesus

In his important work *Jesus – God and Man* (German title: "Foundations of Christology"), Wolfhart Pannenberg (born 1928) argues for the indispensability of engagement with the historical Jesus. He is severely critical of those who he regards as disengaging with history, and includes both Rudolf Bultmann and Paul Tillich among those whom he critiques. In this passage, Pannenberg puts forward a series of considerations which seem to him to make it clear that engagement with the historical figure of Jesus is essential. See also 4.26, 4.29, 4.30, 4.32, 4.35, 4.41

The idea that theology, when it deals with Jesus Christ, must take its starting point in the proclamation of his community has become very influential since Martin Kähler. This idea was not completely original with Kähler. Albrecht Ritschl already had said this about the perception of Jesus: "One can attain the full extent of his historic reality only out of the faith which the Christian community has in him." Such a point of view was suggested earlier by Schleiermacher and by the Erlangen school of theology. Kähler advocated this idea especially in his famous book *The So-called Historical Jesus and the Historic, Biblical Christ* (1892). In this book he attacked the theological claim of the quest for the historical Jesus which was at that time in full bloom. The quest for the historical Jesus sought to lay bare the man Jesus and his message from the later development of the piety and Christology of the Christian community as they are combined in the New Testament writings. The life of Jesus and his religion should have direct, exemplary meaning for Christians today. Jesus was set in opposition to Paul, who, as Harnack thought, had covered up the simple humanness of Jesus with his own bizarre Christology. Such a harsh contrast between Jesus and Paul has recently been advocated anew by Ethelbert Stauffer. Kähler's work opposes that kind of quest for the historical Jesus which makes of him a mere man. Kähler rightly protested against the tendency to drive a cleft between Jesus and the apostles' preaching about Christ. In this sense his statement is correct: "The real Christ is the preached Christ." It is based on the fact that, in general, "the personal effect which survives in a noticeable way for subsequent generations" belongs to the historical reality of any important figure. This personal effect in the case of Jesus is "the faith of his disciples, the conviction that one has in him the conqueror of guilt, sin, the Tempter, and death."

We repeat, Kähler is correct in these statements, insofar as he protests against setting the figure and message of Jesus in opposition to the apostolic preaching in such a way that no sort of continuity between the two would exist any longer. However, it does not follow from the rejection of such false antitheses either (1) that the effects of the person Jesus are to be found only in the apostolic preaching or (2) that what is "truly historic" about Jesus is only his "personal effect." This effect radiated outward into definite and, already in early Christianity, varied historical situations. Therefore, something of the particular intellectual situation of the respective witness, of the questions that moved their times and to which they answered with their confession of Christ, also always adheres to the New Testament accounts of Jesus. This is the basis for the diversity of the New Testament witnesses to Jesus, which is not to be overlooked. Because the New Testament testimony to Christ so clearly bears the stamp of the particular contemporary problematic of the witnesses, one cannot simply equate Jesus himself with the apostles' witness to him, as Kähler expressed it in his formula about "the whole Biblical Christ."

In the sense of such an equation it is false to say that the real Christ is the preached Christ. One can and must get back to Jesus himself from the witness of the apostles by trying to recognize, and thus making allowance for, the relation of New Testament texts to their respective situations. It is quite possible to distinguish the figure of Jesus himself, as well as the outlines of his message, from the particular perspective in which it is transmitted through this or that New Testament witness. What is no longer "possible," according to the insights of the form-critical study of the Gospels, is really only the attempt to exploit the sequence of the presentation in our Gospels as a chronology of Jesus' life and ministry; for the sequence of presentation in all four

Gospels has been proved to be determined by considerations of composition. This does not mean, however, that even the question of evidence in the Gospels for a chronology of Jesus' life is completely settled, not to speak of the question of a history of Jesus in general. Ultimately, Kähler is right on only one point: the historical reconstruction of the figure and proclamation of Jesus is always required to explain how the early Christian proclamation of Christ could emerge from the fate of Jesus. The assertion of an antithesis between Jesus and the primitive Christian kerygma about him remains unsatisfying also from a historical point of view. The continuity between the two must be made understandable.

Going back behind the apostolic kerygma to the historical Jesus is, therefore, possible. It is also necessary. Wilhelm Herrmann properly criticized Kähler at just this point: precisely because the New Testament witnesses proclaimed Jesus as he appeared to faith at that time, "this proclamation alone, if we leave it up to that, cannot protect us from the doubt that we want to base our faith on something that is perhaps not historical fact at all, but is itself a product of faith." To be sure, Herrmann also shies away from basing faith on our historical knowledge about Jesus: "It is a fatal error to attempt to establish the basis of faith by means of historical investigation. The basis of faith must be something fixed; the results of historical study are continually changing. The basis of our faith must be grasped in the same independent fashion by learned and unlearned, by each for himself." In this, Herrmann agrees with Kähler's demand that faith ought not to "depend on scholarly investigation."

In the present revival of the quest of Jesus by Käsemann, Fuchs, Bornkamm, and others, this restriction has been overcome in principle. Whether Jesus himself or someone else was the real bearer of the message handed down by the writers of the Synoptic Gospels is no longer considered, with Bultmann, since it is an incidental question. This position is possible for Bultmann because, for him, "the person of Jesus is absorbed in his word." Over against that, it is recognized today that faith must have "support in the historical Jesus himself." That means, certainly, in Jesus himself as he is accessible to our historical inquiry. One can agree completely with this assertion. The only question that remains is: What is really the decisive factor in Jesus' life and proclamation upon which faith is based? We will return at length to this question later.

To go back behind the New Testament text to Jesus himself is unavoidable for another reason. Only in this way is it possible to see the unity that binds together the New Testament witnesses. As long as one only compares the varied witnesses, one will have to recognize the antitheses that appear even in passages that sound similar. The unity of Scripture will not be grasped in a comparison of the statements of the New Testament witnesses; it consists only in the one Jesus to whom they all refer, and will be recognizable, therefore, only when one has penetrated behind the kerygma of the apostles. The inner unity of the New Testament writings will be visible precisely when they are taken as a "historical source" and not only as a "preaching text." As a historical source they express not only "what was at once believed," but also permit something of Jesus himself, in whom the Christian believes, to be recognized.

Comment

This passage represents an engagement with a continual conversation within Christian theology over the place of history in relation to the figure of Jesus. Christian interest in engaging with questions of history, and especially the philosophy of history, reached a peak during the 1960s. In part, this was due to the need to engage with Marxism, which offered what seemed to be a coherent vision of historical events and the historical process as a whole. One of those who responded to this challenge was Pannenberg, who developed his "revelation in history" approach in response. It was therefore entirely natural that Pannenberg should stress the importance of history in relation to the questions of Christology.

Note that Pannenberg mentions two writers in particular: Willhelm Herrmann and Martin Kähler; it would be helpful to read extracts from these writers as preparation for engaging with this text (see 2.40, 4.29). Pannenberg's argument is very accessible and clear, and requires little in the way of introduction or comment.

Questions for Study

1 Set out the reasons why Pannenberg insists on going "behind the New Testament text to Jesus himself."
2 Pannenberg engages in dialogue with Martin Kähler in this passage. Set out, in your own words, the points at which Pannenberg agrees with Kähler, and those where he departs from him.
3 "The assertion of an antithesis between Jesus and the primitive Christian kerygma about him remains unsatisfying also from a historical point of view. The continuity between the two must be made understandable. "Locate this statement within the text. What does Pannenberg mean by this? Would Martin Kähler agree with this?

4.37

Thomas F. Torrance on the Incarnation and Soteriology

In some of his later writings, the noted Scottish theologian Thomas F. Torrance (born 1913) explored a series of questions relating to Christology and the doctrine of the Trinity with particular reference to the Greek patristic tradition of reflection on these issues. In his major work *The Trinitarian Faith* (1988), Torrance explored the relation of the doctrine of the incarnation to questions of soteriology. See also 4.8, 4.13, 5.25, 5.26, 5.32.

The incarnation, far from being some sort of docetic epiphany of God the Son in the flesh, involves the full reality and integrity of human and creaturely being in space and time. The immediate focus is undoubtedly centred on the *human agency* of the incarnate Son within the essential conditions of actual historical human existence, and therefore on the undiminished actuality of the whole historical Jesus Christ who was born of the Virgin Mary, suffered under Pontius Pilate, was crucified and buried, and rose again from the dead.

It was when this stress on the wholeness and reality of the human nature, being and agency of the incarnate Son was challenged, and heretically dualist notions began to creep back, that Athanasius wrote the highly important letter to Epictetus of Corinth, in which he defended the truth of the birth and descent of Jesus from the seed of David, and yet the unimpaired relation of this historical Jesus to the eternal Son, for while he was physically born of Mary, born of earth, he was not changed into flesh. His conception and birth of the Virgin Mary, apart from a human father, did not alter the fact that the birth of Jesus was truly of the flesh just like that of all other human beings.

Questions had also been raised which troubled the Church for some decades through Apollinarius of Laodicea. Apollinaris taught that the Son or Word of God became man in such a way that "in place of the inward man within us there is a heavenly mind in Christ . . . he took that which is without mind that he might himself be mind in it".

It is to be noted that the defence of the complete reality and integrity of the historical humanity of Christ by Nicene theologians was offered mainly on *soteriological grounds*. It was the *whole man* that the Son of God came to redeem by becoming man himself and effecting our salvation in and through the very humanity he appropriated from us – if the humanity of Christ were in any way deficient, all that he is said to have done in offering himself in sacrifice "for our sakes", "on our behalf" and "in our place" would be quite meaningless. As Athanasius wrote to Epictetus, "The Saviour having in very truth become man, the salvation of the whole man was brought about. . . . Truly our salvation is no myth, and does not extend to the body only – the whole man, body and soul, has truly received salvation in the Word himself." He wrote in similar terms to the Antiochenes: "The body possessed by the Saviour did not lack soul or sense or mind, for it was impossible when the Lord became man that his body should be without mind; nor was the salvation effected in the Word himself only of the body but also of the soul." Thus the whole life of Christ is understood as a continuous vicarious sacrifice and oblation which, as such, is indivisible, for everything he assumed from us is organically united in his one Person and work as Saviour and Mediator. The teaching given here in face of the critical questions that arose after the Council of Nicaea was in fact but an extension of what he had first put forward in his early work *On the incarnation of the Word*, as well as in his debates with the Arians: the redemption of the whole man through the incarnation, and the redemption of the whole man effected in it by way of Christ's vicarious sacrifice for sin and his victory in death and resurrection over corruption and death.

In his incarnation the Son of God took on himself not only the form of man but the form of a *servant* – for his incarnation was an act of utter self-abasement and humiliation in which he assumed our abject servile condition, our state under the slavery of sin, in order to act for us and on our behalf from within our actual existence. It must be noted, however, as Basil insisted, that the Pauline expression "form of a servant" should be taken to mean, not some "likeness" or "resemblance" assumed by Christ in his incarnation, but the actual form of existence which he took over from "the lump of Adam" – it was a "real incarnation". The Nicene theologians could never suppress their utter astonishment at the incredible act of condescension on the part of God in the stark *reality* of the incarnation. Thus Gregory of Nyssa exclaimed: "Why did the divine being descend to such humiliation? Our faith staggers at the thought that God, the infinite, inconceivable and ineffable reality, who transcends all glory and majesty, should be clothed with the defiled nature of man, so that his sublime activities are abased through being united with what is so degraded." The Pauline concept of *kenosis* was not interpreted in any metaphysical way as involving a contraction, diminution or self-limitation of God's infinite being, but in terms of his self-abnegating love in the inexpressible mystery of the *tapeinosis*, impoverishment or abasement, which he freely took upon himself in what he became and did in Christ entirely for our sake.

The Arians, before the Council of Nicaea and afterwards, had made a point of searching the Scriptures for every possible passage or text indicating the creatureliness, human weakness, the mortality of Christ, his subordinate and servile condition, which were stressed in contrast to the transcendent Godhead of the Father. Instead of rejecting these passages, however, Athanasius seized upon them and emphasised them in order to show that it was deliberately in this servile condition that the eternal Son came among us, became one of us and one with us, precisely in order to be *our* Saviour. Here we find closely allied, and knit into each other, the notions of the *servant* and of the *priest* – the teaching of St Paul and that of the Epistle to the Hebrews (which was held to be Pauline) were integrated. The servant form of Christ was discerned to be essential to his priestly oneness with us in virtue of which he could act on our behalf, in our place, and in our stead, before God the Father. As we shall see, this involved an understanding of Christ in which his Person and his act, what he was and what he did, were completely one, for he was himself both the one offered and the one who offered for mankind. This view of the mediatorial and priestly nature of Christ's Person and work, in the unity of his divine and human agency, in virtue of which "he might minister the things of God to us and of us to God", also had the effect of making the whole event of our redemption one which is properly to be understood within the context of worship. Hence it is not surprising that an essential element in redemption was reckoned by the Nicene and post-Nicene fathers to be redemption from "false worship".

Comment

This passage represents an important attempt by a leading western theologian to evaluate and appropriate the emerging Christological consensus of the Greek patristic tradition. The issues debated at that stage in Christian history are here taken as being of perennial importance, requiring attention by each theological generation. The passage can be read at two levels: first, as an overview and synthesis of the Greek patristic Christological tradition; second, as a plea for the contemporary appropriation of the theological legacy of the past.

Questions for Study

1 Torrance clearly regards the Greek patristic debates as having continuing importance. On the basis of this passage, what reasons might be given for such an attitude? What, in your view, are its strengths and its weaknesses?
2 Set out clearly, in your own words, the links that Torrance identifies between the incarnation and salvation.
3 In what way does the theological critique offered by Gregory of Nazianzus in response to Apollinarius of Laodicea feature in Torrance's analysis? You will find it helpful to read 4.9 and 4.10 before answering this question.

4.38

Rosemary Radford Ruether on the Maleness of Christ

Rosemary Radford Ruether's book *Sexism and God-Talk* (1983) established her as one of the most significant feminist theological writers. In the course of this wide-ranging book, Ruether turns to explore the question of whether a male savior can save women. Arguing that the dominant trend within the church has been to develop "masculinist" Christologies, Ruether (born 1936) considers two alternative traditions – "androgynous Christologies" and "spirit Christologies." The extract for study concerns the first of these – an approach which sees "the split between maleness and femaleness overcome on a spiritual plane in the redeemed humanity." (Note: "androgynous" basically means "having the characteristics of both male and female," just as "androgyne" means "a being who has both these characteristics.") See also 2.45, 3.42, 4.39.

Behind the androgynous Christologies, as well as androgynous anthropologies, often lurks the myth of an original androgyne. In this myth Adam originally contained both male and female. The splitting of the female from the male side of Adam signals the downfall of humanity and the advent of sex and sin. Christ, the new androgynous Adam, enables the redeemed to transcend the split of male and female and regain their spiritual humanity. These ideas are suggested in many of the Gnostic Gospels. The Second Epistle of Clement (12:2) says:

> For the Lord himself being asked by someone when his Kingdom would come, said: When the two shall be one, and the outside as the inside, the male with the female, neither male nor female.

Women are seen as equal participants in this spiritual humanity, but only by transcending their identities as sexual persons and mothers. In the Gospel of the Egyptians Jesus declares, "I have come to destroy the works of the female," that is, sexual desire and procreation (9:63), while the Gospel of Thomas vindicates the inclusion of women in the redemptive community by having Jesus say, "Lo, I shall lead her and make her male, so that she too may become a living spirit resembling you males, for every woman who makes herself male will enter the kingdom of heaven" (*Logion* 114). Similar ideas were revived in early modern mystics such as Jacob Boehme and Emanuel Swedenborg. Boehme particularly influenced many mystical Utopian sects, such as the German Rappites, who emigrated to America in the nineteenth century. Notions of an androgynous divinity, an original androgynous humanity, and the restoration of spiritual androgyny in the redeemed are frequently found in these movements.

The Christ figure reinforces the androcentric bias of these concepts of androgyny. Christ represents the male as the normative human person. Femaleness represents the lower instinctual and bodily side of "man," which was originally unified in a spiritual whole. The separation of the female out of the side of Adam represents the disintegration of this original whole, the revolt of the lower against the higher side of "man." The very existence of woman as a separate gender represents the fall of "man." Femaleness is still correlated with the lower side of human nature, which is to be abolished in Heaven.

A somewhat different tradition develops in medieval Jesus mysticism, expressed particularly by Julian of Norwich. Here Jesus is proclaimed both mother and father. Like a mother he feeds us with his own body. He nurtures us with milk, like newborn babes. The ambience of these images of the mothering Jesus is found especially in eucharistic piety. Since both the human and the divine persons of Jesus are established in Catholic thought as male, however, Jesus as a male person is given "mothering" attributes. In Christ the male gains a model of androgyny, of personhood that is both commanding and nurturing. The female mystic gains the satisfaction of relation to a tender and mothering person, but she herself does not gain a comparable androgyny. The Church does not allow her to represent the "masculine" authority of Christ as priest or public teacher.

Nineteenth-century romanticism comes close to reversing these value symbols of masculinity and femininity. With the secularization of society and the privatization of religion, Christianity becomes identified with the shrinking sphere of middle-class femininity. Woman comes to be identified with the spiritual, pious, and altruistic impulses, whose purity can be preserved only by the strictest segregation from the public world of male materialism and power. Many writers come close to identifying woman as the more naturally "Christlike" type. A sweet fragile femininity also comes to characterize the pietistic images of Jesus. But this feminization of Christ, while it makes woman closer to the spiritual pole, still does not liberate her for public influence in society or in the Church.

Horace Bushnell, in his treatise "Women's Suffrage: The Reform Against Nature" (1869), argues that the male nature represents the law, whereas the female nature represents the Gospel. The Gospel is the higher revelation of grace, forgiveness, and altruistic love. Women have a natural affinity for these higher spiritual characteristics. But the Gospel is impractical and incapable of providing the principle of leadership in public society. It is here that males, as representatives of law, must still rule in the public sphere of Church and society. Thus, by a peculiar reversal of classical Christian anthropological reasoning, Bushnell argues that women's Christlike nature makes them unfit for ordained ministry. Femininity and Christ-likeness are both defined into a private realm of altruistic other-worldliness which, while appropriate for redemption, is inappropriate for the exercise of public power, even in the Church.

Reformist feminists draw different conclusions from the thesis of woman's more Christlike nature. For them this suggests a messianic meaning to the emergence of woman. If woman represents the higher human qualities of peace, purity, and reconciliation, then these are too good to keep at home. They are just what the world needs now to redeem it from the various evils that corrupt society. The home and woman's higher feminine nature become the launching pad for a crusade into society to elevate it to the female standards of goodness.

All of these concepts of androgyny, whether they identify woman with the lower material nature and hence with finitude and sin, or whether they identify her with the higher spiritual qualities of altruistic love, never succeed in allowing woman to represent full human potential. The very concept of androgyny presupposes a psychic dualism that identifies maleness with one-half of human capacities and femaleness with the other. As long as Christ is still presumed to be, normatively, a male person, androgynous Christologies will carry an androcentric bias. Men gain their "feminine" side, but women contribute to the whole by specializing in the representation of the "feminine," which means exclusion from the exercise of the roles of power and leadership associated with masculinity.

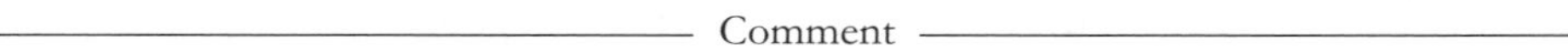

Comment

Ruether's concern throughout this section of her book is that the maleness of Christ is used by traditional Christian groups to defend the idea that Christ can only be represented by males – for example, in the priesthood. The maleness of Jesus, she argues, has been used to perpetuate oppressive social arrangements between men and women. She therefore explores alternative ways of representing the distinctive identity of Christ, including the "androgynous" approach found in Gnosticism and certain medieval mystics. As will be clear from this passage, she finds this approach unsatisfactory. The implicit dualism in these Christologies continues to subordinate femininity, rather than liberate it.

Questions for Study

1 Try to summarize Ruether's assessment of the androgynous approach. What are its merits? And, on the basis of this passage, what are its weaknesses?
2 How does Ruether understand this Christology to impact on women?
3 What precisely is the point being made by Ruether in her criticism of Horace Bushnell?

4.39

Daphne Hampson on the Possibility of a Feminist Christology

Jesus Christ was male. What implications may this have as to his significance? In an important analysis Daphne Hampson (born 1944) argues that this is a complex question but that, at the end of the day, there can be no Christology compatible with human equality. Christian feminists have been considering these questions since about 1975, though have not often thought about the possibilities opened up by the philosophical context in which Christianity arose. Hampson is herself not a Christian. See also 2.45, 3.41, 3.42, 4.38, 6.55, 6.56.

The nub of the question as to whether feminism is compatible with Christianity is that of whether a Christology can be found of which it may be said that at least it is not incompatible with feminism. By Christology is meant the portrayal of Jesus as the Christ. I have suggested that a meaningful way to set the limits as to what may rightly be called a Christian position, is that Christians are those who proclaim Jesus to have been unique. Such a definition does not only include those Christians who construe their belief in orthodox terms; who proclaim of Christ (following the definition of the Council of Chalcedon) that he was fully God and fully human, these two natures existing in one person. It includes also those who wish to speak of uniqueness in some other way. For example I shall later consider Bultmann, who has no classical two-nature Christology, but who says of Jesus, as of no other, that this was the man whom God raised from the dead; so that for him this man's resurrection becomes the pivot of history. I do not intend to have a restrictive but rather an expansive definition. To say of persons however who simply believe of Jesus that he had a very fine moral teaching, but who wish to say nothing of Jesus himself, that they are Christian surely does not make sense theologically – whatever they may say of themselves. Such a position should rightly be called humanist. Christians have always proclaimed not simply Jesus' teaching, but something about Jesus. There can rightly be no Christianity without a Christology.

The question of the compatibility of feminism and Christianity then is that of whether there can be a way of speaking of Christ's uniqueness which is not incompatible with feminism. (Let us take also a minimalist definition of feminism, as meaning the proclaimed equality of women and men.) The problem of course with Christology for feminists is that Jesus was a male human being and that thus as a symbol, as the Christ, or as the Second Person of the trinity, it would seem that "God" becomes in some way "male." It should be noted at the outset what is the nature of the problem with which we are concerned. It is not a question of whether feminists have something against "men." Whether or not that is the case, the problem here is not that Jesus was a man, but that this man has been considered unique, symbolic of God, God Himself – or whatever else may be the case within Christianity. The Godhead, or at least Christology, then appears to be biased against women. Feminists have been very aware of the power of symbolism and ideology. It is no small matter then to suggest that western religious thought, which has been so fundamental to western culture, has been ideologically loaded against women.

Before we proceed to consider the question as to whether there can be a Christology which is not incompatible with feminism, I should like to point to the significance of this question for Christians. It is not simply that it is a vital matter for some small group of people (as some may think them to be) called "Christian feminists" who would reconcile their feminism with their Christian faith. For Christianity has always proclaimed Christ to be an inclusive concept. In him, it is said, there is no East nor West, he is the new Adam, the first-born of all humanity; there is in Christ no Jew nor Greek, no more male and female. The question which feminists are raising then strikes at the very core of Christology. For it is being questioned whether a symbol which would appear to be necessarily male can be said to be inclusive of all humanity. Does it not give male human beings privilege within the religion? As far as women who would be Christian are concerned, how may they see in the Godhead an image of themselves? The contention that Christology is not inclusive represents the undoing of what, classically, has been claimed of Christ.

Why has this question now come upon the scene? What has changed in human relations between men and women, or how is it that women sense themselves differently, such that this matter has become urgent? It would be difficult to give a definitive answer, but we may have some clue. In other ages, the female seemed in some sense to be "included" in the male, in a way in which this is no longer the case. This made Christology seem natural. Men were normally held to represent women also. Humanity could then as a whole be thought to be summed up in Christ. Mistaken biological beliefs, such that the male alone was thought to be a full human being, underlay western culture, making this seem the more plausible. Today men are not in the same way held to represent women: there are two sexes and women represent themselves.

It may then be that today situations where men alone are priests, or equally the fact that Christ is a male symbol and God is conceptualized using male metaphors, may make God appear to be "male" in a way in which this was not earlier the case. If we see a procession of only men we ask "where are the women?" As we have said, in an age when men alone filled the professions, it appeared only natural that those who led the church were likewise male. When this is no longer so, the fact of a male priesthood makes God appear to be in some way peculiarly male, such that He needs a male priesthood to represent Him. The belief that men alone represent humanity, whereas a woman is an individual who only represents herself, never absolute, does not wash any longer. A symbol which is a male symbol appears in our culture to represent maleness, in a way in which earlier this may not necessarily have been the case. Hence the urgency of the question as to whether Christ is an inclusive symbol, and the feeling of many women that it is not.

Comment

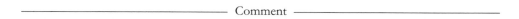

The issues which Daphne Hampson brings together in this passage may be seen as a useful general overview of central feminist concerns about the implications of the maleness of Christ. Hampson does not regard herself as a Christian; nevertheless, the line of thought developed in this extract has had considerable impact within Christian feminist circles since about 1975. The issues are so clearly presented that no additional comment is required.

Questions for Study

1 Set out, in your own words, the issues raised by the maleness of Jesus, according to Hampson.
2 Christian theology has always recognized that Jesus discloses God. Does this mean that a male Jesus discloses a male God?
3 "There can rightly be no Christianity without a Christology." Locate this passage within the text. What does Hampson do with this affirmation? How does it function within her overall argument?

4.40

Morna D. Hooker on Chalcedon and the New Testament

The relationship between the highly developed Christological ideas of the Council of Chalcedon and the more restrained statements of the New Testament has been the subject of much discussion in the last two centuries. Morna Hooker (born 1931), Lady Margaret Professor of Divinity Emerita at the University of Cambridge, here offers an accessible, informed reflection on what she terms "the great gulf between the thought-world" of the New Testament and that of Chalcedon. She offers three reasons which help explain why the language of Chalcedon is so different from that of the New Testament, while at the same time arguing that the Chalcedonian way of thinking about the identity of Christ was "an inevitable development." See also 2.38, 4.16, 4.17, 4.32, 4.34.

First of all, Chalcedon was primarily intended as a bastion against heresy. Definition was necessary in order to make quite clear which heretical views were being excluded. In the days of the New Testament, on the other hand, Christianity was itself the heresy. This is something which is frequently forgotten by exegetes, who tend to read back later situations into the New Testament and suppose that our writers were defending the true Christian gospel against this or that heresy. But for most of the time they were not; they were propagating a message which was itself heretical, and were still in the process of working out its significance. The orthodoxy was Judaism; the Christian sect was trying to work out its position *vis-à-vis* the parent body and to reconcile faith in Jesus as God's Messiah with the conviction that God was indeed the God who had revealed himself to his people in the past. What our writers say about Christ has to be seen in this context. By the time of the Chalcedonian Council, the statements which had once been heresy had become orthodoxy, and were therefore handled in a completely different way.

Secondly, our New Testament writers were primarily concerned to describe the activity of God: he had acted, he had redeemed his people. They used a great variety of imagery – anything and everything available to them – in order to describe this activity; it was natural to them to employ narrative and metaphor. Their concern was not to offer definitions of the being of God or the being of Christ. The nature of God is known by what he does: many of the most important New Testament christological passages are hymns extolling God for what he has done through Christ. This is what is meant by describing New Testament christology as "functional" rather than as "ontological"; it seems to me to be a valid distinction. Nor is this simply an aberration on the part of our New Testament writers: it is part of the biblical tradition. Nowhere in the Old Testament does one find God being spoken of in terms of pure being: even in Deutero-Isaiah, where the description of God is at its most majestic, God is still celebrated as the one who acts. He is the God who reveals himself to his people and acts on their behalf, "the God of Abraham, Isaac and Jacob", the "Lord your God, who brought you out of the land of Egypt" (Exodus 3: 6; 20: 2). But by the time of Chalcedon things had changed radically; after four centuries in which Christians had grown accustomed to the idea of a divine Father and a divine Son and were used to speaking of them as peers, the Fathers of the Church approached the questions of christology in a very different way. What had been for our New Testament authors helpful images used to describe their experience of God have now become doctrines which themselves need to be defined and analysed.

Thirdly, leading on from there, our New Testament authors write from within a Jewish context and not a Greek philosophical one. One hesitates these days to make contrasts between Greek and Hebrew language, but in spite of the pitfalls involved in easy contrasts it is still true to say that there are differences in outlook. Paul, for example, could never have spoken of Christ as "consisting of a reasonable soul and a body". He speaks of man as *sōma psuchikon*, and the contrasts he uses are not between God and man, but between spirit and flesh. The debate at Chalcedon makes no sense to those accustomed to think in Jewish terms. Most important of all, the issues were quite different: our New Testament authors were wrestling with the question: "How do our new beliefs about Christ relate to what we have always believed about God – about the creation of the universe, his election of Israel, and his promises to his people?" Their concern was to show that it was the same God who had been at work in the past who was now at work in Christ, and that his new work in Christ was the fulfilment of everything that had gone before: hence the importance of showing his superiority to Moses.

The idea of an incarnate God is, we suggest, foreign to Jewish thinking. Remember the prayer of Solomon: "Will God indeed dwell on the earth? Behold, heaven and the highest heaven cannot contain thee" (1 Kings 8: 27). To be sure, the Shekinah dwelt on earth, but the Shekinah was a particular manifestation of God's universal presence, and like other manifestations (angels, wisdom, the Spirit, the Word) was a way of speaking of God's self-revelation. Again, individuals were accorded divine honours: Moses, in particular, was said by Philo, elaborating Exodus 7: 1, to have been given the name of god and king (e.g. *Mas. i.* 158; *De som. 2.* 189). Ezekiel the Tragedian relates a dream of Moses, in which he is enthroned by God on his own throne and given the emblems of rule – symbols of his future authority over men (68–89); the passage is reminiscent of that in 1 Enoch 45, where it is said that the Elect One (i.e. the Son of man) will sit on God's throne of glory. In these passages and others, five men share in divine honour because they are given divine authority, but this does not mean that they are themselves "divine" beings: rather their authority and honour are manifestations of the fact that God is revealing his power and purpose through them.

Comment

In this essay, Hooker was interested in understanding the transition from the New Testament ways of speaking about Jesus Christ to the more elaborate approach, heavily influenced by Greek philosophy, found in the Council of Chalcedon. Some scholars had argued that Chalcedon represented a distortion of the New Testament for this reason. Hooker, however, rejects this, seeing the transition as representing a change in *emphasis* and a change in *context*. In particular, she notes the biblical emphasis on the actions of God, which becomes an emphasis on the identity of Christ as a result of the church's shift over time from a Jewish to a Greek context. Note that the Greek phrase *sōma psuchikon*, used by Paul at 1 Corinthians 15: 44, means "spiritual body."

Questions for Study

1 Summarize in your own words the three points that Hooker makes. How do you assess her argument?
2 What does she mean by "functional" and "ontological" approaches to Christology? How is this related to her point about a shift in emphasis from actions to being?
3 Hooker argues that the idea of incarnation is foreign to Jewish thinking. How might this help us understand the fact that it took the church something like three hundred years to confirm that this was the best way of explaining the significance of Jesus Christ?

4.41

N. T. Wright on History and Christology

N. T. Wright (born 1948) has caused considerable interest in both New Testament and theological circles in recent years through his massive engagement with the question of Christian origins, including issues relating to the "historical Jesus." Wright is alert to both the historical and theological aspects of this question, and offers important reflections on the role of historical inquiry in contemporary New Testament study and Christological reflection. In this passage he explains why such historical engagement is essential. See also 4.26, 4.29, 4.30, 4.33, 4.36, 4.40.

This almost instinctive, and quite understandable, reticence has been considerably fortified by a whole string of other more subtle motivations. Albert Schweitzer was passionately concerned to restore the conception of Jesus' "*overwhelming historical greatness*" against those who, like Renan and Schopenhauer, had "stripped off his halo and reduced him to a sentimental figure". Schweitzer tore down the sentimental portraits of Jesus and, like a revolutionary replacing the monarch's portrait on the schoolroom wall with that of the new leader, put up instead the sharp, indeed shocking, drawing of Jesus the towering prophetic genius, the enigmatic hero-figure, totally unlike "modern man", yet strangely summoning him to follow in the noble path that would bring in the kingdom. One might point out that Blake had said similarly iconoclastic things eighty years before; but now it was being said by a highly learned and respected teacher in one of the strongholds of academic theology.

Bultmann wrestled mightily with the multiple ambiguities of German theology after the First World War, and achieved the status of a prince among exegetes, even if his theology limps as a result of the struggle. He and his followers in their way, and Barth in his, found this Jesus too remote, and actually a *misguided* hero (since he hoped for a kingdom that never came). They therefore determined to strip off the layers of paint which even Jesus himself, as a child of his time, could not help superimposing on his real message, and to uncover the original fresco, which turned out to be a message whose etiolated content seemed to be a necessary condition of its required timelessness: a constant invitation from the creator to live in faith and obedience, open to the future. With that, the bulk of the gospel records can safely be put on one side as relevant merely for establishing the views of the early church or the evangelists, whose apparent desire to express their faith by telling stories about Jesus we cannot, or must not, emulate. The powerful theological constructs of Barth and Bultmann formed an alliance with the fears of ordinary people as to what might happen to orthodox Christianity if history was scrutinized too closely. The icon and the silhouette ruled, and ruled powerfully, at the popular and at the academic level.

Schweitzer and Bultmann are of vital, if negative, importance to contemporary work on the New Testament. This is not merely because of their direct influence. Schweitzer, in fact, has never had a "school" of disciples. One could argue that he deserved one more than Bultmann, whose children and grandchildren are yet with us, reinforcing their ancestral heritage by telling and retelling their story (sometimes wrongly called "the history of modern New Testament Studies" or some such) as though it were the only family story, or tracing, in the fashion of those Jewish apocalyptic works they are so careful to disdain, the line of great events from the founding of their clan up to the present moment, when by implication the final revelation is about to dawn in some grand seminar or colloquium. No: Schweitzer and Bultmann are important because they saw, arguably more clearly than anyone else this century, the fundamental shape of the New Testament jigsaw, and the nature of the problems involved in trying to put it together. They thus established fundamental hypotheses for lesser lights to test, elaborate and modify. They are the giants, a pair of Colossi bestriding the narrow world of learned articles, seminar papers, and textual variants.

The jigsaw they perceived is first and foremost an historical one. The oddity of this particular puzzle consists in the fact that the shape of the pieces is indeterminate: each must be cut and trimmed to fit with the others, with none being automatically exempt from the process. The outside limits – themselves a matter of fierce debate – are pre-Christian Judaism and the second-century church; and the puzzle involves fitting together the bits in the middle to make a clear historical sequence all the way across. How did this new movement arise, and why did it arise in this way? The central pieces are, of course, John the Baptist (or does he belong with pre-Christian Judaism?), Jesus, the earliest church, Paul, the churches he and others founded, and the other writers of the New Testament, particularly John (or do some of them belong with the second-century church?). The way in which we shape any one bit of the puzzle will determine, and/or be determined by, the shape we give the others. What we say about Jesus is thus inextricably intertwined with what we say about the first century as a whole. That is why I dealt with the first century in some detail in *The New Testament and the People of God* Parts III and IV.

Twentieth-century scholarship has at least one great advantage over its predecessors. Since Weiss and Schweitzer at the turn of the century, it has been realized that Jesus must be understood in his Jewish context. The only sense in which the old nineteenth-century "Quest" had really attempted this was by producing a sharp contrast. The Jews had the wrong sort of religion; Jesus came to bring the right sort. The game was then to cut off all those bits of the "Jesus" piece that appeared too Jewish, too ethnically restricted, leaving the hero as the founder of a great, universal, "spiritual" religion, so nobly recaptured now by Protestantism, at least since Kant and Hegel. The other bits of the puzzle would then drop into place. Weiss and Schweitzer, however, rightly insisted that the historical jigsaw must portray Jesus as a credible and recognizable first-century Jew, relating comprehensibly in speech and action to other first-century Jews. No solution which claims to be talking about history can ever undo this basic move.

But what does it involve? Here there is still no agreement. We shall see below that the relation of Jesus to his Jewish context is the first question that faces any serious attempt to understand him historically. I shall suggest that there are possibilities that have not been sufficiently explored, and which can give a more rigorously historical shape to the central piece of the jigsaw and, ultimately, a new and more satisfactory solution to the entire puzzle.

The giants who set us this puzzle, and offered such cautious and apparently negative answers to it themselves, were not interested in history simply for its own sake. Though several scholars have claimed to write as "mere historians", there is, as we saw in *The New Testament and the People of God*, no such thing as "mere history". Schweitzer and Bultmann both had in mind a reconstruction of first-century Christian origins which would possess significance for contemporary Christian faith and life. Schweitzer's Jesus set the example for all those who (like Schweitzer himself) would devote themselves to the cause of the kingdom, crazy though it might seem. History itself, in which Jesus' message was an apparent failure, prompts us (he said) to take this unhistorical step of active reinterpretation. Schweitzer thus anticipated by a matter of decades one key element in Bultmann's famous "demythologization" programme: the historical husk of the "real" message must be identified *and then thrown away*. But if for Schweitzer, Jesus was "as one unknown", one could be forgiven for thinking that for Bultmann he was even less: Bultmann's Jesus was "unknown" in the sense that one could not know his "personality" at all, whereas for Schweitzer it was precisely his "personality" that was unexpectedly shocking. Schweitzer claimed that his predecessors had painted the portrait wrong; Bultmann, that no portrait was possible. Bultmann therefore drew his silhouette: Jesus the preacher of existentialist decision, calling to all those who (like Bultmann himself) lived in the midst of social chaos, and who needed to trust and follow their god day by day without being able to see, in the darkness of the present, what was going to happen in the future. Both Schweitzer and Bultmann, to complete their schemes, needed to show how Paul in particular had taken Christianity in the form in which Jesus left it (about which they disagreed) and had made it relevant for the gentile world.

Even where neither of these solutions has held any appeal, almost every book on Jesus has carried the implicit presupposition that when we "really" find what Jesus was like we will have discovered the pearl of great price, the buried treasure that will set us up for life – even if the treasure turns out to be the truth that Jesus was quite an ordinary and unremarkable person and that we are thus set free from the church's arrogant claims about him. History, not least this bit of history, can never be done in a vacuum. There is thus a second jigsaw, connected somehow or other to the first, consisting this time of the questions asked not only by Christians but by all who seek a worldview which might include so obviously attractive a figure as Jesus: what should we believe, and how should we behave, in the modern world? I have no desire to avoid, or to pretend to be uninterested in, such questions; I shall attempt to address them when appropriate. But we must recognize that, for all the necessary interconnections, they are not the *same* questions as the first ones.

The legacy of the giants has meant, however, that the relation between the two jigsaws ("Who was Jesus? "and "so what?") appears very tenuous. *That* we must relate them is clear (at least, to all writers on the subject known to me, without exception): *how* we are to do so is not. This has meant a lot of split-level writing about Jesus. A good example is the massive book of Edward Schillebeeckx, who spends hundreds of pages investigating a merely human Jesus, only to move at the end, without much help from the preceding argument, to a confession of faith in Jesus as the Son of God. It is a measure of the extent to which the split between history and theology has dominated recent western Christian thought that writers of all shades of opinion, from extreme orthodox to extreme radical, have tacitly affirmed that it is difficult, if not impossible, to hold the two together, especially in talking about Jesus. Either we "know" ahead of time that Jesus is "divine" (it is usually assumed that the force of this predicate is already understood), in which case the writing of the history of his life "must" reflect this fact: the portrait then becomes an icon, useful for devotion but probably unlike the original subject. Alternatively, we commit ourselves to ruthless historical investigation, and expect, whether gladly or fearfully, that we will thereby "disprove", or at least seriously undermine, orthodox theology. If we dislike these two options, we can still withdraw to the silhouette, lest we compromise or damage our faith; or we can leap, without explanation, from one side to the other. [. . .] the split is not warranted: that rigorous history (i.e. open-ended investigation of actual events in first-century Palestine) and rigorous theology (i.e. open-ended investigation of what the word "god", and hence the adjective "divine", might actually refer to) belong together, and never more so than in discussion of Jesus. If this means that we end up needing a new metaphysic, so be it. It would be pleasant if, for once, the historians and the theologians could set the agenda for the philosophers, instead of vice versa.

Comment

This extract is taken from *Jesus and the Victory of God* (1996), the second in Wright's projected five-volume series dealing with "Christian origins and the question of God." The first volume in the series, entitled *The New Testament and the People of God* (1992), is alluded to at several points in this extract. Wright here offers a critical survey of trends within New Testament scholarship, especially as this relates to the question of the historical Jesus, engaging with the major landmarks in doing so. The text is very clearly written, and requires little in the way of comment.

Questions for Study

1 Why does Wright believe that historical engagement is essential? Write down a quotation from the text which seems to you to make this point most clearly.
2 Why does Wright single out the writings of Rudolf Bultmann and Albert Schweitzer as being of especial importance to his task?
3 Wright develops the image of two "jigsaws" in this text. What are these two jigsaws? In what way are they related? You might like to consult 4.31 and 10.19 at this point.

For Further Reading

Colin Brown, *Jesus in European Thought 1778–1860* (Durham, NC: Labyrinth Press, 1985).

Raymond E. Brown, *An Introduction to New Testament Christology* (New York: Paulist Press, 1994).

Peter Carnley, *The Structure of Resurrection Belief* (Oxford: Clarendon Press, 1987).

Richard Cross, *The Metaphysics of the Incarnation: Thomas Aquinas to Duns Scotus* (Oxford: Oxford University Press, 2005).

Stephen T. Davis, Daniel Kendall, and Gerald O'Collins (eds), *The Incarnation: An Interdisciplinary Symposium on the Incarnation of the Son of God* (Oxford: Oxford University Press, 2004).

Gregory W. Dawes, *The Historical Jesus Quest: Landmarks in the Search for the Jesus of History* (Louisville, KY: Westminster John Knox Press, 2000).

J. D. G. Dunn, *Christology in the Making* (London: SCM Press, 1980).

J. D. G. Dunn, *A New Perspective on Jesus: What the Quest for the Historical Jesus Missed* (London: SPCK, 2005).

C. Stephen Evans, *The Historical Christ and the Jesus of Faith: The Incarnational Narrative as History* (Oxford: Clarendon Press, 1996).

Aloys Grillmeier, *Christ in Christian Tradition*, 2nd edn (London: Mowbrays, 1975).

Larry W. Hurtado, *Lord Jesus Christ: Devotion to Jesus in Earliest Christianity* (Grand Rapids, MI: Eerdmans, 2003).

Luke Timothy Johnson, *The Real Jesus: The Misguided Quest for the Historical Jesus and the Truth of the Traditional Gospels* (San Francisco: HarperSanFrancisco, 1996).

John Macquarrie, *Jesus Christ in Modern Thought* (London: SCM Press; Philadelphia: Trinity Press International, 1990).

I. H. Marshall, *The Origins of New Testament Christology*, 2nd edn (Leicester, UK: Inter-Varsity Press, 1992).

G. E. Michalson, *Lessing's Ugly Ditch: A Study of Theology and History* (University Park: Pennsylvania State University Press, 1985).

Thomas V. Morris. *The Logic of God Incarnate* (Ithaca, NY: Cornell University Press, 1986).

C. F. D. Moule, *The Origin of Christology* (Cambridge, UK: Cambridge University Press, 1977).

Gerald O'Collins, *Christology: A Biblical, Historical and Systematic Study of Jesus* (Oxford: Oxford University Press, 1995).

Richard Swinburne, *The Resurrection of God Incarnate* (Oxford: Clarendon Press, 2003).

Rowan Williams, *Arius: Heresy and Tradition* (London: Darton, Longman and Todd, 1987).

5

Salvation in Christ

Introduction

Soteriology – that is, the section of Christian theology which deals with the question of what salvation (Greek: *sōtēria*) is, and how it is acquired – has always been of central importance to Christian thought, particularly in relation to evangelism and mission. The following collection of readings explores the ways in which salvation is conceived, and especially the manner in which it is connected with the death and resurrection of Jesus Christ. The term "atonement" is often used in this connection, meaning either "the benefits resulting from the death of Christ," or "specific ways of understanding the meaning of the death of Christ." This term will be encountered frequently in this set of readings, especially those from English-language sources.

Several themes are of particular importance. The relation of Christology and soteriology has been the subject of continuing debate within the Christian tradition. It is clear that there is a close connection between the identity and the significance, between the person and the work, of Christ. But how is this to be understood? The positions outlined by Athanasius, F. D. E. Schleiermacher, Charles Gore, and Wolfhart Pannenberg illustrate both the importance of this point, as well as the different approaches to the issue.

The Relation of Christology and Soteriology	
4.37	Thomas F. Torrance on the Incarnation and Soteriology
5.5	Athanasius on the Relation of Christology and Soteriology
5.25	F. D. E. Schleiermacher on Christology and Soteriology
5.26	Charles Gore on the Relation of Christology and Soteriology
5.28	James Denney on Atonement and Incarnation
5.32	Wolfhart Pannenberg on Soteriological Approaches to Christology

In the early church, the idea of Christ gaining a cosmic victory over sin, death, and Satan through his death and resurrection became very influential. This theme found new importance in the twentieth century, largely through the writings of Gustaf Aulén. However, other themes are also of considerable importance. Among these, particular attention should be paid to the theme of the death of Christ providing a "satisfaction" by which the redemption of humanity was made possible. This is especially associated with Anselm of Canterbury. Other themes of importance include the idea, especially associated with the Greek churches, of salvation as deification, and approaches to the death of Christ which focus on its demonstrating the love of God for humanity.

Models of Atonement

5.1	Irenaeus on the "Ransom" Theory of the Atonement
5.2	Irenaeus on "Recapitulation" in Christ
5.3	Clement of Alexandria on Christ's Death as an Example of Love
5.6	Pseudo-Hippolytus on the Cosmic Dimensions of the Cross
5.7	Rufinus of Aquileia on the "Mousetrap" Theory of the Atonement
5.8	An Ancient Liturgy on Christ's Descent into Hell
5.9	Theodoret of Cyrrhus on the Death of Christ
5.10	Augustine on Redemption in Christ
5.12	Simeon the New Theologian on Salvation as Deification
5.13	Anselm of Canterbury on the Atonement
5.14	Peter Abelard on the Love of Christ in Redemption
5.15	Hugh of St Victor on the Death of Christ
5.17	Thomas Aquinas on the Satisfaction of Christ
5.27	Hastings Rashdall on Christ as a Moral Example
5.29	Gustaf Aulén on the Classic Theory of the Atonement
5.30	Vladimir Lossky on Redemption as Deification
5.33	James I. Packer on Penal Substitution
5.35	Colin E. Gunton on the Language of Atonement

5.1

Irenaeus on the "Ransom" Theory of the Atonement

In this extract from *adversus haereses* ("Against the Heresies"), written in the second half of the second century, Irenaeus of Lyons (c.130–c.200) argues that the death of Christ is to be regarded as a ransom, by which God justly liberated humanity from Satanic captivity. Irenaeus avoids any suggestion that the redemption of humanity took place by force, insisting that only persuasion was used. See also 5.2, 5.4, 5.6, 5.7, 5.8.

Thus the powerful Word and true human being, ransoming us by his own blood in a rational manner, gave himself as a ransom for those who have been led into captivity. The apostate one unjustly held sway over us, and though we were by nature the possession of Almighty God, we had been alienated from our proper nature, making us instead his own disciples. Therefore the almighty Word of God, who did not lack justice, acted justly even in the encounter with the apostate one, ransoming from him the things which were his own, not by force, in the way in which [the apostate one] secured his dominion over us at the beginning, by greedily snatching what was not his own. Rather, it was appropriate that God should obtain what he wished through persuasion, not by the use of force, so that the principles of justice might not be infringed, and, at the same time, that God's original creation might not perish. The Lord therefore ransomed us by his own blood, and gave his life for our life, his flesh for our flesh; and he poured out the Spirit of the Father to bring about the union and fellowship of God and humanity, bringing God down to humanity through the Spirit while raising humanity to God through his incarnation, and in his coming surely and truly giving us incorruption through the fellowship which we have with him.

Comment

Irenaeus here develops an approach to the doctrine of the atonement which seeks to maintain justice, while maintaining the existing tradition which spoke of humanity as being under Satanic dominion as a result of sin. Note that the Latin terms such as *redimens* and *redemptio* here have the more technical sense of "ransom" rather than "redemption," and I have translated them to bring out this point clearly.

Questions for Study

1 What reasons does Irenaeus offer for humanity being under the authority of the devil?

2 In what way does the divine justice show itself in the work of redemption?
3 What motivations does Irenaeus offer for the work of redemption?

5.2

Irenaeus on "Recapitulation" in Christ

In this passage Irenaeus explores his distinctive idea of "recapitulation." For Irenaeus, this term means something like "going over again." Christ "recapitulates" the history of Adam, except he succeeds at every point at which Adam failed. Thus Adam's disobedience is matched by Christ's obedience. Thus the salvation of humanity, which was lost in Adam, was regained in Christ. See also 5.1, 5.9, 5.29.

Now it has been clearly shown that the Word which exists from the beginning with God, through whom all things were made, who was also always present with the human race, has in these last times, according to the time appointed by the Father, been united to his own creation and has been made a human being capable of suffering [*passibilem hominem factum*]. This disposes of the objection of those who say, "If he was born at that time, it follows that Christ did not exist before then." For we have shown that the Son of God did not begin to exist at that point, because he had always existed with the Father. But when he was incarnate and became a human being, he recapitulated in himself [*in seipso recapitulavit*] the long history of the human race, obtaining salvation for us, so that we might regain in Jesus Christ what we had lost in Adam, that is, being in the image and likeness of God [*secundum imaginem et similitudinem esse Dei*].

Comment

Irenaeus uses the term "recapitulation" to refer to the idea of Christ, in his work of redemption, going over again the main points at which Adam failed. Notice the way in which redemption is understood as restoring humanity to the situation which existed prior to the entry of sin into the world.

Questions for Study

1 For what reasons, according to this passage, did God become incarnate?
2 How does Irenaeus deal with the objection that the Son of God came into being only with the incarnation?
3 Irenaeus speaks of redemption in terms of regaining "in Jesus Christ what we had lost in Adam." What does he mean by this?

5.3

Clement of Alexandria on Christ's Death as an Example of Love

Clement of Alexandria (c.150–c.215) wrote a much-admired exposition of Mark 10: 17–31, in which he extends the passage to include the apostle John converting the young man "who wished to be saved." In the course of this exposition, which probably dates from the first decade of the third century, Clement deals with the manner in which Christ can be said to demonstrate the love of God for humanity. See also 5.14, 5.21, 5.27.

Consider the mysteries of love, and you will then have a vision of the bosom of the Father, whom the only-begotten God alone has declared. God himself is love, and for the sake of this love he made himself known. And while the unutterable nature of God is as a Father, his sympathy with us is as a Mother. It was in his love that the Father became the nature which derives from woman, and the great proof of this is the Son whom he begot from himself, and the love that was the fruit produced from his love. For this he came down, for this he assumed human nature, for this he willingly endured the sufferings of humanity, that by being reduced to the measure of our weakness, he might raise us to the measure of his power. And just before he poured out his offering, when he gave himself as a ransom, he left us a new testament: "I give you my love" (John 13: 34). What is the nature and extent of this love? For each of us he laid down his life, the life which was worth the whole universe, and he requires in return that we should do the same for each other.

Comment

It must be realized that this is only one aspect of Clement's discussion of the meaning of the death of Christ, so that it would be quite wrong to suggest, on the basis of this passage, that he reduces salvation to a demonstration of God's love. However, there is no doubt that this is a highly important aspect of Clement's teaching, and the passage makes it clear that it illuminates many aspects of his theology.

Questions for Study

1 How does Clement bring together paternal and maternal aspects of the love of God in this passage?
2 "Being reduced to the measure of our weakness, he might raise us to the measure of his power." Locate this statement within the passage. What does Clement mean by this?

5.4

Athanasius on the Death of Christ

Athanasius of Alexandria (c.296–373) was one of the most vigorous defenders of the doctrine of the incarnation of the Word against its Arian critics. At some point before 318, while still a young man, Athanasius wrote *de incarnatione Verbi* ("On the Incarnation of the Word"), which is now regarded as a classic statement of orthodoxy on this matter. In the passage below, Athanasius argues that human redemption is dependent upon the incarnation. It was only by taking on a real human body, capable of dying, that God was able to redeem fallen human nature. This passage indicates the close connection between Christology and soteriology. See also 4.8, 4.34, 4.37, 5.5, 5.25, 5.26.

Therefore, assuming a body like ours, because all people were liable to the corruption of death, [the Word] surrendered it to death for all humanity, and offered it to the Father. He presented it to the Father as an act of pure love for humanity, so that by all dying in him the law concerning the corruption of humanity might be abolished (inasmuch as its power was fulfilled in the Lord's body, and no longer has capacity against human beings who are like him), and that he might turn back to a state of incorruption those who had fallen into a state of corruption, and bring them to life by the fact of his death, by the body which he made his own, and by the grace of his resurrection. [. . .] The Word thus takes on a body capable of death, in order that, by partaking in the Word that is above all, this body might be worthy to die instead for all humanity, and remain incorruptible through the indwelling Word, and thus put an end to corruption through the grace of his resurrection. [. . .] Hence he did away with death for all who are like him by the offering of the body which he had taken on himself. The Word, who is above all, offered his own temple and bodily instrument as a ransom for all, and paid their debt through his death. Thus the incorruptible Son of God, being united with all humanity by likeness to them, naturally clothed all humanity with incorruption, according to the promise of the resurrection.

Comment

This passage casts important light on Athanasius's understanding of the death of Christ. Note in particular the way in which atonement and incarnation are seen virtually as two sides of the same coin.

Questions for Study

1 "Thus the incorruptible Son of God, being united with all humanity by likeness to them, naturally clothed all humanity with incorruption." Locate this passage

within the text. What does Athanasius mean by this? And how does he arrive at this conclusion?

2 Set out, in your own words, the way in which Athanasius deals with and makes use of the concepts of "corruption" and "incorruptibility."

5.5

Athanasius on the Relation of Christology and Soteriology

Athanasius defended the doctrine of the incarnation of Christ on a number of grounds, including the soteriological argument that humanity could only be redeemed by God himself. Therefore unless Christ was God, the redemption of humanity through Christ was an impossibility. In this passage, Athanasius stresses the close link between the person and work of Christ, noting in particular the soteriological aspects of the incarnation. See also 5.4, 5.25, 5.26.

If the works of the divinity of the Word had not taken place through a body, humanity would not have been made divine. And again, if the properties of the flesh had not been ascribed to the Word, humanity would not have been thoroughly freed from them. [...] But now the Word became human and took as his own the properties of the flesh. Thus, because of the Word which has come in humanity, these attributes [death and corruption] no longer pertain to the flesh, but have been destroyed in the body by the Word. Henceforth people no longer remain sinful and dead according to their own attributes, but they rise in accordance with the Word's power, and remain immortal and incorruptible. And just as the flesh is said to have been begotten from Mary the *Theotokos* [god-bearer], he himself is said to have been begotten, he who brings to birth all others so that they come into being. This is in order that he may transfer our birth to himself, that we may no longer return as earth to earth, but, being joined with the Word from heaven, we may be carried up with him into heaven.

Comment

Athanasius has no doubt that there is the closest of connections between the person and work of Christ. What Christ does is grounded in who Christ is. The functional aspects of the incarnation are thus dependent upon its ontological foundations. See 4.40.

Questions for Study

1 Set out, in your own words, the basic ideas which Athanasius develops in this passage.
2 How does Athanasius understand salvation? How is this linked with the incarnation?

5.6

Pseudo-Hippolytus on the Cosmic Dimensions of the Cross

The means by which the death of Christ on the cross enabled humanity to be redeemed was the subject of considerable speculation in the early patristic period. This anonymous fourth-century writing, which cannot be dated with any certainty, views the cross against a cosmic background, arguing that the redemption achieved by Christ affected every aspect of the universe. Note in particular the way in which the cross is seen as of central importance to the well-being of the cosmos. See also 5.1, 5.7, 5.8, 5.9.

This tree is for me a plant of eternal salvation. By it I am nourished, by it I am fed. By its roots, I am firmly planted. By its branches, I am spread out, its perfume is a delight to me, and its spirit refreshes me like a delightful wind. I have pitched my tent in its shadow, and during the heat I find it to be a haven full of fragrance. [. . .] This tree of heavenly proportions rises up from the earth to heaven. It is fixed, as an eternal growth, at the midpoint of heaven and earth. It sustains all things as the support of the universe, the base of the whole inhabited world, and the axis of the earth. Established by the invisible pegs of the Spirit, it holds together the various aspects of human nature in such a way that, divinely guided, its nature may never again become separated from God. By its peak which touches the height of the heavens, by its base which supports the earth, and by its immense arms subduing the many spirits of the air on every side, it exists in its totality in every thing and in every place.

Comment

This text takes the form of a short sermon or homily, delivered at Easter, which sets out the importance of the cross for Christian life and thought. The important point to note is that the meaning of the cross is not limited to individual human beings, but is understood to extend to the entire order of the cosmos. This reflects ideas which have always had some importance within the Greek patristic tradition – namely, that salvation is a cosmic, not simply a personal, notion.

Questions for Study

1 How is the analogy of the cross as a plant developed?
2 In what way does the cross have cosmic dimensions, according to the passage?

5.7

Rufinus of Aquileia on the "Fish-hook" Theory of the Atonement

In this passage, which dates from around the year 400, Rufinus of Aquileia (c.345–410) sets out a classic statement of the "fish-hook" or "mousetrap" theory of the atonement, which held that Christ's death on the cross was an elaborate trap laid for Satan. Satan, it was argued, held humanity so securely captive that God was unable to liberate them by any legitimate means, and thus resorted to divine deception. The humanity of Christ was the bait, and his divinity the hook. Unaware of Christ's divinity, Satan was trapped through his humanity. The highly questionable morality of this theory was the subject of intense criticism by many medieval writers. See also 5.1, 5.9, 5.10.

[The purpose of the incarnation] was that the divine virtue of the Son of God might be like a kind of hook hidden beneath the form of human flesh [. . .] to lure on the prince of this world to a contest; that the Son might offer him his human flesh as a bait and that the divinity which lay underneath might catch him and hold him fast with its hook. [. . .] Then, just as a fish when it seizes a baited hook not only fails to drag off the bait but is itself dragged out of the water to serve as food for others; so he that had the power of death seized the body of Jesus in death, unaware of the hook of divinity which lay hidden inside. Having swallowed it, he was immediately caught. The gates of hell were broken, and he was, as it were, drawn up from the pit, to become food for others.

Comment

This is thought to be one of the earliest statements of the "fish-hook" theory of the atonement. Rufinus clearly develops the idea of the humanity of Christ being the bait, and the divinity of Christ the hook, which together entrap Satan.

Questions for Study

1 Set out, in your own words, the idea that Rufinus develops in this passage.
2 Why, according to Rufinus, did Satan need to be trapped in this manner?

5.8

An Ancient Liturgy on Christ's Descent into Hell

This homily (or sermon) was probably written towards the end of the fourth century. The identity of the author is unknown, although some traditions suggest that it was Epiphanius of Constantia. The homily pictures the cosmic dimensions of the cross, particularly the impact which Christ had upon those who were held prisoner in hell. The liberation of the imprisoned dead is described in vivid and realistic terms. See also 5.2, 5.7, 5.9, 5.10.

Today, there is a great silence on earth – a great silence and a great stillness. There is a great silence because the king is sleeping. The earth trembled and is still because God has fallen asleep in the flesh, and he has raised up all who have fallen asleep ever since the beginning of the world. God has appeared in the flesh, and Hades has swallowed him. God will sleep for a short time, and then raise those who are in Hades. [. . .] He has gone to search out Adam, our first father, as if he were a lost sheep. Earnestly longing to visit those who live in darkness and the shadow of death, he – who is both their God and the son of Eve – has gone to liberate Adam from his bonds, and Eve who is held captive along with him. [. . .] "I am your God. For your sake I have become your son [. . .] I order you, O sleeper, to awake. I did not create you to be a prisoner in hell. Rise from the dead, for I am the life of the dead! Arise, my seed! Arise, my form [*morphē*], who has been made in my image [*eikōn*]!"

Comment

This homily was intended to be preached on Holy Saturday – that is, the day which separates the commemoration of the crucifixion (Good Friday) and resurrection (Easter Day) of Christ. In popular thought, this period of time represented the moment at which Christ descended into hell, in order to achieve redemption for those who were imprisoned there.

Questions for Study

1 The passage makes use of the image of "sleeping" at several points. Locate all the references. What point is being made by this imagery?
2 Adam and Eve are here treated as representatives of humanity. What conclusions does the author of this homily wish us to draw from his treatment of them?

5.9

Theodoret of Cyrrhus on the Death of Christ

Theodoret of Cyrrhus (c.393–c.460) became bishop of the Syrian city of Cyrrhus in 423, and established a reputation as a vigorous defender of the doctrine of the incarnation, which he interpreted on the basis of the Antiochene model. He fell foul of Dioscoros in the aftermath of the Council of Ephesus, and was deposed and forced into exile by the so-called "Robber Council" of Ephesus in 449. Relatively few of Theodoret's works have survived; one of them is a treatise on providence, consisting of 10 orations. The following extract is taken from the 10th and final oration. See also 5.7, 5.10.

Therefore the Lord takes upon himself the curse that lay on all humanity and removes it by a death which was not required by justice. He himself was not under the curse [. . .] but he endured the death of sinners; and he contends in judgment with the vengeful foe of all our human nature, becoming the champion and advocate of our nature. He says, with justice, to our harsh tyrant: "You are trapped, you villain, and ensnared in your own nets. [. . .] Why have you nailed my body to the cross and handed me over to death? What kind of sin have you found in me? What breach of the law did you detect? [. . .] If the smallest fault is found in me, you would have every right to hold me, in that death is the punishment of sinners. But if you find nothing in me which God's law forbids, but rather everything which it demands, I will not allow you to hold me wrongfully. What is more, I will open the prison of death for others also: and I will confine you there alone, for transgressing the law of God. [. . .] And since you have taken one prisoner unjustly, you will be deprived of all those who are in fact justly subject to you. Since you have eaten what was not to be eaten, you will vomit all that you have swallowed. [. . .] I have paid the debt, and it is right that those who were imprisoned on account of that debt should now be set free to enjoy their former liberty and return to their own homeland." With those words the Lord raised his own body, and sowed in human nature the hope of resurrection, giving the resurrection of his own body to humanity as a guarantee. Let no one suppose that this is an idle tale. We have been taught from the holy Gospels and the apostolic teachings that this is indeed a fact. We have heard the Lord himself say: "The ruler of this world is coming, and he finds nothing in me" (John 14: 30) [. . .] and in another place: "Now is the judgment of this world: now will the ruler of this world be cast out" (John 12: 31).

Comment

This interesting passage offers a more extensive reflection on the nature of redemption through the cross of Christ. In particular, it should be noted how the text engages with the moral and legal aspects of the atonement, offering explanations of how the death of Christ can be seen as the grounds of human liberation from Satanic oppression.

Questions for Study

1. Set out, in your own words, the general argument of the passage. What seems to you to be the author's main interest?
2. Theodoret places the following words into the mouth of Christ: "I have paid the debt, and it is right that those who were imprisoned on account of that debt should now be set free to enjoy their former liberty and return to their own homeland." What does he mean by this? And how does this statement merge the ideas of "ransom" and "return from exile"?

5.10

Augustine on Redemption in Christ

While Augustine (354–430) never became embroiled in any controversies concerning the significance of the death of Christ, he addressed the topic regularly in the course of his preaching. What follows is an extract from one of his later sermons, in which he offers an explanation of how that death secured human salvation. See also 5.6, 5.7, 5.9.

If Christ had not been put to death, death would not have died. The devil was conquered by his own trophy of victory. The devil jumped for joy, when he seduced the first man, and cast him down to death. By seducing the first man, he killed him; by killing the last man, he lost the first from his snare. The victory of our Lord Jesus Christ came when he rose again from the dead, and ascended into heaven. It was at this point that the text from the Book of Revelation, which you heard read today, was fulfilled:

"The lion of the tribe of Judah has won the day" (Revelation 5: 5). The one who was slain as a lamb is now called a lion – a lion on account of his courage, a lamb on account of his innocence; a lion, because he was unconquered: a lamb, because of his gentleness. By his death, the slain lamb has conquered the lion who "goes around seeking someone to devour" (1 Peter 5: 8). The devil, on the other hand, is here called a lion for his savagery, rather than his bravery. [...] The devil jumped for joy when Christ died; and by the very death of Christ the devil was overcome: he took, as it were, the bait in the mousetrap. He rejoiced at Christ's death, believing himself to be the commander of death. But that which caused his joy dangled the bait before him. The Lord's cross was the devil's mousetrap: the bait which caught him was the death of the Lord.

Comment

This passage develops the "mousetrap" model of the atonement, found in the writings of Rufinus of Aquileia (5.7). It is interesting to note the imagery that Augustine uses, especially his development of the theme of the "lion of Judah." This would become a standard feature of medieval hymnody and preaching.

Questions for Study

1 What point does Augustine make with reference to the image of a lion?
2 "The Lord's cross was the devil's mousetrap." Locate this passage within the text. What does Augustine mean by this?

5.11

Maximus of Constantinople on the Economy of Salvation

Maximus of Constantinople – also known as Maximus the Confessor – (c.580–662) is widely regarded as one of the most significant Greek Christian writers, whose ideas continue to play an important role in modern Greek and Russian Orthodox theology. He is often thought of as the last great Christian Neoplatonist, and is particularly valued for his writings on the incarnation. Maximus's writings are often quite difficult to understand, making it difficult to identify short passages suitable for study. However, his responses to a number of questions raised by his colleague Thalassius of Caesarea are relatively accessible. Our extract, taken from these responses, deals with the place of the incarnation in history. See also 5.2, 5.6, 5.12, 5.30.

The one who brought all of creation into existence, visible and invisible, according to the sole decision of prompting of his will, beyond all the ages and the very creation of all things that were created, had a supreme goodness of the will towards them. This was that he should be united, without change, with the nature of humanity, without change, through a true union of existence, so that he himself would become a human being, as he himself knows, and he would make humanity divine on account of this union with him. He therefore divided the ages wisely, and allocated one part of them to the work of his becoming a human being, and the other to the work of making humanity divine.

Of the ages that were appointed to the work of his becoming a human being, the last part has come to us, when the divine intention was fulfilled by actuality of the incarnation, which is exactly what the divine apostle studied; in the actual incarnation of God and Word he saw the fulfillment of this divine intention of God to become a human being. For this reason, he says that the end of ages has come to us (1 Corinthians 10: 11). Obviously, he does not mean by this that all the ages ended with us, but rather that the part of them which was appointed to the work of God becoming a human being has had its proper end according to the intention of God.

Since, then, the ages appointed to the work of God becoming a human being have come to fulfillment in us, and since God worked truly to complete his perfect incarnation, we should accept that the ages to come are appointed to the work of the mystical and ineffable deification of humanity, when God will reveal the supreme wealth of his goodness upon us (Ephesians 2: 7), having worked perfectly to make us worthy of such deification. Because, if he himself has completed the mystical work of the incarnation, having become like us in all manners except for sin, and having descended even to the lowest parts of the earth, where the tyranny of sin had expelled and exiled humanity, it is certain that the mystical work of the deification of humanity will also be completed in every respect, except obviously in the single respect of our identity of essence with him.

Comment

The basic theme of this passage is the divine preparation for the redemption of humanity through the incarnation. Maximus argues that Christ's incarnation must be understood to be the ultimate purpose of history because it restores the original equilibrium between God and humanity which was destroyed by Adam's fall. If Christ is not fully God and fully man, argues Maximus, salvation is impossible. The passage sets out an understanding of the economy of salvation which proposes the incarnation happening in the fullness of time, followed by a period allocated to the divinization of humanity as a result of the incarnation.

Questions for Study

1 Summarize Maximus's argument in your own words. What is the main point he wants to make? How does Maximus understand the relationship of incarnation and redemption?

2 Consider the following passage from the New Testament: "But when the fullness of time had come, God sent his Son, born of a woman, born under the law" (Galatians 4: 4). How does Maximus develop this Pauline idea?

5.12

Simeon the New Theologian on Salvation as Deification

Simeon the New Theologian (949–1022) is one of the more important early Byzantine theologians, noted for his emphasis upon the divinization of humanity through Christ. In this poem, which dates from around the year 1000, Simeon sets out the full implications of the believer being united with Christ. See also 4.23, 5.30.

But your nature is your essence, and your essence your nature.
So uniting with your body, I share in your nature,
and I truly take as mine what is yours,
uniting with your divinity, and thus becoming an heir,
superior in my body to those who have no body.
As you have said, "I have become a son of God,
not for the angels, but for us, who you have called gods."
I have said: "You are gods and are all sons of the Most High."
Glory be to your kindness and to the plan [*oikonomia*],
by which you became human, you who by nature are God,
without change or confusion, remaining the same,
and that you have made me a god, a mortal by my nature,
a god by your grace, by the power of your Spirit,
bringing together as god a unity of opposites.

Comment

Simeon is one of the Greek patristic writers regarded with especial favor by modern Orthodox theologians. In this passage he explores the nature of salvation and sets out the characteristically eastern Christian view of salvation as "deification."

Questions for Study

1 "You have made me a god, a mortal by my nature, a god by your grace." Locate this passage within the text. What does Simeon mean by this?
2 Why is the concept of union with God so important to Simeon?

5.13

Anselm of Canterbury on the Atonement

In this classic text, originally written in Latin in 1098, Anselm of Canterbury (c.1033–1109) sets out his understanding of the reason why God became human. The text as printed here is basically a series of short extracts from the work, which sum up its central themes. The most important point to note is its emphasis that, on account of sin, humanity has an obligation to offer God an infinite satisfaction, which only God can meet. Therefore a God-man would have both the ability (as God) and obligation (as a human) to pay this satisfaction, and thus obtain forgiveness of sins. See also 5.10, 5.17, 5.19, 5.29, 5.33.

The problem is, how can God forgive human sin? To clear our thoughts let us first consider what sin is, and then what a satisfaction for sin is. [. . .] To sin is to fail to render to God what God is entitled to. What is God entitled to? Righteousness, or rectitude of will. Anyone who fails to render this honor to God robs God of that which belongs to God, and thus dishonors God. And what is satisfaction? It is not enough simply to restore what has been taken away; but, in consideration of the insult offered, more than what was taken away must be rendered back. Let us consider whether God could properly remit sin by mercy alone without satisfaction. So to remit sin would be simply to abstain from punishing it. And since the only possible way of correcting sin, for which no satisfaction has been made, is to punish it; not to punish it, is to leave it uncorrected. But God cannot properly leave anything uncorrected in His kingdom. Furthermore, to leave sin unpunished would be tantamount to treating the sinful and the sinless alike, which would be inconsistent with God's nature. And this inconsistency is injustice. It is necessary, therefore, that either the honor taken away should be repaid, or punishment should be inflicted. Otherwise one of two things follows: either God is not just to his own nature; or God is powerless to do what ought to be done, which is a blasphemous supposition. The satisfaction ought to be in proportion to the sin.

Yet you have not yet duly estimated the gravity of sin. Suppose that you were standing in God's presence, and some one said to you "look over there." And God said, "I am altogether unwilling that you should look." Ask yourself whether there could be anything in the whole universe for the sake of which you would allow yourself that one look against the will of God. You should not act against the will of God, not even to prevent the whole creation from perishing. And if you were to act in this way, what could you pay for this sin? You could not make satisfaction for it, unless you were to pay something greater than the whole creation. All that is created, that is, all that is not God, cannot compensate for the sin in question.

It is necessary that God should fulfill His purpose respecting human nature. And this cannot be except there be a complete satisfaction made for sin; and this no sinner can make. Satisfaction cannot be made unless there is someone who is able to pay to God for the sin of humanity. This payment must be something greater than all that is beside God. [. . .] Now nothing is greater than all that is not God, except God. So nobody can make this satisfaction except God. And nobody ought to make it except human beings themselves. If, then, it is necessary that the kingdom of heaven should be fulfilled by the admission of humanity, and if we cannot be admitted unless this satisfaction for sin is first made, and if God only *can*, and only humanity *ought* to make this satisfaction, then it is necessary that someone must make it who is both God and a human being.

This person must have something to offer to God which is greater than all that is lower than God, and something that can be given to God voluntarily, and not as a matter of obligation. Mere obedience would not be a gift of this kind; for every rational creature owes this obedience as a duty to God. But Christ was in no way under any obligation to suffer death, in that Christ never sinned. So death was an offering that he could make as a matter of free will, rather than of debt.

Now anyone who could freely offer so great a gift to God, clearly ought to be rewarded in some way. [. . .] But what reward could be given to someone who needed nothing, someone who demanded neither a gift nor needed a pardon? [. . .] If the Son chose to make over the claim he had on God to humanity, could the Father justly forbid Him doing so, or refuse to humanity what the Son willed to give him? What greater mercy can be conceived than that God the Father should say to sinners, condemned to eternal torment and unable to redeem themselves: "Receive my only Son, and offer him for yourselves," while the Son himself said: "Take me, and redeem yourselves"? And what greater justice than that One who receives a payment far exceeding the amount due, should, if it be paid with a right intention, remit all that is due?

Comment

This passage sets out the basic features of Anselm's approach to the meaning of Christ's death, especially the concept of the "satisfaction." It may be helpful to offer a summary of the argument, which will cast light on certain aspects of this passage. The argument is complex, and can be summarized as follows.

1 God created humanity in a state of original righteousness, with the objective of bringing humanity to a state of eternal blessedness.
2 That state of eternal blessedness is contingent upon human obedience to God. However, through sin, humanity is unable to achieve this necessary obedience, which appears to frustrate God's purpose in creating humanity in the first place.
3 In that it is impossible for God's purposes to be frustrated, there must be some means by which the situation can be remedied. However, the situation can only be remedied if a satisfaction is made for sin. In other words, something has to be done, by which the offense caused by human sin can be purged.
4 There is no way in which humanity can provide this necessary satisfaction. It lacks the resources which are needed. On the other hand, God possesses the resources needed to provide the required satisfaction.
5 A "God-man" would possess both the ability (as God) and the obligation (as a human being) to pay the required satisfaction. Therefore the incarnation takes

place, in order that the required satisfaction may be made, and humanity redeemed.

Questions for Study

1 Why does Anselm take sin so seriously? And how do you think he evaluates the contributions of earlier writers, especially those who developed the "fish-hook" or "mousetrap" theories of the atonement?
2 "It is not enough simply to restore what has been taken away; but, in consideration of the insult offered, more than what was taken away must be rendered back." What is Anselm talking about here? And how does he develop this idea?
3 "So nobody can make this satisfaction except God. And nobody ought to make it except human beings themselves." Locate this passage within the text. How does Anselm arrive at this point? And where does he go from here?

5.14

Peter Abelard on the Love of Christ in Redemption

The French theologian Peter Abelard (also spelled "Abailard," 1079–1142) was one of Anselm's earliest critics. In his commentary on Romans, dating from the early decades of the twelfth century, Abelard argued that one of the chief consequences of the death of Christ was its demonstration of the love of God for humanity. It is through our response of love to Christ that we are joined to him, and benefit from his passion. See also 5.3, 5.10, 5.13, 5.16, 5.17, 5.19, 5.27.

Love is increased by the faith which we have concerning Christ on account of the belief that God in Christ has united our human nature to himself, and that by suffering in that same nature he has demonstrated to us that supreme love (*in ipsa patiendo summam illam charitatem nobis exhibuisse*) of which Christ himself speaks: "Greater love has no one than this" (John 15: 13). We are thus joined through his grace to him and our neighbor by an unbreakable bond of love. [. . .] Just as all have sinned, so they are justified without respect of person [*indifferenter*] by this supreme grace which has been made known to us by God. And this is what [Paul] declares: "For all have sinned, and all need the grace of God" (Romans 3: 23), that is, they need to glorify the Lord as a matter of obligation [. . .] Now it seems to us that we have been justified by the blood of Christ and reconciled to God in this way: through this singular act of grace made known in us (in that his Son has taken our nature on himself, and persevered in this nature, and taught us by both his word and his example, even to the point of death) he has more fully bound us to himself by love. As a result, our hearts should be set on fire by such a gift of divine grace, and true love should not hold back from suffering anything for his sake. [...] Therefore, our redemption through the suffering of Christ is that deeper love within us which not only frees us from slavery to sin, but also secures for us the true liberty of the children of God, in order that we might do all things out of love rather than out of fear – love for him who has shown us such grace that no greater can be found.

Comment

This passage has often been cited as demonstrating that Abelard held to a purely exemplarist approach to the doctrine of the atonement. In fact, the reality is rather more complex. While Abelard did indeed place considerable emphasis on the subjective aspects of atonement, that is, Christ died to become an example to humanity of God's love, he set this emphasis within a context which included a full incorporation of sacrificial understandings of the cross. This passage is of especial importance in that it demonstrates Abelard's awareness of the importance of the interior impact of the love of God for individuals, but should not be taken to imply that he therefore denied other ideas.

Questions for Study

1 Examine the role which Abelard allots to "love" in this passage. In particular, consider Abelard's understanding of how the love of God evokes a response on our part.
2 In what ways could Abelard's approach be seen as an attempt to compensate for a perceived deficiency in Anselm's?

5.15

Hugh of St Victor on the Death of Christ

This important passage, written in Latin in the first decades of the twelfth century, represents a development of the theology of atonement associated with Anselm. Hugh of St Victor (died 1142) here mingles Anselmian ideas with other motifs, including some of an explicitly sacrificial nature. Note in particular the explicit declaration that God could have redeemed humanity in another manner. See also 5.9, 5.10, 5.13, 5.14, 5.16, 5.17, 5.28.

God became a human being so that he might liberate the humanity which he had created, in order that he might be both the creator and redeemer of humanity. [...] From our nature, he took a victim for our nature, so that the whole burnt offering which was offered up might come from that which is ours. He did this so that the redemption to be offered might have a connection with us, through its being taken from what is ours. We are truly made to be partakers in this redemption if we are united through faith to the redeemer who has entered into fellowship with us through his flesh. Now human nature had become corrupted by sin, and had thus become liable to condemnation on its account. But grace came, and chose some from the mass of humanity through mercy for salvation, while it allowed others to remain for condemnation through justice. Those who grace saved through mercy were not saved without justice, in that it was in its power to do this justly; yet even if it had not saved them, it would still have acted justly, in that in terms of their merit, it would not have been unjust to have acted in this way. [...]

God, however, would have been able to achieve the redemption of humanity in a totally different manner, if he had wanted to. It was, however, more appropriate to our weakness that God should become a human being, and that he should transform humanity for the hope of immortality by taking its mortality upon himself. In this way, humanity might have the hope of ascending to the good things of the one who descended to bear its evils, and the humanity which has been glorified in God might be an example of glorification to us.

Comment

Hugh of St Victor here brings together a number of important themes relating to the meaning of the death of Christ. Note especially the way in which Hugh is concerned to show continuity between the human predicament and the redemption which was achieved by Christ.

Questions for Study

1 "From our nature, he took a victim for our nature, so that the whole burnt offering which was offered up might come from that which is ours." Locate this passage in the text. What does Hugh mean by this? And why does he regard it as being important that Christ should in some sense be the "representative" of humanity in this sacrifice?
2 Hugh makes it clear that it was appropriate, rather than necessary, that God should become incarnate in order to redeem us. In what ways was the incarnation "appropriate" for this purpose?

5.16

Rupert of Deutz on the Incarnation as God's Response to Sin

Rupert of Deutz (c.1075–1129) was a Benedictine monk who was educated and spent most of his life in the diocese of Liège, before becoming abbot of Deutz, near Cologne. He was one of the greatest biblical commentators of his age, producing works on the four books of Kings, Job, the Song of Solomon, the 12 minor prophets, Matthew, John, and Revelation. His discussion of major issues of theology is often set within the context of the exposition of biblical passages. Rupert is noted for his defense of the view that Christ would have become incarnate irrespective of the Fall of humanity. The extract for study is taken from his comments on the 13th chapter of Matthew's Gospel. See also 4.21, 4.22.

Here it is first proper to ask whether or not the Son of God, whom this discourse concerns, would have become incarnate, without the intervention of sin, on account of which all shall die. There is no doubt that he would not have become mortal and assumed a mortal body if sin had not occurred and caused humanity to become mortal; only an infidel could be ignorant about this. The real question is this: would this have occurred, and would it somehow have been necessary for humanity that God became incarnate, the Head and King of all, as He now is? What will be the answer? [. . .] Since, with regard to the saints and all the elect there is no doubt but that they will all be found, up to the number appointed in God's plan, about which he speaks in blessing them, before sin, "Increase and multiply," and it is absurd to think that sin was necessary in order to achieve that number, what must be thought about the very Head and King of all the elect, angels and men, but that he had indeed no necessary cause for becoming man, other than that his love's "delights were to be with the children of men" (Proverbs 8:31).

Comment

Like his near-contemporary Honorius of Autun, Rupert was unpersuaded by the theological consensus of his day, according to which the coming of Christ was precipitated by human sin. Rupert's brief discussion of this matter makes it clear that he believes the incarnation of the Son of God to be the result of God's wish to dwell among his people, so that the incarnation can be seen as the climax of the work of creation, rather than a reaction to human sin.

Questions for Study

1 Set out, in your own words, Rupert's argument for the incarnation. What role does sin play in his reasoning?
2 A similar conclusion concerning the logic of the incarnation is reached by Honorius of Autun (4.21). Compare the two writers' arguments on this question. Their conclusions are analogous – but what about the arguments that lead to them?

5.17

Thomas Aquinas on the Satisfaction of Christ

The *Summa Theologiae* ("The Totality of Theology"), which Aquinas began to write in Latin in 1265 and left unfinished at the time of his death, is widely regarded as the greatest work of medieval theology. In this important and influential analysis, Aquinas (c.1225–74) develops the Anselmian theme of satisfaction, dealing with a number of objections which had been raised against it. Note in particular his response to the criticism that the dignity of Christ was not sufficient to obtain God's forgiveness of human sin. See also 5.10, 5.13, 5.14, 5.15, 5.16, 5.27.

1. It seems that the passion of Christ did not effect our salvation by way of satisfaction. For it seems that to make satisfaction is the responsibility of the one who sins, as is clear from other aspects of penance, in that the one who sins is the one who must repent and confess. But Christ did not sin. As St Peter says, "he committed no sin" (1 Peter 2: 22). He therefore did not make satisfaction through his passion.

2. Furthermore, satisfaction can never be made by means of a greater offense. But the greatest offense was perpetrated in the passion of Christ, since those who put him to death committed the most grievous of sins. For this reason, satisfaction could not be made to God through the passion of Christ.

3. Furthermore, satisfaction implies a certain equality with the fault, since it is an act of justice. But the passion of Christ does not seem to be equal to all the sins of the human race, since Christ suffered according to the flesh, not according to his divinity. As St Peter says, "Christ has suffered in the flesh" (1 Peter 4: 1). [. . .] Christ therefore did not make satisfaction for our sins by his passion. [. . .]

I reply that a proper satisfaction comes about when someone offers to the person offended something which gives him a delight greater than his hatred of the offense. Now Christ by suffering as a result of love and obedience offered to God something greater than what might be exacted in compensation for the whole offense of humanity; firstly, because of the greatness of the love, as a result of which he suffered; secondly, because of the worth of the life which he laid down for a satisfaction, which was the life of God and of a human being; thirdly, because of the comprehensiveness of his passion and the greatness of the sorrow which he took upon himself. [...] And therefore the passion of Christ was not only sufficient but a superabundant satisfaction for the sins of the human race. As John says, "he is a propitiation for our sins, not only for ours, but also for those of the whole world" (1 John 2: 2).

Hence, in reply to the first point, the head and the members are as it were one mystical person; and thus the satisfaction of Christ belongs to all the faithful as to his members. [...] In reply to the second, the love of Christ in his suffering outweighed the malice of them that crucified him. [...] In reply to the third, the worth of Christ's flesh is to be reckoned, not just according to the nature of flesh [*solum secundum carnis naturam*], but according to the person who assumed it [*secundum personam assumentem*], in that it was the flesh of God, from whom it gained an infinite worth.

Comment

Anselm was responsible for the introduction of the notion of the "satisfaction" to help account for the mechanics of the atonement (5.13). In this important discussion Aquinas aimed to clarify a number of critical issues relating to this concept, especially the question of what it was about Christ that made this "satisfaction" so intrinsically worthy.

Questions for Study

1 Set out in your own words the three issues Aquinas considers, making sure that you have accurately summarized both the points at issue and the responses that Aquinas makes.
2 "The worth of Christ's flesh is to be reckoned, not just according to the nature of flesh, but according to the person who assumed it." Locate this passage in the text. What does Aquinas mean by this? And how does this assertion allow him to deal with a potential difficulty concerning the satisfaction?

5.18

Nicholas Cabasilas on the Death of Christ

This fourteenth-century work, which incorporates some of the major representive strands of Byzantine theology, deals with the purpose of Christ's death. Nicholas Cabasilas (born c.1322) here argues that Christ's death took place in such a way that he was able to deal with each of the three afflictions of sinful humanity. See also 5.4, 5.9, 5.27.

Just as humanity was cut off from God in three ways – by nature, sin, and death – so the Savior operated in such a way that it might come to him directly, without any obstacles. He did this by successively removing everything which stood in its way; the first, by sharing in human nature; the second, by undergoing death on the cross; and finally, the third dividing barrier by rising from the dead, and banishing the tyranny of death totally from our nature.

Comment

This very brief extract needs little comment, in that the point is made very clearly. Cabasilas clarifies the nature of sin and, in so doing, is able to demonstrate how there is a direct correlation between sin and redemption.

Questions for Study

1 What are the "three ways" in which humanity is alienated from God?
2 In what way does the specific mode of redemption in Christ relate to each of these "three ways"?

5.19

John Calvin on the Grounds of Redemption

In this letter Calvin (1509–64) provides a very brief summary of his general position concerning the doctrine of redemption. A fuller treatment may be found in his *Institutes of the Christian Religion*, book 2, chapters 1–17. The style used by Calvin in his brief "letter of advice" (*consilium*) is much lighter and simpler than that adopted in the *Institutes*, making this extract unusually easy to follow and understand. See also 5.13, 51.4, 5.15, 5.16, 5.17, 5.22, 5.28, 5.33.

The first man of all was created by God with an immortal soul and a mortal body. God adorned him with his own likeness [*similitudo*], so that he was free from any evil, and he commanded him to enjoy all that was in his pleasant garden, with the exception of the tree in which all life was hidden. He was so concerned that he should keep his hand away from this tree that he told him that he would die when he first touched its fruit. However, he did touch it. As a result, he died and was no longer like God. This was the primary origin of death. That this is true is proved by the following words: "As often as you eat of it, you will die." [...] Man was therefore driven into exile, along with his descendants, in order that, having lost "the horn of plenty," he should be miserable and experience all kinds of work and every ill; seeking food, sweating, and suffering cold; often hungry, often thirsty, always wretched. Finally, God took pity upon this unfortunate and thoroughly unhappy man. Although the sentence which he passed upon him was correct, he nevertheless gave his only and much-loved Son as a sacrificial victim for such sins. By reason of this amazing and unexpected mercy [*admirabili et inusitata misericordiae ratione*], God commended his own love towards us more greatly than if he had rescinded this sentence. Therefore Christ, the Son of God, was both conceived through the overshadowing of the Holy Spirit and born of the virgin. He was finally raised up on the cross, and through his own death delivered the human race from eternal death.

Comment

In this very compressed discussion Calvin sets out to explain how sin entered into the world, and the manner in which God chose to respond to this development. It is important to note how Calvin affirms that the quality of the redeemed life exceeds that of the innocent life. Note especially how Calvin argues that God's bearing the penalty for sin was a far more effective demonstration of the love of God for humanity than the mere rescinding of any penalty that was due.

Questions for Study

1 According to Calvin, how did sin enter into the world? And what were its effects?
2 What images of salvation can you discern within this passage?

5.20

The Socinian Critique of the Idea of Satisfaction

The Socinian critique of the idea of satisfaction gained influence during the sixteenth century. *The Racovian Catechism*, published in Polish in 1605 at the city of Racow (from which it takes its name), argued that God was perfectly capable of forgiving human sin without the need for the death of Christ, and vigorously opposed the idea of Christ's death representing any form of satisfaction. This extract is taken from the English translation of Thomas Rees, first published in London in 1818. See 5.10, 5.13, 5.17, 5.19, 5.27.

But did not Christ die also, in order, properly speaking, to purchase our salvation, and literally to pay the debt of our sins? Although Christians at this time commonly so believe, yet this notion is false, erroneous, and exceedingly pernicious; since they conceive that Christ suffered an equivalent punishment for our sins, and by the price of his obedience exactly compensated our disobedience. There is no doubt, however, but that Christ so satisfied God by his obedience, as that he completely fulfilled the whole of his will, and by his obedience obtained, through the grace of God, for all of us who believe in him, the remission of our sins, and eternal salvation.

How do you make it appear that the common notion is false and erroneous?

Not only because the Scriptures are silent concerning it, but also because it is repugnant to the Scriptures and to right reason. [. . .] They who maintain this opinion never adduce explicit texts of Scripture in proof of it, but string together certain inferences by which they endeavour to maintain their assertions. But, besides that a matter of this kind, whereon they themselves conceive the whole business of salvation to turn, ought certainly to be demonstrated not by inferences alone but by clear testimonies of Scripture, it might easily be shown that these inferences have no force whatever. [. . .] The Scriptures every where testify that God forgives men their sins freely, and especially under the New Covenant (2 Corinthians 5: 19; Romans 3: 24, 25; Matthew 18: 23; &c.). But to a free forgiveness nothing is more opposite than such a satisfaction as they contend for, and the payment of an equivalent price. For where a creditor is satisfied, either by the debtor himself, or by another person on the debtor's behalf, it cannot with truth be said of him that he freely forgives the debt. [. . .] It would follow that Christ, if he has satisfied God for our sins, has submitted to eternal death; since it appears that the penalty which men had incurred by their offences was eternal death; not to say that one death, though it were eternal in duration, – much less one so short, – could not of itself be equal to innumerable eternal deaths. For if you say that the death of Christ, because he was a God infinite in nature, was equal to the infinite deaths of the infinite race of men, – besides that I have already refuted this opinion concerning the nature of Christ, – it would follow that God's infinite nature itself suffered death. But as death cannot any way belong to the infinity of the divine nature, so neither, literally speaking (as must necessarily be done here where we are treating of a real compensation and payment), can the infinity of the divine nature any way belong to death. In the next place, it would follow that there was no necessity that Christ should endure such sufferings, and so dreadful a death; and that God – be it spoken without offence, – was unjust, who, when he might well have been contented with one drop (as they say) of the blood of Christ, would have him so severely tormented. Lastly, it would follow that we were more obliged to Christ than to God, and owed him more, indeed owed him every thing; since he, by this satisfaction, showed us much kindness; whereas God, by exacting his debt, showed us no kindness at all. [. . .]

They endeavour to [maintain this] first by a certain reason, and then by the authority of Scripture. [. . .] They say that there are in God, by nature, justice and mercy: that as it is the property of mercy to forgive sins, so is it, they state, the property of justice to punish every sin whatever. But since God willed that both his mercy and justice should be satisfied together, he devised this plan, that Christ should suffer death in our stead, and thus satisfy God's justice in the human nature, by which he had been offended; and that his mercy should at the same time be displayed in forgiving sin. [. . .] This reason bears the appearance of plausibility, but in reality has in it nothing of truth or solidity; and indeed involves a self-contradiction. For although we confess, and hence exceedingly rejoice, that our God is wonderfully merciful and just, nevertheless we deny that there are in him the mercy and justice which our adversaries imagine, since the one would wholly annihilate the other. For, according to them, the one requires that God should punish no sin; the other, that he should leave no sin unpunished. If then it were naturally a property of God to punish no sin, he could not act against his nature in order that he might punish sin: in like manner also, if it were naturally a property of God to leave no sin unpunished, he could not, any more, contrary to his nature, refrain from punishing every sin. For God can never do any thing repugnant to those properties which pertain to him by nature. For instance, since wisdom belongs naturally to God, he can never do any thing contrary to it, but whatever he does he does wisely. But as it is evident that God forgives and punishes sins whenever he deems fit it appears that the mercy which commands to spare, and the justice which commands to destroy, do so exist in him as that both are tempered by his will, and by the wisdom, the benignity, and holiness of his nature. Besides, the scriptures are not wont to designate the justice, which is opposed to mercy, and is discernible in punishments inflicted in wrath, by this term, but style it the *severity*, the *anger*, and *wrath* of God.

[. . .] Since I have shown that the mercy and justice which our adversaries conceive to pertain to God by nature, certainly do not belong to him, there was no need of that plan whereby he might satisfy such mercy and justice, and by which they might, as it were by a certain tempering, be reconciled to each other: which tempering nevertheless is such that it satisfies neither, and indeed destroys both; – For what is that justice, and what too that mercy, which punishes the innocent, and absolves the guilty? I do not, indeed, deny that there is a natural justice in God, which is called rectitude, and is opposed to wickedness: this shines in all his works, and hence they all appear just and right and perfect; and that, no less when he forgives than when he punishes our transgressions.

Comment

Earlier, we noted how Thomas Aquinas had developed some of the themes first set out by Anselm of Canterbury in relation to the concept of "satisfaction" (5.17). The present passage offers a sustained and strongly rationalist critique of the idea. The fundamental theme of the passage is that God requires no intermediaries in order to forgive sin.

Questions for Study

1 What specific criticisms does the passage direct against the idea that the death of Christ is necessary in order to secure divine forgiveness of sins? You will find it helpful to summarize the passage in your own words.

2 "It is repugnant to the Scriptures and to right reason." To what does the Catechism refer at this point? What reasons does it offer for this judgment? And what alternative does it set forth?

5.21

John Donne on the Work of Christ

John Donne (1571–1631) established a reputation as one of England's finest secular and religious poets. This poem, taken from the collection known as the "Holy Sonnets," indicates the approaches to the incarnation and atonement which were prevalent in the high noon of Anglican theology, just before the period of the Civil War. In this early edition, the sonnet appears as the 11th in a collection of 12; later editions treat it as the 15th in a collection of 19. The original orthography has been retained. See also 5.10, 5.13, 5.14, 5.15, 5.16, 5.17, 5.19.

Wilt thou love God, as he thee? then digest,
My Soul, this wholesome meditation,
How God the Spirit, by Angels waited on
In heaven, doth make his Temple in thy breast.
The Father having begot a Son most blest,
And still begetting, (for he ne'r begonne)
Hath deign'd to choose thee by adoption,
Coheir to his glory, and Sabbath's endlesse rest;
And, as a robbed man, which by search doth find
His stolen stuff sold, must lose or buy it again:
The Son of glory came down, and was slain,
Us whom he had made, and Satan stole, to unbind.
'Twas much, that man was made like God before,
But, that God should be made like man, much more.

Comment

Donne's poetry is widely regarded as representing one of the most important styles of theological discourse in Elizabethan England. This sonnet deals with the divine motivation for redemption, and its implications for our understanding of the love of God. Note in particular Donne's argument that Christ's incarnation and death can be seen as a counterweight to the work of Satan. What Satan stole, Christ legitimately and justly purchased.

Questions for Study

1 The sonnet can be regarded as an exploration of the nature of the love of God for humanity. What are the main points that Donne makes in this respect?
2 Read again the concluding couplet of the sonnet. What does Donne mean by these words?

'Twas much, that man was made like God before,
But, that God should be made like man, much more.

5.22

George Herbert on the Death of Christ and Redemption

George Herbert (1593–1633) was one of the most important Anglican poets of the seventeenth century, and regularly incorporated theological reflections within his poetry. In this poem, which forms part of the collection known as "The Temple," composed around 1633, the poet explores the associations of the term "redemption." See also 5.13, 51.4, 5.15, 5.16, 5.17, 5.28, 5.33.

Having been tenant long to a rich Lord,
Not thriving, I resolved to be bold,
And make a suit unto him, to afford
A new small-rented lease, and cancel th'old,

In heaven at his manor I him sought:
They told me there, that he was lately gone
About some land, which he had dearly bought,
Long since on earth, to take possession.

I straight returned, and knowing his great birth,
Sought him accordingly in great resorts;
In cities, theatres, gardens, parks, and courts:
At length I heard a ragged noise and mirth

Of thieves and murderers: there I him espied,
Who straight, *Your suit is granted,* said, & died.

Comment

Alluding to the Old Testament notion of "redeeming land," Herbert develops the idea of the death of Christ as the price by which God takes legitimate possession of a precious piece of land. While also exploring the idea of the shame and humility of the cross, Herbert is able to bring out the legal and financial dimensions of redemption. Note in particular the way in which Herbert brings out the costliness of redemption, and also the way in which he develops the idea of the humility of God in the incarnation.

Questions for Study

1 Set out, in ordinary English prose, the basic line of argument of the poem. In particular, try to identify the various ways in which Herbert uses the idea of "redemption."
2 What does Herbert mean by the following lines of the poem?

> I straight returned, and knowing his great birth,
> Sought him accordingly in great resorts;
> In cities, theatres, gardens, parks, and courts.

5.23

Charles Wesley on Salvation in Christ

On May 21, 1738, Charles Wesley (1707–88) underwent a profound conversion experience through the ministry of the Moravian Peter Böhler. In this hymn, written a year after this experience, Wesley put into verse his understanding of the significance of the death of Christ for Christian believers. See also 5.3, 5.4, 5.12, 5.13, 5.14, 5.15, 5.19, 5.21.

> And can it be that I should gain
> An int'rest in the Saviour's blood!
> Dy'd he for me? – who caus'd his pain?
> For me? – who Him to Death pursued?
> Amazing love! How can it be
> That Thou, my God, shouldst die for me?
>
> 'Tis mystery all! Th'Immortal dies!
> Who can explore his strange Design?

In vain the first-born Seraph tries
   To sound the Depths of Love divine.
'Tis mercy all! Let earth adore;
Let Angel Minds inquire no more.

He left his Father's throne above
   (So free, so infinite his grace!)
Empty'd himself of All but Love,
   And bled for *Adam's* helpless Race.
'Tis Mercy all, immense and free,
For, O my God! it found out Me!

Long my imprison'd Spirit lay,
   Fast bound in Sin and Nature's Night
Thine Eye diffus'd a quickning Ray;
   I woke; the Dungeon flam'd with Light.
My Chains fell off, my Heart was free,
I rose, went forth, and follow'd Thee.

Still the small inward Voice I hear,
   That whispers all my Sins forgiv'n;
Still the atoning Blood is near,
   That quench'd the Wrath of hostile Heav'n:
I feel the Life his Wounds impart;
I feel my Saviour in my Heart.

No Condemnation now I dread,
   Jesus, and all in Him, is mine.
Alive in Him, my Living Head,
   And clothed in Righteousness Divine,
Bold I approach th'Eternal Throne,
And claim the Crown, thro' CHRIST my own.

Comment

Note the way in which the hymn brings together a range of images relating to salvation, including liberation and enlightenment. The hymn, originally entitled "Free Grace," can be seen as a summary of the "economy of salvation," placing considerable emphasis upon the self-humiliation of Christ. Notice also the explicit references to the suffering and death of God, most notably in the exclamation "th'Immortal dies"! The original English text (which differs significantly from later versions) is here reproduced without any alterations. Note that the theologically significant fifth verse, which deals with the subjective assurance of salvation and the experiential aspects of Christian existence, is omitted in modern versions. Two points should be noted about Wesley's English: "'Tis" is an archaic version of "It is"; "quickning" is an archaic form of "life-giving."

Questions for Study

1 How many images of sin and salvation can you discern in this hymn? Why do you think Wesley uses such richly visual imagery here?
2 Are there any sections of this hymn which point to the idea of a "suffering God"?

5.24

F. D. E. Schleiermacher on Christ as a Charismatic Leader

In the second edition of his *Christian Faith* (1834), F. D. E. Schleiermacher (1768–1834) set out an account of the role of Jesus as the founder of the Christian community. Aware of the rationalist challenge to traditional Christian teachings concerning the work of Christ, Schleiermacher sought to give an account of the supreme significance of Jesus for the Christian church which avoided concepts and values which were known to be objectionable to the Enlightenment. The model of Christ as a charismatic community leader seemed to offer Schleiermacher precisely such a way of explaining the significance of Jesus. See also 4.27, 5.25.

An analogy to this relation may be pointed out in a sphere which is universally familiar. As contrasted with the condition of things existing before there was any law, the civil community within a defined area is a higher vital potency. Let us now suppose that some person for the first time combines a naturally cohesive group into a civil community (legend tells of such cases in plenty); what happens is that the idea of the state first comes to consciousness in him, and takes possession of his personality as its immediate dwelling-place. Then he assumes the rest into the living fellowship of the idea. He does so by making them clearly conscious of the unsatisfactoriness of their present condition by effective speech. The power remains with the founder of forming in them the idea which is the innermost principle of his own life, and of assuming them into the fellowship of that life. The result is, not only that there arises among them a new corporate life, in complete contrast to the old, but also that each of them becomes in themselves new persons – that is to say, citizens. And everything resulting from this is the corporate life – developing variously with the process of time, yet remaining essentially the same – of this idea which emerged at that particular point of time, but was always predestined in the nature of that particular racial stock. The analogy might be pushed even further, to points of which we shall speak later. But even this presentation of it will seem mystical to those who admit only a meagre and inferior conception of the civic state.

Let us be content, then, that our view of the matter should be called mystical in this sense; naturally everything to be derived from this main point will be called mystical too. But just as this mystical view can substantiate its claim to be the original one, so too it claims to be the true mean between two others, of which I shall call the one the magical way, and the other the empirical. The former admits, of course, that the activity of Christ is redemptive, but denies that the communication of His perfection is dependent on the founding of a community; it results, they maintain, from His immediate influence upon the individual: and for this some take the written word to be a necessary means, others do not. The latter show themselves the more consistent, but the more completely they cut themselves loose from everything originating in the community the more obvious becomes the magical character of their view. This magical character lies in an influence not mediated by anything natural, yet attributed to a person. This is completely at variance with the maxim everywhere underlying our presentation, that the beginning of the Kingdom of God is a supernatural thing, which, however, becomes natural as soon as it emerges into manifestation; for this other view makes every significant moment a supernatural one. Further, this view is completely separatist in type, for it makes the corporate life a purely accidental thing; and it comes very near being docetic as well. For if Christ exerted influence in any such way as this – as a person, it is true, but only as a heavenly person without earthly presence, though in a truly personal way – then it would have been possible for Him to work in just the same way at any time, and His real personal appearance in history was only a superfluous adjunct. But those who likewise assume an immediate personal influence, but mediate it through the word and the fellowship, are less magical only if they attribute to these the power of evoking a mood in which the individual becomes susceptible to that personal influence. They are more magical still, if these natural elements have the power of disposing Christ to exert His influence; for then their efficacy is exactly like that attributed to magic spells. The contrary empirical view also, it is true, admits a redemptive activity on the part of Christ, but one which is held to consist only in bringing about an increasing perfection in us; and this cannot properly occur otherwise than in the forms of teaching and example. These forms are general; there is nothing distinctive in them. Even suppose it admitted that Christ is distinguished from others who contribute in the same way to our improvement, by the pure perfection of His teaching and His example, yet if all that is achieved in us is something imperfect, there remains nothing but to forgo the idea of redemption in the proper sense – that is, as the removal of sin – and, in view of the consciousness of sin still remaining even in our growing perfection, to pacify ourselves with a general appeal to the divine compassion. Now, teaching and example effect no more than such a growing perfection, and this appeal to the divine compassion occurs even apart from Christ. It must therefore be admitted that His appearance, in so far as intended to be something special, would in that case be in vain. At most it might be said that by His teaching He brought people to the point of giving up the effort, previously universal, to offer God substitutes for the perfection they lacked. But since the uselessness of this effort can be demonstrated, already in our natural intelligence we have the divine certainty of this, and had no need to obtain it elsewhere. And probably this view is chiefly to blame for the claim of philosophy to set itself above faith and to treat faith as merely a transitional stage. But we cannot rest satisfied with the consciousness of growing perfection, for that belongs just as much to the consciousness of sin as to that of grace, and hence cannot contain what is peculiarly Christian. But, for the Christian, nothing belongs to the consciousness of grace unless it is traced to the Redeemer as its cause, and therefore it must always be a different thing in His case from what it is in the case of others – naturally, since it is bound up with something else, namely, the peculiar redemptive activity of Christ.

Comment

Schleiermacher locates the significance of Jesus of Nazareth in terms of the impact which he has upon the church, or "community of faith." Reacting against the rationalism and moralism of the Enlightenment, Schleiermacher stressed the importance of religious feeling, particularly a "feeling of absolute dependence" on God. This feeling, he argued, is brought about by Jesus Christ. But how? In this passage, Schleiermacher suggests that Jesus of Nazareth relates to the church in much the same way as a charismatic leader relates to his or her people. Note in particular the emphasis placed upon the role of the community, and the criticism of the traditional language of "satisfaction," which Schleiermacher here refers to as "magical."

Questions for Study

1 What difficulties does Schleiermacher note with what he terms the "magical" understanding of the work of Christ? Which of the writers considered in this chapter of *The Christian Theology Reader* do you think might fall into this category?
2 Set out, in your own words, the model that Schleiermacher wishes to commend. Assuming that its intended readership was rationalist in nature, how would this have been received? And how is this approach to be viewed today, now that the constraints of a rationalist worldview have been removed?

5.25

F. D. E. Schleiermacher on Christology and Soteriology

In this highly influential discussion of the relation of Christology and soteriology, Schleiermacher argues that the doctrines of the person and work of Christ are inseparable. The "activity" and "dignity" of Christ are mutually related concepts, which cannot be discussed in isolation from each other. Previously, dogmatic textbooks had tended to regard these two areas of theology as distinct; since Schleiermacher, they have generally been discussed together. See also 5.5, 5.24, 5.26.

The peculiar activity and the exclusive dignity of the Redeemer imply each other, and are inseparably one in the self-consciousness of believers.

1. Whether we prefer to call Christ the Redeemer, or to regard Him as the one in whom the creation of human nature, which up to this point had existed only in a provisional state, was perfected, each of these points of view means only that we ascribe to Him a peculiar activity, and that in connexion with a peculiar spiritual content of His person. For if His influence is only of the same kind as that of others, even if it is ever so much more complete and inclusive, then its result also, that is, the salvation of humanity, would be a work common to Him and the others, although His share might be the greater; and there would be, not one Redeemer over against the redeemed, but many, of whom one would only be the first among those like Him. Nor would the human creation then be completed through Him, but through all of those redeemers together, who, in so far as their work implies in them a peculiar quality of nature, are all alike distinguished from the rest of humanity. It would be just the same, if His activity were indeed peculiar to Himself, but this less in virtue of an inner quality belonging to Him than of a peculiar position in which He had been put. The second form of expression, that the human creation had been completed in Him, would then be altogether without content, since it would be more natural to suppose that there are many like Him, only they did not happen to occupy the same position. In that case He would not even be properly Redeemer, even though it could be said that humanity had been redeemed through His act or His suffering, as the case might be. For the result, namely, salvation, could not be something communicated from Him (since He had nothing peculiar to Himself); it could only have been occasioned or released by Him.

   Just as little could the approximation to the condition of blessedness be traced to Him, if He had indeed had an exclusive dignity, but had remained passive in it, and had exercised no influence corresponding to it. For (apart from the fact that it is incomprehensible how His contemporaries, and we after them, should ever have come to attribute such an influence to Him, especially when the manner of His appearance was what it was), supposing that the blessedness could have been communicated merely through people observing this dignity, although there were united with it no influence acting on others, then in the observers there must have been something more than receptivity; His appearance would have to be regarded rather as merely the occasion for this idea, spontaneously produced by themselves.
2. Thus the approximation to blessedness, out of the state of misery, cannot be explained as a fact mediated through Jesus, by reference to either of these elements without the other. It follows, therefore, that they must be most intimately related and mutually determined. So that it is vain to attribute to the Redeemer a higher dignity than the activity at the same time ascribed to Him demands, since nothing is explained by this surplus of dignity. It is equally vain to attribute to Him a greater activity than follows naturally from the dignity which one is ready to allow to Him, since whatever results from this surplus of activity cannot be traced to Him in the same sense as the rest. Therefore every doctrine of Christ is inconsistent, in which this equality (of dignity and activity) is not essential, whether it seeks to disguise the detraction from the dignity by praising in Him great but really alien

activities, or, conversely, seeks to compensate for the lesser influence which it allows Him by highly exalting Him, yet in a fashion which leads to no result.

3. If we hold fast to this rule, we could treat the whole doctrine of Christ either as that of His activity, for then the dignity must naturally follow from that, or as that of His dignity, for the activity must then result of itself. This is indicated by the two general formulae above. For that the creation of human nature has been completed in His person is in and by itself only a description of His dignity, greater or less, according as the difference between the condition before and after is regarded as greater or less; but the activity follows of itself, if indeed the creation is to continue to exist. Again, that He is the Redeemer similarly describes His activity, but the dignity follows of itself to just the same degree.

Comment

Schleiermacher's insistence that Christ's "activity" and "dignity" cannot be considered in isolation from one another has been widely accepted within modern theology. The most fundamental statement within this passage which should be noted is the following: "The peculiar activity and the exclusive dignity of the Redeemer imply each other, and are inseparably one in the self-consciousness of believers." Note the dual grounding of this statement: first, they are related on account of their inner nature and interconnectedness; second, they are related in the experience of believers, in that who Jesus *is* cannot be separated from what Jesus is *experienced* as having done.

Questions for Study

1 "Who Jesus Christ is becomes known in his saving action" (Philip Melanchthon). How might Schleiermacher respond to this statement?

2 Set out, in your own words, the trajectory of Schleiermacher's argument in this text. Given that the intended readership of this passage would have been inclined to be sympathetic to rationalism, how does Schleiermacher seek to establish the "peculiar activity and dignity" of Christ?

5.26

Charles Gore on the Relation of Christology and Soteriology

In this review of a series of somewhat mediocre English works dealing with aspects of Christology, Charles Gore (1853–1932) turns to discuss the relation between what human nature requires and the identity of Jesus Christ. After an analysis of the weaknesses of moral understandings of the person of Christ, Gore famously declares that "the Nestorian Christ is the fitting Saviour of the Pelagian man." See also 5.5, 5.25.

Inadequate conceptions of Christ's person go hand in hand with inadequate conceptions of what human nature wants. The Nestorian conception of Christ [...] qualifies Christ for being an example of what man can do, and into what wonderful union with God he can be assumed if he is holy enough; but Christ remains one man among many, shut in within the limits of a single human personality, and influencing man only from outside. He can be a Redeemer of man if man can be saved from outside by bright example, but not otherwise. The Nestorian Christ is logically associated with the Pelagian man. [...] The Nestorian Christ is the fitting Saviour of the Pelagian man.

Comment

Gore's argument is very clear and requires no comment. However, it must be noted that Gore was writing at a time when "Nestorianism" was widely equated with a view of the person of Jesus Christ which stressed his moral example. Modern scholarship has modified this judgment, on account of the subsequent discovery of some of Nestorius's works. Gore's point could perhaps be better expressed as: "The exemplarist Christ is the fitting saviour of the Pelagian person."

Questions for Study

1 "Inadequate conceptions of Christ's person go hand in hand with inadequate conceptions of what human nature wants." Gore here implies a close linkage between concepts of sin and concepts of salvation. Do you think that he is right?
2 What is the basic point that Gore wishes to make concerning the deficiencies of an exemplarist Christology?

5.27

Hastings Rashdall on Christ as a Moral Example

In this sermon, preached at Oxford in 1892, the noted English modernist Hastings Rashdall (1858–1924) argued that the new intellectual climate in England demanded a new statement of traditional Christian teachings. The area of theology which he singled out for special mention in this respect is the doctrine of the atonement; or, more specifically, approaches to this doctrine which seem to make irrational claims and judgments. Rashdall argues that a more congenial approach to the cross lies in the exemplarism offered by Peter Abelard, and proceeds to explore its utility for a modern age. Rashdall sets out this position by examining Matthew 20: 28, which speaks of Christ offering his life "as a ransom for many." See also 5.3, 5.13, 5.14, 5.20.

The history of the interpretation of this text [Matthew 20: 28] is indeed a melancholy example of the theological tendency to make systems out of metaphors. [...] In Origen, and still more clearly in later Fathers, it appears that Satan was deliberately deceived by God. He was somehow or other induced to believe that in bringing about the death of Christ he would get possession of his soul. But there he over-reached himself; he found that there was one soul which could not be held in Hades. The very device by which he had hoped to complete his triumph became the means of his own ruin, and the whole body of his ancient subjects escaped his wrath.

Such, in brief outline, was the theory of the Atonement which on the whole held possession of Christian Theology throughout the patristic period. [...] I wish to call attention to the work of the great men to whom Christendom owes its emancipation from this grotesque absurdity. Among all the enormous services of Scholasticism to human progress, none is greater than this; none supplies better evidence that in very many respects the scholastic age was intellectually in advance of the patristic. The demolition of this time-honoured theory was effected principally by two men [...] the attack on the received theology was begun by St Anselm; the decisive victory was won by Abelard. [...]

[After citing from Abelard's comments on Romans 2, noting his emphasis upon the arousal of God's love within us, Rashdall continues:] Three points may be noted in this Abelardian view of the Atonement.

1. There is no notion of vicarious punishment, and equally little of any vicarious expiation or satisfaction, or objectively valid sacrifice, an idea which is indeed free from some of the coarse immorality of the idea of vicarious punishment, but is somewhat difficult to distinguish from it.
2. The atoning efficacy of Christ's work is not limited to his death. [...] The whole life of Christ, the whole revelation of God which is constituted by that life, excites the love of man, moves his gratitude, shows him what God would have him be, enables him to be in his imperfect way what Christ alone was perfectly, and so makes at-one-ment, restores between God and man the union which sin has destroyed.
3. And it follows from this view of the Atonement that the justifying effect of Christ's work is a real effect, not a mere legal fiction. Christ's work really does make men better, instead of supplying the ground why they should be considered good or be excused the punishment of sin, without being really made any better than before. [...]

Even from the slight specimen that I have given you of Abelard's teaching you may be struck with the modernness of his tone. Abelard, in the twelfth century, seems to stretch out his hands to F. D. Maurice and Charles Kingsley and Frederick Robertson in the nineteenth. At least, I know not where to look for the same spirit of reverent Christian rationalism in the intervening ages, unless it be in the Cambridge Platonists.

Comment

In this sermon Rashdall argued that Matthew 20: 28 ("For the Son of Man came not to be served, but to serve, and to give his life as a ransom for many") had been grossly misunderstood during the patristic period. The patristic *Christus Victor* theory is thus little more than an overelaboration of a metaphor. Rashdall finds a more acceptable approach in the writings of Abelard, who he misunderstands to teach a purely exemplarist doctrine of the Atonement, in which Christ is nothing more than an outstanding moral example (5.14). This idea would receive more substantial exposition in his later work, *The Idea of Atonement in Christian Thought* (London: Macmillan, 1921).

Questions for Study

1 Set out, in your own words, the three advantages that Rashdall believes result from adopting an Abelardian approach to the atonement.
2 "Even from the slight specimen that I have given you of Abelard's teaching you may be struck with the modernness of his tone." How would you account for this observation?

5.28

James Denney on Atonement and Incarnation

James Denney (1856–1917) was professor of theology at the Glasgow Free Church College from 1897 until his death. Denney was a noted exponent of a traditional approach to the atonement, and was convinced that there was the closest of connections between the doctrines of the person and work of Christ. This excerpt comes from his book *The Christian Doctrine of Reconciliation* (published in the year of his death), where Denney explored the reasons lying behind this connection. See also 5.4, 5.5, 5.25, 5.26.

It is natural at this point to refer to a subject which has been much discussed in this connection, though the New Testament hardly raises it in the form in which it is most familiar – the relation of the atonement, or of the work of reconciliation, to the incarnation. There are those who hold that the incarnation is too great a thing to be contingent upon anything else, and especially upon such an unhappy chance as the appearance of sin in the world. It would have taken place in any case: the Son of God would have become man even if man had never fallen; He would have come in flesh to consummate creation and give the human race its true head and a true unity. There is an ideal or metaphysical necessity for the incarnation which is independent of sin. In spite of the fascination which this view has had for some speculative or quasi-speculative minds, it may be doubted whether it has any Christian interest. There are hypothetical questions which it is idle to discuss, and they include those in which the hypothesis is that the world might have been something quite other than we know it to be. We know the world only as a sinful world, and we know the relation of Christ to it, experimentally, only as that of its Saviour from sin. Whether we can draw inferences, on the basis of this, to an original relation of the Son of God to nature and to the human race is, of course, an open question; and assuming that we could do so, it would be again an open question, but a very remote one, whether we could base on these inferences still further conclusions as to the probability or the inevitableness of the incarnation of the Son of God in a sinless world. The New Testament writers are not afraid to base the most far-reaching inferences on their experience of reconciliation. The Christ who has won eternal redemption, who has reconciled them to God with a perfect reconciliation, who has made all things theirs, is a Being by relation to whom all things have to be determined: they even say of Him, "In Him were all things created"; yes, in Him, and through Him, and for Him; He is the centre in which all have their unity (Colossians 1: 16). But they stick to the actual. They feel, as all serious thinkers feel, that the task of the mind is to understand and interpret what is, not to wander off into what might have been, as though it might find there truths sublime or more profound. The world we live in is the only world, and it is not thinking, but some other intellectual exercise, which concerns itself with a world we have never known and can never know. Probably this is why the New Testament ignores the question referred to, and when it speaks of Christ's coming connects it with His work of reconciliation, and contemplates it in no other light. He came to seek and to save that which was lost. He came to give His life a ransom. The meaning of all these expressions is that He came for us, and it is a Christian instinct which confines the New Testament to this point of view. [. . .] though the work of reconciliation has its source in the character of God, so that it may be said that God would not have done Himself justice unless He had manifested Himself as He has done in Christ, this is not a mode of statement which has apostolic support; it approaches too closely to the feeling that the Christian revelation of God is a thing on which the sinner can of course presume. It is the same with the point which is now before us. An incarnation which would have taken place in any event is an incarnation which does not put the sinner under that obligation to Christ under which he is put by an incarnation which is necessitated and determined by the loving will to save sinners by bearing their sins.

Schleiermacher, who takes both sides on every question, and is of all philosophers least exposed to the charge of being right in what he asserts and wrong in what he denies, tries to combine both points of view. The incarnation is natural, and it is also supernatural; it involves the redemption of man from sin, and at the same time the carrying out of the original idea of His creation; it consummates creation, as well as saves the human race. But he would be a bold man who ventured to maintain that the total impression made by Schleiermacher is in keeping with the total impression made by the New Testament. There is as much of Spinoza in his intellectual atmosphere as of Paul or John, and in his moral atmosphere there is more. But the real objection to the speculative theories of an incarnation independent of sin is that they assume us to know, in independence of the Saviour and of His sin-bearing work, what incarnation means. But this we do not know at all. What the writer understands, and alone can understand, by the incarnation, is the actual historical life and death of Christ. What many of those who use the term understand by it is the taking up of human nature into union with a divine person. In this sense, the incarnation is the presupposition of the life of Jesus, it is not identical with that life. There is a deep gulf between these two views, and when they express themselves, as they sometimes do, in similar language, it is apt to lead to misunderstanding. Nothing is commoner, for instance, than for those who conceive the incarnation as the taking up of human nature into union with the divine, to say that the incarnation is itself the atonement; in the person of the God-man humanity as such is reconciled to God. To the writer such expressions are as good as meaningless, and neither for the evangelist nor the theologian can he see that they have any value. But looking at the actual life and death of Jesus as the proper definition of the term incarnation – the sum of reality apart from which incarnation is an empty sound – he would have no difficulty in saying that the incarnation and the atonement, or the incarnation and the work of reconciling man to God, were all one. The traditional dogmatic conception of the incarnation, with which the idea of an incarnation independent of sin, and designed to consummate creation, is usually connected, does not lift us into a region of eternal or ideal truth; it does not enlighten our minds in the knowledge of Christ; it only lifts us out of the region of historical and moral reality. We have the practical interest of Christianity as well as the broad sense of the New Testament with us when we stand by the view that Christ Jesus came into the world to save sinners.

Comment

Denney's staunch defense of this issue makes reference to the views of Schleiermacher (5.24, 5.25), and is generally critical of the approach offered by the German liberal Protestant theologian. Yet Denney also has another target for his criticism: those who defend the idea of the incarnation, yet fail to link this with the atonement. Denney probably has in mind here some Anglican writers of the 1890s and early 1900s, who argued that the fact that God had become incarnate was, in itself, quite adequate as a statement of the Christian gospel. Denney denies this, insisting that there must be a link with the cross before the full richness of the gospel can be proclaimed.

Questions for Study

1 Denney argues that the "traditional dogmatic conception of the incarnation, with which the idea of an incarnation independent of sin, and designed to consummate creation" is inadequate. Locate this statement in the text. Why does he critique this viewpoint? And what alternative does he propose?
2 "We know the world only as a sinful world, and we know the relation of Christ to it, experimentally, only as that of its Saviour from sin." Locate this statement. What does Denney mean by this? How does he defend it? And what conclusions does he draw from it?

5.29

Gustaf Aulén on the Classic Theory of the Atonement

In this seminal and highly influential study, originally published as an article in a German theological journal in 1930, the Swedish Lutheran theologian Gustaf Aulén (1879–1978) rehabilitated what he termed the "classic" or *Christus Victor* ("Christ the Victor") approach to the atonement. This approach, he argued, avoided the weaknesses of the approaches associated with Anselm and Abelard. In the passage here reprinted, he sets out his anxieties concerning traditional approaches to the atonement. See also 5.1, 5.4, 5.12, 5.13, 5.14, 5.15, 5.30.

My work on the history of Christian doctrine has led me to an ever-deepening conviction that the traditional account of the history of the idea of the Atonement is in need of thorough revision. The subject has, indeed, received a large share of attention at the hands of theologians; yet it has been in many important respects seriously misinterpreted. It is in the hope of making some contribution to this urgently needed revision that this work has been undertaken.

The Traditional Account

Let us first take a rapid survey of the history of the idea of the Atonement, according to the generally accepted view. The early church had, it is said, no developed doctrine of the Atonement, properly so called. The contributions of the patristic period to theology lie in another direction, being chiefly concerned with Christology and the doctrine of the Trinity; in regard to the Atonement, only hesitating efforts were made along a variety of lines, and the ideas which found expression were usually clothed in a fantastic mythological dress. The real beginnings of a thought-out doctrine of the Atonement are found in Anselm of Canterbury, who thus comes to hold a position of first-rate importance in the history of dogma. By the theory of satisfaction developed in the *Cur Deus homo?* he repressed, even if he could not entirely overcome, the old mythological account of Christ's work as a victory over the devil; in place of the older and more "physical" idea of salvation he put forward his teaching of a deliverance from the guilt of sin; and, above all, he clearly taught an "objective" Atonement, according to which God is the object of Christ's atoning work, and is reconciled through the satisfaction made to His justice. Needless to say, it is not implied that

Anselm's teaching was wholly original. The stones lay ready to hand; but it was he who erected them into a monumental building.

A typical expression of the view which we have described is that of Ritschl, in *The Christian Doctrine of Justification and Reconciliation*. The very full historical section of this book begins with an introductory chapter on certain aspects of "the doctrine of salvation in the Greek church"; the use of the term "salvation" indicates that, in his view, the history of the doctrine of the Atonement proper had not yet begun. This chapter is immediately followed by one entitled "The Idea of Atonement through Christ in Anselm and Abelard".

Typical again is the collocation of the names of Anselm and Abelard. These two are commonly contrasted as the authors respectively of the "objective" and "subjective" doctrines of the Atonement; the latter term is used to describe a doctrine which explains the Atonement as consisting essentially in a change taking place in men rather than a changed attitude on the part of God.

In the subsequent history of the doctrine, it is held that a continuous line may be traced from Anselm, through medieval scholasticism, and through the Reformation, to the Protestant Orthodoxy of the seventeenth century. It is not implied that the teaching of Anselm was merely repeated, for differences of view are noted in Thomas Aquinas and in the Nominalists, and the post-Reformation statements of the doctrine have a character of their own; nevertheless, there is a continuity of tradition, and the basis of it is that which Anselm laid. It must specially be noted that the Reformation is included in this summary, and that it is treated as self-evident that Luther had no special contribution to make, but followed in all essentials the Anselmian tradition. Those writers, however, who are opposed to that tradition readily allow an unsolved contradiction in Luther's world of ideas, between the medieval doctrine of Atonement which he left unchanged, and the religious outlook which inspired his reforming work and his teaching of justification by faith.

Finally, according to the traditional account, the last two centuries have been marked by the coexistence of these two types, the "objective" and the "subjective", and by the controversies between them. The subjective type has connections with Abelard, and with a few other movements here and there, such as Socinianism; but its rise to power came during the period of the Enlightenment. The nineteenth century is characterised by the conflict of this view with what was left of the "objective" doctrine, as well as by a variety of compromises; Ritschl regards the period of the Enlightenment as that of the disintegration of the "objective" doctrine, and gives as a chapter heading "The Revival of the Abelardian type of Doctrine by Schleiermacher and his Disciples". Naturally, both sides found support for their respective views in the New Testament. Those who sought to uphold, with or without modifications, the tradition of Protestant Orthodoxy, contended vigorously for the "biblical basis" of this type of Atonement-theory; the other side sought to show that the New Testament could not possibly be made to cover the teaching which was readily allowed the name of "the church doctrine". In this controversy the exegesis of Scripture suffered cruelly and long. Such is the common account of the history of the doctrine of the Atonement. But we may well question whether it is satisfactory.

The Classic Idea of the Atonement

There is a form of the idea of the Atonement which this account of the matter either ignores altogether or treats with very much less than justice, but whose suppression falsifies the whole perspective, and produces a version of the history which is seriously misleading. This type of view may be described provisionally as the "dramatic." Its central theme is the idea of the Atonement as a Divine conflict and victory; Christ – *Christus Victor* – fights against and triumphs over the evil powers of the world, the "tyrants" under which mankind is in bondage and suffering, and in Him God reconciles the world to Himself. Two points here require to be pressed with special emphasis: first, that this is a doctrine of Atonement in the full and proper sense, and second, that this idea of the Atonement has a clear and distinct character of its own, quite different from the other two types.

First, then, it must not be taken for granted that this idea may rightly be called only a doctrine of salvation, in contrast with the later development of a doctrine of Atonement properly so called. Certainly it describes a work of salvation, a drama of salvation; but this salvation is at the same time an atonement in the full sense of the word, for it is a work wherein God reconciles the world to Himself, and is at the same time reconciled. The background of the idea is dualistic; God is pictured as in Christ carrying through a victorious conflict against powers of evil which are hostile to His will. This constitutes Atonement, because the drama is a cosmic drama, and the victory over the hostile powers brings to pass a new relation, a relation of reconciliation, between God and the world; and, still more, because in a measure the hostile powers are regarded as in the service of the will of God the Judge of all, and the executants of His judgment. Seen from this side, the triumph over the opposing powers is regarded as a reconciling of God Himself; He is reconciled by the very act in which He reconciles the world to Himself.

Secondly, it is to be affirmed that this "dramatic" view of the Atonement is a special type, sharply distinct from both the other types. We shall illustrate its character fully in the course of these lectures; for the present a preliminary sketch must suffice.

The most marked difference between the "dramatic" type and the so-called "objective" type lies in the fact that it represents the work of Atonement or reconciliation as from first to last a work of God Himself, a continuous Divine work; while according to the other view, the act of Atonement has indeed its origin in God's will, but is, in its carrying-out, an offering made to God by Christ as man and on man's behalf, and may therefore be called a discontinuous Divine work.

On the other hand, it scarcely needs to be said that this "dramatic" type stands in sharp contrast with the "subjective" type of view. It does not set forth only or chiefly a change taking place in men; it describes a complete change in the situation, a change in the relation between God and the world, and a change also in God's own attitude. The idea is, indeed, thoroughly "objective"; and its objectivity is further emphasised by the fact that the Atonement is not regarded as affecting men primarily as individuals, but is set forth as a drama of a world's salvation.

Since, then, the objective character of the "dramatic" type is definite and emphatic, it can hardly help to a clear understanding of the history of the idea of Atonement to reserve the term "objective Atonement" for the type of view which commonly bears that name. The result can only be a confusion of two views of the Atonement which need to be clearly distinguished. I shall therefore refer to the type of view commonly called objective as the "Latin" type, because it arose and was developed on Western, Latin soil, and to the dualistic-dramatic view as "the classic idea" of the Atonement.

The classic idea has in reality held a place in the history of Christian doctrine whose importance it would not be easy to exaggerate. Though it is expressed in a variety of forms, not all of which are equally fruitful, there can be no dispute that it is the dominant idea of the Atonement throughout the early church period. It is also in reality, as I hope to show, the dominant idea in the New Testament; for it did not suddenly spring into being in the early church, or arrive as an importation from some outside source. It was, in fact, the ruling idea of the Atonement for the first thousand years of Christian history. In the Middle Ages it was gradually ousted from its place in the theological teaching of the church, but it survived still in her devotional language and in her art. It confronts us again, more vigorously and profoundly expressed than ever before, in Martin Luther, and it constitutes an important part of his expression of the Christian faith. It has therefore every right to claim the title of the *classic Christian idea of the Atonement*. But if this be the case, any account of the history of the doctrine which does not give full consideration to this type of view cannot fail to be seriously misleading.

Comment

Aulén's article of 1930 was originally published in German and attracted relatively little attention. However, the article was then translated into English and published in book form. The work had an influence far beyond its merits, not least because Aulén's exposition of the *Christus Victor* model is colored by a severely critical, and often inaccurate, account of the alternative theories associated with Anselm and Abelard. One of the reasons why Aulén's approach to the atonement may have proved so attractive was a renewed interest in the imagery of conflict, following the events of World War I, as well as a growing skepticism concerning the liberal Protestant approaches to the issue, which had dominated academic theological discussion up to that point.

Questions for Study

1 Outline, in your own words, the differences between what Aulén terms the "dramatic," "objective," and "subjective" approaches to the atonement.

2 Aulén states that the "dramatic" theory of the atonement "describes a complete change in the situation, a change in the relation between God and the world, and a change also in God's own attitude." How does Aulén himself respond to this? And how does he distinguish this from the "objective" approach?

5.30

Vladimir Lossky on Redemption as Deification

In this passage, originally published in French in 1953, the Russian émigré theologian Vladimir Lossky (1904–58) sets out the fundamental importance of the notion of deification to Orthodox theology. See also 4.23, 5.4, 5.5, 5.8, 5.12.

"God made Himself man, that man might become God." These powerful words, which are found for the first time in St Irenaeus, can be found again in the writings of St Athanasius, St Gregory of Nazianzen and St Gregory of Nyssa. The Fathers and Orthodox theologians have repeated them with this same emphasis in every century, wishing to sum up in this striking sentence the very essence of Christianity – an ineffable descent of God to the ultimate limit of our fallen human condition, even unto death – a descent of God which opens to men a path of ascent to the unlimited vision of the union of created beings with the divinity.

The descent (*katabasis*) of the divine person of Christ makes human persons capable of an ascent (*anabasis*) in the Holy Spirit. It was necessary that the voluntary humiliation, the redemptive self-emptying (*kenosis*) of the Son of God should take place, so that fallen men might accomplish their vocation of *theosis*, the deification of created beings by uncreated grace. Thus the redeeming work of Christ – or rather, more generally speaking, the Incarnation of the Word – is seen as directly related to the ultimate goal of creatures: to know union with God. If this union has been accomplished in the divine person of the Son, who is God become man, it is necessary that each human person should in turn become god by grace, or become "a partaker in the divine nature," according to St Peter's expression (2 Peter 1: 4).

[...] The Son of God came down from heaven to accomplish the work of our salvation, to liberate us from the captivity of the devil, to destroy the dominion of sin in our nature, and to undo death, which is the wages of sin. The Passion, Death and Resurrection of Christ, by which his redemptive work was accomplished, thus occupy a central place in the divine dispensation for the fallen world. From this point of view it is easy to understand why the doctrine of the redemption has such a great importance in the theological thought of the Church.

Nevertheless, when the dogma of the redemption is treated in isolation from the general body of Christian teaching, there is always a risk of limiting the tradition by interpreting it exclusively in terms of the work of the Redeemer. Then theological reflection develops in three directions: original sin, its reparation on the cross, and the appropriation of the saving results of the work of Christ to Christians. In these constricting perspectives of a theology dominated by the idea of "redemption," the patristic sentence "God made Himself man, that man might become God" seems to be strange and abnormal. The thought of union with God is forgotten because of our preoccupation solely with our own salvation; or rather, union with God is seen only negatively, in contrast with our present wretchedness.

Comment

Lossky sets out the characteristic Orthodox emphasis upon the redemptive descent (*katabasis*) of God in the incarnation, and the resulting ascent (*anabasis*) of humanity into God, as a result of its being enabled to share in the divine nature. Lossky is particularly critical of the tendency in western theology, which he traces back to Anselm of Canterbury, to treat redemption as a single aspect of theology, rather than its unifying theme.

Questions for Study

1 Why is Lossky so critical of approaches to the atonement which focus "exclusively in terms of the work of the Redeemer"?
2 Explain what Lossky means by these theological terms: *kenosis*, *anabasis*, *katabasis*.

5.31

Bernard Lonergan on the Intelligibility of Redemption

One of the most distinguished Canadian theologians of the twentieth century was the Jesuit writer Bernard J. F. Lonergan (1904–84). Lonergan is best known for his discussions of theological method, especially his *Method in Theology* (1973). However, his interests ranged more widely. The passage here reprinted is an extract of a lecture given in 1958 at the Thomas More Institute, Montreal, on the general topic of "redemption." The ideas presented in this lecture are developed more fully – though not necessarily more clearly – in his later work *De verbo incarnato* (1960). Lonergan here considers the question of how we may be said to "understand" redemption, and offers five points of reflection on this theme. See also 5.11, 5.13, 5.16, 5.17, 5.28.

1. Not a Necessity

The first point to be noted is that, while the redemption is an intelligibility, it is not to be thought of as a necessity.

The early Protestants, the orthodox Lutherans and the orthodox Calvinists, mainly the thinkers who succeeded the first Reformers, flatly affirmed that God in his justice could not possibly forgive the sins of mankind, unless Christ became man and suffered and died. Calvin had even gone further. He was not content with the sufferings that Christ endured at the hands of the soldiers and of Pilate, but also required that the phrase in the creed "He descended into hell" be taken to mean that Christ also suffered the punishment of the damned.

The doctrine – not Calvin's, but the doctrine – that suffering is a necessary condition limiting God's goodness can in some way be attributed to St Anselm. He frequently seems to be offering a theory that would explain why Christ's suffering and death were necessary. On the other hand, he also qualifies what he means by necessary. And it requires very nuanced interpretive efforts to determine what precisely St Anselm thought. As a matter of fact, his thinking, at the end of the eleventh century, was prior to any developed systematic distinction between philosophy and theology or any systematic attempt at determining the precise nature of theological thinking and the intelligibility that theology can grasp.

The Catholic tradition on the necessity of redemption by Christ is clear and uniform. St Augustine flatly stated that there were many other ways in which God could redeem man apart from the suffering and death of Christ. The same view was repeated by Peter Lombard, whose Sentences were the basic text in theology for about three or four centuries. It was repeated by St Thomas and Scotus and subsequently by all theologians. And so, while there is something to be understood in connection with the redemption, this understanding is not grasping a necessity. It is not like understanding that 2 and 2 must be 4. It is like understanding the law of gravitation, which, is a constant acceleration but might without any contradiction be some other mathematical formula. Intelligibility, then, is not the same as necessity.

2. A Dynamic Intelligibility

In the second place, that intelligibility is not static but dynamic, not a matter of deductive but rather of dialectical thought. Its fundamental element is a reversal of roles. In the book of Genesis, we read that God said to Adam when forbidding him to eat of the fruit of the tree, "On whatever day thou eatest thereof, thou shalt die" (2. 17). Death is presented in the book of Genesis, and in the book of Wisdom, as the penalty for sin. The same doctrine is repeated by St Paul in Romans 5. 12: "By one man sin entered into the world, and by sin death." And again in chapter 6, verse 23, "The wages of sin are death." Yet death is not simply and solely the wages of sin. It is by the death of Christ that we are saved. And our salvation through the death of Christ is reaffirmed continuously throughout the New Testament. As St Paul says in 1 Corinthians 15. 21, "A man has brought us death, and a man should bring us resurrection from the dead; just as all have died with Adam, so with Christ all will be brought to life." The theme of death and resurrection takes many forms and is constantly returning in St Paul. And the meaning of that recurrence is that death is swallowed up in victory (the words in 1

Corinthians 15. 54), that what was the consequence of sin became the means of salvation. [...]

3. An Incarnate Intelligibility

Again, the intelligibility to be reached in considering the redemption is not an abstract but an incarnate intelligibility. It exploits all the subtle relations that hold between body and mind, between flesh and spirit. Christ crucified is a symbol of endless meaning, and it is not merely a symbol but also a real death. It is again in the concrete, in the flesh of Christ, in his blood, and in his death that punishment is transfigured into satisfaction. And as you no doubt are aware, the notion of punishment is an extremely difficult notion to philosophize upon. The notion of the satisfaction of Christ contains all those difficulties and the transformation of them. [...]

4. A Complex Intelligibility

Again, the redemption is not a simple but a complex intelligibility; and I use the word "complex" in the sense that the mathematician speaks of "complex numbers." The mathematician uses not only rational but also irrational numbers, not only real numbers but also imaginary numbers. And everything goes well, provided he does not mix them up, provided he does not consider that they are all numbers in exactly the same sense and manner. Similarly with regard to the redemption, we must not think of it as something that will fall into a single intelligible pattern. [...]

Consequently, in thinking about the redemption one must make an effort – and it requires an effort – to avoid the tendency to think that an explanation casts everything one can think of into a single intelligible pattern. It does that insofar as what one is considering is intelligible, has a reason. But the redemption regards sin, it presupposes sin, and it is the transformation of the situation created by sin. Consequently, in a consideration of the redemption one has to have in mind the existence not of a simple intelligibility but of the transcendent intelligibility of God meeting the unintelligibility of sin.

5. A Multiple Intelligibility

Finally, the intelligibility to be reached in the consideration of the redemption is not a single but a multiple intelligibility. It is not something that is going to be fitted into some single formula, some neat reason. St Anselm's *Cur Deus homo?* does illustrate the tendency to try to reduce everything to a single formula. But it was followed by a much less celebrated work about a century and a half later, about the beginning of the first quarter of the thirteenth century, by William of Auvergne, Bishop of Paris, the title of which was not *Cur Deus homo?* why a God-man? but *De causis cur Deus homo*, on the causes or the reasons why God was made man. What William wanted to put forward was that the redemption is not a matter of some single reason but of many reasons. [...]

Such, then, are the general characteristics, the precautions that one must take, I think, in seeking a total view of the redemption. There is an intelligibility to be grasped, but that intelligibility is not a necessity. It is an expression of what God thought wise, what God thought good, and that is intelligible, but it is not an expression of what simply had to be. It is like an empirical law, not a mathematical necessity.

Comment

This is an important passage, which raises many important questions. While Lonergan insists that we may legitimately speak about the redemption as being "intelligible," he criticizes attempts to reduce the complexity of redemption to a single theological principle. He is particularly critical of the approach introduced by Anselm of Canterbury (5.13), which he believes reduces the mystery of atonement to one theological formula. While affirming the intelligibility of redemption, he insists that it is to be approached, not as a mathematical or logical truth, but as an empirical law.

Questions for Study

1 Summarize, in your own words, the five points that Lonergan makes. How do you react to each of them?
2 At what points does Lonergan engage with Anselm? What issues does he raise? Do you think he is right?
3 What does Lonergan mean by contrasting deductive and dialectical approaches to redemption?

5.32

Wolfhart Pannenberg on Soteriological Approaches to Christology

In his influential 1964 essay on Christological method entitled *Grundzüge der Christologie* ("Foundations of Christology"), published in English as *Jesus – God and Man*, Wolfhart Pannenberg (born 1928) set out the case for returning to history in order to establish the foundations of Christology. He expressed a particular concern about the soteriological approach to Christology – in other words, the approach which determines the identity of Jesus on the basis of his saving significance for humanity. For Pannenberg, the identity of Jesus must be established on the basis of the history of Jesus of Nazareth. See also 5.5, 5.25, 5.26, 9.2.

The two designations "God" and "savior" form the content of the basic confession of the World Council of Churches, which was formulated at Amsterdam in 1948. The divinity of Jesus and his freeing and redeeming significance for us are related in the closest possible way. To this extent, Melanchthon's famous sentence is appropriate: 'Who Jesus Christ is becomes known in his saving action." Nevertheless, the divinity of Jesus does not consist in his saving significance for him. Divinity and saving significance are interrelated as distinct things. The divinity of Jesus remains the *presupposition* of his saving significance for us, and, conversely, the saving significance of his divinity is the reason why we take *interest* in the question of his divinity. Since Schleiermacher the close tie between Christology and soteriology has won general acceptance in theology. This is particularly to be seen in one characteristic feature of modern Christology. One no longer separates the divine–human person and the redemptive work of Jesus Christ, as was done in medieval Scholastic theology and, in its wake, in the dogmatics of sixteenth- and seventeenth-century Protestant orthodoxy, but rather, with Schleiermacher, both are conceived as two sides of the same thing. [. . .]

A separation between Christology and soteriology is not possible, because in general the soteriological interest, the interest in salvation, in the *beneficia Christi*, is what causes us to ask about the figure of Jesus. [. . .] However, the danger that is involved in this connection between Christology and soteriology has emerged at the same time. Has one really spoken there about Jesus himself at all? Does it not perhaps involve projections onto Jesus' figure of the human desire for salvation and deification, of human striving after similarity to God, of the human duty to bring satisfaction for sins committed, of the human experience of bondage in failure, in the knowledge of one's own guilt, and, most clearly in neo-Protestantism, projections of the idea of perfect religiosity, of perfect morality, of pure personality, of radical trust? Do not human desires only become projected upon the figure of Jesus, personified in him? [. . .]

The danger that Christology will be *constructed* out of the soteriological interest ought to be clear. Not everywhere is this so unreservedly expressed as by Tillich: "Christology is a function of soteriology." However, the tendency that is expressed here plays a part, more or less consciously and to a greater or lesser extent, in all the types of Christological thought considered here. The danger becomes acute when this procedure is elevated to a program, as by Melanchthon and later by Schleiermacher, who constructed his Christology by inference from the experience of salvation. [. . .]

Therefore Christology, the question about Jesus himself, about his person, as he lived on earth in the time of the Emperor Tiberius, must remain prior to all questions about his significance, to all soteriology. Soteriology must follow from Christology, not vice versa. Otherwise, faith in salvation loses any real foundation.

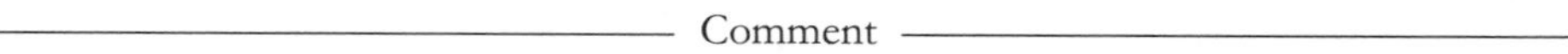

Comment

It is clear from this passage that Pannenberg regards Christology and soteriology as closely linked. However, he urges caution in proceeding directly from soteriology to Christology. Pannenberg's chief concern is that an approach to Christology which sets out from Christ's impact upon humanity runs the risk of losing contact with history, and hence might become little more than a projection reflecting perceived human needs. Focusing on history keeps Christology firmly moored to reality.

Questions for Study

1 Pannenberg quotes, more or less approvingly, Philip Melanchthon's famous dictum: "Who Jesus Christ is becomes known in his saving action." Yet he is clearly worried by aspects of Paul Tillich's related statement: "Christology is a function of soteriology." How can these observations be accounted for?
2 What criticism of Schleiermacher's theological program is offered by Pannenberg?

5.33

James I. Packer on Penal Substitution

In this published lecture, originally given at Tyndale House, Cambridge, in 1973, James I. Packer (born 1926), one of the most widely read evangelical theologians, argues for an Anselmian approach to the atonement which lays an emphasis upon the substitutionary character of Christ's death. In arguing his case, he deals with the way in which "substitution" is to be understood. See also 5.13, 5.14, 5.15, 5.16, 5.19, 5.28, 5.31.

The first thing to say about penal substitution has been said already. It is a Christian theological model, based on biblical exegesis, formed to focus a particular awareness of what Jesus did at Calvary to bring us to God. If we wish to speak of the "doctrine" of penal substitution, we should remember that this model is a dramatic, kerygmatic picturing of divine action, much more like Aulén's "classic idea" of divine victory (though Aulén never saw this) than it is like the defensive formula-models which we call the Nicene "doctrine" of the Trinity and the Chalcedonian "doctrine" of the person of Christ. Logically, the model is put together in two stages: first, the death of Christ is declared to have been *substitutionary*; then the substitution is characterized and given a specific frame of reference by adding the word *penal*. We shall examine the two stages separately.

Stage one is to declare Christ's death *substitutionary*. What does this mean? The *Oxford English Dictionary* defines substitution as "the putting of one person or thing in the place of another". One oddity of contemporary Christian talk is that many who affirm that Jesus' death was vicarious and representative deny that it was substitutionary; for the *Dictionary* defines both words in substitutionary terms! Representation is said to mean "the fact of standing for, or in place of, some other thing or person, esp. with a right or authority to act on their account; *substitution* of one thing or person for another". And vicarious is defined as "that takes or supplies the place of another thing or person; *substituted* instead of the proper thing or person". So here, it seems, is a distinction without a difference. Substitution is, in fact, a broad idea that applies whenever one person acts to supply another's need, or to discharge his obligation, so that the other no longer has to carry the load himself. As Pannenberg says, "in social life, substitution is a universal phenomenon . . . Even the structure of vocation, the division of labour, has substitutionary character. One who has a vocation performs this function for those whom he serves". For "every service has vicarious character by recognizing a need in the person served that apart from the service that person would have to satisfy for himself". In this broad sense, nobody who wishes to say with Paul that there is a true sense in which "Christ died for us" (once, on our behalf, for our benefit), and "Christ redeemed us from the curse of the law, having become a curse for us" [. . .] and who accepts Christ's assurance that he came "to give his life a ransom for many" [. . .] should hesitate to say that Christ's death was substitutionary. Indeed, if he describes Christ's death as vicarious he is actually saying it. [. . .]

Broadly speaking, there have been three ways in which Christ's death has been explained in the church. Each reflects a particular view of the nature of God and our plight in sin, and of what is needed to bring us to God in the fellowship of acceptance on his side and faith and love on ours. It is worth glancing at them to see how the idea of substitution fits in with each.

There is, first, the type of account which sees the cross as having its effect entirely on men, whether by revealing God's love to us, or by bringing home to us how much God hates our sins, or by setting us a supreme example of godliness, or by blazing a trail to God which we may now follow, or by so involving mankind in his redemptive obedience that the life of God now flows into us, or by all these modes together. It is assumed that our basic need is lack of motivation Godward and of openness to the inflow of divine life; all that is needed to set us in a right relationship with God is a change in us at these two points, and this Christ's death brings about. The forgiveness of our sins is not a separate problem; as soon as we are changed we become forgivable, and are then forgiven at once. This view has little or no room for any thought of substitution, since it goes so far in equating what Christ did for us with what he does to us.

A second type of account sees Christ's death as having its effect primarily on hostile spiritual forces external to us which are held to be imprisoning us in a captivity of which our inveterate moral twistedness is one sign and symptom. The cross is seen as the work of God going forth to battle as our champion, just as David went forth as Israel's champion to fight Goliath. Through the cross these hostile forces, however conceived – whether as sin and death, Satan and his hosts, the demonic in society and its structures, the powers of God's wrath and curse, or anything else – are overcome and nullified, so that Christians are not in bondage to them, but share Christ's triumph over them. The assumption here is that man's plight is created entirely by hostile cosmic forces distinct from God; yet, seeing Jesus as our champion, exponents of this view could still properly call him our substitute, just as all the Israelites who declined Goliath's challenge in 1 Samuel 17: 8–11 could properly call David their substitute. Just as a substitute who involves others in the consequences of his action as if they had done it themselves is their representative, so a representative discharging the obligations of those whom he represents is their substitute. What this type of account of the cross affirms (though it is not usually put in these terms) is that the conquering Christ, whose victory secured our release, was our representative substitute.

The third type of account denies nothing asserted by the other two views save their assumption that they are complete. It agrees that there is biblical support for all they say, but it goes further. It grounds man's plight as a victim of sin and Satan in the fact that, for all God's daily goodness to him, as a sinner he stands under divine judgment, and his bondage to evil is the start of his sentence, and unless God's rejection of him is turned into acceptance he is lost for ever. On this view, Christ's death had its effect first on God, who was hereby *propitiated* (or, better, who hereby propitiated himself), and only because it had this effect did it become an overthrowing of the powers of darkness and a revealing of God's seeking and saving love. The thought here is that by dying Christ offered to God what the West has called *satisfaction* for sins, satisfaction which God's own character dictated as the only means whereby his "no" to us could become a "yes". Whether this Godward satisfaction is understood as the homage of death itself, or death as the perfecting of holy obedience, or an undergoing of the Godforsakenness of hell, which is God's final judgment on sin, or a perfect confession of man's sins combined with entry into their bitterness by sympathetic identification, or all these things together (and nothing stops us combining them together), the shape of this view remains the same – that by undergoing the cross Jesus expiated our sins, propitiated our Maker, turned God's "no" to us into a "yes," and so saved us. All forms of this view see Jesus as our representative substitute in fact, whether or not they call him that, but only certain versions of it represent his substitution as penal.

[Packer then makes three points, of which the first two are of especial relevance here:]

First, it should be noted that though the two former views regularly set themselves in antithesis to the third, the third takes up into itself all the positive assertions that they make; which raises the question whether any more is at issue here than the impropriety of treating half-truths as the whole truth, and of rejecting a more comprehensive account on the basis of speculative negations about what God's holiness requires as a basis for forgiving sins. Were it allowed that the first two views might be misunderstanding and distorting themselves in this way, the much-disputed claim that a broadly substitutionary view of the cross has always been the mainstream Christian opinion might be seen to have substance in it after all. It is a pity that books on the atonement so often take it for granted that accounts of the cross which have appeared as rivals in historical debate must be treated as intrinsically exclusive. This is always arbitrary, and sometimes quite perverse.

Second, it should be noted that our analysis was simply of views about the death of Christ, so nothing was said about his resurrection. All three types of view usually agree in affirming that the resurrection is an integral part of the gospel; that the gospel proclaims a living, vindicated Saviour whose resurrection as the firstfruits of the new humanity is the basis as well as the pattern for ours is not a matter of dispute between them. It is sometimes pointed out that the second view represents the resurrection of Jesus as an organic element in his victory over the powers of death, whereas the third view does not, and hardly could, represent it as an organic element in the bearing of sin's penalty or the tasting and confessing of its vileness (however the work of Calvary is conceived); and on this basis the third view is sometimes criticized as making the resurrection unnecessary. But this criticism may be met in two ways. The first reply is that Christ's saving work has two parts, his dealing with his Father on our behalf by offering himself in substitutionary satisfaction for our sins and his dealing with us on his Father's behalf by bestowing on us through faith the forgiveness which his death secured, and it is as important to distinguish these two parts as it is to hold them together. For a demonstration that part two is now possible because part one is finished, and for the actual implementing of part two, Jesus' resurrection is indeed essential, and so appears as an organic element in his work as a whole. The second reply is that these two ways of viewing the cross should in any case be synthesized, following the example of Paul in Colossians 2: 13–15, as being complementary models expressing different elements in the single complex reality which is the mystery of the cross.

Comment

The concept of "penal substitution" has long been associated with various forms of conservative evangelicalism. The concept, however, came under increasing criticism within evangelical circles in the United Kingdom and North America in the late 1960s and early 1970s. Packer's lecture, entitled "What did the Cross Achieve? The Logic of Penal Substitution," is to be seen as a vigorous defense of the centrality of the concept of penal substitution against some of the criticisms from within evangelicalism. The lecture is to be seen as a piece of constructive theology, showing a shrewd and critical awareness of the theological trends of the 1960s. Packer opened the lecture by noting the importance of his theme. "The task which I have set myself in this lecture is to focus and explicate a belief which, by and large, is a distinguishing mark of the world-wide evangelical fraternity; namely, the belief that Christ's death on the cross had the character of *penal substitution*, and that it was in virtue of this fact that it brought salvation to mankind."

Questions for Study

1 Outline the three approaches which Packer sets out, using your own words. Packer argues that "the third type of account denies nothing asserted by the other two views save their assumption that they are complete." Do you agree?
2 How does Packer incorporate the resurrection of Christ into his preferred model of the atonement?

5.34

Dorothee Sölle on Suffering and Redemption

The German theologian Dorothee Sölle (1929–2003), whose surname is often printed as "Soelle" in English-language contexts, is widely regarded as one of the most interesting twentieth-century theologians. She was influential both in her native Germany and her adopted United States, with particular interests in feminist, liberationist, and political theology. Her book *Suffering* (1975) sets out to dismantle what Sölle regards as inappropriate Christian views on suffering, and replace them with something more appropriate. To regard human suffering as the demonstration of divine strength or as a Christian calling fails to provide adequate answers to two basic questions: "What are the causes of suffering, and how can these conditions be eliminated?"; and "What is the meaning of suffering and under what conditions can it make us more human?" The passage extracted for study interacts with the cross as a symbol of suffering, and its implications for suffering humanity. See also 3.21, 3.23, 3.33, 3.38.

The symbol for the religion of slaves is the cross, the kind of punitive death reserved for slaves. Is it necessary for this symbol of suffering, of failure, of dying, to stand at the mid-point of the Christian religion? Has not an overemphasis on the cross in theology and piety resulted in the fact that a "God who justifies misery" was and is worshipped in society? Ulrich Hedinger has attacked the "alliance between antiquity and Christianity" because of their fundamental doctrine that "a supreme Providence rules over or by harsh fate," and radically rejected any commendation of submission. The cross cannot be made the center of a messianically understood theology that abolishes misery. Jesus' death was first and foremost a religio-political and political assassination, and love, "even Jesus' forgiving love, does not require assassination by crucifixion in order to be authentic." In this context Hedinger criticizes theological thinking that elevates the paradox, the unresolved contradiction to suffering-filled reality, to the central theological category. "Where God is the paradox in an absolute sense, there he clouds the distinction between love and misery."

But the question whether love requires the cross in order to be authentic appears to me to be posed falsely. In the context of this question Hedinger understands the cross either as a "metaphysic of punitive death," that is, from the perspective of the God who ordains suffering, who finally has a chance to complete Abraham's sacrifice, or he takes it as a "mysticism of consolation for death," which people receive for their own suffering and dying in view of the cross. But the cross is neither a symbol expressing the relationship between God the Father and his Son nor a symbol of masochism which needs suffering in order to convince itself of love. It is above all a symbol of reality. Love does not "require" the cross, but *de facto* it ends up on the cross. *De facto* Jesus of

Nazareth was crucified; *de facto* the crosses of the rebellious slaves under Spartacus adorned the streets of the Roman empire. The cross is no theological invention but the world's answer, given a thousand times over, to attempts at liberation. Only for that reason are we able to recognize ourselves in Jesus' dying on the cross. We observe the ideology of the rulers who supported the prevailing order. We see the brutality and sadism of the soldiers, who had a hand in it, following orders. We are confronted by the behavior of friends. All these are possibilities for our behavior toward the stricken. And when we ourselves are struck by affliction, then we can try to learn from the story of Jesus. The question whether love needs the cross for its actualization holds only a speculative and not an existential interest. Nor does God's *doxa*, his splendor, his self-revealing glory, his happiness, "need" the dreadful paradoxes of the destruction and mutilation of life if one considers God in that light. But *de facto* love ends up on the cross and within visible reality God chooses to act paradoxically.

Comment

In this passage, Sölle interacts with the German writer Ulrich Hedinger in exploring the meaning of suffering. She argues that, while it is possible to "demystify" suffering by offering some kind of theoretical interpretation of it, this "speculation" is of limited importance compared with the existential importance of the cross. The cross represents an affirmation of life in all its dimensions and conditions. The reality of suffering is affirmed, while at the same time, it is humanized on account of Christ's incarnational solidarity with believers.

Questions for Study

1 Set out the two positions that Sölle believes to represent inadequate understandings of suffering.
2 "Love does not 'require' the cross, but de facto it ends up on the cross." What does Sölle mean by this?

5.35

Colin E. Gunton on the Language of Atonement

In this important study of the atonement, the British theologian Colin Gunton (1941–2003) argues that a proper appreciation of the status of the language used in relation to the cross of Christ is fundamental to a correct understanding of its meaning.

He illustrates this point by considering some aspects of the *Christus Victor* theory, especially associated with Gustaf Aulén (see 5.29), noting its metaphorical status. See also 1.30.

As the Christian tradition took shape during the early centuries, the way in which Satan and the demonic realm came to be understood underwent some changes. In particular, there was a tendency to personify the devil as an individual being defeated by Christ on the cross. On the whole, as time passes, there is rather less restraint shown in the way in which the devil is depicted. As Aulén has noticed, there is a real contrast between Paul's treatment of the matter and that of later thinkers, in that he makes considerably less mention of the devil than most of the Fathers. This relative lack of restraint in the later period is revealed also in a tendency to picture the defeat of the devil as a kind of deceit, in which the devil, believing that Jesus is merely a human victim, swallows him, only to be impaled on the hidden hook of his divinity. Gregory of Nyssa is clearly uncomfortable, though not uncomfortable enough, with such a conception. [. . .] But the problem with Gregory's way of putting the matter is revealed by [. . .] its tendency to be what has come to be called mythological. The battle is to be conceived to be fought in a sphere outside the course of concrete divine–human relations. We can contrast here two features of the gospel narratives we have noted: both the temptations and the healings are actual human encounters with evil, theologically conceived. In Gregory, on the other hand, the metaphorical dimension has fallen into the background, the victory is understood too literally, and the result is that *too much* is known about what is supposed to have happened.

The reference to the tendency of the tradition to become mythological brings us to a distinction of immense importance: that between metaphor and myth. Those who spoke too *literally* of the devil having obtained rights over mankind of which he was deprived by deceit had, in effect, failed to appreciate the metaphorical nature of the language they were using. It is as if, when Mark reports Jesus as saying that he had come to give his life as a ransom for many, we were to speculate about how much money was to be handed over, and to whom (Mark 10: 45). We have here an example of what some thinkers have claimed to happen when a metaphor is taken too literally: it becomes a myth. [. . .]

What, then, is to be made of biblical and other theological language which uses language of this kind? G. B. Caird speaks as follows about the principalities and powers in the New Testament:

> They stand, as their names imply, for the political, social, economic and religious structures of power . . . of the old world order which Paul believed to be obsolescent. When therefore he claims that on the cross Christ has disarmed the powers and triumphed over them, he is talking about earthly realities, about the impact of the crucifixion on the corporate life of men and nations. He is using mythical language of great antiquity and continuing vitality to interpret the historic event of the cross.

On such an account we can understand Paul to be using mythical language in a non-mythological way. If Caird is right, we have discovered another qualification of Aulén's account. The victory is not over forces which inhabit a transcendent world, separate from ours, and intervene from outside, as Aulén's account might appear to suggest. Paul is speaking about "earthly realities [. . .] the corporate life of men and nations." But they are not forces which can adequately be described in everyday empirical terms. The forces are "cosmic" in the sense that they *as a matter of fact affect the way things are on earth*, but not simply as aspects, but as qualifications of them. These biblical metaphors, then, are ways of describing realistically what can be described only in the indirect manner of this kind of language. But an indirect description is still a description of what is really there.

Comment

This important study addresses the question of the status of the language traditionally used in accounts of the atonement. Gunton argues for the need to appreciate that metaphorical language is being used to describe something that is really there. In other words, the use of nonliteral modes of speaking is not to be taken to imply that reality is not being depicted reliably. Gunton makes this point most forcibly through his observation that "biblical metaphors . . . are ways of describing realistically what can be described only in the indirect manner of this kind of language. But an indirect description is still a description of what is really there."

Questions for Study

1 Gunton suggests that some theologians of the patristic era may have been incautious in their use of theological language, perhaps through a failure to appreciate its metaphorical status. What theologians has he in mind? And what doctrines did they teach?

2 Note the important citation from George Caird's masterly study, *The Language and Imagery of the Bible*, published in 1980. What use does Gunton make of Caird's approach?

For Further Reading

D. M. Baillie, *God was in Christ: An Essay in Incarnation and Atonement* (London: Faber & Faber, 1956).

Vincent Brümmer, *Atonement, Christology, and the Trinity: Making Sense of Christian Doctrine* (Aldershot, UK: Ashgate, 2005).

F. W. Dillistone, *The Christian Understanding of Atonement* (London: SCM Press, 1984).

Everett Ferguson, *Doctrines of Human Nature, Sin, and Salvation in the Early Church* (New York: Garland Publishing, 1993).

R. S. Franks, *The Work of Christ: A Historical Study* (London/New York: Nelson, 1962).

E. M. B. Green, *The Meaning of Salvation* (London: Hodder & Stoughton, 1965).

L. W. Grensted, *A Short History of the Doctrine of the Atonement* (Manchester, UK: Manchester University Press, 1920).

Charles E. Hill and Frank A. James, *The Glory of the Atonement: Biblical, Historical and Practical Perspectives* (Downers Grove, IL: Inter-Varsity, 2004).

Lars Koen, *The Saving Passion: Incarnational and Soteriological Thought in Cyril of Alexandria's Commentary on the Gospel according to St. John* (Uppsala: Acta Universitatis Uppsaliensis, 1991).

Leon Morris, *The Apostolic Preaching of the Cross* (Leicester, UK: Inter-Varsity Press, 1965).

Philip Quinn, "Aquinas on Atonement," in Ronald Feenstra and Cornelius Plantinga (eds), *Trinity, Incarnation, and Atonement* (Notre Dame, IN: University of Notre Dame Press, 1989), pp. 153–77.

Peter Schmiechen, *Saving Power: Theories of Atonement and Forms of the Church* (Grand Rapids, MI: Eerdmans, 2005).

S. W. Sykes (ed.), *Sacrifice and Redemption* (Cambridge, UK: Cambridge University Press, 1991).

Leanne Van Dyk, *The Desire of Divine Love: John McLeod Campbell's Doctrine of the Atonement* (New York: Peter Lang, 1995).

Geoffrey Wainwright, *For Our Salvation: Two Approaches to the Work of Christ* (Grand Rapids, MI: William B. Eerdmans, 1997).

Dietrich Wiederkehr, *Belief in Redemption: Concepts of Salvation from the New Testament to the Present Time* (London: SPCK, 1979).

6

Human Nature, Sin, and Grace

Introduction

This chapter brings together a substantial body of material which focuses on the Christian understanding of human nature and the means by which it is restored to fellowship with God. While these issues have always been important to Christian theology, they assumed an especially high profile during two major controversies within the Christian tradition – the Pelagian controversy, and the Reformation.

The Pelagian controversy of the early fifth century, which featured Pelagius of Rome and Augustine of Hippo as the chief protagonists, focused on the question of grace and sin. This can be studied from a number of texts, as follows.

The Pelagian Controversy and its Aftermath

The Reformation of the sixteenth century also focused on the issue of grace, but with particular reference to the doctrine of justification by faith. It is of considerable importance to appreciate the different positions adopted within the Reformation, as well as the definitive Catholic response to the Reformation, provided by the Council of Trent. This debate can be followed from the following readings:

The Reformation Debates on Grace	
6.32	Martin Luther's Discovery of the "Righteousness of God"
6.33	Martin Luther on Justifying Faith
6.34	Martin Luther on Sin and Grace
6.35	Philip Melanchthon on Justification by Faith
6.36	John Calvin on Predestination
6.37	John Calvin on Faith and the Promises of God
6.38	John Calvin on the Concept of Justification
6.39	The Council of Trent on Justification

Other debates of considerable interest include the long-standing discussion of the nature and causes of predestination – an issue of importance during the Pelagian controversy, but which has continued to fascinate theologians throughout Christian history.

The Debate over Predestination	
6.8	Ambrose on the Unmerited Character of Salvation
6.11	Augustine on the Divine Election
6.12	Augustine on the Nature of Predestination
6.15	Augustine on Irresistible Grace and Perseverance
6.16	Pelagius on Human Responsibility
6.17	Pelagius on Human Freedom
6.19	The Council of Carthage on Grace
6.20	The Synod of Arles on Pelagianism
6.21	The Second Council of Orange on Grace and Freedom
6.29	Gregory of Rimini on Predestination
6.36	John Calvin on Predestination
6.40	Theodore Beza on the Causes of Predestination
6.42	James Ussher on the Grounds of Assurance
6.43	The Westminster Confession on Predestination
6.51	Karl Barth on Election in Christ
6.52	Emil Brunner on Barth's Doctrine of Election

This chapter also deals with aspects of the doctrine of creation, especially the place of humanity within creation. This has often been discussed in terms of what it means for humanity to be created in the image of God. This theme can be studied with profit from the readings provided.

The "Image of God" in Humanity	
6.4	Tertullian on the Image of God
6.5	Origen on the Image of God
6.7	Lactantius on Political Aspects of the Image of God
6.10	Gregory of Nyssa on Human Longing for God
6.23	Hildegard of Bingen on the Creation of Man and Woman
6.27	Mechthild of Magdeburg on Humanity's Longing for God
6.50	Emil Brunner on the Image of God
6.56	Mary Hayter on Human Sexuality and the Image of God

A final topic of interest within this chapter is the theological discussion of the origins and nature of sin. This question has close links with both the doctrine of grace and also that of creation in the "image of God."

The Origin and Nature of Sin	
6.1	Irenaeus on Human Progress
6.2	Tertullian on the Origin of Sin
6.3	Tertullian on Inherited Guilt
6.6	Origen on Inherited Sin
6.9	Ambrosiaster on Original Sin
6.10	Gregory of Nyssa on Human Longing for God
6.13	Augustine on Fallen Human Nature
6.18	Pelagius's Rejection of Original Sin
6.19	The Council of Carthage on Grace
6.20	The Synod of Arles on Pelagianism
6.21	The Second Council of Orange on Grace and Freedom
6.34	Martin Luther on Sin and Grace
6.47	Jonathan Edwards on Original Sin
6.53	Reinhold Niebuhr on Original Sin
6.55	Daphne Hampson on Feminist Approaches to Sin

6.1

Irenaeus on Human Progress

In this passage, which dates from the later part of the second century, Irenaeus of Lyons (c.130–c.200) develops the idea that humanity was created with the potential for perfection. Humanity was not created perfect; that perfection had to take place through a process of moral and spiritual growth. Ireneaus thus locates the origin of evil in human weakness and frailty, rather than in any defect on the part of God. See also 3.2.

Here, someone may raise an objection. "Could not God have made humanity perfect from the beginning?" Yet one must know that all things are possible for God, who is always the same and uncreated. But created beings, and all who have their beginning of being in the course of time, are necessarily inferior to the one who created them. Things which have recently come into being cannot be eternal; and, not being eternal, they fall short of perfection for that very reason. And being newly created they are therefore childish and immature, and not yet fully prepared for an adult way of life. And so, just as a mother is able to offer food to an infant, but the infant is not yet able to receive food unsuited to its age, in the same way, God, for his part, could have offered perfection to humanity at the beginning, but humanity was not capable of receiving it, being nothing more than an infant.

Comment

Irenaeus is concerned to address the question of why God did not create humanity in a state of total perfection. Irenaeus's answer is important, and can be summarized as follows: because humanity was simply not able to receive this gift of perfection. Perfection was something that came about through personal growth.

Questions for Study

1 How does Irenaeus understand the capacities of human nature? And how does this relate to the notion of "perfection"?
2 How does Irenaeus relate his understanding of human nature to the issue of the origin of evil (3.2)?

6.2

Tertullian on the Origin of Sin

In this passage, originally written in Latin in the first decade of the third century, Tertullian (c.160–c.225) locates the origin of sin in Satanic temptation of humanity. Note the emphasis placed on the notion of "discontent," which Tertullian regards as underlying all rebellion against God. See also 3.2, 3.6, 6.6.

I find the origin of discontent [*impatientia*] in the devil himself since from the beginning he was discontented and annoyed that the Lord God had subjected the whole of the world to the one who he had created in his own image, that is to humanity. Now if the devil had tolerated that patiently, he would not have grieved; had he not grieved he would not have envied man: and envy was the cause of his deceiving the man. [...] Then when [the devil] met the woman, I may say that with good reason that as a result of their conversation she was filled with a spirit infected with discontent; for it is certain that she would never have sinned, had she contentedly persisted in obedience to the divine command! Furthermore, she did not stop there, after her meeting with the devil, but she was too discontented to keep silence in the presence of Adam, though he was not yet her husband and therefore not bound to listen: but she passed on to him what she had learned from the evil one. Thus another human perishes through the discontent of the one; and [Adam] himself soon perished through his own discontent. [...] Here is the primal source of judgment and of sin; God was aroused to anger and man is induced to sin. [...] What offence is ascribed to humanity before the sin of discontent? Humanity was blameless, the intimate friend of God and the steward of paradise [*Deo de proximo amicus et paradisi colonus*]. But when he succumbed to discontent he ceased to care for God, and ceased to have the power to be content with heavenly things. From that moment, humanity was sent out on the earth, and cast out from God's sight. As a result, discontent had no difficulty in gaining the upper hand over humanity, and causing it to do things which were offensive to God.

Comment

Tertullian locates the origins of human sin in the actions of the devil, who is here personified. The passage is interesting on account of the way it portrays the interaction of Satan, Adam, and Eve, as well as the reflections which it offers on the original state of human nature.

Questions for Study

1 How does Tertullian depict the original created state of humanity?
2 Set out, in your own words, Tertullian's account of the progress of sin.

6.3

Tertullian on Inherited Guilt

Tertullian here warns his readers against thinking of sin or redemption in purely individualist terms. Both sin and grace relate to the whole body of humanity. Tertullian points out that sin is inherited from our forebears, and passed down from one generation to another. Although he does not develop a doctrine of original sin in the strict sense of the phrase, some of the foundational ideas of this doctrine may be found in this passage. See also 6.6, 6.9, 6.13.

But if the blessing of the fathers was destined to be transmitted to their posterity, without any merit on their part, why should not the guilt of the fathers be passed on to their sons, so that the transgression as well as the grace should spread through the whole human race? (Except for the point, which was to be made known later, that men shall not say, "The fathers have eaten a sour grape and the children's teeth have been set on edge" (Jeremiah 31: 29) that is, the father shall not take upon himself the transgression of his son, nor the son the transgression of his father, but each shall be guilty of their own transgression.) This means that after the hardness of the people and the hardness of the law had been overcome, God's justice should then judge individuals and not the whole race. If you would receive the gospel of truth you would discover to whom that saying refers which speaks of bringing home to the sons the transgressions of their fathers. It applies to all those who of their own accord applied to themselves the saying: "may his blood be on our heads and on the heads of our sons" (Matthew 27: 25). That is why the providence of God, having already heard this, established it [i.e. the gospel of truth] for them.

Comment

Sin is a complex notion, and in this passage, Tertullian explores some of its many aspects. Perhaps the most important is the *corporate* nature of guilt – an idea which is difficult for many modern readers to make sense of, on account of the strongly individualist assumptions of the Enlightenment, which still exercise considerable influence over western thinking.

Questions for Study

1 How does Tertullian explore the corporate dimensions of sin? What criticisms does he offer of purely individualist ways of thinking? And what difficulties does he anticipate?
2 Look at the two biblical passages cited in support of his approach by Tertullian: Jeremiah 31: 29 and Matthew 27: 25. You might like to look these up in their original contexts. How do you respond to the way in which Tertullian uses them?

6.4

Tertullian on the Image of God

In this important treatise, written in Latin in the first decade of the third century, Tertullian draws a distinction between the "image" and "likeness" of God. Note how Tertullian regards the Fall as involving the loss of the indwelling presence of the Holy Spirit, which is restored through baptism. See also 6.5, 6.7, 6.50.

[In baptism] death is abolished by the washing away of sins: for the removal of guilt also removes the penalty. Thus humanity is restored to God into "his likeness," for he had originally been "in his image." The state of being "in the image of God" relates to his form; "in the likeness" refers to his eternity: for humanity receives back that Spirit of God which at the beginning was received from God's inbreathing, but which was afterwards lost through falling away.

Comment

In this brief passage, Tertullian deals primarily with the effects of baptism. In enumerating these, he deals with the question of the theological role of the "image of God." The important distinction between "image" and "likeness" rests upon part of the first Genesis creation account, which speaks of God making humanity in God's "image and likeness" (Genesis 1: 26).

Questions for Study

1 Set out, in your own words, the way in which Tertullian explores the difference between the terms "image" and "likeness."
2 What specific understanding does Tertullian set out of the relation of the "image of God" and the "Spirit of God"?

6.5

Origen on the Image of God

Origen (c.185–c.254) here draws a distinction between the "image" and "likeness" of God, arguing that the image refers to the status of humanity, and the likeness to the final perfection of the human race at the resurrection. See also 6.4, 6.7, 6.50, 10.6.

"And God said, 'Let us make man in our image and likeness' " (Genesis 1: 26). He then adds: "In the image of God he made him" (Genesis 1: 27), and is silent about the likeness. This indicates that in his first creation man received the dignity of the image of God, but the fulfillment of the likeness is reserved for the final consummation; that is, that he himself should obtain it by his own effort, through the imitation of God. The possibility of perfection given to him at the beginning by the dignity of the image, and then in the end, through the fulfillment of his works, should bring to perfect consummation the likeness of God. The Apostle John defines this state of things more clearly when he declares: "My little children, we do not yet know what we shall be but if it shall be revealed to us concerning the Savior, without doubt you will say: We shall be like him" (1 John 3: 2).

Comment

Notice again how the distinction between "image" and "likeness" (Genesis 1: 26) is of importance within this passage. Origen sets out an important eschatologically orientated understanding of the relation between these concepts, which links together the moment of creation and the final consummation of humanity.

Questions for Study

1 Set out, in your own words, the way in which Origen explores the difference between the terms "image" and "likeness."
2 What role does Origen assign to individual humans in bringing about this transition from image to likeness?

6.6

Origen on Inherited Sin

Origen here argues that humanity is contaminated by sin from the moment of its entry into the world, with the sole exception of Jesus Christ. Note how Origen sees a link between the virginity of Mary as the mother of Christ and the sinlessness of Christ. See also 6.3, 6.9.

Everyone who enters the world may be said to be affected by a kind of contamination [*in quadam contaminatione effici dicitur*]. [. . .] By the very fact that humanity is placed in its mother's womb, and that it takes the material of its body from the source of the father's seed, it may be said to be contaminated in respect of both father and mother. [. . .] Thus everyone is polluted in father and mother. Only Jesus my Lord was born without stain. He was not polluted in respect of his mother, for he entered a body which was not contaminated. [. . .] For Joseph played no part in his birth other than his devotion and his affection, and it is on account of his faithful devotion that Scripture allows him the name "father."

Comment

Although Origen does not use the language of "original sin" – which became fully developed in the writings of Augustine – he nevertheless appears to have held beliefs about the original state of humanity which bear some resemblance to this later idea. Notice especially how Origen insists that Jesus Christ is exempt from this common human state of sinfulness.

Questions for Study

1 How, according to Origen, does human nature become contaminated by sin?
2 On the basis of Origen's approach, how is the doctrine of the sinlessness of Christ linked with the doctrine of the virgin birth? You might like to compare this with the ideas of Duns Scotus (6.28).

6.7

Lactantius on Political Aspects of the Image of God

In this passage from his *Divine Institutes*, Lactantius (c.240–c.320) develops the political and ethical aspects of the doctrine of creation. As all human beings are made by the same God, bear his image, and were created from the same original human being – a reference to Adam – they must hold each other in respect. Lactantius uses the Latin term *simulacrum* for "image" instead of the more customary *imago*. This term is often used to refer to idols or statues of gods, and emphasizes the degree of likeness between the image and its object. See also 6.4, 6.5, 6.50.

I have spoken about what is due to God; now I shall speak about what is due to other people, although what is due to people still equally relates to God, since humanity is the image of God [*homo dei simulacrum est*]. The first duty of justice concerns God and binds us to him; the second concerns humanity. The name of the first is religion; the name of the second is mercy or humanity. Religion is a characteristic of the righteous and those who worship God. It alone is life. God made us naked and fragile in order to teach us wisdom. In particular he gave us this affection of piety in order that we might protect our fellow human beings, love them, cherish them, defend them against all dangers, and give them help. The strongest bond which unites us is humanity. Anyone who breaks it is a criminal and a parricide. Now it was from the one human being that God created us all, so that we are all of the same blood, with the result that the greatest crime is to hate humanity or do them harm. That is why we are forbidden to develop or to encourage hatred. So if we are the work of the same God, what else are we but brothers and sisters? The bond which unites our souls is therefore stronger than that which unites our bodies. So Lucretius does not err when he declares:

> Finally, we are all the offspring of heavenly seed.
> To everyone that same one is Father.

[...] We must therefore show humanity if we want to deserve the name of human beings. And showing humanity means loving our fellow human beings because they are human beings, just as we are ourselves.

Comment

Lactantius was concerned to explore the implications of Christian faith for public life, as well as exploring aspects of Christian theology. The passage lays a theological foundation for the assertion that all human beings share a common dignity on account of having been created in the image of God.

Questions for Study

1 Notice how Lactantius develops the idea that humanity was created in weakness. What conclusion does he draw from this? And how does this relate to the views of Irenaeus on this matter (3.2, 6.1)?

6.8

Ambrose on the Unmerited Character of Salvation

In this fourth-century commentary on the opening words of the Lord's Prayer (Matthew 6: 9), Ambrose of Milan (c.339–97) stresses the unmerited nature of the privilege of being able to address and approach God in this way. See also 6.11, 6.12.

O man, you did not dare to raise your face to heaven; you lowered your eyes to the earth – and suddenly you have received the grace of Christ, and all your sins have been forgiven! From being a wicked servant, you have become a good son! And do not suppose that this is due to any action on your part; it is due to the grace of Christ. [...] So raise your eyes to the Father who has redeemed you through his Son, and say: "Our Father..." But do not claim any privilege. He is the Father in a special way only of Christ; he is the common Father of us all, in that although he has created all of us, he has begotten none but Christ. Then also say by his grace, "Our Father," so that you may merit being his son.

Comment

Ambrose here stresses that being able to call God "Father" – as, for example, in the Lord's Prayer – must itself be regarded as a privilege to which we are not strictly entitled. Its use is a matter of divine graciousness.

Questions for Study

1 How does Ambrose base his argument, in part, on the postures adopted in prayer?
2 What point does Ambrose seek to make through comparing the relationship of Christ to the Father, and believers to the Father?

6.9

Ambrosiaster on Original Sin

The Old Latin translation of Romans 5: 12, on which Ambrosiaster here depends, mistranslates Paul's Greek, interpreting a reference to "in that all have sinned" to mean "in whom [that is, Adam] all have sinned." On the basis of this misunderstanding, Ambrosiaster develops a notion of original sin which had a considerable impact on Augustine's teaching on the matter. Little is known of this fourth-century theologian, including his true name. See also 6.2, 6.3, 6.6, 6.18, 6.47, 6.53.

"In whom – that is, in Adam – all have sinned" (Romans 5: 12). Notice that he uses the masculine (*in quo*) though he is speaking about the woman, because his reference was not to the sex, but to the race. So it is clear that all have sinned in Adam collectively, as it were (*quasi in massa*). He was himself corrupted by sin, and all that were born were therefore all born under sin. From him therefore all are sinners, because we are all produced from him.

Comment

This text is important because it illustrates how a translation mistake can have important theological implications. The Latin term *in quo* can be treated as masculine or neuter. The Greek text of Paul's letter to the Romans, which it translates, makes it clear that the neuter meaning is intended. Thus a text which meant something like "in what all have sinned" is interpreted as a reference to Adam "in whom all have sinned." Ambrosiaster thus interprets this text as meaning that all of humanity have corporately and originally sinned in the person of Adam, the first man. While the doctrine of original sin rests on other texts as well, this was widely regarded as an important textual foundation for the doctrine.

Questions for Study

1 Set out, in your own words, the translation issue at stake here. Make sure that you can understand the point at issue.
2 In what way can all be said to have "sinned in Adam collectively"?

6.10

Gregory of Nyssa on Human Longing for God

Gregory of Nyssa (c.330–c.395) made extensive use of Platonic ideas (such as the notion of "the Good") in his exposition and defense of the Christian faith. His more spiritual writings stress the inability of the human mind to fully comprehend or penetrate into the mystery of God. In this passage, which takes the form of an exposition of Matthew 5: 4, Gregory explores the sense of human longing for God, resulting from alienation from the true good and goal of humanity. See also 6.4, 6.5, 6.50.

The more that we believe that "the Good," on account of its nature, lies far beyond the limits of our knowledge, the more we experience a sense of sorrow that we have to be separated from this "Good," which is both great and desirable, and yet cannot be embraced fully by our minds. Yet we mortals once had a share in this "Good" which so eludes our attempts to comprehend it. This "Good" – which surpasses all human thought, and which we once possessed – is such that human nature also seemed to be "good" in some related form, in that it was fashioned as the most exact likeness and in the image of its prototype. For humanity then possessed all those qualities about which we now speculate – immortality, happiness, independence and self-determination, a life without drudgery or sorrow, being caught up in divine matters, a vision of "the Good" through an unclouded and undistracted mind. This is what the creation story hints at briefly (Genesis 1: 27), when it tells us that humanity was formed in the image of God, and lived in Paradise, enjoying what grew there (and the fruit of those trees was life, knowledge, and so on). So if we once possessed those gifts, we can only grieve over our sadness when we compare our previous happiness to our present misery. What was high has been made low; what was created in the image of heaven has been reduced to earth; the one who was ordained to govern the earth has been reduced to a slave; what was created for immortality has been destroyed by death; the one who lived in the joys of Paradise has ended up in this place of drudgery and illness. [...] Our tears would flow even more if we were to list all those physical sufferings that are an inevitable part of our human conditions (by this, I mean all the different sorts of illnesses), and when we reflect on the fact that humanity was originally free from all of these, and when we compare the joys that we once knew with our present misery by setting our sadness alongside that better life. So when our Lord says: "Blessed are those who mourn" (Matthew 5: 4), I believe his hidden teaching to be this: the soul should fix its gaze on "the true Good," and not be immersed in the illusion of this present life.

Comment

Gregory's basic argument is that humanity enjoyed the life of paradise before losing this through disobedience. Gregory thus argues that it is inevitable that we will feel sad and miserable when we compare our present situation with that which existed in paradise. Yet the Beatitude affirms that those who mourn *shall be comforted* (Matthew 5: 4). This allows Gregory to draw hope from our present sorrow. It is important to appreciate that Gregory's general theological outlook brings together the past, present, and future. The past is about paradise; the present is about a loss of God's immediate presence and all the joys of paradise; the future, however, is about the potential recovery of those joys of paradise in heaven. Gregory's argument is that we can set our minds and hearts firmly on the recovery of that lost state of innocence and joy in the world to come. His analysis thus encourages his readers to contemplate the future restoration of what was lost in Eden through sin. (For Gregory, incidentally, one of the leading themes of the doctrine of redemption is that Christ restores what Adam lost.)

Questions for Study

1 Read Genesis 1: 26–7. Note that the passage refers to humanity being created in the image and likeness of God. How does Gregory make use of this point in his argument? What difference does this insight make to our understanding of human nature and destiny?
2 According to this passage, for what is humanity mourning?

6.11

Augustine on the Divine Election

Augustine of Hippo (354–430) here argues that all humanity are contaminated by sin, with the result that salvation is a human impossibility. In his grace, God chose to save some from this "mass of perdition." Note the appeal to the analogy of the potter and the clay (Romans 9: 21), which becomes a frequent element in Augustinian and Reformed discussions of election and predestination. See also 6.12, 6.29, 6.36, 6.40, 6.43.

There was one lump of perdition [*massa perditionis*] out of Adam to which only punishment was due; from this same lump, vessels were made which are destined for honor. For the potter has authority over the same lump of clay (Romans 9: 21). What lump? The lump that had already perished, and whose just damnation was already assured. So be thankful that you have escaped! You have escaped the death certainly due to you, and found life, which was not due to you. The potter has authority over the clay from the same lump to make one vessel for honor and another for contempt. But, you say, why has He made me to honor and another to contempt? What shall I answer? Will you listen to Augustine, if you will not listen to the Apostle [Paul] when he says "Who are you who argues with God?" (Romans 11: 33).

Two little children are born. If you ask what is due to them, the answer is that they both belong to the lump of perdition. But why does its mother carry the one to grace, while the other is suffocated by its mother in her sleep? Will you tell me what was deserved by the one which was carried to grace, and what was deserved by the one whom its sleeping mother suffocated? Both have deserved nothing good; but the potter has authority over the clay, of the same lump to make one vessel for honor, and the other for contempt.

Comment

In this sermon Augustine stresses the priority of God in both creation and redemption. Humanity simply does not have any right to challenge or call into question the wisdom of God, which it is not in a position to understand fully. Notice in particular the use of the biblical analogy of the potter and the clay, and the conclusions which Augustine draws from it.

Questions for Study

1 Set out, in your own words, Augustine's understanding of the human predicament and the manner in which God deals with this.
2 Read the section of the passage dealing with the two children. What point does Augustine want to make in this way? How successful is he?

6.12

Augustine on the Nature of Predestination

Augustine here develops the idea that predestination involves God withholding or making available, according to the divine will, the means by which salvation is possible. Augustine stresses that the divine judgment which determines who will be allowed to be saved in this manner is beyond human understanding. See also 6.8, 6.15, 6.29, 6.36, 6.40, 6.43.

This is the predestination of the saints, and nothing else: the foreknowledge and preparation of the benefits of God, whereby whoever are set free are most certainly set free. And where are the rest left by the just judgment of God, except in that mass of perdition, in which the inhabitants of Tyre and Sidon were left? Now they would have believed, if they had seen the wonderful signs of Christ. However, because it was not given to them to believe, they were not given the means to believe [*quoniam ut crederent, non erat eis datum, etiam unde crederent est negatum*]. From this, it seems that certain people have naturally in their minds a divine gift of understanding, by which they may be moved to faith, if they hear the words or see the signs which are adapted to their minds [*si congrua suis mentibus*]. But if, by virtue of a divine judgment which is beyond us, these people have not been predestined by grace and separated from the mass of perdition, then they must remain without contact with either these divine words or deeds which, if heard or seen by them, would have allowed them to believe.

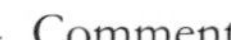

Comment

Augustine opens this passage with a definition of predestination. Notice how predestination is here defined in purely positive terms. Predestination concerns salvation. God does not predestine to condemnation; rather, God omits to predestine all to salvation. The contrast with Calvin is of particular interest (6.36), in that predestination is there defined as God's decision to save some and condemn others. Notice how Augustine here suggests that salvation depends upon certain "means of grace"; predestination involves making those "means of grace" available only to the elect.

Questions for Study

1 What does Augustine mean by the "means to believe"? How does he illustrate this idea? And what conclusions does he draw from this?
2 What are the implications of Augustine's statements concerning "a divine judgment which is beyond us"?

6.13

Augustine on Fallen Human Nature

In this important discussion of fallen human nature, originally written in Latin in 415, Augustine identifies the consequences of the Fall upon human nature. Originally created without any fault, human nature is now contaminated by sin, and can only be redeemed through grace. See also 6.2, 6.3, 6.4, 6.6, 6.9, 6.10, 6.11, 6.51, 6.54.

Human nature was certainly originally created blameless and without any fault [*vitium*]; but the human nature by which each one of us is now born of Adam requires a physician, because it is not healthy. All the good things, which it has by its conception, life, senses, and mind, it has from God, its creator and maker. But the weakness which darkens and disables these good natural qualities, as a result of which that nature needs enlightenment and healing, did not come from the blameless maker but from original sin [*ex originali peccato*], which was committed by free will [*liberum arbitrium*]. For this reason our guilty nature is liable to a just penalty. For if we are now a new creature in Christ, we were still children of wrath by nature, like everyone else. But God, who is rich in mercy, on account of the great love with which He loved us, even when we were dead through our sins, raised us up to life with Christ, by whose grace we are saved. But this grace of Christ, without which neither infants nor grown persons can be saved, is not bestowed as a reward for merits, but is given freely [*gratis*], which is why it is called grace [*gratia*]. [. . .]

For this reason it is that those who are not made free by that blood (whether because they have not been able to hear, or because they were not willing to obey, or were not able to hear on account of their youth, and have not received the bath of regeneration which they might have done and through which they might have been saved) who are most justly condemned because they are not without sin, whether they derived from their origins or were acquired by evil actions. For all have sinned, whether in Adam or in themselves, and have fallen short of the glory of God (Romans 3: 23).

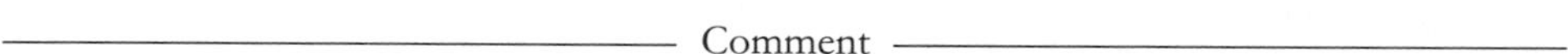

Augustine here clarifies the nature of human sin, resulting from the Fall of humanity in Adam. Notice how sin is defined or illustrated in a number of ways, including the idea of a defect or fault, and the state of being guilty or liable to some penalty. For Augustine, sin is a complex notion, having many aspects; the present passage casts some light on how Augustine understands both sin itself, and God's chosen remedy for that sin.

Questions for Study

1 "And when Jesus heard it, he said to them, 'Those who are well have no need of a physician, but those who are sick; I came not to call the righteous, but sinners' " (Mark 2: 17). In what way does this text lie behind Augustine's comments in the early part of this passage?
2 Augustine clearly sees a link between the Latin terms *gratis* ("freely" or "without cost") and *gratia* ("grace" or "gift"). How would you explain this?

6.14

Augustine on Human Freedom

Augustine's emphasis on grace occasionally seems to suggest that he denies human freedom. In this passage, originally written in Latin at some point during the period 413–26, Augustine discusses the relation of sin, grace, and free will in some detail, noting the various types of freedom which humanity possesses, from the freedom enjoyed by Adam to that which will be enjoyed by those who finally inhabit the heavenly Jerusalem. See also 6.17.

Nor will they not have free choice because sins will have no power to attract them. Far from it; it will be more truly free, when it has been set free from the delight of sinning, to enjoy the steadfast delight of not sinning. For the first free will [*liberum arbitrium*] which was given to humanity when it was created upright [*rectus*], gave not just the ability not to sin, but also the ability to sin. This new freedom is all the more powerful precisely because it will not have power to sin; and this, not by its unaided natural ability, but by the gift of God. It is one thing to be God, and another to share in God. God is unable to sin; anyone who shares in God has received from God the inability to sin. [. . .] The first immortality, which Adam lost by sinning, was the ability not to die [*posse non mori*], the new immortality will be the inability to die [*non posse mori*]. In the same way, the first freedom of choice conferred the ability not to sin [*posse non peccare*]; the new freedom will confer the inability to sin [*non posse peccare*]. [. . .] It surely cannot be said that God does not have any freedom of choice, just because God is unable to sin?

Thus the freedom of that city will be one single will, present in everyone, freed from all evil and filled with every good, enjoying continually the delight of eternal joy. Although sins and punishments will be forgotten, this will not lead to forgetting its liberation, or being ungrateful to its liberator.

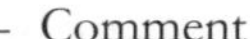

Comment

Augustine is often referred to as the *doctor gratiae* ("the teacher of grace") on account of his emphasis upon the grace of God. In this passage he shows that his emphasis upon the priority of grace does not entail the denial of human freedom. In the course of this important discussion, he sets out his understanding of the various freedoms which human nature has possessed, and now possesses. In particular, note his discussion of the relationship between the Latin phrases *posse non peccare* and *non posse peccare*.

Questions for Study

1 How does Augustine understand the freedom enjoyed by Adam in paradise? What issues might this raise for the question of the origins of sin and evil?
2 "I found that God made humans upright, but they have sought out many devices" (Ecclesiastes 7: 29). How does this text feature in Augustine's reflections on sin and grace?

6.15

Augustine on Irresistible Grace and Perseverance

Augustine here argues that God bestows a gift of perseverance on those whom he has elected to this end. The nature of this gift is such that it is irresistible, and will ensure that its recipient remains in grace. The distinction Augustine draws between different types of divine assistance had a considerable impact on medieval thinking on this issue. See also 6.29, 6.40, 6.43.

Now two kinds of assistance are to be distinguished. On the one hand, there is an assistance without which something does not come about [*adiutorium sine quo non fit*], and on the other there is the assistance by which something does come about [*adiutorium quo fit*]. We cannot live without food, but the fact that food is available will not keep people alive if they want to die. [. . .] But in the case of blessedness, when it is bestowed on people who are without it, they become perpetually blessed. [. . .] Thus this is an assistance both *sine quo non* and *quo*. [. . .] Now Adam was created upright, in a state of good; he was given the possibility of not sinning [*posse non peccare*], the possibility of not dying [*posse non mori*], the possibility of not losing that state of good: and in addition he was given the assistance of perseverance, not so that by this assistance it might come about that he should in fact persevere, but because without it he could not persevere through his own free will. Now in the case of the saints who are predestined to the kingdom of God by the grace of God, the assistance of perseverance which is given is not that [granted to the first man], but that kind which brings the gift of actual perseverance. It is not just that they cannot persevere without this gift; once they have received this gift, they can do nothing except persevere.

Comment

In this influential account of the way in which God relates to humanity, Augustine distinguishes between two different modes of divine assistance, and explores their implications for perseverance in faith, and the final achievement of eternal life. Notice again how a specific text is used to illuminate the original human nature: "I found that God made humans upright, but they have sought out many devices" (Ecclesiastes 7: 29). In Latin translation, the word "upright" is rendered as *rectus*, which has some overtones of "rightness" or "righteousness."

Questions for Study

1 Set out, in your own words, the two types of divine assistance which Augustine identifies. Why do you think he wishes to draw this distinction?
2 Compare this passage with 6.14. How do these two passages link the ideas of *posse non peccare* and *posse non mori*?

6.16

Pelagius on Human Responsibility

In this letter written to Demetrias, a Roman woman of high social status who eventually became a nun, Pelagius (c.355–c.435) argues that the divine commands are unconditionally binding upon Christians. God knows the abilities of humanity, and the commands reflect the ability with which God endowed humanity at creation. There is no defect in human nature which prevents them from achieving what God commands people to do. See also 6.17, 6.18, 6.19, 6.20.

[Instead of regarding God's commands as a privilege . . .] we cry out at God and say, "This is too hard! This is too difficult! We cannot do it! We are only human, and hindered by the weakness of the flesh!" What blind madness! What blatant presumption! By doing this, we accuse the God of knowledge of a twofold ignorance – ignorance of God's own creation and of God's own commands. It would be as if, forgetting the weakness of humanity – God's own creation – God had laid upon us commands which we were unable to bear. And at the same time – may God forgive us! – we ascribe to the righteous One unrighteousness, and cruelty to the Holy One; first, by complaining that God has commanded the impossible, second, by imagining that some will be condemned by God for what they could not help; so that – the blasphemy of it! – God is thought of as seeking our punishment rather than our salvation. [. . .] No one knows the extent of our strength better than the God who gave us that strength. [. . .] God has not willed to command anything impossible, for God is righteous; and will not condemn anyone for what they could not help, for God is holy.

Comment

The fundamental point being made by Pelagius is this: God made humanity and is therefore fully apprised of human capacities. It is therefore inconceivable that God would ask anything of humanity, unless humanity already had the capacity to achieve it. For Augustine, however, the commands served the purpose of disclosing the human inability to keep the law of God without divine grace.

Questions for Study

1 "No one knows the extent of our strength better than the God who gave us that strength." Locate this passage within the text. What does Pelagius mean by this?
2 How does Pelagius estimate the human capacity to fulfill the law?

6.17

Pelagius on Human Freedom

This extract is taken from what remains of an otherwise lost writing of Pelagius, which is cited by Augustine in order to criticize Pelagius's views. For this reason it cannot be regarded as totally reliable; it may have been cited out of context, for example. The Pelagian idea to which Augustine takes particular exception is that humanity can exist without sin. However, he also criticizes Pelagius for ascribing the will to perform good works to human nature; for Augustine, such a will can only be a divine gift, in that fallen human nature inclines to do evil rather than good. See also 6.13, 6.14, 6.18, 6.20.

We distinguish three things and arrange them in a certain order. We put in the first place "possibility" [*posse*]; in the second, "will" [*velle*]; in the third, "being" [*esse*]. The *posse* we assign to nature, the *velle* to will, the *esse* to actual realization. The first of these, *posse*, is properly ascribed to God, who conferred it on his creatures; while the other two, *velle* and *esse*, are to be referred to the human agent, since they have their source in the divine will. Therefore human praise lies in being willing and in doing a good work; or rather this praise belongs both to humanity and to the God who has granted the possibility of willing and working, and who by the help of grace assists [*gratiae suae adiuvat semper auxilio*] exactly this possibility. The fact that someone has this possibility of willing and doing any good work is due to God alone. [. . .]

Therefore (and this must be often repeated because of your foolishness), when we say that it is possible for someone to be without sin, we are even then praising God by acknowledging the gift of possibility which we have received. It is God who has bestowed this *posse* on us, and there is no occasion for praising the human agent when we are treating of God alone; for the question is not about *velle* or *esse*, but solely about what is possible [*potest esse*].

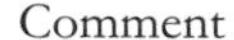

Comment

This extract is taken from Pelagius's lost writing *pro libero arbitrio* ("for the free will"). In this work, Pelagius argues that God has endowed human beings with certain abilities – for example, the ability to avoid sin. When someone avoids sin, therefore, Pelagius argues, praise and thanks are due to God, for having given such an ability to the one who merely exercised, rather than achieved or created, such a talent. Note especially Pelagius's assumption that human nature, as we now know it, is more or less the same as when God originally created it – an idea which Augustine opposed, believing that the Fall had radically distorted and weakened the original state of humanity.

Questions for Study

1 Pelagius here explores the relation of three Latin verbs: *posse, velle, esse* ("to be able," "to wish," and "to be"). How does their relationship help him make his points?
2 "This praise belongs both to humanity and to the God who has granted the possibility of willing and working." Locate this passage within the text. What does Pelagius mean by this?

6.18

Pelagius's Rejection of Original Sin

This passage, taken from a lost writing of Pelagius, is cited in a work of Augustine, who quotes it in order to discredit it. Note the distinctive Pelagian idea that humanity is born with a capacity for good or evil, rather than being intrinsically evil. For Augustine, original sin contaminates humanity from its moment of conception, so that humanity is born sinful. See also 6.2, 6.3, 6.6, 6.9, 6.13, 6.17, 6.19.

"Everything," [Pelagius] says, "good and evil, concerning which we are either worthy of praise or of blame, is done by us, not born with us [*non nobiscum oritur sed agitur a nobis*]. We are not born in our full development, but with a capacity for good and evil; we are begotten without virtue as much as without fault [*sine virtute ita et sine vitio*], and before the activity of the individual will there is nothing in humans other than what God has placed in them."

Comment

This is an important passage, in that it casts light on Pelagius's understanding of human nature. Basically, Pelagius argues that God endows humanity with certain capacities and abilities. It is then up to individual human beings to use these abilities appropriately. They may use them for good or evil, but Pelagius is clear that they are *intended* to be used for good, and that, when rightly used, they will achieve the good goals which God purposed.

Questions for Study

1 Pelagius asserts that we are born "with a capacity for good and evil." What does he mean by this? And how does it illuminate his understanding of human nature?
2 Building on this point, Pelagius argued that we are born "without virtue as much as without fault." What are the implications of this statement? In what ways would Augustine have disagreed?

6.19

The Council of Carthage on Grace

The Pelagian controversy was officially ended by the Council of Carthage (418), which laid down a series of propositions which it defined as the teaching of the catholic church on this matter. It explicitly condemned as heretical a series of eight teachings, as below. In the original document, each of these statements is prefaced with a condemnation, generally of the form "if anyone says . . . let him be condemned (*anathema sit*)." See also 6.13, 6.14, 6.16, 6.18, 6.20.

1. That Adam, the first human being, was created mortal, so that, whether he sinned or not, he would have died from natural causes, and not as the wages of sin [...]

2. That new-born children need not be baptized, or that they are baptized for the remission of sins, but that no original sin is derived from Adam to be washed away in the laver of regeneration, so that in their case the baptismal formula "for the remission of sins" is not understood in its true sense, but rather in a false sense [*non vera sed falsa intelligatur*] [...]

3. That the grace of God, by which we are justified through Jesus Christ our Lord, avails only for the remission of sins already committed, and not for assistance to prevent the sins being committed [...]

4. That this grace [...] only helps us to avoid sin in this way; that by it we are given by revelation an understanding of God's commands that we may learn what we ought to strive for and what we ought to avoid, but that it does not give us also the delight in doing, and the power to do, what we have recognized as being good [...]

5. That the grace of justification is given to us so that we may more easily perform by means of grace that which we are commanded to do by means of our free will [*per liberum arbitrium*]; as if we could fulfill those commands even without the gift of grace, though not so easily [...]

6. That the words of the Apostle John, "If we say that we have no sin, etc." (1 John 1: 8) are to be taken as meaning that we should say that we have sin not because it is true, but on account of humility on our part [...]

7. That in the Lord's Prayer the saints say "Forgive us our trespasses" not for themselves, because for them this prayer is unnecessary, but for others among their people who are sinners [...]

8. That in the Lord's Prayer the saints say "Forgive us our trespasses" out of humility and not because they are true [...]

Comment

The Council of Carthage – which took place at the leading city of Roman north Africa – sought to put an end to the Pelagian controversy through the eight explicit condemnations here presented. It is essential to realize that each of the eight statements is condemned, not affirmed! The statements are easily understood and require little in the way of comment.

Questions for Study

1 What general understanding of the relation of grace and human free will is condemned by this Council?

2 What understanding of original sin leads to these condemnations?

6.20

The Synod of Arles on Pelagianism

The condemnation of Pelagianism continued in the fifth century, with southern France emerging as a region in which the issue was of particular importance. The southern Gallic city of Arles was the venue for a synod which confirmed a series of condemnations of Pelagianism. The precise date of this synod is not known; however, it is referred to in a letter of Faustus of Regium to Lucidus, dated 473, suggesting that the synod met shortly before the letter was written. The synod condemned a series of Pelagian statements, while offering positive statements of its own. A representative selection is printed below. See also 6.16, 6.17, 6.18, 6.19.

[The following statements are condemned:]

1. That after the fall of Adam, human free choice [*arbitrium voluntatis*] was extinguished;
2. That Christ, our Lord and Savior, did not die for the salvation of all people;
3. That the foreknowledge of God forces people violently towards death, or that those who perish, perish on account of the will of God;

[The following statements are affirmed:]

1. Human effort and endeavor is to be united with the grace of God;
2. Human freedom of will [*libertas voluntatis*] is not extinct but attenuated and weakened [*non extinctam sed adtenuatam et infirmatam esse*];
3. Those who are saved could still be lost, and those that have perished could have been saved.

Comment

The Council of Carthage was intended to bring the Pelagian controversy to an end. In fact, a number of issues remained contested, so that the next few centuries saw continued discussion and debate, especially in the south of France. The Synod of Arles attempted to clarify a number of matters, especially the effect of the Fall upon human freedom.

Questions for Study

1 According to this synod, does human freedom remain after the Fall?
2 Can any statements of this synod be seen as implying criticism of Augustine's doctrine of irresistible grace (6.15)?

6.21

The Second Council of Orange on Grace and Freedom

In 529 a local gathering of bishops convened in the southern Gallic city of Orange to deal with further issues which had arisen as a result of the Pelagian controversy. The Council made 25 rulings, in which it condemned a series of positions which it regarded as failing to do justice to the priority of God's grace. The text for study consists of the first seven rulings or "canons," which condemned viewpoints regarded as unacceptable. See also 6.19, 6.20.

1. If anyone says that it is not the whole human person – that is, both body and soul – that was changed for the worse through the offense of Adam's sin, but believes that the freedom of the soul remains unimpaired, and that only the body is subject to corruption, he is deceived by the error of Pelagius and opposes the Scriptures which say, "The soul that sins shall die" (Ezekiel 18: 20), and "Do you not know that if you yield yourselves to anyone as obedient slaves, you are the slaves of the one whom you obey?" (Romans 6: 16), and, "For whatever overcomes someone, to that he is enslaved" (2 Peter 2: 19).

2. If anyone declares that Adam's sin affected him alone and not also his descendants; or that it is only the death of the body which is the punishment for sin, and not also that sin, which is the death of the soul, passed through one man to the whole human race; he does injustice to God and contradicts the Apostle, who says, "Therefore as sin came into the world through one man and death through sin, and so death spread to all men because all have sinned" (Romans 5: 12; cf. Augustine).

3. If anyone says that the grace of God can be conferred as a result of human prayer, but that it is not grace itself which makes us pray to God, he contradicts the prophet Isaiah, or the Apostle who says the same thing, "I have been found by those who did not seek me; I have shown myself to those who did not ask for me" (Romans 10: 20; cf. Isaiah 65: 1).

4. If anyone holds that God waits for our will to be cleansed from its sin, but does not admit that our will to be cleansed comes to us through the infusion and working of the Holy Spirit, he resists the Holy Spirit himself who says through Solomon, "The will is prepared by the Lord" (Proverbs 8: 35), and the sound words of the Apostle, "For God is at work in you, both to will and to work for his good pleasure" (Philippians 2: 13).

5. If anyone says that not only the increase of faith but also its beginning and the very desire for faith, by which we believe in the one who justifies the ungodly and

comes to the regeneration of holy baptism – if anyone says that this belongs to us by nature and not by a gift of grace, that is, by the inspiration of the Holy Spirit which corrects our will and turns it from unbelief to faith, and from godlessness to godliness, it is proof that he is opposed to the teaching of the Apostles, for the blessed Paul says, "And I am sure that he who began a good work in you will bring it to completion at the day of Jesus Christ" (Philippians 1: 6). And again, "For by grace you have been saved through faith; and this is not your own doing, it is the gift of God" (Ephesians 2: 8). For those who declare that the faith by which we believe in God is natural declare that all who are separated from the Church of Christ are believers, at least to some extent (cf. Augustine).

6. If anyone holds that God has mercy upon us when, apart from his grace, we believe, will, desire, strive, labor, pray, watch, study, seek, ask, or knock; but does not admit that it is by the infusion and inspiration of the Holy Spirit within us that we have this faith, will, or strength to do all these things as we ought; or if anyone makes the assistance of grace dependent upon the humility or obedience of humanity, and does not agree that we are obedient and humble through a gift of grace, he contradicts the Apostle who says, "What have you that you did not receive?" (1 Corinthians 4: 7), and, "But by the grace of God I am what I am" (1 Corinthians 15: 10; cf. Augustine and Prosper of Aquitaine).

7. If anyone affirms that we can, through our natural powers, form any right opinion or make any right choice which relates to salvation and eternal life, as is expedient for us; or that we can be saved, that is, assent to the preaching of the gospel without the illumination and inspiration of the Holy Spirit, who makes all people gladly assent to and believe in the truth; he is led astray by a heretical spirit, and does not understand the voice of God who says in the Gospel, "For apart from me you can do nothing" (John 15: 5), and the word of the Apostle, "Not that we are able in ourselves to claim anything as coming from us; our sufficiency is from God" (2 Corinthians 3: 5; cf. Augustine).

Comment

For reasons which are not fully understood, the decisions of this Council were overlooked by the Middle Ages and were apparently rediscovered in the early sixteenth century. The Council's condemnations of certain positions are clear and precise, and are generally regarded as having brought the western patristic discussion of the doctrine of grace, arising from the Pelagian controversy, to a close.

Questions for Study

1 The Council condemns anyone who teaches "that Adam's sin affected him alone and not also his descendants." What reasons are given for this condemnation? And what view does the Council hold on this matter?

2 "For by grace you have been saved through faith; and this is not your own doing, it is the gift of God" (Ephesians 2: 8). How does the Council make use of this text?

6.22

John Scotus Eriugena on the Nature of Paradise

In this passage the Irish theologian John Scotus Eriugena (c.810–c.877) spiritualizes the notion of paradise, denying that it is a place. Unlike writers such as Augustine, who understood paradise as a specific location in place and time, Eriugena argues that paradise is in reality perfect human nature. A similar line of thought can be found in writers such as Origen, Gregory of Nyssa, and Maximus the Confessor. See also 10.1, 10.6, 10.13.

[Therefore] the praise of the life of humanity in paradise must refer to the future life that would have been ours if Adam had remained obedient, rather than to the life which he had only just begun, and in which he did not continue. For if he had continued in it for even a brief period, he must have achieved some degree of perfection, and in that case perhaps his master would not have said, "He began to live [*vivebat*]" but "He lived [*vixit*]," or "He had lived [*vixerat*]." However, if he had used the past or pluperfect tenses in this way, or if he used them like this somewhere else, I would have thought that he was using the past tense to refer to the future, rather than meaning that Adam had continued for a space of time in the blessedness of paradise before the Fall. My reason for doing so is that he was giving expression to the predestined and foreordained blessedness, which was to be ours if Adam had not sinned, as though it had already happened – when, as a matter of fact, it was still among the things which were predestined to be perfect in the future, and which have yet to take place. Now I say this because often when he is writing about paradise, he does not use the past and pluperfect tenses. [...] This is not surprising, in that the most wise divine authority often speaks of the future as though it had already taken place.

Comment

This is an unusual text, in that its argument rests largely on an appeal to the specific tenses associated with the verbs found in Scripture. The general principle being affirmed is that paradise is not to be interpreted geographically, but theologically – that is, in a perfect relationship with God, which was the original state of humanity, and to which redeemed humanity will finally be restored again at the end of time.

Questions for Study

1 What does this passage tell us about its author's view of human nature and destiny?
2 According to the passage, what are the consequences of the original human sin for humanity?

6.23

Hildegard of Bingen on the Creation of Man and Woman

Hildegard of Bingen (1098–1179) was Abbess of Rupertsberg, near the city of Bingen. She established a reputation as a theological and spiritual writer of considerable originality, and developed a particular interest in the spirituality of creation. One of her most important works is the *Liber Divinorum Operum* ("Book of Divine Works"), which was written in Latin over the period 1163–73. This represents an exploration of the universe, the earth, and all created things. The text for study is taken from the "fourth vision," which deals with the human body. See also 6.4, 6.5, 6.50, 6.55.

Now when God looked at the man, he was well pleased, in that God had created him according to God's image and likeness, and declared him to be the greatest of God's miracles. Man is the work of God perfected, because God is known through him, and also since God created all creatures for man, and allowed man to proclaim and praise God through the quality of his mind, in the embrace of true love. Yet man needed a helper in his likeness. God therefore gave him such a helper in the form of his mirror image [*speculativa forma*] – woman – in whom the whole of the human race lay concealed. This was to be brought forth through the power and in the strength of God, just as God produced the first man. The man and the woman were thus complementary, in that one works through the other. Man cannot be called "man" without the woman, in the same way as the woman cannot be called "woman" without the man. Woman is thus the work of man, and man the consolation of the woman. Neither can exist without the other. Man signifies the divinity of the Son of God, in the same way as the woman signifies his humanity.

Comment

Hildegard here offers an account of the relation of male and female, based partly on her reading and interpretation of the second Genesis creation account. The passage offers a view of the relation of male and female which is complementary; they are meant to assist each other, and bring each other to their intended goals. Note especially Hildegard's suggestion that woman is the "mirror image" of the male.

Questions for Study

1 "Woman is thus the work of man, and man the consolation of the woman." Locate this passage in the text. What does Hildegard mean by this?

2 How does Hildegard draw a Christological conclusion from her analysis of the nature of man and woman? And how do you think she justifies this?

6.24

Alan of Lille on Penitence as a Cause of Grace

Alan of Lille (died 1203) argued that penitence on the part of someone was the means by which that person received grace. However, the penitence itself could not strictly be seen as the cause of grace, but merely the occasion or means by which it was received. See also 6.30.

Penitence is indeed a necessary cause [of grace], in that unless someone is penitent, God will not forgive that person's sins. It is like the sun, which illuminates a house when a shutter [*fenestra*] is opened. The opening of that shutter is not the efficient cause of that illumination, in that the sun itself is the efficient cause of that illumination. However, it is nevertheless its occasion.

Comment

The point that Alan of Lille is making can be summarized as follows. The sun is always radiating its illumination. Nevertheless, for that light to enter into and illuminate a room in the house, a shutter must be opened. The opening of that shutter does not cause the sun to shine, in that this is already happening. Rather, the opening of the shutter is the means by which that light enters and illuminates the house. The removal of an obstacle to illumination thus serves a real role in the lighting up of that dark room. In the same way, human beings can remove obstacles to God's grace, so that they may develop and progress in the spiritual life. This action does not cause God's grace, but is the occasion or means by which grace may enter into a person's life.

Questions for Study

1 What types of causes does Alan distinguish in this passage? And how does he use this distinction?
2 Set out, in your own words, the theological point that Alan wishes to make by using the analogy of the sun illuminating a room when a shutter is opened.

6.25

Francis of Assisi on the Creation

Francis of Assisi's *Canticle of the Sun* represents an important affirmation of a positive attitude towards the creation, typical of Franciscan spirituality. Francis (1181–1226) probably composed this during the winter of 1224–5 at the Church of San Damiano, Assisi. Traditional English translations of this familiar poem have been heavily influenced by the need to ensure rhyming. My prose translation of the original Italian ignores such considerations in order to convey the basic sense of the poem. The lines of the original have been retained. See also 2.31, 2.32, 2.37.

The Song of Brother Sun; or, The Praises of the Creatures

1. Most high, all-powerful and good Lord,
   To you are due the praises, the glory, the honor, and every blessing.

2. To you only, O highest one, are they due
   and no human being is worthy to speak of you.

3. Be praised, my Lord, with all your creatures
   especially by brother sun, by whom we are lightened every day

4. He is fair and radiant with great splendor
   and bears your likeness, O highest one.

5. Be praised, my Lord, for sister moon and the stars
   which you have set in heaven, precious, fair, and bright.

6. Be praised, my Lord, by brother wind,
   and by air and cloud and sky and every weather,
   through whom you give life to all your creatures.

7. Be praised, my Lord, by sister water
   for she is most useful and humble and precious and chaste.

8. Be praised, my Lord, by brother fire,
   by him we are lightened at night
   and he is fair and cheerful and sturdy and strong.

9. Be praised, my Lord, by our sister, mother earth
who sustains and governs us
and brings forth many fruits and colored flowers and plants.

10. Be praised, my Lord, by those who have been pardoned by your love
and who bear infirmity and tribulation.

11. Blessed are those who suffer them in peace
for they shall be crowned by you, O highest one.

12. Be praised, my Lord, by our sister, physical death [*morte corporale*]
from whom no one who lives can escape.

13. Woe to those who die in mortal sin,
but blessed are those who are found in your most holy will
for the second death [*morte secunda*] can do them no harm.

14. May I bless and praise you, my Lord,
and give you thanks and serve you with great humility.

Comment

Francis was noted for his concern for the animal kingdom, which was regarded as somewhat eccentric by many at the time. In this famous poem Francis sets out a vision of the entire creation praising its creator. Note especially the underlying theology of providence, in which the benefit of each aspect of creation for humanity is identified. The most famous feature of the canticle is its use of the terms ''brother'' and ''sister'' to refer to various aspects of the created order.

Questions for Study

1 Why do you think that Francis personifies the various aspects of creation in this way?
2 Francis finds something positive to say about every aspect of creation. Why? What point does he make in doing this?

6.26

Thomas Aquinas on the Nature of Grace

The *Summa Theologiae* (''The Totality of Theology''), which Aquinas began to write in Latin in 1265 and left unfinished at the time of his death, is widely regarded as the greatest work of medieval theology. In this section Aquinas (c.1225–74) deals with various ways in which the word "grace" may be understood, while affirming that in its proper sense, grace designates something supernatural implanted by God within the human soul. See also 6.19, 6.34, 6.39.

As used in everyday language, "grace" is commonly understood to mean three things. First, it can mean someone's love, as when it is said that a soldier has the king's favor – that is, that the king holds him in favor. Secondly, it can mean a gift which is freely given, as when it is said: "I do you this favor." Thirdly, it can mean the response to a gift which is freely given, as when we are said to give thanks for benefits which we have received. Now the second of these depends upon the first, as someone freely bestows a gift on someone else on account of their love for them. And the third depends upon the second, since thankfulness is appropriate to gifts which are freely given.

Now if "grace" is understood in either the second or third sense of the word, it will be clear that it leaves something in the one who receives it – whether it is the gift which is freely given, or the acknowledgement of that gift. [. . .] To say that someone has the grace of God is to say that there is something supernatural in humanity, coming forth from God [*quiddam supernaturale in homine a Deo proveniens*].

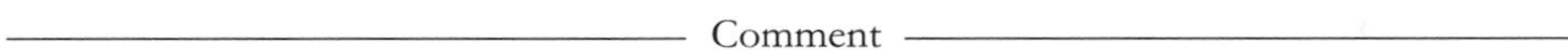

Comment

In addition to offering clarification of the meaning of the theological term "grace," this passage also allows us to see Aquinas reflecting on the relation of words in their everyday sense, and more specifically religious senses. This reflects Aquinas's doctrine of analogy, which holds that, on account of God's work as creator, there is some kind of inbuilt correspondence between the things in the world and their divine creator. It should therefore not be a cause for surprise that words can play this kind of dual role. Note also that Aquinas understands grace in *ontological*, rather than relational, terms. "To say that someone has the grace of God is to say that there is something supernatural in the soul, coming forth from God." This contrasts with the Reformation viewpoint, which understands grace as the "favor of God" (*favor Dei*).

Questions for Study

1 Set out, in your own words, the three main everyday senses of the word "grace." How does Aquinas apply these theologically? Are all equally useful?

2 What, according to Aquinas, is grace?

6.27

Mechthild of Magdeburg on Humanity's Longing for God

Mechthild of Magdeburg (c.1210–c.1282) is widely celebrated as one of the most important women spiritual writers of the thirteenth century. Her *Vliessende lieht miner gotheit in allu die herzen die da lebent ane valscheit* ("Light of my divinity, flowing into all hearts that live without falsehood") includes her visionary experiences, as well as letters of advice and criticism, allegories, reflections, and prayers. Our extract is taken from the first of its seven books, probably written in the 1250s, and takes the form of a dialogue between God and the believing soul. The section of the dialogue extracted for study concerns the longing of humanity for God. See also 6.10, 6.23, 6.50, 10.13.

GOD: You are hunting desperately for the one that you love; tell me, what do you bring me, O my Queen?

SOUL: Lord, I bring you my treasure; It is greater than the mountains; It is wider than the world, deeper than the sea, higher than the clouds, more brilliant than the sun, more numerous than the stars, weighing more than everything.

GOD: O image of my Godhead, ennobled by my own humanity, adorned by my Holy Spirit, what is your treasure called?

SOUL: Lord, it is called my heart's desire, which I have taken out of the world, kept to myself, and denied to all creatures. Now I can bear this no longer. Where, O Lord, shall I lay it

GOD: Your heart's desire you will lay nowhere other than in my own divine heart, and in my human breast. There alone will you find comfort, and be embraced by my Spirit.

Comment

Much of the great medieval mystical tradition was based on a central theme of the Christian understanding of human nature – that humanity was created in order to love God, and is dissatisfied unless this relationship is in place. The idea is found in Augustine of Hippo's famous prayer, "You have made us for yourself, and our heart is restless until it finds its rest in you." Mechthild's spiritual reflections are grounded in this central insight, and can be seen as a variation on this Augustinian theme.

Questions for Study

1 The concept of the "heart's desire" is clearly of considerable importance for Mechthild. What use does she make of it?
2 Martin Luther once commented that "wherever your heart is, and whatever is your security, that has become your God." What does Mechthild's text tell us about the location of her trust and love?

6.28

John Duns Scotus on the Immaculate Conception of Mary

Is Mary, the mother of Jesus Christ, a sinner, requiring redemption along with the rest of the human race? Up to the thirteenth century, this question had been answered predominantly in the affirmative. Mary, it was argued, was herself conceived normally, and hence was contaminated through original sin. This position, traditionally described as the "maculate conception" (from the Latin *macula*, a "defect" or "blemish") is defended by Thomas Aquinas, amongst others. A very different position, however, was set out by the British scholastic theologian John Duns Scotus (c.1266–1308). For Scotus, Mary was preserved from original sin – a position now known as "immaculate conception" – and hence did not require redemption. He defends this position in his commentary on Peter Lombard's standard textbook, *The Four Books of the Sentences*, based on lectures given at Oxford University during the academic year 1298–99. See also 6.2, 6.3, 6.23, 6.55.

Christ was the most perfect mediator. Therefore he exercised the highest degree of mediation in favor of another person. Now he could not be a most perfect mediator and could not repair the effects of sin to the highest degree if he did not preserve his Mother from original sin, as we shall prove. Therefore, since he was the most perfect mediator regarding the person of his mother, it follows from this that he preserved her from original sin. [. . .] It is more noble to forgive one's guilt by preserving that person from it, than by permitting that same person to fall into guilt and than to remit that person's guilt [*obilius est remittere alicui culpam ipsum praeservando ne insit, quam permittere offensam inesse et eam postea remittere*]. [. . .] I say that it was possible that she was not conceived in original sin. It was also possible that she was in the state of original sin only for a brief moment of time and then was in a state of grace for the rest of her life. Lastly it was possible that she was in a state of original sin for some time and then passed into the state of grace.

Comment

Scotus argues that the manner of Mary's conception is such that she is preserved from the common human condition of original sin. The most important part of his argument is that it is fitting that Christ should redeem his own mother in the most fitting manner. Whereas other humans sin, and hence require to be redeemed, Scotus argues that Christ performs a "more noble" act of redemption in her case. She is preserved from the sin which necessitates redemption in the case of others. This, however, raises another question: was Mary conceived in original sin and then immediately purified from it? Scotus notes three possible views on this matter, of which the first is most consistent with his own approach.

Questions for Study

1 What you do think Scotus means by "preserved"? Do you think he is saying that Mary was conceived without original sin? Or that she was conceived in original sin, but somehow preserved from its effects?
2 How persuasive do you find Scotus's argument concerning the unique mode of Mary's redemption?

6.29

Gregory of Rimini on Predestination

Gregory of Rimini (died 1358) was one of the most important Augustinian theologians of the later Middle Ages. Gregory was strongly opposed to what he regarded as the Pelagian tendencies of the dominant theologies of his day, and proposed instead the reappropriation of Augustine's doctrine of grace. The extract is taken from his "Commentary on the Sentences." See also 6.12, 6.36, 6.40, 6.43.

It is clear to me from the statements of Scripture and of the saints that the following conclusions must be accepted as true, and taught and preached as such. First, that no one is predestined on account of the good use of the free will, which God foreknows and considers to their advantage. Second, that no one is predestined because it is foreknown that he will not finally place any obstacle in the path of habitual or actual grace. Thirdly, that whoever God predestines, is predestined in a manner which is gracious and merciful. Fourthly, that no one is condemned on account of the evil use of the free will, which is foreknown by God. Fifthly, that no one is condemned because it is foreseen that he will finally place an obstacle in the path of grace.

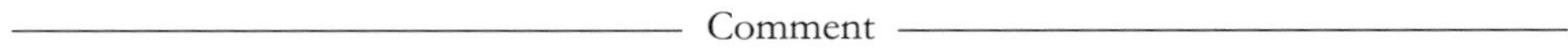

Comment

Gregory is sometimes spoken of as a leading member of the *schola Augustiniana moderna* ("the modern Augustinian school"). This late medieval school of theology, which seems to have had links with the Augustinian monastic order, accepted many of the "modern" philosophical assumptions of the fourteenth century, but insisted that these be affirmed alongside an essentially Augustinian doctrine of grace. In this passage we find a strongly Augustinian stance being taken on the doctrine of predestination.

Questions for Study

1 Gregory offers five statements concerning predestination. Summarize each in your own words.
2 Is "predestination" the same as "foreknowledge," in Gregory's view?

6.28

Gabriel Biel on Merit and Justification

Gabriel Biel (c.1420–95) was one of the most influential scholastic theologians of the fifteenth century. He was closely linked with the Brethren of the Common Life, and was one of those responsible for the founding of the University of Tübingen, where he served as professor of theology. Biel developed an approach to the doctrine of justification which he believed avoided Pelagianism on the one hand, while at the same time doing justice to the need to involve the believer in the process of justification. The passage which follows is taken from his "Commentary on the Sentences." See also 6.24.

The soul, by removing an obstacle towards a good movement to God through the free will, is able to merit the first grace *de congruo*. This may be proved as follows: because God accepts the act of doing "what lies within its powers" [*actum facientis quod in se est*)] as leading to the first grace, not on account of any debt of justice, but on account of God's generosity. The soul, by removing this obstacle, ceases from acts of sin and consent to sin, and thus elicits a good movement towards God as its principal end; and does "what lies within its powers" [*quod in se est*]. Therefore God accepts, out of his generosity [*ex sua liberalitate*], this act of removing an obstacle and a good movement towards God as the basis of the infusion of grace.

Comment

Gabriel Biel sets out an approach to justification which places considerable emphasis upon the divine generosity (*liberalitas*). God does not demand that we succeed in Herculean achievements before giving us grace; rather, we are asked to meet certain rather modest demands – specifically, turning away from sin and towards God. Biel refers to these as doing "what lies within one" (*quod in se est*). Once this is achieved, God supplements this with his gift of grace. Biel argued that his emphasis on God's liberality meant that he had avoided falling into any kind of Pelagianism in this matter. The reformer Martin Luther disagreed, and made Biel the target of some sustained criticisms in 1517. Note that *meritum de congruo* ("congruous merit") is a weak statement of the idea of merit, meaning something like "a gift which reflects the liberality of the giver rather than the claims of the recipient." The normal sense of merit – which scholastic theologians referred to as *meritum de condigno* ("condign merit") – would have the sense of "something which was given on account of the merits of the recipient."

Questions for Study

1 What does Biel require individuals to do before they can receive grace? How does this compare with the view of Alan of Lille (6.24)?
2 What obstacles exist to grace within the human soul? How does Biel believe that they are to be removed?

6.31

Giovanni Pico della Mirandola on Human Nature

Giovanni Pico della Mirandola (1463–94), one of the leading voices of the Italian Renaissance, delivered his "oration on the dignity of humanity" in 1486 at the age of 24. This "Manifesto of the Renaissance," written in a highly polished and elegant Latin style, represents a significant development of the traditional Christian doctrine of creation. Humanity is depicted as a creature with the capacity to determine its own identity, rather than to receive this in any given fixed form. The human creature possesses no determinate image, and is urged by its creator to pursue its own perfection. The ideas of this oration proved to be enormously influential in the late Renaissance, and can be seen as setting the scene for the Enlightenment assertion of human autonomy in the face of God. See also 6.4, 6.5, 6.25, 6.54.

Now God the Father, the supreme Architect, had already constructed this cosmic home that we see, the most august temple of His godhead, by the laws of His mysterious wisdom. He adorned the region above the heavens with minds, he populated the heavenly spheres with eternal souls, and he filled the excrementary and filthy parts of the lower world with a multitude of animals of every kind. But, when this work was finished, the Craftsman wished that there might be someone to admire the plan of so great a work, to love its beauty, and to wonder at its grandeur. Therefore, when everything was done (as Moses and Timaeus bear witness), he finally gave thought to the creation of humanity. But there was nothing among his archetypes from which he could fashion a new creation, nor was there in his treasure houses anything that he could bestow on His new son as an inheritance, nor was there a seat in all the world from where this son might contemplate this universe. Everything was now complete: everything had been assigned to the highest, the middle, and the lowest orders.

Yet it was not in the nature of the power of the Father to fail in this last act of creation; nor was it in the nature of that supreme Wisdom to hesitate through lack of counsel in so crucial a matter; nor, finally, was it in the nature of his beneficent love to compel the creature destined to praise the divine generosity in all other things to find it wanting in himself.

At last the best of artisans ordained that this creature, to whom He could give nothing that was distinctively his own, should have a share in the particular endowment of every other creature. Taking humanity, therefore – this creature of indeterminate image – he set him in the middle of the world and spoke to him: We have given you, Adam, neither a fixed dwelling place, nor a form that is yours alone, nor any function that is peculiar to you alone. This is so that you may have and possess whatever dwelling place, form, and functions that you yourself may desire, according to your longing and judgment. The nature of all other beings is limited and constrained within the bounds of laws prescribed by us. You are constrained by no limits, and shall determine the limits of your nature for yourself, in accordance with your own free will, in whose hand we have placed you. We have set you at the center of the world, in order that you may more easily observe whatever is in the world. We have made you neither of heaven nor of earth, neither mortal nor immortal, in order that you may, as the free and proud shaper of your own being, fashion yourself in whatever form you may prefer. It will be in your power to descend to the lower orders of animals; it will also be in your power to rise again to the higher orders, whose life is divine.

Comment

This elegant, occasionally flamboyant, piece of rhetoric sets out the Renaissance vision of human nature. It includes many Christian elements, most notably the idea of humanity as representing the height of creation, alone possessing the capacity to admire, understand, and revere the created order, and hence its creator. Yet the oration also opens up a new way of thinking about the location of humanity within the created order. Pico della Mirandola insists that humanity is not assigned to any particular location or assigned any specific function within creation. It is the privilege and responsibility of humanity to determine its own place and function, through the proper exercise of its freedom and intelligence. Humanity can thus descend to the level of animals, or rise to the level of God.

Questions for Study

1 A fundamental theme of this oration is that humanity must determine its own identity. How does Pico della Mirandola lay the foundations for this doctrine?
2 In what ways might Pico della Mirandola's understanding of human nature come into conflict with traditional Christian views on this matter?

6.32

Martin Luther's Discovery of the "Righteousness of God"

In this passage, originally written in 1545, the year before his death, the reformer Martin Luther (1483–1546) reflects on his early life, and particularly a major theological difficulty which he experienced as a young man. What was "good news" about the proclamation of the righteousness of God? For Luther, the righteousness of God could only mean the condemnation of sinners, himself included. Luther here relates how, after wrestling with the meaning of Romans 1: 17, he finally came to understand the "righteousness of God" (*iustitia Dei*) in a different way, thus opening the door to his theological reformation. See also 6.33, 6.34.

Meanwhile in that year [1519], I had returned to interpreting the Psalter again, confident that I was better equipped after I had expounded in the schools the letters of St Paul to the Romans and the Galatians, and the letter to the Hebrews. I had certainly been overcome with a great desire to understand St Paul in his letter to the Romans, but what had hindered me thus far was not any "coldness of the blood" so much as that one phrase in the first chapter: "The righteousness of God is revealed in it." For I had hated the phrase "the righteousness of God" which, according to the use and custom of all the doctors, I had been taught to understand philosophically, in the sense of the formal or active righteousness (as they termed it), by which God is righteous, and punishes unrighteous sinners.

Although I lived an irreproachable life as a monk, I felt that I was a sinner with an uneasy conscience before God; nor was I able to believe that I had pleased him with my satisfaction. I did not love (in fact, I hated) that righteous God who punished sinners, if not with silent blasphemy, then certainly with great murmuring. I was angry with God, saying "As if it were not enough that miserable sinners should be eternally damned through original sin, with all kinds of misfortunes laid upon them by the Old Testament law, and yet God adds sorrow upon sorrow through the gospel, and even brings wrath and righteousness to bear through it!" Thus I drove myself mad, with a desperate disturbed conscience, persistently pounding upon Paul in this passage, thirsting most ardently to know what he meant.

At last, God being merciful, as I meditated day and night on the connection of the words "the righteousness of God is revealed in it, as it is written: the righteous shall live by faith," I began to understand that "righteousness of God" as that by which the righteous live by the gift of God, namely by faith, and this sentence, "the righteousness of God is revealed," to refer to a passive righteousness, by which the merciful God justifies us by faith, as it is written, "The righteous live by faith." This immediately made me feel as though I had been born again, and as though I had entered through open gates into paradise itself. From that moment, the whole face of Scripture appeared to me in a different light. Afterwards, I ran through the Scriptures, as from memory, and found the same analogy in other phrases such as the "work of God" (that which God works within us), the "power of God" (by which he makes us strong), the "wisdom of God" (by which he makes us wise), the "strength of God," the "salvation of God," and the "glory of God."

And now, where I had once hated the phrase "the righteousness of God," so much I began to love and extoll it as the sweetest of words, so that this passage in Paul became the very gate of paradise for me. Afterwards, I read Augustine, *On the Spirit and the Letter*, where I found that he too, beyond my expectation, interpreted "the righteousness of God" in the same way – as that which God bestows upon us, when he justifies us. And although this is expressed somewhat imperfectly, and he does not explain everything about imputation clearly, it was nevertheless pleasing to find that he taught that the "righteousness of God" is that by which we are justified.

Comment

In this passage Luther sets out the way in which he arrived at a new understanding of the "righteousness of God." This insight may be regarded as being of fundamental importance to the development of Luther's doctrine of justification by faith. Notice how Luther is especially critical of the understanding of the "righteousness of God" which he received from his scholastic teachers. The text is very clear and easy to follow, and requires nothing additional in the way of comment.

Questions for Study

1 How did Luther initially understand the phrase "the righteousness of God"?
2 What was his final understanding of this concept? How, according to the passage, did he arrive at this understanding?

6.33

Martin Luther on Justifying Faith

In this passage, originally published in German in 1520, Luther develops the idea that faith unites the believer to Christ, in much the same way as marriage unites a bride and bridegroom. The soul is thus made "single and free" from its sin on account of being married to Christ; Luther's language here suggests the image of being "divorced from sin" in order to be "united with Christ." Through this union, the believer shares in all Christ's riches, while Christ swallows up the believer's sin. The passage serves to emphasize that Luther sees faith as far more than intellectual assent to propositions. Faith establishes a living personal relationship between Christ and the believer. See also 1.13, 6.30, 6.32, 6.37.

In the twelfth place, faith does not merely mean that the soul realizes that the divine word is full of all grace, free and holy; it also unites the soul with Christ [*voreynigt auch die seele mit Christo*], as a bride is united with her bridegroom. From such a marriage, as St Paul says (Ephesians 5:31–2), it follows that Christ and the soul become one body, so that they hold all things in common, whether for better or worse. This means that what Christ possesses belongs to the believing soul; and what the soul possesses, belongs to Christ. Thus Christ possesses all good things and holiness; these now belong to the soul. The soul possesses lots of vices and sin; these now belong to Christ. Here we have a happy exchange [*froelich wechtzel*] and struggle. Christ is God and a human being, who has never sinned and whose holiness is unconquerable, eternal, and almighty. So he makes the sin of the believing soul his own through its wedding ring [*braudtring*], which is faith, and acts as if he had done it [i.e. sin] himself, so that sin could be swallowed up in him. For his unconquerable righteousness is too strong for all sin, so that is made single and free [*ledig und frei*] from all its sins on account of its pledge, that is its faith, and can turn to the eternal righteousness of its bridegroom, Christ. Now is not this a happy business [*ein froehliche wirtschafft*]? Christ, the rich, noble, and holy bridegroom, takes in marriage this poor, contemptible, and sinful little prostitute [*das arm vorachte boetzes huerlein*], takes away all her evil, and bestows all his goodness upon her! It is no longer possible for sin to overwhelm her, for she is now found in Christ and is swallowed up by him, so that she possesses a rich righteousness in her bridegroom.

Comment

Luther's concern here is to illuminate how faith is able to deliver such benefits to believers. Luther emphasizes the critical role of faith in establishing an intimate relationship between Christ and the believer (attributing to "faith" many of the qualities which medieval writers tended to attribute to "love"). This relationship has both personal and legal aspects, in the same way as a human marriage possesses both these dimensions. Notice how Luther draws a distinction between believing that certain things are true and a personal trust in God which brings about an intimate and personal union with Christ. In one of Luther's later writings, he refers to a "grasping faith" (*fides apprehensiva*) which "takes hold of this treasure, Jesus Christ." This idea is anticipated in this present text. The passage reflects its sixteenth-century origins, not least in the way it assumes that the dignity of the husband is automatically conferred upon his wife at the time of marriage.

Questions for Study

1 The image of a marriage is used extensively in this passage. What are the main points which Luther bases upon the analogy, or illuminates on its basis?
2 Some scholars suggest that Luther sees the Christian life in terms of a "legal fiction," in that God treats us as if we are righteous when in reality we are sinners. Does the marriage analogy confirm or challenge this interpretation?

6.34

Martin Luther on Sin and Grace

During the academic year 1515–16, Luther delivered a course of lectures in Latin at the University of Wittenberg on Paul's letter to the Romans. A copy of these lectures has survived, allowing insights into Luther's theology at this early stage in his career. In the course of analyzing Romans 4: 7, Luther opens up a discussion of the relation of sin and grace in the life of the believer. His basic argument is that sin and righteousness coexist in the existence of believers, so that they are at one and the same time sinners and righteous people. See also 6.13, 6.17, 6.21.

Since the saints are always conscious of their sin, and seek righteousness from God in accordance with his mercy, they are always reckoned as righteous by God [*semper quoque iusti a Deo reputantur*]. Thus in their own eyes, and as a matter of fact, they are unrighteous. But God reckons them as righteous on account of their confession of their sin. In fact, they are sinners; however, they are righteous by the reckoning of a merciful God [*Re vera peccatores, sed reputatione miserentis Dei iusti*]. Without knowing it, they are righteous; knowing it, they are unrighteous. They are sinners in fact, but righteous in hope (*peccatores in re, iusti autem in spe*). [. . .]

It is like the case of a man who is ill, who trusts the doctor who promises him a certain recovery and in the meantime obeys the doctor's instructions, abstaining from what has been forbidden to him, in the hope of the promised recovery [*in spe promissae sanitatis*], so that he does not do anything to hinder this promised recovery. [...] Now this man who is ill, is he healthy? The fact is that he is a man who is both ill and healthy at the same time [*immo aegrotus simul et sanus*]. As a matter of fact, he is ill; but he is healthy on account of the certain promise of the doctor, who he trusts and who reckons him as healthy already, because he is sure that he will cure him. Indeed, he has already begun to cure him, and no longer regards him as having a terminal illness. In the same way, our Samaritan, Christ, has brought this ill man to the inn to be cared for, and has begun to cure him, having promised him the most certain cure leading to eternal life. [...] Now is this man perfectly righteous? No. But he is at one and the same time a sinner and a righteous person [*simul iustus et peccator*]. He is a sinner in fact, but a righteous person by the sure reckoning and promise of God that he will continue to deliver him from sin until he has completely cured him. And so he is totally healthy in hope, but is a sinner in fact [*sanus perfecte est in spe, in re autem peccator*]. He has the beginning of righteousness, and so always continues more and more to seek it, while realizing that he is always unrighteous.

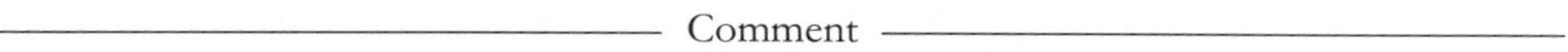

Comment

The issue being addressed here is whether someone has to be perfectly righteous before they can be accepted by God. Luther answers this emphatically in the negative: sinners are accepted on account of Christ's righteousness. Luther's analogy of the doctor accounts both for the persistence of sin in believers, and the gradual transformation of the believer and the future elimination of that sin. But it is not necessary to be perfectly righteous to be a Christian. Sin does not point to unbelief, or a failure on the part of God; rather, it points to the continued need to entrust one's person to the gentle care of God. Luther thus declares, in a famous phrase, that a believer is "at one and the same time righteous and a sinner" (*simul iustus et peccator*); righteous in hope, but a sinner in fact; righteous in the sight and through the promise of God, yet a sinner in reality.

Questions for Study

1 Set out, in your own words, the point which Luther wishes to make using the analogy of the doctor and the patient.
2 "They are sinners in fact, but righteous in hope." What does Luther mean by this statement?

6.35

Philip Melanchthon on Justification by Faith

In the first edition of his *Loci Communes* ("Commonplaces"), published in Latin in 1521, Philip Melanchthon (1497–1560) set out his understanding of justification by faith. The dominant theme of the passage is the relation between faith and works, and especially Melanchthon's response to the suggestion that his approach leaves no place for good works and invalidates the New Testament references to "rewards" for the Christian life. See also 6.32, 6.33, 6.34, 6.38, 6.39.

For what cause is justification attributed to faith alone? I answer that since we are justified by the mercy of God alone, and faith is clearly the recognition of that mercy by whatever promise you apprehend it, justification is attributed to faith alone. Let those who marvel that justification is attributed to faith alone marvel also that justification is attributed only to the mercy of God, and not rather to human merits. For to trust in the divine mercy is to have no confidence in any of our own works. Anyone who denies that the saints are justified by faith insults the mercy of God. For since our justification is a work of divine mercy alone and is not a merit based on our own works, as Paul clearly teaches in Romans 11, justification must be attributed to faith alone: faith is that through which alone we receive the promised mercy.

So what about works that precede justification, works of the free will? All those who are of the cursed tree are cursed fruits. Although they are examples of the most beautiful virtues, comparable to the righteousness of Paul before his conversion, yet they are nothing but deceit and treachery on account of their having their source in an impure heart. Impurity of heart consists of ignorance of God, not fearing God, not trusting God, and not seeking after God, as we have shown above. For the flesh knows nothing but fleshly things, as it says in Romans 8: 5: "Those who live according to the flesh set their minds on the things of the flesh." [. . .] The philosophers list many such things in their definitions of the goal of what is good: one suggests "happiness," and another "lack of pain." It is clear that by nature human beings care nothing for the divine. They are neither terrified by the word of God, nor brought to life in faith. And what are the fruits of such a tree but sin?

But although the works that follow justification have their source in the Spirit of God who has taken hold of the hearts of those who are justified, because they are performed in a still impure flesh, the works themselves are also impure. Although justification has begun, it has not yet been brought to its conclusion. We have the first fruits of the Spirit, but not yet the whole harvest. We are still awaiting with groaning the redemption of our bodies, as we read in Romans 8: 23. Therefore, because there is something unclean even in these works, they do not deserve the name of righteousness, and wherever you turn, whether to the works preceding justification, or to those which follow, there is no room for our merit. Therefore, justification must be a work of the mercy of God alone. This is what Paul says in Galatians 2: 20: "And the life I now live in the flesh I live by faith in the Son of God, who loved me and gave himself for me." He does not say: "I live now in my good works," but "I live by faith in the mercy of God." Moreover, faith is the reason that those works which follow justification are not imputed as sin. This we shall discuss a little later.

Therefore, when justification is attributed to faith, it is attributed to the mercy of God; it is set apart from human efforts, works, and merits. The beginning and growth of righteousness are linked to the mercy of God so that the righteousness of the entire life is nothing else than faith. That is why the prophet Isaiah calls the Kingdom of Christ a kingdom of mercy: "And a throne will be established in steadfast love," etc. (Isaiah 16: 5). For if we were justified by our own works, the kingdom would not be that of Christ, nor of mercy, but it would be our own – a kingdom of our own works. [. . .]

You will say: "so do we then merit nothing? For what reason, then, does Scripture use the word "reward" throughout?" I answer that there is a reward, and it is not because of any merit of ours; but because the Father promised, he has now laid himself under obligation to us and made himself a debtor to those who had deserved nothing at all. [. . .] Paul says in Romans 6: 23: "For the wages of sin is death, but the free gift of God is eternal life." He calls eternal life a "gift," not a "debt" – although as a matter of fact it is a debt because the Father has promised it and he has pledged it in faith.

Comment

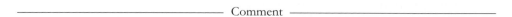

One of the issues arising from Martin Luther's insistence that justification is by faith, not works, is the role of good works in the Christian life. Luther's desire to avoid any suggestion that works contribute to justification occasionally led him to suggest or imply that good works were of no value. In this careful discussion, Melanchthon aims to set out the place of good works in the Christian life, avoiding any suggestion that justification takes place on their account – while at the same time stressing that they have a real and significant role within the context of Christian living.

Questions for Study

1 Set out, in your own words, Melanchthon's understanding of the role of human works before justification and after justification.

2 "Anyone who denies that the saints are justified by faith insults the mercy of God." Locate this statement within the passage. What does Melanchthon mean by this? How does he arrive at this conclusion?

6.36

John Calvin on Predestination

The doctrine of predestination is of major importance to John Calvin (1509–64). In this mature statement of his views, Calvin declares that some people are predestined to eternal life and others to eternal death. This doctrine, known as "double predestination," affirms that only those who are elected to salvation will, in fact, be saved. Note how Calvin draws a clear distinction between "predestination" and "foreknowledge." See also 6.12, 6.19, 6.21, 6.40, 6.43, 6.51.

The covenant of life is not preached equally to all people, and amongst those to whom it is preached, it does not meet with the same acceptance either constantly or in equal degree. In this diversity the unsearchable depths of God's judgment are made known. For there is no doubt that this variety is subordinate to the will of God's eternal election. If it is clear that salvation is freely offered to some while others are barred from access to it, on account of God's pleasure, this raises some major and difficult questions. They can be explained only when election and predestination are rightly understood. Many find this a puzzling subject, in that it seems to be nothing less than capricious, that out of the human community some should be predestined to salvation, others to destruction. But it will become clear in the following discussion that such confusion is needless. In any case, the complexity of this matter makes known both the usefulness of this doctrine and also the very sweet fruit which it brings. We shall never be clearly persuaded, as we ought to be, that our salvation flows from God's free mercy until we come to know his eternal election, which casts light on God's grace by this comparison: he does not indiscriminately adopt all to the hope of salvation but gives to some what he denies to others. [. . .]

Predestination, by which God adopts some to the hope of life, and sentences others to eternal death, is denied by no one who wishes to be thought of as pious. But there are many, especially those who make foreknowledge its cause, who surround it with all kinds of petty objections. Both doctrines are indeed to be located within God, but subjecting one to the other is absurd. In attributing foreknowledge to God, we mean that all things always have been, and always will be, under God's eyes, so that there is nothing future or past to this knowledge, but all things are present – present in such a way that God not only conceives them through ideas, as we have before us those things which our minds remember, but God truly looks upon them and discerns them as things placed before God. And this foreknowledge is extended throughout the universe to every creature. We call predestination God's eternal decree, by which God determined what God willed to become of each human being. For all are not created in equal condition [*non enim pari conditione creantur omnes*]; but eternal life is foreordained for some, and eternal damnation for others. Therefore, as any person has been directed [*conditus*] to one or the other of these ends, we speak of him or her as predestined to life or to death.

Comment

Predestination is occasionally asserted to be the center of Calvin's theological system. It is difficult to defend this, partly because Calvin's system does not seem to have a "center," and partly because other doctrines or themes appear to concern him more passionately. Calvin's special concern for predestination is partly due to a ferocious controversy with Jerome Bolsec, which led to this aspect of Calvin's thought being given a much higher profile within Geneva than he had intended. Note that Calvin explicitly defines predestination in terms of the divine decision to elect some to life, and others to death; this may be contrasted with Augustine's view, which sees predestination as relating only to the divine decision to redeem some (6.12).

Questions for Study

1 "The covenant of life is not preached equally to all people, and amongst those to whom it is preached, it does not meet with the same acceptance either constantly or in equal degree." What does Calvin mean by this opening statement? And what conclusions does he draw?
2 "All are not created in equal condition; but eternal life is foreordained for some, and eternal damnation for others." Locate this statement within the text. What does Calvin mean by this? How does he arrive at this conclusion? What are its implications? And how does this relate to Augustine's teaching on the matter?

6.37

John Calvin on Faith and the Promises of God

In this passage, taken from the 1559 *Institutes of the Christian Religion*, Calvin emphasizes the way in which faith is grounded specifically in the promises of God. Faith is not based on the word of God in general, but more specifically in the promises of God which offer salvation. Calvin also stresses that it is not faith in itself, but being united to Christ through faith, which is of decisive importance. See also 1.13, 6.33.

We make the foundation of faith the gracious promise, because faith properly consists of this. [Faith] is certain that God is true in everything, whether he commands something or forbids it, whether he promises something or threatens it. Faith also obediently receives his commandments, observes his prohibitions, and heeds his threats. Nevertheless, [faith] properly begins with the promise, consists of it, and ends in it. For in God faith seeks life; a life that is not found in commandments or edicts or penalties, but in the promise of mercy, and a promise which is nothing if it is not gracious. [. . .] When we say that faith must rest upon a gracious promise, we do not deny that believers embrace and grasp the Word of God in every respect; but we identify the promise of mercy as the proper object of faith. [. . .]

It is our intention to make only these two points. First, that faith does not stand firm unless a believer attains to the gracious promise; second, that faith does not reconcile us to God by itself, unless it joins us to Christ. Both points are worth noting. We seek a faith which distinguishes the children of God from the wicked, and believers from unbelievers. If people believe that God both justly commands all that he commands and threatens, can they be called believers for that reason? Certainly not. Therefore, there can be no firm foundation of faith unless it rests upon God's mercy.

Comment

Calvin here offers a discussion of the way in which faith relates to the promises of God. It is important to note that faith does not simply believe in the general contents of the Bible; it is grounded specifically in the promises of God which are contained within it.

Questions for Study

1 "We identify the promise of mercy as the proper object of faith." What are the implications of this assertion?
2 "Faith does not reconcile us to God by itself, unless it joins us to Christ." Locate this passage within the text. How does Calvin's statement here relate to the general position set out by Luther (6.33)?

6.38

John Calvin on the Concept of Justification

Up to about the year 1500, the term "justification" was widely understood to mean "to be made righteous." This interpretation, which had its origins in the writings of Augustine, saw justification as both an event and process. The Reformation, however, saw justification defined exclusively in forensic terms – that is, as an event, in which sinners are declared to be righteous before God. Justification is then followed by sanctification, a process in which believers are made righteous. In this passage Calvin provides a classic articulation of this forensic notion of justification. See also 6.32, 6.35, 6.39.

To be justified in God's sight is to be reckoned as righteous in God's judgment, and to be accepted on account of that righteousness. [. . .] The person who is justified by faith is someone who, apart from the righteousness of works, has taken hold of the righteousness of Christ through faith, and having been clothed with it, appears in the sight of God not as a sinner, but as a righteous person. Therefore justification is to be understood simply as the acceptance by which God receives us into his favor as righteous people. We say that it consists of the remission of sins and the imputation of the righteousness of Christ. [. . .]

There is no doubt that we obtain justification in the sight of God only by the intercession of the righteousness of Christ. This is equivalent to saying that believers are not righteous in themselves, but on account of the communication of the righteousness of Christ through imputation, something to be noted carefully. [. . .] Our righteousness is not in us, but in Christ. We possess it only because we participate in Christ; in fact, with him, we possess all his riches.

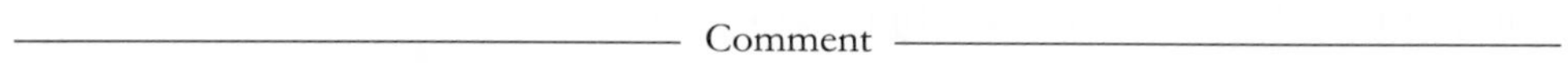

Comment

Calvin here sets out what would be understood to be a "forensic" understanding of justification. Justification is defined in terms of the beginning of the Christian life, in which the believer enters into a right relation with God. The Christian life is then about sanctification, which concerns growth in holiness. For Augustine, in contrast, "justification" means *both* the beginnings of the Christian life *and* the ongoing process of "being made righteous" – an understanding which is developed by the Council of Trent (6.39).

Questions for Study

1 "To be justified in God's sight is to be reckoned as righteous in God's judgment." What does Calvin understand by this opening statement? Notice how there is no reference here to being made righteous.

2 "Believers are not righteous in themselves, but on account of the communication of the righteousness of Christ through imputation." Locate this statement within the text. What does Calvin mean by this? And how does this compare with the Council of Trent's teaching on this matter (6.39)?

6.39

The Council of Trent on Justification

During its sixth session, which ended on January 13, 1547, the Council of Trent set out a definitive statement on the Roman Catholic Church's teaching on justification. Of particular interest is its definition of justification in terms of both an event and process, embracing both the act of God by which the Christian life is begun and the process by which God renews the believer. See also 6.32, 6.35, 6.38.

The justification of the sinner may be briefly defined as a translation from that state in which a human being is born a child of the first Adam [*translatio ab eo statu in quo homo nascitur filius primi Adae*], to the state of grace and of the adoption of the sons of God through the second Adam, Jesus Christ our Savior [*in statum gratiae et adoptionis filiorum Dei per secundum Adam Iesum Christum Salvatore, nostrum*]. According to the gospel, this translation cannot come about except through the cleansing of regeneration, or a desire for this, as it is written, "No one can enter the kingdom of God without being born again of water and the Holy Spirit" (John 3: 5).

Comment

Trent strongly opposes the view of Calvin on the nature of justification (6.38), and vigorously defends the idea, originally associated with Augustine of Hippo, that justification is the process of regeneration and renewal within human nature, which brings about a change in both the outer status and inner nature of the sinner. For Trent, justification thus includes the idea of regeneration. This brief statement is amplified in the seventh chapter of the Decree on Justification, which stresses that justification "is not only a remission of sins but also the sanctification and renewal of the inner person through the voluntary reception of the grace and gifts by which an unrighteous person becomes a righteous person."

Questions for Study

1 "This translation cannot come about except through the cleansing of regeneration." What does Trent mean by this? And how does this statement confirm the divergence of Trent from the teachings of reformers such as Calvin on this matter (6.38)?
2 What confusions might result in debates on justification when Trent means by "justification" what Melanchthon or Calvin mean by "justification" *and* "sanctification"?

6.40

Theodore Beza on the Causes of Predestination

Theodore Beza (1519–1605), one of Calvin's followers in Geneva, achieved considerable fame as a leading exponent of Calvinist ideas. In this letter to Calvin, written at a time at which the issue of predestination was fiercely debated within Geneva, Beza locates the ultimate ground of predestination as lying totally within the sovereign will of God. See also 6.12, 6.21, 6.29, 6.36, 6.43, 6.51.

So if someone asks concerning the cause by which God should have decided from all eternity to elect some and to condemn others, I think that we must reply by saying that this is in order that God's immense power may be made known better. But if they then ask about the "material cause" (as they call it) of this eternal decree, then I have nothing to point to other than the will of God, who has just as much freedom [over the creation] as the potter, by which he can produce one vessel for honor, and the other for disgrace. If someone should ask why God should have predestined some people instead of others to salvation or destruction, I again point to the will of God, in whose power it lies not merely to produce some vessels for honor and others to disgrace from the same mass of clay, but also to express his own unique judgment in that distinction. So, in responding to these questions, I would not appeal to "secondary causes," among which number are included Christ and Adam, but rather to what follows on from this. The question does not concern the degree of election or reprobation, but their *execution*. There are ordained secondary causes for the execution of the divine counsel. A reason can be brought forward as to why and how we are elect – namely, that God, on account of his enormous love and as he sees us in Christ (to whom he determined to give us before all ages), was not able not to love us [*non potuit nos non amare*], so that we might be righteous and holy in him. But if it is asked what caused God to condemn some, I shall reply that the cause is to be located in the people themselves, in that they persist in corruption and sin, which merit the righteous hatred of God. Such people are thus rightly rejected and renounced by God. [. . .] So when we are said to be "elect in Christ before the creation of the world" (Ephesians 1: 4), I understand this [. . .] to mean: God, when predestining us to election from all eternity, at the same time subordinated Christ to this decree [*simul huic decreto substravisse Christum*], in whom God might elect us, and call, justify and glorify the elect. On the other hand, when God predestined some to destruction, God at the same time appointed Adam, in whom those who had been corrupted might be hardened, so that God might declare his supreme power in them.

Comment

Beza here follows the general lines of Calvin's statements on this matter (6.36), stressing that God must be free to deal with creatures. Predestination is seen as the ultimate expression of the divine sovereignty, and is an assertion of the rights and power of the creator over the creation. Predestination does not lie in God's foreknowledge of the use to which his creatures would put grace, but is totally and completely an unconditional divine decision.

Questions for Study

1 What motives, according to Beza, lie behind God's decision to redeem some and condemn others?
2 What "causes" of predestination does Beza identify? And how do these influence his discussion of the grounds of predestination?

6.41

John Donne on the Bondage of the Human Will

John Donne (1571–1631) is widely regarded as one of the most important English poets and preachers of the early seventeenth century, and as the leading "metaphysical" poet. This poem, first published in 1633, deals with a central issue concerning the human free will. Western Christianity, following Augustine, argued that the human free will had been "taken captive" by sin – a notion expressed in the Latin slogan *liberum arbitrium captivatum*, "the captive free will." As a result, the human free will cannot freely respond to God, in that it is entrapped by sin. It is therefore necessary for God to break down a false human freedom – in that the free will is biased towards sin and a turning away from God – if true freedom is to be restored. In this meditation, Donne wrestles with this apparent paradox, using the image of a "usurped town" to make his point. See also 6.13, 6.14, 6.21, 6.34, 6.44.

Batter my heart, three-person'd God; for you
As yet but knock; breathe, shine, and seek to mend;
That I may rise, and stand, o'erthrow me, and bend
Your force, to break, blow, burn, and make me new.
I, like an usurp'd town, to another due,
Labour to admit you, but O, to no end.

Reason, your viceroy in me, me should defend,
But is captived, and proves weak or untrue.
Yet dearly I love you, and would be loved fain,
But am betroth'd unto your enemy;
Divorce me, untie, or break that knot again,
Take me to you, imprison me, for I,
Except you enthrall me, never shall be free,
Nor ever chaste, except you ravish me.

Comment

In this poem, Donne sets out the paradox of the Augustinian concept of the *liberum arbitrium captivatum* – the "enslaved free will." The human free will, which was meant to keep humanity firmly anchored to God, has been seduced or traduced by sin. As a result, it is in revolt against God, despite its own best interests. As a result, it is necessary for God to "batter" the poet's heart, rather than just politely request admission. We see here Donne's poetic reworking and reimagining of Augustine's more medical approach to salvation, which treats fallen human nature as infected with an illness, of which one symptom is the lack of any desire to be cured.

Questions for Study

1 Human reason is described as God's "viceroy" in humanity. A "viceroy" (literally, "in place of a king") refers to an individual to whom authority is entrusted by a monarch. So what point is Donne making here about the role of reason within the purposes of God?
2 In line 11, Donne uses three related images to refer to the breaking of the power of sin over fallen humanity. What are they? And who is doing the breaking? And what does Donne mean by his final assertion that he shall never be chaste, unless God shall ravish him?

6.42

James Ussher on the Grounds of Assurance

In this important analysis of the grounds of assurance, the seventeenth-century Archbishop of Armagh James Ussher (1581–1656) argues that assurance is the result, not the precondition, of justification. He sets out with particular clarity what has come to be known as the *syllogismus practicus* ("practical syllogism"), which argues that anyone who shows the results of justification may be regarded as being justified. See also 6.12, 6.20, 6.29, 6.36, 6.40, 6.43, 6.45.

But is it not necessary to justification, to be assured that my sins are pardoned, and that I am justified? No: that is no act of faith as it justifyeth, but an effect and fruit that followeth after justification. For no man is justified by believing that he is justified; for he must be justified before he can believe it. [. . .] But faith as it justifyeth, is a resting upon Christ to obtain pardon by the acknowledging him to be the onely Saviour, and the hanging upon him for salvation. [. . .] It is the direct act of faith that justifyeth; that whereby I do believe; it is the reflect act of faith that assures; that whereby I do believe, and it comes by way of argumentation thus.

Major: Whosoever relyeth upon Christ the Saviour of the world for justification and pardon [. . .] is actually justified and pardoned.

Minor: But I do truly rely upon Christ for justification and pardon.

Conclusion: Therefore I undoubtedly believe that I am justified and pardoned. But many times both the former propositions may be granted to be true, and yet a weak Christian want strength to draw the conclusion.

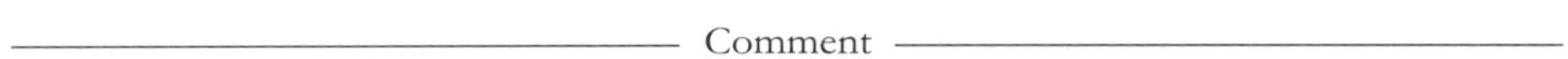

Comment

In this passage Ussher sets out some considerations which were important within English Puritan circles in relation to the question of assurance: "How can I know that I am among the elect?" "How can I know that I am saved?" These questions were raised by the teaching of both Calvin (6.36) and Beza (6.40) on predestination. Ussher offered an answer to these concerns, which he set out in the "practical syllogism" embedded in this passage. The older English prose style has been retained in this passage; readers might find it helpful to know that the phrase to "hang upon" would be rendered as to "depend upon" in modern English.

Questions for Study

1 "No man is justified by believing that he is justified." Locate this statement within the text. What does Ussher mean by this?

2 Set out, in your own words, the syllogism which Ussher believes will lead to assurance of salvation for his readers. Can you discern any problems with the logic of the argument or its theology?

6.43

The Westminster Confession of Faith on Predestination

This leading Reformed confession of faith, formulated in London in 1643 during the period of the Puritan Commonwealth, reaffirms the strongly predestinarian teaching of Calvin and Beza. Predestination is totally grounded in the will of God, and owes nothing to anything in human nature. See also 6.12, 6.20, 6.29, 6.36, 6.40, 6.52.

All those whom God had predestinated unto life, and those only, he is pleased, in his appointed and accepted time, effectually to call, by his word and Spirit, out of that state of sin and death in which they are by nature, to grace and salvation by Jesus Christ: enlightening their minds, spiritually and savingly, to understand the things of God, taking away their heart of stone and giving unto them a heart of flesh; renewing their wills, and by his almighty power determining them to that which is good; and effectually drawing them to Jesus Christ; yet so as they come most freely, being made willing by his grace.

This effectual call is of God's free and special grace alone, not from anything at all foreseen in man, who is altogether passive therein until, being quickened and renewed by the Holy Spirit, he is thereby enabled to answer this call, and to embrace the grace offered and conveyed in it.

Comment

This classic statement of the Reformed doctrine of predestination builds upon the positions of both Calvin (6.36) and Beza (6.40). The text is very clearly written, and requires little, if anything, by way of comment. Note especially how "predestination" is rigorously distinguished from "foreknowledge."

Questions for Study

1 Set out the roles of Jesus Christ and the Holy Spirit in the doctrine of "calling" laid down in this text.

2 "This effectual call is of God's free and special grace alone, not from anything at all foreseen in man, who is altogether passive therein." What does the Confession mean by this? And at what point, and for what reason, is this passive replaced by a more active role?

6.44

Anne Bradstreet on Flesh and Spirit

Anne Bradstreet (1612–72) is one of the most important figures in the history of American literature, and is considered by many to be the first American poet. Her poems, written in a deceptively simple style, are inspired by a Puritan theological foundation, firmly anchored in the realities of American colonial life of that age. Her poem "The Flesh and the Spirit," part of which is reprinted here, deals with the impact of sin on human thought and action. The idea of a dialogue between flesh and spirit was especially popular in medieval literature, and was a common theme in the poetry of the Elizabethan and Jacobean periods. The noted Puritan poet Andrew Marvell, for example, wrote "A Dialogue Between the Soul and Body," which depicts the spirit as being imprisoned in the flesh. Similar themes, along with reflections on how the situation may be transformed, abound in Bradstreet's poem. See also 6.13, 6.14, 6.21, 6.34, 6.41.

Be still, thou unregenerate part,
Disturb no more my settled heart,
For I have vow'd (and so will do)
Thee as a foe still to pursue,
And combat with thee will and must
Until I see thee laid in th' dust.
Sister we are, yea twins we be,
Yet deadly feud 'twixt thee and me,
For from one father are we not.
Thou by old Adam wast begot,
But my arise is from above,
Whence my dear father I do love.
Thou speak'st me fair but hat'st me sore.
Thy flatt'ring shews I'll trust no more.
How oft thy slave hast thou me made
When I believ'd what thou hast said
And never had more cause of woe
Than when I did what thou bad'st do.
I'll stop mine ears at these thy charms
And count them for my deadly harms.
Thy sinful pleasures I do hate,
Thy riches are to me no bait.
Thine honours do, nor will I love,
For my ambition lies above.
My greatest honour it shall be
When I am victor over thee,

And Triumph shall, with laurel head,
When thou my Captive shalt be led.

Comment

The central theme of this section of the poem deals with the impact of the flesh on the spirit. Given that human nature is ensnared, weakened, and misled by sin, what can be done about it? Is there any way in which the situation may be transformed? Bradstreet answers these questions by focusing on the way in which the Christian vision of reality allows the human situation to be seen in a fresh way, pointing to resources that lie outside human powers.

Questions for Study

1 How would you characterize Bradstreet's depiction of the human situation? And what resources does she identify as potential cures?
2 Read the following verses from Ephesians 4: 7–8 in the King James Version of the Bible, which Bradstreet knew well. What use does she make of them? "But unto every one of us is given grace according to the measure of the gift of Christ. Wherefore he saith, When he ascended up on high, he led captivity captive, and gave gifts unto men."

6.45

Nikolaus Ludwig von Zinzendorf on Saving Faith

In September 1746 the leading German Pietist Nikolaus Ludwig von Zinzendorf (1700–60) delivered nine lectures on various aspects of the Christian faith at the Brethren Chapel, London. The first of these, entitled "Concerning Saving Faith," develops the characteristic Pietist notion of a personally assimilated faith, leading to personal conversion. See also 1.13, 5.23, 6.33, 6.37.

No man can create faith in himself. Something must happen to him which Luther calls "the divine work in us," which changes us, gives us new birth, and makes us completely different people in heart, spirit, mind, and all our powers. This is *fides*, faith properly speaking. If this is to begin in us, then it must be preceded by distress, without which men have no ears for faith and trust.

The distress which we feel is the distress of our soul when we become poor, when we see we have no Savior, when we become palpably aware of our misery. We see our corruption on all sides and are really anxious because of it. Then afterward it happens as with patients who have reached the point of crisis; they watch for help, for someone who can help them out of their distress, and accept the first offer of aid without making an exact examination or investigation of the person who helps them. That is the way it went once with the woman whom the Savior healed. For twelve years she had gone to see all kinds of physicians and had endured much from them. And finally she came upon him too and said, "If only I would touch that man's clothes, it would help me; even if I could not get to the man himself, if I could only get hold of a bit of his garment, then I would be helped" (Matthew 9: 21).

This is faith-in-distress. And here I can never wonder enough at the blindness and ignorance of those people who are supposed to handle the divine Word and convert men, for example the Jews and heathen, those abortive so-called Christians (who are indeed as blind as Jews and heathen) who think that if they have them memorize the catechism or get a book of sermons into their heads or, at the most, present all sorts of well-reasoned demonstrations concerning the divine being and attributes, thus funneling the truths and knowledge into their heads, that this is the sovereign means to their conversion. But this is such a preposterous method that if one wanted to convert people that way, reciting demonstrations to them, then it is just as if one wanted to go against wind and current with full sails, or as if one, on the contrary, would run one's boat into an inlet so that one could not find one's way out again.

For that same knowledge of divine things which is taken to be faith, although it appears only, other things being equal, as an adjunct of faith, puffs up and nothing comes of it. And if one has all of that together, says Paul, and does not also have love, and even if one can preach about it to others, still it is nothing more than if a bell in the church rings. As little as the bell gets out of it, as little as it is benefited by the fact that it hangs there and rings, just so little does the fact that a teacher makes the most cogent demonstrations benefit him as far as his own salvation is concerned.

But what results from this faith-in-distress, from this blind faith which one has out of love for one's own salvation? What comes of a bold trust in the physician that he can and shall help, without knowing what his name is and who he is, without having known and seen him before, without having clearly sensed what sort and nature of man he is? Thankful love results from it, as long ago with Manoah and his wife, who so loved the man who came to them; they did not know him, though, for they said, "What is your name? We do not know you, but we love you. We should like to know who you are, that we may praise you when what you have said to us comes true" (Judges 13: 17). So it is exactly with the faith-in-distress: It has to do completely with an unknown man, yet with a man of whom one's heart says, "He likes to help, he likes to comfort, and he can and will help." My heart tells me that it is he of whom I have heard in my youth, of whom I have heard on this or that occasion. They called him the Savior, the Son of God, the Lord Jesus, or however else one has heard him named and however anyone in anxiety and distress thinks of him. In short: "He must help me; oh, if he would only come to my aid! If he would only take my soul into his care, so that it would not perish! *Kyrie Eleison*! Lord have mercy!"

Comment

This is a classic Pietist text, which stresses the importance of the religious feelings of the heart. Many Pietists distrusted academic theology, believing that it allowed "theological correctness" to come in the way of a "living faith" or "personal holiness." Some such concern can be detected in this passage, especially when Zinzendorf turns to deal with those who think that they can convert people by getting them to memorize catechisms. Faith is about a "new birth," a living and trusting relationship with God, not assent to theological propositions. Zinzendorf's primary target here is probably the theology of Lutheran orthodoxy, which he regarded as having lost sight of the experiential aspects of faith, which Luther knew and celebrated. Note especially his allusion to Luther, which was probably intended to annoy orthodox theologians by implying that they had lost sight of part of their heritage.

Questions for Study

1 Faith "changes us, gives us new birth, and makes us completely different people in heart, spirit, mind, and all our powers." Locate this passage in the text. What does Zinzendorf mean by this?
2 Summarize, in your own words, Zinzendorf's criticism of those who think people can be converted through books or sermons or catechisms. What is the fundamental concern that Zinzendorf expresses through this criticism?

6.46

Friedrich Christoph Oetinger on Conversion

In this extract from a dictionary of central biblical terms, as understood within Pietism, originally published in 1776, Friedrich Christoph Oetinger (1702–82) deals with the idea of "conversion." Pietist writers placed considerable stress on the importance of a "living faith" and "new birth," and saw conversion as a hallmark of authentic Christian faith – anticipating the "born-again" Christian phenomenon of recent decades, which has important historical connections with the Pietist tradition. See also 6.45.

What is conversion? Answer: If you turn away from false intentions and customs, and if you turn to the Word and law of God, you will learn as its chief purpose the directions of Psalm 1. If you see how you have been blinded to the way in which you were in darkness and under the power of Satan even though you were learned, then you are on the path of blessedness. All preaching has the intention of showing that people who from their youth upwards have clung to many false intentions and cover up their hearts, so that they might look to Jesus as the highest law to love above all and that in this way they might be free of the hardness of their understanding and the whole web of sinfulness [*Sündengewebe*] with its hundred excuses, and turn about completely toward the righteousness to which they have been called internally and externally. They are to do so, indeed, in such a way that they remain directed with all which they have, with all the powers and impulses of God, toward that which is preserved as beautiful and divine in righteousness. They are to do so until the Word comes fully into them from the kingdom and is a judge of hidden inclinations and revealed thoughts. For this reason, the Proverbs of Solomon and Psalm 119 note that you are not only to be converted generally to the Lord, but also through your whole heart, soul, mind, and powers toward everything which the law testifies of Christ in particular.

Comment

In this passage, Oetinger stresses the importance of the notion of conversion (which had been marginalized within German Lutheranism), and draws out its significance for the renewal of the believer. Note the strong defense of the role of the law, both in convicting people of their sin and also in indicating the extent of internal and external renewal required of them. The element of legalism which often crept into Pietism was regarded with some horror by its Lutheran critics, who accused them of distorting Luther's doctrine of justification by faith.

Questions for Study

1 What exactly does Oetinger understand by "conversion"? What are people converted from?
2 The text makes frequent and approving reference to the Law of God. Locate some of these. (Note that Psalms 1 and 119 are both celebrations of the Law.) Do you think Oetinger is a legalist, teaching that the primary purpose of conversion is to become obedient to the Law of God?

6.47

Jonathan Edwards on Original Sin

The eighteenth-century American writer Jonathan Edwards (1703–58) was a leading exponent of Puritan ideas in North America. One of the themes to which he paid particular attention was the doctrine of original sin, which he regarded as being under threat, due to the pressure of Enlightenment rationalism. The treatise from which this extract is taken was published in 1758, shortly after Edwards' death. See also 6.3, 6.6, 6.9, 6.13, 6.20, 6.21, 6.34, 6.53, 6.55.

By *Original Sin* as the phrase has been most commonly used by divines, is meant the innate sinful depravity of the heart. But yet when the doctrine of original sin is spoken of, it is vulgarly understood in that latitude, which includes not only the depravity of nature, but the imputation of Adam's first sin; or, in other words, the liableness or exposedness of Adam's posterity, in the divine judgment, to partake of the punishment of that sin. So far as I know, most of those who have held one of these, have maintained the other; and most of those who have opposed one, have opposed the other: both are opposed by the Author chiefly attended to in the following discourse, in his book against original sin: And it may perhaps appear in our future consideration of the subject, that they are closely connected; that the arguments which prove the one establish the other, and that there are no more difficulties attending the allowing of one, than the other.

I shall in the first place, consider this doctrine more especially with regard to the corruption of nature; and as we treat of this the other will naturally come into consideration, in the prosecution of the discourse, as connected with it. As all moral qualities, all principles either of virtue or vice, lie in the disposition of the heart, I shall consider whether we have any evidence that the heart of man is naturally of a corrupt and evil disposition. This is strenuously denied by many late writers who are enemies to the doctrine of original sin; and particularly by Dr. TAYLOR. [. . .]

Here I would first consider the *truth* of the proposition; and then would shew the certainty of the *consequences* which I infer from it. If both can be clearly and certainly proved, then I trust none will deny but that the doctrine of original depravity is evident, and so the falseness of Dr. TAYLOR's scheme demonstrated; the greatest part of whose book called *The Scripture Doctrine of Original Sin, &c.* is against the doctrine of *innate depravity*. In p. 107, he speaks of the conveyance of a corrupt and sinful nature to *Adam's* posterity as the *grand point* to be proved by the maintainers of the doctrine of original sin.

In order to demonstrate what is asserted in the proposition laid down, there is need only that these two things should be made manifest: *one* is this fact, that all mankind come into the world in such a state as without fail comes to this issue, namely, the universal commission of sin; or that every one who comes to act in the world as a moral agent, is, in a greater or less degree, guilty of sin. The *other* is, that all sin deserves and exposes to utter and eternal destruction under God's wrath and curse; and would end in it, were it not for the interposition of divine grace to prevent the effect. Both which can be abundantly demonstrated to be agreeable to the word of God, and to Dr. TAYLOR's own doctrine.

That every one of mankind, at least such as are capable of acting as moral agents, are guilty of sin (not now taking it for granted that they come guilty into the world) is most clearly and abundantly evident from the holy scriptures: 1 Kings 8: 46. If any man sin against thee: for there is no man that sinneth not; Ecclesiastes 7: 20. There is not a just man upon earth that doeth good and sinneth not. Job 9: 2–3. I know it is so of a truth, (i.e. as Bildad had just before said, that God would not cast away a perfect man, &c.) but how should man be just with God? If he will contend with him, he cannot answer him one of a thousand. To the like purpose, Psalm 143: 2. Enter not into judgment with thy servant; for in thy sight shall no man living be justified. So the words of the apostle (in which he has apparent reference to those of the Psalmist) Romans 3: 19, 20. "That every mouth may be stopped, and all the world become guilty before God. Therefore by the deeds of the law there shall no flesh be justified in his sight: for by the law is the knowledge of SIN." [...] In this, and innumerable other places, confession and repentance of sin are spoken of as duties proper for ALL; as also prayer to God for pardon of sin: also forgiveness of those that injure us, from that motive, that we hope to be forgiven of God. Universal guilt of sin might also be demonstrated from the appointment, and the declared use and end of the ancient sacrifices; and also from the ransom which every one that was numbered in Israel was directed to pay, to make atonement for his soul. [...] All are represented, not only as being sinful, but as having great and manifold iniquity. [...]

There are many Scriptures which both declare the universal sinfulness of mankind, and also that all sin deserves and justly exposes to everlasting destruction, under the wrath and curse of God; and so demonstrate both parts of the proposition I have laid down. To which purpose that passage in Galatians 3: 10 is exceeding full: For as many as are of the works of the law are under the curse; for it *is* written, cursed is every one that continueth not in all things which are written in the book of the law, to do them. How manifestly is it implied in the apostle's meaning here, that there is no man but what fails in some instances of doing all things that are written in the book of the law, and therefore as many as have their dependence on their fulfilling the law, are under that curse which is pronounced on them that fail of it? And hence the apostle infers in the next verse, that NO MAN is justified by the law in the sight of *God*.

Comment

It is clear from this passage that Edwards dislikes "Dr Taylor" – namely, Jeremy Taylor (1613–97), a noted High Churchman who became Bishop of Down and Dromore in the north of Ireland (see 10.16). Edwards believes that Taylor is a moralist, and that his moralism is based upon either an outright denial of original sin, or a serious weakening of this idea. Both Taylor and the writers of the Enlightenment denied the notion of original sin, but for different reasons. For Taylor, the idea discouraged moral living; for the writers of the Enlightenment – such as Voltaire – it encouraged human subservience to tradition, and discouraged original and critical thought. Edwards' concern is to affirm the doctrine at a time when he believes it is being challenged and abandoned.

Questions for Study

1 What reasons does Edwards offer for affirming the doctrine of original sin?
2 Edwards' defense of the doctrine of original sin is thoroughly biblical. What does this suggest about the intended readership of this work?

6.48

John Wesley on Justification

John Wesley (1703–91) founded the Methodist movement within the Church of England, which subsequently gave birth to Methodism as a denomination in its own right. Convinced that he "lacked the faith whereby alone we are saved," Wesley discovered the need for a "living faith" and the role of experience in the Christian life through his conversion experience at a meeting in Aldersgate Street, London, in May 1738, in which he felt his heart to be "strangely warmed." Wesley's emphasis upon the experiential side of Christian faith, which contrasted sharply with the dullness of contemporary English Deism, led to a major religious revival in England. John Wesley's sermon on justification was first published in 1746. It is an important witness to a Pietist understanding of the nature of the Christian life, which placed considerable emphasis on the ideas of "conversion" and "new birth." See also 6.35, 6.38, 6.39, 6.45, 6.46.

4. Least of all does justification imply that God is deceived in those whom he justifies; that he thinks them to be what, in fact, they are not; that he accounts them to be otherwise than they are. It does by no means imply that God judges concerning us contrary to the real nature of things, that he esteems us better than we really are, or believes us righteous when we are unrighteous. Surely no. The judgement of the all-wise God is always according to truth. Neither can it ever consist with his unerring wisdom to think that I am innocent, to judge that I am righteous or holy, because another is so. He can no more, in this manner, confound me with Christ than with David or Abraham. Let any man to whom God hath given understanding weigh this without prejudice and he cannot but perceive that such a notion of justification is neither reconcilable to Reason or Scripture.

5. The plain scriptural notion of justification is pardon – the forgiveness of sins. It is that act of God the Father whereby, for the sake of the propitiation made by the blood of his Son, he "showeth forth his righteousness (or mercy) by the remission of sins that are past" (Romans 3: 25). This is the easy natural account of it given by St Paul throughout this whole Epistle.

Comment

John Wesley's sermon is notable for its vigorous attack on the idea of "forensic justification," associated with Melanchthon and Calvin. Wesley regards the idea of the "imputed righteousness of Christ" as morally and theologically untenable. It suggests that God is deceived when he justifies individuals, or pretends that we are in reality someone else (in this case, Christ). Wesley argues for a move away from forensic ideas of justification to a more biblical understanding of justification simply as "pardon and forgiveness."

Questions for Study

1 How does Wesley respond to the suggestion that justification involves a "legal fiction"? How does this compare with the approach adopted by Luther (6.33)?
2 "The plain scriptural notion of justification is pardon – the forgiveness of sins." Locate this passage within the text. How does this definition compare with that offered by Calvin (6.38)? Why is there no reference to "imputed righteousness"? What objections might a Pietist have to such an idea?

6.49

Richard Watson on Regeneration and Sanctification

Richard Watson (1781–1833) is one of Methodism's greatest theologians. His *Theological Institutes* (1823) can be seen as an attempt to give a systematic presentation of the ideas of John Wesley, the founder of Methodism, including his distinctive emphasis upon the importance of personal holiness and sanctification. It was the standard textbook in Methodist theological seminaries for many decades, and did much to shape the theological distinctiveness of the movement, especially in the United States. The extract from the *Theological Institutes* deals with regeneration as an integral element of salvation. See also 6.35, 6.45, 6.46, 6.48.

[Regeneration] is that mighty change in man, wrought by the Holy Spirit, by which the dominion which sin has over him in his natural state, amid which he deplores and struggles against in his penitent state, is broken and abolished, so that, with full choice of will and the energy of right affections, he serves God freely, and "runs in the way of his commandments." "Whosoever is born of God doth not commit sin, for his seed remaineth in him, and he cannot sin, because he is born of God." "For sin shall not have dominion over you; for ye are not under the law, but under grace." "But now being made free from sin, and become servants to God, ye have your fruit unto holiness, and the end everlasting life." Deliverance from the bondage of sin, and the power and the will to do all things which are pleasing to God, both as to inward habits and outward acts, are, therefore, the distinctive characters of this state.

That repentance is not regeneration, we have before observed. It will not bear disputing whether regeneration begins with repentance; for if the regenerate state is only entered upon at our justification, then all that can be meant by this, to be consistent with the Scriptures, is, that the preparatory process, which leads to regeneration, as it leads to pardon, commences with conviction and contrition, and goes on to a repentant turning to the Lord. In the order which God has established, regeneration does not take place without this process. Conviction of the evil and danger of an unregenerate state must first be felt. God hath appointed this change to be effected in answer to our prayers; and acceptable prayer supposes that we desire the blessing we ask; that we accept of Christ as the appointed medium of access to God; that we feel and confess our own inability to attain what we ask from another; and that we exercise faith in the promises of God which convey the good we seek. It is clear that none of these is regeneration, for they all suppose it to be a good in prospect, the object of prayer and eager desire. True it is, that deep and serious conviction for sin, the power to desire deliverance from it, the power to pray, the struggle against the corruptions of an unregenerate heart, are all proofs of a work of God in the heart, and of an important moral change; but it is not *this* change, because regeneration is that renewal of our nature which gives us dominion over sin, and enables us to serve God, from love, and not merely from fear, and it is yet confessedly unattained, being still the object of search and eager desire. We are not yet "created anew unto good works," which is as special and instant a work of God as justification, and for this reason, that it is not attained before the pardon of our sins, and always accompanies it.

This last point may be proved, 1. From the nature of justification itself, which takes away the penalty of sin; but that penalty is not only obligation to punishment, but the loss of the sanctifying Spirit, and the curse of being left under the slavery of sin, and under the dominion of Satan. Regeneration is effected by this Spirit restored to us, and is a consequence of our pardon; for though justification in itself is the remission of sin, yet a justified *state* implies a change, both in our condition and in our disposition: in our *condition,* as we are in a state of life, not of death, of safety, not of condemnation; in our *disposition,* as regenerate and new creatures.

2. From Scripture, which affords us direct proof that regeneration is a concomitant of justification, "If any man be in Christ, he is a new creature." It is then the result of our entrance into that state in which we are said to be in Christ; and the meaning of this phrase is most satisfactorily explained by Rom. viii, 1, considered in connection with the preceding chapter, from which, in the division of the chapters, it ought not to have been separated. That chapter clearly describes the state of a person convinced and slain by the law applied by the Spirit. We may discover indeed, in this description, certain moral changes, as consenting to the law that it is good; delighting in it after the inward man; powerful desires; humble confession, &c. The state represented is, however, in fact, one of guilt, spiritual captivity, helplessness, and misery; a state of condemnation; and a state of bondage to sin. The opposite condition is that of a man "in Christ Jesus:" to him "there is no condemnation"; he is forgiven; the bondage to sin is broken; he "walks not after the flesh, but after the Spirit." To be in Christ, is, therefore, to be justified, and regeneration instantly follows. We see then the order of the Divine operation in individual experience: conviction of sin, helplessness and danger; faith; justification; and regeneration. The regenerate state is, also, called in Scripture sanctification; though a distinction is made by the Apostle Paul between that and being "sanctified *wholly,*" a doctrine to be afterward considered. In this regenerate,

or sanctified state, the former corruptions of the heart may remain, and strive for the mastery; but that which characterizes and distinguishes it from the state of a penitent before justification, before he is "in Christ," is, that they are not even his inward *habit;* and that they have no *dominion*. Faith unites to Christ; by it we derive "grace and peace from God the Father, and his Son Jesus Christ," and enjoy "the communion of the Holy Ghost"; and this Spirit, as the sanctifying Spirit, is given to us to "abide with us, and to be in us," and then we walk not after the flesh but after the Spirit.

Comment

Methodism placed an emphasis upon regeneration or sanctification, which became characteristic of the many "holiness" movements to originate in the United States, particularly in the late nineteenth and early twentieth century. Watson stresses that regeneration may be distinguished, but not separated, from justification. The passage establishes a sequential ordering of the components of salvation, namely, "conviction of sin, helplessness and danger; faith; justification; and regeneration." Notice how Watson introduces, but does not develop, the notion of being "sanctified wholly" (sometimes known as "entire sanctification"). This doctrine had been characteristic of early Methodism, being set out in John Wesley's *A Plain Account of Christian Perfection* and his sermon "Of Christian Perfection." It is thought that this notion was not regarded as central by nineteenth-century Methodists, although neither the historical evidence nor the theological and cultural reasons for this are totally clear.

Questions for Study

1. Why do you think Watson places so much emphasis on the connection between justification and regeneration?
2. How does Watson understand the Holy Spirit to be involved in the process of regeneration?

6.50

Emil Brunner on the Image of God

In his later period, the Swiss Reformed theologian Emil Brunner (1889–1966) developed a theology which focused on a dialogue or partnership between God and humanity. Thus Brunner understood revelation to involve a "dialogue" between God and his people. In the passage reprinted here, Brunner develops the idea of an "I–Thou" relationship, grounded in the fact that humanity is created in the image of God (*imago Dei*). See also 6.4, 6.5, 6.23.

God is the One who wills to have from me a free response to His love, a response which gives back love for love, a loving echo, a loving reflection of His glory. I cannot meet the holy loving God in Christ without knowing this about myself. Once more, both are correlated and connected; to be aware of the holy loving God, and to be aware of the fact that my nature is created by God, comes to the same thing. It is thus, and not otherwise, that I am intended to be by the Creator. This generous will which claims me, of the God who wills to glorify Himself, and to impart Himself, is the cause of my being, and the fundamental reason for my being what I am, and as I am. Now we must go into some particular points in greater detail.

(a) God, who wills to glorify Himself and to impart Himself, wills humanity to be a creature who responds to His call of love with a grateful, responsive love. God wills to possess humanity as a free being. God wills a creature which is not only, like other creatures, a mere object of His will, as if it were a reflector of His glory as Creator. He desires from us an active and spontaneous response in our "reflecting"; He who creates through the Word, who as Spirit creates in freedom, wills to have a "reflex" which is more than a "reflex", which is an answer to His Word, a free spiritual act, a correspondence to His speaking. Only thus can His love really impart itself as love. For love can only impart itself where it is received in love. Hence the heart of the creaturely existence of humanity is freedom, selfhood, to be an "I", a person. Only an "I" can answer a "Thou", only a Self which is self-determining can freely answer God. An automaton does not respond; an animal, in contradistinction from an automaton, may indeed react, but it cannot respond. It is not capable of speech, of free self-determination, it cannot stand at a distance from itself, and is therefore not responsible.

The free Self, capable of self-determination, belongs to the original constitution of humanity as created by God. But from the very outset this freedom is limited. It is not primary but secondary. Indeed, it does not posit itself – like the Self of Idealism – but it is posited; it is not *a se* but *a Deo*. Hence although humanity's answer is free, it is also limited. God wills my freedom, it is true, because He wills to glorify Himself, and to give Himself. He wills my freedom in order to make this answer possible; my freedom is therefore, from the outset, a responsible one. Responsibility is restricted freedom, which distinguishes human from divine freedom; and it is a restriction which is also *free* and this distinguishes our human limited freedom from that of the rest of creation. The animals, and God, have no responsibility – the animals because they are below the level of responsibility, and God, because He is above it; the animals because they have no freedom, and God because He has absolute freedom. Humanity, however, has a limited freedom. This is the heart of his being as humanity, and it is the condition on which humanity possesses freedom. In other words, this limited human freedom is the very purpose for which humanity has been created: humanity possesses this "freedom" in order that it may respond to God, in such a way that through this response God may glorify Himself, and give Himself to His creature.

(b) Now, however, it is of the essence of this responsible freedom that its purpose may or may not be fulfilled. This open question is the consequence of freedom. Thus it is part of the divinely created nature of humanity that it should have both a formal and a material aspect. The fact that humanity must respond, that it is responsible, is fixed; no amount of human freedom, nor of the sinful misuse of freedom, can alter this fact.

Humanity is, and remains, responsible, whatever its personal attitude to its Creator may be. Humanity may deny its responsibility, and may misuse its freedom, but it cannot get rid of its responsibility. Responsibility is part of the unchangeable structure of human being. That is: the actual existence of humanity – of every human being, not only those who believe in Christ – consists in the positive fact that they have been made to respond to God.

Whatever kind of response humanity may make to the call of the Creator – in any case it does respond, even if the reply is: "I do not know any Creator, and I will not obey any God." Even this answer is an answer, and it comes under the inherent law of responsibility. This formal essential structure cannot be lost. It is identical with human existence as such, and indeed with the quality of being which all human beings possess equally; it only ceases where true human living ceases – on the borderline of imbecility or madness.

In the Old Testament, the Bible describes this formal aspect of human nature by the concept of "being made in the image of God". In the thought of the Old Testament the fact that humanity has been "made in the Image of God" means something which humanity can never lose; even when they sin, they cannot lose it. This conception is therefore unaffected by the contrast between sin and grace, or sin and obedience, precisely because it describes the "formal" or "structural", and not the "material" aspect of human nature. Then how is it possible to perceive reflected similarity in this formal likeness to God? The similarity consists in being "subject", being "person", freedom. Certainly, humanity has only a limited freedom, because it is responsible, but it *has* freedom; only so *can* it be responsible. Thus the formal aspect of human nature, as beings "made in the image of God", denotes being as Subject, or freedom; it is this which differentiates humanity from the lower creation; this constitutes its specifically *human* quality; it is this which is given to humanity – and to humanity alone – and under all circumstances by Divine appointment.

The New Testament simply presupposes this fact that humanity – in its very nature – has been "made in the image of God"; it does not develop this any further. To the Apostles what matters most is the "material" realization of this God-given quality; that is, that humanity should really give *the* answer which the Creator intends, the response in which God is honoured, and in which He fully imparts Himself, the response of reverent, grateful love, given not only in words, but in its whole life. The New Testament, in its doctrine of the *Imago Dei*, tells us that this right answer has not been given; that a quite different one has been given instead, in which the glory is not given to God, but to human beings and to creatures, in which humanity does not live in the love of God, but seeks itself. Secondly, the New Testament is the proclamation of what God has done in order that he may turn this false answer into the true one.

Here, therefore, the fact that humanity has been "made in the image of God" is spoken of as having been lost, and indeed as wholly, and not partially lost. Humanity no longer possesses this *Imago Dei*; but it is restored through Him, through whom God glorifies and gives Himself: through Jesus Christ. The restoration of the *Imago Dei*, the new creation of the original image of God in humanity, is identical with the gift of God in Jesus Christ received by faith.

The *Imago Dei* in the New Testament, in the "material" sense of the word, is identical with "being-in-the-Word" of God. This means that humanity does not possess its true being in itself, but in God. Thus it is not a fact which can be discovered in humanity, something which can be found through introspection. It is not the "Thou" of Idealistic philosophy, but it is the "I" derived from the "Thou". Hence it cannot be understood by looking at humanity, but only by looking at God, or, more exactly, by looking at the Word of God. To be true humanity, humanity must not be itself, and in order to understand his true being it must not look at itself. Our true being is *extra nos et alienum nobis* (Luther); it is "eccentric" and "ecstatic"; humanity is only truly human when it is in God. Then, and then only, is humanity truly itself.

From the standpoint of sinful humanity, the *Imago Dei* is existence in Jesus Christ, the Word made flesh. Jesus Christ is the true *Imago Dei*, which humanity regains when through faith it is "in Jesus Christ". Faith in Jesus Christ is therefore the *restauratio imaginis*, because He restores to us that existence in the Word of God which we had lost through sin. When humanity enters into the love of God revealed in Christ it becomes truly human. True human existence is existence in the love of God. Thus also the true freedom of humanity is complete dependence upon God. *Deo servire libertas* (Augustine). The words "Whose service is perfect freedom" express the essence of Christian faith. True humanity is not genius but love, that love which humanity does not possess from or in itself but which is received from God, who is love. True humanity does not spring from the full development of human potentialities, but it arises through the reception, the perception, and the acceptance of the love of God, and it develops and is preserved by "abiding" in communion with the God who reveals Himself as Love. Hence separation from God, sin, is the loss of the true human quality, and the destruction of the quality of "being made in the Image of God". When the human heart no longer reflects the love of God, but itself and the world, humanity no longer bears the "Image of God", which simply consists in the fact that God's love is reflected in the human heart.

Since through faith in Jesus Christ humanity once more receives God's Primal Word of love, once more the divine Image (*Urbild*) *is* reflected in it, the lost *Imago Dei* is restored. The *Imago Dei*, in the sense of true humanity – not in the sense of formal or structural humanity – is thus identical with the true attitude of humanity in relation to God, in accordance with God's purpose in Creation. Your attitude to God determines what you are. If your attitude towards God is "right", in harmony with the purpose of Creation, that is, if in faith you receive the love of God, then you *are* right; if your attitude to God is wrong, then you are wrong, as a whole.

It is evident that our thought will become terribly muddled if the two ideas of the *imago Dei* – the "formal" and "structural" one of the Old Testament, and the "material" one of the New Testament – are either confused with one another, or treated as identical. The result will be either that we must deny that the sinner possesses the quality of humanity at all; or, that which makes the sinner a human being must be severed from the *imago Dei*; or, the loss of the *imago* in the material sense *must* be regarded merely as an obscuring, or a *partial* corruption of the *imago*, which lessens the seriousness of sin. All these three false solutions disappear once the distinction is rightly made.

Comment

This long passage is clearly written and requires little in the way of comment. The critically important issue is the way in which Brunner distinguishes various senses of the term "the image of God" and affirms the importance of relationality. Brunner's thinking has been influenced here by the "personalist" philosophy of the Jewish writer Martin Buber. Brunner applies Buber's idea of an "I–You" relationship (see Comment, 2.42) to the Christian life. Brunner applies this idea of an "I–You" relationship to the Christian life, and argues that the objective basis of this relationship between God and believer is the "image of God" in human beings, established in creation and renewed in redemption.

Questions for Study

1 Set out, in your own words, what Brunner understands by the phrase "the image of God." In particular, make sure that you can explain the "formal" and "material" aspects of this concept.
2 Is the image of God destroyed by sin? If not, what difference does sin make, according to Brunner? And how does redemption come into play here?

6.51

Karl Barth on Election in Christ

In this passage from his *Church Dogmatics*, Karl Barth (1886–1968) reinterprets the classic Reformed doctrine of predestination. Noting that the doctrine takes the form of God's pronouncement of "Yes" and "No," Barth argues that the negative aspects of the doctrine relate to Christ, and Christ alone. By taking the negative aspects of predestination upon himself, Christ thus converts predestination into a totally positive and affirming doctrine. See also 6.12, 6.20, 6.21, 6.29, 6.36, 6.40, 6.43, 6.52.

In its simplest and most comprehensive form the dogma of predestination consists, then, in the assertion that the divine predestination is the election of Jesus Christ. But the concept of election has a double reference – to the elector and the elected. And so, too, the name of Jesus Christ has within itself the double reference: the One called by this name is both very God and very man. Thus the simplest form of the dogma may be divided at once into the two assertions that Jesus Christ is the electing God, and that He is also elected man.

In so far as He is the electing God, we must obviously – and above all – ascribe to Him the active determination of electing. It is not that He does not elect as man; i.e., elect God in faith. But this election can only follow His prior election, and that means that it follows the divine electing which is the basic and proper determination of His existence.

In so far as He is man, the passive determination of election is also and necessarily proper to Him. It is true, of course, that even as God he is elected: the Elected of His Father. But because as the Son of the Father, he has no need of any special election, we must add at once that He is the Son of God elected in His oneness with man, and in fulfilment of God's covenant with man. Primarily, then, electing is the divine determination of the existence of Jesus Christ, and election (being elected) the human. [...]

The eternal will of God in the election of Jesus Christ is His will to give Himself for the sake of man as created by Him and fallen from Him. According to the Bible this was what took place in the incarnation of the Son of God, in His death and passion, in His resurrection from the dead. We must think of this as the content of the eternal divine predestination. The election of grace in the beginning of all things is God's self-giving in His eternal purpose. His self-giving: God gave – not only as an actual event but as something eternally foreordained – God gave His only begotten Son. God sent forth his own Word. And in so doing, He gave Himself. He gave Himself up. He hazarded himself. He did not do this for nothing, but for man as created by Him and fallen away from Him. This is God's eternal will. And our next task is to arrive at a radical understanding of the fact and extent that this will, as recognized and expressed in the history of doctrine, is a twofold will, containing within itself both a Yes and a No. We must consider how and how far the eternal predestination is a quality, a *praedestinatio gemina*. [...]

For if God Himself became man, this man, what else can this mean but that He declared himself guilty of the contradiction against Himself in which man was involved; that He submitted Himself to the law of creation by which such a contradiction could be accompanied only by loss and destruction; that He made Himself the object of the wrath and judgment to which man had brought himself; that He took upon Himself the rejection which man had deserved; that he tasted Himself the damnation, death and hell which ought to have been the portion of fallen man? [...]

When we say that God elected as His own portion the negative side of the divine predestination, the reckoning with man's weakness and sin and inevitable punishment, we say implicitly that this portion is not man's portion. In so far, then, as predestination does contain a No, it is not a No spoken against man. In so far as it is directed to perdition and death, it is not directed to the perdition and death of man. [...] Rejection cannot again become the portion or affair of man. The exchange which took place at Golgotha, when God chose as His throne the malefactor's cross, when the Son of God bore what the son of man ought to have borne, took place once and for all in fulfilment of God's eternal will, and it can never be reversed. There is no condemnation – literally none – for those that are in Christ Jesus. For this reason, faith in the divine election as such as *per se* means faith in the non-rejection of man, or disbelief in his rejection. Man is not rejected. In God's eternal purpose it is God Himself who is rejected in His Son. The self-giving of God consists, the giving and sending of His Son is fulfilled, in the fact that He is rejected in order that we might not be rejected. Predestination means that from all eternity God has determined upon man's acquittal at His own cost.

Comment

Barth here offers a radical reworking of the Reformed concept of *praedestinatio gemina* ("double predestination"). According to Barth, God elected to take from us the negative aspects of divine judgment. God rejects Christ in order that we might not be rejected. The negative side of predestination, which ought, Barth suggests, properly to have fallen upon sinful humanity, is instead directed toward Christ as the electing God and elected human being. God willed to bear the "rejection and condemnation and death" which are the inevitable consequences of sin. Thus "rejection cannot again become the portion or affair of humanity." Christ bore what sinful humanity ought to have borne, in order that they need never bear it again. Barth thus eliminates any notion of a "predestination to condemnation" on the part of humanity. The only one who is predestined to condemnation is Jesus Christ who "from all eternity willed to suffer for us." The consequences of this approach are clear. Despite all appearances to the contrary, humanity cannot be condemned. In the end, grace will triumph, even over unbelief. Barth's doctrine of predestination eliminates the possibility of the rejection of humanity. In that Christ has borne the penalty and pain of rejection by God, this can never again become the portion of humanity. Taken together with his characteristic emphasis upon the "triumph of grace," Barth's doctrine of predestination points to the universal restoration and salvation of humanity – a position which has occasioned a degree of criticism from others who would otherwise be sympathetic to his general position.

Questions for Study

1 "In so far, then, as predestination does contain a No, it is not a No spoken against man." Locate this passage within the text. What does Barth mean by this?
2 How does Barth's interpretation of predestination compare with the older Reformed tradition, as seen in Calvin (6.36), Beza (6.40), and the Westminster Confession (6.43)?

6.52

Emil Brunner on Barth's Doctrine of Election

Brunner here reacts against Barth's doctrine of election, by declaring that it amounts to an irresistible imposition of salvation upon humanity. Note especially his analogy of the people in shallow water. They may think that they are in danger of drowning; in reality, they are in no danger at all. See also 6.36, 6.40, 6.43, 6.51.

The monumental presentation of the doctrine of predestination, and that of election in particular, which we find in Karl Barth's *Church Dogmatics*, justifies us in making our own critical estimation of it, in part because it is the most comprehensive discussion of the question in modern theology, but especially because some totally new ideas have been introduced into the discussion of the whole question. [. . .]

The second main article of his doctrine can be expressed as follows: Jesus Christ is the only elect human being. In order to develop this statement further, Barth is obliged to make a third statement: Jesus is "the eternally elect human being," "the pre-existing God-man who, as such, is the eternal ground of all election."

No special proof is required to show that the Bible contains no such doctrine, or that no theologian has ever formulated any theory of this kind. If the eternal pre-existence of the God-man were a fact, then the incarnation could no longer be an *event*. It would no longer be the great miracle of Christmas. In the New Testament, what is new is that the eternal Son of God *became* a human being, and that thereafter, through his resurrection and ascension, humanity has *received* a share of his heavenly glory. Yet according to Barth, all of this is now anticipated, as it were; it is torn out of the sphere of history and set within the pre-temporal sphere, in the pre-existence of the Logos. [. . .]

Karl Barth has been charged with teaching universalism. When he denies this, he is not actually wrong. He knows too much about the not especially illustrious theologians who have maintained this doctrine of *Apokatastasis* in Christian history to be prepared to have himself counted among their number. [. . .] Rather, Barth goes much further. For none of them dared to maintain that through Jesus Christ, everyone – whether believer or non-believer – are saved from the wrath of God and share in redemption through Jesus Christ. But this is precisely what Barth teaches. [. . .] Hell has been blotted out, and condemnation and judgement eliminated. This is not a conclusion *I* have drawn from Barth's statements, but something he has stated himself. [. . .]

There is no doubt that many people today will be glad to hear such a doctrine, and will rejoice that a theologian has finally dared to consign the idea of a final divine judgement, or that someone would finally be "lost", to the rubbish tip. But they cannot dispute one point: that Barth, in making this statement, is in total opposition to the Christian tradition, as well as – and this is of decisive importance – to the clear teaching of the New Testament. [. . .]

Karl Barth, in his transference to the salvation offered to faith to unbelievers, departs from the ground of the biblical revelation, in order to draw a logical conclusion which he finds illuminating. But what is the result? First of all, the result is that the real decision takes place in the objective sphere alone, and not in the subjective sphere. The decision has thus been taken in Jesus Christ – for everyone. It does not matter whether they know it or not, or believe it or not. The main point is that they are saved. They resemble people who seem to be about to sink in a stormy sea. Yet in reality, they are not in a sea in which sinking is a possibility, but in shallow waters in which it is impossible to drown. Only they do not know this. Hence the transition from unbelief to faith is not a transition from "being lost" to "being saved". This transition cannot happen, as it is no longer possible to be lost.

Comment

Brunner's critique of Barth's doctrine of election is widely cited in the literature, and has the immense advantage of being easy to understand. Brunner's fundamental point is that, if Barth is right, nobody can fail to be saved. So it is ultimately not meaningful to talk about "being saved," in that nobody can avoid being saved. Brunner's analysis involves an exploration of the consequences of Barth's reinterpretation of the Reformed concept of *praedestinatio gemina* ("double predestination"), and the use of a good analogy to press his point home. Barth's views on this issue (6.51) should be read before engaging with Brunner's critique.

Questions for Study

1 Summarize, in your own words, Brunner's critique of Barth's position. What are the key points that Brunner makes against Barth?
2 Set out the point that Brunner makes with his analogy of the people in shallow water.

6.53

Reinhold Niebuhr on Original Sin

In his 1939 Gifford Lectures at Edinburgh University, Reinhold Niebuhr (1892–1971) set out his views on the nature and destiny of humanity. By this stage in his career, Niebuhr had gained a reputation as a strong defender of the reality of sin. In the passage reprinted below, Niebuhr explores the notion of original sin, focusing particularly on the issue of how sin can be inevitable, yet still be the responsibility of the individual who sins. See also 6.2, 6.3, 6.12, 6.13, 6.47.

The Christian doctrine of sin in its classical form offends both rationalists and moralists by maintaining the seemingly absurd position that man sins inevitably and by a fateful necessity, but that he is nevertheless responsible for actions which are prompted by an ineluctable fate. The explicit Scriptural foundation for the doctrine is given in Pauline teaching. On the one hand, St Paul insists that man's sinful glorification of himself is without excuse [. . .] and on the other hand, he regards human sin as an inevitable defect, involved in or derived from the sin of the first man. [. . .]

Here is the absurdity in a nutshell. Original sin, which is by definition an inherited corruption, or at least an inevitable one, is nevertheless not to be regarded as belonging to his essential nature and therefore is not outside the realm of human responsibility.

Sin is natural for man in the sense that it is universal but not in the sense that it is necessary. Calvin makes this distinction very carefully. [. . .]

Sin is to be regarded as neither a necessity of man's nature nor yet as a pure caprice of his will. It proceeds rather from a defect of the will, for which reason it is not completely deliberate: but since it is the will in which the defect is found, and the will presupposes freedom, the defect cannot be attributed to a taint in man's nature. Here again Calvin is most precise: "Wherefore, as Plato has been deservedly censured for imputing all sins to ignorance, so also we must reject the opinion of those who maintain that all sins proceed from deliberate malice and pravity. For we too must experience how frequently we fall into error even when our intentions are good. Our reason is overwhelmed with deceptions in so many forms." The doctrine of original sin never escapes the logical absurdities in which these words of Calvin abound. Calvin remains within speaking terms of logic by insisting that sin is "an adventitious quality or accident" rather than a necessity. But if this were true it could not be as inevitable as Calvin's own doctrine assumes. Kierkegaard is more correct in his assertion that "sin comes as neither necessity nor accident." Naturally a position which seems so untenable from a logical standpoint has been derided and scorned not only by non-Christian philosophers but by many Christian theologians.

The whole crux of the doctrine of original sin lies in the seeming absurdity of the conception of free-will which underlies it. The Pauline doctrine, as elaborated by Augustine and the Reformers, insists on the one hand that the will of man is enslaved to sin and is incapable of fulfilling God's law. It may be free, declares Augustine, only it is not free to do good. [. . .] Yet on the other hand the same Augustine insists upon the reality of free-will whenever he has cause to fear that the concept of original sin might threaten the idea of human responsibility. [. . .] One could multiply examples in the thought of theologians of the Pauline tradition in which logical consistency is sacrificed in order to maintain on the one hand that the will is free in the sense that man is responsible for his sin, and on the other hand is not free in the sense that he can, of his own will, do nothing but evil. [. . .]

The full complexity of the psychological facts which validate the doctrine of original sin must be analysed, first in terms of the relation of temptation to the inevitability of sin. Such an analysis may make it plain why man sins inevitably, yet without escaping responsibility for his sin. The temptation to sin, as observed previously, lies in the human situation itself. This situation is that man as spirit transcends the temporal and natural process in which he is involved, and also transcends himself. Thus his freedom is the basis of his creativity but it is also his temptation. Since he is involved in the contingencies and necessities of the natural process on the one hand, and since, on the other, he stands outside of them and foresees their caprices and perils, he is anxious. In his anxiety, he seeks to transmute his finiteness into infinity, his weakness into strength, his dependence into independence. He seeks in other words to escape finiteness and weakness by a quantitative rather than qualitative development of his life. The quantitative antithesis of finiteness is infinity. The qualitative possibility of human life is its obedient subjection to the will of God. This possibility is expressed in the words of Jesus: "he that loseth his life for my sake shall find it" (Matthew 10: 39).

Comment

Niebuhr is often regarded as the North American counterpart to Karl Barth, not least on account of his radical criticism of the assumptions of the dominant liberal Protestant theology of his day. In Niebuhr's case, this critique was especially aimed against optimistic views of human nature. Niebuhr's most important statement of his views on human nature is to be found in his major work *The Nature and Destiny of Man* (1941), which offers both a fresh statement and defense of the notion of original sin.

Questions for Study

1 Niebuhr is clearly aware that many have severe difficulties with the idea of original sin. In what ways does this awareness show itself in the passage?
2 In what way does the concept of "free will" play an especially important role in any discussion of original sin, according to Niebuhr?

6.54

The Second Vatican Council on Human Nature

The Pastoral Constitution *Gaudium et Spes* ("Joy and Hope"), promulgated in December, 1965, was one of the Second Vatican Council's most significant contributions to theological reflection on human nature and dignity. It sets out the traditional Catholic understanding of human nature, paying particular attention to the place of humanity within creation, and the impact of sin upon the human capacity to choose rightly and do good. See also 6.4, 6.5, 6.10, 6.13, 6.23, 6.27, 6.31, 6.50.

12. According to the almost unanimous opinion of believers and unbelievers alike, all things on earth should be related to man as their center and crown.

But what is man? About himself he has expressed, and continues to express, many divergent and even contradictory opinions. In these he often exalts himself as the absolute measure of all things or debases himself to the point of despair. The result is doubt and anxiety. The Church certainly understands these problems. Endowed with light from God, she can offer solutions to them, so that man's true situation can be portrayed and his defects explained, while at the same time his dignity and destiny are justly acknowledged.

For Sacred Scripture teaches that man was created "to the image of God," is capable of knowing and loving his Creator, and was appointed by Him as master of all earthly creatures that he might subdue them and use them to God's glory. "What is man that you should care for him? You have made him little less than the angels, and crowned him with glory and honor. You have given him rule over the works of your hands, putting all things under his feet" (Psalm 8: 5–7).

But God did not create man as a solitary, for from the beginning "male and female he created them" (Genesis 1: 27). Their companionship produces the primary form of interpersonal communion. For by his innermost nature man is a social being, and unless he relates himself to others he can neither live nor develop his potential. Therefore, as we read elsewhere in Holy Scripture God saw "all that he had made, and it was very good" (Genesis 1: 31).

13. Although he was made by God in a state of holiness, from the very onset of his history man abused his liberty, at the urging of the Evil One. Man set himself against God and sought to attain his goal apart from God. Although they knew God, they did not glorify Him as God, but their senseless minds were darkened and they served the creature rather than the Creator. What divine revelation makes known to us agrees with experience. Examining his heart, man finds that he has inclinations toward evil too, and is engulfed by manifold ills which cannot come from his good Creator. Often refusing to acknowledge God as his beginning, man has disrupted also his proper relationship to his own ultimate goal as well as his whole relationship toward himself and others and all created things.

Therefore man is split within himself. As a result, all of human life, whether individual or collective, shows itself to be a dramatic struggle between good and evil, between light and darkness. Indeed, man finds that by himself he is incapable of battling the assaults of evil successfully, so that everyone feels as though he is bound by chains. But the Lord Himself came to free and strengthen man, renewing him inwardly and casting out that "prince of this world" (John 12: 31) who held him in the bondage of sin. For sin has diminished man, blocking his path to fulfillment.

The call to grandeur and the depths of misery, both of which are a part of human experience, find their ultimate and simultaneous explanation in the light of this revelation.

14. Though made of body and soul, man is one. Through his bodily composition he gathers to himself the elements of the material world; thus they reach their crown through him, and through him raise their voice in free praise of the Creator. For this reason man is not allowed to despise his bodily life, rather he is obliged to regard his body as good and honorable since God has created it and will raise it up on the last day. Nevertheless, wounded by sin, man experiences rebellious stirrings in his body. But the very dignity of man postulates that man glorify God in his body and forbid it to serve the evil inclinations of his heart.

Now, man is not wrong when he regards himself as superior to bodily concerns, and as more than a speck of nature or a nameless constituent of the city of man. For by his interior qualities he outstrips the whole sum of mere things. He plunges into the depths of reality whenever he enters into his own heart; God, Who probes the heart, awaits him there; there he discerns his proper destiny beneath the eyes of God. Thus, when he recognizes in himself a spiritual and immortal soul, he is not being mocked by a fantasy born only of physical or social influences, but is rather laying hold of the proper truth of the matter.

15. Man judges rightly that by his intellect he surpasses the material universe, for he shares in the light of the divine mind. By relentlessly employing his talents through the ages he has indeed made progress in the practical sciences and in technology and the liberal arts. In our times he has won superlative victories, especially in his probing of the material world and in subjecting it to himself. Still he has always searched for more penetrating truths, and finds them. For his intelligence is not confined to observable data alone, but can with genuine certitude attain to reality itself as knowable, though in consequence of sin that certitude is partly obscured and weakened.

The intellectual nature of the human person is perfected by wisdom and needs to be, for wisdom gently attracts the mind of man to a quest and a love for what is true and good. Steeped in wisdom, man passes through visible realities to those which are unseen.

Our era needs such wisdom more than bygone ages if the discoveries made by man are to be further humanized. For the future of the world stands in peril unless wiser men are forthcoming. It should also be pointed out that many nations, poorer in economic goods, are quite rich in wisdom and can offer noteworthy advantages to others.

It is, finally, through the gift of the Holy Spirit that man comes by faith to the contemplation and appreciation of the divine plan.

16. In the depths of his conscience, man detects a law which he does not impose upon himself, but which holds him to obedience. Always summoning him to love good and avoid evil, the voice of conscience when necessary speaks to his heart: do this, shun that. For man has in his heart a law written by God; to obey it is the very dignity of man; according to it he will be judged. Conscience is the most secret core and sanctuary of a man. There he is alone with God, Whose voice echoes in his depths. In a wonderful manner conscience reveals that law which is fulfilled by love of God and neighbor. In fidelity to conscience, Christians are joined with the rest of men in the search for truth, and for the genuine solution to the numerous problems which arise in the life of individuals from social relationships. Hence the more right conscience holds sway, the more persons and groups turn aside from blind choice and strive to be guided by the objective norms of morality. Conscience frequently errs from invincible ignorance without losing its dignity. The same cannot be said for a man who cares but little for truth and goodness, or for a conscience which by degrees grows practically sightless as a result of habitual sin.

17. Only in freedom can man direct himself toward goodness. Our contemporaries make much of this freedom and pursue it eagerly; and rightly to be sure. Often however they foster it perversely as a license for doing whatever pleases them, even if it is evil. For its part, authentic freedom is an exceptional sign of the divine image within man. For God has willed that man remain "under the control of his own decisions," so that he can seek his Creator spontaneously, and come freely to utter and blissful perfection

through loyalty to Him. Hence man's dignity demands that he act according to a knowing and free choice that is personally motivated and prompted from within, not under blind internal impulse nor by mere external pressure. Man achieves such dignity when, emancipating himself from all captivity to passion, he pursues his goal in a spontaneous choice of what is good, and procures for himself through effective and skilful action, apt helps to that end. Since man's freedom has been damaged by sin, only by the aid of God's grace can he bring such a relationship with God into full flower. Before the judgement seat of God each man must render an account of his own life, whether he has done good or evil.

Comment

The Constitution sets out a view of human nature which is rigorously grounded both in the Old and New Testaments, and reflects the Christian exploration of these themes in the long subsequent tradition of theological reflection. The influence of Augustine of Hippo is evident at a number of points. Humanity is here portrayed as the height of God's good creation. The constitution speaks of a "split" within human nature, as a result of sin, leading to a weakening of the human will, while at the same time affirming that the law of God is written on human hearts in the conscience.

Questions for Study

1 Set out, in your own words, the main features of the Constitution's understanding of human nature. How does it describe and account for the tensions within human nature? On the basis of this view of humanity, how can we account for humans longing to do good, but often doing evil instead?
2 Compare this understanding of human nature with that set out in the "Manifesto of the Renaissance," Pico della Mirandola's *Oration on Human Dignity* (6.31). What would you judge to be the main points of difference?

6.55

Daphne Hampson on Feminist Approaches to Sin

In this perceptive analysis of the nature of sin Daphne Hampson (born 1944) argues that classic expositions, such as those found in the writings of Reinhold Niebuhr, reflect what sin has been in a masculinist and patriarchal world; such that it is understood in the first instance as a domination of others arising from pride on the part of an isolated and highly individualised self. Hampson argues (as have women of many religious persuasions, Jewish, Christian feminist both Catholic and Protestant, and post-Christian since about 1980) that such an analysis is peculiarly inappropriate to the situation of women, who lack rather self-realization. Hampson is herself a post-Christian theologian. See also 2.45, 3.42, 6.53, 6.54.

The doctrine of sin has always been fundamental to theological anthropology. That this is the case may in itself be significant. Human beings have been seen as in opposition to God. God is considered good; humans, by contrast with God, sinful. [. . .] It has also affected [. . .] the way in which women have been conceived in relation to men. Sin is connected with what is "below" and with our bodily nature; and woman comes to be associated with sexuality. However, the primary understanding of sin in the tradition (which has been a male tradition, for theology has been male) has been that sin is in the first instance not sensuality but rather pride. Here again we may think the conceptualization to have fitted a male dynamic; for men have been the ones who have been in a position to be proud.

In my consideration of sin, I shall look at feminist responses to the conceptualization of sin articulated by Reinhold Niebuhr. I turn to the feminist critique of Niebuhr for two reasons. In the first place there has been a concentration of feminist work here. And secondly, Niebuhr's analysis of sin, particularly as developed in his Gifford lectures *The Nature and Destiny of Man*, is arguably the most profound that there has been. The women who have taken issue with Niebuhr (and this includes myself) have trained in theology in the United States where his thought has been influential. The argument is not that Niebuhr's analysis is false, but that it is inapplicable to the situation of all of humanity, while failing to recognize that this is the case.

The setting for Niebuhr's Gifford lectures was Scotland at the outbreak of the Second World War. Europe was faced, in National Socialist Germany, with the most overweening pride (or hubris) of a people in their desire for expansion and their subjugation of others, which the western world has experienced. Niebuhr's is a multi-faceted analysis, brilliantly interweaving theology with historical, social and psychological insights. Sin he sees in its basic form to be pride, showing convincingly that this has been the major understanding in the western tradition. Sin comes to be, not necessarily but inevitably, in a situation of *Angst*; that anxiety which, having no definite object, consists in a basic disease. In their anxiety human beings are faced with two possibilities. Either they can trust in God; which is what the creator intended – for indeed the anxiety has only arisen through a lack of such trust. Or they fall into sin. Sin can be of two kinds: pride, in which human beings attempt to set themselves up in the place of God, to be gods themselves, subjecting others to their will; or sensuality, in which (rather than having an egotistical sense of self) human beings try to get rid of any sense of themselves and bury themselves in others or the things of this world – for example through the misuse of sexuality.

That Niebuhr's analysis contains deep insights is not in dispute. Indeed feminists might well say that Niebuhr has put his finger on what they find to be so worrying about the male world. He describes a situation in which a man, or a nation, would try to be free of the web of humanity (perhaps through insecurity) and then comes to dominate others. (Again the discussion of the misuse of sexuality as an attempt to escape from self rings true.) But the problem is that of the isolated male who would be free of others. He attempts self-sufficiency at the expense of other life. Women's criticism has thus been twofold. In the first place it is said that this is not a good analysis of the situation in which women find themselves; moreover that women's failings are typically other.

Secondly, it is pointed out that Niebuhr (for all that he is concerned with social analysis) has an extraordinarily individuated concept of the human being, who finds himself essentially caught up in competitive relationships.

That Niebuhr (and Tillich also) do not describe what is typically woman's predicament was first elucidated by Valerie Saiving in an article published in 1960, the article which is often taken to mark the beginning of the current wave of feminist theological writing. Saiving writes:

> It is clear that many of the characteristic emphases of contemporary theology . . . its identification of sin with pride, will-to-power, exploitation, self-assertiveness, and the treatment of others as objects rather than persons . . . it is clear that such an analysis of man's dilemma was profoundly responsive and relevant to the concrete facts of modern man's existence. . . . As a matter of fact, however, this theology is not adequate to the universal human situation. . . . For the temptations of woman *as woman* are not the same as the temptations of man *as man*, and the specifically feminine forms of sin – "feminine" not because they are confined to women or because women are incapable of sinning in other ways but because they are outgrowths of the basic feminine character structure – have a quality which can never be encompassed by such terms as "pride" and "will-to-power." They are better suggested by such items as triviality, distractability, and diffuseness; lack of an organizing center or focus; dependence on others for one's own self-definition; . . . in short, underdevelopment or negation of the self.

One may remark on the fact that Niebuhr, who follows closely the Danish nineteenth-century thinker Søren Kierkegaard in his understanding of the relationship of insecurity, pride and sensuality, does not however take up Kierkegaard's dual articulation of the typically "manly" and "womanly" ways of sinning. Man, says Kierkegaard, would try to be Caesar, whereas woman would be rid of herself. That Kierkegaard's (and Saiving's) analysis is an analysis of women as women are living under patriarchy is of course the case.

Consequently some women have wanted to say that woman's "sin" is – to quote an effective phrase of Judith Plaskow's – "the failure to take responsibility for self-actualization". To name such behaviour "sin" is (as I have discovered when working with groups of women) very effective. For women to hear that it is their right and duty to take themselves seriously, that it matters who they are and what they think, is to turn Christian theology as they have imbibed it upside-down. For it is women largely who have been expected by society to take on board the Christian admonition to be self-effacing. This suggests that the fact that women have had preached to them that self-sacrifice is the message of the gospel has been wholly inappropriate in the situation in which they found themselves. Whether "the failure to take responsibility for self-actualization" should however be called "sin" is another question – as Helen Percy in particular has pointed out to me. If we think of women's typical "failings", as Saiving names them, they can hardly be said (in the way in which this is true of male pride) to be actively destructive of others. Rather have women been destructive of themselves and their own potentialities.

But the feminist criticism is not simply that Niebuhr has described what have been behaviour patterns of men rather than of women. It has seemed to feminist theologians, that in his sense of the individual as highly individuated and "atomic" rather than in relationship to others, Niebuhr has described what is peculiarly a male propensity. When (as I have discovered) it is said by feminists that Niebuhr fails to have a social conception of the human, this may well be misunderstood. For – the response comes back – no theologian more than he has considered the human in society. Of course this is the case. What is being referred to here however is a different level of the word social. Niebuhr sees the human being as monadic rather than as having an essential relationality. In this he is very different from much feminist thought. Very fine work here has been accomplished by Judith Vaughan. Vaughan, in work originally undertaken with Rosemary Ruether, compares Niebuhr's ethics with Ruether's ethics. She shows that their different ethical and political stance relates to a different understanding of the human being. Vaughan, and Ruether, hold what I earlier designated a Marxist–Hegelian perspective. They see persons as caught up in social relationships and believe that the external relations of the self form the understanding which a person has of him or herself. It is from such a position that Vaughan mounts a critique of Niebuhr.

Comment

Hampson here offers a feminist critique of some existing approaches to original sin, especially that which she finds in Reinhold Niebuhr's *Nature and Destiny of Man* (1941). You might like to read an extract from this work (6.53) before engaging with the present text. One of the most fundamental issues raised by Hampson is whether the specific manifestations of sin which Niebuhr and other (male) writers discuss are, in fact, specific to males. Drawing on an important article of Valerie Saiving (first published in *The Journal of Religion*, 1960), Hampson argues that women experience sin in a different manner to males – and that this must have implications for any theological discussion of the issue.

Questions for Study

1 Locate the citation from Valerie Saiving within the text. What specifically male sins does she identify? And how does she characterize specifically female sins?
2 "Niebuhr (for all that he is concerned with social analysis) has an extraordinarily individuated concept of the human being, who finds himself essentially caught up in competitive relationships." What does Hampson mean by this? And how does she illustrate this point?

6.56

Mary Hayter on Human Sexuality and the Image of God

The English theologian and writer Mary Hayter (born 1958) here considers the way in which the biblical doctrine of humanity being created in the "image of God" relates to issues of sexuality and gender. In particular, she deals with the issue of the correct relationship between men and women, in the light of the doctrine of creation. See also 3.41, 3.42, 6.4, 6.5, 6.50, 6.53, 6.55.

We are now in a position to examine specific issues regarding the relation of male and female in God's image. In the past, several deductions have been made from the Genesis passages which seem to me to be based upon misinterpretations of the text. There is need, therefore, for a reappraisal of the biblical material if it is to be used correctly by modern doctrinal scholars in the debate about the role of women in the Church.

First, there has been a persistent tradition which declares that while the "whole man" as male is in God's image, *woman does not participate* in the *Imago Dei*, or that woman is only in the divine image in a *secondary sense*. Diodore of Tarsus, for instance, in his commentary on Genesis, states that woman is not in God's image but is under man's dominion. Again, by "the image of God" in man, John Chrysostom understands Adam's sovereignty over the rest of creation, including woman. [...] An unbiased exegesis of Genesis 1: 26–27 and 5: 1–2 provides no grounds for holding that woman participates in the image of God in a different way from man. It is as false to say that only the male is created in the divine image as it would be to make the same claim for the female. [...]

Second, it has been suggested that *originally humanity was sexless or androgynous* and that *the fact of the two sexes was a result of the Fall*. Sexuality in general, and femininity in particular, came to be regarded with fear and suspicion by many Christians. This tallied with some of the motives behind ascetic and monastic movements and the effort to bring man to the level of an angelic, sexless life. Through subversive influences from Gnosticism and Platonic Hellenistic mysticism large sections of the early Church were permeated with the idea that the sex element is something low and unworthy of intelligent man – an idea which, as Emil Brunner points out, has "more or less unconsciously and secretly ... determined the thought of Christendom down to the present day".

A notable twentieth-century spokesman for the view that man's sexual duality is an expression of fallen nature is N. Berdyaev, who refers with approval to the androgynous ideal which he finds in Plato's *Symposium*. As with most supporters of the androgynous ideal, in the end it is not sexuality as such that Berdyaev despises, but femininity. For example, more than a hint of misogyny characterizes the remark that "Man's slavery to sex is slavery to the feminine element, going back to the image of Eve."

I believe that Genesis 1: 26–28 provides no evidence to support such views. The subject of this passage, "man," *'adam*, is referred to by the collective Hebrew noun for "mankind." Genesis 5: 2 confirms that male and female together were named Adam, man, when they were created. In Genesis 5: 3, "Adam" is used as a proper name; but this is not the case in Chapter 1, nor in 5: 1–2. Therefore, efforts to harmonize the first Creation narrative with the ancient Greek myth of the androgyne or hermaphrodite cannot be sustained. [. . .]

This has important implications for our thinking about the role of women, and their relative position to men in the created order, since it stresses both the unity and the differentiation of the sexes. First, the singular word *'adam* with its singular pronoun, "him", *'oto* (Genesis 1: 27), indicates God's intention for the harmony and community of males and females in their shared humanity and joint participation in the image and likeness of God. Second, sexuality is presented as fundamental to what it means to be human and procreation is the subject of a positive command (Genesis 1: 28); the differentiation between the sexes and the means of procreation were not retrograde steps away from an ideal androgyny. This accords with the positive value ascribed to marriage and sexual love in other parts of the Old Testament. For the Hebrews reproduction, and so sexual life, too, are a special gift to all living creatures. Third, since man and woman were created together, with no hint of temporal or ontological superiority, the difference between the sexes cannot be said to affect their equal standing before God and before one another. Sexual differentiation does not mean hierarchy. There is no sexual stereotyping of roles regarding procreation and dominion here; male and female are blessed together and together are commanded to "fill the earth and subdue it" (Genesis 1: 28); neither sex is given dominion over the other. If there is any relationship between the image of God and dominion it must be noted that the record ascribes the image of God to man and woman indiscriminately.

Thus, Genesis 1: 26–28 does away with any justification for the view that sexuality resulted from sinfulness. Furthermore, by stating that men and women were together created after God's image, the passage forbids us to hold the female half of the human race in contempt as inferior, or in some way closer to the animals, or as needing redemption in the form of a transformation of feminine nature into the "more noble" spirituality of the masculine or the asexual.

Partly in reaction against the low view of sexuality and theories of divine androgyny, and partly as a result of a distinctive exegesis of the Genesis material, a *third* approach to the relation of male and female in God's image has been to say that human *sexuality is part of what it means to be like God*. It must now be asked, therefore, whether or not the fact of the two sexes in humankind tells us anything about the deity. [. . .] Some people have asserted that the use of divine plurals in Genesis 1 [. . .] and the subsequent creation of mankind as male and female indicate the presence of sexuality in the Godhead. It has been maintained that, in common with the Canaanite divinization of sex, the Hebrew believed that the human capacity for reproduction was a means by which man could become aware of kinship with God and gain access to divine power. The employment of divine plurals by Old Testament writers poses a problem with which exegetes have frequently wrestled. It is beyond the scope of this study to evaluate each of the possible interpretations, but the one which bears directly upon the subject of divine and human sexuality must be taken into account here. Is it possible that the divine plural expresses a Hebrew belief in the sexual duality of the Godhead? And is it true to say that the *Imago Dei* resides in human sexual polarity?

According to Karl Barth, the basis of the *Imago Dei* doctrine is to be found in the relationship between man and woman, particularly in the marriage relationship: "By the divine likeness of man in Genesis 1: 27–28 there is understood the fact that God created them male and female, corresponding to the fact that God himself exists in relationship and not in isolation." This definition has been much criticized by other scholars. [. . .] To such scholars it is preferable to see the *Imago* as in some sense finding its existential expression in the interrelatedness of man with others, regardless of whether the "other" is male or female. The seat of the image is then the "person" as distinguished from the solipsist individual.

Again, it may be said that Barth's stress upon the importance of marriage as the "crucial expression" of human I–Thou relationships is more the result of a reading into the text of his own ideas than of objective Old Testament exegesis. Although it was probably against Barth's intentions, his hypothesis can lead to the view that *only* in marriage or at least through sexual experience does a person become fully human. Vital as marriage might be in the Barthian doctrinal schemata, Genesis 1 itself treats of sexuality in general and is not concerned first and foremost with the institution of marriage.

It may be justifiable to say that the use of divine plurals for God, such as the term *'elohim*, shows that the fullness of deity is comprehended in Yahweh. Whatever the origin of this practice, the Old Testament usage may be interpreted in an inclusive sense: Yahweh, as *'elohim*, embraces the whole range of divinity, including any facets of masculinity or femininity which may legitimately be predicated of deity. Above and beyond the feminist term God/Goddess, the term *'elohim* as applied to Yahweh can denote that the God of Israel incorporates and transcends masculinity and femininity. Thus, John Macquarrie believes that if the image of God is represented by male and female, then:

> This implies that already in the divine Being there must be, though in an eminent way beyond what we can conceive, whatever is affirmative in sexuality and sociality, in masculinity and femininity. . . . God transcends the distinction of sex, but he does this not by sheer exclusion, but by prefiguring whatever is of value in sexuality on an altogether higher level.

Such a sensitive and carefully worded statement marks the limit to which we may go in making deductions about sexuality in God from Genesis 1: 26–27 and 5: 1–2. By contrast, when Frazer declares that we gather from Genesis 1 "that the distinction of the sexes, which is characteristic of humanity, is shared also by the divinity", he seems to be reading back human male- and female-ness on to God. As James Barr reminds us, the question behind Genesis 1: 26–28 is not so much "What is God like?" but "What is man like?" The Priestly theologian "is saying not primarily that God's likeness is man, but that man is in a relation of likeness to God". It is incorrect therefore, to state bluntly that the *Imago* concept and the divine plurals in Genesis are illustrative of a sexual distinction in God.

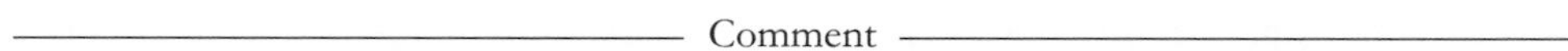

Comment

Mary Hayter here offers a lucid and learned exploration of what it means to say that humanity is created "in the image of God." The text is interesting in many respects. It represents a creative exploration of the meaning of Genesis 1: 26–8, and an attempt to apply this to the present theological debates over gender identity. Note in particular Hayter's insistence that gender distinction is limited to the created order, and cannot be read back into the Godhead. The passage also offers some important reflections on the issue of whether God should be represented in a gender-neutral manner. The text is very clearly written, and requires no additional comment.

Questions for Study

1 Set out, in your own words, Hayter's interpretation of the concept of the "image of God."
2 According to Hayter, should the term "God/dess" be used to refer to God? What reasons can you identify for her judgment on this matter?

For Further Reading

William O. Amy and James B. Recob, *Human Nature in the Christian Tradition* (Washington, DC: University Press of America, 1982).

Ian G. Barbour, *Nature, Human Nature, and God* (Minneapolis, MN: Fortress, 2002).

John Behr, *Asceticism and Anthropology in Irenaeus and Clement* (Oxford: Oxford University Press, 2000).

Warren S. Brown, Nancey C. Murphy, and H. Newton Malony (eds), *Whatever Happened to the Soul?: Scientific and Theological Portraits of Human Nature* (Minneapolis, MN: Fortress Press, 1998).

José Comblin, *Retrieving the Human: A Christian Anthropology* (Maryknoll, NY: Orbis Books, 1990).

Dennis R. Creswell, *St. Augustine's Dilemma: Grace and Eternal Law in the Major Works of Augustine of Hippo* (New York: Peter Lang, 1997).

Julian N. Hartt, "Creation and Providence," in P. Hodgson and R. King (eds), *Christian Theology* (Philadelphia: Fortress Press, 1982), pp. 115–40.

Philip J. Hefner, "Creation," in C. E. Braaten and R. W. Jenson (eds), *Christian Dogmatics*, 2 vols (Philadelphia: Fortress Press, 1984), vol. 1, pp. 269–357.

David H. Kelsey, "Human Being," in P. Hodgson and R. King (eds), *Christian Theology* (Philadelphia: Fortress Press, 1982), pp. 141–67.

Peter Langford, *Modern Philosophies of Human Nature: Their Emergence from Christian Thought* (Dordrecht: Kluwer Academic, 1986).

Alister E. McGrath, *Iustitia Dei: A History of the Christian Doctrine of Justification*, 3rd edn (Cambridge, UK: Cambridge University Press, 2005).

John Randall Sachs, *The Christian Vision of Humanity: Basic Christian Anthropology* (Collegeville, MN: Liturgical Press, 1991).

Paul R. Sponheim, "Sin and Evil," in C. E. Braaten and R. W. Jenson (eds), *Christian Dogmatics*, 2 vols (Philadelphia: Fortress Press, 1984), vol. 1, pp. 363–463.

Basil Studer, *The Grace of Christ and the Grace of God in Augustine of Hippo: Christocentrism or Theocentrism?* (Collegeville, MN: Liturgical Press, 1997).

Elsa Tamez, *The Amnesty of Grace: Justification by Faith from a Latin American Perspective* (Nashville, TN: Abingdon Press, 1993).

N. P. Williams, *The Ideas of the Fall and Original Sin* (London: Longmans, 1927).

R. R. Williams, "Sin and Evil," in P. Hodgson and R. King (eds), *Christian Theology* (Philadelphia: Fortress Press, 1982), pp. 168–95.

Richard Worsley, *Human Freedom and the Logic of Evil: Prolegomenon to a Christian Theology of Evil* (New York: St. Martin's Press, 1996).

7

The Church

Introduction

Ecclesiology is the section of Christian theology dealing with the nature and tasks of the church (Greek: *ekklēsia*). Once more, major debates on the issue erupted in the patristic and Reformation periods. A landmark debate concerning the church broke out in the fourth century, centering on the churches of North Africa. Both Augustine and his Donatist opponents saw themselves as safeguarding the heritage of the martyr Cyprian of Carthage. However, they chose to emphasize different aspects of that heritage. Augustine stressed the priority of Christ as redeemer over his church and its ministers, while the Donatists emphasized the need for personal purity of church members and ministers. At the time of the Reformation, a related debate broke out. However, the main debate associated with the Reformation centered on the identifying characteristics of a church.

The doctrine of the church continues to be an area of discussion today, with particular emphasis being placed upon the role and tasks of local churches.

Several themes of importance can be studied from this chapter, including the following:

What Does it Mean to Say that the Church is "Catholic"?

7.4 Cyril of Jerusalem on the Catholicity of the Church
7.9 Thomas Aquinas on the Catholicity of the Church
7.14 Philip Melanchthon on the Nature of Catholicity
7.27 John D. Zizioulas on Local and Universal Churches
7.29 Avery Dulles on the Meanings of "Catholicity"

How Does the Church Relate to the State?

7.8 Innocent III on the Church and State
7.10 Boniface VIII on Papal Primacy: *Unam Sanctam*
7.22 The First Vatican Council on Papal Primacy in the Church
7.24 The Barmen Confession on the Identity of the Church
7.26 The Second Vatican Council on the Nature of the Church

What is the Place of Priests in the Church?

7.5 Petrilian of Cirta on the Purity of Ministers
7.6 Augustine on the Mixed Nature of the Church
7.7 Leo the Great on Ministry within the Church
7.13 Martin Luther on Priests and Laity
7.21 F. D. E. Schleiermacher on the Church as a Fellowship of Believers
7.25 Yves Congar on the Hierarchy of the Church
7.26 The Second Vatican Council on the Nature of the Church

7.1

Irenaeus on the Function of the Church

In this passage, which dates from the late second century, Irenaeus of Lyons (c.130–c.200) stresses the importance of the church as the living body which has been entrusted with the Christian tradition and proclamation. Note the emphasis placed upon the historic institution of the church, which is seen as a living body within which the proper interpretation of Scripture is kept alive. See also 2.2, 2.5.

True knowledge is the teaching of the Apostles, the order of the church as established from the earliest times throughout the world, and the distinctive stamp of the body of Christ, passed down through the succession of bishops in charge of the church in each place, which has come down to our own time, safeguarded without any spurious writings by the most complete exposition [i.e. the Creed], received without addition or subtraction; the reading of the Scriptures without falsification; and their consistent and careful exposition, avoiding danger and blasphemy; and the special gift of love, which is more precious than knowledge, more glorious than prophecy, and which surpasses all other spiritual gifts.

Comment

In this passage we see Irenaeus stressing the role of the church as the bearer of the apostolic tradition. For Irenaeus, the gospel had been corrupted by those outside the church; in order to be assured of the integrity of the Christian proclamation, it was essential to be able to demonstrate that the church had faithfully preserved and proclaimed the apostolic preaching. Note the close link between the institution of the church and the preaching of the gospel which this approach fosters.

Questions for Study

1 Why does Irenaeus place such stress upon the historical credentials of the institution of the church?
2 What role does Irenaeus ascribe to bishops in this matter? How does this compare with the position adopted by Tertullian (2.5)?

7.2

Origen on the Church and Salvation

Origen (c.185–c.254) here comments on the reference to the prostitute Rahab in Joshua 2, seeing in the promise that those inside her house would be saved from destruction a prophecy or "type" of the Christian church. Only those inside the house of God will be saved. The scarlet thread hung in the window of the prostitute Rahab's house, by which it was identified, is seen as anticipating the identification of the house of God by the scarlet sign of the blood of Christ. See also 2.3, 2.8, 2.11, 7.3.

If anyone wishes to be saved, let them come to this house, just as they once came to that of the prostitute. If anyone of that people wished to be saved, they could come to that house, and they could have salvation as a result. Let them come to this house where the blood of Christ is a sign of redemption. For that blood was for condemnation among those who said, "His blood be on us and on our children" (Matthew 27: 25). Jesus was "for the fall and resurrection of many" (Luke 2: 34) and therefore in respect of those who "speak against his sign" his blood is effective for punishment, but effective for salvation in the case of believers. Let no one therefore be persuaded or deceived: outside this house, that is, outside the Church, no one is saved [*extra hanc domum, id est extra ecclesiam, nemo salvatur*]. [. . .] The sign of salvation was given through the window because Christ by his incarnation gave us the sight of the light of godhead as it were through a window; that all may attain salvation by that sign who shall be found in the house of her who once was a harlot, being made clean by water and the Holy Spirit, and by the blood of our Lord and Savior Jesus Christ, to whom be glory and power for ever.

Comment

This passage is of especial interest on account of the type of biblical exegesis involved, and the development of the idea that there is no salvation outside the "house of the church." The reference is to Joshua 2, which describes how two Israelite spies enter Jericho, and are cared for in a safe house by the prostitute Rahab. The spies offer her safety in return; she is to mark her house by a "scarlet cord" in her window. Origen sees this as an allegorical reference to the church, which is marked out as a place of safety by the scarlet mark of the blood of Christ.

Questions for Study

1. What type of biblical exegesis does Origen employ in linking the "scarlet cord" with the blood of Christ? How does he establish a connection between Rahab's house and the church?
2. Note the Latin phrase *extra hanc domum, id est extra ecclesiam, nemo salvatur*. This is translated in the passage; what does it mean?

7.3

Cyprian of Carthage on the Unity of the Church

In this discussion of the unity of the church, written in 251, Cyprian of Carthage (martyred 258) stresses the indivisibility of the catholic church, and its essential role in obtaining salvation. Salvation is not possible outside the church. It is not possible to have God as a father unless you also have the church as your mother. See also 7.2, 8.3, 8.7, 8.8.

This unity we ought to hold and preserve, especially the bishops who preside in the Church, so that we may demonstrate that the episcopate itself is united and undivided. Let no one deceive the brotherhood [*fraternitas*] with falsehood or corrupt our faith in the truth by faithless transgression. The episcopate is one, and each [individual member] has a part in the whole. The Church is one, and by her fertility she has extended by degree into many. In the same way, the sun has many rays, but a single light; a tree has many branches but a single trunk resting on a deep root; and many streams flow out from a single source. However many may spread out from the source, it retains its unity. Cut off a ray from the orb of the sun; the unity of light cannot be divided. Break off a branch from the tree, and the broken branch cannot come into bud. Sever the stream from its source, and the severed section will dry up. So it is also with the Church. She is flooded with the light of the Lord, and extends her rays all over the globe. Yet it is the one light which is diffused everywhere, without breaking up the unity of the body. She stretches forth her branches over the whole earth in rich abundance; she spreads widely her flowing streams. Yet there is but one head, one source, one mother, abounding in the increase of her fruitfulness. We are born of her womb, we are nourished by her milk, and we are given life from her breath.

The bride of Christ cannot be made an adulteress; she is undefiled and chaste. She has one home, and guards with virtuous chastity the sanctity of one chamber. She serves us for God, who enrolls into his Kingdom the children to whom she gives birth. Anyone who is cut off from the Church and is joined to an adulteress is separated from the promises of the Church, and anyone who leaves the Church of Christ behind cannot benefit from the rewards of Christ. Such people are strangers, outcasts, and enemies. You cannot have God as father unless you have the Church as mother [*Habere iam non potest Deum patrem qui ecclesiam non habet matrem*]. [. . .]

This sacrament of unity, this inseparable bond of peace, is shown in the gospel when the robe of the Lord Jesus Christ was neither divided at all or torn, but they cast lots for the clothing of Christ [. . .] so the clothing was received whole and the robe was taken unspoilt and undivided. [. . .] That garment signifies the unity which comes "from above," that is, from heaven and from the Father, a unity which could not be ruptured at all by those who receive and possess it, in that it was received undivided in its unbreakable entirety. Anyone who rends and divides the Church of Christ cannot possess the clothing of Christ [*possidere non potest indumentum Christi qui scindit et dividit ecclesiam Christi*].

Comment

In this passage Cyprian argues for the unity of the church using a number of important and influential images. The first is that of "God as Father, church as mother." Cyprian here makes use of the fact that the Latin word *ecclesia* ("church") is feminine. The developed ecclesiological vocabulary of the catholic tradition includes phrases such as "holy mother church," which can be traced back to Cyprian. The second is that of the "seamless robe" of Christ, a reference to John 19: 23–4: "When the soldiers had crucified Jesus they took his garments and made four parts, one for each soldier; also his tunic. But the tunic was without seam, woven from top to bottom; so they said to one another, 'Let us not tear it, but cast lots for it to see whose it shall be.' " Cyprian argues that this "robe" or "tunic" is a type of the church.

Questions for Study

1 What point does Cyprian wish to make by his appeal to John 19: 23–4? How persuasive do you find him at this point? In what other ways does he make this point?
2 In what ways does Cyprian develop the imagery of the sun, trees, and streams to develop his thinking on the nature of the church?

7.4
Cyril of Jerusalem on the Catholicity of the Church

In this important lecture Cyril of Jerusalem (c.315–86) argues that the church may be referred to as "catholic" on account of the universality of its teaching and relevance, and also to distinguish it from the sectarian gatherings of heretics. See also 7.9, 7.14, 7.29.

The church is called "catholic" because it extends through all the world, from one end of the earth to another; and because it teaches completely, and without any omissions, all the doctrines which ought to be known to humanity concerning both things that are visible and invisible, and things that are earthly and heavenly; and because it brings all kinds of people – whether rulers or subjects, learned or ignorant – under the influence of true piety; and because it universally treats and cures every kind of sin, whether committed by the soul or the body; and possesses in itself every kind of virtue which can be named relating to words, deeds, or spiritual gifts of every kind. [...] Now the word "church" has different senses. It can refer to the crowd which filled the theatre at Ephesus (Acts 19: 41) [...] or to gatherings of heretics. [...] And because of this variation in the use of the word "church," the article of faith "and in one holy catholic church" has been given to you, so that you can steer clear of the meetings [of the heretics] and remain within the holy catholic church within which you have been born again. If you ever have cause to visit a strange town, do not ask simply [...] "Where is the church?" Instead, ask: "Where is the *catholic* church?" This is the distinctive name of this, the holy church and mother of us all. She is the bride of our Lord Jesus Christ, the only-begotten Son of God.

Comment

In this passage, Cyril brings together four different understandings of the word "catholic":

1 Found throughout the world in its entirety;
2 Preaches the gospel in its entirety;
3 Directed towards the human race in its entirety;
4 Makes available a universal cure for the ills of the human race in its entirety.

In addition to clarifying the various senses of the term "catholic," Cyril notes its usefulness in distinguishing Christian gatherings and assemblies from those of their sectarian and heretical rivals.

Questions for Study

1 Set out, in your own words, the various senses of the word "catholic," as these are distinguished by Cyril. Why is this matter of such importance to him?
2 What additional titles does Cyril use to refer to the church? What do they suggest as to his understanding of its nature and role?

7.5

Petilian of Cirta on the Purity of Ministers

Petilian, the Donatist Bishop of Cirta (born c.365), circulated a letter to his priests warning against the moral impurity and doctrinal errors of the catholic church. Augustine's reply, dated 401, led Petilian to write against Augustine in more detail. In this letter, dating from 402, from which Augustine quotes extracts, Petilian sets out fully the Donatist insistence that the validity of the sacraments is totally dependent upon the moral worthiness of those who administer them. Petilian's words are included within quotation marks in Augustine's text. See also 7.15.

"What we look for is the conscience" [Petilian] says, "of the one who gives [the sacraments], giving in holiness, to cleanse the conscience of the one who receives. For anyone who knowingly receives 'faith' from the faithless does not receive faith, but guilt." And he will then go on to say: "so how do you test this? For everything consists of an origin" he says, "and a root; if it does not possess something as its head, it is nothing. Nor can anything truly receive a second birth, unless it is born again [*renaneretur*] from good seed."

Comment

This passage sets out clearly the Donatist concerns over the catholic view that it is not the personal qualities of the minister, but the merits of Christ, which give spiritual efficacy to the sacraments. For Petilian, how can someone who is unworthy or corrupt be allowed to administer these sacraments? And how can anyone benefit from receiving such sacraments, when they have been tainted in the process of administration?

Questions for Study

1 Summarize, in your own words, the points which Petilian makes against Augustine.
2 What point is Petilian making through the analogy of the seed?

7.6

Augustine on the Mixed Nature of the Church

Augustine of Hippo (354–430) was of the view that the church is a "mixed body," consisting of both the righteous and unrighteous. His reading of the Parable of the Tares (Matthew 13: 24–30) convinced him that the church was like a field, in which both wheat and weeds grew side by side. ("Tares" is an archaic English word for "weeds," used in the King James Version of the Bible.) They would finally be separated at the time of the harvest; in the meantime, the wheat and the weeds coexist within the same field. In this passage Augustine explores this understanding of the nature of the church using imagery from the Song of Songs. See also 7.3, 7.5, 7.18.

In the Song of Songs the Church is described as "an enclosed garden, my sister and bride, a sealed fountain, a well of living water, an orchard of choice fruit" (Song of Songs 4: 12–13). I dare not interpret this except as applying only to the holy and righteous, not to the greedy, the fraudulent, the grasping, the usurers, the drunken, or the envious. Those share a common baptism with the righteous: they do not, however, share a common charity. [...] How have they penetrated into the "enclosed garden, the sealed fountain?" As Cyprian says, they have renounced the world only in word, not in deed; and yet he admits that they are within the Church. If they are within, and form "the Bride of Christ," is this really that bride "without any blemish or wrinkle?" (Ephesians 5: 27). Is that "beautiful dove" (Song of Songs 6: 9) defiled by such a part of her members? Are those the "brambles" in the midst of which she is "like a lily?" (Song of Songs 2: 2). As a lily, she is the enclosed garden, the sealed fountain: that is, as she exists in the persons of the righteous, who are "Jews in secret, through the circumcision of the heart" (Romans 2: 29). "All the beauty of the king's daughter is within her" (Psalm 45: 13). In them is found the fixed number of the saints, foreordained before the creation of the world. That host of brambles surrounds her on the outside, above that number, whether openly or secretly separated from her. "I have proclaimed and spoken: they have been multiplied beyond number" (Psalm 40: 5). [...] There are some in that number who now live wickedly; they may even be sunk in heresies or in pagan superstitions: yet even there "The Lord knows those who belong to him" (2 Timothy 2: 19). For in the ineffable foreknowledge of God, many who seem to be outside are actually within, just as many who seem to be within are in reality outside.

Comment

The text reflects Augustine's conviction that the church is, on the one hand, separated from the world and distinguished from it; on the other hand, however, there are those within the church who seem to behave as if they really belong to the world. Augustine argues that there will always be an element of mystery here. Who is truly a believer, and who not? Purely moral criteria are not good enough. Someone's behavior is not good enough to identify them as a Christian. For Augustine, God alone is the judge and arbiter of who is a true Christian, and God's judgment on this matter cannot be fully known in advance. This idea would be developed by a number of writers, including John Calvin, who insisted that no human being was in a position to make a judgment on this matter.

Questions for Study

1 Summarize, in your own words, the point that Augustine is making in this passage.
2 "Many who seem to be outside are actually within, just as many who seem to be within are in reality outside." Locate this passage within the text. What does Augustine mean by this? What are its implications?

7.7

Leo the Great on Ministry within the Church

Writing in the middle of the fifth century, Pope Leo I (usually known as "Leo the Great," died 461) affirms that all Christian believers are sharers in the priestly office of Christ, anticipating aspects of the Reformation doctrine of the priesthood of all believers. See also 7.13, 7.25.

The sign of the cross makes all those who are born again in Christ kings, and the anointing of the Holy Spirit consecrates them all as priests. As a result, apart from the particular service of our ministry, all spiritual and rational Christians are recognized as members of this royal people and sharers in the priestly office [of Christ]. What is there that is as "royal" for a soul to govern in obedience to God as the body? And what is there that is as "priestly" as to dedicate a pure conscience to the Lord, and to offer the unstained offerings of devotion [*immaculatas pietatis hostias*] on the altar of the heart?

Comment

This important passage sets out an understanding of the role of the laity within the church in terms of their sharing in its "royal" and "priestly" attributes. The biblical passage which lies behind this text is 1 Peter 2: 9, which reads as follows: "But you are a chosen race, a royal priesthood, a holy nation, God's own people, that you may declare the wonderful deeds of him who called you out of darkness into his marvelous light." The text picks up on the idea of the church as "a royal priesthood." This biblical passage also lies behind Martin Luther's reflections on the "priesthood of all believers" (7.13).

Questions for Study

1 In what way does Leo believe that Christians are kings and priests? And how do they achieve this status?
2 Set out, in your own words, what functions Leo associates with being a "royal priesthood."

7.8

Innocent III on the Church and State

Under Innocent III, who was pope from 1198 to 1216, the medieval papacy reached a hitherto unprecedented level of political authority in western Europe. This was given theological justification in the decree *Sicut universitatis conditor*, issued in October 1198, in which Innocent III set out the principle of the subordination of the state to the church in the following way. The decree is of major importance in relation to medieval ecclesiology. See also 7.10.

Just as the creator of the universe established two great lights in the firmament of heaven (the greater one to rule the day, and the lesser one to rule the night), so he also appointed two dignitaries for the firmament of the universal church (which is referred to as "heaven"). The greater of these rules human souls (the "days"), and the lesser of them rules human bodies (the "nights"). These dignitaries are the authority of the pope and the power of the king. And just as the moon derives her light from the sun, and is inferior to the sun in terms of its size and its quality, so the power of the king derives from the authority of the pope.

Comment

This text needs to be seen against the growing authority of the pope at this important juncture in European history, and especially the increasing tendency of the papacy to act as a mediator in international disputes. The text itself represents an unambivalent assertion of the priority of ecclesiastical authority over the secular power.

Questions for Study

1 The text includes an interpretation and application of Genesis 1: 14–17. Read this passage. How does Innocent defend his interpretation of the sun and moon, and days and nights?
2 What were the practical implications of this text for church–state relations in western Europe at this time?

7.9

Thomas Aquinas on the Catholicity of the Church

In the course of his exposition of the articles of the Apostles' creed, Thomas Aquinas (c.1225–74) analyzes the concept of "catholicity," identifying three key elements of the notion. See also 7.4, 7.14, 7.29.

Concerning the third point, it is known that the church is catholic, that is, universal, first with respect to place, because it is throughout the entire world [*per totum mundum*], against the Donatists. See Romans 1: 8: "Your faith is proclaimed in all the world"; Mark 16: 15: "Go into all the world and preach the gospel to the whole creation." In ancient times, God was known only in Judea, but now throughout the entire world. This church, moreover, has three parts. One is on earth, another is in heaven, and the third is in purgatory. Secondly, the Church is universal with respect to the condition of people, because no one is rejected, whether master or slave, male or female. See Galatians 3: 28: "There is neither male nor female." Thirdly, it is universal with respect to time. For some have said that the church should last until a certain time, but this is false, because this church began from the time of Abel and will last to the end of the world. See Matthew 28: 20: "And I am with you always, to the close of the age." And after the close of the age it will remain in heaven.

Comment

The text is very clear, and requires little in the way of comment. The biblical texts which Aquinas uses to underpin his assertions should be noted, as they had by this stage become standard proof texts of the points in question. This text should be compared with Cyril of Jerusalem's exposition of the concept of the "catholicity" of the church (7.4), as it represents a development of some of his lines of thinking. The remarks on those who say that the church has only been allowed to function "until a certain time" is a reference to writers such as Joachim of Fiore, who argued that a new era in human history would begin in 1260, with the church ceasing to have its former role.

Questions for Study

1 Set out, in your own words, Aquinas's understanding of what it means to refer to the church as "catholic."
2 Find Galatians 3: 28. What use does Aquinas make of this text? And what bearing does this text have on the notion of "universality" or "catholicity"?

7.10

Boniface VIII on Papal Primacy: *Unam Sanctam*

On November 18, 1302, Pope Boniface VIII (c.1234–1303) issued the bull *Unam Sanctam*, which set out his understanding of the relation of church and state. The bull explicitly affirms the priority of the spiritual authority over the temporal authority. The bull also reaffirms the dictum, associated with Cyprian of Carthage, that "there is no salvation outside the church." See also 7.3, 7.8.

We are obliged by the faith to believe and to hold – as we do indeed firmly believe and simply confess – that the Church is one, holy, catholic, and apostolic, and that outside her there is neither salvation nor the remission of sins. [. . .] She represents the one and only mystical body whose head is Christ, and the head of Christ is God (1 Corinthians 11: 3), in whom there is one Lord, one faith, and one baptism (Ephesians 4: 5). There was only one ark of Noah at the time of the flood, prefiguring the one Church; this ark, having been finished to a single cubit, had only one helmsman and captain, that is Noah himself, and we read that, outside of this ark, all that existed on the earth was destroyed.

We honor this Church as one, the Lord having said by the mouth of the prophet: "Deliver, O God, my soul from the sword and my only one from the hand of the dog" (Psalm 22: 20). He has prayed for his soul, that is for himself, heart and body; and this body, that is to say, the Church, he has called "one" because of the unity of the Bride, the faith, the sacraments, and the charity of the Church. This is the seamless robe (*tunicum*) of the Lord, which was not torn, but for which lots were cast (John 19: 23–4). Therefore, there is one body, and one head of the one and only Church, not two heads like some monster; that is, Christ and the Vicar of Christ, Peter and the successor of Peter, since the Lord speaking to Peter himself said: "Feed my sheep" (John 21: 17) meaning, "my sheep in general," not these, nor those in particular. For this reason, we understand that he [Christ] entrusted all his people to him [Peter]. Therefore, if the Greeks or others should say that they have not been entrusted to Peter and to his successors, they must also declare that they are not the sheep of Christ, since our Lord says in John's Gospel that "there is one sheepfold and one shepherd" (John 10: 16).

We learn in the words of the gospels that in this Church and in her power there are two swords; namely, the spiritual and the temporal. [. . .] Both – that is to say, the spiritual and the material sword – therefore, are in the power of the Church; the former, however, is to be administered *for* the Church and the latter *by* the Church [*sed is quidem pro ecclesia, ille vero ab ecclesia exercendus*]; the former in the hands of the priest; the latter by the hands of kings and soldiers, but at the will and permission of the priest. However, one sword ought to be subordinated to the other, so that temporal authority is to be subjected to the spiritual power. For since the Apostle said: "There is no power except from God and the things that are ordained by God" (Romans 13: 1–2), it follows that they would not be ordained if one sword were not subordinated to the other and if the inferior one, as it were, were not led upwards by the other. [. . .] Hence we must recognize clearly that spiritual power surpasses in dignity and in nobility any temporal power whatsoever, just as spiritual things surpass the temporal. [. . .] Therefore, if the earthly authority were to err, it is to be judged by the spiritual authority; but if a lower spiritual authority were to err, it would be judged by a superior spiritual power; but if the highest authority of all were to err, it can be only judged by God, and not by human authority, according to the testimony of the Apostle: "The spiritual person judges all things, is judged by no person" (1 Corinthians 2: 15).

This authority, however (though it has been given to humanity and is exercised by humanity), is not in itself human but is rather divine, having been granted to Peter by a divine word and reaffirmed to him and his successors by the One whom Peter confessed, when the Lord spoke to Peter himself: "Whatsoever you shall bind on earth shall be bound also in Heaven" etc. (Matthew 16: 19). Therefore whoever resists this power, which has been ordained by God, resists the command of God (Romans 13: 2), unless, like Manicheus, we invent two origins of all things, which is false and judged by us to be heretical, since according to the testimony of Moses, it is not in the "beginnings" but in the "beginning" that God created heaven and earth (Genesis 1: 1).

Furthermore, we declare, proclaim, and define that it is absolutely necessary for salvation that every human creature should be subject to the Roman Pontiff.

Comment

This is an important document for the history of the relationship of church and state in western Europe in the later Middle Ages; it is also important as a powerful statement of an institutional model of the church. This idea is expressed elsewhere in this document in the Latin phrase *extra hanc domum, id est extra ecclesiam, nemo salvatur* ("outside this house, that is, outside the church, no-one is saved"), which we first noted in Origen (7.2) but was developed more fully in the writings of Cyprian of Carthage.The image of the "seamless robe" of Christ, also associated with Cyprian, is developed further here. This is based on a reference to John 19: 23–4. Cyprian argues that this "robe" or "tunic" is a type of the church; *Unam Sanctam* develops the theme further. Notice also the way in which the interaction of spiritual and temporal authority is discussed with particular reference to a series of biblical texts.

Questions for Study

1 Set out, in your own words, the way in which this text relates the authority of the church and state.
2 "Whatsoever you shall bind on earth shall be bound also in Heaven" etc. (Matthew 16: 19). Locate this text within the reading. How does Boniface interpret this statement? And how does this affect the balance of power between church and state?

7.11

Jan Hus on the Church

The issue of the doctrine of the church was debated extensively in the Middle Ages, especially by those anxious to reduce the power of the papacy or establish local or regional churches. In the early fifteenth century, the Bohemian writer Jan Hus (or "Huss," c.1372–1415) criticized the power of the pope and argued for a national church. Our text is taken from his treatise on the church, written in Latin in 1413. See also 7.12, 7.17.

[In response to what has just been said], we may go beyond what is normally reckoned to be the church, and say that the church may be defined in three ways. First, the church is defined as the congregation or convocation of the faithful [*congregacio vel convocacio fidelium*], the faithful, understood as those who are faithful in the sense of being righteous for the present. According to this definition those who are reprobate, yet who possess grace for the present, do belong in the church. But such a church is not the mystical body of Christ nor the holy catholic church nor any part of it. The second definition understands the church to contain a mixture of those who are reprobate, who possess grace and righteousness only for the present, and those who are truly predestined. This church coincides partially but not totally with the holy church of God. It is called "mixed" [*mixtim*] because it contains both grain and chaff, wheat and weeds, just as the kingdom of heaven is like a net cast into the sea which gathers up fish of all kinds, and the kingdom of heaven is like the ten virgins, five of whom were foolish and five of whom were wise. [. . .]

But the third definition understands the church as the whole convocation of those who are predestined, regardless of whether or not they are in grace or righteousness for the present. This was the definition used by the Apostle Paul when he said, "Christ loved the Church and gave Himself up for her that He might sanctify her by the washing of water with the word, that the Church might be presented before him without spot or wrinkle or any such thing, that she might be holy and without blemish" (Ephesians 5: 25–7).

Comment

In this treatise, Hus offers three definitions of the church. The first corresponds to the Donatist idea of the church as a body of perfect saints, the second to Augustine's concept of a "mixed body" of saints and sinners, and the third to a concept of the church as it will be when it is purified by God on the last day. Hus, who clearly prefers this third approach, appears to have derived it from the writings of John Wycliffe, from which this section borrows heavily. It is interesting to contrast this view of the church with that set out in *Unam Sanctam* (7.10).

Questions for Study

1 Set out, in your own words, the various models of the church which Hus considers in this passage.
2 What model of the church does Hus prefer and for what reasons?

7.12

Martin Luther on the Marks of the Church

In this treatise, first published in early modern German in 1539, Luther (1483–1546) lays down seven distinguishing marks of a true Christian church, including the preaching and hearing of the word of God; the true Christian sacraments of baptism and the sacrament of the altar; the office of the keys and ministry; proper public worship; and the bearing of the cross. The first of these is clearly the most important, and is here explored in some detail. See also 7.17.

First, this holy Christian people [*dis Christlich heilig Volck*] is to be recognized as having possession of the holy word of God, even if all do not possess it in equal measure, as St Paul says (1 Corinthians 3: 12–14). Some possess it completely purely, others not so purely. Those who possess it purely are called those who "build on the foundation with gold, silver, and precious stones"; those who do not possess it purely are those who "build on the foundation with wood, hay, and straw," and yet will be saved through fire. More than enough was said about this above. This is the main thing, and the most holy thing of all, by reason of which the Christian people are called holy; for God's word is holy and sanctifies everything it connects with; it is indeed the very holiness of God (Romans 1: 16): "It is the power of God for salvation to every one who has faith," and 1 Timothy 4: 5: "Everything is consecrated by the word of God and prayer." For the Holy Spirit himself administers it and anoints or sanctifies the Christian church with it, and not with the pope's chrism, with which he anoints or consecrates fingers, clothes, cloaks, chalices, and stones. These objects will never teach one to love God, to believe, to praise, or to be pious. They may adorn this bag of maggots [*madensack*], but afterward they fall apart and decay, along with the chrism and whatever holiness it contains, and the bag of maggots itself.

Yet this holy thing [*heiligthum*] is the true holy thing, the true anointing that anoints with eternal life, even though you may not have a papal crown or a bishop's hat, but will die bare and naked, just like children (as we all are), who are baptized naked and without any such adornment. But we are speaking of the external word, preached orally by people like you and me, for this is what Christ left behind as an external sign [*eusserlich zeichen*], by which his church, or his Christian people in the world, should be recognized. We also speak of this external word as it is sincerely believed and openly confessed before the world, as Christ says, "Every one who acknowledges me before people, I also will acknowledge before my Father and his angels" (Matthew 10: 32). There are many who know it in their hearts, but will not profess it openly. Many possess it, but do not believe in it or act on it, for the number of those who believe in and act on it is small. The parable of the seed (Matthew 13: 4–8) says that three sections of the field receive and contain the seed, but only the fourth section, the fine and good soil, bears fruit with patience.

Now, anywhere you hear or see such a word preached, believed, confessed, and acted upon [*Wo du nu solch wort hoerest odder sihest predigen, gleuben, bekennen und darnach thun*], do not doubt that the true *ecclesia sancta catholica*, a "holy Christian people" must be there, even though there are very few of them. For God's word "shall not return empty" (Isaiah 55: 11), but must possess at least a fourth or a part of the field. And even if there were no other sign than this alone, it would be enough to prove that a holy Christian people must exist there, for God's word cannot be without God's people and conversely, God's people cannot be without God's word. For who would preach the word, or hear it preached, if there were no people of God? And what could or would God's people believe, if there were no word of God?

Comment

Luther had been formally excommunicated from the Catholic church at this stage in his career. So what was the status of the group of people who gathered around Luther, and sought to promote his teaching? Did they constitute a Christian church? Or were they a heretical or schismatic gathering? To answer this question, it was essential to have a definition of the church which was not dependent upon institutional continuity with the medieval church. Luther's key theme in this passage is that, wherever the word of God is truly preached, a Christian church exists. Historical and institutional continuity with the medieval church is not a necessary component of the definition of the church. Note that a "chrism" is a form of anointing with oil.

Questions for Study

1 "Now, anywhere you hear or see such a word preached, believed, confessed, and acted upon, do not doubt that the true *ecclesia sancta catholica*, a 'holy Christian people' must be there, even though there are very few of them." Locate this text within the passage. What are its implications for Luther's program of reform?
2 What use does Luther make of the image of a "bag of maggots"?

7.13

Martin Luther on Priests and Laity

In his major reforming treatise *Appeal to the Nobility of the German Nation*, written in early modern German in 1520, Luther argues that there is no fundamental distinction in status between priests and laity. The ideas set out in this passage underlie the Protestant notion of the "priesthood of all believers." See also 7.7.

The Romanists have very cunningly built three walls around themselves, preventing any reformation. As a result, the whole of Christianity has fallen grievously. In the first place, when they have been pressed by the secular authorities, they have laid down laws which declare that the secular authority [*weltlicher gewalt*] has no rights over them; in fact, quite the reverse – the spiritual power has authority over the secular. In the second place, when someone tries to correct them on the basis of Holy Scripture, they lay down that nobody except the Pope can interpret Scripture. And in the third place, when someone threatens them with a Council, they protest that nobody can convene a Council, except the Pope. [. . .]

Let us first assault the first wall. It is an invention that the Pope, bishop, priests, and monks are called "the spiritual estate" [*geistlich stand*], while princes, lords, craftsmen, and farmers are called "the secular estate" [*weltlich stand*]. This is a spurious idea, and nobody should fear it for the following reason. All Christians truly belong to the spiritual estate, and there is no difference among them apart from their office [*ampt*]. [...] We all have one baptism, one gospel, one faith, and are all alike Christians, in that it is baptism, gospel, and faith which alone make us spiritual and a Christian people. [...] We are all consecrated priests through baptism, as St Peter says: "You are a royal priesthood and a priestly kingdom" (1 Peter 2: 9). [...]

So a bishop's consecration is nothing other than this: in the place and stead of the whole congregation [*der gantzen samlung*], who all alike have the same power, he takes a person and authorizes him to exercise this power on behalf of the others. [...]

Since the secular power has been baptized with this same baptism, and has the same faith and the same gospel as the remainder of us, we must concede that they are priests and bishops, and must accept their office as one which has a lawful and useful place in the Christian community [*gemeyne*]. [...] Therefore someone who bears the status of a priest [*ein priester stand*] is nothing other than an officeholder [*amptman*]. He takes priority for as long as he holds this office; when he is deposed, he becomes a peasant or citizen like all the others. It is thus most true that a priest is never a priest when he has been deposed. But now the Romanists have invented the idea of *characteres indelebiles*, and prattle on about a deposed priest being different from an ordinary lay person. [...]

It follows from this that there is no basic true difference between lay people, priests, princes, and bishops, between the spiritual and the secular, except for their office and work [*den des ampts odder wercks halben*] and not on the basis of their status (*stand*). All are of the spiritual estate, and all are truly priests, bishops, and popes, although they are not the same in terms of their individual work.

Comment

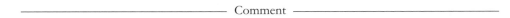

This passage sets out the idea now generally known as the "priesthood of all believers." All Christians are priests by virtue of their baptism, faith, and the gospel – a doctrine which is often referred to as the "priesthood of all believers." The only distinction that can be recognized between them relates to the different "office" or "function" (*ampt*) and "work" or "responsibility" (*werck*) with which they are entrusted. Notice that Luther is quite clear that, once priests retire or are dismissed, they revert to the role of lay people. The contrast with the views set out in *Unam Sanctam* (7.10) is especially significant. Note that the term *characteres indelebiles* (indelible characters) refers to the medieval teaching that an ordained priest is permanently and irreversibly marked with the nature and dignity of priesthood.

Questions for Study

1. Set out, in your own words, what Luther means when he refers to the clergy of the church as "office-holders." Office-holders can be fired. What conclusions might Luther draw from this about the status of clergy?
2. Does Luther intend to abolish a professional ministry within the church? If not, what changes did he wish to introduce?

7.14

Philip Melanchthon on the Nature of Catholicity

In this treatise on the use of the word "catholic," the German Lutheran writer Philip Melanchthon (1497–1560) emphasizes the importance of doctrinal correctness as its defining element. Although the church may be dispersed throughout the world, it nevertheless remains universally faithful to the same teaching. See also 7.4, 7.7, 7.29.

What does "catholic" mean? It means the same as universal. *Kath' holou* means "universally" and "in general." [...] throughout all ages from the beginning until the very end. [...] It is one thing to be called catholic, something else to be catholic in reality. Those are truly called catholic who accept the doctrine of the truly catholic church, i.e., that which is supported by the witness of all time, of all ages, which believes what the prophets and apostles taught, and which does not tolerate factions, heresies, and heretical assemblies. We must all be catholic, i.e., accept this word which the rightly thinking church holds, separate from, and unentangled with, sects warring against that Word.

Comment

The text is very clear, and needs little comment. Melanchthon's concern is to explore the meaning of the term "catholicity," while at the same time insisting that the churches of the Reformation have every right to use this term to refer to themselves, despite having broken away from the medieval catholic church. The Greek phrase *kath' holou*, used extensively in this context, means something like "according to the whole."

Questions for Study

1 Why does Melanchthon place such emphasis on the notion of theological correctness in this passage?
2 What rival conceptions of "catholicity" do you think Melanchthon wishes to oppose?

7.15

Sebastian Franck on the True Church

The Radical Reformation, here represented by Sebastian Franck (c.1499–c.1542), was severely critical of any attempt to invest the patristic period with theological or ecclesiological significance. In a letter originally written in Latin in 1531, only fragments of which have survived, Franck sets out the characteristic radical view that the true church ceased to exist after the apostles. See also 7.3, 7.11.

I maintain, against all the doctors, that all external things which were in use in the church of the apostles have been abolished [*abrogata*], and none of them are to be restored or reinstituted, even though they have gone beyond their authorization or calling and attempted to restore these fallen sacraments [*lapsa sacramenta*]. For the church will remain scattered among the heathen until the end of the world. Indeed, the Antichrist and his church will only be defeated and swept away at the coming of Christ, who will gather together in his kingdom Israel, which has been scattered to the four corners of the world. [...] The works [of those who understood this] have been suppressed as godless heresies and rantings, and pride of place has instead been given to foolish Ambrose, Augustine, Jerome, Gregory – of whom not even one knew Christ, nor was sent by God to teach. But rather all were and shall remain the apostles of Antichrist. [...] Since experience teaches us that the power of the churches and all external things have fallen into decay, and that this church is dispersed among the heathen, it is my definite opinion that no persons on earth (unless they have received a personal divine call to do so) can gather this dispersed church together again or bring its concealed rites [*obruta symbola*] back into the light again. [...] The external things of the church ought not to be re-established unless Christ himself commands it.

Comment

This passage can be seen as a classic Radical Reformation critique of any institutional definition of the church, as well as those who hold that patristic writers, such as Augustine, can be regarded as theological authorities today. Franck is here criticizing both the doctrines of the church associated with the papacy, and reformers such as Luther. Franck's frequent reference to "external things" (*externa*) is a reference to external ceremonies, including the sacraments, which he regards as being "fallen" (*lapsus*). The true church will only come into being at the end of time, when Christ returns in glory to gather the scattered people of his church into his kingdom. Until then, the true church will remain concealed.

Questions for Study

1 Why is Franck so critical of patristic writers such as Ambrose and Augustine?
2 Franck prefers to speak of the future "restoration" of the church, rather than its present "reformation." Does this passage help us to understand why?

7.16

The First Helvetic Confession on the Nature of the Church

The First Helvetic Confession, which was written in Swiss-German in 1536, set out an early Reformed view of the church, which placed emphasis on the importance of outward signs of church ordering and government. See also 7.12, 7.15, 7.17.

A holy, universal Church is, we affirm, built and gathered together from living stones built upon this living rock [Christ]. It is the fellowship and congregation of all saints which is Christ's bride and spouse, and which He washes with His blood and finally presents to the Father without blemish or any stain. And although this Church and congregation of Christ [*dise kilchen und samlung Christi*] is only open and known to God's eyes, yet it is not only known but also gathered and built up by visible signs, rites, and ordinances, which Christ Himself has instituted and appointed by the Word of God as a universal, public, and orderly discipline. Without these marks (speaking generally and without a special permission revealed by God) no one is numbered with this Church.

Comment

This text takes up the Reformation idea that the church is the community which is brought into being by the Word of God, and is sustained by teaching and preaching. Note the emphasis placed upon the church as founded upon and grounded in Christ, and the absence of any suggestion that the church is an institution defined by certain structures.

Questions for Study

1 Locate all the references to Christ in this passage. In what way does this text link the church to Christ?
2 What are the "marks" by which a church is defined, according to this passage?

7.17

John Calvin on the Marks of the Church

John Calvin (1509–64) here defines the essential features or "marks" of the true church as the preaching of the Word of God, and the proper administration of the sacraments. This definition became widely accepted within the mainline Reformation. Calvin argues that a degree of failure or diversity on other matters may be permitted, providing that these two essential features are present. See also 7.12, 7.18, 7.19.

Wherever we see the Word of God purely preached and listened to, and the sacraments administered according to Christ's institution, it is in no way to be doubted that a church of God exists. For his promise cannot fail: "Wherever two or three are gathered in my name, there I am in the midst of them" (Matthew 18: 20). [...] If the ministry has the Word and honors it, if it has the administration of the sacraments, it deserves without doubt to be held and considered a church. For it is certain that such things are not without fruit. In this way the unity of the universal church is preserved, which diabolical spirits have always tried to tear apart; and we do not deny authority to those lawful assemblies which have been set up in accordance with the opportunities of different places in mind [*pro locorum opportunitate distributi sunt*].

We have identified that the distinguishing marks of the church are the preaching of the Word and the observance of the sacraments. These can never happen without bringing forth fruit and prospering through God's blessing. I do not say that wherever the Word is preached there will be immediate results, but that wherever it is received and takes root [*statam habere sedem*], it shows its effectiveness. When the preaching of the gospel is reverently heard and the sacraments are not neglected, there for the time being no false or ambiguous form [*facies*] of the church is seen; and no one is permitted to ignore its authority, flout its warnings, resist its counsels, or make light of its chastisements – much less to break away from it and wreck its unity. For the Lord values the fellowship of his church so highly that all those who arrogantly leave any Christian society (provided that it holds fast to the true ministry of Word and sacraments) are regarded by him as deserters. He so values the authority of the church that when it is violated he believes that his own authority has been diminished. [...]

When we say that the pure ministry of the Word and pure mode of celebrating the sacraments are a sufficient pledge and guarantee by which we may recognize as a church any society, we mean where both these marks exist, it is not to be rejected, even if it is riddled with faults in other respects [*etiamsi multis alioqui vitiis scateat*]. What is more, some shortcoming may find its way into the administration of either doctrine or sacraments, but this ought not to estrange us from communion with this church. For not all articles of true doctrine are of equal weight. Some are so necessary to know that they should be certain and unquestioned by everyone as proper to religion, such as: God is one; Christ is God and the Son of God; our salvation rests in God's mercy; and the like. There are other [articles of doctrine] disputed among the churches which still do not break the unity of faith. [. . .] I am not condoning error, no matter how insignificant it may be, nor do I wish to encourage it. But I am saying that we should not desert a church on account of some minor disagreement, if it upholds sound doctrine over the essentials of piety, and maintains the use of the sacraments established by the Lord.

Comment

This passage maintains and develops the Reformation view that the church is not defined by institutional continuity with the apostolic church, but by upholding the teaching of the apostles, as found in the New Testament. Note that Calvin stresses that the foundations of a true Christian church are ultimately theological, rather than historical. Where the word of God is truly preached, and the sacraments properly administered, a true Christian church exists. Note also Calvin's willingness to tolerate disagreement on issues which are not essential to Christian integrity.

Questions for Study

1 What, according to Calvin, are the two defining characteristics of a Christian church?
2 Why does Calvin consider preaching to be of such importance in determining whether a true church exists?

7.18

Richard Hooker on the Purity of the Church

In this passage, published in 1594, the English writer Richard Hooker (c.1554–1600) defends an Augustinian view of the visible church, which he distinguished from the "mystical" or invisible church. The passage can be regarded as a theological defense of the existence and establishment of the Church of England at this time, as a result of the Elizabethan "Settlement of Religion" of 1559. See also 7.5, 7.15, 7.17.

7. [. . .] We speak now of the visible Church, whose children are signed with this mark, "One Lord, one Faith, one Baptism". In whomsoever these things are, the

Church doth acknowledge them for her children; them only she holdeth for aliens and strangers, in whom these things are not found. For want of these it is that Saracens, Jews and Infidels are excluded out of the bounds of the Church. Others we may not deny to be of the visible Church, as long as these things are not wanting in them. For apparent it is, that all men are of necessity either Christians or not Christians. If by external profession they be Christians, then are they of the visible Church of Christ: and Christians by external profession they are all, whose mark of recognizance hath in it those things which we have mentioned, yea, although they be impious idolaters, wicked heretics, persons excommunicable, yea, and cast out for notorious improbity. Such withal we deny not to be the imps and limbs of Satan, even as long as they continue such.

8. Is it then possible, that the selfsame men should belong to the synagogue of Satan and to the Church of Jesus Christ? Unto that Church which is his mystical body, not possible; because that body consisteth of none but only true Israelites, true sons of Abraham, true servants and saints of God. Howbeit of the visible body and Church of Jesus Christ those may be and oftentimes are, in respect of the main parts of their outward profession, who in regard of their inward disposition of mind, yea, of external conversation, yea, even of some parts of their very profession, are most worthily hateful in the sight of God himself, and in the eyes of the sounder part of the visible Church most execrable. Our Saviour therefore compareth the kingdom of heaven to a net, whereunto all which cometh neither is nor seemeth fish (Matthew 13: 47): his Church he compareth to a field, where tares manifestly known and seen by all men do grow intermingled with good corn (Matthew 13: 24), and even so shall continue till the final consummation of the world. God hath ever and ever shall have some Church visible upon earth. When the people of God worshipped the calf in the wilderness, when they adored the brazen serpent (2 Kings 18: 4), when they bowed their knees to Baal, when they burned incense and offered sacrifice unto idols [. . .] Howbeit retaining the law of God and the holy seal of his covenant, and sheep of his visible flock they continued even in the depth of their disobedience and rebellion.

Comment

Hooker adopts a series of biblical images used originally by Augustine – such as the net with a variety of fish, and the field in which grew both wheat and "tares" (an older English word for "weeds") – to bring out the mixed character of the visible church. For this reason, Hooker insists that perfect holiness of life is not a "mark" or defining characteristic of the church, which is defined instead by its doctrine and sacraments.

Questions for Study

1 What use does Hooker make of the Parable of the Tares in this passage?
2 "If by external profession they be Christians, then are they of the visible Church of Christ." Locate this statement within the passage. What does Hooker mean by this? What conclusions does he draw from it?

7.19

The Westminster Confession of Faith on the Church

This important Reformed Confession of Faith, drawn up in London in 1643, sets out a Reformed view of the church, which makes a distinction between the "invisible" and "visible" church. Note how the individual "particular churches" are to be judged in terms of their doctrine and sacraments, rather than the morals of their members. See also 7.4, 7.12, 7.17.

The catholic or universal church, which is invisible, consists of the whole number of the elect that have been, are, or shall be gathered into one, under Christ the head thereof. [. . .] The visible church, which is also catholic or universal under the gospel (not confined to one nation as before under the law), consists of all those throughout the world that profess the true religion, together with their children. [. . .] Unto this catholic visible church, Christ hath given the ministry, oracles, and ordinances of God, for the gathering and perfecting of the saints in this life, to the end of the world; and doth by his own presence and Spirit, according to his promise, make them effectual thereunto. [. . .] Particular churches, which are members [of this catholic church] are more or less pure, according as the doctrine of the gospel is taught and embraced, ordinances administered, and public worship performed more or less purely in them. The purest churches under heaven are subject both to mixture and error; and some have so degenerated as to become apparently no churches of Christ. Nevertheless, there shall always be a church on earth, to worship God according to his will.

Comment

By the time of the Westminster Confession it was clear that the use of the word "catholic" was beginning to cause some difficulties. In seventeenth-century England it was becoming increasingly common to regard "catholic" and "Roman Catholic" as synonymous. To avoid misunderstandings, many Protestant writers began to use the word "universal" in their discussions of the catholicity of the church; this practice can be seen reflected in the present passage. Notice that the use of the word "catholic" is not abandoned. The passage defends a generally Augustinian view of the church.

Questions for Study

1 Why does the Confession concede that even the "purest churches" have been subject to "mixture and error"?
2 Set out, in your own words, the distinction made within this passage between the "visible" and "invisible" church. Why do you think this distinction is important?

7.20

John Owen on the Nature of a Gospel Church

In this statement on the "nature of a gospel church," which had considerable influence within contemporary Puritanism, John Owen (1616–83) sets out the distinguishing characteristics of such a church, which gained widespread assent within English and American Puritanism. Note how the church is understood to be a body which has separated from the world, and whose members are distinguished by their explicit public profession of faith, and their holiness of life. See also 7.3, 7.5, 7.12, 7.15, 7.16, 7.17, 7.18, 7.19, 7.24.

The church may be considered either as unto its *essence*, constitution and being, or as unto its *power* and *order*, when it is organized. As unto its essence and being, its constituent parts are its *matter* and *form*. These we must inquire into.

By the matter of the church, we understand the persons whereof the church doth consist, with their qualifications; and by its form, the reason, cause, and way of that kind of relation among them which gives them the being of a church, and therewithal an interest in all that belongs unto a church, either privilege or power, as such.

Our first inquiry being concerning what sort of persons our Lord Jesus Christ requireth and admitteth to be the visible subjects of his kingdom, we are to be regulated in our determination by respect unto his honour, glory, and the holiness of his rule. To reckon such persons to be subjects of Christ, members of his body, such as he requires and owns (for others are not so), who would not be tolerated, at least not approved, in a well-governed kingdom or commonwealth of the world, is highly dishonourable unto him. [. . .] But it is so come to pass, that let men be never so notoriously and flagitiously wicked, until they become pests of the earth, yet are they esteemed to belong to the church of Christ; and not only so, but it is thought little less than schism to forbid them the communion of the church in all its sacred privileges. Howbeit, the Scripture doth in general represent the kingdom or church of Christ to consist of persons called *saints*, separated from the world, with many other things of an alike nature, as we shall see immediately. And if the honour of Christ were of such weight with us as it ought to be, – if we understood aright the nature and ends of his kingdom, and that the peculiar glory of it above all the kingdoms in the world consists in the holiness of its subjects, such a holiness as the world in its wisdom knoweth not – we would duly consider whom we avow to belong thereunto. Those who know aught of these things will not profess that persons openly profane, vicious, sensual, wicked, and ignorant, are approved and owned of Christ as the subjects of his kingdom, or that it is his will that we should receive them into the communion of the church, 2 Timothy 3: 1–5. But an old opinion of the unlawfulness of separation from a church on the account of the mixture of wicked men in it is made a scarecrow to frighten men from attempting the reformation of the greatest evils, and a covert for the composing churches of such members only.

Some things, therefore, are to be premised unto what shall be offered unto the right stating of this inquiry; as –

1. That if there be no more required of any, as unto *personal qualifications*, in a visible, uncontrollable profession, to constitute them subjects of Christ's kingdom and members of his church, Ezekiel 22: 26, but what is required by the most righteous and severe laws of men to constitute a good subject or citizen, the distinction between his visible kingdom and the kingdoms of the world, as unto the principal causes of it, is utterly lost. Now, all negative qualifications, as, that men are not oppressors, drunkards, revilers, swearers, adulterers, etc., are required hereunto; but yet it is so fallen out that generally more is required to constitute such a citizen as shall represent the righteous laws he liveth under than to constitute a member of the church of Christ.

2. That whereas *regeneration* is expressly required in the gospel to give a right and privilege unto an entrance into the church or kingdom of Christ, John 3: 3, Titus 3: 3–5, whereby that kingdom of his is distinguished from all other kingdoms in and of the world, unto an interest wherein never any such thing was required, it must of necessity be something better, more excellent and sublime, than any thing the laws and polities of men pretend unto or prescribe. Wherefore it cannot consist in any outward rite, easy to be observed by the worst and vilest of men. Besides, the Scripture gives us a description of it in opposition unto its consisting in any such rite, 1 Peter 3: 21; and many things required unto good citizens are far better than the mere observation of such a rite.

3. Of this regeneration baptism is the symbol, the sign, the expression, and representation, John 3: 5; Acts 2: 38; 1 Peter 3: 21. Wherefore, unto those who are in a due manner partakers of it, it giveth all the external rights and privileges which belong unto them that are regenerate, until they come unto such seasons wherein the personal performance of those duties whereon the continuation of the estate of visible regeneration doth depend is required of them. Herein if they fail, they lose all privilege and benefit by their baptism. [. . .] Verily it profiteth, if a man stand unto the terms of the covenant which is tendered therein between God and his soul, for it will give him a right unto all the outward privileges of a regenerate state; but if he do not, as in the sight of God, his baptism is no baptism, as unto the real communication of grace and

acceptance with him, Philippians 3: 18–19; Titus 1: 15–16. So, in the sight of the church, it is no baptism, as unto a participation of the external rights and privileges of a regenerate state.

4. God alone is judge concerning this regeneration, as unto its *internal, real principle and state* in the souls of men, Acts 15: 8, Revelation 2: 23, whereon the participation of all the spiritual advantages of the covenant of grace doth depend. The church is judge of its evidences and fruits in their external demonstration, as unto a participation of *the outward privileges of a regenerate state*, and no farther, Acts 8: 13. And we shall hereon briefly declare what belongs unto the forming of a right judgment herein, and who are to be esteemed fit members of any gospel church-state, or have a right so to be:

1. Such as from whom we are obliged to *withdraw* or *withhold communion* can be no part of the matter constituent of a church, or are not meet members for the first constitution of it. [. . .] But such are all habitual sinners, those who, having prevalent habits and inclinations unto sins of any kind unmortified, do walk according unto them. Such are profane swearers, drunkards, fornicators, covetous, oppressors, and the like, "who shall not inherit the kingdom of God," 1 Corinthians 6: 9–11. [. . .] As a man living and dying in any known sin, that is, habitually, without repentance, cannot be saved, so a man known to live in sin cannot regularly be received into any church. To compose churches of habitual sinners, and that either as unto sins of commission or sins of omission, is not to erect temples to Christ, but chapels unto the devil.

2. Such as, being in the fellowship of the church, are to be *admonished of any scandalous sin*, which if they repent not of they are to be cast out of the church, are not meet members for the original constitution of a church, Matthew 18: 15–18; 1 Corinthians 5: 11. This is the state of them who abide obstinate in any known sin, whereby they have given offence unto others, without a professed repentance thereof, although they have not lived in it habitually.

3. They are to be such as *visibly answer* the description given of gospel churches in the Scripture, so as the titles assigned thereto unto the members of such churches may on good grounds be appropriated unto them. To compose churches of such persons as do not visibly answer the character given of what they were of old, and what they were always to be by virtue of the law of Christ or gospel constitution, is not church edification but destruction. And those who look on the things spoken of all church-members of old, as that they were saints by calling, lively stones in the house of God, justified and sanctified, separated from the world, etc., as those which were in them, and did indeed belong unto them, but even deride the necessity of the same things in present church-members, or the application of them unto those who are so, are themselves no small part of that woeful degeneracy which Christian religion is fallen under. Let it then be considered what is spoken of the church of the Jews in their dedication unto God, as unto their typical holiness, with the application of it unto Christian churches in real holiness, 1 Peter 2: 5, 9, with the description given of them constantly in the Scripture, as faithful, holy, believing, as the house of God, as his temple wherein he dwells by his Spirit, as the body of Christ united and compacted by the communication of the Spirit unto them, as also what is said concerning their ways, walkings, and duties, and it will be uncontrollably evident of what sort our church-members ought to be. [. . .]

4. They must be such as do *make an open profession of the subjection of their souls and consciences unto the authority of Christ in the gospel, and their readiness to yield obedience unto all his commands*, Romans 10: 10; 2 Corinthians 8: 5. [. . .] This, I suppose, will not be denied; for not only doth the Scripture make this profession necessary unto the participation of any benefit or privilege of the gospel, but the nature of the things themselves requires indispensably that so it should be: for nothing can be more unreasonable than that men should be taken into the privileges attending obedience unto the laws and commands of Christ, without avowing or professing that obedience.

Comment

This is one of the most important statements within the Puritan literature of an approach to the doctrine of the church which resisted a close link between the English church and state. Notice how Owen stresses the importance of both right faith and personal discipline as marks of both a true Christian believer and a true Christian church. Although Puritanism is rightly regarded as representing a form of Reformed theology, Owen's understanding of the nature of the church appears somewhat stricter than that envisaged by the Westminster Confession of Faith (7.19).

Questions for Study

1 How would Owen respond to the arguments of Augustine (7.6) and Richard Hooker (7.18) to the effect that a visible church includes both saints and sinners?
2 Owen makes an extensive appeal to the concept of "regeneration." What does he understand by this idea? And how does he use it in his discussion of the nature of the church and its sacraments, especially baptism?

7.21

F. D. E. Schleiermacher on the Church as a Fellowship of Believers

In this analysis of the nature and function of the church, originally published in German in 1834, Schleiermacher (1768–1834) explores the relation between those who are regenerate and the community of faith. See also 7.6.

All that comes to exist in the world through redemption is embraced in the fellowship of believers, within which all regenerate people are always found. This section, therefore, contains the doctrine of the Christian Church.

In reckoning the two expressions – the fellowship of believers and the Christian Church – as equivalent, our proposition seems to be in opposition to the Roman Symbol; but neither earlier versions of the latter nor the Nicene Creed know anything of using the two side by side yet with a distinction. What is evident is that fellowship may be taken in a narrower or a wider sense. For, if the regenerate find themselves already within it, they must have belonged to it even before regeneration, though obviously in a different sense from actual believers.

If this were not so, no accession to or extension of the Church could be imagined except by an absolute breach of continuity – that is, in a way unknown to history. But the truth is that the new life of each individual springs from that of the community, while the life of the community springs from no other individual life than that of the Redeemer. We must therefore hold that the totality of those who live in the state of sanctification is the inner fellowship; the totality of those on whom preparatory grace is at work is the outer fellowship, from which by regeneration members pass to the inner, and then keep helping to extend the wider circle. It would, however, be quite a novel and merely confusing use of terms to try to assign the two expressions in question respectively to the two forms of fellowship.

Further, no particular form of fellowship is here definitely asserted or excluded; every form, perfect and imperfect, that has ever been or that may yet appear, is included. This, and this only, is assumed, that wherever regenerate persons are within reach of each other, some kind of fellowship between them is bound to arise. For if they are in contact, their witness to the faith must in part overlap, and must necessarily involve mutual recognition and a common understanding as to their operation within the common area. What was stated at the beginning of our treatment of the consciousness of grace, namely, that it always proceeds from a common life, was meant exclusively in this far-reaching sense; but now that very statement finds for the first time its full explanation. For if, when regenerate, we did not find ourselves already within a common life, but had to set out to discover or constitute it, that would mean that just the most decisive of all the works of grace was not based on a life in common. [. . .]

The Christian self-consciousness expressed in our proposition is the general form, determined by our faith in Christ, taken by our fellow-feeling with human things and circumstances. This becomes all the clearer if we combine with it the corresponding negative expression. For if, leaving redemption out of account, the world is, relatively to humanity, the place of original perfection of men and things which yet has become the place of sin and evil; and if, with the appearance of Christ a new thing has entered the world, the antithesis of the old; it follows that only that part of the world which is united to the Christian Church is for us the place of attained perfection, or of the good, and – relatively to quiescent self-consciousness – the place of blessedness. This is so, not in virtue of the original perfection of human nature and the natural order, though of course it is thus conditioned, but in virtue solely of the sinless perfection and blessedness which has come in with Christ and communicates itself through him. With this goes the converse; that the world, so far as it is outside this fellowship of Christ, is always, in spite of that original perfection, the place of evil and sin. No one, therefore, can be surprised to find at this point the proposition that salvation or blessedness cannot enter from without, but can be found within the Church only by being brought into existence there, the Church alone saves. For the rest, it is self-evident that the antithesis between what is realized in the world by redemption and all the rest of the world is acute in proportion to the completeness with which the peculiar dignity of Christ and the full content of redemption is apprehended. It disappears or loses itself in a vague distinction between better and worse only where the contrast between Christ and sinful man is similarly obliterated or toned down.

This, too, affords the best proof that our proposition is simply an utterance of the Christian self-consciousness. For if the Christian Church were in its essential nature an object of outward perception, that perception might be passed on without involving attachment to the fellowship. But the fact is that those who do not share our faith in Christ do not recognize the Christian fellowship in its antithesis to the world. Wherever the feeling of need of redemption is entirely suppressed, the Christian Church is misconstrued all round; and the two attitudes develop *pari passu*. With the first stirrings of preparatory grace in consciousness, there comes a presentiment of the divine origin of the Christian Church; and with a living faith in Christ awakens also a belief that the Kingdom of God is actually present in the fellowship of believers. On the other hand, an unalterable hostility to the Christian Church is symptomatic of the highest stage of insusceptibility to redemption; and this hostility hardly admits even of outward reverence for the person of Christ. But faith in the Christian Church as the Kingdom of God not only implies that it will ever endure in antithesis to the world, but also – the fellowship having grown to such dimensions out of small beginnings, and being inconceivable except as ever at work – contains the hope that the Church will increase and the world opposed to it decrease. For the incarnation of Christ means for human nature in general what regeneration is for the individual. And just as sanctification is the progressive domination of the various functions, coming with time to consist less and less of fragmentary details and more and more to be a whole, with all its parts integrally connected and lending mutual support, so too the fellowship organizes itself here also out of the separate redemptive activities and becomes more and more co-operative and interactive. This organization must increasingly overpower the unorganized mass to which it is opposed.

Comment

Schleiermacher lived through a period of considerable religious turbulence in Prussia, in which questions of church and state became increasingly contentious. This tension is reflected in his discussion of the nature of the church, which sidesteps the question of how the church should relate to the state. Instead, we find a cautious discussion of the nature of the church as a community of believers. Note that the term "Symbol" here means something like "statement of faith."

Questions for Study

1 "No particular form of fellowship is here definitely asserted or excluded; every form, perfect and imperfect, that has ever been or that may yet appear, is included."

What does Schleiermacher mean by this? And how do you think this relates to the ecclesiastical controversies which were going on around Schleiermacher at the time?

2 What specific role does Schleiermacher ascribe to the church?

7.22

The First Vatican Council on Papal Primacy in the Church

The First Vatican Council met to consolidate the position and teachings of the Roman Catholic Church at a time of crisis and uncertainty, largely brought about by political and social developments in Europe. The position of the Roman Catholic Church appeared increasingly insecure. Part of the achievement of Vatican I was the reassertion of the authority of the church. "The First Dogmatic Constitution of the Church," also known as *Pastor Aeternus*, from which this extract is taken, was drawn up during the fourth session of the Council, on July 18, 1870. It includes the famous declaration on papal infallibility. See also 7.8, 7.10.

1. We teach and declare that, according to the testimony of the gospels, a primacy of jurisdiction over the whole church of God was immediately and directly promised to the blessed apostle Peter, and that this was conferred on him by Christ the Lord. It was to Simon alone – to whom the Lord had already said "You shall be called Cephas" (John 1: 42) – that the Lord spoke these words, after [Peter's] confession, "You are the Christ, the son of the living God":

> Blessed are you, Simon Bar-Jona. For flesh and blood has not revealed this to you, but my Father who is in heaven. And I tell you, you are Peter, and on this rock I will build my church, and the gates of the underworld shall not prevail against it. I will give you the keys of the kingdom of heaven, and whatever you bind on earth shall be bound in heaven, and whatever you loose on earth shall be loosed in heaven.
>
> *(Matthew 16: 16–19)*

And it was to Peter alone that Jesus, after his resurrection, entrusted the jurisdiction of the supreme pastor and ruler [*pastor et rector*] of his whole flock, saying: "Feed my lambs" and "feed my sheep" (John 21: 15).

The distorted opinions of those who misrepresent the form of government which Christ the Lord established in his church, and who deny that Peter, in preference to the rest of the apostles (singly or collectively) was endowed by Christ with a true and proper primacy of jurisdiction are in total opposition to this completely clear teaching of the Holy Scriptures, as it has always been understood by the catholic church. The same may be said of those who assert that this primacy was not conferred immediately and directly on Peter himself, but rather on the church, and that it was through the church that it was transmitted to him in his capacity as her minister.

Canon: Therefore, if anyone says that Peter the apostle was not appointed by Christ the Lord as the head [*princeps*] of all the apostles and visible head of the whole church militant; or that this was only a primacy of honor, and not one of true and proper jurisdiction, that he directly and immediately received from our lord Jesus Christ himself: let that person be condemned. [. . .]

4. [. . .] The Roman pontiffs, as the circumstances of the time or the state of affairs may indicate, may define certain things which, through God's aid, they knew to be in keeping with Holy Scripture and the apostolic traditions, as doctrines which must be held. This may be done from time to time by summoning ecumenical councils, or consulting the opinion of the churches scattered throughout the world. At some times it may be achieved by special synods; at others by taking advantage of other useful means made available by divine providence.

For the Holy Spirit was promised to the successors of Peter not so that they might, by his revelation, make known some new doctrine, but rather that, by his assistance, they might guard as sacred and faithfully expound the revelation or deposit of faith passed down by the apostles. Indeed, their apostolic teaching was embraced by all the venerable fathers, and honored and followed by all the holy orthodox teachers, for they knew that the see of St Peter must always remain unblemished by any error, in accordance with the divine promise of our Lord and Savior to the chief of his disciples: "I have prayed for you that your faith may not fail; and when you have turned again, strengthen your brethren" (Luke 22: 32).

This gift of truth and unfailing faith was therefore divinely conferred on Peter and his successors in this see, so that they might discharge their exalted office for the salvation of all people, and so that the whole flock of Christ might be kept away by them from the poisonous food of error, and be nourished with the sustenance of heavenly doctrine. Thus the tendency to schism is removed and the whole church is preserved in unity, and, resting on its foundation, can stand firm against the gates of hell.

But since in this very age when the sound influence of the apostolic office is most especially needed, and when some are to be found who disparage its authority, we judge it absolutely necessary to affirm solemnly the prerogative which the only-begotten Son of God was pleased to attach to the supreme pastoral office.

Therefore, faithfully adhering to the tradition received from the beginning of the Christian faith, to the glory of God our Savior, for the exaltation of the catholic religion and for the salvation of Christian people, with the approval of the sacred council, we teach and define as a divinely revealed dogma that when the Roman pontiff speaks *ex cathedra* (that is, when he defines a doctrine concerning faith or morals to be held by the whole church in the exercise of his office as shepherd and teacher of all Christians, by virtue of his supreme apostolic authority), he possesses, by the divine assistance promised to him in Peter, that infallibility which the divine

Redeemer willed his church to enjoy in defining doctrine concerning faith or morals. Therefore, such definitions of the Roman pontiff are of themselves, and not by the consent of the church, irreformable.

Canon: So then, should anyone, which God forbid, have the effrontery to reject this definition of ours: let this person be condemned.

Comment

This is one of the most important ecclesiological statements of the modern era, and deserves close study. The text concerns not merely the authority of the church, but also the specific role of the pope, as the successor of Peter, within that church. The text, making veiled references to the political uncertainties of the time, makes it clear that the church remains unmoved by the uncertainties of the day; it is a divinely established institution, charged with the responsibility of defining and defending catholic truth.

Questions for Study

1 What understanding of the role of the pope is set forth in this document? And how is this developed and defended?
2 How is the concept of "papal infallibility" defined? What are its implications?

7.23

Henry Barclay Swete on the Apostolicity of the Church

The later nineteenth century saw considerable interest in discussion of the doctrine of the church within England. In part, this reflected an awareness of the need to offer a definition of the distinctive position of the Church of England which went beyond the simple fact of its establishment as the English national church. In part, the re-establishment of Roman Catholicism within England occasioned a new interest in clarifying the position of the two churches. In this passage, H. B. Swete (1835–1917), Regius Professor of Divinity at Cambridge University, explores what it means to assert that the church is "apostolic." See also 2.2, 2.5, 2.10.

The Catholic Church is Apostolic in three respects: as planted in the world by the Apostles; as adhering to the teaching of the Apostles; as carrying on the succession of Apostolic ministry.

(1) Before the Ascension our Lord charged the Apostles with the work of preaching the Gospel in Judaea and Samaria and to the uttermost part of the earth. This evangelization of Judaea and Samaria was carried out by the Twelve and their company, as the Acts relate; the Gentile missions, so far as the West was concerned, fell chiefly into other hands. But the mission of St Paul was undertaken with the full approval of the original Apostolate, and was in fact a fulfilment of a part of their task with which they were themselves not qualified to deal. By agreement and fellowship with St Paul the Twelve "were enabled to feel that they were in effect carrying out through him that extension of their sphere which it is incredible that they should ever have dismissed from their minds". Thus Gentile Christendom was ultimately of Apostolic planting, even if we limit the Apostolic college to the Twelve. The churches founded by St Paul and his associates were Apostolic foundations, not only because St Paul was an Apostle, but because his work was done with the concurrence of the original Apostles.

As Tertullian points out in the passage already quoted, not all the churches of his day owed their origin either to the Twelve or to St Paul. After the end of the Apostolic age, and the passing of all their immediate disciples, new Christian brotherhoods sprang up in regions hitherto unevangelized. The same process is going forward at this present time through the missionary labours of the modern Church. Do these churches partake the apostolicity which the Creed attributes to the Catholic Church? The African father answers that they do, if they inherit the Apostolic doctrine.

(2) The earliest converts, it is noted in Acts, "continued steadfastly in the Apostles' teaching" (Acts 2: 42). On their teaching and the teaching of St Paul there was built up a tradition, or as the Pastorals put it, a " 'deposit' was formed, which remained as an abiding treasure of the Church" (2 Thessalonians 2: 15; 3: 6). Its substance was known as the "rule of faith", and found expression in the early creeds. This Apostolic tradition was held to be preserved with especial purity in churches which could claim Apostolic founders, and more particularly in the Roman church, which had for its founders both St Peter and St Paul. But, in fact, the whole Catholic Church in all parts of the world possessed one and the same faith of Apostolic origin. The tradition was not simply oral; it was embodied also in the Apostolic writings, which by the end of the second century had been collected into a New Testament or "Instrument." Written or unwritten, the witness of the Apostolic age was the heritage of the Catholic Church; she claimed all Apostolic teaching as her own, and admitted no other body of truth.

(3) Besides Apostolic tradition, the Catholic Church possessed also an Apostolic ministry. The orderly devolution of ministerial authority from the Apostolate is a clearly marked principle of the first age. The Seven were chosen by the whole body of the disciples, but on their election they were set before the Apostles, and by them admitted to their office. In the new churches among the Gentiles, elders (presbyters) were appointed by Barnabas and Saul. Later on, at Ephesus and in Crete, in the absence of the Apostle, the ordination of presbyter-bishops and deacons was entrusted by St Paul to his delegates, Timothy and Titus. Timothy himself had received the gift of ministerial grace through the laying on of the Apostle's hands (2 Timothy 1: 6).

The principle of succession was maintained in the sub-Apostolic age. We have already seen how Clement of Rome points out to the Corinthians who had deposed their presbyters, that the men had been appointed either by the Apostles, or, according to a provision made by the Apostles, "by other men of repute with the consent of the whole church". The language is not technical, but it sufficiently indicates that some kind of ministerial succession was maintained after the death of the Apostolic founders and by their desire. As soon as the monarchical episcopate emerges, one of its functions is to secure the maintenance of this succession. "We can count up", writes Irenaeus, "those who were appointed by the Apostles to be bishops in the several churches, and their successors to our own time" (i.e., to about AD 180) "It would be tedious", he adds, "to count up the successions in all the churches", and so he selects the Roman succession as an example. The moral is: "We must obey the elders in the churches who derive their succession from the Apostles or men who, with their succession to the episcopal office, have received the sure gift of truth." Those who hold aloof from the succession are to be held suspect. Hippolytus, a junior contemporary and disciple of Irenaeus, attaches the same importance to Apostolical succession; "the Apostles (he says) imparted the Holy Spirit to men who held the right faith, and we, their successors, have partaken of the same grace, high priesthood, and office of teaching, and are accounted guardians of the Church." "Christ", writes Cyprian in the next generation and amid other surroundings, "says to the Apostles, and thereby to all heads of churches who succeed to the Apostles by an ordination which puts them in their place, 'He who heareth you, heareth me, and he who heareth me heareth him that sent me'."

Thus, as the Catholic Church was planted by Apostolic hands and inherits Apostolic teaching, her ministry succeeds in an unbroken line to the Apostolic office, so far as the latter is perpetuated in the *life* of later Christendom. This is not to say that the Bishops are in all respects successors of the Apostles, or even that monarchical episcopacy dates back to the lifetime of St John. But a succession of some kind there clearly was from the first, and thus the principle of continuity was in any case maintained. In other words, the authority to minister in the ancient Church came not from the Church itself, or from Christ acting directly through the Church, but from the Apostles or their delegates or successors, in virtue of Christ's original gift to the Twelve. The people elected their clergy, but the clergy received authority from the hands of those who ultimately derived their commission from the Apostles. Thus in the Catholic Church every ministerial act is linked by historical sequence with the work of the first age, with the ministry of the Twelve and of St Paul, with the ministry of Christ Himself.

Comment

There is little doubt that most discussions of the doctrine of the church have focused on questions of "unity" and "catholicity," on account of their importance in the Donatist and Reformation debates. As a result, the notion of "apostolicity" was somewhat neglected. In this useful discussion, Swete explores three main aspects of the concept. Swete was a noted patristic scholar, and his interest and competence in this field are clearly reflected in this passage.

Questions for Study

1 Set out, in your own words, the three elements of "apostolicity" identified by Swete in this passage.
2 "The Catholic Church was planted by Apostolic hands and inherits Apostolic teaching." Locate this passage within the text. How would you evaluate this statement?

7.24

The Barmen Confession on the Identity of the Church

This historically and theologically important document, first published in 1934 at the height of the "German church crisis," insists upon the distinctiveness of the church in relation to the state. At a time at which a Nazi government seemed poised to take over the church and subvert it for its own ends, theologians and church leaders (including Karl Barth) insisted that the church found its identity and purpose only in relation to Jesus Christ. See also 2.41.

1. Jesus Christ, as he is attested for us in Holy Scripture, is the one Word of God which we have to hear and which we have to trust and obey in life and in death. We reject the false teaching, that the church could and should acknowledge any other events and powers, figures and truths, as God's revelation, or as a source of its proclamation, apart from or in addition to this one Word of God. [. . .]

3. The Christian church is the congregation of brothers and sisters in which Jesus Christ acts presently as the Lord in Word and sacrament, through the Holy Spirit. As the church of forgiven sinners, it has to bear witness in the midst of a sinful world, with both its faith and its obedience, with its proclamation as well as its order, that it is the possession of him alone, and that it lives and wills to live only from his comfort and his guidance in the expectation of his appearance. We reject the false teaching, that the church is free to abandon the form of its proclamation and order in favor of anything it pleases, or in response to prevailing ideological or political beliefs [*der jeweils herrschenden weltanschaulichen und politischen Überzeugungen*]. [. . .]

5. Scripture declares that the state has, by divine appointment [*nach göttlicher Anordnung*] the task of providing for justice and peace in the as yet unredeemed world in which the church also exists, by means of the threat and exercise of force, according to the measure of human judgment and ability. The church acknowledges before God the benefit of this divine appointment in gratitude and

reverence. It recalls the Kingdom of God, God's command and his righteousness, and through this, the responsibilities both of those who rule and those who are ruled. It trusts and obeys the power of the Word of God, by which God upholds all things. We reject the false teaching, that the state, over and beyond its special commission, should or could become the sole and supreme authority in human life, thus fulfilling the vocation of the church as well as its own. We reject the false teaching, that the church, over and beyond its special commission, could or should appropriate the distinctive features, tasks or authority of the state, thus becoming itself an organ of the state.

Comment

The "Theological Clarification of the Present State of the German Evangelical Churches" (1934) was concerned to defend the integrity of German Protestant churches in the face of what many regarded as compromises on the part of "German Christians" with the Nazi regime. The document insists that true Christian churches owe their allegiance to Jesus Christ, and not to any secular figures, norms, or values. Especial attention is devoted to clarifying the role of the state in affairs of the church. German Lutheranism had been influenced to no small extent by Luther's "doctrine of the two kingdoms," which to its critics gave the state an excessively influential role in the church – and hence allowed Adolf Hitler to shape German Christianity to meet his own agenda.

Questions for Study

1 This document addresses a series of concerns which arose through Adolf Hitler's rise to power at this time. At what points can you discern these concerns?
2 Note that each section of the document consists of an affirmation of positive teaching, followed by a rejection of views which are regarded as unacceptable. In each of the three sections, identify the relationship between the positions which are affirmed, and those which are rejected.

7.25

Yves Congar on the Hierarchy of the Church

The French Dominican writer Yves Congar (1904–95) played a major role as a theological advisor at the Second Vatican Council. Congar's influence was particularly significant in relation to twentieth-century Catholic reflection on the nature of the church. In this extract from a major theological work dealing with the place of the laity in the life of the church, first published in French in 1951, Congar reflects on why the church possesses a hierarchical structure. See also 7.5, 7.7, 7.13, 7.22, 7.26.

The Church can be compared to a building under construction, say a place of worship. The world is the quarry that supplies the stone. A whole organization is necessary to bring the rough stone to its final state in the finished building: hammer and chisels, means of transport, scaffolding and ladders, cranes, an architect to give orders and industrious workmen. When the church is finished, every stone in its place according to the architect's design, the scaffolding and everything else that is no longer wanted is taken away, and the workmen have a rest. When the Body of Christ has reached its final state in Heaven there will no longer be any mediating activity of the hierarchical priesthood, no magisterium of the faith, no ruling authority, no 'dogma', no law, no sacrament: for God will be all in all (1 Corinthians 15: 28). For man now saved and reborn, external things will have ceased, there will be an end to the machinery of the earthly Church, her hierarchy, temples, powers, her aspect of law and synagogue, all the things that belonged to a time of waiting and change, when the *sacramentum* was not yet completely *res*. Or, if there be still some outward expression of spiritual realities, it will not be in order to procure those realities, by a movement from, without to within, making them dependent on an external thing for their existence: rather will it be by supererogation, in order to instruct and enlighten, or by way of manifestation and as an element of glory: that is, by a movement from within to without, and so in no wise opposed to the perfect inwardness of truth and life. That is why St John describes the Heavenly Jerusalem (which is perfectly free: Galatians 4: 26) thus: 'I saw no sanctuary therein, for the Lord God almighty is the sanctuary thereof, and the Lamb. And the city hath no need of the sun or of the moon to shine upon it, for the glory of the Lord enlighteneth it, and the lamp thereof is the Lamb' (Revelation 21: 22–23; cf. 22: 3–5). There we see the full realization of the messianic promises (Isaiah 40: 1–9) and the effects of the New Covenant as declared by Jeremiah: 'I will give my law in their bowels and I will write it in their heart: and I will be their God, and they shall be my people. And they shall teach no more every man his neighbour, and every man his brother, saying: Know the Lord. For all shall know me from the least of them even to the greatest . . . ' (Jeremiah 31: 33–34; cf. Hebrews 8: 10–11).

But Jerusalem below is only the beginning and an earnest of Jerusalem above. In as much as it is in a state of becoming and men are on their pilgrimage to God, it has an element of outwardness and, in this sense, of 'law' (though this word would raise certain difficulties in regard to some passages of the Epistle to the Galatians). Metaphysically, the relevant principle is this: so far as action does not coincide with its norm, a rule exterior to it is at work: a law or a pedagogy, so far as good does not fully reside in our freedom; an instruction, so far as truth does not fill the mind; a nourishing from without, so far as the fountain of Life does not gush forth from the living person himself. Theologically and Christianly, we are here only interpreting God's design, the law of his saving economy. Its object is that he shall be all in all, that his creation shall be his temple and men the associates of his life; and to realize it he has adopted a means in our world, or more accurately, in the depth of human nature – the incarnation. So from the start he has joined the oneness of the communion we must have with him to the means of realizing it: the mediation of the man Jesus Christ (1 Timothy 2: 5). Thus in communicating his life to us, God acts not according to his mode, but according to ours. Whatever is given us of the final reality of divine life is through the *sacramentum humanitatis (Christi)*: there will be nothing in Omega that has not come from Alpha, that is, from what Christ has been and has done and has suffered for us in his incarnation.

And so it will be until Christ shall have given back all things to the Father, in a '*Consummatum est*' of which that uttered alone on the Cross is only the 'sacrament'; only then will God be truly all in all; only then will there be an end to the regime of mediation under which men live so long as the night shall last, *donec auferetur luna*.

The Church as institution has no other meaning than to carry on this mediation (in traditional symbolism she is compared to the moon). Those people who misunderstand the Church as institution are the same people who misunderstand the existence of an element of externality or 'law', and their misjudgement arises from the same basic attitude. It is for the same reason that they completely misunderstand the meaning of the hierarchical fact, which is an aspect of the Church as institution and of the existing regime of mediation.

Comment

The hierarchical structure of the church was frequently criticized in the period after World War II, as shifting social attitudes led to a growing suspicion of the idea of "authority" and "power." Although Congar believed that the laity had a vitally important role to play in a renewed Catholic church, he did not see this as entailing the abolition of its hierarchy of priests, bishops, and the Pope. Drawing a distinction between the "structure" and the "life" of the church, Congar argued that the structure of the church was bestowed upon it by Christ as a means of grace, to make the life of the church possible.

Questions for Study

1 What point does Congar want to make through his image of the church as a work in progress? How persuasive do you find this to be?
2 What is the purpose of Congar's contrast between the church as it now exists on earth, and as it will exist in heaven? Why should not the heavenly form of the church exist now on earth?

7.26

The Second Vatican Council on the Nature of the Church

The Second Vatican Council (1962–5) set out to address issues of major concern to the Roman Catholic Church in the modern world. The third session of the council (September 14–November 21, 1964) dealt with a series of matters, including the nature and mission of the church. The resulting "Dogmatic Constitution on the Church" – often known by its Latin title of *Lumen Gentium* ("A light to the nations") – is widely regarded as one of the most important ecclesiological documents of recent times. See also 7.8, 7.10.

6. In the Old Testament the revelation of the kingdom is often made under the forms of symbols. In similar fashion the inner nature of the Church is now made known to us in various images. Taken either from the life of the shepherd or from cultivation of the land, from the art of building or from family life and marriage, these images have their preparation in the books of the prophets.

The Church is, accordingly, a sheepfold, the sole and necessary gateway to which is Christ (John 10: 1–10). It is also a flock, of which God foretold that he would himself be the shepherd (cf. Isaiah 40: 11; Exodus 34: 11–12), and whose sheep, although watched over by human shepherds, are nevertheless at all times led and brought to pasture by Christ himself, the Good Shepherd and prince of shepherds (cf. John 10: 11; 1 Peter 5: 4), who gave his life for his sheep (cf. John 10: 11–16).

The Church is a cultivated field, the tillage of God (1 Corinthians 3: 9). On that land the ancient olive tree grows whose holy roots were the prophets and in which the reconciliation of Jews and Gentiles has been brought about and will be brought about again (Romans 11: 13–26). That land, like a choice vineyard, has been planted by the heavenly cultivator (Matthew 21: 33–43; cf. Isaiah 5: 1–2). Yet the true vine is Christ who gives life and fruitfulness to the branches, that is, to us, who through the Church remain in Christ without whom we can do nothing (John 15: 1–5).

Often, too, the Church is called the building of God (1 Corinthians 3: 9). The Lord compared himself to the stone which the builders rejected, but which was made into the corner stone (Matthew 21: 42; cf. Acts 4: 11; 1 Peter 2: 7; Psalm 117: 22). On this foundation the Church is built by the apostles (cf. 1 Corinthians 3: 11) and from it the Church receives solidity and unity. This edifice has many names to describe it: the house of God in which his family dwells – the household of God in the Spirit (Ephesians 2: 19, 22); the dwelling-place of God among men (Revelation 21: 3); and, especially, the holy temple. This temple, symbolized in places of worship built out of stone, is praised by the Fathers and, not without reason, is compared in the liturgy to the Holy City, the New Jerusalem. As living stones we here on earth are built into it (1 Peter 2: 5). It is this holy city that is seen by John as it comes down out of heaven from God when the world is made anew, prepared like a bride adorned for her husband (Revelation 21: 1–2).

The Church, further, which is called "that Jerusalem which is above" and "our mother" (Galatians 4: 26; cf. Revelation 12: 17), is described as the spotless spouse of the spotless lamb (Revelation 19: 7; 21: 2 and 9; 22: 17). It is she whom Christ "loved and for whom he delivered himself up that he might sanctify her" (Ephesians 5: 26). It is she whom he unites to himself by an unbreakable alliance, and whom he constantly "nourishes and cherishes" (Ephesians 5: 29). It is she whom, once purified, he willed to be joined to himself, subject in love and fidelity (cf. Ephesians 5: 24), and whom, finally, he filled with heavenly gifts for all eternity, in order that we may know the love of God and of Christ for us, a love which surpasses all understanding (cf. Ephesians 3: 19). While on earth she journeys in a foreign land away from the Lord (cf. 2 Corinthians 5: 6), the Church sees herself as an exile. She seeks and is concerned about those things which are above, where Christ is seated at the right hand of God, where the life of the Church is hidden with Christ in God until she appears in glory with her Spouse (cf. Colossians 3: 1–4).

7. In the human nature united to himself, the son of God, by overcoming death through his own death and resurrection, redeemed man and changed him into a new creation (cf. Galatians 6: 15; 2 Corinthians 5: 17). For by communicating his Spirit, Christ mystically constitutes as his body those brothers of his who are called together from every nation.

In that body the life of Christ is communicated to those who believe and who, through the sacraments, are united in a hidden and real way to Christ in his passion and glorification. Through baptism we are formed in the likeness of Christ: "For in one Spirit we were all baptized into one body" (1 Corinthians 12: 13). In this sacred rite fellowship in Christ's death and resurrection is symbolized and is brought about: "For we were buried with him by means of baptism into death"; and if "we have been united with him in the likeness of his death, we shall be so in the likeness of his resurrection also" (Romans 6: 4–5). Really sharing in the body of the Lord in the breaking of the eucharistic bread, we are taken up into communion with him and with one another. "Because the bread is one, we, though many, are one body, all of us who partake of the one bread" (1 Corinthians 10: 17). In this way all of us are made members of his body (cf. 1 Corinthians 12: 27), "but severally members one of another' " (Romans 12: 4).

As all the members of the human body, though they are many, form one body, so also are the faithful in Christ (cf. 1 Corinthians 12: 12). Also, in the building up of Christ's body there is engaged a diversity of members and functions. There is only one Spirit who, according to his own richness and the needs of the ministries, gives his different gifts for the welfare of the Church (cf. 1 Corinthians 12: 1–11). Among these gifts the primacy belongs to the grace of the apostles to whose authority the Spirit himself subjects even those who are endowed with charisms (cf. 1 Corinthians 14). Giving the body unity through himself, both by his own power and by the interior union of the members, this same Spirit produces and stimulates love among the faithful. From this it follows that if one member suffers anything, all the members suffer with him, and if one member is honored, all the members together rejoice (cf. 1 Corinthians 12: 26).

The head of this body is Christ. He is the image of the invisible God and in him all things came into being. He is before all creatures and in him all things hold together. He is the head of the body which is the Church. He is the beginning, the firstborn from the dead, that in all things he might hold the primacy (cf. Colossians 1: 15–18). By the greatness of his power he rules heaven and earth, and with his all-surpassing perfection and activity he fills the whole body with the riches of his glory (cf. Ephesians 1: 18–23).

All the members must be formed in his likeness, until Christ be formed in them (cf. Galatians 4: 19). For this reason we, who have been made like to him, who have died with him and risen with him, are taken up into the mysteries of his life, until we reign together with him (cf. Philippians 3: 21; 2 Timothy 2: 11; Ephesians 2: 6; Colossians 2: 12, etc.). On earth, still as pilgrims in a strange land, following in trial and in oppression the paths he trod, we are associated with his sufferings as the body with its head, suffering with him, that with him we may be glorified (cf. Romans 8: 17).

From him "the whole body, supplied and built up by joints and ligaments, attains a growth that is of God" (Colossians 2: 19). He continually provides in his body, that is, in the Church, for gifts of ministries through which, by his power, we serve each other unto salvation so that, carrying out the truth in love, we may through all things grow unto him who is our head (cf. Ephesians 4: 11–16, original Greek text).

In order that we might be unceasingly renewed in him (cf. Ephesians 4: 23), he has shared with us his Spirit who, being one and the same in head and members, gives life to, unifies and moves the whole body. Consequently, his work could be compared by the Fathers to the function that the principle of life, the soul, fulfills in the human body.

Christ loves the Church as his bride, having been established as the model of a man loving his wife as his own body (cf. Ephesians 5: 25–28); the Church, in her turn, is subject to her head (Ephesians 5: 23–24). "Because in him dwells all the fullness of the Godhead bodily" (Colossians 2: 9), he fills the Church, which is his body and his fullness, with his divine gifts (cf. Ephesians 1: 22–23) so that it may increase and attain to all the fullness of God (cf. Ephesians 3: 19).

8. The one mediator, Christ, established and ever sustains here on earth his holy Church, the community of faith, hope and charity, as a visible organization through which he communicates truth and grace to all men. But, the society structured with hierarchical organs and the mystical body of Christ, the visible society and the spiritual community, the earthly Church and the Church endowed with heavenly riches, are not to be thought of as two realities. On the contrary, they form one complete reality which comes together from a human and a divine element. For this reason the Church is compared, not without significance, to the mystery of the incarnate Word. As the assumed nature, inseparably united to him, serves the divine Word as a living organ of salvation, so, in a somewhat similar way, does the social structure of the Church serve the Spirit of Christ who vivifies it, in the building up of the body (cf. Ephesians 4: 15).

This is the sole Church of Christ which in the Creed we profess to be one, holy, catholic and apostolic, which our Savior, after his resurrection, entrusted to Peter's pastoral care (John 21: 17), commissioning him and the other apostles to extend and rule it (cf. Matthew 28: 18, etc.), and which he raised up for all ages as "the pillar and mainstay of the truth" (1 Timothy 3: 15). This Church, constituted and organized as a society in the present world, subsists in the Catholic Church, which is governed by the successor of Peter and by the bishops in communion with him. Nevertheless, many elements of sanctification and of truth are found outside its visible confines. Since these are gifts belonging to the Church of Christ, they are forces impelling towards Catholic unity.

Comment

This section of *Lumen Gentium* brings together a number of biblical ideas and images, as it sets out a catholic understanding of the nature and task of the church. The extensive appeal to Scripture is characteristic of Vatican II, and indicates a new concern to ensure that the catholic teaching on this matter is rigorously grounded in the New Testament. The extract is taken from the first chapter of *Lumen Gentium*, entitled "The Mystery of the Church."

Questions for Study

1. "While on earth she journeys in a foreign land away from the Lord (cf. 2 Corinthians 5: 6), the Church sees herself as an exile." Locate this passage. This is a reaffirmation of the notion of the *ecclesia in via* ("the church in transit"), which affirms that the church, though located in the world, has a goal and destiny which lie beyond this world. Summarize this aspect of the doctrine of the church, based on the text.
2. "The society structured with hierarchical organs and the mystical body of Christ, the visible society and the spiritual community, the earthly Church and the Church endowed with heavenly riches, are not to be thought of as two realities." Locate this passage within the text. What point is being made here? What possible criticisms or misunderstandings of the doctrine of the church are being countered?

7.27

John D. Zizioulas on Local and Universal Churches

John D. Zizioulas (born 1931), a leading contemporary Orthodox theologian, here sets out an understanding of "catholicity" and explores its relevance for local churches. In the course of his discussion he identifies a number of characteristics which determine whether a local congregation can be said to be a part of the catholic church as a whole. See also 7.28.

From what has just been said it follows that the "catholicity" of the Church is not to be juxtaposed to locality: it is rather an indispensable aspect *of the local Church*, the ultimate criterion of ecclesiality for any local body. Universality, however, is a different notion and can certainly be contrasted with locality. How does the concept of universality affect our understanding of the local Church?

It is in the nature of the eucharist to transcend not only divisions occurring within a local situation but also the very division which is inherent in the concept of geography: the division of the world into local places. Just as a eucharist which is not a transcendence of divisions within a certain locality is a false eucharist, equally a eucharist which takes place in conscious and intentional isolation and separation from other local communities in the world is not a true eucharist. From that it follows inevitably that a local Church, in order to be not just local but also Church, must be in full communion with the rest of the local Churches in the world.

For a local Church to be in full communion with the rest of local Churches the following elements are involved:

(a) That the problems and concerns of all local Churches should be the objects of prayer and active care by a particular local Church. If a local Church falls into indifference as to what is going on in the rest of the world, it is certainly not a Church.

(b) That a certain common basis of the vision and understanding of the Gospel and the eschatological nature of the Church exist between a local Church and the rest of the local Churches. This requires a constant vigilance concerning the true faith in all local Churches by every single local Church.

(c) That certain structures be provided which will facilitate this communion. On this point some further explanations become necessary.

If the locality of the Church is not to be absorbed and in fact negated by the element of universality, the utmost care must be taken so that the structures of ministries which are aimed at facilitating communion among the local Churches do not become a superstructure over the local Church. It is extremely significant that in the entire course of church history there has never been an attempt at establishing a super-local eucharist or a super-local bishop. All eucharists and all bishops are local in character – at least in their primary sense. In a eucharistic view of the Church this means that the local Church, as defined earlier here, is the only form of ecclesial existence which can be properly called Church. All structures aiming at facilitating the universality of the Church create a *network of communion of Churches, not a new form of Church*. This is not only supported by history, but rests also upon sound theological and existential ground. Any structural universalization of the Church to the point of creating an ecclesial entity called "universal Church" as something parallel to or above that of the local Church would inevitably introduce into the concept of the Church cultural and other dimensions which are foreign to a particular local context. Culture cannot be a monolithically universal phenomenon without some kind of demonic imposition of one culture over the rest of cultures. Nor is it possible to dream of a universal "Christian culture" without denying the dialectic between history and eschatology which is so central, among other things, to the eucharist itself. Thus, if there is a transcendence of cultural divisions on a universal level – which indeed must be constantly aimed at by the Church – it can only take place *via* the local situations expressed in and through the particular local Churches and not through universalistic structures which imply a universal Church. For a universal Church as an entity besides the local Church would be either a culturally disincarnated Church – since there is no such a thing as universal culture – or alternatively it would be culturally incarnated in a demonic way, if it either blesses or directly or indirectly imposes on the world a particular culture.

In conclusion, all church structures aiming at facilitating communion between local Churches (e.g., synods, councils of all forms etc.) do possess ecclesiological significance and must be always viewed in the light of ecclesiology. But they cannot be regarded as forms of *Church* without the serious dangers I have just referred to.

Comment

Zizioulas here articulates an Orthodox vision of the church, which is critical of centralized and hierarchical approaches to understanding the church. The church must be "incarnated" in a manner which is sensitive to the local culture, rather than being seen as a centralized universal body. The basic model of the church which he aims to counter is that set out by Vatican I. It should be noted that Vatican II is much less vulnerable to the criticisms made here.

Questions for Study

1 What exactly does Zizioulas mean by a "local church"? How is it defined? What are its characteristics? And how can its "catholicity" or "universality" be understood and maintained?
2 Zizioulas clearly regards the eucharist as being of central importance to a right understanding of the nature of the church. Set out, in your own words, his "eucharistic" understanding of the church.

7.28

Leonardo Boff on the Nature of Local Churches

The Brazilian Roman Catholic theologian Leonardo Boff (born 1938) here offers a major discussion of the identity and role of the church, which brings together a number of insights characteristic of Latin American liberation theology. Notice the importance attached to the "base communities" and the "bottom-upwards" model of authority which they embody. The passage raises the question of whether an ordained ministry, or any form of properly constituted sacramental worship, is essential if such a community can be regarded as a church. The issues addressed in this passage call into question some of the more conservative understandings of church and ministry which were typical of Latin American Catholicism until recently. See also 1.31, 3.35, 7.26, 7.27.

The church comes into being as church when people become aware of the call to salvation in Jesus Christ, come together in community, profess the same faith, celebrate the same eschatological liberation, and seek to live the discipleship of Jesus Christ. We can speak of church *in the proper sense* only when there is question of this ecclesial consciousness. Hence the crucial importance of explicit Christian motivation. We are united and we pursue our social objectives of liberation *because* we react to the call of Christ, and the call of other communities that transmit his call to us and that have preceded us in the living experience of this same community faith. We can speak of a *church* community, therefore, only when a given community has this explicit religious and Christian character. Otherwise it will be some other kind of community, however it may actualize the same values as the church pursues. For an authentic, contemplative Christian, this other community indeed verifies the essential definition of church in its ontic reality. But the presence of the ontic ecclesial reality is not enough. In order formally to be church, the *consciousness* of this reality must be there, the profession of explicit faith in Jesus Christ who died and was raised again.

Having clarified this point, we are now in a position to move on to the next – once more, one of special importance.

Differing Opinions

We speak of "basic church communities." Are these communities themselves actually church, or do they merely contain elements of church?

Many different answers are proposed to this question, but this scarcely deprives it of its importance either for ecclesiology or for the actual members of the basic communities. Opinions tend to vary with the position their subjects occupy in the church structure, or with the model of church they adopt as key to the interpretation of total church reality. Thus those within the actual basic communities will tend to consider these communities as church, while those whose orientation is toward the historically established churches will reserve the minimum requirement for church to the parish community. The hierarchy, as we see from Vatican Council II, will define "a church" in terms of diocesan reality, with bishop and Eucharist. Let us consider each of these opinions in turn, and attempt to establish the theological value of each.

First, we shall examine what the basic church community itself says. There is a study carried out by the Centro de Estatística Religiosa e Investigações Sociais (CERIS), in which Father Alfonso Gregory catalogues various responses to the question of the ecclesiality of various experiences. When he comes to the basic communities, he records the following reasons explaining why the basic church community is properly denominated "church":

1 "Because it is founded on the common faith, and its objectives bear on a deepening and an increase of this faith, with all that this implies."
2 "Because there is a direct connection with the ecclesiastical framework, a sense of church-of-the-people." Or, as another respondent put it: "Because it feels its oneness with the parish, diocese, and church universal."
3 "Because in religious activities only Catholics participate, while other activities are ecumenical" – that is, socioeconomic activities. Here we may add what another respondent said: "When you consider yourselves a church community, you can't work when your religious motives are different, or opposite."
4 "Because the strictly religious activities are basic, while all the others are as a consequence of accepting God's word." Or again: "Christianity is the activating of integral humanism."
5 "Because we are working at the grassroots for a communion in faith, through humanization."

But Gregory also documents the contrary view: The basic communities "are not churches (or, as some would say, they are churches only *juxta modum*), because, though there may be priests and nuns here, these communities are just beginning. In other cases, their activities are oriented consciously and mainly to the social area."

The vast majority of those responsible for these experiments – the respondents in this research project – feel that they are in contact with actual, genuine church, and not just with ecclesial elements or parachurch communities. José Marins, who is in the front line of defense of the basic communities, puts it well in his reformulation of the thinking of the communities:

> For us, the basic church community is the church itself, the universal sacrament of salvation, as it continues the mission of Christ – Prophet, Priest, and Pastor. This is what makes it a community of faith, worship, and love. Its mission is explicitly expressed on all levels – the universal, the diocesan, and the local, or basic.

Elsewhere we read that the basic community is genuine church because it has "the same goals" as the universal church: "to lead all men and women to the full communion of life with the Father and one another, through Jesus Christ, in the gift of the Holy Spirit, by means of the mediating activity of the church." These few citations are representative of the thinking of the great majority of pastoral leaders and theologians directly involved with the basic communities, particularly in Latin America. Most of them consider that the basic church communities constitute the true and authentic presence of the Catholic Church.

Once upon a time the populations in the interior of the Latin American countries, cut off by thick rain forests or other wild territory and scattered over the vast expanses of these empty lands, met together only when the priest came to them – once a year, perhaps, or every six months. Only for this brief moment did they feel themselves to be living church united by the word, together with their ordained minister, around the same altar, celebrating and offering the same sacred Victim. Then came the basic communities, and these same people began to meet every week – or twice a week or every day – to celebrate the presence of the risen One and of his Spirit, to hear and meditate on his word, and to renew their commitment to liberation, together with their community leaders who are the principle of unity and communion with other basic communities and with the parish and diocesan community. Are we now going to tell these people that they are not church, that they have certain "ecclesial elements," but that these do not actually constitute the essence of church?

We must ask ourselves: Are they not baptized? Do they not possess the same faith as the church universal? The same love? The same hope? Do they not read the same Scriptures? Do they not live the same Christian praxis? Are they not fully united to Christ, and are they not the body of Christ? We are not dealing with some mere point of sentimentality here. Let us face the actual ecclesiological problem, and face it objectively. If we are to develop a new ecclesiology, we shall need more than just theological perspicacity and historico-dogmatic erudition. We must face the new experiences of church in our midst. We in Brazil and Latin America are confronted with a new concretization of church, without the presence of consecrated ministers and without the eucharistic celebration. It is not that this absence is not felt, is not painful. It is, rather, that these ministers do not exist in sufficient numbers. This historical situation does not cause the church to disappear. The church abides in the people of God as they continue to come together, convoked by the word and discipleship of Jesus Christ. Something is new under the sun: a new church of Christ.

As a result, even those theologians who restrict the definition of church to a community presenting constitutive, essential elements of church such as word, sacrament, the presence of the bishop, and communion with all the other churches – and who therefore pronounce the basic community "not fully church" – are forced nonetheless to conclude: "From the pastoral viewpoint, these basic groups or communities must be considered authentic ecclesial reality – needing development, doubtless, but surely integrated into the one communion of the Father, in Christ, through the Holy Spirit."

The theological problem of the ecclesial character of the basic community must be seen within a context of the recovery by these communities of a true ecclesiological dimension. This is the process now under way in many places. We know that the ninth century saw the rise of papal supremacy. The absolutist ideology of the Gregorian reform two centuries later served to reinforce this development. Then came conciliarism, Gallicanism, and episcopalism, with their attendant polemics. Finally, with the development of the ultramontane ecclesiology and its triumph under Pius IX, the church acquired a unitarian organization, as if it were one great, worldwide diocese, with one sole liturgy, one visible head, one embodiment. [...] Vatican II transcended this state of affairs, recognizing the local or particular church as genuine church, but without developing a complete theology of the local church. An important step has been taken, then, in the process of defining what it is to be a particular or local church, and restoring to it its proper evaluation. Vatican II defined the particular church as

> that portion of God's people which is entrusted to a bishop to be shepherded by him with the cooperation of the presbytery. Adhering thus to its pastor and gathered together by him in the Holy Spirit through the gospel and the Eucharist, this portion constitutes a particular church in which the one, holy, catholic, and apostolic church of Christ is truly present and operative.

The particular church, then, is defined in diocesan terms. Unity is secured through the presence of the bishop and the celebration of the Eucharist. The capacity to represent the church universal is not, however, reserved to the diocese gathered around the bishop in the celebration of the Eucharist. *Lumen Gentium* says:

> This church of Christ is truly present in all legitimate local congregations of the faithful . . . united with their pastors. . . . In them the faithful are gathered together by the preaching of the gospel of Christ, and the mystery of the Lord's Supper is celebrated, "that by the flesh and blood of the Lord's body the whole brotherhood may be joined together. . . . In these communities, though frequently small and poor, or living far from any other, Christ is present. By virtue of Him the one, holy, catholic, and apostolic Church gathers together.

In all cases, then, the essential constitutive element of a particular church as church, for Vatican Council II, is always the gospel, the Eucharist, and the presence of the apostolic succession in the person of the bishop.

Medellin, in 1968, could already testify to an evolution in the ecclesial experience of the postconciliar era, with the rise of basic communities all over the South American continent:

> Thus the Christian base community is *the first and fundamental ecclesiastical nucleus*, which on its own level must make itself responsible for the richness and expansion of the faith, as well as of the cult which is its expression. This community becomes then the *initial cell* of the ecclesiastical structures and the focus of evangelization, and it currently serves as the most important source of human advancement and development. The essential element for the existence of Christian base communities are their leaders or directors. These can be priests, deacons, men or women religious, or laymen.

There is no mention here of the elements of bishop and Eucharist. The church is not being thought of from the top down, but from the bottom up, from the grassroots, from the "base." The church – "God's family" – takes form by "means of a nucleus, although it be small, which creates a community of faith, hope and charity." Truly another step has been taken in a grasp of the church dimension of the basic communities.

Comment

This text represents an important (and somewhat controversial) application of Vatican II's "Dogmatic Constitution on the Church" (see 7.26) to the Latin American situation.

Boff, along with other Latin American liberation theologians, has encouraged reflection on "base ecclesial communities" (or simply "base communities") – that is, individual gatherings of Christians which understand their identity in local, rather than centralized, terms. In this important passage, Boff argues for a rethinking of traditional models of the church in the light of the realities of the Latin American situation. Boff interprets *Lumen Gentium* as being broadly supportive to – or at least not being opposed to – his own position on this matter. This interpretation of *Lumen Gentium* has not found official sanction.

Questions for Study

1 "Are we now going to tell these people that they are not church, that they have certain 'ecclesial elements,' but that these do not actually constitute the essence of church?" Locate this text within the passage. What is the point that Boff is making here? What is the "essence of the church" which is not reflected in the base communities?
2 How does Boff understand the relation between the following two concepts: "a community of believers" and "the church"?

7.29

Avery Dulles on the Meanings of "Catholicity"

At the conclusion of a detailed analysis of the notion of the "catholicity" of the church, the American Catholic theologian Avery Dulles (born 1918) sets out five general ways in which the term "catholic" has been used in Christian history. See also 7.4, 7.9, 7.14.

The term "catholic," with or without an initial capital, has various levels of meaning. [. . .] The following five usages may now be enumerated:

1. The adjectival form of "catholicity." [. . .] To be catholic in this sense is to share in the universal community, rooted in cosmic nature, that transcends the barriers of time and place and has its source in God's self-communication. The opposite of "catholic" in this sense is sectarian.
2. Universal as opposed to local or particular. This seems to be the primary meaning of "catholic" as used in a number of important texts from the early Fathers of the

Church, notably Ignatius of Antioch and the Martyrdom of Polycarp, though there is some disagreement about the precise interpretation of these texts.

3. True or authentic as contrasted with false or heretical. This polemical use of the term is found in many church Fathers, especially after AD 150, and is much in use among Greek Orthodox theologians of our own time.
4. The type of Christianity that attaches particular importance to visible continuity in space and time and visible mediation through social and institutional structures, such as creeds, sacraments, and the historic episcopate. This sense of the word "Catholic" (with a capital C) was prominent at the Amsterdam Assembly of the World Council of Churches (1948). The opposite was taken to be "Protestant," although a good case could be made for regarding "charismatic" or "mystical" as the opposite.
5. The title of the church which, organized in the world as a society, is governed by the bishop of Rome, as successor of Peter, and by the bishops in communion with him. In ecumenical circles it has become common to use the term "Roman Catholic" to designate this sociological group, partly because the term "Catholic" has the various other meanings listed above.

Comment

This passage is so clear that it needs no comment. Dulles sets out five interpretations of the term "catholicity" with precision and clarity.

Questions for Study

1 Study the passage from Cyril of Jerusalem (7.4) on the theme of catholicity. Which of Dulles's five points are reflected in his discussion? What themes are absent?

2 Now repeat this process by considering the views of Thomas Aquinas (7.9) and Philip Melanchthon (7.14). How do you account for your observations?

7.30

Stanley Hauerwas on the Importance of the Church

The movement often known as "postliberalism" places a particular emphasis upon the importance of the church as a community, identified by its own distinctive set of ideas and values. Stanley Hauerwas (born 1940) is widely regarded as the leading representative of this approach, especially in the field of Christian ethics. In this extract from his early book *A Community of Character*, published in 1981, Hauerwas sets out his views on the importance of the church to ethics, and how its distinctive ethos is to be maintained through the Christian story. See also 7.1, 7.2, 7.12, 7.16, 7.24

To insist on the significance of narrative for theological reflection is not, however, just to make a point about the form of biblical sources, but involves claims about the nature of God, the self, and the nature of the world. We are "storied people" because the God that sustains us is a "storied God," whom we come to know only by having our character formed appropriate to God's character. [. . .]

The existence of the church, therefore, is not an accidental or contingent fact that can be ignored in considerations of the truth of Christian convictions. The church, and the social ethic implied by its separate existence, is an essential aspect of why Christians think their convictions are true. For it is a central Christian conviction that even though the world is God's creation and subject to God's redemption it continues eschatologically to be a realm that defies his rule. The church, which too often is unfaithful to its task, at the very least must lay claim to being the earnest of God's Kingdom and thus able to provide the institutional space for us to rightly understand the disobedient, sinful, but still God-created character of the world. The ethical significance of Christian convictions depends on the power of those convictions to shape a community sufficient to face truthfully the nature of our world.

Christian social ethics should not begin with attempts to develop strategies designed to make the world more "just," but with the formation of a society shaped and informed by the truthful character of the God we find revealed in the stories of Israel and Jesus. The remarkable richness of these stories of God requires that a church be a community of discourse and interpretation that endeavors to tell these stories and form its life in accordance with them. The church, the whole body of believers, therefore cannot be limited to any one historical paradigm or contained by any one institutional form. Rather the very character of the stories of God requires a people who are willing to have their understanding of the story constantly challenged by what others have discovered in their attempt to live faithful to that tradition. For the church is able to exist and grow only through tradition, which – as the memory sustained over time by ritual and habit – sets the context and boundaries for the discussion required by the Christian stories. As Frank Kermode has recently reminded us, the way to interpret a narrative is through another narrative; indeed, a narrative is already a form of interpretation, as the power of a narrative lies precisely in its potential for producing a community of interpretation sufficient for the growth of further narratives.

Inevitably, calling attention to the narrative shape of Christian convictions means that Christian ethics must be taken seriously as Christian. To do that seems to risk the cooperation Christians have achieved with those who do not share their convictions; or worse, it might provide justification for the church to withdraw into a religious ghetto no longer concerned to serve the world. Such a result would indeed be a new and not even very sophisticated form of tribalism. The church, however, is not and cannot be "tribal"; rather the church is the community that enables us to recognize that, in fact, it is the world we live in which has a splintered and tribal existence.

The ability of the church to interpret and provide alternatives to the narrow loyalties of the world results from the story – a particular story, to be sure – that teaches us the significance of lives different from our own, within and without our community.

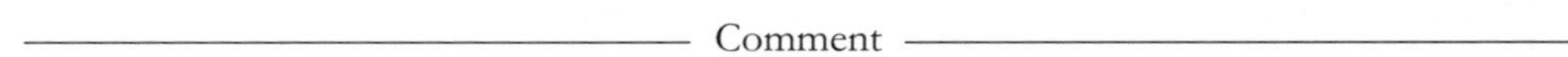

Comment

Hauerwas's central argument is that the church is a community whose ideas and values are shaped by the Christian story. The Christian narrative possesses a capacity to generate a community of people who are able to witness to their ideas and values, and tell the truth about the way things are. An ethic does not begin with agreement about what is "just," but with discernment of the character of God as this is revealed in the Christian story. A Christian ethic is fundamentally an attempt to shape one's life in accordance with the truth of God, as disclosed in this way.

Questions for Study

1. How does Hauerwas establish the relationship of the church and its story? Why is narrative so importance to Hauerwas's analysis at this point? What does he mean when he says we are a "storied people"?
2. What do you think Hauerwas means by "tribalism"? Does he think his approach leads the church to become 'tribal,' or to retreat into some kind of ghetto? Do you agree?

For Further Reading

Raymond F. Collins, *The Many Faces of the Church: A Study in New Testament Ecclesiology* (New York: Crossroad Publishing, 2004).

Avery Dulles, *Models of the Church* (Dublin: Gill & Macmillan, 1976).

Roger Haight, *Christian Community in History: Historical Ecclesiology* (London: Continuum, 2004).

Philip J. Hefner, "The Church," in C. E. Braaten and R. W. Jenson (eds.), *Christian Dogmatics*, 2 vols (Philadelphia: Fortress Press, 1984), vol. 2, pp. 183–247.

Michael J. Himes, *Ongoing Incarnation: Johann Adam Möhler and the Beginnings of Modern Ecclesiology* (New York: Crossroad Publications, 1997).

Peter Hodgson, "The Church," in P. Hodgson and R. King (eds.), *Christian Theology* (Philadelphia: Fortress Press, 1982), pp. 223–47.

Mark Husbands and Daniel J. Trier (eds.), *The Community of the Word: Toward an Evangelical Ecclesiology* (Downers Grove, IL: InterVarsity, 2005).

Michael Jinkins, *The Church Faces Death: Ecclesiology in a Post-Modern Context* (New York: Oxford University Press, 1999).

Veli-Matti Karkkainen, *An Introduction to Ecclesiology: Ecumenical, Historical & Global Perspectives* (Downers Grove, IL: InterVarsity Press, 2002).

Hans Küng, *The Church* (New York and London: Sheed & Ward, 1968).

Paul McPartlan, *Sacrament of Salvation: An Introduction to Eucharistic Ecclesiology* (Edinburgh: T&T Clark, 1995).

Jürgen Moltmann, *The Church in the Power of the Spirit: A Contribution to Messianic Ecclesiology* (Minneapolis: Fortress Press, 1993).

Bernard P. Prusak, *The Church Unfinished: Ecclesiology Through the Centuries* (New York: Paulist Press, 2004).

Arne Rasmusson, *The Church as Polis: From Political Theology to Theological Politics as Exemplified by Jürgen Moltmann and Stanley Hauerwas* (Lund, Sweden: Lund University Press, 1994).

Herwi Rikhof, *The Concept of Church : A Methodological Inquiry into the Use of Metaphors in Ecclesiology* (London: Sheed and Ward, 1981).

Juan Luis Segundo, *The Community Called Church* (Maryknoll, NY: Orbis Books, 1978).

George H. Tavard, *The Church, Community of Salvation: An Ecumenical Ecclesiology* (Collegeville, MN: Liturgical Press, 1992).

J. M. R. Tillard, *Church of Churches: The Ecclesiology of Communion* (Collegeville, MN: Liturgical Press, 1992).

G. G. Willis, *Saint Augustine and the Donatist Controversy* (London: SPCK, 1950).

8

The Sacraments

Introduction

The theology of the sacraments represents an area of Christian thought in which there is substantial divergence between the various Christian traditions. Whereas the Roman Catholic and the Orthodox churches recognize seven sacraments, and generally regard them as causing what they signify, Protestant churches generally accept only two sacraments (baptism and the Lord's Supper), often regarding them as signifying – but not causing – grace. The readings presented in this chapter allow the reader to gain an impression of the considerable differences within the Christian tradition over these issues, and assess their importance. In addition to these, other questions may be noted as being of importance, including the specific role of baptism, and the general question of what the sacraments actually do.

How are Sacraments to be Defined?

How is the "Real Presence" to be Understood?

What Benefits does Baptism Offer?

8.1

Clement of Alexandria on Faith as Feeding on Christ

In this second-century text, Clement of Alexandria (c.150–c.215) explores the meaning of Paul's statement "I fed you with milk, not meat, for you were not ready for meat" (1 Corinthians 3: 2). He interprets the text to refer to various types of nourishment for the soul. He then links the idea of spiritual food with the sacramental idea of feeding on Jesus Christ, which he especially associates with John's Gospel. See also 8.2.

We may understand "milk" (1 Corinthians 3: 2) as meaning the preaching which has been spread far and wide, "meat" as the faith which as a result of instruction has been consolidated to form a foundation. In that faith is more solid than hearing, it is likened to "meat," since it provides analogous nourishment for the soul. In another place the Lord also expressed that by a different symbolism, when, in John's Gospel, he says "Eat my flesh and drink my blood" (John 6: 53–55). The metaphor of drinking, applied to faith and the promise, clearly means that the church, consisting (like a human being) of many members, is refreshed and grows, is consolidated and welded together, by both of these, faith being the body and hope the soul: just as the Lord was made of flesh and blood. In reality, hope is the blood of faith, as it gives cohesion to faith, as with the soul.

Comment

Clement here develops the idea of "meat" (1 Corinthians 3: 2) as a way of reflecting on the issue of spiritual sustenance. Note especially the way in which the imagery of "eating" and "drinking" is developed as a means of embedding the sacraments, especially the Eucharist, within the normal Christian life.

Questions for Study

1 Why does Clement find the image of "drinking" so useful? How does he ground this image? And what use does he make of it?
2 What images of faith do you find in this passage? And how does Clement develop them?

8.2

Clement of Alexandria on the Results of Baptism

Clement here develops a strongly physical and realistic understanding of the effects of baptism. Note especially the emphasis upon "enlightenment" (*phōtisma*). See also 8.1, 8.5, 8.9.

Being baptized, we are enlightened: being enlightened, we are adopted as sons: being adopted, we are made perfect; being made complete, we are made immortal. The Scripture says "I said, You are gods, and are all sons of the Highest" (Psalm 28: 6). This operation has many names; gift of grace, enlightenment, perfection, and washing (*charisma kai phōtisma kai teleion kai loutron*). Washing, by which we are cleansed from the filth of our sins; gift of grace, by which the penalties of our sins are cancelled; enlightenment, through which that holy light which saves us is perceived, that is, by which our eyes are made alert to see the divine; perfection means the lack of nothing, for what is still lacking to anyone who has the knowledge of God? It would clearly be absurd to give the name of "grace" of God to a gift which is not complete. Being perfect, we may be assured that God will bestow perfect graces.

Comment

Clement here sets out a chain or sequence of concepts, which he holds to be closely linked within the economy of salvation. Notice how the entire sequence is dependent upon baptism.

Questions for Study

1 Set out the various terms and images which Clement uses to refer to baptism. What ideas are conveyed in this manner?
2 Set out, in your own words, the point that Clement makes concerning grace not being an "incomplete gift."

8.3

Cyprian of Carthage on Heretical Baptism

In this letter to his colleague Quintus in the third century, Cyprian (martyred 258) argues that heretical baptism has no validity. To concede any validity to such baptisms would be to destroy the distinctiveness and uniqueness of the Christian church. See also 7.3, 7.4, 8.7, 8.8.

I do not know by what presumption some of our colleagues have been led to suppose that those who have been dipped [*tincti*] among the heretics ought not to be baptized when they join us; because, they say, there is "one baptism." Yes, but that one baptism is in the catholic church. And if there is one church, there can be no baptism outside it. There cannot be two baptisms: if heretics really baptize, then baptism belongs to them. And anyone who, asserting their own authority, grants them this privilege admits, by conceding their claim, that the enemy and adversary of Christ should appear to possess the power of washing, purifying, and sanctifying humanity [*abluendi et purificandi et sanctificandi hominis potestatem*]. We declare that those who come to us out of heresy are not rebaptized by us; they are baptized. They do not receive anything there; there is nothing there for them to receive. They come to us so that they may receive here, where there is all grace and truth; for grace and truth are one.

Comment

One of the major issues raised for the early church by the rise of heresy was whether heretical baptism was valid. Heresy is perhaps best regarded as a distortion of the Christian faith, rather than its denial. So what are the implications of baptism from a position which holds to some Christian beliefs, but rejects others? Cyprian here sets out the view that sacraments have their true and effective sphere of operation within the catholic church, and not elsewhere. The issue would be raised again during the Donatist controversy, when Cyprian's position was re-evaluated.

Questions for Study

1 Set out, in your own words, exactly why Cyprian rejects the validity of heretical baptism.

2 Read again Cyprian's views on the nature of the church (7.3). Then trace the connection between his teaching on the identity and function of the church and the efficacy of baptism.

8.4

Cyril of Jerusalem on the Meaning of Baptism

This is an extract from the first of a series of catechetical lectures given by Cyril of Jerusalem (c.315–86) in which he explains the significance of baptism. The lecture is of value in several respects, including its documentation of early Christian baptismal practices. The lecture is prefaced by the reading of 1 Peter 5: 8–11. See also 8.2, 8.6.

For a long time I have wished, true born and long-desired children of the church, to speak to you about these spiritual and heavenly mysteries. However, knowing very well that seeing is believing, I waited until the present occasion, knowing that after what you have experienced you would be a more receptive audience, now that I am to lead you to the brighter and more fragrant meadows of this paradise. In particular, you are now able to understand the more divine mysteries of divine and life-giving baptism. So now that the time has come to prepare for you the table of more perfect instruction, let me explain what happened to you on the evening of your baptism.

First you entered the antechamber of the baptistery [*proaulios tou baptismatos oikon*], and turned westwards. When you were told to stretch out your hands, you renounced Satan as though he were there in person. Now you should know that ancient history provides a type of this. When Pharaoh, the harshest and most cruel of all tyrants, oppressed the free and noble people of the Hebrews, God sent Moses to deliver them from this harsh slavery which had been imposed on them by the Egyptians. They anointed their doorposts with the blood of a lamb, so that the destroyer might pass over the houses which bore the sign of this blood, and miraculously set the Hebrew people free from their bondage. After their liberation the enemy pursued them, and on seeing the sea open in front of them, they still continued to pursue them, only to be engulfed in the Red Sea.

Let us now pass from the old to the new, from the type to the reality. There Moses is sent by God to Egypt; here Christ is sent by the Father into the world. There, he was to lead an oppressed people from Egypt; here he was to deliver those who are under the tyranny of sin. There the blood of the lamb turned away the destroyer; here the blood of the unblemished lamb, Jesus Christ, puts the demons to flight. In the past, the tyrant pursued the Hebrew people right to the sea; in your case, the devil, the arch-evil one, followed each one of you up to the edge of the streams of salvation. This first [tyrant] was engulfed in the sea; this one disappears in the waters of salvation.

Comment

This passage is important for two reasons. In the first, it offers us some insights into the way in which the early church at Jerusalem baptized its converts. Second, it explains the way in which early Christian thinkers interpreted the exodus from Egypt as an anticipation or forerunner of baptism. (In more exact terms, the exodus is being proposed as a "type" of baptism.)

Questions for Study

1 Set out, in your own words, the parallel between the personages and the events of the exodus and those of baptism.
2 What interpretation does Cyril offer of the meaning of the Passover celebration?

8.5

Cyril of Jerusalem on the Body and Blood of Christ

This address explains the meaning of the bread and wine to those who have recently been baptized. It is preceded by the reading of 1 Corinthians 11: 23–5. Note especially the emphasis on the real change in the bread and wine as a result of their consecration. See also 8.1, 8.9, 8.10, 8.11, 8.12, 8.16, 8.18, 8.22, 8.23.

[Jesus Christ], by his own will, once changed water into wine at Cana in Galilee. So why should we not believe that he can change wine into blood? [. . .]

We should therefore have full assurance that we are sharing in the body and blood of Christ. For in the type of bread, his body is given to you, and in the type of wine, his blood is given to you, so that by partaking of the body and blood of Christ you may become of one body and one blood with him. [. . .] In the words of Peter, "we are made to share in the divine nature" (2 Peter 1: 4). [. . .]

So do not think of them just as bread and wine. As the Lord himself has declared, they are body and blood. And if your senses suggest otherwise, then let faith, and be assured beyond doubt that you have received the body and blood of Christ.

Comment

Cyril here offers a simple defense of the transformation of the bread and wine into the body and blood of Christ, based on John 2: 1–11, along with a discussion of the importance of this change. Note especially the link between feeding on the eucharistic elements and the promise of divinization.

Questions for Study

1 According to Cyril, what benefits result from the eucharistic bread and wine?
2 Read the Bible passage which precedes this: 1 Corinthians 11: 23–5. In what way do Cyril's words relate to this biblical text?

8.6

Hilary of Poitiers on the Effects of Baptism

In these comments on the baptism of Jesus, as recorded in Matthew's Gospel, Hilary of Poitiers (c.315–67) draws out the parallels between the work of the Father and Spirit in Jesus's baptism and that of ordinary believers. See also 8.3, 8.8.

Everything that happened to Christ lets us know that, after the washing of water [*post aquae lavacrum*], the Holy Spirit descends upon us from the heights of heaven, and that we become sons of God, having been adopted by the voice of the Father.

Comment

This brief text takes the form of a commentary on Matthew 3: 16–17: "And when Jesus was baptized, he went up immediately from the water, and behold, the heavens were opened and he saw the Spirit of God descending like a dove, and alighting on him; and there was a voice from heaven, saying, 'This is my beloved Son, with whom I am well pleased.' "

Questions for Study

1 What specific benefits does Hilary understand to be conferred by baptism?
2 In what way does Hilary's analysis reflect the structure of the text on which he is commenting?

8.7

Augustine on Donatist Approaches to the Sacraments

Augustine's view of the church accepts that congregations and priests will include sinners as well as saints. So does this invalidate the sacraments? This passage provides his answer. See also 7.3, 7.4, 7.15, 8.3, 8.8.

Now as it is possible that the sacrament of Christ may be holy, even among those who are on the side of the devil [. . .] and even if they are such in heart when they received the sacrament [. . .] the sacrament is not to be readministered; [. . .] to my mind it is abundantly clear that in the matter of baptism we have to consider not who he is that gives it, but what it is that he gives; not who he is that receives, but what it is that he receives [*non esse cogitandum quis det sed quid det, aut quis accipiat sed quid accipiat, aut quis habeat sed quid habeat*] [. . .] wherefore, any one who is on the side of the devil cannot defile the sacrament, which is of Christ. [. . .] When baptism is administered by the words of the gospel, however great the evil of either minister or recipient may be, the sacrament itself is holy on account of the one whose sacrament it is. In the case of people who receive baptism from an evil person [*per hominum perversum*], if they do not receive the perverseness of the minister but the holiness of the mystery, being united to the church in good faith and hope and charity, they will receive the forgiveness of their sins. [. . .] But if the recipients themselves are evil, then that which is administered does not avail for their salvation while they remain in their errors. On the other hand, that which they receive remains holy in the recipients, and need not be repeated if they are subsequently corrected [*et sanctum tamen in eo permanet quod accipitur nec ei si correctus fuerit iteratur*].

Comment

Against the Donatist view, which declared that only the righteous can administer and profitably receive the sacraments (an *ex opere operantis* view of sacramental efficacy), Augustine argues that the efficacy of the sacraments rests on Christ himself, not the merits of either the administrator or recipient (an *ex opere operato* view of sacramental efficacy).

Questions for Study

1 Set out in your own words the point that Augustine makes with the following statement: "in the matter of baptism we have to consider not who he is that gives it,

but what it is that he gives; not who he is that receives, but what it is that he receives."

2 According to Augustine, what are the effects that a faithful recipient of a sacrament may expect to gain if the one who offers the sacrament is evil?

8.8

Augustine on the "Right to Baptize"

The issue of who had the authority to baptize became of especial importance during the Donatist controversy. This debate raised a number of issues. For example, was the efficacy of a sacrament dependent upon the morality of the one who baptized, or the faithfulness of the one to whom baptism points? And are sacraments valid outside the sphere of the church? In this passage, Augustine (354–430) explores some of there issues. See also 7.3, 7.4, 7.15, 8.3, 8.7.

We deal with these matters in case the unity of the harvest should be abandoned on account of evil dispensers of the sacraments – not their own, but the Lord's – who must, of necessity, be mixed among us, until the winnowing of the Lord's field [*ad tempus ventilationis areae dominicae*]. Now to make a schism from the unity of Christ, or to be in schism, is indeed a great evil. And it is not possible in any way that Christ should give to the schismatics what is his own – not faith, that is, but a sacrilegious error; or that a schismatic should cleave, in Christ, to the root; or that Christ should be the fountain head to schismatics. And yet, if [a schismatic] gives the baptism of Christ, if it is given and if it is received, it will be received, not to eternal life but to eternal damnation of those who persevere in sacrilege, not by converting a good thing into evil but by having a good thing to their evil, so long as he receives evil.

Comment

Augustine lays down a fundamental distinction between an "irregular" and "invalid" administration of a sacrament. What makes a sacrament invalid is not sin on the part of the one who administers or receives it, but a deliberate breaking away from the body of Christ in schism. Augustine's view of the church as a "mixed body" recognizes that the church will include sinners as well as saints; however, he insists that schism leads to a break with the church and its sacraments, with the result that the latter are no longer of any benefit to their recipients. The sacraments are valid only within the church.

Questions for Study

1 What kind of theology of the church is set out in the opening sentences of this passage? In what way does the Parable of the Tares (Matthew 13: 24–30) lie behind the ideas and imagery of this section?
2 Set out, in your own words, the specific reasons why Augustine opposes schismatic baptism.

8.9

John of Damascus on the Holy Spirit and Eucharist

In this important work, written in Greek in the first half of the eighth century, John of Damascus (c.675–c.749) recognizes the central role of the Holy Spirit in bringing about the transformation of the bread into the body of Christ. The incarnation is seen as a further illustration of the same principle. See also 3.19, 4.20, 8.1.

And now you ask how the bread becomes the body of Christ, and the wine and the water become the blood of Christ. I shall tell you. The Holy Spirit comes upon them, and achieves things which surpass every word and thought. [...] Let it be enough for you to understand that this takes place by the Holy Spirit, just as the Lord took flesh, in and through himself, of the Holy *Theotokos* and by the Holy Spirit.

Comment

This brief passage sets out an understanding of the role of the Holy Spirit in the eucharist. Technically, the issue under consideration is known as the "epiclesis" (from the Greek term *epiklēsis* meaning "calling down" or "invocation"). John is here referring to the section of the liturgy which calls upon the Father to send down the Holy Spirit upon the bread and wine.

Questions for Study

1 What points does John wish his readers to appreciate, on the basis of this passage?
2 Set out, in your own words, the parallel between the incarnation and the eucharistic real presence.

8.10

Paschasius Radbertus on the Real Presence

The monastery of Corbie in Picardy was the scene for some theological fireworks during the ninth century, focusing on the doctrine of predestination and the nature of the real presence. The two extracts which follow are from the writings of Paschasius Radbertus (c.790–865) and Ratranmus of Corbie (died 868), who were both monks at Corbie during this period. Each wrote a work with the same title: *De corpore et sanguine Christi*, yet developed very different understandings of the real presence. Radbertus, whose work was completed around 844, developed the idea that the bread and the wine become the body and blood of Christ in reality; Ratranmus, whose work was written shortly afterwards, defended the view that they were merely symbols of body and blood (see 8.11). See also 8.12.

A sacrament is something which is passed down to us in any divine celebration as a pledge of salvation, when what is done visibly achieves something very different and holy inwardly. [...]

We feed upon and drink the sacrament of the body and blood only during the journey through this life, so that, nourished by it, we may be made one in Christ, who sustains us this way so that we may be made ready for immortal and eternal things, while being nourished by angelic grace, we may be made alive spiritually. The Holy Spirit who works in all these sacraments will do this. [...] In baptism through water, we are all born again through him; afterwards, we daily feed upon Christ's body and drink his blood by his power. The same Spirit who created the human being Jesus Christ in the womb of the Virgin without any human seed daily creates the flesh and the blood of Christ by his invisible power through the consecration of this sacrament, even though this cannot be understood outwardly by either sight or taste. [...]

No one who believes the divine words of the Truth declaring "For my flesh is truly food, and my blood is truly drink" (John 6: 55–56)" can doubt that the body and blood are truly created by the consecration of the mystery. [...] Because it is not seemly to devour Christ with our teeth, he willed that, in this mystery, the bread and wine should truly be made his body and blood through their consecration by the power of the Holy Spirit, who daily creates them so that they might be sacrificed mystically for the life of the world. Just as through the Spirit true flesh was created without sexual union from the Virgin, so the same body and blood of Christ are created by mystical consecration out of the substance of bread and wine. It is clearly about this flesh and blood that Christ declares: "Truly, truly I say to you, unless you eat of the flesh of the Son of Man and drink his blood, you will not have eternal life within you" (John 6: 53). There he is certainly speaking about nothing other than the true flesh and the true blood.

Comment

In this, and the reading which follows, we consider the eucharistic debate at the monastery of Corbie. Paschasius may be regarded as a supporter of what was by now the traditional viewpoint – namely, that there was a real change in both bread and wine. The term "transubstantiation" had yet to be invented; there is no doubt, however, that Paschasius's general position could be described in this manner. For Paschasius, the eucharistic body of Christ was to be defined precisely as the flesh born of Mary, which was crucified and rose again, and which was miraculously multiplied by God at each consecration. Paschasius's emphatically realistic view of the transformation of the bread and the wine met with critical responses from a number of writers, including Rabanus Maurus.

Questions for Study

1 Set out Paschasius's understanding of the role of the Holy Spirit in the eucharistic transformation.
2 What role does human reason play in this understanding of the sacramental transformation?

8.11

Ratranmus of Corbie on the Real Presence

As noted in the previous reading, an important debate developed at the monastery of Corbie during the ninth century. Paschasius Radbertus developed the idea that the bread and the wine become the body and blood of Christ in reality (see 8.10); we now turn to consider the views of Ratranmus, who defended the view that they were merely symbols of the body and blood. See also 8.10, 8.12, 8.13.

Certain of the faithful say that [in the mystery] of the body and blood of Christ, which is celebrated daily in the church, nothing happens in the form of a figure or under a hidden symbol, but that it is an open manifestation of truth. Others, however, hold that these elements take the form of a mystery, so that it is one thing which appears to the physical senses, and something different which is discerned by faith. [...] There is no small difference between these two. And although the apostle writes to believers, telling them that they should all hold the same opinions and say the same things, and that no schism should appear among them, yet when they state such totally different views on the mystery of the body and blood of Christ, they are indeed divided by a schism. [. . .] The bread which, through the ministry of the priest, becomes the body of Christ, exhibits one thing externally to human senses, and points to something different inwardly to the minds of believers. Externally, the bread has the same shape, color, and flavor as before; inwardly, however, something very different, something much more precious and excellent, is made known, because something heavenly and divine – that is, the body of Christ – is revealed. This is not perceived or received or consumed by the physical senses, but only in the sight of the believer. The wine also becomes the sacrament of the blood of Christ through priestly consecration. Superficially, it shows one thing; yet inwardly, it contains something else. What can be seen on the surface other than the substance of wine? Taste it, and it has the flavor of wine; smell it, and it has the aroma of wine; look at it, and see the color of wine. [. . .] Since nobody can deny that this is the case, it is clear that the bread and wine are the body and blood of Christ in a figurative sense. After the mystical consecration, when they are no longer called bread and wine, but the body and blood of Christ, as far as the external appearance is concerned, the likeness of flesh cannot be discerned in that bread, just as the actual liquid of blood cannot be seen. [. . .] How then can they be called the body and blood of Christ when no change can be seen to have taken place? [. . .] As far as the physical appearance of both are concerned, they seem to be things which have been physically created. However, as far as their power is concerned, in that they have been created spiritually, they are the mysteries of the body and blood of Christ.

Comment

Offended and puzzled by what he clearly regarded as the unacceptable position of Paschasius Radbertus, Ratranmus set out a rival position, in direct response to Paschasius. An important distinction is drawn between the physical reality of the elements, and their spiritual impact. Ratranmus attracted no criticism at the time for his insistence that there was no ontological change in the bread and the wine; however, by about 1050 there was increasing concern over his views, given the growing sympathy for the view which would later be known as "transubstantiation."

Questions for Study

1 "The bread which, through the ministry of the priest, becomes the body of Christ, exhibits one thing externally to human senses, and points to something different inwardly to the minds of believers." Locate this statement within the text. What is meant by this? Is Ratranmus denying a real change, or suggesting that there are various ways of understanding what is going on?
2 "As far as the physical appearance of both are concerned, they seem to be things which have been physically created. However, as far as their power is concerned, in that they have been created spiritually, they are the mysteries of the body and blood of Christ." What point is being made here? And how does this distinction help Ratranmus critique Paschasius?

8.12

Candidus of Fulda on "This is My Body"

The Benedictine monastery of Fulda, founded in 744, became a leading center of theological reflection under the influential Carolingian writer Rabanus Maurus, who held the position of abbot during the period 822–42. One of the most noted theologians associated with the monastery during this period was Candidus of Fulda (died 845), whose views on the nature of the eucharistic bread attracted some debate. See also 8.10, 8.11, 8.13.

"Take up and eat." That is, my people, make my body – which you now are. This is the body which was given for you. He took this body from the mass of humanity, broke it in the passion, and, having broken it, raised it again from the dead. [. . .] What he took from us, he has now given to us. And you are to "eat" it. That is, you are to make perfect (*perficite*) the body of the church, so that it might become the entire, perfect one bread, whose head is Christ.

Comment

Candidus's interpretation of the phrase "this is my body" (Matthew 26: 26) is quite remarkable. Candidus understands this phrase to refer to the "body of Christ" in the sense of *the church*. The purpose of the sacrament of the body and blood of Christ is to nourish and bring to perfection the church as the body of Christ.

Questions for Study

1 Set out, in your own words, Candidus's understanding of the nature of the bread after its consecration.
2 How does the view set out by Candidus differ from rival Carolingian views (see 8.10, 8.11). What are the main points of difference?

8.13

Lanfranc of Bec on the Mystery of the Sacraments

Lanfranc of Bec (1010–89), who preceded Anselm of Canterbury both as Abbot of the monastery of Bec in Normandy, and as Archbishop of Canterbury, was outraged by what he regarded as totally improper logical explanations of the eucharist, especially that offered by Berengar of Tours. See also 8.10, 8.11, 8.12.

On the one hand, there is the "sacrament" [*sacramentum*]; on the other, there is the "thing of the sacrament" [*res sacramenti*]. The "thing" (or the "reality") of the sacrament is the body of Christ. Yet Christ is risen from the dead. He does not die, and death has no more power over him (Romans 6: 9). So, as the apostle Andrew says, while the bits of [Christ's] flesh [*carnes*] are really eaten and his blood is really drunk, he himself nevertheless continues in his totality [*integer*], living in the heavens at the right hand of the Father until such time as when all will be restored. If you ask me how this is possible, I can only reply briefly as follows: it is a mystery of faith. To believe it can be healthy; to investigate it cannot be of any use.

Comment

Lanfranc here directs his wrath against Berengar of Tours (c.1010–88) – regarded by many medieval writers as something of a maverick – who had argued that it was ridiculous to suppose that the eucharistic bread could be the body of Christ. How could a piece of bread become the body of Christ, when that body had been in heaven for the last thousand years? In this treatise, written around 1070, Lanfranc vigorously defended the mystery of the sacraments, drawing a sharp distinction between the sacrament itself, and the thing which the sacrament signified. Without really providing an explanation of the point, Lanfranc insists that it is possible to eat "bits of Christ's flesh," while Christ's body remains intact in heaven.

Questions for Study

1 Berengar was regarded by many medieval theologians as having discredited the use of reason in theology. Is there anything in this passage which suggests that Lanfranc shares this view?
2 Describe in your own words the distinction between *sacramentum* and *res sacramenti* set out in this passage.

8.14

Hugh of St Victor on the Definition of a Sacrament

In this comprehensive account of the theology of the sacraments, written in Latin at Paris in the first half of the twelfth century, Hugh of St Victor (died 1142) attempts to bring together the various ideas which he believes are essential to the definition of a sacrament. See also 8.15, 8.17, 8.21.

Not every sign of a sacred thing can properly be called a sacrament (for the letters in sacred writings, or statues and pictures, are all "signs of sacred things," but cannot be called sacraments for that reason). [. . .] Anyone wanting a fuller and better definition of a sacrament can define it as follows: "a sacrament is a physical or material element set before the external senses, representing by likeness, signifying by its institution, and containing by sanctification, some invisible and spiritual grace." This definition is recognized as being so appropriate and perfect that it turns out to be appropriate in the case of every sacrament, yet only the sacraments. For everything that has these three elements is a sacrament; and everything that lacks these three cannot be considered as a sacrament. For every sacrament ought to have a kind of likeness to the thing of which it is the sacrament, according to which it is capable of representing the same thing. It ought also to have been instituted in such a way that it is ordained to signify this thing. And finally, it ought to have been sanctified in such a way that it contains that thing, and is efficacious in conferring the same on those who are to be sanctified.

Comment

Hugh of St Victor set out a definition of a sacrament which included the need for a physical element which bore some resemblance to the grace it signified. This had the important consequence of excluding penance from the list of sacraments; it was only when Peter Lombard modified this definition (see 8.15) that the medieval formulation of the list of seven sacraments was standardized.

Questions for Study

1 Set out, in your own words, the essential elements to the definition of a sacrament which Hugh offers.
2 On the basis of Hugh's definition, which of the following count as "sacraments": baptism, ordination, penance, the eucharist?

8.15

Peter Lombard on the Definition of a Sacrament

In this major theological work, compiled at Paris during years 1155–8, Peter Lombard (c.1100–60) brought together a series of quotations – known as "Sentences" – from patristic writers such as Augustine, and attempted to reconcile them and offer a theological synthesis based upon them. In this passsage he reflects on the nature of a sacrament and offers his own definition. See also 8.14.

A sacrament bears a likeness to the thing of which it is a sign. "For if sacraments did not have a likeness of the things whose sacraments they are, they would not properly be called sacraments" (Augustine). [. . .] Something can properly be called a sacrament if it is a sign of the grace of God and a form of invisible grace, so that it bears its image and exists as its cause. Sacraments were therefore instituted for the sake of sanctifying, as well as of signifying. [. . .] Those things which were instituted for the purpose of signifying alone are nothing more than signs, and are not sacraments, as in the case of the physical sacrifices and ceremonial observances of the Old Law, which were never able to make those who offered them righteous.

[. . .] Now let us consider the sacraments of the New Law, which are baptism, confirmation, the bread of blessing (that is, the Eucharist), penance, extreme unction, ordination, and marriage. Some of these, such as baptism, provide a remedy against sin and confer the assistance of grace; others, such as marriage, are only a remedy; and others, such as the Eucharist and ordination, strengthen us with grace and power. [. . .] So why were these sacraments not instituted soon after the fall of humanity, since they convey righteousness and salvation? We reply that the sacraments of grace were not given before the coming of Christ, who is the giver of grace, in that they receive their virtue from his death and suffering.

Comment

Peter Lombard sets out a definition of a sacrament which differed from that offered by Hugh of St Victor (see 8.14) by avoiding any reference to any physical element (such as bread, wine, or water.) Penance could now be reckoned among the sacraments. Using this definition, Peter was able to set out a list of seven sacraments, which became definitive for medieval catholic theology.

Questions for Study

1 Set out, in your own words, the essential elements to the definition of a sacrament which Peter offers.
2 In what way does the definition offered by Peter differ from that provided by Hugh of St Victor? And what are the outcomes of this difference?

8.16

Thomas Aquinas on Transubstantiation

The *Summa Theologiae* ("The Totality of Theology"), which Aquinas began to write in Latin in 1265 and left unfinished at the time of his death, is widely regarded as the greatest work of medieval theology. In this discussion of the doctrine of transubstantiation, Aquinas (c.1225–74) sets out an approach which would become normative for medieval catholic theology. See also 8.5, 8.10, 8.11, 8.12, 8.22, 8.23, 8.28.

2. *Whether the substance of bread and wine remain in this sacrament after consecration.*

[...] It has been held that the substance of bread and wine remain in this sacrament after consecration. But this position cannot be maintained, for in the first place it destroys the reality of this sacrament, which demands that in the sacrament there should be the true body of Christ, which was not there before consecration. Now a thing cannot be in a place where it was not before except either by change of position, or by the conversion of some other thing into it; as a fire begins to be in a house either because it is carried there or because it is kindled. But it is clear that the body of Christ does not begin to be in the sacrament through change of position. [...] Therefore it remains that the body of Christ can only come to be in the sacrament by means of the conversion of the substance of bread into his body; and that which is converted into anything does not remain after the conversion. [...] This position is therefore to be avoided as heretical.

3. *Whether the substance of bread or wine is annihilated after the consecration of this sacrament.*

[...] As the substance of bread or wine does not remain in the sacrament, some have thought it impossible that their substance should be converted into that of the body or blood of Christ, and therefore have maintained that through the consecration the substance of bread or wine is either resolved into underlying matter (that is, the four elements) or annihilated. [. . .] But this is impossible, because it is impossible to suppose the manner in which the true body of Christ begins to be in the sacrament, unless by conversion of the substance of bread; and this conversion is ruled out by the supposition of the annihilation of the substance of bread, or its resolution into underlying matter. [. . .]

4. *Whether bread can be changed into the body of Christ.*

[. . .] This conversion is not like natural conversions but is wholly supernatural, brought about only by the power of God. [. . .] All conversion which takes place according to the laws of nature is formal. [. . .] But God [. . .] can produce not only a formal conversion, that is, the replacement of one form by another in the same subject, but also the conversion of the whole being, that is, the conversion of the whole substance of A into the whole substance of B. And this is done in this sacrament by the power of God, for the whole substance of bread is converted into the whole substance of Christ's body. [. . .] Hence this conversion is properly called transubstantiation. [. . .]

5. *Whether the accidents of bread and wine remain in the sacrament after this conversion.*

[. . .] It is obvious to our senses that after consecration all the accidents of bread and wine remain. And, by divine providence, there is a good reason for this. First, because it is not normal for people to eat human flesh and to drink human blood; in fact, they are revolted by this idea. Therefore Christ's flesh and blood are set before us to be taken under the appearances of those things which are of frequent use, namely bread and wine. Secondly, if we ate our Lord under his proper appearance, this sacrament would be ridiculed by unbelievers. Thirdly, in order that, while we take the Lord's body and blood invisibly, this fact may avail towards the merit of faith.

Comment

This important discussion of the nature of the eucharistic real presence can be seen as a definitive statement of the concept of transubstantiation. Note that the passage makes an important distinction, based on Aristotelian philosophy, between the "accidents" (outward appearances) and "substance" (inward reality) of the bread and wine.

Questions for Study

1 Explain exactly what happens in the process of consecration, according to Aquinas. What does Aquinas mean by the term "transubstantiation"?
2 According to Aquinas, why is it that, after consecration, all the accidents of the bread and the wine remain unchanged?

8.17

Martin Luther on the Number of Sacraments

In this opening part of his 1520 writing *The Babylonian Captivity of the Church*, Martin Luther (1483–1546) allowed that penance was a sacrament. By the end of the same work, he had changed his mind, and denied the sacramental character of penance, apparently on the basis of the fact that there was no sacramental sign associated with it. Luther here seems to base himself on the Vulgate version of 1 Timothy 3: 16, which refers to Christ as a *sacramentum*. See also 8.18, 8.19, 8.26.

To begin with, I must deny that there are seven sacraments, and for the present maintain that there are but three: baptism, penance, and the bread. All three have been subjected to a miserable captivity by the Roman curia, and the church has been robbed of all her liberty. Yet if I were to speak according to the usage of the Scriptures, I should have only one single sacrament, but with three sacramental signs.

Comment

In this brief passage Luther sets out a number of points. First, he insists that a sacrament is something which points to Christ. At this stage, he does not regard a physical sign as being of decisive importance. By the end of the work, he has come to the view that there are three essential elements to the definition of a sacrament:

1 a divine promise;
2 authorization from Jesus Christ;
3 a physical sign.

As a result, penance ceased to be, in Luther's view, sacramental.

Questions for Study

1 On the basis of Luther's definition of a sacrament, comment on the grounds on which the following are denied sacramental status: extreme unction, marriage, ordination.
2 What does Luther mean when he speaks of "one single sacrament" and "three sacramental signs"?

8.18

Martin Luther on the Doctrine of Transubstantiation

In this 1520 criticism of the teachings of the medieval church concerning the sacraments, again taken from *The Babylonian Captivity of the Church*, Luther argued that the concept of "transubstantiation" is untenable. While Luther maintains a doctrine of the real presence of Christ in the eucharist, he refuses to accept the specifically Aristotelian interpretation of it associated with transubstantiation. See also 8.16, 8.28.

Therefore it is an absurd and new imposition upon the words to understand "bread" to mean "the form or accidents" of bread, and "wine" to mean "the form or accidents of wine." Why do they not also understand all other things to mean their "forms or accident?" And even if this might be done with everything else, it would still not be right to weaken the words of God in this way, and to cause so much harm by depriving them of their signification.

But for more than twelve hundred years the church believed rightly, during which time the holy fathers never, at any time or place, mentioned this "transubstantiation" (a pretentious word and idea) until the pseudo-philosophy of Aristotle began to make its inroads into the church in these last three hundred years, in which many things have been incorrectly defined, as for example, that the divine essence is neither begotten nor begets; or that the soul is the substantial form of the human body. These and like assertions are made without any reason or cause, as the Cardinal of Cambrai himself admits.

They may want to argue that the danger of lapsing into idolatry demands that the bread and wine should not be truly present. This is ridiculous. The laity have never heard of their subtle philosophy of substance and accidents, and could not make sense of it even if they were taught about it. Anyway, the same danger is just as much present with the accidents which they can see, as with the substance which they cannot see. If they do not worship the accidents, but the Christ hidden under them, why should they worship the [substance of the] bread, which they do not see?

But why could not Christ include his body in the substance of the bread just as well as in the accidents? In red-hot iron, for example, the two substances, fire and iron, are so mingled that every part is both iron and fire. Why should it not be even more possible that the glorious body of Christ be contained in every part of the substance of the bread? [. . .] I rejoice greatly that the simple faith of this sacrament is still to be found, at least among ordinary people. For as they cannot understand the matter, neither do they dispute whether accidents are present without substance, but believe with a simple faith that Christ's body and blood are truly contained there, and leave the argument about what contains them to those who have nothing else to do with their time. [. . .]

What is true concerning Christ is also true concerning the sacrament. In order for the divinity to dwell in a human body, it is not necessary for the human nature to be transubstantiated and the divinity contained under the accidents of the human nature. Both natures are simply there in their entirety, and it is true to say: "This man is God; this God is man." Even though philosophy is not capable of grasping this, faith is. And the authority of God's Word is greater than the capacity of our intellect to grasp it. In the same way, it is not necessary in the sacrament that the bread and wine be transubstantiated and that Christ be contained under their accidents in order that the real body and real blood may be present. But both remain there at the same time, and it is truly said: "This bread is my body; this wine is my blood," and vice versa. (I will understand it in this way for the time being on account of the honor of the holy words of God, to which I will allow no violence to be done by petty human arguments, nor will I allow them to be twisted into meanings which are foreign to them.)

Comment

This passage indicates that Luther rejected the concept of transubstantiation on the grounds that it represented the intrusion of Aristotle's "pseudo-philosophy" into theology. Yet although Luther is hostile to the *term* transubstantiation, his own views on the real presence are actually quite similar to those which it expresses. Note that the "Cardinal of Cambrai" is a reference to Pierre d'Ailly, a noted late medieval theologian, who Luther studied while preparing for the priesthood.

Questions for Study

1 On exactly what grounds does Luther reject transubstantiation?
2 "In red-hot iron, for example, the two substances, fire and iron, are so mingled that every part is both iron and fire. Why should it not be even more possible that the glorious body of Christ be contained in every part of the substance of the bread?" Locate this text within the passage. What does Luther mean by this? What view of the real presence is being set out here?

8.19

Martin Luther on the Bread and Wine as a Testament

In this discussion of the function of the communion service, again taken from the 1520 writing *The Babylonian Captivity of the Church*, Luther argues that it acts like a "last will" or "testament," in which certain goods are promised to named heirs, once the testator has died. Note in particular how Luther insists that the incarnation means that it is perfectly proper to say that "God can die." The concept of a faith "which clings to the Word of the promising God" is characteristic of Luther and other reformers. See also 6.33, 6.37.

Let this stand, therefore, as our first and infallible proposition: the mass or Sacrament of the Altar [*missam seu sacramentum altaris*] is Christ's testament [*testamentum Christi*], which, when he was dying, he left to be distributed among believers. For that is the meaning of his words, "This cup is the new testament in my blood" (Luke 22: 20; 1 Corinthians 11: 25). Let this truth stand, I say, as the immovable foundation on which we shall base all that we have to say. You will see that we are going to undermine every human impiety to have been brought into this most precious sacrament. Christ, who is the truth, truly says that this is the new testament in his blood, poured out for us (Luke 22: 20). Not without reason do I dwell on this sentence; this is no minor matter, and it demands our full attention.

Were we to enquire what a testament is, we shall learn at the same time what the mass is, and what constitutes its use, benefits, and abuse. A testament is, without doubt, a promise made by someone who is about to die, in which a bequest is identified and heirs are appointed. A testament, therefore, involves first, the death of the testator; and second, the promise of an inheritance and the identification of the heirs. Thus Paul discusses at length the nature of a testament in Romans 4, Galatians 3 and 4, and Hebrews 9. We see the same thing clearly also in these words of Christ. Christ testifies concerning his death when he says: "This is my body, which is given, this is my blood, which is poured out" (Luke 22: 19–20). He names and designates the bequest when he says "for the forgiveness of sins" (Matthew 26: 28). And he appoints the heirs when he says "For you (Luke 22: 19–20; 1 Corinthians 11: 24) and for many" (Matthew 26: 28; Mark 14: 24), that is, for those who accept and believe the promise of the testator. For it is faith that makes heirs, as we shall see.

So you see that what we call the mass is a promise of the forgiveness of sins, made to us by God, and such a promise as has been confirmed [*firma sit*] by the death of the Son of God. For a promise and a testament differ only in that a testament involves the death of the one who makes it. A testator is someone who promises and is about to die [*testator idem est quod moriturus promissor*], while someone who promises (if I may put it thus) is a testator who is not about to die. This testament of Christ is foreshadowed in all the promises of God from the beginning of the world; indeed, whatever value those ancient promises possessed derived totally from this new promise that was to come in Christ. Hence the words "compact," "covenant," and "testament of the Lord" [*pactum, foedus, testamentum domini*] occur so often in Scripture, by which it was signified that God would one day die. "For where there is a testament, the death of the testator must of necessity occur" (Hebrews 9: 16). Now God made a testament; therefore, it was necessary that he should die. But God could not die unless he became a human. Thus the incarnation and the death of Christ are both to be understood as being in this one enormously rich word, "testament."

From this, it can be seen what constitutes the right and what is the wrong use of the mass, and what constitutes worthy and what the unworthy preparation for it. If the mass is a promise, as has been said, then access to it is to be gained, not with any works, or powers, or merits of one's own, but by faith alone. For where there is the Word of the promising God, there must necessarily be the faith of the accepting person [*Ubi enim est verbum promittendis dei, ibi necessaria est fides acceptantis hominis*], so that it is clear that the beginning of our salvation is a faith which clings to the Word of the promising God [*fides quae pendeat in verbo promittendis dei*], who, without any effort on our part, in free and unmerited mercy goes before us and offers us the word of his promise. "He sent forth his word, and thus healed them" (Psalm 107: 20) not: "He accepted our work, and thus healed us." The Word of God is first of all. After it follows faith; after faith, love [*charitas*]; then love does every good work, for it does no wrong, indeed, it is the fulfilling of the law (Romans 13: 10). Humanity can only come to God or deal with him through faith.

Comment

Luther's insight here is that a "testament" involves the making of promises which become operational only after the death of the person who made those promises in the first place. The liturgy of the mass, or communion service, thus makes three vitally important points.

1 It affirms the promises of grace and forgiveness.
2 It identifies those to whom those promises are made.
3 It declares the death of the one who made those promises.

The mass thus dramatically proclaims that the promises of grace and forgiveness are now in effect. It is a promise of the forgiveness of sins made to us by God, and such a promise as has been confirmed by the death of the Son of God. By proclaiming the death of Christ, the community of faith affirms that the precious promises of forgiveness and eternal life are now effective for those with faith.

Questions for Study

1 Set out, in your own words, the general manner in which Luther uses the notion of a "testament" in this passage.
2 "For where there is the Word of the promising God, there must necessarily be the faith of the accepting person." Locate this statement within the passage. What does Luther mean by this?

8.20

Martin Luther on Baptism

This extract from Luther's *Lesser Catechism*, written in German in 1529, brings out the close relation between Word and sacrament in Luther's thought. Notice the distinctive "question and answer" format of the Catechism, designed to aid learning its contents by heart. See also 6.33, 8.19.

Q. What is baptism?
A. Baptism is not just water on its own, but it is water used according to God's command and linked with God's Word.
Q. What is this Word of God?
A. Our Lord Christ, as recorded in Matthew 28: 19, said, "Go therefore and make disciples of all nations, baptizing them in the name of the Father and of the Son and of the Holy Spirit."
Q. What gifts or benefits does Baptism bring?
A. It brings about the forgiveness of sins, saves us from death and the devil, and grants eternal blessedness to all who believe, as the Word and promise of God declare.
Q. What is this Word and promise of God?
A. Our Lord Christ, as recorded in Mark 16: 16, said, "Anyone who believes and is baptized will be saved; but those who do not believe will be condemned."
Q. How can water bring about such a great thing?
A. Water does not; but it is the Word of God with and through the water, and our faith which trusts in the Word of God in the water. For without the Word of God, that water is nothing but water, and there is no Baptism. But when it is linked with the Word of God, it is a Baptism, that is, a gracious water of life [*gnadenreych wasser desz lebens*] and a bath of new birth in the Holy Spirit [*ain bad der neuwen geburt im heyligen geyst*]. [. . .]
Q. What does such washing with water mean?
A. It means that the old Adam in us should be drowned by daily sorrow and repentance, and put to death, along with all sins and evil lusts, and that a new person [*neuwer-mensch*] should come forth daily and rise up in righteousness and purity [*reynigkeyt*], to live forever before God.

Comment

The format of this work is as interesting as its contents. This passage takes the question-and-answer format typical of the catechisms of the Reformation, and aims to offer simple answers which could be memorized by children. The passage in question sets out a brief theology of baptism, in which the theme of trust in the divine promises plays a major role.

Questions for Study

1 Set out in your own words what benefits Luther understands baptism to bring.
2 How does Luther deal with the objection that the benefits which are brought by baptism seem out of all proportion to the humble and ordinary water that is used in baptism?

8.21

Philip Melanchthon on Sacramental Signs

In this extract from the *Loci Communes* ("Commonplaces"), written in Latin in 1521, the German Lutheran theologian Philip Melanchthon (1497–1560) sets out his understanding of the relation of Word and Sacrament, and particularly between faith and the promises of God. Note the emphatic insistence that sacraments do not justify in themselves; they are merely signs of the justifying grace of God. Nevertheless, they serve the vital function of reassuring believers of God's grace and goodness. See also 6.33, 6.37, 8.19, 8.28.

We have said that the gospel is the promise of grace. The *locus* on signs is very closely related to promises. For in the Scriptures these signs are added to the promises as seals which remind us of the promises, and are certain witnesses to the divine will toward us, testifying that we shall certainly receive what God has promised. Major errors have resulted from the use of signs. For when the [medieval theological] schools dispute about the difference between the sacraments of the Old and New Testaments, they say that there is no power to justify in the sacraments of the Old Testament. They attribute the power to justify to the sacraments of the New Testament, which is clearly an error. For faith alone justifies. The nature of signs is best understood from Paul in Romans 4: 10–12, where he speaks of circumcision. He says that Abraham was not justified *by* circumcision but *before* circumcision and without merit of circumcision. But afterward he received circumcision as a "seal of righteousness" – that is, a seal that God declared Abraham to be righteous, and declared that Abraham was righteous before God, so that his troubled conscience might not despair. And what can be more pleasing than this use of signs? It is not enough for signs to remind us of the divine promises. The great fact is that they are a testimony of God's will toward you. Thus Moses calls circumcision a "sign" in Genesis 17: 11: "And it shall be a sign of the covenant between me and you." The fact that circumcision is a sign reminds Abraham and all who are circumcised of the divine promise. The fact that circumcision is a sign of the covenant, strengthens the conscience of Abraham so that he does not doubt at all that what has been promised will come to pass, that God will furnish what he promised. And what was it that God promised to Abraham? Was it not that he would be Abraham's God: that he would cherish, justify, and preserve him, and so on? Abraham did not doubt that these things were certain, since he had been strengthened by circumcision as by a seal. [. . .]

Signs do not justify, as the apostle says: "circumcision counts for nothing" (1 Corinthians 7: 19), so that baptism is nothing, and participation in the Lord's Supper [*mensa domini*] is nothing, but they are testimonies and "seals" of the divine will toward you which give assurance to your conscience if it doubts God's grace or benevolence toward you. [. . .] You ought not to doubt that you have experienced mercy when you have heard the gospel and received the signs of the gospel, baptism, and the body and blood of the Lord. Hezekiah could have been restored without a sign if he had been willing to believe the bare promise of God, and Gideon would have overcome without a sign if he had believed. So you can be justified without a sign, provided you believe. Therefore, signs do not justify, but the faith of Hezekiah and Gideon had to be secured, strengthened, and confirmed by such signs. In the same way our weakness is strengthened by signs, lest it despair of the mercy of God amid so many attacks from sin. If God himself were to speak with you face to face or show you some special pledge of his mercy as, for example, a miracle, you would consider it nothing else than a sign of divine favor. As for these signs, then, you ought to believe with as much certainty that God is merciful to you when you receive baptism and participate in the Lord's Supper as you would if God himself were to speak with you or to show forth some other miracle that would relate directly to you. Signs are given for the purpose of stimulating faith. Those who call such things into question have lost both faith and the use of signs. The knowledge of signs is very healthful, and I have no idea whether there is anything else that consoles the conscience and strengthens it more effectively than this use of signs.

Those things which others call "sacraments" we call "signs," or, if you prefer, "sacramental signs." For Paul calls Christ himself a "sacrament" (Colossians 1: 27; 1 Timothy 3: 16). If you do not like the term "sign," you may call the sacraments "seals," for this term comes closer to the nature of the sacraments. Those who have compared these signs with symbols or military passwords are to be commended for doing so, because signs were only marks by which those to whom the divine promises pertained could be known. Although he had already been justified, Cornelius was baptized that he might be reckoned in the number of those to whom the promise of the Kingdom of God and eternal life pertained. I have given this instruction on the nature of signs that you may understand what a godly use of the sacraments is, lest anyone follow the Scholastics, who have attributed justification to the signs by a terrible error.

There are two signs, however, instituted by Christ in the gospel: baptism and participation in the Lord's Supper. For we judge that sacramental signs are only those which have been divinely handed down as signs of the grace of God. For we human beings can neither institute a sign of the divine will toward us nor can we adapt those signs which Scripture has employed in other ways as signifying that will. Therefore, we are all the more amazed at how it ever came into the minds of the Sophists to include among the sacraments things which the Scriptures do not mention by so much as a word, especially when they attributed justification to signs.

Comment

The key theological issue to be explored in this passage is the relation between the sign and what is being signified. Melanchthon is especially concerned to explain that it is not signs in themselves which justify individuals, or confer spiritual benefits, but the greater spiritual reality which they represent. In particular, Melanchthon stresses that sacraments serve to reinforce trust in the divine promises.

Questions for Study

1 What does Melanchthon mean when he speaks of sacraments as "sealing" the promises of God?
2 "For where there is the Word of the promising God, there must necessarily be the faith of the accepting person." Locate this statement within Luther's discussion of the eucharist (8.19). In what way does Melanchthon's discussion help clarify what Luther might mean by this, and how the sacraments can work to deepen faith and trust in God?

8.22

Kornelius Hendriks Hoen on "This is My Body"

In this letter, which circulated widely in 1525, the Dutch humanist writer Kornelius Hendriks Hoen (died 1524) argued for a symbolical or metaphorical interpretation of the Latin words *hoc est corpus meum* ("this is my body"). Although ignored by Luther, Hoen's letter was read with enthusiasm by Zwingli (8.23), whose own view of the matter subsequently strongly resembled Hoen's. See also 8.11, 8.23.

For if we adore and worship this consecrated bread, honoring it in every way as if it were God, even though it is not God, how, I ask you, do we differ from those heathens who worshiped wood and stones? They believed that there was some divinity [*numen*] in them, which there was not, for they would not have wished to adore stones unless perhaps they had first believed that these stones were gods.

Now someone might say: "We have the Word of God which says, 'This is My Body.' " That is true, you do have this Word of the Lord. In just the same way, you also have that word which encourages Roman tyranny: "Whatever you shall bind on earth is bound in heaven" (Matthew 16: 19). But if you were to study this carefully, you will find it does not provide any basis at all for such tyranny. So let us examine these matters facing us, so that we may not be like those with blind guides, who fall together with them into a pit (Matthew 15: 14). For the Lord prohibits us from believing anyone who says, "Here is Christ" or "There is Christ" (Matthew 24: 23). For this reason, I should not have faith in those who say that Christ is in the bread: I could not excuse myself as having been deceived, since I have refused to listen to the warning voice of Christ. For now those dangerous times have come, during which he predicted this would happen.

Nor did the apostles speak of the sacrament in this way: they *broke* bread, and they *called* it bread: they were silent about this Roman belief. Nor is this contradicted by St Paul who, although he says, "The bread which we break, is it not a sharing in the body of Christ?" (1 Corinthians 10: 16), does not say that the bread *is* the body of Christ. It is therefore obvious that the word "is" [*est*] in this text should be interpreted as meaning "signifies" [*significat*)]. [. . .]

But let us first see on what foundation the Romanists build their doctrine, a teaching that is so singular and wonderful that nothing like it is found in Scripture. We read that Christ became flesh [*incarnatus*] – but that was once only, in the womb of the virgin. And this incarnation was predicted by many prophetic oracles; it was demonstrated in Christ's life, death, and whole way of life, and preached by the apostles. But that idea that Christ would daily become bread [*impanatus*], so to speak, in the hands of anyone conducting this sacrifice [*in manibus cuiusvis sacrificuli*] was neither foretold by the prophets nor preached by the apostles, but rests only on what Christ said: "This is my body; do this in remembrance of me."

Comment

Historically, the kind of arguments set out by Hoen in this letter proved to be very influential. Huldrych Zwingli clearly believed that the points raised by Hoen were unanswerable, and developed a theology of the "real presence" (which, in his case, is perhaps better described as a "real absence") based upon Hoen's approach. Note especially that Hoen's arguments can be directed against Luther's view of the real presence as much as against the idea of transubstantiation.

Questions for Study

1. What use does Hoen make of Paul's comments in 1 Corinthians 10? Why do you think he concentrates upon this passage, rather than the Gospel accounts of the Last Supper?
2. What point is Hoen making in his critical comparison of the Latin words *incarnatus* and *impanatus*, both of which are translated in this passage?

8.23

Huldrych Zwingli on "This is My Body"

In this work, first published in Swiss-German on February 23, 1526 under the title *Eine klare Unterrichtung vom nachtmal Christi* ("A clear instruction concerning the supper of Christ"), the Swiss Protestant reformer Huldrych Zwingli (1484–1531) sets out his "memorialist" view of the Lord's Supper. According to Zwingli, Christ is remembered in his absence. See also 8.10, 8.11, 8.22.

But there are two clear flaws in the argument [that the words "this is my body" refer to the bread being the physical body of Christ]. The first is that we are not given any reason to believe that when the Pope or some other human person says: "This is my body," the body of Christ is necessarily present. It is useless to say that Christ himself said: "Do this in remembrance of me": therefore the body of Christ is there. [. . .] The second flaw is a failure to see that before we use the Word of God to justify anything, we must first understand it correctly. For example, when Christ says: "I am the vine" (John 15: 5), we have to consider that he is using figurative speech in the first place. In other words, he is *like* a vine, just as the branches are nourished by the vine and cannot bear fruit without it, so believers are in him, and without him they can do nothing. Now if you object against this interpretation of Christ's saying "I am the vine," and argue that therefore he must be a physical vine, you end up by making Christ into a piece of vine wood. In the same way, when you come to the words: "This is my body," you must first make sure that he intended to give his flesh and blood in physical form. Otherwise it is quite pointless to argue that he said it, and therefore it is so. For it is so only as he himself understood it to be so, and not as you misunderstand it. [. . .] Let us consider the basis of the doctrine. If in Christ's saying: "This is my body," we take the little word "is" in a substantive manner, that is literally, then it necessarily follows that the substance of the body or the flesh of Christ is literally and essentially present. But this gives rise to two obvious mistakes.

The first is this: if he is literally and essentially present in the flesh, then he is actually torn apart by the teeth and tangibly masticated in human mouths. We cannot get round the issue by saying: "With God all things are possible." [. . .] It is evident, then, that the flesh is not present literally and corporally. For if it were, its mass and substance would be perceived, and it would be pressed with the teeth. [. . .] Therefore, if the "is" is to be taken literally, the body of Christ must be visibly, essentially, physically and tangibly present [*so müßte der lychnam Christi sichtbar, wesenlich, lyplich, empfindlich da sin*]. For that reason even in this erroneous teaching itself there is a proof that the words cannot possibly mean that we partake physically of flesh and blood: for if God says literally: "This is my body," then the body ought to be there literally and physically [. . .] And since we do not experience or perceive any such presence, it follows that the words of Christ cannot refer to physical flesh and blood. For if that were the meaning, we should constantly perceive them, for he cannot lie. You see, then, that the argument for a literal presence merely works against them.

The second error resulting from a literal interpretation corresponds to that second opinion which we mentioned alongside the first, namely, that we eat the body of Christ in or under the bread, the bread itself remaining bread. If we take the word "is" in a substantive way, that is literally, then it is an obvious mistake to say that the bread remains bread and to deny transubstantiation, the changing of the substance of bread into that of flesh. And for this reason: I apply the argument used in the first error. The Word of God is living. He said: "This is my body." Therefore it is his body. But if we take the word "is" literally, as the second error obstinately maintains, then necessarily the substance of bread has to be changed completely into that of flesh. But that means that the bread is no longer there. Therefore it is impossible to maintain that the bread remains, but that in or under the bread flesh is eaten. Notice how utterly unreasonable this position is. On no account will it allow that Christ's words: "This is my body," are figurative or symbolical. It insists that the word "is" must be taken literally. But it then proceeds to ignore that word and to say: "The body of Christ is eaten *in* the bread." Yet Christ did not say: "Take, eat, my body is eaten in the bread." He said: "This is my body." How dreadful a thing it is to get out of one's depth! If it were I who perverted the words of Christ in that way, surely the ax of judgment would strike me down. The second error is easily perceived, then, and we have only to compare the two and they cancel each other out. For the first maintains that the flesh and blood are present on account of the word "is." But if we take that word literally, it destroys the second, which tries to take it literally but still asserts that the bread remains bread. For if the word is taken literally, the bread is not bread but flesh. On the other hand, the second error at least recognizes that the substance of bread is not turned into the substance of flesh. It thus safeguards the truth that the word "is" cannot be taken literally. If it were literal, the flesh would be no less perceptible than the bread. For just as, before the consecration (as they term it), the bread is perceptible as bread, so from the moment of consecration [*wyhung*] it would have to be perceptible as flesh. Hence the first error is destroyed, and we may conclude that they are both obviously false. For when the second maintains that the "is" is to be taken literally, it is adopting a quite indefensible position, as we have seen: for there is no other way of avoiding a figurative interpretation. Yet when we forcibly expose this defect, pointing out that there is no foundation for such ideas, they simply cry: "We remain faithful to the simple words of Christ, trusting that those Christians who follow the simple words of Christ will not go astray." But what you call the simple meaning of those words is actually the most doubtful, the most obscure, the least intelligible of all. If the simple meaning of Scripture is that which we maintain through a misunderstanding of the letter, then Christ is a piece of vine wood, or a silly sheep, or a door, and Peter is the foundation-stone of the Church. The simple or natural sense of these words is that which obtains in all similar instances, that which the minds of all believers find the most natural and the most easily understood.

Comment

Zwingli here deals with the true meaning of the Latin phrase *hoc est corpus meum*, "this is my body" (Matthew 26: 26). Using arguments which clearly reflect familiarity with Kornelius Hoen's letter on the subject (see 8.22), Zwingli argues that the only acceptable meaning of the word "is" in this phrase must be acknowledged to be "signifies." The unstated object of Zwingli's criticism here is Martin Luther's view of the real presence, which Zwingli regarded as being inconsistent with his reforming principles.

Questions for Study

1 Set out, in your own words, Zwingli's argument against the notion of the "real presence."
2 Why does Zwingli insist that the word "is," as it occurs in Christ's words "this is my body" (Matthew 26: 26), is not to be interpreted literally?

8.24

Huldrych Zwingli on the Nature of Sacraments

This work, published on May 27, 1525 in Swiss-German as *von dem touff* ("On baptism"), opens with an important discussion of the nature of sacraments in general, before moving on to a more detailed analysis of baptism itself. Zwingli here develops an understanding of sacraments which focuses on their symbolic role, and particularly the way in which they function as signs of public commitment on the part of individuals to the church as a whole. He draws an analogy with the annual pilgrimage to the battle site of Nähenfels – the "Näfelser Fahrtfeier" – which commemorated a major Swiss victory over the Austrians in April 1388. Just as a loyal Swiss citizen would commemorate this great victory as a sign of loyalty to the nation, so the Christian celebrates Christ's death as a sign of loyalty to the church. See also 8.14, 8.15, 8.17, 8.19, 8.26.

Now [Christ] has left behind to us, his fellow members, two ceremonies, that is, two external things or signs: baptism and the thanksgiving or remembrance [*dancksagung oder widergedächtnus*], undoubtedly as a concession to our weakness. [. . .] By the first of these signs, baptism, we are initially marked off to God, as we shall see later. In the other, the Lord's Supper or thanksgiving, we give thanks to God because he has redeemed us by his Son.

Before we speak about baptism, we must first identify the meaning of the word "sacrament." To us Germans, the word "sacrament" suggests something that has power to take away sin or to make us holy. But this is a serious error. For only Jesus Christ and no external thing can take away the sins of us Christians or make us holy. [...] As used in this context the word "sacrament" means a sign of commitment [*Pflichtszeichen*]. If a man sews on a white cross, he proclaims that he is a [Swiss] Confederate [*Eydgnoß*]. And if he makes the pilgrimage to Nähenfels and gives God praise and thanksgiving for the victory delivered to our forefathers, he testifies from his heart that he is a Confederate. Similarly the man who receives the mark of baptism is the one who is resolved to hear what God says to him, to learn the divine precepts and to live his life in accordance with them. And the man who, in the remembrance or supper, gives thanks to God in the congregation declares that he heartily rejoices in the death of Christ and thanks him for it. So I ask these quibblers that they allow the sacraments to be real sacraments, and that they do not describe them as signs [*zeichen*] which are identical with the things which they represent. For if they are the things which they represent, they are no longer signs: for the sign and the thing which is represented cannot be the same thing. Sacraments – as even the papists maintain – are simply the signs of holy things. Baptism is a sign which pledges us to the Lord Jesus Christ. The remembrance shows us that Christ suffered death for our sake. They are the signs and pledges [*zeichen und verpflichtungen*] of these holy things. You will find ample proof of this if you consider the pledge of circumcision and the thanksgiving of the Passover lamb.

Comment

The passage refers to the victory of the Swiss over the Austrians in 1388 near Nähenfels. This victory is usually regarded as marking the beginning of the Swiss (or Helvetic) Confederation, and it was commemorated by a pilgrimage to the site of the battle on the first Thursday in April. Zwingli makes two points on the basis of this analogy. First, the Swiss soldier wears a white cross (now incorporated into the Swiss national flag, of course) as a *Pflichtszeichen*, demonstrating publicly his allegiance to the Confederacy. Similarly, Christians demonstrate their allegiance to the church publicly, initially by baptism, and subsequently by participating in the Eucharist. Baptism is thus the "visible entry and sealing into Christ." Second, the historical event which brought the Confederacy into being is commemorated as a token of allegiance to that same Confederacy. Similarly, Christians commemorate the historical event which brought the Christian church into being (the death of Jesus Christ) as a token of their commitment to that church. The Eucharist is thus a memorial of the historical event leading to the establishment of the Christian church, and a public demonstration of the believer's allegiance to that church and its members.

Questions for Study

1 What does Zwingli say about baptism in this passage? And how does the Nähenfels analogy illustrate this?
2 What does Zwingli say about the Lord's Supper in this passage? And how does the Nähenfels analogy illustrate this?

8.25

The First Helvetic Confession on the Efficacy of the Sacraments

This important early statement of Reformed theology, formulated by Swiss theologians in 1536, sets out a view of the sacraments which regards them as efficacious signs. Note the emphatic assertion that the efficacy of these is totally due to God, rather than anything which is inherent within those signs. The fact that they are able to bring about what they signify is due to the power of God, not to the power of the signs themselves. See also 8.18, 8.19, 8.26, 8.29.

The signs [*zeychen*], which are called sacraments, are two, namely, Baptism and the Lord's Supper. These sacraments are significant, holy signs of elevated and secret things [*hoher und heymlicher dingen*]. However, they are not merely empty signs, but consist of both the sign and substance. For in baptism the water is the sign, but the substance and spiritual thing is rebirth and admission into the people of God. In the Lord's Supper the bread and wine are the signs, but the spiritual substance is the communion of the body and blood of Christ, the salvation acquired on the cross, and forgiveness of sins. As the signs are physically received, so these substantial, invisible, and spiritual things are received in faith. In addition, the entire power, efficacy, and fruit of the sacraments lies in these spiritual and substantial things. For this reason, we confess that the sacraments are not simply outward signs of Christian fellowship. On the contrary, we confess them to be signs of divine grace by which the ministers of the Church work with the Lord for the purpose and to the end which He Himself promises, offers and efficaciously provides. We confess, however, that all sanctifying and saving power is to be ascribed to God, the Lord alone.

Comment

This is a very clearly worded passage, which needs little comment. The basic point is that a sacrament is indeed affirmed to be a sign – but more than just a sign. The basic idea is probably best conceived as an "efficacious sign" – that is, something that somehow brings about what is signified.

Questions for Study

1. What, according to this passage, do sacraments achieve?
2. Why, according to this passage, is it inadequate to refer to sacraments simply as "signs"?

8.26

John Calvin on the Nature of Sacraments

In this passage from the 1559 edition of the *Institutes of the Christian Religion*, John Calvin (1509–64) explores the relation between a sacramental sign and the grace which it signifies. Notice the emphasis placed on God's deliberate accommodation to human weakness. See also 8.21, 8.25, 8.29.

To start with, we must consider what a sacrament is. It seems to me that a simple and proper definition is that it is an outward sign by which the Lord seals on our consciences the promises of his good will toward us in order to sustain the weakness of our faith; and by which we in turn bear witness to our piety toward him in the presence of the Lord and of his angels, and before human beings. More briefly, it is a testimony of divine grace toward us, confirmed by an outward sign, with mutual attestation of our piety towards him [*cum mutua nostrae erga ipsum pietatis testificatione*]. Whichever of these definitions is preferred, its sense does not differ from that given by Augustine, who teaches that a sacrament is "a visible sign of a sacred thing" or "a visible form of an invisible grace"; however, it explains the thing itself better and more clearly. [...]

Now, from this definition we understand that a sacrament is never without a prior promise but is joined to it as a sort of appendix [*tanquam appendicem quandam adiungi*], with the objective of confirming and sealing the promise itself, and of making it clearer to us and, so to speak, ratifying it. God thus makes allowance first for our ignorance and slowness, then for our weakness. Yet, properly speaking, it is not so much needed to strengthen his holy Word as to support our faith in it. For God's truth is of itself firm and sure enough; nor can it receive better confirmation from any source other than from itself. But as our faith is slight and feeble unless it is supported at every point and sustained by every means, it trembles, wavers, totters, and finally falls down. So our merciful Lord, by his infinite kindness, adjusts himself to us in such a way that, since we are creatures who always creep on the ground, cleave to the flesh, and do not think about or even conceive of anything spiritual, uses these earthly elements, and sets before us in the flesh a mirror of spiritual blessings. For if we were incorporeal (as Chrysostom says), he would give us these very things naked and incorporeal. Now, because we have souls inserted into our bodies, he imparts spiritual things under visible ones. This does not mean that the gifts set before us in the sacraments are bestowed with the natures of those things; rather, that they have been given this signification by God.

Comment

The basic point made in this passage is that humanity needs reassurance and reminding of the promises of God. The sacraments provide such reassurance, not because of any shortcoming in God's goodness, but because of human weakness and frailty. Sacraments are thus intended to confirm to a doubting humanity the trustworthiness of the promises of a gracious God.

Questions for Study

1 What definition of a sacrament does Calvin offer in this passage? How does this definition differ from that offered by Peter Lombard (8.15)?
2 "So our merciful Lord, by his infinite kindness, adjusts himself to us in such a way that, since we are creatures who always creep on the ground, cleave to the flesh, and do not think about or even conceive of anything spiritual, uses these earthly elements, and sets before us in the flesh a mirror of spiritual blessings." Locate this important statement. What does Calvin mean by this? And how does it illuminate Calvin's understanding of (a) theological language, and (b) the purpose of sacraments?

8.27

Martin Bucer on the Sacraments

In *de regno Christi* ("On the reign of Christ"), a work of Reformed pastoral theology written during his final years, spent in England (1549–51), the German reformer Martin Bucer (1491–1551) sets out his understanding of the place of sacraments in the life of a Reformed church. In the course of this analysis, Bucer brings out the pastoral function of the sacraments, particularly in relation to reassurance. See also 8.26.

Another part of the sacred ministry is the administration of the sacraments. There are two sacraments explicitly instituted and commanded for us by Christ. Moreover, the apostles so religiously used the sacrament of the imposition of hands in ordaining the ministry of the churches, as we read in Acts 13: 3, the First Letter to Timothy 4: 14 and 5: 22, and the Second Letter, 1: 6, that it appears very likely that they did this at the command of the Lord. For Paul writes about the use of this sign to Timothy as if he was writing about a sacrament which was permanently established, in that he warns him not to lay hands on anyone as a matter of haste. But we have no explicit command of Christ to this effect in Scripture, as we do in the case of Baptism and the Eucharist.

We further read that the early churches used the sign of the laying on of hands in the reconciliation of penitents, as well as in the confirmation of the baptized in the faith of Christ. This the bishops normally did according to the example of the apostles, who by this sign bestowed the Holy Spirit on those who had been baptized (Acts 8: 17–18). Those who desire that the Kingdom of Christ should be established correctly among them once more must therefore take special care to re-establish the legitimate administration of Baptism and the Eucharist.

But this involves the following matters. First, holy and blameless ministers should administer each sacrament, only to those whom they know to be holy and blameless according to the Word of the Lord.

For by Baptism people must be washed from sins, regenerated and renewed for eternal life, incorporated in Christ the Lord, and clothed with him, and all of these things are reserved only to those chosen for eternal life (Acts 22: 16; Titus 3: 5; 1 Corinthians 12: 12–13; Galatians 3: 27). Concerning the baptizing of the infants of believers, the Word of the Lord is sufficient: "I will be your God, and of your seed" (Genesis 17: 7), and "Your children are holy" (1 Corinthians 7: 14). But adults, as has been said above, ought to be catechized before they are baptized and carefully examined as to whether they believe in their hearts what they profess with their lips. [...]

Secondly, since remission of sins and the holy communion of Christ are imparted through these sacraments, and the covenant of eternal salvation is thereby sealed and confirmed [*foedusque aeternae salutis obsignatur et confirmatur*], it is necessary that these mysteries be explained to those about to receive such sacraments in the presence of the whole church and that they be celebrated as reverently as possible. Hence the ancient churches spent an entire octave in celebrating the mysteries of Baptism. To accomplish this more effectively, they administered Baptism only at Easter and Pentecost, unless someone was in danger of death. [...]

At the administration of each of these sacraments, appropriate lessons from Holy Scripture should be read and explained as reverently as possible, and then the people should be exhorted earnestly to a worthy reception of the sacraments. There ought also to be added most ardent prayers and thanksgivings to the Lord, and also devout offerings. For since people receive the supreme benefits of God through these sacraments – the forgiveness of sins and inheritance of eternal life – they should certainly not appear before God with empty hands (Exodus 23: 15).

Comment

Martin Bucer here offers a systematic reflection on the role of the sacraments in relation to the Christian community. The basic themes which Bucer explores are already familiar; nevertheless, Bucer's reflections are important, in that they aim to make some pastoral applications of what might otherwise be simply abstract theological speculation.

Questions for Study

1 Bucer lays down some specific guidelines for the administration of the sacraments. What theological or biblical principles can be argued to lie behind these guidelines?
2 Why does Bucer place such emphasis on the need to explain the place and purpose of the sacraments?

8.28

The Council of Trent on Transubstantiation

During the course of its 13th session, which ended on October 11, 1551, the Council of Trent set out a definitive statement on its understanding of the nature of the real presence of Christ in the Eucharist, affirming that the term "transubstantiation" was appropriate to refer to the change in the substance of the bread and wine resulting from their consecration. See also 8.5, 8.9, 8.10, 8.11, 8.12, 8.16, 8.31, 8.32.

To begin with, the sacred Council teaches and confesses, openly and clearly, that in the noble sacrament of the holy Eucharist, after the consecration of the bread and wine, our Lord Jesus Christ, true God and human being, is truly, really, and substantially contained under the species of those sensible things. For neither are these things mutually opposed to one another: that our Savior himself always sits at the right hand of the Father in heaven, according to the natural mode of existing; and that, nevertheless, he is, in many other places, sacramentally present to us in his own substance, by a manner of existing, which, though we cannot express it fully in words, yet we can, by understanding illuminated by faith, conceive that this is possible for God (as we ought most firmly to believe).

For thus all our forebears, as many as were in the true Church of Christ, who have treated of this most holy sacrament, have most openly professed, that our Redeemer instituted this truly admirable sacrament at the last supper; when, after the blessing of the bread and wine, he testified, in unambiguous and clear words, that he gave them his own true body and blood. These words were recorded by the holy Evangelists, and afterwards repeated by Saint Paul. For this reason, they carry with them that proper and most obvious meaning in which they were understood by the Fathers. It is totally unworthy that they should be distorted, by certain contentious and wicked people, into fictitious and imaginary figures of speech, whereby the reality of the flesh and blood of Christ is denied, contrary to the universal sense of the Church. [. . .]

Because Christ our Redeemer declared that it was truly his body that he was offering under the species of bread, it has always been the belief of the Church of God, which this sacred council reaffirms, that by the consecration of the bread and wine a change takes place in which the entire substance of the bread becomes the substance of the body of Christ our Lord, and the whole substance of the wine becomes the substance of his blood. This change the holy Catholic Church has fittingly and correctly called "transubstantiation" [*quae conversio convenienter et proprie a sancta catholica Ecclesia transubstantiatio est appellata*].

Comment

The Council of Trent believed that the sacramental theology of the Protestant Reformation was seriously deficient. While some of those present at the Tridentine debates appear to have realized that there was a diversity of perspectives within the Reformation, ranging from the more catholic views of Luther, especially on the "real presence," to the more radical views of Zwingli, this is not reflected in the final Tridentine decree. The text vigorously defends both the theology and the terminology of transubstantiation.

Questions for Study

1 Set out, in your own words, the views of the Council of Trent on the real presence of Christ in the Eucharist.
2 Why does Trent reaffirm the doctrine of transubstantiation so firmly?

8.29

Theodore Beza on Sacramental Signs

In this work, published in Latin in 1570, Theodore Beza (1519–1605) set out a view of the nature and function of the sacraments which develops the views of Calvin. The most important feature of this discussion is its affirmation that sacramental signs are efficacious, in that they are able to bring about what they signify. Beza provides an illustration, based on a wax seal, which brings out the point at issue. See also 8.21, 8.24, 8.26.

We use the word "sign" in explaining the sacraments, not to designate something ineffective, as if something were represented to us merely by a picture or memorial or figure, but to declare that the Lord, by his singular goodness, in order to help our weakness, uses external and physical things to represent to our external senses the greatest and most divine things, which he truly communicates to us internally through his Spirit. In this way, he does not give us the reality which is signified to any lesser extent than he gives us the external and physical signs. [. . .] In the sacraments, therefore, neither the substance of the signs nor their natural qualities and quantities are changed, but they are changed with regard to the purpose and use for which they were given to the church of God. They now begin to signify truly heavenly and divine realities for us, not only on the basis of their own intrinsic nature, but also on the basis of their institution by the Son of God. Therefore water, in terms of its natural use, may be used to wash away bodily stains, just as the bread and wine may be used to sustain life. But these things are applied in the sacraments for a very different purpose, namely to bring before our eyes the mystery of salvation. [. . .] To illustrate these very sacred matters, we may take an example from human affairs. The principle involved is like that which underlies the use of wax which is usually stamped with the seal of a prince or magistrate to confirm a public document. In this case, the nature or substance of the wax does not differ at all from any other wax. In terms of its use, however, it is very different. [. . .] The promises to which the sacraments are attached in this way in the manner of authentic seals concern Christ only. That is why it is first Jesus Christ himself and then all the riches which he has in himself, which are the only reality which the most compassionate Father gives us to bring us to eternal life. He signifies them to us truly and certainly by visible signs and by the word joined to the signs, so that faith, by which alone we can receive that offered treasure, is more and more increased and confirmed. And since this concerns our union with Christ as individual members of the Church, the sacraments have another purpose: to enhance that mutual union which the members of the same body should have with one another.

Comment

In this passage Beza sets out the idea of an "efficacious sign." The idea is not especially easy to understand, and it is possible to argue that Beza's discussion in this passage does not illuminate the matter as much as might be hoped. The key section of the passage is that which deals with the analogy of the wax seal, which Beza regards as an excellent illustration for the theological point which is at issue.

Questions for Study

1 Set out, in your own words, the analogy of the wax seal. What does Beza hope to prove or illuminate through this?
2 How does Beza's position differ from that of (a) Huldrych Zwingli (8.24) and (b) the First Helvetic Confession (8.25)?

8.30

John Wesley on the Eucharist and Salvation

John and Charles Wesley were noted for their ability to express theology in the form of hymns, and for using these hymns as a means of educating their congregations theologically. In this important hymn, published in 1786, John Wesley (1703–91) stressed the connection between the actuality of salvation in Christ and its commemoration in the communion service. See also 5.23.

Victim divine, thy grace we claim,
While thus thy precious death we show,
Once offer'd up, a spotless Lamb,
In thy great temple here below,
Thou didst for all mankind atone,
And standest now before the throne.

Thou standest in the holiest place,
As now for guilty sinners slain,
Thy blood of sprinkling speaks and prays
All prevalent for helpless man;
Thy blood is still our ransom found,
And spreads salvation all around.

The smoke of thy atonement here,
Darken'd the sun, and rent the veil,
Made the new way to heaven appear
And show'd the great Invisible:
Well pleased in thee, our God looked down,
And called his rebels to a crown.

He still respects thy sacrifice,
Its savour sweet doth always please,
The offering smokes through earth and skies,
Diffusing life, and joy, and peace:
To these thy lower courts it comes,
And fills them with divine perfumes.

We need not now go up to heaven
To bring the long-sought Saviour down,
Thou art to all already given,
Thou dost e'en now thy banquet crown:
To every faithful soul appear,
And shew thy real presence here.

Comment

John and Charles Wesley made the hymn into a theological essay in miniature. Hymns were seen as important means of furthering the goals of Christian education. In this hymn, we find John Wesley setting out his reflections on the nature of the Eucharist. While touching on the issue of the real presence (see the final verse), Wesley's real concern is to stress the close link between the sacrificial work of Christ on the cross and its proclamation and calling to mind in the Eucharist.

Questions for Study

1 How would you describe the general approach of Wesley to the Eucharist? What is his main concern? What does he want to draw attention to?
2 What parallels does Wesley see between the Old Testament sacrificial system and the Eucharist?

8.31
The Second Vatican Council on the Eucharist

The Second Vatican Council (1962–5) set out to address issues of major concern to the Roman Catholic Church in the modern world. The second session of the council (September 29–December 4, 1963) dealt with a series of matters, including the complex issue of liturgical revision. The resulting "Constitution on the Sacred Liturgy" – often known by its Latin title *Sacrosanctum Concilium* – was published on the final day of this session. The section of this Constitution reprinted here is entitled "The Most Sacred Mystery of the Eucharist." See also 8.5, 8.9, 8.10, 8.11, 8.12, 8.16, 8.28, 8.32.

47. At the Last Supper, on the night he was betrayed, our Savior instituted the eucharistic sacrifice of his Body and Blood. This he did in order to perpetuate the sacrifice of the Cross throughout the ages until he should come again, and so to entrust to his beloved Spouse, the Church, a memorial of his death and resurrection: a sacrament of love, a sign of unity, a bond of charity, a paschal banquet in which Christ is consumed, the mind is filled with grace, and a pledge of future glory is given to us.

48. The Church, therefore, earnestly desires that Christ's faithful, when present at this mystery of faith, should not be there as strangers or silent spectators. On the contrary, through a good understanding of the rites and prayers they should take part in the sacred action, conscious of what they are doing, with devotion and full collaboration. They should be instructed by God's word, and be nourished at the table of the Lord's Body. They should give thanks to God. Offering the immaculate victim, not only through the hands of the priest but also together with him, they should learn to offer themselves. Through Christ, the Mediator, they should be drawn day by day into ever more perfect union with God and each other, so that finally God may be all in all.

49. For this reason the sacred Council having in mind those Masses which are celebrated with the faithful assisting, especially on Sundays and holidays of

obligation, has made the following decrees so that the sacrifice of the Mass, even in the ritual forms (of its celebration), have full pastoral efficacy.

Decrees

50. The rite of the Mass is to be revised in such a way that the intrinsic nature and purpose of its several parts, as well as the connection between them, may be more clearly manifested, and that devout and active participation by the faithful may be more easily achieved.

For this purpose the rites are to be simplified, due care being taken to preserve their substance. Parts which with the passage of time came to be duplicated, or were added with little advantage, are to be omitted. Other parts which suffered loss through accidents of history are to be restored to the vigor they had in the days of the holy Fathers, as may seem useful or necessary.

51. The treasures of the Bible are to be opened up more lavishly so that a richer fare may be provided for the faithful at the table of God's word. In this way a more representative part of the sacred scriptures will be read to the people in the course of a prescribed number of years.

52. By means of the homily the mysteries of the faith and the guiding principles of the Christian life are expounded from the sacred text during the course of the liturgical year. The homily, therefore, is to be highly esteemed as part of the liturgy itself. In fact at those Masses which are celebrated on Sundays and holidays of obligation, with the people assisting, it should not be omitted except for a serious reason.

53. The "common prayer" or "prayer of the faithful" is to be restored after the gospel and homily, especially on Sundays and holidays of obligation. By this prayer in which the people are to take part, intercession will be made for holy Church, for the civil authorities, for those oppressed by various needs, for all mankind, and for the salvation of the entire world.

54. A suitable place may be allotted to the vernacular in Masses which are celebrated with the people, especially in the readings and "the common prayer," and also, as local conditions may warrant, in those parts which pertain to the people, according to the rules laid down in Article 36 of this Constitution.

Nevertheless care must be taken to ensure that the faithful may also be able to say or sing together in Latin those parts of the Ordinary of the Mass which pertain to them.

Wherever a more extended use of the vernacular in the Mass seems desirable, the regulation laid down in Article 40 of this Constitution is to be observed.

55. The more perfect form of participation in the Mass whereby the faithful, after the priest's communion, receive the Lord's Body from the same sacrifice, is warmly recommended.

The dogmatic principles which were laid down by the Council of Trent remaining intact, communion under both kinds may be granted when the bishops think fit, not only to clerics and religious but also to the laity, in cases to be determined by the Apostolic See. For example,

To the newly ordained in the Mass of their ordination;
To the newly professed in the Mass of their religious profession;
To the newly baptized in the Mass which follows their baptism.

56. The two parts which in a sense go to make up the Mass, viz. the liturgy of the word and the eucharistic liturgy, are so closely connected with each other that they form but one single act of worship. Accordingly this sacred Synod strongly urges pastors of souls that, when instructing the faithful, they insistently teach them to take their part in the entire Mass, especially on Sundays and holidays of obligation.

57. (1) Concelebration, whereby the unity of the priesthood is appropriately manifested, has remained in use to this day in the Church, both in the East and in the West. For this reason it has seemed good to the Council to extend permission for celebration to the following cases:

1. (a) On the Thursday of the Lord's Supper (not only at the Mass of the Chrism, but also at the evening Mass.)
   (b) At Masses during Councils, Bishops' Conferences and Synods.
   (c) At the Mass for the Blessing of an Abbot.

2. (a) Also with permission of the Ordinary, to whom it belongs to decide whether concelebration is opportune:
   (a) at conventual Mass, and at the principal Mass in churches, when the needs of the faithful do not require that all the priests available should celebrate individually;
   (b) at Mass celebrated at any kind of priests' meetings whether the priests be secular or religious.

(2) 1. The regulation, however, of the discipline of concelebration in the diocese pertains to the bishop.
   2. Each priest shall always retain his right to celebrate Mass individually, though not at the same time in the same church as a concelebrated Mass nor on the Thursday of the Lord's Supper.

58. A new rite for Concelebration is to be drawn up and inserted into the Pontifical and into the Roman Missal.

Comment

This is one of the most important documents of the Second Vatican Council, setting out the basis for a new approach to the liturgical life of the church. Notice that the constitution set out, not merely its understanding of the eucharist, but a series of specific practical recommendations to ensure that the theological foundations of the sacramental life of the church are firmly linked with the everyday life of the church.

Questions for Study

1 What specific functions does the Council ascribe to the Eucharist?
2 What is the practical effect of the specific recommendations for change set out in this text?

8.32

Edward Schillebeeckx on Understanding the Real Presence

The Dutch Roman Catholic theologian Edward Schillebeeckx (born 1914) gained a reputation during the 1960s as a proponent of nonontological approaches to the dogma of transubstantiation. For Schillebeeckx, the eucharistic bread can be understood to have changed the manner in which it represented or "signified" the spiritual realities to which it points. In the extended passage which follows, Schillebeeckx sets out the interesting and much-discussed concept of "transsignification." See also 8.16, 8.28, 8.31.

When I was studying in France in 1945 and 1946, transubstantiation was a subject of animated discussion among the students. The professor of dogmatic theology, a man well on in years but nevertheless very openminded, observing that the students could no longer find a place for his Thomistic doctrine of transubstantiation (which was itself a reaction against the post-Tridentine theology), allowed them to air their own views in seminars. Even then, words like "transfunctionalisation" and even "transfinalisation" could be heard in these discussions – the idea being that it was not the physical reality of the bread, but its function and meaning that were substantially changed. These discussions were not yet connected with modern phenomenology, which had, at that time, hardly begun to influence Catholic thought, but were prompted by the difficulties experienced in connection with the Aristotelian concept of substance as a result of modern physics and Bergson's criticisms.

The first theologian to rise above both the physical and the purely ontological interpretations and to situate the reality of the eucharistic presence in the sacramental presence was, without any doubt, J. de Baciocchi. He accepted an ontological depth in transubstantiation, but placed this on the sacramental level. He did in fact use the terms transfunctionalisation, transfinalisation and transsignification. The ultimate reality of things is not what they are for our senses or for the scientific analysis that is based on this, but what they are for Christ. Christ's power as Lord makes all things be for him. If, therefore, Christ really gives *himself* in bread and wine, God's good gifts, then an objective and fundamental change has taken place, a transubstantiation – bread and wine become *signs* of Christ's real gift of himself. De Baciocchi was reacting here against the concept of a substance situated *behind* the phenomenal world. "The gift of bread and wine is changed by Christ into the gift of his body and blood," and this changes the reality of the bread. This was the first attempt by a Catholic theologian to synthesise "realism" (transubstantiation) and "the sacramental symbolism in its full depth of meaning".

It would seem that, with these views, the interpretation based on the Aristotelian philosophy of nature was completely superseded and the anthropological approach was already recognisable. It is, however, remarkable that this reinterpretation was not worked out until after 1950. This was the year in which the encyclical *Humani Generis* appeared, which denounced the opinion of certain theologians who maintained that transubstantiation was based on an outdated philosophical concept of substance and therefore had to be corrected in such a way that the real presence of Christ was reduced to a kind of symbolism, in which the consecrated hosts were simply efficacious signs of the *spiritual* presence of Christ and of his intimate union with his mystical body and its members. But I have never been able to discover a purely symbolical interpretation of the Eucharist in Catholic theology prior to 1950. Rome's criticism is probably based on a misunderstanding. Together with other theologians of the *Nouvelle Théologie* who favoured the practice of going back to original sources, Henri de Lubac had shown that both the early scholastic theologians and those of the High Middle Ages stressed not Christ's eucharistic presence (*res et sacramentum*), but the unity of all believers on the basis of a eucharistic communion with Christ (*res sacramenti*), the mystical body. Thomas Aquinas also explicitly postulated that the saving power of this sacrament is ultimately situated in the real presence of Christ in the believing community itself. The rediscovery of this datum has in fact supported the new interpretations. Whatever the case may be, De Baciocchi was radically opposed to any purely symbolic interpretation. Post-war Catholic theologians, who had rediscovered the sacrament as a sign, have never again left the path that was first followed by De Baciocchi, the path of synthesis between realism and sacramentality – two poles between which theologians have been trying to find an equilibrium since the ninth century.

In Belgium, A. Vanneste, clearly inspired by De Baciocchi and by Leenhardt's *Ceci est mon corps*, tried to make transubstantiation intelligible, but without appealing either to philosophy or to cosmology or even to phenomenology. His point of departure was the creation, the fact that the ultimate meaning of things comes from God. He made a distinction, not between substance and accidents or between the *noumenon* and the *phenomenon*, but between what things are for God (and for the believer) and what they are for our secular experience as men. Man does not give things their ultimate meaning. If God gives a different destination to this bread, then it *is* metaphysically something different: "philosophically too, the bread is no longer bread".

In Germany, a new approach to transubstantiation was more fully explored in a symposium on the Eucharist held at Passau on the seventh to tenth of October, 1959. In the published account of the lectures and discussions, the papers read by L. Scheffczyk and B. Welte are especially representative. Scheffczyk took as his point of departure the biblical belief in creation, which related the material reality as well as the spiritual to salvation, maintaining that at the deepest level the *being* of things was, in the Bible, a sign and symbol of spiritual and divine realities. This is worked out especially in connection with man and applied in all its depth to the man Jesus, the Son of God, so that the material substance in the Eucharist is fully sign. Although he did not use the word, Scheffczyk, like De Baciocchi, stated that a real transubstantiation must be a transsignification, which is a transfinalisation. B. Welte offered a more fully worked out analysis. His starting-point was that personal and spiritual relationships are more real than physical and material relationships. He therefore viewed bread and wine in the Eucharist in the light of their relationships. Being, being true and being good ("having meaning for") are, in the authentically Thomistic view, interchangeable. In their own *being*, things have a meaning for someone (God, man), an original meaning which belongs to the reality itself, since, without this "having meaning for", something is not what it *is*. This transcendental "having meaning for" is made particular in concrete forms. A chemical substance may be nourishment, but it may also be fuel. If this relationship is changed, the being itself of a thing changes. A Greek temple is something different for its builders, for those who worship in it and for modern tourists. Man himself is essentially involved in this change of relationship, but it is not completely dependent on him – the *being* itself of things changes when the relationship is altered. It is therefore possible to say that the temple has undergone a "historical transubstantiation". There are also relationships which are *brought about* by man. In such cases, *what* the being concerned really *is* is authoritatively determined. A coloured cloth is purely decorative, but if a government decides to raise it to the level of a national flag, then the same cloth is really and objectively no longer the same. Physically, nothing has been changed, but its being is essentially changed. Indeed, a new meaning of this kind is more real and more profound than a physical or chemical change. In the case of the Eucharist too, a new meaning is given to the bread and wine, not by any man, but by the Son of God. The relationship which is brought about by the Son of God is, because it is divine, binding in the absolute sense and determines the being of the Eucharist for the believer. Anyone who does not believe, and consequently does not see it in this way, places himself outside the reality which is *objectively* present – he is outside the order of being.

Welte put forward this idea as a working hypothesis. He was in any case the first to elaborate in some detail a modern interpretation of transubstantiation – a change of the being itself (*conversio entis*) that is much more objective than physical changes, but on the level of giving meaning.

In the Netherlands in 1960, J. Moiler, without looking for an ontological basis, put forward an existential and phenomenological interpretation in which the reality of Christ's "giving of himself in the gift" was for the first time painstakingly analysed phenomenologically. Although these analyses were not closely enough related to the specifically eucharistic context, they are nonetheless worthy of careful consideration by theologians.

The years 1964 and 1965 marked the beginning of a new phase in the reinterpretation of Christ's real presence in the Eucharist. By this, I mean above all that it was then that the new ideas which had been developed in different countries, especially during the ten years following the publication of *Humani Generis* in 1950, became widely known in the Church as a whole. Various theologians presented their views to the Catholic world, in England and the Netherlands especially, in a less academic way and with new shades of meaning.

In England, Charles Davis cautiously suggested a new anthropological interpretation that was in harmony with that of De Baciocchi. In accordance with the general tendency away from the categories of natural philosophy and towards anthropological thinking, he based his argument concerning both grace and the sacramental life not on objective categories, but on interpersonal categories. Davis attempted to define more precisely the distinctive character of the eucharistic presence, which had, in his opinion, also to be interpreted in personal terms – that is, within the category of the interpersonal encounter between Christ and the believer – and to determine in this light what, so to speak, the "real presence" is *in itself* (directed, of course, towards this personal encounter) in the eucharistic bread and wine. It is the first stage of what must become a *reciprocal* presence and of what *de facto* also makes this reciprocal presence possible. Expressed in scholastic terms, it is the *res et sacramentum*, the first stage of the real presence, of which the *res tantum* is the completion. There is therefore an identification with the *object* and not with an action, although this is certainly assumed. It is a substantial identity and therefore a "substantial presence". "Substantial" here means the manner of being present which has its origin in the identity with an object. This object, the eucharistic bread, is Christ. "As symbolic it embodies the reality it manifests." The reality itself of an object undergoes a change and, for this reason, there is no "consubstantiation", but a real transubstantiation. The identity is, however, not complete. Nothing is changed visibly and empirically, and what we perceive is not a deception. If the reality were changed empirically, there could be no question of sacramentality.

Davis does not, however, explain this by using the Aristotelian twin concept of substance and accidents. The change cannot, in his opinion, be situated at a non-empirical, physical level, separate from the personal and sacramental encounter with Christ, and he therefore proposes that the change concerns the reality the bread has as a "human object". There are objects which only have reality and meaning *for man* and are as such made by him for his needs, plans, self-expression and communication with others. These remain "external" realities (in this sense, an "ontological" reality as bread), but they are no longer "things of nature". Thus, the unity that we call bread is unintelligible without its relationship to man – it is only an agglomeration of diverse constituent parts. To this agglomeration transubstantiation gives a new *human unity*, a new meaning or relationship to man. The real, ontological meaning of the bread, that is, the bread itself, is thus radically changed – it is no longer orientated towards man as bread. A new pattern of unity is brought about, a new relationship to man, even though nothing is changed physically and the elements nourish the body as all bread does. A new object comes into being – the sacrament in which the reality of Christ is the *formally* constitutive element ("the substance as it were") together with the other elements which, subordinated to this new reality of Christ, are the *sign* of this reality and the *medium* by which it becomes accessible to us. The "new object" is thus the sacrament of Christ's body and blood.

Davis insists that the datum of Christ's presence in the Eucharist does not mean that he is, as far as we are concerned, absent outside the Eucharist. He is close to us in an even more intimate manner in the life of grace than he is in the tabernacle. Christ's real presence in the Eucharist therefore only finds its completion in the reciprocal encounter that takes place between Christ and ourselves. Davis' view thus amounts to an *ontological* "transfinalisation" and "transsignification," even though he does not in fact use these words. The basic meaning of the dogma of transubstantiation is guaranteed by Davis, but without the Aristotelian wording.

In the Netherlands, the theologians P. Schoonenberg and L. Smits have moved in rather a different direction, which they prefer to characterise, as equivalent to transubstantiation, as "transsignification" or "transfinalisation". Schoonenberg stresses above all that personal presence, in contrast to spatial presence, is identical with personal communication and is brought about by this. It is a self-communication of a person and a corresponding reception of this communication – in other words, a reciprocal self-communication in which the one person is himself for the other. This is reflected even in spatial presence – it always implies *activity*, the influence of one on the other. Personal presence is corporeally "mediated". It is visibly realised in signs. It is free self-disclosure and spiritual openness in bodiliness. Thus "the material activities of human bodies or things acquire a new dimension – they become *signs* of persons. All making known or perception becomes a sign of revelation and faith, an active sign of human community, the manifestation and cause of personal presence."

This interpretation properly stresses the fact that there are different degrees of personal presence. The two basic forms of personal presence are the presence that is *only offered* and the presence that is *also received* as a gift. "The only complete personal presence is that which is both given and accepted. That which is only offered, but is not (yet) accepted is a secondary presence, which is orientated towards the first as its aim and completion." There is also personal presence which does not come about directly by "mediation" of the human body, but by mediation of even more alien material things, such as a letter, a souvenir or a gift. In this context, however, these things become *signs*. "They have a new and deeper being, being as signs, which communicates the personal presence. It is almost possible to say that they are transubstantiated."

Schoonenberg's analysis, of which I have given only a summary of a few main points, may be regarded as generally acceptable to modern existential thought. It is quite possible to say that the contemporary image of man and the world is taken as much for granted in modern theology as the Aristotelian image of man and the world was, broadly speaking, in the theology of the second half of the thirteenth century. This new understanding of man and the world forms, in a less thematised way, the background to all attempts to reinterpret the Tridentine dogma, including, for example, those of Charles Davis and Luchesius Smits.

Comment

Schillebeeckx offers both a historical reflection and theological analysis of the concept of transubstantiation, dealing with the contributions of writers such as Piet

Schoonenberg, Charles Davis, and Luchesius Smits to the debate. The fundamental points which he makes can be summarized as follows. First, ontological ways of thinking are found exceptionally difficult by many, and ought therefore to be reconsidered. Second, there are other acceptable ways of understanding the spiritual changes which result in the bread and the wine at their consecration, especially the view that there is a change in their manner of signification.

Questions for Study

1 Set out clearly, in your own words, the reasons why Schillebeeckx believes that ontological approaches to the concept of transubstantiation are no longer viable.
2 Set out clearly, using your own words but citing from the passage as appropriate, the alternative that Schillebeeckx proposes. How do you assess his proposal?

8.33

The World Council of Churches on Baptism

In 1982 the Faith and Order Commission of the World Council of Churches published a highly influential theological statement entitled "Baptism, Eucharist and Ministry." The statement was the outcome of several years of ecumenical study and dialogue, mainly between Protestant denominations, to identify what sacramental beliefs can be affirmed together by the churches of the Reformed, Lutheran, Methodist, Anglican, and Orthodox traditions. The document proved highly influential in catalyzing ecumenical discussions on issues relating to the sacraments and Christian ministry. See also: 8.2, 8.3, 8.4, 8.6, 8.8, 8.20.

I. The Institution of Baptism

B1. Christian baptism is rooted in the ministry of Jesus of Nazareth, in his death and in his resurrection. It is incorporation into Christ, who is the crucified and risen Lord; it is entry into the New Covenant between God and God's people. Baptism is a gift of God, and is administered in the name of the Father, the Son, and the Holy Spirit. St Matthew records that the risen Lord, when sending his disciples into the world, commanded them to baptize (Matt. 28: 18–20). The universal practice of baptism by the apostolic

Church from its earliest days is attested in letters of the New Testament, the Acts of the Apostles, and the writings of the Fathers. The churches today continue this practice as a rite of commitment to the Lord who bestows his grace upon his people.

II. The Meaning of Baptism

B2. Baptism is the sign of new life through Jesus Christ. It unites the one baptized with Christ and with his people. The New Testament scriptures and the liturgy of the Church unfold the meaning of baptism in various images which express the riches of Christ and the gifts of his salvation. These images are sometimes linked with the symbolic uses of water in the Old Testament. Baptism is participation in Christ's death and resurrection (Rom. 6: 3–5; Col. 2: 12); a washing away of sin (1 Cor. 6: 11); a new birth (John 3:5); an enlightenment by Christ (Eph. 5: 14); a reclothing in Christ (Gal. 3: 27); a renewal by the Spirit (Titus 3: 5); the experience of salvation from the flood (1 Peter 3: 20–21); an exodus from bondage (1 Cor. 10: 1–2) and a liberation into a new humanity in which barriers of division whether of sex or race or social status are transcended (Gal. 3: 27–28; 1 Cor. 12: 13). The images are many but the reality is one.

A. Participation in Christ's death and resurrection

B3. Baptism means participating in the life, death and resurrection of Jesus Christ. Jesus went down into the river Jordan and was baptized in solidarity with sinners in order to fulfil all righteousness (Matt. 3:15). This baptism led Jesus along the way of the Suffering Servant, made manifest in his sufferings, death and resurrection (Mark 10: 38–40, 45). By baptism, Christians are immersed in the liberating death of Christ where their sins are buried, where the "old Adam" is crucified with Christ, and where the power of sin is broken. Thus those baptized are no longer slaves to sin, but free. Fully identified with the death of Christ, they are buried with him and are raised here and now to a new life in the power of the resurrection of Jesus Christ, confident that they will also ultimately be one with him in a resurrection like his (Rom. 6: 3–11; Col. 2: 13, 3: 1; Eph. 2: 5–6).

B. Conversion, pardoning and cleansing

B4. The baptism which makes Christians partakers of the mystery of Christ's death and resurrection implies confession of sin and conversion of heart. The baptism administered by John was itself a baptism of repentance for the forgiveness of sins (Mark 1: 4). The New Testament underlines the ethical implications of baptism by representing it as an ablution which washes the body with pure water, a cleansing of the heart of all sin, and an act of justification (Heb 10: 22; 1 Peter 3: 21; Acts 22: 16; 1 Cor. 6: 11). Thus those baptized are pardoned, cleansed and sanctified by Christ, and are given as part of their baptismal experience a new ethical orientation under the guidance of the Holy Spirit.

C. The gift of the Spirit

B5. The Holy Spirit is at work in the lives of people before, in and after their baptism. It is the same Spirit who revealed Jesus as the Son (Mark 1: 10–11) and who empowered and united the disciples at Pentecost (Acts 2). God bestows upon all baptized persons the anointing and the promise of the Holy Spirit, marks them with a seal and implants in their hearts the first instalment of their inheritance as sons and daughters of God. The Holy Spirit nurtures the life of faith in their hearts until the final deliverance when they will enter into its full possession, to the praise of the glory of God (2 Cor. 1: 21–22; Eph, 1: 13–14).

D. Incorporation into the body of Christ

B6. Administered in obedience to our Lord, baptism is a sign and seal of our common discipleship. Through baptism, Christians are brought into union with Christ, with each other and with the Church of every time and place. Our common baptism, which unites us to Christ in faith, is thus a basic bond of unity. We are one people and are called to confess and serve one Lord in each place and in all the world. The union with Christ which we share through baptism has important implications for Christian unity. "There is . . . one baptism, one God and Father of us all . . . " (Eph. 4: 4–6). When baptismal unity is realized in one holy, catholic, apostolic Church, a genuine Christian witness can be made to the healing and reconciling love of God. Therefore, our one baptism into Christ constitutes a call to the churches to overcome their divisions and visibly manifest their fellowship.

Comment

The World Council of Churches paper "Baptism, Eucharist and Ministry" (sometimes known as the "Lima Text," after the Peruvian city which hosted the 1982 meeting of its Faith and Order Commission) is widely regarded as marking a landmark in ecumenical discussions of its themes. Baptism is here presented in a way which remains close to the language and imagery of the New Testament (note how often this text is cited), while responding to some of the debates that have subsequently divided Christians. Although there is wide variation in baptismal practices, particularly within Protestant denominations, this document attempts to identify the common themes and beliefs that underlie Christian doctrine and practice at this point.

Questions for Study

1 According to the Lima Text, what does baptism actually do? What difference does it make to someone when they are baptized?
2 The Lima Text makes particular reference to the role of the Holy Spirit in baptism, and the importance of the church community. How would you summarize its teaching on both these points?

8.34

Alexander Schmemann on the Eucharist

Alexander Schmemann (1921–83) is one of the most important voices in twentieth-century Orthodox theology. He served as dean of St Vladimir's Theological Seminary in New York State, during which time he acquired his reputation as a leading representative of Orthodoxy. In this important passage, Schmemann sets out some of the features of an Orthodox approach to the Eucharist. See also 3.18, 8.9.

Now we can ask, what is the specific function of the *epiklesis*, the prayer for the sending down of the Holy Spirit, which we find to be the concluding part of the anamnesis in the Orthodox liturgy?

Above all it is what the very text of the *epiklesis*, which begins in both the liturgies of St John Chrysostom and St Basil the Great with the words "remembering therefore," testifies to: the organic connection of this prayer with the remembrance.

I cited Chrysostom's text in the very beginning of this chapter, and therefore I will limit myself here to citing the parallel prayer, the *epiklesis* in the liturgy of St Basil the Great:

> Therefore, we also, O Master, remembering His (i.e., Christ's) saving Passion and life-creating Cross, His three-day Burial and Resurrection from the dead, His Ascension into heaven and Sitting at Thy right hand of the God and Father, and His Glorious and awesome Second Coming, Thine own of Thine own we offer to Thee, in behalf of all, and for all.... We now dare to approach Thy holy altar and, offering to Thee the antitypes of the holy Body and Blood of Thy Christ, we pray Thee and call upon Thee, O Holy of Holies, that by the favor of Thy goodness Thy Holy Spirit may come upon us and upon the gifts now offered.

As we see, the prayer of the *epiklesis* constitutes the conclusion of the *remembrance*. In the categories of the *new time* in which the eucharist is accomplished, it unites "all those things which have come to pass for us," the entire mystery of salvation accomplished by Christ, the mystery of Christ's love, which embraces the whole world and has been granted to us. The remembrance is the confession of the *knowledge* of this mystery, its *reality*, and likewise faith in it as the salvation of the world and man. Like the entire eucharist, the remembrance is not a *repetition*. It is the manifestation, gift and experience, in "this world" and therefore again and again, of the eucharist offered by Christ once and for all, and of our ascension to it.

The eucharist is accomplished from beginning to end over the bread and wine. Bread and wine are the *food* that God created from the beginning as *life*: "you shall have them for food" (Genesis 1: 29). But the meaning, essence and joy of life is not in food, but in

God, in communion with him. Man, and in him "this world," fell away from this food, "in paradise the food of immortality" (Liturgy of St Basil the Great). Food came to reign in him, but this reign is not unto life, but unto death, disintegration and separation. And that is why Christ, when he had come into the world, called himself "the bread of God . . . which comes down from heaven, and gives life to the world" (John 6: 33). "I am the bread of life; he who comes to me shall not hunger, and he who believes in me shall never thirst" (John 6: 35).

Christ is the "bread of heaven," for this definition contains the entire content, the entire reality of our faith in him as Savior and Lord. He is life, and therefore food. He offered this life in sacrifice "on behalf of all and for all," in order that we might become communicants of his own life, the new life of the new creation, and that we might manifest him as his body.

To all this the Church answers *amen*, she receives all this through faith, she fulfills all this in the eucharist through the Holy Spirit. All the *rites* of the liturgy are a manifestation, one after the other, of the *realities* of which the saving work of Christ is comprised. But, I shall repeat once more, the *progression* here is not in the accomplishment but in the manifestation. For what is manifested is not something *new*, that did not exist before the manifestation. No – in Christ all is already *accomplished*, all is *real*, all is granted. In him we have obtained access to the Father and communion in the Holy Spirit and anticipation of the new life in his kingdom.

And here the *epiklesis*, which we find at the end of the eucharistic prayer, is also this manifestation and this gift, and likewise the *Church's acceptance of them*. "Send down Thy Holy Spirit upon us and upon these Gifts here offered." For the invocation of the Holy Spirit is not a separate act whose one and only object is the bread and wine. Immediately after the invocation of the Holy Spirit the celebrant prays: "And unite all of us to one another who become partakers of the one Bread and Cup in the communion of the Holy Spirit" (St Basil the Great). "That they may be to those who partake for the purification of soul, for the remission of sins, for the communion of Thy Holy Spirit, for the fulfillment of the Kingdom of Heaven."

Furthermore, again without interruption, the prayer goes on to the *intercession*, of which we shall speak later. The purpose of the eucharist lies not in the change of the bread and wine, but in our partaking of Christ, who has become our food, our life, the manifestation of the Church as the body of Christ.

This is why the holy gifts themselves never became in the Orthodox East an object of special reverence, contemplation and adoration, and likewise an object of special theological "problematics": how, when, in what manner their change is accomplished. The eucharist – and this means the changing of the holy gifts – is a mystery that cannot be revealed and explained in the categories of "this world" – time, essence, causality, etc. It is revealed only to faith: "I believe also that this is truly Thine own most pure Body, and that this is truly Thine own precious Blood." Nothing is explained, nothing is defined, nothing has changed in "this world." But then whence comes this light, this joy that overflows the heart, this feeling of fullness and of touching the "other world"?

We find the answer to these questions in the *epiklesis*. But the answer is not "rational," built upon the laws of our "one-storied" logic; it is disclosed to us by the Holy Spirit. In almost every order of the eucharist that has reached us, the Church prays in the text of the *epiklesis* that the eucharist will be for those who partake "*for the communion of the Holy Spirit*": "And unite all of us to one another who become partakers of the one Bread and Cup in the communion of the Holy Spirit," and, further, "for the fulfillment of the Kingdom of Heaven." These two definitions of the purpose of the eucharist are in essence synonyms, for both manifest the eschatological essence of the sacrament, its orientation to the kingdom of God, which is to come but in the Church is already manifested and granted.

Thus the *epiklesis* concludes the *anaphora*, the part of the liturgy that encompasses the "assembly as the Church," the entrance, the proclamation of the good news of the word of God, the offering, the oblation, the thanksgiving and the remembrance. But with the *epiklesis* begins the consummation of the liturgy, whose essence lies in *communion*, in the distribution to the faithful of the holy gifts, the body and blood of Christ.

Comment

Schmemann places considerable emphasis on the role of the Holy Spirit, following here the general lines of the approach set out by John of Damascus in his *de fide orthodoxa*, which we considered earlier (8.9). The *epiklesis* – that is, the moment in the eucharistic liturgy when the Holy Spirit is called down on the bread and the wine – is seen as being of critical theological importance.

Questions for Study

1 Set out in your own words the theological function of the Holy Spirit, according to Schmemann.
2 Schmemann is critical of what he discerns as excessively rationalist approaches to the eucharistic mystery. What does he mean by this? Are there any writers represented in this chapter who you could consider to be potential targets of his criticisms?

8.35

Rowan Williams on the Nature of a Sacrament

Rowan Williams (born 1950), formerly Lady Margaret Professor of Divinity at Oxford University, and more recently Archbishop of Canterbury, has written extensively on various theological themes, and is widely regarded as one of the world's most important living theologians. Although a noted academic theologian, Williams has always recognized and valued the connection between theology and the life of the church, and many of his published writings deal with such themes. The extract is taken from a lecture given at a London church, dealing with the manner in which Jesus of Nazareth instituted signs for the Christian community. See also 8.14, 8.15, 8.21, 8.26, 8.34.

It is clear that the tradition of [Jesus of Nazareth's] deeds and words is heavily influenced by the sense that he was a sign-maker of a disturbingly revolutionary kind. He worked – we are led to understand – on the assumption that a time of crisis had begun in which the people of God would be both summoned to judgement and restored under God's kingship so as to become a people bound to God in unprecedented closeness. The covenanted faithfulness of God would once and for all overcome and cast out the unfaithfulness of the people. Thus Jesus acts for a community that does not yet exist, the Kingdom of God: he chooses rabbis and judges for the twelve tribes of the future, he heals and forgives, he takes authority to bring the outcasts of Israel into this new world by sharing their tables. His strange isolation, the suspicion and incomprehension he meets, have to do with the fact that his acts are signs of a form of human life yet to be realized and standing at odds with the political and cultic status quo. The 'sense' he is making is entirely rooted in the fundamental Jewish conviction that God is the God who, by his free commitment, brings a people into being; yet the 'people' in whose name he acts, whose forms and signs he constructs in his healing and fellowship, both is and is not identical with the Israel that now exists.

This paradox is most evident in the last of the 'signs' of the kingdom which he performs, the unexpected variation on the passover theme in which he announces a new covenant sealed in his forthcoming death. The Last Supper is not a simple, primitive fellowship meal; as far back as we can go in the tradition about Jesus, it is seen as 'intending', meaning, the event that finally sets Jesus and his followers apart from the continuities of Israel and makes the beginnings of a new definition of God's people. Maundy Thursday *means* Good Friday and Easter, the sealing of the new and everlasting covenant. In the costly gift of his chosen and beloved to the risk of rejection and death, God uncovers the scope of his commitment in a way that alters the whole quality of human trust and commitment to him: he creates *faith.* And he creates a community of faith called, exactly as Israel is called, to show his nature in their life by following out the logic of Torah itself. Every act must speak of God, but not in such a way as to suggest a satisfying of divine demands, an *adequacy* of response to God's creative act. What we do is now to be a sign, above all, of a gift given for the deepening of solidarity - or, in Paul's language, ethics is about 'the building up of the body of Christ'. If our acts with one another speak of mutual gift and given-ness, they are signs of the radical self-gift which initiates the Church.

So, it is readily intelligible that the most characteristic (i.e. self-identifying) acts of the Church from its beginnings should be the signs of the paschal event. Baptism is already, in the tradition about Jesus, something that stands not only for commission and empowerment, but for the specific commission to die at the hands of the powerful of this earth, to realize God's power through the gift of one's own life to him (Mark 10.38–39, cf. Luke 12.50), so that the washing of the convert becomes an identification with this death, this gift and this empowering. The supper draws us into the event of the covenant's sealing, placing us with the unfaithful disciples at table whose unfaithfulness is to be both judged and set aside by God – for the supper is also celebrated as the meal shared with the risen Jesus.

Comment

Williams argues that a normal part of human communal life is to create signs, and that it is therefore to be expected that such actions or signs should play an important role in the life of the Christian community. For Williams, these actions are linked with the "paschal event" (the cross), both demonstrating and enhancing the believer's identification with Jesus of Nazareth and the redemption and transformation which he or she achieves.

Questions for Study

1 How does Williams understand the relationship between the church and Israel? And how is this related to his understanding of the role of sacraments?
2 Explain, in your own words, how Williams understands baptism and the Eucharist to relate to the "paschal event."

8.36

John Paul II on the Eucharist as a Sign of Hope

The encyclical letter *Evangelium Vitae* ("The Gospel of Life") was issued on 25 March, 1995, after four years of consultations with the world's Roman Catholic bishops. The primary concern of the letter was the use of capital punishment. Pope John Paul II (1920–2005) declared that execution is only appropriate "in cases of absolute necessity." The letter, however, also included significant passages offering theological reflection on areas of theology touching on issues of life and death, including the Eucharist as a means of relating the death of Christ to the gospel declaration of eternal life. What follows is an extract which sets out a brief, powerful statement of the Eucharist as a symbol of hope in a world of death. See also 8.9, 8.19, 8.35, 10.10, 10.13.

25. "The voice of your brother's blood is crying to me from the ground" (Gen 4: 10). It is not only the voice of the blood of Abel, the first innocent man to be murdered, which

cries to God, the source and defender of life. The blood of every other human being who has been killed since Abel is also a voice raised to the Lord. In an absolutely singular way, as the author of the Letter to the Hebrews reminds us, the voice of the blood of Christ, of whom Abel in his innocence is a prophetic figure, cries out to God: "You have come to Mount Zion and to the city of the living God . . . to the mediator of a new covenant, and to the sprinkled blood that speaks more graciously than the blood of Abel" (12: 22, 24).

It is the sprinkled blood. A symbol and prophetic sign of it had been the blood of the sacrifices of the Old Covenant, whereby God expressed his will to communicate his own life to men, purifying and consecrating them (cf. Ex 24: 8; Lev 17: 11). Now all of this is fulfilled and comes true in Christ: his is the sprinkled blood which redeems, purifies and saves; it is the blood of the Mediator of the New Covenant "poured out for many for the forgiveness of sins" (Mt 26: 28). This blood, which flows from the pierced side of Christ on the Cross (cf. Jn 19: 34), "speaks more graciously" than the blood of Abel; indeed, it expresses and requires a more radical "justice", and above all it implores mercy, it makes intercession for the brethren before the Father (cf. Heb 7: 25), and it is the source of perfect redemption and the gift of new life.

The blood of Christ, while it reveals the grandeur of the Father's love, shows how precious man is in God's eyes and how priceless the value of his life. The Apostle Peter reminds us of this: "You know that you were ransomed from the futile ways inherited from your fathers, not with perishable things such as silver or gold, but with the precious blood of Christ, like that of a lamb without blemish or spot" (1 Pt 1: 18–19). Precisely by contemplating the precious blood of Christ, the sign of his self-giving love (cf. Jn 13: 1), the believer learns to recognize and appreciate the almost divine dignity of every human being and can exclaim with ever renewed and grateful wonder: "How precious must man be in the eyes of the Creator, if he 'gained so great a Redeemer' (*Exsultet* of the Easter Vigil), and if God 'gave his only Son' in order that man 'should not perish but have eternal life' (cf. Jn 3: 16)!".

Furthermore, Christ's blood reveals to man that his greatness, and therefore his vocation, consists in the sincere gift of self. Precisely because it is poured out as the gift of life, the blood of Christ is no longer a sign of death, of definitive separation from the brethren, but the instrument of a communion which is richness of life for all. Whoever in the Sacrament of the Eucharist drinks this blood and abides in Jesus (cf. Jn 6: 56) is drawn into the dynamism of his love and gift of life, in order to bring to its fullness the original vocation to love which belongs to everyone (cf. Gen 1: 27; 2: 18–24).

It is from the blood of Christ that all draw the strength to commit themselves to promoting life. It is precisely this blood that is the most powerful source of hope, indeed it is the foundation of the absolute certitude that in God's plan life will be victorious. "And death shall be no more", exclaims the powerful voice which comes from the throne of God in the Heavenly Jerusalem (Rev 21: 4). And Saint Paul assures us that the present victory over sin is a sign and anticipation of the definitive victory over death, when there "shall come to pass the saying that is written: 'Death is swallowed up in victory'. 'O death, where is your victory? O death, where is your sting?' " (1 Cor 15: 54–55).

Comment

The pasage deals with the question of how a symbol of death – the blood of Christ – can come to have such a positive significance, with such immense importance for a series of ethical and social issues relating to matters of life and death. The passage is very clearly written, and requires no additional comment.

Questions for Study

1 Summarize the argument by which Pope John Paul II identifies the eucharist as a sign of hope, and especially an incentive to work for the preservation of life.
2 Locate the following statement within the passage: "How precious must man be in the eyes of the Creator, if he 'gained so great a Redeemer'." What is meant by this? How does this relate to the death of Christ? You might like to look at two additional readings relating to this point: 4.21, 5.16.

For Further Reading

Johann Auer, *A General Doctrine of the Sacraments and the Mystery of the Eucharist* (Washington, DC: Catholic University of America Press, 1995).

Lyle D. Bierma, *The Doctrine of the Sacraments in the Heidelberg Catechism: Melanchthonian, Calvinist, or Zwinglian?* (Princeton, NJ: Princeton Theological Seminary, 1999).

Marian Bohen, *The Mystery of Confirmation: A Theology of the Sacraments* (London: Darton, Longman & Todd, 1966).

Francis Clark, *Eucharistic Sacrifice and the Reformation* (London: Darton, Longman and Todd, 1960).

Robert W. Jenson, *Visible Words* (Philadelphia: Fortress Press, 1978).

Aidan Kavanagh, *The Shape of Baptism* (New York: Pueblo Publishing, 1978).

Bernard Leeming, *Principles of Sacramental Theology* (Westminster, MD: Newman Press, 1960).

Paul McPartlan, *Sacrament of Salvation: An Introduction to Eucharistic Ecclesiology* (Edinburgh: T&T Clark, 1995).

Kenan B. Osborne, *Christian Sacraments in a Postmodern World: A Theology for the Third Millennium* (New York: Paulist Press, 1999).

Paul F. Palmer, *Sacraments and Forgiveness: History and Doctrinal Development of Penance, Extreme Unction and Indulgences* (London: Darton, Longman & Todd, 1959).

David N. Power, *The Sacrifice We Offer: The Tridentine Dogma and Its Reinterpretation* (Edinburgh: T&T Clark, 1987).

Hugh M. Riley, *Christian Initiation* (Washington, DC: Catholic University of America Press, 1974).

Alexander Schmemann, *The Eucharist* (Crestwood, NY: St Vladimir's Seminary Press, 1988).

Bryan D. Spinks, *Two Faces of Elizabethan Anglican Theology: Sacraments and Salvation in the Thought of William Perkins and Richard Hooker* (London: Scarecrow Press, 1999).

Herbert Vorgrimler, *Sacramental Theology* (Collegeville, MN: Liturgical Press, 1992).
James F. White, *The Sacraments in Protestant Practice and Faith* (Nashville, TN: Abingdon Press, 1999).
World Council of Churches, *Baptism, Eucharist and Ministry* (Geneva: World Council of Churches, 1982).

9

Christianity and Other Religions

Introduction

The issue of the relation of Christianity to other religions became of particular importance in the twentieth century. However, as this set of readings will indicate, a debate was underway long before this. This chapter includes three major readings relating to the nature of religion itself. Ludwig Feuerbach regarded religion as an expression of human longing; Karl Marx, as the result of social and economic alienation; and Karl Barth, as an expression of human defiance in the face of God. Each of these views is influential, and worth careful consideration.

However, it is the issue of Christian theological responses to religious pluralism which was of chief importance in the twentieth century, which was without question *the* most significant period of theological reflection on this theme. This chapter provides some extended readings relating to this theme, as follows:

Christian Approaches to Other Religions

9.1

Justin Martyr on Christianity before Christ

The question of the relation of Christianity to other religions was an issue at the time of the New Testament, and continued to be so into the second and third centuries. Christian writers found themselves confronted with demands to clarify the relation between Christianity and the imperial cult of emperor-worship, the gods of classical paganism, and Gnostic and other forms of religions of the later classical period. In this important second-century text, the apologist Justin Martyr (c.100–c.165) sets out the foundations of what he believes to be a viable approach. See also 2.16, 2.17, 9.5, 9.6, 9.7.

It is unreasonable to argue, by way of refutation of our teachings, that we assert Christ was born a hundred and fifty years ago, under Cyrenius, and to have given his teaching somewhat later, under Pontius Pilate; and to accuse us of implying that everyone who was born before that time was not accountable. To refute this, I will dispose of the difficulty by anticipation. We are taught that Christ is the first-born of God, and [. . .] he is the Word of whom all of humanity has a share, and those who lived according to the Logos [*hoi meta logou biōsantes*] are therefore Christians, even though they were regarded as atheists; among Greeks, Socrates, and Heraclitus; and among non-Greeks, Abraham, Ananias, Azanas, and Misad, and Elijah, and many others.

Comment

Justin, writing in the second century, solved the problem of the relation between Christianity and other religions (and he had the Greek religions particularly in mind) by arguing that anyone who "lived according to the Logos" is a Christian. Justin regarded the Logos to have dispersed its seeds throughout the world (see 1.1), with the result that it is to be expected that peoples living in every culture and at every time could become Christians.

Questions for Study

1 How does Justin defend his view of the status of those who lived before Christ?
2 What difficulties are raised by the suggestion that Heraclitus was a Christian?

9.2

Ludwig Feuerbach on the Origins of Religion

In his *Essence of Christianity*, published in 1841, the German atheist writer and critic Ludwig Feuerbach (1804–72) argued that the basic elements of religion were fundamentally due to the projection of human longings and fears onto an imaginary transcendent place. The consciousness of God (a leading theme in the writings of F. D. E. Schleiermacher) is thus nothing more than human self-consciousness. See also 9.3.

Consciousness of God is human self-consciousness; knowledge of God is human self-knowledge. By the God you know the human, and conversely, by the human, you know the God. The two are one. What God is to a person that too is the spirit, the soul; and what the spirit, the soul, are to a person, that is the God. God is the revealed and explicit inner self of a human being. Religion is the ceremonial unveiling of the hidden treasures of humanity, the confession of its innermost thoughts, and the open recognition of its secrets of love.

However, to characterize the consciousness of God as human self-consciousness in this manner does not mean that religious people are themselves immediately aware of the fact that their consciousness of God is simply their own self-consciousness. In fact, the absence of such an awareness is the distinctive mark of religion. In order to avoid this misunderstanding, it should be said that religion is the *earliest* and *truly indirect* form of human *self-consciousness*. For this reason, religion precedes philosophy in the history of humanity in general, as well as in the history of individual human beings. Initially, people mistakenly locate their essential nature as if it were *outside* of themselves, before finally realizing that it is actually within them. [. . .] The historical progress of religion consists therefore in this: that what an earlier religion took to be objective, is later recognized to be subjective; what formerly was taken to be God, and worshiped as such, is now recognized to be something human. What was earlier religion is later taken to be idolatry: humans are seen to have adored their own nature. Humans objectified themselves but failed to recognize themselves as this object. The later religion takes this step; every consolidation in religion is therefore a deeper self-knowledge.

Comment

Feuerbach here argues that religious beliefs do not concern an external and objective deity, but relate to internal and subjective human feelings and hopes which are improperly "projected" or "objectified."

Questions for Study

1 "Every consolidation in religion is therefore a deeper self-knowledge." Locate this passage within the text. What does Feuerbach mean by this? And how does he arrive at this conclusion?
2 Sigmund Freud later argued that religion was a kind of "wish-fulfillment." In what way does this view build on Feuerbach's approach?

9.3

Karl Marx on Feuerbach's Views on Religion

The German political philosopher and social critic Karl Marx (1818–83) believed that Feuerbach had shown that religious beliefs arose through an improper objectification of human feelings. However, he believed that Feuerbach had failed to press his points home adequately. In particular, he had failed to appreciate the importance of the socioeconomic situation to the way in which individuals generated religious emotions. See also 1.31.

1 The chief defect of all previous materialism (including Feuerbach's) is that things, reality, the sensible world are conceived only in the form of objects of observation, not as human sense activity [*sinnlich menschliche Tätigkeit*], not as practical activity; not subjectively. [...] In the *Essence of Christianity*, Feuerbach regards the theoretical attitude as the only genuine human attitude, while practical activity is apprehended only in its dirty Jewish manifestation. For this reason, he fails to grasp the significance of "revolutionary," "practical–critical," activity. [...]

4 Feuerbach sets out from the fact of religious self-alienation [*religiösen Selbstentfremdung*], the replication of the world in religious and secular forms. His achievement has therefore consisted in resolving the religious world into its secular foundation. [...]

6 Feuerbach resolves the essence of religion into the essence of *humanity*. But the essence of humanity is not an abstraction which inheres in each individual [*keim dem einzelnen Individuum inwohnendes Abstraktum*]. Real human nature is a totality of social relations [*das ensemble der gesellschaftlichen Verhältnisse*]. As Feuerbach does not deal with this point, he is obliged to:

(i) abstract from the historical process, to hypostatize religious feeling, and to postulate an abstract – isolated – human individual;
(ii) to conceive human nature only in terms of a "genus," as something inner and silent, which is the natural common link connecting many individuals.

7 Feuerbach therefore fails to see that "religious feeling" is itself a social product, and that the abstract individual who he is analyzing belongs to a particular form of society [*einer bestimmten Gesellschaftsform*]. [. . .]

11 The philosophers have only *interpreted* the world in different ways; the point is to change it [*Die Philosophen haben die Welt nur verschieden interpretiert, es kömmt drauf an sie zu verändern*].

Comment

In the 11 theses directed against Feuerbach's criticisms of Christianity (see 9.2), Marx argues that he has failed to go far enough. It is not enough to explain religion; the point is that social and economic changes must be introduced which will eliminate the causes of religion in the first place. Marx locates the human tendency to "invent" God in socioeconomic alienation, and thus places an emphasis upon practical action in the world, rather than just theoretical reflection. This insight has subsequently been taken up once more within some sections of Latin American liberation theology.

Questions for Study

1 Set out, in your own words, what Marx makes of Feuerbach's approach. Make sure that you can identify their points of agreement and disagreement.
2 "The philosophers have only *interpreted* the world in different ways; the point is to change it." What does Marx mean by this? And in what way can this be seen as the climax of his critique of Feuerbach?

9.4

Karl Barth on Christianity and Religion

Karl Barth(1886–1968) addresses the question of the relation of Christianity and other religions by arguing that "religion" is basically a human invention, a category to which Christianity ought not to belong. Barth sets up a distinction between "religion" and "revelation," arguing that the former is a human attempt at self-justification, and the latter is God's contradiction of human ideas. See also 2.41, 3.32.

A theological evaluation of religion and religions must be characterized primarily by the great cautiousness and charity of its assessment and judgments. It will observe and understand and take man in all seriousness as the subject of religion. But it will not be man apart from God, in a human *per se*. It will be man for whom (whether he knows it or not) Jesus Christ was born, died, and rose again. It will be man who (whether he has already heard it or not) is intended in the Word of God. It will be man who (whether he is aware of it or not) has in Christ his Lord. It will always understand religion as a vital utterance and activity of this man. It will not ascribe to this life-utterance and activity of his a unique "nature", the so-called "nature of religion". [. . .]

Revelation singles out the Church as the locus of true religion. But this does not mean that the Christian religion as such is the fulfilled nature of human religion. It does not mean that the Christian religion is the true religion, fundamentally superior to all other religions. We can never stress too much the connection between the truth of the Christian religion and the grace of revelation. We have to give particular emphasis to the fact that through grace the Church lives by grace, and to that extent it is the locus of true religion. And if this is so, the Church will as little boast of its "nature", i.e., the perfection in which it fulfils the "nature" of religion, as it can attribute that nature to other religions. We cannot differentiate and separate the Church from other religions on the basis of a general concept of the nature of religion. [. . .]

We begin by stating that religion is unbelief. It is a concern, indeed, we must say that it is the one great concern, of godless man. [. . .] Where we want what is wanted in religion, i.e., justification and sanctification as our own work, we do not find ourselves – and it does not matter whether the thought and representation of God has a primary or only a secondary importance – on the direct way to God, who can then bring us to our goal at some higher stage on the way. On the contrary, we lock the door against God, we alienate ourselves from him, we come into direct opposition to him. God in his revelation will not allow man to try to come to terms with life, to justify and sanctify himself. God in his revelation, God in Jesus Christ, is the one who takes on himself the sin of the world, who "wills that all our care should be cast upon him, because he careth for us. . . . "

Religion is never true in itself and as such. The revelation of God denies that any religion is true, i.e., that it is in truth the knowledge and worship of God and the reconciliation of man with God. For as the self-offering and self-manifestation of God, as the work of peace which God himself has concluded between himself and man, revelation is the truth beside which there is no other truth, over against which there is only lying and wrong. If by the concept of a "true religion" we mean truth which belongs to religion in itself and as such, it is just as unattainable as a "good man", if by goodness we mean something which man can achieve on his own initiative. No religion is true. It can only become true, i.e., according to that which it purports to be and for which it is upheld. And it can become true only in the way in which man is justified, from without; i.e., not of its own nature and being but only in virtue of a reckoning and adopting and separating which are foreign to its own nature and being, which are quite inconceivable from its own standpoint, which come to it quite apart from any qualifications or merits. Like justified man, true religion is a creature of grace. But grace is the revelation of God. No religion can stand before it as true religion. No man is righteous in its presence. It subjects us all to the judgment of death. But it can also call dead men to life and sinners to repentance. And similarly in the wider sphere where it shows all religion to be false, it can also create true religion. The abolishing of religion by revelation need not mean only its negation: the judgment that religion is unbelief. Religion can just as well be exalted in revelation, even though the judgment still stands. It can be upheld by it and concealed in it. It can be justified by it, and – we must at once add – sanctified. Revelation can adopt religion and mark it off as true religion. And it not only can. How do we come to assert that it can, if it has not already done so? There is a true religion: just as there are justified sinners. If we abide strictly by that analogy – and we are dealing not merely with an analogy, but in a comprehensive sense with the thing itself – we need have no hesitation in saying that the Christian religion is the true religion.

Comment

Barth here takes a principled stand against the notion of "religion" as a human construction, rather than a datum of divine revelation. He insists that "religion" will continue until the end of time, as a necessary prop or support to faith. Barth's concern here is to emphasize that, by the grace of God, this "religion" is transcended and surpassed by God. It is something neutral, not negative. Barth uses the word *Aufhebung* (abolition) in the original German, but his references to the *Aufhebung* of religion do not make much sense, if these are translated as referring to the simple *abolition* of religion. In fact, these comments should be interpreted in terms of the "transformation" or even "sublimation" of religion. Religion, seen as a human construction, and contrasted with divine revelation, certainly needs to be critiqued – yet it serves a useful role.

Questions for Study

1 Set out, in your own words, the relation between "religion" and "unbelief" which Barth advocates in this passage.
2 What does Barth mean by "abolishing" religion?

9.5

C. S. Lewis on Myth in Christianity and Other Faiths

How does Christianity relate to other faiths? For the Oxford literary critic J. R. R. Tolkien, all religions and worldviews rest on myths – an attempt to account for reality, expressed in many different ways, as splintered fragments of light, each reflecting only some aspects of a greater whole. For Tolkien, Christianity takes the structural form of such a myth – but is the real myth, to which all other myths only approximate. His Oxford colleague C. S. Lewis (1898–1963) took a similar view. In this extract, taken from a paper entitled "Is Theology Poetry?," delivered to the Socratic Club at Oxford in 1945, Lewis sets out why occasional similarities between Christianity and other religions is to be expected, on the basis of the overarching nature of the Christian view of reality. See also 1.1, 2.17, 2.37, 9.1, 9.7.

There are, however, two other lines of thought which might lead us to call Theology a mere poetry, and these I must now consider. In the first place, it certainly contains elements similar to those which we find in many early, and even, savage, religions. And those elements in the early religions may now seem to us to be poetical. The question here is rather complicated. We now regard the death and return of Balder as a poetical idea, a myth. We are invited to infer thence that the death and resurrection of Christ is a poetical idea, a myth. But we are not really starting with the datum "Both are poetical" and thence arguing "Therefore both are false". Part of the poetical aroma which hangs about Balder is, I believe, due to the fact that we have already come to disbelieve in him. So that disbelief, not poetical experience, is the real starting point of the argument. But this is perhaps an over-subtlety, certainly a subtlety, and I will leave it on one side.

What light is really thrown on the truth or falsehood of Christian Theology by the occurrence of similar ideas in Pagan religion? I think the answer was very well given a fortnight ago by Mr. Brown. Supposing, for purposes of argument, that Christianity is true, then it could avoid all coincidence with other religions only on the supposition that all other religions are one hundred per cent erroneous. To which, you remember, Professor Price replied by agreeing with Mr. Brown and saying: Yes. From these resemblances you may conclude not "so much the worse for the Christians" but "so much the better for the Pagans". The truth is that the resemblances tell nothing either for or against the truth of Christian Theology. If you start from the assumption that the Theology is false, the resemblances are quite consistent with that assumption. One would expect creatures of the same sort, faced with the same universe, to make the same false guess more than once. But if you start with the assumption that Theology is true, the resemblances fit in equally well. Theology, while saying that a special illumination has been vouchsafed to Christians and (earlier) to Jews, also says that there is some divine illumination vouchsafed to all men. The Divine light, we are told, "lighteneth every man". We should, therefore, expect to find in the imagination of great Pagan teachers and myth-makers some glimpse of that theme which we believe to be the very plot of the whole cosmic story – the theme of incarnation, death and rebirth. And the differences between the Pagan Christs (Balder, Osiris, etc.) and the Christ Himself is much what we should expect to find. The Pagan stories are all about someone dying and rising, either every year, or else nobody knows where and nobody knows when. The Christian story is about a historical personage, whose execution can be dated pretty accurately, under a named Roman magistrate, and with whom the society that He founded is in a continuous relation down to the present day. It is not the difference between falsehood and truth. It is the difference between a real event on the one hand and dim dreams or premonitions of that same event on the other. It is like watching something come gradually into focus: first it hangs in the clouds of myth and ritual, vast and vague, then it condenses, grows hard and in a sense small, as a historical event in first-century Palestine. This gradual focussing goes on even inside the Christian tradition itself. The earliest stratum of the Old Testament contains many truths in a form which I take to be legendary, or even mythical – hanging in the clouds: but gradually the truth condenses, becomes more and more historical. From things like Noah's Ark or the sun standing still upon Ajalon, you come down to the court memoirs of King David. Finally you reach the New Testament and history reigns supreme, and the Truth is incarnate. And "incarnate" is here more than a metaphor. It is not an accidental resemblance that what, from the point of view of being, is stated in the form "God became Man"; should involve, from the point of view of human knowledge, the statement "Myth became Fact". The essential meaning of all things came down from the "heaven" of myth to the "earth" of history. In so doing, it partly emptied itself of its glory, as Christ emptied Himself of His glory to be Man. That is the real explanation of the fact that Theology, far from defeating its rivals by a superior poetry is, in a superficial but quite real sense, less poetical than they. That is why the New Testament is, in the same sense, less poetical than the Old. Have you not often felt in Church, if the first lesson is some great passage, that the second lesson is somehow small by comparison – almost, if one might say so, humdrum? So it is and so it must be. This is the humiliation of myth into fact, of God into Man: what is everywhere and always, imageless and ineffable, only to be glimpsed in dream and symbol and the acted poetry of ritual, becomes small, solid – no bigger than a man who can lie asleep in a rowing boat on the Lake of Galilee.

Comment

Lewis's argument is that, throughout its history, humanity has developed myths which can be seen as glimpsing something of the true situation. These myths can be seen as approximations to truth. The reality to which all myths bear witness, however partially and inadequately, is to be found in the incarnation, which Lewis suggests can be understood as "myth become fact".

Questions for Study

1 What does Lewis understand by the word "myth"? And how does he understand Christian and pagan myths to relate to each other?
2 Lewis ends this paper with the following comment: "I believe in Christianity as I believe that the sun has risen; not only because I see it, but because by it, I see everything else." How does this statement illuminate his approach to other religions?

9.6

Karl Rahner on Christianity and the Non-Christian Religions

The Jesuit writer Karl Rahner (1904–84) devoted considerable attention to the relation between Christianity and other religions. In his analysis of the subject, Rahner maintains the distinctiveness of Christianity, while maintaining that the other religions are capable of offering their adherents genuine salvation. Rahner argues that the grace of God can be found in other religions, and suggests that their members may be regarded as "anonymous Christians." See also 9.7.

1st Thesis: We must begin with the thesis which follows, because it certainly represents the basis in the Christian faith of the theological understanding of other religions. This thesis states that Christianity understands itself as the absolute religion, intended for all men, which cannot recognize any other religion beside itself as of equal right. This proposition is self-evident and basic for Christianity's understanding of itself. There is no need here to prove it or to develop its meaning. After all, Christianity does not take valid and lawful religion to mean primarily that relationship of man to God which man himself institutes on his own authority. Valid and lawful religion does not mean man's own interpretation of human existence. It is not the reflection and objectification of the experience which man has of himself and by himself. Valid and lawful religion for Christianity is rather God's action on men, God's free self-revelation by communicating himself to man. It is God's relationship to men, freely instituted by God himself and revealed by God in this institution. *This* relationship of God to man is basically the same for all men, because it rests on the Incarnation, death and resurrection of the one Word of God become flesh. Christianity is God's own interpretation in his Word of this relationship of God to man founded in Christ by God himself. And so Christianity can recognize itself as the true and lawful religion for all men only where and when it enters with existential power and demanding force into the realm of another religion and – judging it by itself – puts it in question. Since the time of Christ's coming – ever since he came in the flesh as the Word of God in absoluteness and reconciled, i.e. united the world with God by his death and resurrection, not merely theoretically but really – Christ and his continuing historical presence in the world (which we call "Church") is *the* religion which binds man to God. Already we must, however, make one point clear as regards this first thesis (which cannot be further developed and proved here). It is true that the Christian religion itself has its own pre-history which traces this religion back to the beginning of the history of humanity – even though it does this by many basic steps. It is also true that this fact of having a pre-history is of much greater importance, according to the evidence of the New Testament, for the theoretical and practical proof of the claim to absolute truth made by the Christian religion than our current fundamental theology is aware of. Nevertheless, the Christian religion as such has a beginning in history; it did not always exist but began at some point in time. It has not always and everywhere been *the* way of salvation for men – at least not in its historically tangible ecclesio-sociological constitution and in the reflex fruition of God's saving activity in, and in view of, Christ. As a historical quantity Christianity has, therefore, a temporal and spatial starting point in Jesus of Nazareth and in the saving event of the unique Cross and the empty tomb in Jerusalem. It follows from this, however, that this absolute religion – even when it begins to be this for practically all men – must come in a historical way to men, facing them as the only legitimate and demanding religion for them. It is therefore a question of whether this moment, when the existentially real demand is made by the absolute religion in its historically tangible form, takes place really at the same chronological moment for all men, or whether the occurrence of this moment has itself a history and thus is not chronologically simultaneous for all men, cultures and spaces of history. [. . .]

2nd Thesis: Until the moment when the gospel really enters into the historical situation of an individual, a non-Christian religion (even outside the Mosaic religion) does not merely contain elements of a natural knowledge of God, elements, moreover, mixed up with human depravity which is the result of original sin and later aberrations. It contains also supernatural elements arising out of the grace which is given to men as a gratuitous gift on account of Christ. For this reason a non-Christian religion can be recognized as a *lawful* religion (although only in different degrees) without thereby denying the error and depravity contained in it. This thesis requires a more extensive explanation.

We must first of all note the point up to which this evaluation of the non-Christian religions is valid. This is the point in time when the Christian religion becomes a historically real factor for those who are of this religion. Whether this point is the same, theologically speaking, as the first Pentecost, or whether it is different in chronological time for individual peoples and religions, is something which even at this point will have to be left to a certain extent an open question. We have, however, chosen our formulation in such a way that it points more in the direction [illegible] the opinion which seems to us the more correct one in the matter although th[illegible] for a more exact determination of this moment in time must again [illegible] question.

The thesis itself is divided into two parts. It means firs[illegible] possible to suppose that there are supernatural, gr[illegible] religions. Let us first of all deal with this staten[illegible] the elements of a polytheistic conception of [illegible] ethical and metaphysical aberrations containe[illegible] be or may be treated as harmless either in the[illegible] constant protests against such elements through[illegible] throughout the history of the Christian interpretat[illegible] starting with the Epistle to the Romans and followin[illegible] against the religion of the "heathens". Every one of th[illegible] was really meant and expressed by them. Every such protest remains a part of the message which Christianity and the Church has to give to the peoples who profess such religions. Furthermore, we are not concerned here with an *a posteriori* history of religions. Consequently, we also cannot describe empirically what should not exist and what is opposed to God's will in these non-Christian religions, nor can we represent these things in their many forms and degrees. We are here concerned with dogmatic theology and so can merely repeat the universal and unqualified verdict as to the unlawfulness of the non-Christian religions right from the moment when they came into real and historically powerful contact with Christianity (and at first only thus!). It is clear, however, that this condemnation does not mean to deny the very basic differences within the non-Christian religions especially since the *pious*, God-pleasing pagan was already a theme of the Old Testament, and especially since this God-pleasing pagan cannot simply be thought of as living absolutely outside the concrete socially constituted religion and constructing his own religion on his native foundations – just as St Paul in his speech on the Areopagus did not simply exclude a positive and basic view of the pagan religion. The decisive reason for the first part of our thesis is basically a theological consideration. This consideration (prescinding from certain more precise qualifications) rests ultimately on the fact that, if we wish to be Christians, we must profess belief in the universal and serious salvific purpose of God towards all men which is true even within the post-paradisean phase of salvation dominated by original sin. We know, to be sure, that this proposition of faith does not say anything certain about the *individual* salvation of man understood as something which has in fact been reached. But God desires the salvation of everyone. And this salvation willed by God is the salvation won by Christ. [. . .]

3rd Thesis: If the second thesis is correct, then Christianity does not simply confront the member of an extra-Christian religion as a mere non-Christian but as someone who can and must already be regarded in this or that respect as an anonymous Christian. It would be wrong to regard the pagan as someone who has not yet been touched in any way by God's grace and truth. If, however, he has experienced the grace of God – if, in certain circumstances, he has already accepted this grace as the ultimate, unfathomable entelechy of his existence by accepting the immeasurableness of his dying existence as opening out into infinity – then he has already been given revelation in a true sense even before he has been affected by missionary preaching from without. For this grace, understood as the *a priori* horizon of all his spiritual acts, accompanies his consciousness subjectively, even though it is not known objectively. And the revelation which comes to him from without is not in such a case the proclamation of something as yet absolutely unknown, in the sense in which one tells a child here in Bavaria, for the first time in school, that there is a continent called Australia. Such a revelation is [illegible]hen the expression in objective concepts of something which this person has already [illegible]ained or could already have attained in the depth of his rational existence. It is not [illegible]ble here to prove more exactly that this *fides implicita* is something which dog[illegible]lly speaking can occur in a so-called pagan. We can do no more here than to [illegible] thesis and to indicate the direction in which the proof of this thesis might be [illegible] if it is true that a person who becomes the object of the Church's missionary efforts is or may be already someone on the way towards his salvation, and someone who in certain circumstances finds it, without being reached by the proclamation of the Church's message – and if it is at the same time true that this salvation which reaches him in this way is Christ's salvation, since there is no other salvation – then it must be possible to be not only an anonymous theist but also an anonymous Christian. [. . .]

4th Thesis: It is possibly too much to hope, on the one hand, that the religious pluralism which exists in the concrete situation of Christians will disappear in the foreseeable future. On the other hand, it is nevertheless absolutely permissible for the Christian himself to interpret this non-Christianity as Christianity of an anonymous kind which he does always still go out to meet as a missionary, seeing it as a world which is to be brought to the explicit consciousness of what already belongs to it as a divine offer or already pertains to it also over and above this as a divine gift of grace accepted unreflectedly and implicitly. If both these statements are true, then the Church will not so much regard herself today as the exclusive community of those who have a claim to salvation but rather as the historically tangible vanguard and the historically and socially constituted explicit expression of what the Christian hopes is present as a hidden reality even outside the visible Church. To begin with, however much we must always work, suffer and pray anew and indefatigably for the unification of the whole human race, in the one Church of Christ, we must nevertheless expect, for theological reasons and not merely by reason of a profane historical analysis, that the religious pluralism existing in the world and in our own historical sphere of existence will not disappear in the foreseeable future. [. . .]

Comment

In the fifth volume of his *Theological Investigations* Rahner develops four theses, setting out the view, not merely that individual non-Christians may be saved, but that the non-Christian religious traditions in general may have access to the saving grace of God in Christ. While asserting that Christianity is the absolute religion, founded on the unique event of the self-revelation of God in Christ, Rahner allows that non-Christian religious traditions are valid and capable of mediating the saving grace of God, until the gospel is made known to their members. After the gospel has been proclaimed to the adherents of such non-Christian religious traditions, they are no longer legitimate, viewed from the standpoint of Christian theology. Note especially Rahner's suggestion that other religious traditions will not be displaced by Christianity. Religious pluralism will therefore, he argues, continue to be a feature of human existence.

Questions for Study

1 What does Rahner mean by the phrase "anonymous Christians"? What difficulties does it raise?
2 Set out, in your own words, how Rahner defends the view that non-Christian religions offer salvation through Christ.

9.7

The Second Vatican Council on Non-Christian Religions

The Second Vatican Council issued its landmark statement on the relation between Christianity and other religions on October 28, 1965. The statement affirms the distinctiveness of Christianity, while at the same time affirming that God can be known, to a limited extent, in other religious traditions. It is widely regarded as one of the most important twentieth-century Christian discussions of the relationship of Christianity and other religions, especially Judaism. See also 1.1, 2.17, 2.37, 9.1, 9.6.

1. In this age of ours, when men are drawing more closely together and the bonds of friendship between different peoples are being strengthened, the Church examines with greater care the relation which she has to non-Christian religions. Ever aware of her duty to foster unity and charity among individuals, and even among nations, she reflects at the outset on what men have in common and what tends to promote fellowship among them.

All men form but one community. This is so because all stem from the one stock which God created to people the entire earth (cf. Acts 17: 26), and also because all share a common destiny, namely God. His providence, evident goodness, and saving designs extend to all men (cf. Wisdom 8: 1; Acts 14: 17; Romans 2: 6–7; 1 Timothy 2: 4) against the day when the elect are gathered together in the holy city which is illumined by the glory of God, and in whose splendor all peoples will walk (cf. Apocalypse 21: 23 ff.).

Men look to their different religions for an answer to the unsolved riddles of human existence. The problems that weigh heavily on the hearts of men are the same today as in the ages past. What is man? What is the meaning and purpose of life? What is upright behavior, and what is sinful? Where does suffering originate, and what end does it serve? How can genuine happiness be found? What happens at death? What is judgment? What reward follows death? And finally, what is the ultimate mystery, beyond human explanation, which embraces our entire existence, from which we take our origin and towards which we tend?

2. Throughout history even to the present day, there is found among different peoples a certain awareness of a hidden power, which lies behind the course of nature and the events of human life. At times there is present even a recognition of a supreme being, or still more of a Father. This awareness and recognition results in a way of life that is imbued with a deep religious sense. The religions which are found in more advanced civilizations endeavor by way of well-defined concepts and exact language to answer these questions. Thus, in Hinduism men explore the divine

mystery and express it both in the limitless riches of myth and the accurately defined insights of philosophy. They seek release from the trials of the present life by ascetical practices, profound meditation and recourse to God in confidence and love. Buddhism in its various forms testifies to the essential inadequacy of this changing world. It proposes a way of life by which men can, with confidence and trust, attain a state of perfect liberation and reach supreme illumination either through their own efforts or by the aid of divine help. So, too, other religions which are found throughout the world attempt in their own ways to calm the hearts of men by outlining a program of life covering doctrines, moral precepts and sacred rites.

The Catholic Church rejects nothing of what is true and holy in these religions. She has a high regard for the manner of life and conduct, the precepts and doctrines which, although differing in many ways from her own teaching, nevertheless often reflect a ray of that truth which enlightens all men. Yet she proclaims and is in duty bound to proclaim without fail, Christ who is the way, the truth and the life (John 14: 6). In him, in whom God reconciled all things to himself (2 Corinthians 5: 18–19), men find the fullness of their religious life.

The Church, therefore, urges her sons to enter with prudence and charity into discussion and collaboration with members of other religions. Let Christians, while witnessing to their own faith and way of life, acknowledge, preserve and encourage the spiritual and moral truths found among non-Christians, also their social life and culture.

3. The Church has also a high regard for the Muslims. They worship God, who is one, living and subsistent, merciful and almighty, the Creator of heaven and earth, who has also spoken to men. They strive to submit themselves without reserve to the hidden decrees of God, just as Abraham submitted himself to God's plan, to whose faith Muslims eagerly link their own. Although not acknowledging him as God, they worship Jesus as a prophet, his virgin Mother they also honor, and even at times devoutly invoke. Further, they await the day of judgment and the reward of God following the resurrection of the dead. For this reason they highly esteem an upright life and worship God, especially by way of prayer, alms-deeds and fasting.

Over the centuries many quarrels and dissensions have arisen between Christians and Muslims. The sacred Council now pleads with all to forget the past, and urges that a sincere effort be made to achieve mutual understanding; for the benefit of all men, let them together preserve and promote peace, liberty, social justice and moral values.

4. Sounding the depths of the mystery which is the Church, this sacred Council remembers the spiritual ties which link the people of the New Covenant to the stock of Abraham.

The Church of Christ acknowledges that in God's plan of salvation the beginning of her faith and election is to be found in the patriarchs, Moses and the prophets. She professes that all Christ's faithful, who as men of faith are sons of Abraham (cf. Galatians 3: 7), are included in the same patriarch's call and that the salvation of the Church is mystically prefigured in the exodus of God's chosen people from the land of bondage. On this account the Church cannot forget that she received the revelation of the Old Testament by way of that people with whom God in his inexpressible mercy established the ancient covenant. Nor can she forget that she draws nourishment from that good olive tree onto which the wild olive branches of the Gentiles have been grafted (cf. Romans 11: 17–24). The Church believes that Christ who is our peace has through his cross reconciled Jews and Gentiles and made them one in himself (cf. Ephesians 2: 14–16).

Likewise, the Church keeps ever before her mind the words of the apostle Paul about his kinsmen: "they are Israelites, and to them belong the sonship, the glory, the covenants, the giving of the law, the worship, and the promises; to them belong the patriarchs, and of their race according to the flesh, is the Christ" (Romans 9: 4–5), the son of the virgin Mary. She is mindful, moreover, that the apostles, the pillars on which the Church stands, are of Jewish descent, as are many of those early disciples who proclaimed the Gospel of Christ to the world.

As holy Scripture testifies, Jerusalem did not recognize God's moment when it came (cf. Luke 19: 42). Jews for the most part did not accept the Gospel; on the contrary, many opposed the spreading of it (cf. Romans 11: 28). Even so, the apostle Paul maintains that the Jews remain very dear to God, for the sake of the patriarchs, since God does not take back the gifts he bestowed or the choice he made. Together with the prophets and that same apostle, the Church awaits the day, known to God alone, when all people will call on God with one voice and "serve him shoulder to shoulder" (Soph. 3: 9; cf. Isaiah 66: 23; Psalm 65: 4; Romans 11: 11–32).

Since Christians and Jews have such a common spiritual heritage, this sacred Council wishes to encourage and further mutual understanding and appreciation. This can be obtained, especially, by way of biblical and theological enquiry and through friendly discussions.

Even though the Jewish authorities and those who followed their lead pressed for the death of Christ (cf. John 19: 6), neither all Jews indiscriminately at that time, nor Jews today, can be charged with the crimes committed during his passion. It is true that the Church is the new people of God, yet the Jews should not be spoken of as rejected or accursed as if this followed from Holy Scripture. Consequently, all must take care, lest in catechizing or in preaching the Word of God, they teach anything which is not in accord with the truth of the Gospel message or the spirit of Christ.

Indeed, the Church reproves every form of persecution against whomsoever it may be directed. Remembering, then, her common heritage with the Jews and moved not by any political consideration, but solely by the religious motivation of Christian charity, she deplores all hatreds, persecutions, displays of antisemitism leveled at any time or from any source against the Jews.

The Church always held and continues to hold that Christ out of infinite love freely underwent suffering and death because of the sins of all men, so that all might attain salvation. It is the duty of the Church, therefore, in her preaching to proclaim the cross of Christ as the sign of God's universal love and the source of all grace.

5. We cannot truly pray to God the Father of all if we treat any people in other than brotherly fashion, for all men are created in God's image. Man's relation to God the Father and man's relation to his fellow-men are so dependent on each other that the Scripture says "he who does not love, does not know God" (1 John 4: 8).

There is no basis therefore, either in theory or in practice for any discrimination between individual and individual, or between people and people arising either from human dignity or from the rights which flow from it.

Therefore, the Church reproves, as foreign to the mind of Christ, any discrimination against people or any harassment of them on the basis of their race, color, condition in life or religion. Accordingly, following the footsteps of the holy apostles Peter and Paul, the sacred Council earnestly begs the Christian faithful to "conduct themselves well among the Gentiles" (1 Peter 2: 12) and if possible, as far as depends on them, to be at peace with all men (cf. Romans 12: 18) and in that way to be true sons of the Father who is in heaven (cf. Matthew 5: 45).

Comment

This important text sets out a framework within which Christian distinctiveness may be maintained, while dialogues with other religions can be encouraged. Note in particular the way in which the text stresses the importance of good relations with the Jewish community, and repudiates any suggestions that Jews collectively are guilty of the death of Christ. Note that the Council declined to follow Karl Rahner's suggestion that all religions should be regarded as having the ability to save their members (see 9.6). Rahner is both revelationally and soteriologically inclusive; Vatican II tends to be revelationally inclusive, yet soteriologically particularist.

The text cites and alludes to many biblical passages. Note that "Apocalypse" is synonymous with "Revelation." "Soph." is an abbreviated form of an older name for "Zephaniah," one of the Old Testament prophets. The phrase "serve him shoulder to shoulder," cited from this source, is often translated as "serve him with one accord."

Questions for Study

1 In what ways, according to Vatican II, does the revelation of God make itself known outside the church? And what is the effect of such revelation?
2 What point is being made through the analogy of the wild olive tree?

9.8

Clark Pinnock on Pluralists and Christology

Clark Pinnock (born 1937), a noted Canadian evangelical theologian, here argues that a commitment to religious pluralism generally leads to a weak Christology, in which Jesus is regarded as little more than one among many other religious personalities. He outlines the various strategies adopted by pluralists in dealing with this problem, and provides an assessment of their merits and deficiencies. See also 9.6; 9.7; 9.9; 9.11.

Theological pluralists have a problem with Christology. Were Jesus to be decisive for all nations, that would be unconducive to dialogue and cooperation among the religions. Therefore, ways must be found to reinterpret historical data so as to eliminate finality claims from Christology. They must be diminished so they do not constitute a barrier to interreligious peace. Pluralists hope there is a way to read the New Testament without coming up with a Christ who has to be normative for everybody in the world. They need a way for Jesus to be unique for his followers, but not necessarily for others. If his uniqueness could be relational, for example, this would create fewer problems. Pluralists think that belief in the finality of Jesus Christ stands in the way of our appreciating other religions and getting along smoothly with them. They intend to correct the problem.

Different solutions have been proposed. The least radical involves shifting the emphasis away from metaphysics in the direction of action/functional categories. The problem could be eased, in the minds of theological pluralists, if we would just learn to view Jesus as God's love in action and present him as one who assists people to find access to the grace of God. Why not put the emphasis on Christ's prophetic office, then stress the way he reveals the Father's character and will for humans in his own life and teachings? This would shift the emphasis away from Jesus as a metaphysical oddity and toward the impact he had on people, the way he shaped people's understanding of what God is like. Instead of repeating the idea that God entered history in Jesus from the outside in a miraculous way, we could explain how Jesus functions as a window into God's very nature. [. . .] The late J. A. T. Robinson took this tack. He claimed that it was God's love that was incarnate in Jesus of Nazareth, not the divine substance. Jesus was special because God was acting in and through him. He became the image for us of who God is. Incarnation imagery supplies an effective mythic expression of the way we relate to God through him. Jesus is the clue to the nature of God as personal love, not the absolutely unique embodiment of God's being. He is unique in degree but not in kind.

The idea of Jesus embodying God's love for us is true as far as it goes. But not going farther creates severe difficulties. First, unwanted claims of finality tend to attach themselves to action Christology, even though the claims are functional. Even when the Christ-event is taken only as disclosure, it is still viewed as decisive disclosure. But if decisive for us, why not for others? If it is decisive for us in our cultural setting, why not also in other people's settings? Second, functional Christology has a way of not remaining functional. Edward Schillebeeckx also places emphasis on Jesus' role in communicating God's love, but then he goes on to posit an ontological bond between Jesus and God his Father also. Substance and action categories are brought together in his final assessment. For, he reasons, if Jesus presents us with God most human, are we not also in the presence of unfathomable mystery? Third, there are texts that present ontological teaching about the person of Jesus elsewhere in the New Testament, so that moving to action Christology does not really get one off the hook. It cannot account for the entire biblical witness, even though it can account for some of it.

A second possible way to correct the "problem" of high Christology in the New Testament allows one to accept the higher-than-functional claims that are made for Jesus and still dispense with universal normativeness. With reference to the "once and for all" language of the New Testament for the decisive work of Jesus, Paul Knitter comments that, "To close one's eyes to such proclamation is either psychologically to repress or dishonestly to deny what one does not wish to face." We cannot prevent the biblical witnesses from saying what they meant to say.

Nevertheless, Knitter does try to evade the proclamation in another way. First, he explains the expressions in terms of the culture of the early Christians, saying it was natural for them to speak of their religious experiences in the ways that they did. Being a culturally conditioned way of speaking, their words tell us more about their social setting than about the actual person of Jesus. Second, their high praise of Jesus is more an expression of love and devotion to him than truth claims as such. It is rather like our saying, "My wife (or my husband) is the kindest and most loving person in the world." This is not a scientific statement based on research but rather love language. By looking at these claims in this way, Jesus can be relationally unique (like a spouse is relationally unique), unique in the way Christians experience God – but not unique in a universal sense, in the sense of being normative for other people who may experience God in different religious contexts. The confession, "Jesus is Lord," would express what Jesus means to us without carrying any implication that everybody in the world must worship him or come to God by way of him. This confession is our way to honor God, but need not be taken as a judgment on other confessions made by other people.

This approach allows one to admit that the New Testament witnesses make extraordinarily high claims for Jesus. Yet, one does not have to deny or excise them. The key is to reinterpret their significance in the experiential and confessional terms of love. Because they are culturally conditioned and psychologically rendered, the claims for Jesus turn out not to be truth claims in the ordinary sense, in which the church has understood them historically. The problem of high Christology vanishes.

The approach is ingenious and possible, if not entirely plausible. But there are problems in the following areas. First, the New Testament writers appear to be stating, as far as one can tell, what they consider to be facts and truths. They are not only sharing religious feelings, but conveying what they took to be information as well. [. . .] Second, there is also something of a justice issue involved here. What right does a modern interpreter have to alter what the biblical witnesses intend, so as to make it mean something else? What right has he or she to change and reduce the meaning in this way? To transmute claims about Jesus, as Savior of the world and risen from the dead, into a description of what was going on in their culturally conditioned psyches is illegitimate. Suppose one turned this same argument on pluralists and reduced their claims in this same way? Are their claims for God similarly derivative from the psyche? Is it their love for God that makes them think there actually is a God? To argue in this way constitutes an unacceptable put-down. People have the right to make claims others do not like or accept without having others change and distort their meaning to suit themselves. New Testament claims for Jesus ought to be taken seriously, the same way Knitter's claim about God ought to be. It is inconsistent to apply a noncognitivist bias to claims for Jesus and not to claims for God.

Third, the suggestion is very dubious that Christians might confess a non-normative Jesus without losing anything important in their faith. Knitter posits our living, and even dying, for Christ with the knowledge that the truth of the gospel is our truth, but not necessarily the truth for the world. It is as though we could confess that Jesus is Lord while harboring the reservation that maybe he is, and maybe he isn't. How can Christ's resurrection be true for us and not for the world? The faith of Christians would be fatally damaged if it came to be accepted that the risen Lord were our myth of meaning and not more than that.

A more radical approach to the problem of high Christology in the New Testament is adopted by John Hick. First, he outright denies any uniqueness claims on the part of Jesus. He realizes that hesitating on this point would leave a thread of continuity between Jesus and the later developments, giving it a toehold of plausibility. This is certainly a wise move methodologically, if a risky one exegetically. Second, like Knitter he transposes all the uniqueness claims made on behalf of Jesus by the New Testament witnesses onto the level of noncognitive love language. Third, he attempts to locate the Christology of the Incarnation in a hypothetical context of the development of traditions. Using Buddhism as an example, he points to the process by which religious leaders are deified over time out of respect. Fourth, he adds that there are various insuperable logical problems with belief in Incarnation. This supplies a philosophical backup objection should all else fail.

Unfortunately, none of his points sticks firmly. First, one cannot deny Jesus' claims to uniqueness on the basis of critical exegesis. While granting his point about Jesus not making explicit claims to Incarnation, the implicit claims Jesus does make solidly ground the more-developed views of his person after the Resurrection. Not easily sidestepped, they entail the high view of Jesus which issued in the faith of the church. Second, transposing claims for Jesus' uniqueness made by the biblical witnesses onto the level of noncognitive love language is an unacceptable put-down of their sincerely held beliefs. It is rooted in hostile presuppositions against the truth of what they are declaring. Neither just nor fair, it refuses to take them seriously. Third, there is Christological development in early doctrine, and the Incarnation is noticeable in that development. But the Christology being developed there is already very high, with the event of Jesus' Resurrection, and constitutes an unpacking of what is implicit from the beginning. The centuries of development envisaged by the Buddhist analogy do not exist in this case. Fourth, as to whether belief in the Incarnation is rational or not, two things can be said. First, the problem of finality is much larger than belief in the Incarnation. In many other ways the biblical witnesses lift up Jesus as Lord of the universe. Second, not everyone is as impressed as Hick by the logical problems of believing in the Incarnation. A large number of thoughtful Christians find the belief coherent, even true and magnificent.

The New Testament quite effectively resists attempts of this type to rid it of the unwanted belief in the finality of Jesus Christ. Efforts to revise Christology downward are difficult to accept because they go against the evidence, and they appear to be based on special pleading and hostile presuppositions. It is impossible to bring it off in an exegetically convincing way. One cannot make the New Testament teach a non-normative Christology. There may be nothing wrong with trying – one learns a lot from conducting exegetical experiments. But in terms of results, the effort to rid the New Testament of the doctrine of the finality of Christ must be pronounced a failure.

Comment

Pinnock, while wishing to offer a more "inclusivist" approach to other religions than many of his evangelical colleagues, is nevertheless highly critical of the pluralist approach to the issue of Christianity and other faiths advocated by John Hick. For Pinnock, these cannot be justified intellectually. It is helpful to compare this text with Hick's exposition of a pluralist position (9.9) and offer a critical comparison of the two.

Questions for Study

1 Set out, in your own words, the objections which Pinnock raises to the pluralist paradigm.
2 What specific difficulties does Pinnock see with the idea of a "non-normative Jesus"?

9.9

John Hick on Complementary Pluralism

John Hick (born 1922) is the leading representative of a pluralist approach to the world's religions, seeing each as a distinctive and valid embodiment of "the infinite transcendent divine Reality." Note in particular the argument which leads to the conclusion that the religions "constitute different 'lenses' through which the divine Reality is differently perceived." See also 9.5, 9.6, 9.7, 9.8.

Now it seems to many of us today that we need a Copernican revolution in our understanding of the religions. The traditional dogma has been that Christianity is the centre of the universe of faiths, with all the other religions seen as revolving at various removes around the revelation in Christ and being graded according to their nearness to or distance from it. But during the last hundred years or so we have been making new observations and have realized that there is deep devotion to God, true sainthood, and deep spiritual life within these other religions; and so we have created our epicycles of theory, such as the notions of anonymous Christianity and of implicit faith. But would it not be more realistic now to make the shift from Christianity at the centre to God at the centre, and to see both our own and the other great world religions as revolving around the same divine reality?

Indeed, if we are to understand the entire range of human awarenesses of the divine, including those enshrined in the Buddhist, Hindu and Taoist, as well as the Christian,

Jewish and Muslim traditions, we shall need an even wider framework of thought. Such a framework can perhaps best be approached through a distinction which is found in one form or another within some strand of each of the great traditions. Its Christian form is the distinction between, on the one hand, God as he is in himself, in his infinite self-existing being, independently of and "before" creation, and on the other hand God in relation to and as experienced by his human creatures. In its Hindu form it is the distinction between Nirguna Brahman, i.e. the absolute Reality beyond the scope of human thought and language, and Saguna Brahman, i.e. Brahman humanly experienced as a personal God with describable characteristics. In Buddhism there is the distinction between the incarnate and the heavenly Buddhas (comprising the Nirmanakaya and the Sambhogakaya), and on the other hand the infinite and eternal Dharmakaya or cosmic-Buddha-nature. Again, the Taoist Scriptures begin by saying that "The Tao that can be expressed is not the eternal Tao". Within Jewish mysticism (in the *Zohar*) there is the distinction between En Soph, as the infinite divine ground, and the God of the Bible; and within Muslim mysticism (for example, in Ibn Arabi) between Al Haqq, the Real, and our concrete conceptions of God. Likewise, the Christian mystic Meister Eckhart distinguished between the Godhead (*deitas*) and God (*deus*) in a way which closely parallels the Nirguna–Saguna polarity in Hindu thought. And in the present century Paul Tillich has spoken of "the God above the God of theism". Contemporary process theology likewise distinguishes between the eternal and temporal natures of God. In all these ways we have a distinction between the infinite transcendent divine Reality *an sich*, or in its/his/her-self, and that same Reality as thought, imagined and experienced by finite human beings.

This distinction enables us to acknowledge both the one unlimited transcendent divine Reality and also a plurality of varying human concepts, images, and experiences of and response to that Reality. These different human awarenesses of and response to the Real are formed by and reciprocally inform the religious traditions of the earth. In them are reflected the different ways of thinking, feeling and experiencing which have developed within the world-wide human family. Indeed these cultural variations amount, on the large scale, to different ways of being human – for example, the Chinese, the Indian, the African, the Semitic, the Graeco-Roman way or ways, and the way of our contemporary technological Atlantic civilization. We do not know at all fully why the life of our species has taken these various forms, though geographical, climatic and economic factors have clearly played their parts.

However, given these various cultural ways of being human we can I think to some extent understand how it is that they constitute different "lenses" through which the divine Reality is differently perceived. For we know that all human awareness involves an indispensable contribution by the perceiver. The mind is active in perception, organizing the impacts of the environment in ways made possible both by the inherent structure of consciousness and by the particular sets of concepts embedded in particular consciousnesses. These concepts are the organizing and recognitional capacities by which we interpret and give meaning to the data which come to us from outside. And this general epistemological pattern, according to which conscious experience arises out of the interpretative activity of the mind, also applies to religious experience.

The wide range of the forms of human religious experience seems to be shaped by one or other of two basic concepts: the concept of God, or of the Real as personal, which presides over the theistic religions, and the concept of the Absolute, or of the Real as non-personal, which presides over the non-theistic religious hemisphere. These basic concepts do not, however, enter, in these general and abstract forms, into our actual religious experience. We do not experience the presence of God in general, or the reality of the Absolute in general. Each concept takes the range of specific concrete forms which are known in the actual thought and experience of the different religious traditions.

Thus the concept of deity is concretized as a range of divine *personae* – Yahweh, the Heavenly Father, Allah, Krishna, Shiva, etc. Each of these *personae* has arisen within human experience through the impact of the divine Reality upon some particular stream of human life. Thus Yahweh is the face of God turned towards and perceived by the Jewish people or, in more philosophical language, the concrete form in which the Jews have experienced the infinite divine Reality. As such, Yahweh exists essentially in relation to the Hebrews, the relationship being defined by the idea of covenant. He cannot be extracted from his role in Hebrew historic experience. He is part of the history of the Jews, and they are a part of his history. And as such Yahweh is a quite different divine *persona* from Krishna, who is God's face turned towards and perceived by hundreds of millions of people within the Vaishnavite tradition of India. Krishna is related to a different strand of human history from Yahweh, and lives within a different world of religious thought and experience. And each of these divine *personae*, formed at the interface between the divine Reality and some particular human faith community, has inevitably been influenced by human imaginative construction and sinful human distortion as well as by the all-important impact of the transcendent Reality; there is an element of human projection as well as of divine revelation. How otherwise can we account for the ways in which the various divine *personae* have sometimes validated cruel massacres, savage punishments, ruthless persecutions, oppressive and dehumanizing political regimes? God, as imaged and understood by the masses of believers within any of the great traditions, must be partly a human construction in order, for example, for God the Father to have been on both sides of the conflict in Europe in the Second World War, and for Allah to have been on both sides of the recent Iraq–Iran conflict. But it does not follow that the divine *personae* are purely human projections. On the contrary, the theory that I am outlining is that they constitute the concrete forms in which the transcendent divine Reality is known to us. Each *is* the Real as perceived and experienced (and partly misperceived and misexperienced) from within a particular strand of the human story.

And essentially the same is to be said concerning the various *impersonae* in terms of which the Real is known in the non-theistic religious traditions. Here the concept of the Absolute is made concrete as Brahman, Nirvana, the Dharma, the Dharmakaya, Sunyata, the Tao. And according as an individual's thoughts and practices are formed by the advaitic Hindu tradition, or the Theravada or Mahayana Buddhist tradition, he or she is likely to experience the Real in the distinctive way made possible by this conceptuality and meditational discipline.

But can the divine Reality possibly be such as to be authentically experienced by millions of people as a personal God, and also by millions of others as the impersonal Brahman or Tao or Sunyata? Perhaps there is a helpful analogy in the principle of complementarity in modern physics. Electromagnetic radiation, including light, is sometimes found to behave like waves and sometimes like particles. If we experiment upon it in one way we discover a wave-like radiation, whilst if we experiment upon it in another way we discover a procession of particles. The two observations have both had to be accepted as valid and hence as complementary. We have to say that the electromagnetic reality is such that, in relation to human observation, it is wave-like or particle-like according to how the observer acts upon it. Analogously, it seems to be the case that when humans "experiment" with the Real in one kind of way – the way of theistic thought and worship – they find the Real to be personal and when other humans approach the Real in a different kind of way – the way for example of Buddhist or Hindu thought and meditation – they find the real to be non-personal. This being so, we may well emulate the scientists in their realistic acceptance of the two sets of reports concerning the Real as complementary truths.

Such a theory has the merit that it does not lead us to play down the differences between the various forms of religious experience and thought. It does not generate any pressure to think that God the Father and Brahman, or Allah and the Dharmakaya, are phenomenologically, i.e. as experienced and described, identical; or that the human responses which they evoke, in spiritual practices, cultural forms, life-styles, types of society, etc., are the same. The theory – arrived at inductively by observation of the range of human religious experiences – is that the great world faiths embody different perceptions and conceptions of, and correspondingly different responses to, the Real or the Ultimate from within the major variant cultural ways of being human. Such a theory, I would suggest, does justice both to the fascinating differences between the religious traditions and to their basic complementarity as different human responses to the one limitless divine Reality.

This complementarity is connected with the fact that the great world traditions are fundamentally alike in exhibiting a soteriological structure. That is to say, they are all concerned with salvation/liberation/enlightenment/fulfilment. Each begins by declaring that our ordinary human life is profoundly lacking and distorted. It is a "fallen" life, immersed in the unreality of *maya*, or pervaded by *dukkha*, sorrow and unsatisfactoriness. But each then declares that there is another Reality, already there and already open to us, in relation to or in identity with which we can find a limitlessly better existence. And each proceeds to point out a path of life which leads to this salvation/liberation. Thus they are all concerned to bring about the transformation of human existence from self-centredness to Reality-centredness. Salvation/liberation occurs through a total self-giving in faith to God as he has revealed himself through Jesus Christ; or by the total self-surrender to God which is *islam*: or by transcending self-centredness and experiencing an underlying unity with Brahman; or by discovering the unreality of self and its desires and thus experiencing *nirvana*, or by becoming part of the flow of life which in its emptiness–fullness (*sunyata*) is found to be itself *nirvana*. Along each path the great transition is from the sin or error or self-enclosed existence to the liberation and bliss of Reality-centredness.

Comment

In this passage Hick suggests that the aspect of God's nature of central importance to the question of other faiths is his universal saving will. If God wishes everyone to be saved, it is inconceivable that the divine self-revelation should be effected in such a way that only a small portion of humanity could be saved. Hick thus draws the conclusion that it is necessary to recognize that all religions lead to the same God. Christians have no special access to God, who is universally available through all religious traditions. Note especially his emphasis upon what he believes to be the common soteriological structure of the world's religions.

Questions for Study

1 Set out, in your own words, Hick's argument for the common structure of all religions. What points does he hope to make by doing this? And how successful do you judge him to be in this matter?
2 "This complementarity is connected with the fact that the great world traditions are fundamentally alike in exhibiting a soteriological structure." Locate this statement within the passage. What does Hick mean by this? And what conclusions does he draw from it?

9.10

C. S. Song on the Cross and the Lotus

The Taiwanese theologian C. S. Song (born 1920) here reflects on the relation of Christianity and Buddhism, using the imagery of the cross and the lotus as a stimulus to his reflection. Note in particular the comparison between Jesus and the Buddha. See also 9.5, 9.6.

The question we must now ask is: what has the cross to do with the lotus? As early as the third century, Tertullian raised this question in relation to Jerusalem and Athens: what has Jerusalem to do with Athens? His answer was negative. Jerusalem – the city of the holy temple, the place where Jesus was crucified, the symbol of salvation revealed to the world in Christ in Tertullian's mind – had nothing to do with Athens. Athens stood for reason whereas Jerusalem was the embodiment of the sacred. Athens was a "secular" city in contrast to Jerusalem, a "holy" city. Furthermore, with its many gods and shrines Athens was a center of paganism in the ancient Mediterranean world. There St Paul had delivered his famous sermon on the unknown God before the Court of Areopagus. "Men of Athens," he declared:

> I see that in everything that concerns religion you are uncommonly scrupulous. For as I was going round looking at the objects of your worship, I noticed among other things an altar bearing the inscription "To an Unknown God." What you worship but do not know – this is what I now proclaim.
>
> (Acts 17: 22–23)

Thus it was Paul who in his missionary zeal sought to penetrate the depth of Greek spirituality which had blossomed into art, literature, and philosophy on the one hand and worship of every conceivable deity on the other. Paul's effort in Athens was a dramatic demonstration of the fact that Jerusalem had much to do with Athens. It can even be said to have foreshadowed the Hellenization of Christianity by leaps and bounds in the subsequent history of the development of Christian thought in the West. Tertullian's verdict was wrong. The history of Christian thought was in a true sense a history of how Greek philosophy, especially that of Plato and Aristotle, became integrated into the mainstream of Christian faith. As has been pointed out, through the whole history of Christianity in the West there runs the dynamic of the Gospel's course from the Jew to the Greek, from the Greek to the barbarian.

However that may be, the cross and the lotus seem to have little in common, at first sight at any rate. The lotus springs from the surface of the water. When the wind blows and the water moves, the lotus also moves. It seems in perfect harmony with nature around it. In short, it gives the appearance of being at peace with itself. In contrast, the cross strikes out powerfully, painfully, and defiantly from the earth. It penetrates space and is incongruous with nature. The lotus appeals to our aesthetic feelings, whereas the cross is revolting to the eyes of the beholder. The lotus is soft in texture and graceful in shape, while the cross is hard and harsh. The lotus moves with nature, whereas the cross stands ruggedly and tragically out of the barren earth. The lotus distinguishes itself in gentleness, while the cross is the epitome of human brutality. The lotus beckons and the cross repels. Indeed, what has the cross to do with the lotus? They represent two entirely different spiritualities which seem to be totally incompatible. They seem to have nothing in common.

But the contrast between the cross and the lotus may be deceptive. Essentially, they are two different answers to some basic questions about life and death. They seek to unravel problems and difficulties that beset us in our earthly pilgrimage. They also try to point to the fulfillment of human destiny in the eternal and blissful presence of the divine. They are not primarily concerned with a metaphysical solution to these very important problems, but with practical, day-to-day struggles in the harsh reality of society. Neither the cross nor the lotus, fundamentally speaking, is a system of thought, a set of rituals, or an institution of devotion. Originally they sprang out of the midst of the daily life of the people. They are religions of the people, but theologians – both in Christianity and Buddhism – have taken them away from the people and turned them into theological systems and religious principles bearing little relationship to the genuine fears and aspirations of the people. It is thus not surprising that the cross and the lotus do not intersect in their theological systems or ecclesiastical structures. In fact, these systems and structures only pull the two spiritualities further apart. The place for the cross and the lotus to intersect and intercommunicate is the people – the people who have to fight both spiritual and physical fears, the people who have to live and die without knowing why. Then and only then can the cross and the lotus begin to intercommunicate; they can then begin to point to the mystery that surrounds human destiny. Thus intercommunication and inter-communion of different spiritualities should begin with the people, and with the ways in which they try to cope with the problems of life and the world in sociopolitical and religious terms.

This can be illustrated, first of all, by the way Jesus and Buddha tried to communicate their message through stories and parables. Jesus gave the following reason for using parables to his disciples: "It has been granted to you to know the secrets of the kingdom of Heaven; but to those others it has not been granted" (Matthew 13: 11). Then he went on to explain the meaning of the parable of the sower. An abstruse mystery should not remain the monopoly of a few. Jesus mingled with the crowd and took pains to communicate the message of the Gospel to them. He definitely broke away from the religious elitism of his day and brought religion back to the people. In a sense he was the leader of a new religious movement around which the farmers and workers, the illiterate and the oppressed, could gather. He thus posed a threat to the official religion consolidated on hierarchical structures of religious orders and teachings not readily accessible or intelligible to outsiders.

In the rise of Buddhism in India we also see something of a religious reformation that returned religion from a religious elite to the people in the street. The religious and social situation of India at the time of Buddha in the sixth century BC was similar to that of the Jewish community in Palestine during the life of Jesus. "At the time of the Buddha," writes Kenneth Ch'en, "the dominant position in Indian society was held by the brahmans. They held the key to knowledge, and the power that went with that knowledge." Brahmanism, like Judaism in Jesus' day, was the privilege of the religious leaders and the burden of the masses. As a reformer who ended up by founding a new religion, Buddha repudiated the brahmanical claims that the *Vedas* were the sole and infallible source of religious truth. He also rejected correct performance of the rituals as means of salvation, and he disapproved of the Upanishadic emphasis on intellectual means to attain emancipation. He also protested against the iniquities of the caste system, especially the high pretensions of the brahman class, and welcomed among his followers members from not only the four castes but also from among the outcasts. Buddha was thus the first in the history of India to revolt against the caste system as the chief misfortune of Indian society.

It is therefore not surprising that Buddha tried to communicate a message of emancipation from the suffering of the world in plain language. We can hear him saying something like this:

> I have taught the truth which is excellent in the beginning, excellent in the middle, and excellent in the end; it is glorious in its spirit and glorious in its letter. *But* simple as it is, the people cannot understand it. I must speak to them in their own language. I must adapt my thoughts to their thoughts. They are like unto children and love to hear tales. Therefore, I will tell them stories to explain the glory of the dharma. If they cannot grasp the truth in the abstract arguments by which I have reached it, they may nevertheless come to understand it, if it is illustrated in parables.

It is clear from this that Buddha fully grasped the dynamics of people in religion. As Buddhism spread to China, Japan, and Southeast Asia, it became a religion of the people that created popular culture and cultivated a sense of solidarity among ordinary men and women in all walks of life. To be sure, the teachings of Buddha in their high and lofty forms never filtered down to the people unadulterated. But what is important is that Buddha brought to common men and women a sense of well-being, security, and above all a sense of destiny.

In this way a religious faith can become alive and genuine if it casts aside ecclesiastical pretensions and formidable theological systems and touches the lives and hearts of the people. As previously mentioned, both Jesus and Buddha labored to bring the light of a new faith into the lives of the people. They were close to the people, used popular language, and told stories and parables that came right out of the everyday experiences of the people. No wonder that we find in the Sutra of the Lotus Flower of the Wonderful Law the story of the lost son that bears a remarkable resemblance to the parable of the prodigal son in Luke 15: 32.

According to the Buddhist story of the lost son, a young man left his father and went to another city where he became extremely poor. He was reduced to begging for his food. In contrast, his father grew rich and moved to a big estate where he lived in great luxury. But all the time he grieved over his lost son and said to himself:

> I am old and well advanced in years, and though I have great possessions I have no son. Alas that time should do its work upon me, and that all this wealth should perish unused. [. . .] It would be bliss indeed if my son might enjoy all my wealth.

One day the son wandered into his father's land, and the drama of the reunion of the father and son gradually unfolded:

> Then the poor man, in search of food and clothing, came to the rich man's home. And the rich man was sitting in great pomp at the gate of his house, surrounded by a large throng of attendants. [. . .] When he saw him the poor man was terrified [. . .] for he thought that he had happened on a king or on some high officer of state, and had no business there. [. . .] So he quickly ran away. But the rich man [. . .] recognized his son as soon as he saw him and he was full of joy [. . .] and thought: "This is wonderful! I have found him who shall enjoy my riches. He of whom I thought of constantly has come back, now that I am old and full of years!" Then, longing for his son, he sent swift messengers, telling them to go and fetch him quickly.

The story goes on to describe how the father, who lived in a highly class-conscious society, was not able to disclose his identity to his own son and take him back into his household. The poor man had to go away without realizing that he had been in his own father's house. The father then contrived to have his son hired to work in his own household as a servant. Every day he watched with compassion as his son cleared away a refuse heap. Then one day the rich man came down, took off his wreath and jewels and rich clothes, put on dirty garments, covered his body with dust, and, taking a basket in his hand, went up to his son. And he greeted him at a distance and said, "Take this basket and clear away the dust at once!" By this means he managed to speak to his son.

In this way, the old man made every attempt to make his son feel at home but did not reveal his own identity. In the meantime, the son proved to be a frugal, honest, and industrious man. Finally, knowing that his end was near, the old man sent for the poor man again, presented him before a gathering of his relatives, and, in the presence of the king, his officers, and the people of town and country, he said: "Listen, gentlemen! This is my son, whom I begot. [. . .] To him I leave all my family revenues, and my private wealth he shall have as his own." Consequently, through the father's painful and patient effort the son was reinstated in society and accepted into his father's blessing.

It goes without saying that the ethos of this Buddhist story is quite different from that of the biblical story of the prodigal son. It is Asian through and through in its emphasis on class distinctions that affect even family relations, on accumulation of wealth as a moral and social virtue, and on inheritance as a chief factor affecting the father–son relationship. These are the elements that are part and parcel of a traditional Asian society. For the people in the street such social factors provide a background against which a religious truth can be apprehended. There is in this story no reference to the son's repentance, no mention of the elder son's protest against the father's treatment of the lost son. Despite all these differences in ethos and details, the story points up the father's compassion for his son, the expression of which is very Asian in its reserve and its respect for social conventions. It stresses the acceptance of the son by the father through a ceremony in accordance with the father's social status. The resemblance of the Buddhist story of the lost son to the biblical story of the prodigal son may be accidental. But it is evidence of the fact that deep in people's spirituality is a reflection of God's love and compassion for the world. Jesus Christ, we must admit, is not merely a reflection of God's love. He is the embodiment of that love. In any case, the father's compassion for the son in the Buddhist story may be seen as a reflection, however imperfect, of God's passionate love in the parable of the prodigal son.

Comment

This passage represents a serious and significant attempt to relate Christianity and Buddhism by exploring their values, as well as their beliefs. Song avoids the confident overgeneralizations which are typical of some writers in this field, and instead offers an interesting set of comparisons which merit further attention.

Questions for Study

1 Set out clearly, in your own words, the point that Song is making through his comparison of "parables" in Buddhism and Christianity. How does this relate to the approach developed by C. S. Lewis (9.5)?

2 "The lotus beckons and the cross repels." Locate this statement within the text. What does Song mean by this? And how does he move on from here to achieve some kind of reconciliation between the two?

9.11

John B. Cobb Jr. on Religious Pluralism

In this essay John B. Cobb (born 1925), who has developed a particular interest in the relation between Christianity and Buddhism, raises some penetrating questions concerning certain pluralist assumptions about the religions. In particular, he questions whether there is a universal category called "religion," and points to the way in which Buddhism and Confucianism coexisted in China, one relating to spirituality and the other to morality, as an illustration of the complexity of the issue. See also 9.4, 9.5, 9.6, 9.7, 9.8, 9.9.

How odd I find it to be writing for a collection of essays in criticism of theologies espousing religious pluralism! Yet I have agreed to do so because of the very narrow way – indeed an erroneous way, I think – in which pluralism has come to be defined. By *that* definition of pluralism, I am against pluralism. But I am against pluralism for the sake of a fuller and more genuine pluralism. Let me explain.

I declined to write a paper for the conference that led to the publication of the book, *The Myth of Christian Uniqueness*, because I did not share in the consensus that conference was supposed to express and promote. In the minds of the organizers, that consensus was to be around the view that the several major religions are, for practical purposes, equally valid ways of embodying what religion is all about. The uniqueness that is rejected is any claim that Christianity achieves something fundamentally different from other religions. From my point of view, the assumptions underlying these formulations are mistaken and have misled those who have accepted them.

Probably the most basic assumption is that there is an essence of religion. This essence is thought to be both a common characteristic of all "religions" and their central or normative feature. Hence, once it is decided that Buddhism, Confucianism, or Christianity is a religion, one knows what it is all about and how it is to be evaluated. The next step is then the one about which the consensus was to be formed. Given the common essence, let us agree to acknowledge that it is realized and expressed more or less equally well in all the great religions. It is hoped in this way to lay to rest once and for all Christian arrogance and offensive efforts to proselytize. Christians could then contribute to that peace among religions that is an indispensable part of the peace the world so badly needs.

If, as in my case, one rejects this whole view of religion, then it is very difficult to take part in the discussion as thus posed. I do believe there is a family of traits or characteristics that guides the use of the term *religion* for most people. But the term is used even when only some, not all, the traits are present. For example, most people in the sphere of dominance of the Abrahamic faiths think of worship of a Supreme Being or deity as a religious trait. Yet when they find this absent in most Buddhist traditions, they do not automatically deny that Buddhism is a religion. They notice that it is permeated by a spirit of deep reverence or piety, that it aims to transform the quality and character of experience in a direction that appears saintly, that it manifests itself in such institutions as temples and monasteries in which there are ritual observances, and so forth. The overlap of characteristics suffices for most people, so that Buddhism is almost always included among the world's religions.

If one turns to Confucianism one finds a different set of overlaps with Abrahamic assumptions about religion and a different set of discrepancies. By a certain stretch of terms one can find in it a worship of a Supreme Being, but the function this plays is far less central than in Judaism, Christianity, and Islam. There is great concern for the right ordering of human behavior, but much less interest in transforming the quality and character of experience. So is Confucianism a religion? This question divided Jesuits and their opponents in the seventeenth century, and the vacillation by Rome prevented what might otherwise have been the conversion of the Chinese court to Catholicism.

In the twentieth century the more acute issue is whether communism is a religion. Those who take their cue from the Abrahamic faiths notice at once the denial of God, but such denial does not exclude Buddhism. They notice also the evangelistic fervor, the selfless devotion evoked, the totalistic claims, the interest in the transformation of the human being, the confidence that a new age is coming. And in all this they see religious characteristics. One might judge that communism actually resembles Christianity, at least in its Protestant form, more closely than does Buddhism, yet the features it omits or rejects seem the most "religious" aspects of Christianity. A popular solution is to call communism a *quasi-religion*, whatever that may mean.

It would be possible to draw up a long list of characteristics that one person or another associates with the word *religion*. A list drawn up by a Buddhist would be likely to overlap with, but differ from, a list drawn up by a Muslim. Does that mean that one list would be more accurate than the other? That would imply that there is some objective reality with which the lists more or less correspond. But there is no Platonic idea of "Religion" to which the use of the term *ought* to conform. The term means what it has come to mean through use in varied contexts. Each user should be at some pains to clarify his or her meaning. But arguments as to what religion truly is are pointless. There is no such thing as religion. There are only traditions, movements, communities, people, beliefs, and practices that have features that are associated by many people with what they mean by religion.

One meaning of religion derived from its Latin root deserves special attention here. *Religion* can mean "a binding together"; it can be thought of as a way of ordering the whole of life. All the great traditions *are*, or can be, religions in this sense. So is communism. All are, or can be, ways of being in the world. In most instances they designate themselves, or are readily designated, as Ways. If this were all that were meant by calling them religions, I would have no objection to designating them as such. But we would need to recognize that this use does not capture all the meanings of religion that are important to people. In fact, we do not cease thinking of these traditions as religious when they fail to function as the overarching ways of life for people who identify themselves with them. In the case of Buddhism in China, most people who identified themselves as Buddhists also identified themselves as Confucianists. Neither constituted an inclusive way of being in the world. For many people, being Chinese provided the comprehensive unity of meaning, the basic way of being, in the context of which they could adopt Buddhism for certain purposes and Confucianism for others. When religion is taken to mean the most foundational way of being in the world, then being Chinese is the religion of most of the Chinese people. This meaning of religion needs to be kept in mind along with others, but in most discourse it functions more as one of the characteristics that may or may not be present than as the decisive basis of use of the term.

If one views the situation in this way, as I do, the question, so important to the editors of *The Myth of Christian Uniqueness*, can still arise as to whether all the great traditions are of roughly equal value and validity. But the requisite approach to an answer to this question is then much more complex than it is for those who assume that all these traditions have a common essence or purpose just because they are religions. The issue, in my view, is not whether they all accomplish the same goal equally well – however the goal may be defined. It is first of all whether their diverse goals are equally well-realized.

Consider the case of Buddhism and Confucianism in China. What of their relative value and validity? They coexisted there through many centuries, not primarily as alternate routes to the same goal, but as complementary. In crude oversimplification, Confucianism took care of public affairs, while Buddhism dealt with the inner life. Perhaps one might go on to say that they were about equally successful in fulfilling their respective roles, but that statement would be hard to support and does not seem especially important.

Questions about the relative value of the great religious traditions can all be asked, and asked with less confusion, if the category "religion" is dropped. Both Buddhism and Confucianism are traditions that are correctly characterized in a variety of ways. By most, but not all, definitions of "religious," both can be characterized as religious. But to move from the fact that they are, among other things, "religious," to calling them religions is misleading and has in fact misdirected most of the discussion. It is for this reason that I am belaboring what appears to me an all-too-obvious point. The horse I am beating is not dead. It is alive as an assumption of the editors of *The Myth of Christian Uniqueness*. The assumption is so strong that, so far as I can discover, no argument is given in its support, and arguments against it, such as mine, are systematically ignored rather than debated.

I oppose the "pluralism" of the editors of (and some of the contributors to) *The Myth of Christian Uniqueness*, not for the sake of claiming that only in Christianity is the end of all religion realized, but for the sake of affirming a much more fundamental pluralism. Confucianism, Buddhism, Hinduism, Islam, Judaism, and Christianity, among others, are religious traditions, but they are also many other things. Further, of the family of characteristics suggested by "religious," they do not all embody the same ones.

Few of the supporters of either "pluralism" or "anti-pluralism" deny the fact of diversity. Our difference is that they discern within and behind the diversity some self-identical element, perhaps an *a priori*, that they call religion. It is this that interests them and that functions normatively for them. The issue among the Christians who espouse this view is whether Christians should claim superiority.

What strikes the observer of this discussion is that among those who assume that religion has an essence there is no consensus as to what the essence may be. Even individual scholars often change their mind. The variation is still greater when the scholars represent diverse religious traditions. Yet among many of them the assumption that there is an essence continues unshaken in the midst of uncertainty as to what that essence is.

I see no *a priori* reason to assume that religion has an essence or that the great religious traditions are well understood as religions, that is, as traditions for which being religious is the central goal. I certainly see no empirical evidence in favor of this view. I see only scholarly habit and the power of language to mislead. I call for a pluralism that allows each religious tradition to define its own nature and purposes and the role of religious elements within it.

Comment

In this important discussion Cobb poses a powerful challenge to those who believe that there is some universal or global reality called "religion," the essence of which can be identified and defined. On this view, individual religions would be particular instances of the general phenomenon of "religion." Cobb argues that this approach is completely fallacious, and that any attempt to ground a "theology of religions" upon it is untenable. It is instructive to compare Cobb with Song (9.10), in that both give careful consideration to the relation of Christianity and Buddhism, yet come to differing conclusions.

Questions for Study

1 Set out, in your own words, the reasons why Cobb resists the general approach adopted by writers such as John Hick.
2 "There is no such thing as religion. There are only traditions, movements, communities, people, beliefs, and practices that have features that are associated by many people with what they mean by religion." Locate this statement within the text. How does Cobb arrive at this conclusion? And what are its implications?

9.12

Lesslie Newbigin on the Gospel in a Pluralist Culture

In a series of lectures given at Glasgow University in 1988, the British theologian and missionary Lesslie Newbigin (1909–98) explored a number of major difficulties he detected in the pluralist approaches to religion associated with writers such as John Hick, Wilfrid Cantwell Smith, and Gordon Kaufman, and other contributors to the volume *The Myth of Christian Uniqueness*. The discussion opens with a response to the suggestion that acknowledging the equal validity of all religions would make the world a more peaceful place. See also 9.5, 9.6, 9.7, 9.8, 9.9.

There is a longing for unity among all human beings, for unity offers the promise of peace. The problem is that we want unity on our terms, and it is our rival programs for unity which tear us apart. As Augustine said, all wars are fought for the sake of peace. The history of the world could be told as the story of successive efforts to bring unity to the world, and of course the name we give to these efforts is "imperialism." The Christian gospel has sometimes been made the tool of an imperialism, and of that we have to repent. But at its heart it is the denial of all imperialisms, for at its center there is the cross where all imperialisms are humbled and we are invited to find the center of human unity in the One who was made nothing so that all might be one. The very heart of the biblical vision for the unity of humankind is that its center is not an imperial power but the slain Lamb.

The truth, of course, is that every program for human unity has implicit in it some vision of the organizing principle which is to make this unity possible. As Andrew Dumas has pointed out, if this is not clearly recognized and stated, as it is in the Christian vision of the cross of Jesus as the place where all peoples may find reconciliation, then we shall find that the interests and intentions of the proposer are the hidden center. If there is no explicit statement of the center of unity, then the assumptions and interests of the proposer become the effective center. This becomes very clear in *The Myth of Christian Uniqueness*. Professor Gordon Kaufman of Harvard begins with the need for human unity, assumes without argument that the Christian gospel cannot furnish the center for such unity, and goes on to say that "modern historical consciousness" requires us to abandon the claim to Christ's uniqueness, and to recognize that the biblical view of things, like all other human views, is culturally conditioned. This same "modern historical consciousness" will enable us to enter into the mental worlds of the other religions without supposing that we can impose our Christian norms on them. But to a person living in another culture it is not obvious that the modern historical consciousness of twentieth-century Western intellectuals provides us with a vantage point which can displace the one provided by the Christian story, or that it can furnish a basis for human unity. It is true that modern historical studies enable us to see that people in other times and places were looking at the world through culturally conditioned lenses and that their claim to "see things as they really are" is relativized by our studies in the history of cultures. But to suppose that modern historical consciousness gives us a privileged standpoint where we really do see things as they are, is of course unsupported dogma. Modern historical consciousness is also the product of a particular culture and can claim no epistemological privilege. Kaufman's theology of religions is thus similar to that of the Christian in that it finally rests on an ultimate faith-commitment which does not and cannot seek validation from some more ultimate ground. In this case the ultimate faith-commitment is to the validity of the "modern historical consciousness."

The same is true for the often made claim that all religions are variants of one central human experience, namely that which has been explored most fully by the great mystics. It is indeed true that mystical experience has played a very important role in all the world's great religions, including Christianity. But in no religious tradition is it the only reality. There is much else in all religious traditions, much about the conduct of human life, about justice, freedom, obedience, and mutual charity. To select the mystical element in religion as the core reality is a decision which can be questioned in the name of other elements in the religious life. And the claim that the mystical experience is that which provides the primary clue to what is real, and therefore the one road to salvation for all humanity, is – once again – to choose a particular faith-commitment among others which are possible. It does not enable one to evade the question: Why this, rather than that?

Wilfred Cantwell Smith in the same volume restates his familiar view that all the religions have as their core some experience of the Transcendent; that whether we speak of images made of wood and stone or images made in the mind, or even of such an image as the man Jesus, all are equally the means used by the Transcendent to make himself, herself, or itself present to us humans. To claim uniqueness for one particular form or vehicle of this contact with the Transcendent is preposterous and even blasphemous. Much rather accept the truth so beautifully stated in the *Bhagavad Gita* and in the theology of Ramanuja, that God is so gracious that he (or she or it) accepts everyone who worships whatever be the form through which that worship is offered.

It is clear that in Smith's view "The Transcendent" is a purely formal category. He, she, or it may be conceived in any way that the worshipper may choose. There can therefore be no such thing as false or misdirected worship, since the reality to which it is directed is unknowable. Smith quotes as "one of the theologically most discerning remarks that I know" the words of the *Yogavasistha*: "Thou art formless. Thy only form is our knowledge of Thee." Any claim for uniqueness made for one concept of the Transcendent, for instance the Christian claim that the Transcendent is present in fullness in Jesus (Colossians 1: 19), is to be regarded as wholly unacceptable. There are no criteria by which different concepts of the Transcendent may be tested. We are shut up to a total subjectivity: the Transcendent is unknowable. [. . .]

I venture to offer two concluding comments on the pluralist position as it is set out in *The Myth of Christian Uniqueness*. One is from the perspective of the sociology of knowledge. The culture in which this type of thinking has developed is one in which the most typical feature is the supermarket. In a society which has exalted the autonomous individual as the supreme reality, we are accustomed to the rich variety offered on the supermarket shelves and to the freedom we have to choose our favorite brands. It is very natural that this mentality should pervade our view of religion. One may stick to one's favorite brand and acclaim its merits in songs of praise; but to insist that everyone else should choose the same brand is unacceptable.

And that leads to a second point which is more fundamental. The *Myth* volume celebrated a decisive move beyond exclusivism, and beyond the inclusivism which acknowledges the saving work of Christ beyond Christianity, to a pluralism which denies any uniqueness to Jesus Christ. This move, the "crossing of the Rubicon," is the further development of what was described by John Hick as a Copernican revolution – the move from a christocentric view of reality to a theocentric one. The further move is described as "soteriocentric" – it has its center in the common quest for salvation. Even the word "God" excludes some concepts of the Transcendent Reality and is therefore exclusivist. But what is "salvation"? It is, according to Hick, "the transformation of human experience from self-centredness to God – or Reality – centredness." The Christian tradition affirms that this salvation has been made possible because God, the creator and sustainer of all that is, has acted in the historical person of the man Jesus to meet us, take our burden of sin and death, invite us to trust and love him, and so to come to a life centered in God and not in the self. The authors of the *Myth* deny this. "Reality" is not to be identified with any specific name or form or image or story. Reality "has no form except our knowledge of it." Reality is unknowable, and each of us has to form his or her own image of it. There is no objective reality which can confront the self and offer another center – as the concrete person of Jesus does. There is only the self and its need for salvation, a need which must be satisfied with whatever form of the unknown Transcendent the self may cherish. The movement, in other words, is exactly the reverse of the Copernican one. It is a move away from a center outside the self, to the self as the only center. It is a further development of the move which converted Christian theology from a concern with the reality of God's saving acts, to a concern with "religious experience," the move which converts theology into anthropology, the move about which perhaps the final word was spoken by Feuerbach who saw that the "God" so conceived was simply the blown-up image of the self thrown up against the sky. It is the final triumph of the self over reality. A "soterio-centric" view makes "reality" the servant of the self and its desires. It excludes the possibility that "reality" as personal might address the self with a call which requires an answer. It is the authentic product of a consumer society.

It is not easy to resist the contemporary tide of thinking and feeling which seems to sweep us irresistibly in the direction of an acceptance of religious pluralism, and away from any confident affirmation of the absolute sovereignty of Jesus Christ. It is not easy to challenge the reigning plausibility structure. It is much easier to conform. The overwhelming dominance of relativism in contemporary culture makes any firm confession of belief suspect. To the affirmation which Christians make about Jesus, the reply is, "Yes, but others make similar affirmations about the symbols of their faith; why Jesus and not someone or something else?" Thus a reluctance to believe in something leads to a state of mind in which the *Zeitgeist* becomes the only ruling force. The true statement that none of us can grasp the whole truth is made an excuse for disqualifying any claim to have a valid clue for at least the beginnings of understanding. There is an appearance of humility in the protestation that the truth is much greater than any one of us can grasp, but if this is used to invalidate all claims to discern the truth it is in fact an arrogant claim to a kind of knowledge which is superior to the knowledge which is available to fallible human beings. We have to ask, "How do you know that the truth about God is greater than what is revealed to us in Jesus?" When Samartha and others ask us, "What grounds can you show for regarding the Bible as uniquely authoritative when other religions also have their sacred books?" we have to ask in turn, "What is the vantage ground from which you claim to be able to relativize all the absolute claims which these different scriptures make? What higher truth do you have which enables you to reconcile the diametrically opposite statements of the Bible and the Qur'an about Jesus? Or are you in effect advising that it is better not to believe in anything?" When the answer is, "We want the unity of humankind so that we may be saved from disaster," the answer must be, "We also want that unity, and therefore seek the truth by which alone humankind can become one." That truth is not a doctrine or a worldview or even a religious experience; it is certainly not to be found by repeating abstract nouns like justice and love; it is the man Jesus Christ in whom God was reconciling the world. The truth is personal, concrete, historical. To make that confession does not mean, as critics seem to assume, that we believe that God's saving mercy is limited to Christians and that the rest of the world is lost.

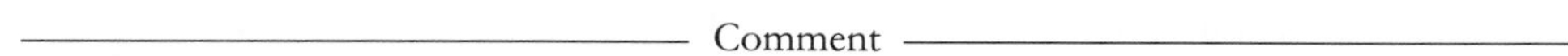

Comment

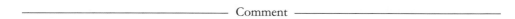

Newbigin is a seasoned interpreter of both Christianity and the religions of the Indian subcontinent, where he served for many years. In this passage, Newbigin sets out his misgivings concerning the "pluralist" paradigm offered by writers such as John Hick and Wilfrid Cantwell Smith. While affirming that there does indeed exist a plurality of religions within the world, and that it is important to increase understanding between them in order to reduce global tension (which often centers on religious issues), Newbigin is adamant that it is unjustifiable to treat all religions as equally valid aspects of some greater whole.

Questions for Study

1 Set out clearly, using your own words and citations from this text, why Newbigin rejects the approach adopted by Wilfrid Cantwell Smith. What appears to be the critical consideration for Newbigin?
2 Newbigin criticizes a "soteriocentric" approach to religion. From this passage, establish what he means by this term. Now examine the exposition of this idea found in the extract from John Hick (9.9). What does Hick mean by this approach? What are its advantages? And why does Newbigin believe him to be mistaken?

For Further Reading

Adnan Aslan, *Religious Pluralism in Christian and Islamic Philosophy: The Thought of John Hick and Seyyed Hossein Nasr* (Richmond, UK: Curzon, 1998).

Carl E. Braaten, *No Other Gospel!: Christianity among the World's Religions* (Minneapolis: Fortress Press, 1992).

Carl Reinhold Bråkenhielm, *How Philosophy Shapes Theories of Religion: An Analysis of Contemporary Philosophies of Religion with Special Regard to the Thought of John Wilson, John Hick and D.Z. Phillips* (Lund, Sweden: Gleerup, 1975).

David Cheetham, *John Hick: A Critical Introduction and Reflection* (Aldershot, UK: Ashgate, 2003).

John B. Cobb, *Christ in a Pluralistic Age* (Philadelphia: Westminster Press, 1975).

John B. Cobb, "The Religions," in P. Hodgson and R. King (eds), *Christian Theology* (Philadelphia: Fortress Press, 1982), pp. 299–322.

Gavin D'Costa, *Theology and Religious Pluralism* (Oxford: Blackwell Publishers, 1986).

Gavin D'Costa (ed.), *Christian Uniqueness Reconsidered: The Myth of a Pluralistic Theology of Religions* (Maryknoll, NY: Orbis Books, 1990).

George E. Griener, *Ernst Troeltsch and Herman Schell: Christianity and the World Religions – An Ecumenical Contribution to the History of Apologetics* (Frankfurt am Main: Peter Lang, 1990).

John Hick, *An Interpretation of Religion* (London: Macmillan, 1989).
John Hick and Paul Knitter (eds), *The Myth of Christian Uniqueness* (Maryknoll, NY: Orbis Books, 1987).
Charles B. Jones, *The View from Mars Hill: Christianity in the Landscape of World Religions* (Cambridge, MA: Cowley Publications, 2005).
Hendrik Kraemer, *The Christian Message in a Non-Christian World* (London: Harpers, 1938).
Harold A. Netland, *Dissonant Voices: Religious Pluralism and the Question of Truth* (Grand Rapids, MI: Eerdmans, 1991).
William Lloyd Newell, *The Secular Magi: Marx, Freud, and Nietzsche on Religion* (Lanham, MD: University Press of America, 1995).
Wilfrid Cantwell Smith, *Towards a World Theology* (London: Macmillan, 1981).

10

The Last Things

Introduction

This final chapter focuses on Christian understandings of what happens at the end of history – an area of theology usually referred to as "eschatology" (Greek: *ta eschata* – "the last things"). There has been a general reluctance within many sections of Christian theology to indulge in speculation over these matters. However, there has been no shortage of statements and explorations concerning the Christian understanding of the last things.

A number of themes are of interest, and are singled out as worth detailed study.

The Christian Hope	
10.1	Irenaeus on the Final Restoration of Creation
10.6	Methodius of Olympus on the Resurrection
10.10	Augustine on the Christian Hope
10.13	Benedict XII on Seeing God in Heaven
10.15	John Donne on the Resurrection
10.16	Jeremy Taylor on Death and Heaven
10.18	John Wesley on Universal Restoration
10.25	Kathryn Tanner on Eternal Life

The Nature of the Resurrection Body	
10.5	Origen on the Resurrection Body
10.6	Methodius of Olympus on the Resurrection
10.8	Gregory of Nyssa on the Resurrection Body
10.12	Peter Lombard on the Appearance of Humanity in Heaven

Purgatory	
10.7	Cyril of Jerusalem on Prayers for the Dead
10.9	John Chrysostom on Prayers for the Dead
10.10	Augustine on the Christian Hope
10.11	Gregory the Great on Purgatory
10.14	Catherine of Genoa on Purgatory

10.1

Irenaeus on the Final Restoration of Creation

In the final book of his "Against Heresies," the second-century writer Irenaeus of Lyons (c.130– c.200) turns to the theme of the Christian hope. In the course of this discussion he sets out his vision of the final restoration of God's creation. See also 10.4, 10.12.

For some people allow themselves to be induced into error by heretical writings, and are ignorant of the way in which God works and of the mystery of the resurrection of the righteous, and of the kingdom, which is the beginning of immortality [*principium incorruptelae*], the kingdom by which such as have proved worthy are gradually accustomed to receive God. For this reason it is necessary to say something on this matter, and to explain that in the restored creation the righteous must first rise at the appearing of the Lord to receive their promised inheritance, promised by God to the fathers, and to reign therein; after that the judgment will come. For it is only right that they should receive the reward of their endurance in that created order [*conditio*] in which they labored or suffered affliction, and were tested by suffering in all kinds of ways; that they should be brought to life in that created order in which they were put to death for the love of God; and to reign where they had endured bondage. For God is "rich in all things" (Romans 10: 12) and all things are his. Therefore this created order must be restored to its first condition and be made subject to the righteous without hindrance; and this the Apostle shows in the Epistle to the Romans, when he says, "The earnest expectation of the creation awaits the revelation of the sons of God" (Romans 8: 19–21). [...]

[After citing the words of Jesus in Matthew 26: 29, "I will no more drink the fruit of the vine until I drink it anew in my Father's kingdom," Irenaeus continues:] It is certain that he will drink it in the heritage of the earth, which he himself will renew and restore to the service of the glory of the sons of God. As David says, he "shall renew the face of the earth" (Psalm 104: 30). He promised to "drink of the fruit of the vine" with his disciples (Matthew 26: 29), and by doing this, he indicated two things: the inheritance of the earth in which the new fruit of the vine will be drunk, and the physical resurrection of his disciples. For it is the body which is raised in a new condition which receives the new drink. Now this should not be understood to mean that he will drink the fruit of the vine with his disciples in some higher region above the heavens [*in supercaelesti loco*]. Nor does it mean that those who drink it are disembodied, as the drink from the vine is more proper to the body rather than to the spirit.

Comment

In this passage Irenaeus sets out his belief in a restored earthly realm, which will be set up at the second coming of Christ, and will last for a thousand years (the "millennium"). After this time, the final judgment will take place. This idea of a worldly millennium is, for Irenaeus, confirmed by a number of considerations, especially Christ's promise to drink wine again with his disciples. How can this happen, he asks, if they are disembodied spirits? The reference to the future drinking of wine is a sure indication that there will be a kingdom of God established upon earth before the final judgment.

Questions for Study

1 How does Irenaeus understand the doctrine of creation to be linked with the eschatological hope?
2 Set out, in your own words, the way in which Irenaeus interprets the remarks of Jesus in Matthew 26: 29.

10.2

Theophilus of Antioch on Conditional Immortality

Theophilus of Antioch, about whom very little is known, composed his treatise *ad Autolycum* shortly after 180. It represents a defense of Christianity against the objections of the pagan Autolycus. In the course of his argument, he turns to deal with the idea of immortality. See also 5.12, 10.24.

Was humanity created merely mortal in nature? Certainly not. So is humanity therefore immortal? We do not accept this either. So maybe humanity is nothing? We do not say this either. What we do say is that humanity was by nature neither mortal nor immortal. If God had created humanity mortal, God would therefore be the author of human death. So God did not create humanity as either mortal or immortal, but, as we have said above, with the capacity for them both. If humanity inclined towards those things which relate to immortality by keeping the commandments of God, then it would receive immortality as a reward from God, and thus become divine. On the other hand, if humanity should incline towards those things which relate to death by disobeying God, then humanity would be the cause of its own death. For God created humanity free [*eleutheros*] and with power over itself [*autexousios*].

Comment

Theophilus, in common with other writers of this period, such as Justin Martyr and Irenaeus, argued that the immortality of the human soul was conditional, rather than intrinsic. In other words, the immortality of the soul was not an integral part of human nature; immortality was to be understood as being conditional upon total obedience to God. A similar assumption underlies the argument in Anselm of Canterbury's *Cur Deus homo*.

Questions for Study

1 What reasons does Theophilus offer for his views on conditional immortality?
2 What role does the notion of human "freedom" or "autonomy" (a good translation of the Greek word *autexousia*) play in this passage?

10.3

Tertullian on Hell and Heaven

The *Apologeticus* is one of Tertullian's earliest writings, dating from around 197. In this passage Tertullian (c.160–c.225) offers both an explanation and defense of the Christian view of judgment and immortality in the face of criticisms made against it by some pagan writers. See also 10.9, 10.10, 10.13, 10.17, 10.18.

And so we are also ridiculed because we proclaim that God is going to judge the world. Yet even the poets and philosophers place a judgment seat in the underworld. In the same way if we threaten Gehenna, which is a store of hidden underground fire for purposes of punishment, we are received with howls of derision. Yet they likewise have the river Pyriphlegethon in the place of the dead. And if we mention paradise, a place of divine delight appointed to receive the spirits of the saints, cut off from the knowledge of this everyday world by a kind of barrier consisting of that zone of fire [*maceria quadam igneae illius zonae a notitia orbis communis segregatum*], then the Elysian Fields have anticipated the faith in this respect. So how, I ask you, do these resemblances to our doctrines on the part of the philosophers or poets come about? They are just taken from our mysteries. And our mysteries, being earlier, are more trustworthy, and more to be believed than these mere copies! If they invented these mysteries subsequently out of their senses, then our mysteries would have to be reckoned as copies [*imagines*] of what came later. For the shadow never preceded the body, nor the copy before the truth [*Nunquam enim corpus umbra aut veritatem imago praedecit*].

Comment

The argument here is that pagan philosophers have no right to criticize Christian ideas of heaven and hell, in that these are already anticipated in pagan Greek writings. Tertullian implies that these pagan writings may have plagiarized Old Testament sources, a common view among Christian writers of this early period.

Questions for Study

1 Set out, in your own words, the use that Tertullian makes of the pagan notion of the Elysian Fields. What point does he make in this way?
2 "The shadow never preceded the body, nor the copy before the truth." What does Tertullian mean by this? And how does he use this consideration in his argument?

10.4

Tertullian on the Millennium

The work from which this extract is taken is a polemic against the heretic Marcion, dating from 207–8. Tertullian sets out the basic features of the Christian hope, and focuses on the idea of the millennium. See also 10.18.

For we also hold that a kingdom has been promised to us on earth, but before heaven: but in another state than this, as being after the resurrection. This will last for a thousand years, in a city of God's own making, the Jerusalem which has been brought down from heaven which the Apostle also designates as "our mother from above" (Galatians 4: 26). When he proclaims that "our *politeuma*," that is, citizenship, "is in heaven" (Philippians 3: 20), he is surely referring to a heavenly city. [...] We affirm that this is the city established by God for the reception of the saints at the resurrection, and for their refreshment with an abundance of all blessings, spiritual blessings to be sure, in compensation for the blessings we have despised or lost in this age. For indeed it is right and worthy of God that his servants should also rejoice in the place where they suffered hardship for his name. This is the purpose of that kingdom, which will last a thousand years, during which period the saints will rise sooner or later, according to their merit [*sanctorum resurrectio pro meritis maturius vel tardius resurgentium*]. When the resurrection of the saints is completed, the destruction of the world and the conflagration of judgment will be effected; we shall be "changed in a moment" into the angelic substance, by the "putting on of incorruption" (1 Corinthians 15: 52–3), and we shall be transferred to the heavenly kingdom.

Comment

The millennium here refers to an earthly reign of God, lasting for a thousand years, in which evil is eliminated from the earth. After enjoying the pleasures of this earthly paradise, believers are then finally raised to heaven. Tertullian uses the word "resurrection" to refer both to the entry into this kingdom, and subsequently entry into heaven.

Questions for Study

1 What role does the millennium play in Tertullian's thought?
2 What is the relation between this millennial kingdom and the final heavenly kingdom of God?

10.5

Origen on the Resurrection Body

In this passage, dating from the first half of the third century, Origen (c.185–c.254) sets out his distinctive view that the resurrection body is totally spiritual in character. See also 10.6, 10.8, 10.12.

Now we ask how can anyone imagine that our animal body is to be changed by the grace of the resurrection and become spiritual? [. . .] It is clearly absurd to say that it will be involved in the passions of flesh and blood. [. . .] By the command of God the body which was earthly and animal will be replaced by a spiritual body, such as may be able to dwell in heaven; even on those who have been of lower worth, even of contemptible, almost negligible merit, the glory and worth of the body will be bestowed in proportion to the deserts of the life and soul of each. But even for those destined for eternal fire or for punishment there will be an incorruptible body through the change of the resurrection.

Comment

Origen here sets out a view of the resurrection body which is partly shaped by the writings of Paul in the New Testament, and partly by Platonic ideas of perfection. Notice how he excludes any form of "passion" as a matter of principle.

Questions for Study

1 How does Origen understand the relation between our earthly and spiritual bodies?
2 What relation does Origen appear to envisage between personal merit and the degree of glory which is achieved?

10.6

Methodius of Olympus on the Resurrection

This work by Methodius of Olympus (died c.311), which was originally written in Greek around the year 300, takes the form of a discussion set in the house of the physician Aglaophon. The book is concerned to refute Origen's idea that the resurrection necessarily involves a spiritual body. See also 10.5, 10.8.

So it seems that it is as if some skilled artificer had made a noble image, cast in gold or other material, which was beautifully proportioned in all its features. Then the artificer suddenly notices that the image had been defaced by some envious person, who could not endure its beauty, and so decided to ruin it for the sake of the pointless pleasure of satisfying his jealousy. So the craftsman decides to recast this noble image. Now notice, most wise Aglaophon, that if he wants to ensure that this image, on which he has expended so much effort, care and work, will be totally free from any defect, he will be obliged to melt it down, and restore it to its former condition. [. . .]

Now it seems to me that God's plan was much the same as this human example. He saw that humanity, his most wonderful creation, had been corrupted by envy and treachery. Such was his love for humanity that he could not allow it to continue in this condition, remaining faulty and deficient to eternity. For this reason, God dissolved humanity once more into its original materials, so that it could be remodeled in such a way that all its defects could be eliminated and disappear. Now in the melting down of a statue corresponds to the death and dissolution of the human body, and the remolding of the material to the resurrection after death.

Comment

Origen had argued that human flesh was simply a prison for the eternal spirit, which was liberated at death, and would be raised again in a purely spiritual manner. Methodius argues that the resurrection is like the recasting of a damaged metal statue.

The Bonwetsch edition, used here, includes material which has been recovered from rediscovered Slav versions of this document; as a result, the numbering of the sections differs from that of older editions. In the edition provided by J. P. Migne in his *Patrologia Graeca*, the section is numbered I.6.

Questions for Study

1 What criticisms are made of Origen? You may find it helpful to read his views again (10.5) before answering this.
2 Set out clearly, in your own words yet with citations from the text, exactly what points Methodius makes through the analogy of the defaced image.

10.7

Cyril of Jerusalem on Prayers for the Dead

In the course of his explanation of aspects of Christian worship, Cyril of Jerusalem (c.315–86) turns to deal with a section of the liturgy which offers prayers for the dead in the Eucharist. See also 10.8, 10.9.

Following this, we pray for the holy fathers and bishops who have fallen asleep, and in general for all those who have fallen asleep before us, in the belief that it is a great benefit to the souls for whom the prayers are offered, while the holy and magnificent victim himself is present. [. . .] In the same way, by offering to God our prayers for those who have fallen asleep and who have sinned, we [. . .] offer Christ sacrificed for the sins of all, and by doing so, obtain the loving God's favor for them and for ourselves.

Comment

The central argument of this passage is that offering such prayers in the presence of Christ lends them an efficacy which they might not possess in other contexts.

Questions for Study

1 What purpose does Cyril believe is served by praying for the dead?
2 Compare this text with the views of John Chrysostom (10.9); what points of similarity can you discern?

10.8

Gregory of Nyssa on the Resurrection Body

After discussing Paul's teaching on the resurrection in 1 Corinthians 15: 35–9, Gregory of Nyssa (c.330–c.395) sets out his own ideas on the matter, and compares them with Paul's (who he refers to as "the Apostle"). See also 10.5, 10.6, 10.12.

It seems clear that the argument of the Apostle agrees in every way with our understanding of the notion of resurrection, and shows the same basic ideas that are contained in our definition of this matter – namely, that the resurrection is nothing other than the reconstitution of our nature to its pristine state. For we read in Scripture that, in the first act of creation, the earth initially brought forth the green plant; then seed was produced from this plant; and from this seed, when it had been scattered on the earth, the same form of the original growth sprang up. Now the inspired Apostle says that this is precisely what also happens at the resurrection. Thus we learn from him not only that human nature is changed into a far nobler state, but also that we are to hope for the return of human nature to its primal condition. The original process was not that of an ear of corn resulting from the seed, but of the seed resulting from the ear, after which the ear grew from the seed.

Comment

Gregory here develops the idea that the concept of "resurrection" can be understood in terms of "restoration" or "repristination" – in other words, the restoration of things to the state in which they were created.

Questions for Study

1 What role does the analogy of the seed play in Gregory's argument?
2 "We are to hope for the return of human nature to its primal condition." Locate this statement within the text. What does Gregory mean by this? And how does he justify this statement?

10.9

John Chrysostom on Prayers for the Dead

In this homily, one of a major series composed during the period 386–98, John Chrysostom (c.347–407) provides theoretical justification for the practice of praying for the dead, noting its important place in Christian liturgical practice at the time. See also 10.7.

Let us help and commemorate them. After all, if the children of Job were purified by the sacrifice of their father (Job 1: 5), why should we doubt that our offerings for the dead bring them any comfort? [. . .] Let us not hesitate to help those who have died, and to offer our prayers on their behalf.

Comment

The passage is brief and clear, and requires little comment. The analogy from the book of Job is not quite as straightforward as the passage suggests; a reading of Job 1: 4–5 may help make the situation clearer.

Questions for Study

1 What purpose does Chrysostom indicate for prayers for the dead?
2 Compare this text with the views of Cyril of Jerusalem (10.7); what points of similarity can you discern?

10.10

Augustine on the Christian Hope

Although Augustine of Hippo (354–430) is remembered for his contributions to the great controversies of his day – such as the Pelagian and Donatist debates – it is important to recall that he wrote and preached on many topics which were not in themselves controversial. In this extract from his *City of God* he sets out the theme of the Christian hope. See also 10.12, 10.13.

The souls of the departed saints [*sanctorum animae defunctorum*] are not troubled by the death by which they are separated from their bodies. This is because their "flesh rests in hope" (Psalm 16: 9). Whatever humiliations it may seem to have suffered, it is now unable to feel them. For they do not (as Plato supposed) desire that their bodies should be forgotten; rather, they remember the promise given them by the one who always keeps his word, and who has given them the assurance of the preservation of the hairs of their head (Luke 21: 18). For this reason, they look forward with patient yearning to the resurrection of the bodies in which they endured many hardships, but in which they will never again feel any pain. If they did not "hate their own flesh" (Ephesians 5: 29) when they subdued it by the law of the spirit (since through its weakness it opposed their will), how much more do they love it when it is itself destined to be spiritual. The spirit when subservient to the flesh is not inappropriately called fleshly: so the flesh in subservience to the spirit is rightly called spiritual, not because it is converted into spirit, as some infer from the scriptural text, "It is sown as a natural body, it will rise as a spiritual body" (1 Corinthians 15: 42), but because it will be subdued to the Spirit, readily offering complete and marvelous obedience. And this will lead to the fulfillment of their desire, with the safe attainment of a secure immortality, with the removal of all feelings of discomfort, corruptibility, and slowness. For this body will not only be better than it was here in its best estate of health; it will far surpass the bodies of the first human beings before sin [*in primis hominibus ante peccatum*].

Comment

The text is interesting in many respects, including the way in which it shows Augustine exploring the relation of "flesh" and "spirit," which may owe as much to the neo-Platonist writer Plotinus as to St Paul. Yet Augustine clearly distinguishes the Christian view of death and immortality from the view he associates with Plato.

Questions for Study

1 How does Augustine understand the relation of "flesh" and "spirit" in the resurrection?
2 Many patristic writers interpreted the last things in terms of the restoration of creation. Would Augustine agree? In particular, what does he mean when he declares that the resurrection body "will far surpass the bodies of the first human beings before sin"?

10.11

Gregory the Great on Purgatory

This important early reference to the idea of purgatory, dating from 593 or 594, is grounded on Gregory's (c.540–604) exposition of Matthew 12: 32, especially its references to sins which can be forgiven "in the age to come." Note especially the reference to the "purifying fire." See also 10.7, 10.8, 10.14.

As for certain lesser faults, we must believe that, before the final judgment, there is a purifying fire [*purgatorius ignis*], for he who is the truth declares that "whoever utters blasphemy against the Holy Spirit will not be pardoned either in this age, or in the age which is to come" (Matthew 12: 31–2). From this statement, it is to be understood that certain offences can be forgiven in this age, whereas certain others will be forgiven in the age which is to come.

Comment

This is not a developed exposition of the concept of purgatory, but an early anticipation of both its *ideas* and its *vocabulary*.

Questions for Study

1 Set out, in your own words, the point which Gregory makes with reference to Matthew 12: 32: "whoever speaks against the Holy Spirit will not be forgiven, either in this age or in the age to come."
2 What are the implications of Gregory's references to a "purifying fire"? What other kinds of fire might there be?

10.12

Peter Lombard on the Appearance of Humanity in Heaven

One of the questions that has greatly vexed Christian theologians concerns the age of those who are resurrected. If someone dies at the age of 60, will they appear in the streets of the New Jerusalem looking like a 60-year-old? And if someone dies at the age of 10, will they appear as a child? This issue caused the spilling of much theological ink, especially during the Middle Ages. By the end of the thirteenth century, an emerging consensus can be discerned. As each person reaches their peak of perfection around the age of 30, they will be resurrected as they would have appeared at that time – even if they never lived to reach that age. Peter Lombard (c.1100–60) discusses the matter in a manner typical of his age: "A boy who dies immediately after being born will be resurrected in that form which he would have had if he had lived to the age of thirty years." The New Jerusalem will thus be populated by men and women as they would appear at the age of 30 (about the age, of course, at which Christ was crucified) – but with every blemish removed. See also 10.1, 10.2, 10.6, 10.15.

A boy who dies immediately after being born will be resurrected in that form which he would have had if he had lived to the age of thirty years, hindered by no defect of his body. So it can be seen that this substance, which is so small in birth, becomes so great in the resurrection, on account of its being multiplied in itself and of itself. From this, it can be seen that, even if he had lived, the substance would not have come from another source, but would have increased by itself, just as Adam's rib, from which the woman was made, and as the loaves were multiplied in the Gospels.

Comment

The question of the apparent age of the occupants of heaven was important beyond the theological community. For example, many medieval and Renaissance artists were asked to paint murals of heaven to decorate private chapels, cathedrals, and monasteries. How should they represent the saints in heaven? Peter Lombard's answer proved highly influential. Since Christ was aged about 30 at the time of his death, this is to be regarded as a perfect age – and is hence the apparent age of those raised to glory in heaven.

Questions for Study

1 Peter is troubled by the question of where the additional material needed to expand the earthly body of a young boy to that of an adult man would come from. What answer does he give?
2 Peter emphasizes that the resurrection body will be perfect, and sees its apparent age of 30 as one aspect of that perfection. What other points does he identify as part of this process of the perfection of the heavenly body?

10.13

Benedict XII on Seeing God in Heaven

In the document *Benedictus Deus*, published on January 29, 1336, and also known as *De visione Dei beatifica* ("On the Beatific Vision of God"), from which the following extract is taken, Pope Benedict XII (died 1342) set out an authoritative statement of the Christian hope. See also 10.1, 10.3, 10.10.

By virtue of our apostolic authority, we define the following point. According to the general disposition of God, since the ascension of our Lord and Savior Jesus Christ into heaven the souls of all the saints [...] and other believers who died after receiving Christ's holy baptism (provided that they were not in need of purification when they died [...] or, if they did need, or will need, such purification, when they have been purified after death) [...] have been, are, and will be in heaven, in the heavenly kingdom and celestial paradise with Christ, and are joined with the company of the angels, already before they take up their bodies once more and before the general judgment. Since the passion and death of our Lord Jesus Christ, these souls have seen and do see the divine essence with an intuitive vision, and even face to face, without the mediation of any creature.

Comment

The passage deals specifically with what is known as the "beatific vision" – that is, with the direct apprehension of God by those in heaven, without the need for any intermediary. Traditional theology insisted that human nature, by virtue of its weakness, could not behold God; Benedict argues that this weakness is abolished through the resurrection, allowing those who have been raised to see God face to face.

Questions for Study

1 What does Benedict understand to happen to believers after death?
2 Consider the following Pauline passage: "For now we see in a mirror dimly, but then face to face" (1 Corinthians 13: 12). How is this passage reflected in Benedict's thoughts in this text?

10.14

Catherine of Genoa on Purgatory

The date of composition of Catherine of Genoa's *Treatise on Purgatory* is not known for certain, although it may date from the 1490s. In this work, written in Italian, Catherine (1447–1510) sets out her influential understanding of the basis and purpose of purgatory, stressing the importance of the notion of being purged from sin. See also 10.11.

The basis of all the pains [of purgatory] is sin, whether original or actual. God created the soul pure, simple, and clean from all stain of sin, with a beatific instinct towards the one from whom original sin, in which the soul presently finds itself, draws it away. When actual sin is added to this original sin, the soul is drawn still further from him. [. . .]

When a soul draws near to the pure and clear state in which it was at its first creation, its beatific instinct is rediscovered and grows continually stronger with such force that any obstacle preventing the soul from finally reaching its goal appears to be unbearable. The more it glimpses this vision, the greater its pain.

Because the souls in purgatory are without the guilt of sin, there is no obstacle between them and God except their pain, which holds them back so that they cannot reach perfection through this instinct. They can also see that this instinct is held back by a need for righteousness. For this reason, a fierce fire [*un tanto extreme foco*] comes into being, which is like that of Hell, with the exception of guilt. This is what makes evil the wills of those who are condemned to Hell, on whom God does not bestow his goodness; they therefore remain in their evil wills, and opposed to the will of God. [. . .]

The souls in purgatory have wills which are in all things in accord with the will of God himself. For this reason, God bestows upon them his goodness. As a result they are joyful and cleansed of all their sin.

And as for guilt, these souls are just as they were when they were originally created by God, in that God forgives immediately the guilt of those who have passed from this life distressed by their sins, and having confessed them and resolved not to commit them any more. Only the corrosion of sin is left, and they are cleansed from this by pain in the fire.

When they have been cleansed for all guilt, and united in their wills with God, they may see him clearly (to the extent that he makes himself known to them), and see also how much it means to enjoy him, which is the goal for which they have been created.

Comment

One of Catherine's concerns in this passage is to explain how guilt is purged by fire in purgatory. This involves a careful consideration of the nature of guilt, and especially its effects upon the vision of God.

Questions for Study

1 According to Catherine, what are the effects of guilt? Why is it essential that this guilt should be purged? And what means of purging does she propose?
2 In what way does the theme of the "beatific vision" appear in this passage? How does this relate to Benedict XII's statements on this matter (10.13)?

10.15

John Donne on the Resurrection

John Donne (1571–1631) is perhaps one of the greatest spiritual poets in the English language. The poem which follows is taken from the collection of "Holy Sonnets," which deal with a range of theological and spiritual issues. See also 5.21, 10.10.

Death be not proud, though some have called thee
Mighty and dreadful, for thou art not so;
For those whom thou think'st, thou dost overthrow,
Die not, poor Death, nor yet canst thou kill me.
From rest and sleep, which but thy pictures be,
Much pleasure; then from thee, much more must flow,
And soonest our best men with thee do go,
Rest of their bones, and soul's delivery.
Thou art slave to Fate, Chance, kings, and desperate men,
And dost with poison, war, and sickness dwell;
And poppy or charms can make us sleep as well
And better than thy stroke; why swell'st thou then?
One short sleep past, we wake eternally,
And death shall be no more; Death, thou shalt die.

Comment

The poem personifies death, and argues that it has been overthrown through the resurrection of Christ. The poem ends with the assertion of the final defeat and death of death.

Questions for Study

1 Read the following verse from the King James Version of the Bible: "The last enemy that shall be destroyed is death" (1 Corinthians 15: 26). How is this theme of death as an enemy incorporated into the poem?
2 Now read the following verses from the King James Version of the Bible: "Then shall be brought to pass the saying that is written, Death is swallowed up in victory. O death, where is thy sting? O grave, where is thy victory? The sting of death is sin; and the strength of sin is the law. But thanks be to God, which giveth us the victory through our Lord Jesus Christ" (1 Corinthians 15: 54–7). How is the theme of victory over death developed in the poem?

10.16

Jeremy Taylor on Death and Heaven

Jeremy Taylor (1613–67) is widely regarded as one of the finest spiritual writers of the seventeenth century. He is often referred to as a "Caroline Divine," meaning a religious writer of the Church of England who was active during the reigns of Charles I and Charles II. His best-known works include *The Rules and Exercises of Holy Living* (1650) and *The Rules and Exercises of Holy Dying* (1651), from which this extract is taken. See also 10.10, 10.13.

If thou wilt be fearless of death endeavour to be in love with the felicities of saints and angels, and be once persuaded to believe that there is a condition of living better than this; that there are creatures more noble than we; that above there is a country better than ours; that the inhabitants know more and know better, and are in places of rest and desire; and first learn to value it, and then learn to purchase it, and death cannot be a formidable thing, which lets us into so much joy and so much felicity. And, indeed, who would not think his condition mended if he passed from conversing with dull tyrants and enemies of learning, to converse with Homer and Plato, with Socrates and Cicero, with Plutarch and Fabricius? So the heathens speculated, but we consider higher. "The dead that die in the Lord" shall converse with St Paul, and all the college of the apostles, and all the saints and martyrs, with all the good men whose memory we preserve in honour, with excellent kings and holy bishops, and with the great Shepherd and Bishop of our souls, Jesus Christ, and with God himself.

Comment

Holy Dying – to use the shorter version of the title of this work – is among Taylor's best-known works. "It is a great art to die well," commented Taylor; the work to which these words are prefaced aims to set out the means by which a Christian can die with dignity and peace. One of the chief means by which Taylor believes that Christians can deal with the fear of death is to contemplate the hope of what lies beyond death. We can see here a clear statement of the impact of Christian beliefs about heaven on Christian living. Taylor clearly believes that the contemplation of the Christian hope serves as a solace and balm to those who fear the end of life, by reminding them that something more wonderful awaits them beyond.

Questions for Study

1 In what way does Taylor see the Christian hope of heaven as being a support and encouragement to those who are dying?
2 Believers in heaven "shall converse with St Paul, and all the college of the apostles, and all the saints and martyrs, with all the good men whose memory we preserve in honour, with excellent kings and holy bishops, and with the great Shepherd and Bishop of our souls, Jesus Christ, and with God himself." What does Taylor mean by this? And why does he find it consoling?

10.17

Jonathan Edwards on the Reality of Hell

In his famous sermon "Sinners in the Hands of an Angry God," originally preached during the Great Awakening in eighteenth-century Massachusetts, Jonathan Edwards (1703–58) presents a vigorous defense of a traditional idea of hell, designed to shock his audiences into repentance. See also 10.3, 10.22, 10.24.

There is no want of *power* in God to cast wicked men into hell at any moment. Men's hands cannot be strong when God rises up. The strongest have no power to resist him, nor can any deliver out of his hands. He is not only able to cast wicked men into hell, but he can most easily do it. Sometimes an earthly prince meets with a great deal of difficulty to subdue a rebel, who has found means to fortify himself, and has made himself strong by the numbers of his followers. But it is not so with God. There is no fortress that is any defence from the power of God. Though hand join in hand, and vast multitudes of God's enemies combine and associate themselves, they are easily broken in pieces. They are as great heaps of light chaff before the whirlwind; or large quantities of dry stubble before devouring flames. We find it easy to tread on and crush a worm that we see crawling on the earth; so it is easy for us to cut or singe a slender thread that any thing hangs by: thus easy is it for God, when he pleases, to cast his enemies down to hell. What are we, that we should think to stand before him, at whose rebuke the earth trembles, and before whom the rocks are thrown down?

They *deserve* to be cast into hell; so that divine justice never stands in the way, it makes no objection against God's using his power at any moment to destroy them. Yea, on the contrary, justice calls aloud for an infinite punishment of their sins. Divine justice says of the tree that brings forth such grapes of Sodom, "Cut it down, why cumbereth it the ground?" (Luke 13: 7). The sword of divine justice is every moment brandished over their heads, and it is nothing but the hand of arbitrary mercy, and God's mere will, that holds it back.

They are already under a sentence of *condemnation* to hell. They do not only justly deserve to be cast down thither, but the sentence of the law of God, that eternal and immutable rule of righteousness that God has fixed between him and mankind, is gone out against them, and stands against them; so that they are bound over already to hell. John 3: 18 "He that believeth not is condemned already." So that every unconverted man properly belongs to hell; that is his place; from thence he is, John 8: 23 "Ye are from beneath." And thither he is bound; it is the place that justice, and God's word, and the sentence of his unchangeable law assign to him.

They are now the objects of that very same *anger* and wrath of God, that is expressed in the torments of hell. And the reason why they do not go down to hell at each moment, is not because God, in whose power they are, is not then very angry with them; as he is with many miserable creatures now tormented in hell, who there feel and bear the fierceness of his wrath. Yea, God is a great deal more angry with great numbers that are now on earth: yea, doubtless, with many that are now in this congregation, who it may be are at ease, than he is with many of those who are now in the flames of hell.

So that it is not because God is unmindful of their wickedness, and does not resent it, that he does not let loose his hand and cut them off. God is not altogether such an one as themselves, though they may imagine him to be so. The wrath of God burns against them, their damnation does not slumber; the pit is prepared, the fire is made ready, the furnace is now hot, ready to receive them; the flames do now rage and glow. The glittering sword is whet, and held over them, and the pit hath opened its mouth under them.

The *devil* stands ready to fall upon them, and seize them as his own, at what moment God shall permit him. They belong to him; he has their souls in his possession, and under his dominion. The scripture represents them as his goods (Luke 11: 21–2). The devils watch them; they are ever by them at their right hand; they stand waiting for them, like greedy hungry lions that see their prey, and expect to have it, but are for the present kept back. If God should withdraw his hand, by which they are restrained, they would in one moment fly upon their poor souls. The old serpent is gaping for them; hell opens its mouth wide to receive them; and if God should permit it, they would be hastily swallowed up and lost. [. . .]

All wicked men's pains and *contrivance* which they use to escape hell, while they continue to reject Christ, and so remain wicked men, do not secure them from hell one moment. Almost every natural man that hears of hell, flatters himself that he shall escape it; he depends upon himself for his own security; he flatters himself in what he has done, in what he is now doing, or what he intends to do. Every one lays out matters in his own mind how he shall avoid damnation, and flatters himself that he contrives well for himself, and that his schemes will not fail. They hear indeed that there are but few saved, and that the greater part of men that have died heretofore are gone to hell; but each one imagines that he lays out matters better for his own escape than others have done. He does not intend to come to that place of torment; he says within himself, that he intends to take effectual care, and to order matters so for himself as not to fail. But the foolish children of men miserably delude themselves in their own schemes, and in confidence in their own strength and wisdom; they trust to nothing but a shadow. The greater part of those who heretofore have lived under the same means of grace, and are now dead, are undoubtedly gone to hell; and it was not because they were not as wise as those who are now alive: it is not because they did not lay out matters as well for themselves to secure their own escape.

Comment

This is widely regarded as one of the classic texts to deal with a traditional view of hell. In this sermon – which it is estimated took two hours to deliver – Edwards sets out the inevitability and eternity of hell for those who fail to amend their ways. Note especially the assumption that the human soul is immortal, and must therefore spend eternity in either heaven or hell.

Questions for Study

1 Set out, in your own words, the general theme of this passage. What do you think Edwards wished his congregation to do, after hearing this sermon?
2 What difference would it make to Edwards' argument if the human soul were created with the capacity for immortality, which is only actualized through faith? You might find it helpful to read Theophilus of Antioch (10.2) and P. E. Hughes (10.24) on this to help clarify the issues.

10.18

John Wesley on Universal Restoration

In this sermon, John Wesley (1703–91) sets out his vision of a universal final restoration of the creation, including the animal and plant worlds. Note Wesley's admission than he cannot justify any assertion that God holds humanity and the remainder of the creation in equal esteem. See also 10.1.

But will "the creature", will even the brute creation, always remain in this deplorable condition? God forbid that we should affirm this; yea, or even entertain such a thought. While "the whole creation groaneth together" (whether men attend or not), their groans are not dispersed in idle air, but enter the ears of Him that made them. While his creatures "travail together in pain", he knoweth all their pain, and is bringing them nearer and nearer to the birth, which shall be accomplished in its season. He seeth the "earnest expectation" wherewith the whole animated creation "waiteth for" that final "manifestation of the sons of God", in which "they themselves also shall be delivered" (not by annihilation; annihilation is not deliverance) "from the present bondage of corruption into" a measure of "the glorious liberty of the children of God". [...]

A general view of this is given us in the twenty-first chapter of the Revelation. When He that "sitteth on the great white throne" hath pronounced "Behold, I make all things new", when the word is fulfilled, "the tabernacle of God is with men, and they shall be his people, and God himself shall be with them, and be their God" – then the following blessing shall take place (not only on the children of men; there is no such restriction in the text; but) on every creature according to its capacity. [...]

To descend to a few particulars. The whole brute creation will then, undoubtedly, be restored, not only to the vigour, strength, and swiftness which they had at their creation, but to a far higher degree of each than they ever enjoyed. They will be restored, not only to that measure of understanding which they had in paradise, but to a degree of it as much higher than that, as the understanding of an elephant is beyond that of a worm. And whatever affections they had in the garden of God, will be restored with vast increase; being exalted and refined in a manner which we ourselves are not able to comprehend. The liberty they then had will be completely restored, and they will be free in all their motions. They will be delivered from all irregular appetites, from all unruly passions, from every disposition that is either evil in itself, or has any tendency to evil. No rage will be found in any creature, no fierceness, no cruelty, or thirst for blood. So far from it that "the wolf shall dwell with the lamb, the leopard shall lie down with the kid, the calf and the young lion together; and a little child shall lead them. The cow and the bear shall feed together, and the lion shall eat straw like an ox. They shall not hurt not destroy in all my holy mountain" (Isaiah 11: 6–7). [...]

But though I doubt not that the Father of All has a tender regard for even his lowest creatures, and that, in consequence of this, he will make them large amends for all they suffer while under their present bondage; yet I dare not affirm that he has an *equal* regard for them and for the children of men.

Comment

Wesley clearly sees redemption in terms of the final restoration of the creation. For Wesley, the vision set out in Isaiah 11: 6–9 is of controlling importance. Heaven, on this view, will include elephants and worms. Wesley's main concern, however, is to establish what degree of priority is to be given to humanity itself in this restored creation. His answer is slightly delphic, but intriguing.

Questions for Study

1. On the basis of what considerations does Wesley affirm that the "whole animated creation" will be finally restored? Which biblical texts seem to be of especial importance to Wesley?
2. Which does Wesley believe will have the greater status in the restored creation: elephants or people? How does he reach this conclusion?

10.19

Rudolf Bultmann on the Existential Interpretation of Eschatology

In his book *History and Eschatology* (1957), which represents the published form of the 1955 Gifford Lectures at Edinburgh University, Rudolf Bultmann (1884–1976) argues for an existentialist reinterpretation of the last things, in which the traditional understanding of judgment is perceived in terms of a personal existential decision in the present. See also 2.43.

[The gospel] message knows itself to be legitimated by the revelation of the grace of God in Jesus Christ. According to the New Testament, *Jesus Christ is the eschatological event*, the action of God by which God has set an end to the old world. In the preaching of the Christian Church the eschatological event will ever again become present and does become present ever and again in faith. The old world has reached its end for the believer; he is "a new creature in Christ". For the old world has reached its end with the fact that he himself as "the old man" has reached his end and is now "a new man" and a free man.

It is the paradox of the Christian message that the eschatological event, according to Paul and John, is not to be understood as a dramatic cosmic catastrophe but as happening within history, beginning with the appearance of Jesus Christ and in continuity with this occurring again and again in history, but not as the kind of historical development which can be confirmed by any historian. It becomes an event repeatedly in preaching and faith. Jesus Christ is the eschatological event not as an established fact of past time but as repeatedly present, as addressing you and me here and now in preaching.

Preaching is address, and as address it demands answer, *decision*. This decision is obviously something other than the decisions in responsibility over against the future which are demanded in every present moment. For in the decision of faith I do not decide on a responsible action, but on a new understanding of myself as free from myself by the grace of God and as endowed with my new self, and this is at the same time the decision to accept a new life grounded in the grace of God. In making this decision I also decide on a new understanding of my responsible acting. This does not mean that the responsible decision demanded by the historical moment is taken away from me by faith, but it does mean that all responsible decisions are born of love. For love consists in unreservedly being for one's neighbour, and this is possible only for the man who has become free from himself.

It is the paradox of Christian being that the believer is taken out of the world and exists, so to speak, as unworldly and that at the same time he remains within the world, within his historicity. To be historical means to live from the future. The believer too lives from the future; first because his faith and his freedom can never be possession; as belonging to the eschatological event they can never become facts of past time but are reality only over and over again as event; secondly because the believer remains within history. In principle, the future always offers to man the gift of freedom; Christian faith is the power to grasp this gift. The freedom of man from himself is always realized in the freedom of historical decisions. [. . .]

In the New Testament the eschatological character of the Christian existence is sometimes called "sonship". F. Gogarten says: "sonship is not something like an habitus or a quality, but it must be grasped ever and again in the decisions of life. For it is that towards which the present temporal history tends, and therefore it happens within this history and nowhere else." Christian faith just "by reason of the radical eschatological character of the salvation believed in never takes man out of his concrete worldly existence. On the contrary, faith calls him into it with unique sobriety. . . . For the salvation of man happens only within it and nowhere else."

We have no time to describe how Reinhold Niebuhr in his stimulating book *Faith and History* (1949) endeavours to explain the relation between faith and history in a similar way. Nor have we time to dispute with H. Butterfield's thought, developed in his book *Christianity and History*. Although I do not think he has clearly seen the problem of historicism and the nature of historicity, his book contains many important statements. And I agree with him when he says: "Every instant is eschatological". I would prefer, however, to say: every instant has the possibility of being an eschatological instant and in Christian faith this possibility is realized.

The paradox that Christian existence is at the same time an eschatological unworldly being and an historical being is analogous with the Lutheran statement *simul iustus, simul peccator*. In faith the Christian has the standpoint above history which Jaspers like many others has endeavoured to find, but without losing his historicity. His unworldliness is not a quality, but it may be called *aliena* (foreign), as his righteousness, his *iustitia* is called by Luther *aliena*.

We started our lectures with the question of meaning in history, raised by the problem of historicism. We have seen that man cannot answer this question as the question of the meaning in history in its totality. For man does not stand outside history. But now we can say: the meaning in *history* lies always in the present, and when the present is conceived as the eschatological present by Christian faith the meaning in history is realized. Man who complains: "I cannot see meaning in history, and therefore my life, interwoven in history, is meaningless," is to be admonished: do not look around yourself into universal history, you must look into your own personal history. Always in your present lies the meaning in history, and you cannot see it as a spectator, but only in your responsible decisions. In every moment slumbers the possibility of being the eschatological moment. You must awaken it.

Comment

"Judgment" is here interpreted by Bultmann to refer to the moment of existential crisis, as human beings are confronted with the divine *kerygma* (or "proclamation") addressed to them. The "realized eschatology" of the fourth Gospel arises, according to Bultmann, through the fact that it presents the *parousia* not as some future event, but as something which has already taken place, in the confrontation of the believer with the *kerygma*.

Questions for Study

1 What does Bultmann mean when he affirms that "Jesus Christ is the eschatological event"?
2 This passage stresses the importance of a personal "decision." Why? How does Bultmann relate an existential decision to the final judgment?

10.20

Helmut Thielicke on Ethics and Eschatology

The noted German Lutheran ethicist and theologian Helmut Thielicke (1908–86) devoted much of his career to writing a three-volumed *Theological Ethics*, in which he set out to reinterpret the traditional Lutheran teaching of the "two kingdoms" in eschatological terms. The text below is taken from this major writing, and sets out the importance of eschatology for ethics. See also 10.19.

The result of all this can be expressed only in the paradoxical statement that Christian ethics is an impossible possibility. What this statement means becomes clear the moment we view the matter in terms of the eschatological perspective sketched by the Sermon on the Mount. The Sermon on the Mount radicalizes the Mosaic nomos. It imposes on us a total demand by forbidding not merely the results of anger but anger itself, not merely the act of adultery but adulterous thoughts (Matthew 5: 22, 28). In so doing it calls in question not merely our conduct but our very being. It insists not simply that we do differently but that we *be* different. It lays claim to us, so to speak, as if the fall had never taken place, as if our whole existence were not determined by this aeon. It imposes its demand upon us as if we were still in the primal state, as when we first came from the hands of God. It imposes its demand upon us as if the new aeon had already come and replaced the old. As a result, everything that we do, and hence also every ethics which would determine our action, is challenged eschatologically.

Christian ethics is an impossible enterprise inasmuch as it lies under the disruptive fire of the coming world. Yet it is also a necessary enterprise inasmuch as we live in that field of tension between the two aeons and must find a *modus vivendi*. In order to characterize this tension by which the whole ethical enterprise is sustained – and at the same time repeatedly shattered – we would list three of its distinctive features.

First, the mystery of Christian ethics is an eschatological mystery. It rests on an irresolvable tension between time and eternity, between this aeon and the coming aeon. This tension cannot be removed by means of a parallelogram of forces which in effect is a compromise. To seek a timeless solution of that kind, in terms of "resultants," would require that time be no longer viewed as hastening toward its end. It would mean looking for that which lasts, searching for those things that can be accepted as of "permanent" validity, even if only by way of compromise.

Second, the mystery of Christian ethics is a christological mystery. It rests on an irresolvable tension between deity and humanity in Christ. Just as I cannot represent logically the togetherness of the divine and the human natures in Christ, coordinating them with one another in a static and timeless way in terms of logic, so I cannot find a formula for the unity of the Christian's existence, which on the one hand is lived out in this aeon and yet at the same time participates in the heavenly commonwealth. Ethics cannot and must not try to resolve this tension by providing rules which on the surface appear to be wise and prudent, satisfying both the law of continuity and that of discontinuity. In such an attempt it would come up against the same impossibility as does the doctrine of the two natures when it tries to show that Christ does justice to the claims of both natures, when it goes so far as to try to present Christ as the true middle-point between the two natures, and hence as a kind of demi-god.

The fact that the tension cannot be resolved is a sign that what takes place when we are called into the kingdom of God, and so exist in the zone of tension between the two worlds, is an inscrutable miracle whose mode is concealed from us. We can no more explain how it happens than we can explain the how of the incarnation and the miracle of Christ's person. In like manner we cannot explain how the new ego is related to the old. "I live, yet not I, but Christ lives in me" (Galatians 2: 20). Here it is said of both the ego "according to the flesh" and the ego "according to the Spirit" that it is "I." Here an identity is asserted similar to that declared by the *est* in Luther's understanding of the identity of the eucharistic elements with the body and blood of Christ. But this identity can be maintained only in faith. To state the matter negatively, it is impossible to make the identification in a statistically objective sense, either by speaking of a congruence of the two forms of the ego or by referring to them as intersecting circles in which the zones that overlap and the zones that do not can be determined. One can speak only of a paradoxical identity which may nonetheless be differentiated in terms of perspective: the ego of the first part (the "I live") is seen *coram se ipso*, and the ego of the second part (the "Christ lives in me") is seen from the divine standpoint.

There is first the mystery of the new being. This mystery of being imparts also to the action which proceeds from it the character of mystery. This is true not merely in the sense that the action takes place in the power of the Holy Spirit – and hence in the name of yet another mystery – but also in the sense that the norms of this action participate in the mystery of the situation between the two aeons.

Third, the mystery of Christian ethics is a sacramental mystery. It rests on an irresolvable tension between the sign and the thing signified, like that we know in the sacraments. It is impossible for me in my concrete existence, by loving, by acting or allowing myself to be acted upon, to express the new existence; in adequate *res* form. I can express it only by means of signs, through demonstrative actions which point beyond themselves. As the body of the Lord is hidden under the signs of bread and wine, so the obedience involved in true love of neighbor is hidden in the highly complex act of my loving, an act made up of such diverse motives as sympathy, generosity, and a self-interest which is on the one hand egoistic no matter how sublimated, and on the other a true seeking of the neighbor. Indeed, my act is complex because it includes "opposition to" as well as "support for" (think for instance of the problems involved in expressing love within the orders, e.g., in war or litigation, as touched upon in Luther's doctrine of the "two kingdoms").

Consequently the aim of ethics cannot be to overcome the tension by suggesting compromises which would supposedly do justice to both elements in the tension. Ethics must rather follow the way which leads into and through the tension. With respect to concrete tasks requiring action, ethics can show wherein that tension consists. Beyond that it can show, in a context where every action stands in need of and under the promise of forgiveness, what those actions should be like which are to demonstrate the fact that a Christian is the citizen of a new aeon and that at the same time he also honors the old aeon as the *kairos* of God, as the "acceptable time" which by the patience of God is still permitted to continue. The theme of ethics is this "walking between two worlds." It is in the strict sense the theme of a "wayfarers' theology," a *theologia viatorum*. It lives under the law of the "not yet" but within the peace of the "I am coming soon" (Revelation 22: 20). Theological ethics is eschatological or it is nothing.

Thielicke here argues that the traditional Lutheran doctrine of the "two kingdoms" is to be restated eschatologically. Instead of thinking of the "earthly kingdom" and the "heavenly kingdom" as two overlapping spheres of authority in the present, we must recast this imagery in terms of the breaking in of the new era of God into the present era. There is thus an eschatological tension between the "now" and the "not yet," which must be fully acknowledged in ethical thinking and decision making.

Questions for Study

1 In what way, according to Thielicke, does Christian ethics "rest on an irresolvable tension between time and eternity, between this aeon and the coming aeon"? You will find it helpful to locate this statement, and examine it in its context.

2 Thielicke also suggests that Christian ethics is Christological. What does he mean by this? Is this an additional consideration, or an aspect of its eschatological nature?

10.21

Richard Bauckham on Jürgen Moltmann's Eschatology

Jürgen Moltmann established himself as one of the most important and stimulating writers on eschatology in the later twentieth century. This passage consists of a lucid summary of and commentary on Moltmann's eschatology, as developed by Moltmann in *The Theology of Hope*. See also 10.10.

One of the most important achievements of Moltmann's theology has been to rehabilitate future eschatology. This was in part a response to the demonstration by modern biblical scholarship that future eschatology is of determinative significance for biblical faith. Whereas Schweitzer, Dodd, Bultmann and many others had thought biblical eschatology unacceptable to the modern mind unless stripped of its reference to the real temporal future of the world, Moltmann, along with some other German theologians in the 1960s, saw in future eschatology precisely the way to make Christian faith credible and relevant in the modern world. He wished to show how the modern experience of history as a process of constant and radical change, in hopeful search of a new future, need not be rejected by the church, as though Christianity stood for reactionary traditionalism, nor ignored, as though Christianity represented a withdrawal from history into purely subjective authenticity. Rather, the eschatological orientation of biblical Christian faith towards the future of the world requires the church to engage with the possibilities for change in the modern world, to promote them against all tendencies to stagnation, and to give them eschatological direction towards the future Kingdom of God. The gospel proves relevant and credible today precisely through the eschatological faith that truth lies in the future and proves itself in changing the present in the direction of the future.

Christian hope, for Moltmann, is thoroughly christological since it arises from the resurrection of Jesus. His famous claim that "from first to last, and not merely in the epilogue, Christianity is eschatology, is hope" was possible only because it was a claim about the meaning of the resurrection of Jesus. It also depends on setting the resurrection of Jesus against its Old Testament and Jewish theological background – a recovery of the Jewish roots of Christian theology which is very characteristic of Moltmann's work. The God of Israel revealed himself to Israel by making promises which opened up the future: against this background God's act of raising the crucified Jesus to new life is to be understood as the culminating and definitive event of divine promise. In it God promises the resurrection of all the dead, the new creation of all reality, and the coming of his kingdom of righteousness and glory, and he guarantees this promise by enacting it in Jesus' person. Jesus' resurrection entails the eschatological future of all reality.

When this concept of the resurrection as promise is related to Moltmann's dialectic of cross and resurrection, important aspects of his eschatology emerge. In the first place, the contradiction between the cross and the resurrection creates a dialectical eschatology, in which the promise contradicts present reality. The eschatological kingdom is no mere fulfillment of the immanent possibilities of the present, but represents a radically new future: life for the dead, righteousness for the unrighteous, new creation for a creation subject to evil and death. But secondly, the identity of Jesus in the total contradiction of cross and resurrection is also important. The resurrection was not the survival of some aspect of Jesus which was not subject to death: Jesus was wholly dead and wholly raised by God. The continuity was given in God's act of new creation. Similarly God's promise is not for another world, but for the new creation of this world, in all its material and worldly reality. The whole of creation, subject as it is to sin and suffering and death, will be transformed in God's new creation.

Christian eschatology is therefore the hope that the world will be different. It is aroused by a promise whose fulfillment can come only from God's eschatological action transcending all the possibilities of history, since it involves the end of all evil, suffering, and death in the glory of the divine presence indwelling all things. But it is certainly not therefore without effect in the present. On the contrary, the resurrection set in motion a historical process in which the promise already affects the world and moves it in the direction of its future transformation. This process is the universal mission of the church. This is the point at which Moltmann's *Theology of Hope* opened the church to the world as well as to the future. Authentic Christian hope is not that purely other-worldly expectation which is resigned to the unalterability of affairs in this world. Rather, because it is hope for the future of this world, its effect is to show present reality to be not yet what it can be and will be. The world is seen as transformable in the direction of the promised future. In this way believers are liberated from accommodation to the status quo and set critically against it. They suffer the contradiction between what is and what is promised. But this critical distance also enables them to seek and activate those present possibilities of world history which lead in the direction of the eschatological future. Thus by arousing active hope the promise creates anticipations of the future kingdom within history. The transcendence of the kingdom itself beyond all its anticipations keeps believers always unreconciled to present conditions, the source of continual new impulses for change.

Comment

Moltmann argued for the rediscovery of the corporate Christian conception of hope as a central motivating factor in the life and thought of the individual and the church. Eschatology needed to be rescued from its position as "a harmless little chapter at the conclusion of a Christian dogmatics" (Karl Barth), and given pride of place. Moltmann thus argues that eschatology is of central importance to Christian thinking. Christian theology provides a vision of hope through the transforming work of God, which stands in sharp contrast to secular ideas of hope and social transformation.

Questions for Study

1 How would you evaluate the significance of Moltmann's demand that Christian theology rediscover eschatology? What benefits might result?

2 Bauckham writes of the "dialectic of cross and resurrection." What does he mean by this? How does the theme of "hope" relate to the grim realities of the cross of Christ, according to Moltmann?

10.22

Hans Urs von Balthasar on Hell

In one of his most interesting works, Hans Urs von Balthasar (1905–88) offers a theological exploration of the events of Holy Week. In addition to considering the importance of Good Friday (the crucifixion) and Easter Day (the resurrection), von Balthasar also explores the significance of the intervening Holy Saturday – the moment when Christ descended to the dead. See also 10.3, 10.17.

As a Trinitarian event, the going to the dead is necessarily also an event of salvation. It is poor theology to limit this salvific happening in an *a priori* manner by affirming – in the context of a particular doctrine of predestination and the presumed identification of Hades (Gehenna) with Hell – that Christ was unable to bring any salvation to "Hell properly so called", *infernus damnatorum*. Following many of the Fathers, the great Scholastics set up just such *a prioristic* barriers. Once agreed that there were four subterranean "reception areas" – pre-Hell, Purgatory, the Hell of unbaptized infants, and the true Hell of fire – theologians went on to ask just how far Christ had descended and to just what point his redemptive influence extended, whether by his personal presence, *praesentia*, or merely by a simple effect, *effectus*. The most frequent reply was that he showed himself to the damned in order to demonstrate his own power, even in Hell; that in the Hell of infants he had nothing to achieve; that in Purgatory an amnesty could be promulgated, its precise scope a matter of discussion. The pre-Hell remained the proper field of play of the redemptive action. [. . .] This whole construction must be laid to one side, since before Christ (and here the term "before" must be understood not in a chronological sense but in an ontological), there can be neither Hell nor Purgatory – as for a Hell for infants, of that we know nothing – but only that Hades (which at the most one might divide speculatively into an upper and a lower Hades, the inter-relationship of the two remaining obscure) whence Christ willed to deliver "us" by his solidarity with those who were (physically and spiritually) dead.

But the desire to conclude from this that all human beings, before and after Christ, are henceforth saved, that Christ by his experience of Hell has emptied Hell, so that all fear of damnation is now without object, is a surrender to the opposite extreme. [. . .] Here the distinction between Hades and Hell acquires its theological significance. In rising from the dead, Christ leaves behind him Hades, that is, the state in which humanity is cut off from access to God. But, in virtue of his deepest Trinitarian experience, he takes "Hell" with him, as the expression of his power to dispose, as judge, the everlasting salvation or the everlasting loss of man.

Comment

In this difficult passage, von Balthasar interacts with a traditional Roman Catholic understanding of hell in assessing the significance of the doctrine of Christ's descent into hell. Notice especially the distinction drawn between "Hades" as the place of the dead, and "Hell" as a place of divine judgment. Von Balthasar argues that the implicit identification of these two notions in earlier theology led to considerable confusion.

Questions for Study

1 Set out, in your own words, the distinction that is made between "the place of the dead" and "Hell." What is the point of this distinction? What purpose does it serve?
2 Why do you think von Balthasar is critical of those who speculate on the precise geography and topography of hell?

10.23

Gabriel Fackre on the Last Things

Christians have always enjoyed speculating about the nature and timing of the "last things." When will Christ come again? What will happen to those who are still alive at the time? And will the final judgment take place before or after a period of tribulation? In this passage the American theologian Gabriel Fackre (born 1926) urges caution in discussing these matters, and offers some guidance to those who feel able to be precise about such complex issues. See also 10.1, 10.3, 10.4, 10.6, 10.11, 10.13.

What does the Christian message have to say about the end? First we must be clear about what it does *not* say. In periods of uncertainty and peril, there is a temptation to claim to know far more about the times and seasons than befits the modesty of classical Christian Faith (1 Thessalonians 5: 1–2). The history of the Church is replete with movements that responded to crisis times or circumstances with detailed forecasts of the how, when, where, and who of the end. Thus eschatology becomes *apocalypticism* with its blueprint, timetable, map, and cast of characters, all in a soon arriving cataclysmic conclusion. Most often, the lush imagery of contemporary apocalyptic takes the form of a *premillennialist* scenario in which identifiable pretribulationary events in the present move toward the "rapture" of believers, a tribulation of holocaust proportions, the return of Christ to establish a thousand-year kingdom in this world, succeeded by a final revolt of the powers of evil, their overthrow, the coming of a new heaven and a new earth, and the going of the damned to the everlasting fires. *Postmillennialist* views read the same texts differently, forecasting the Kingdom within history before Christ's final return. And *amillennialist* conceptions less sanguine about both the postmillennialist possibilities of history and the premillennialist claims to a God's-eye view of the consummation construe the apocalyptic imagery symbolically and see sin and evil persisting to the End. Here we follow in the tradition of the latter while respecting the insights of the other views. "Travelogue eschatologies" (Hans Schwarz) do not represent the mainstream of Christian teaching about the future, for Jesus' own counsel has been decisive: "About that day and hour no one knows" (Mark 13: 32). Tellers of the Christian Story are at their best when they observe this counsel and acknowledge that "We see through a glass darkly" (1 Corinthians 13: 12 KJV). The glass is not transparent, giving us a full and clear view, but translucent. We have enough light by which to see and to discern some of the shape of things to come.

While the Christian epic does not yield up encyclopedic knowledge about the *how, when, where,* and *who* of the Consummation, it does give us bold affirmations about the *that* and *what* of the matter. In this respect the doctrine of the End is much like the doctrine of the Beginning. The factuality and form of creation and Consummation are the things of interest to the Storyteller. *That* God shall fulfill the divine Intention, *that* history moves toward its Omega is fundamental to the meaning of the Christian saga. *What* the dimensions of that fulfillment are is equally important. The latter is summarized in the classic creeds of the Church. The Storytelling community has sifted through the Storybook in its own struggle age after age with human questioning and has fixed upon certain biblical refrains: the resurrection of the *dead, the return of Christ, the last judgment, everlasting life*. These comprise the kernel of Christian teaching about the End. These are the last things.

The kernel is surrounded by a husk. The color and sheen of this covering have a way of attracting the seeker, sometimes causing him or her to settle too quickly for the surface instead of probing to the center. There is a range of rich metaphors and images – the Anti-Christ, a thousand-year reign of peace, golden streets and pearly gates, numerology, the conversion of Israel – in which the great affirmations are housed. Three things should be noted about them: (1) They are not dominant or ubiquitous New Testament motifs, but random assertions. (2) They rise out of particular historical circumstances (Nero, Rome, etc.) and are often calculated to shore up the faith of the early Christians faced with oppression and martyrdom. (3) Most of them fall short of being eschatological affirmations since they do not deal with the transfiguration *of* the world, but with events *in* the world. Christian eschatology is not secular forecasting but the futurology of the World to Come. While these exuberant scenarios provide material for the armchair speculations and sometimes frenzied imaginations so popular in periods of travail in human history, Christian thought about the End has in the main chosen to be reserved about the details, focusing rather on the centralities of resurrection, return, judgment, and eternal life.

Comment

In this discussion Gabriel Fackre points out what he sees as being the dangers of overprecise speculation concerning the last things. He argues that it is possible to discern some basic themes lying beneath the complex network of images and terms used in Christian eschatological language, and enters a plea for moderation in relation to this kind of speculation.

Questions for Study

1 Why do you think Fackre is concerned to avoid overprecision in regard to the end-time?
2 Set out, in your own words, what Fackre understands to be "the kernel of Christian teaching about the End."

10.24

Philip E. Hughes on Everlasting Death

In this passage from one of his final works, Philip E. Hughes (1915–90) raises a series of questions concerning the traditional idea of "everlasting death." He notes a number of difficulties with this traditional approach, before offering his own understanding of conditional immortality, which he regards as avoiding the difficulties of the traditional approach. See also 10.2, 10.22.

The difficulty (if such it is) of equating everlasting death with everlasting existence was compounded in the case of Augustine by reason of the fact that he took the unquenchable flames of eternal fire to be meant in a literal sense. In facing the question how it would be possible for resurrected persons of body and soul to be kept from being consumed by these flames he invoked the support of scientific fact, as he thought it to be, that certain lower creatures, and in particular the salamander, "can live in the fire, in burning without being consumed, in pain without dying." It was decidedly shaky support, however, because the naturalists known to him of his own and earlier periods reported this competence of the salamander with skepticism as a traditional or legendary notion. But in any case the supposed ability of the salamander was irrelevant, because it is not a capacity shared by human beings with salamanders, and Augustine had perforce to resort to the hypothesis that in the flames of hell the wicked would in this respect become salamander-like: "Although it is true," he wrote, "that in this world there is no flesh which can suffer pain and yet cannot die, yet in the world to come there will be flesh such as there is not now, as there will also be death such as there is not now."

Augustine, in short, found it necessary to introduce a change in the meaning of *death* if his belief in the endlessness of the torments of hellfire was to be sustained; and this is a necessity for all who understand eternal destruction in this way, whether or not they consider the flames of hell to be intended in a literal sense. Such persons can indeed claim to be in good company; but they should be aware that their interpretation is open to serious questioning. Apart from the fact that it involves a drastic change in the meaning of death so that, in this eschatological perspective, it signifies being kept alive to suffer punishment without the power of dying, some other considerations must be taken into account.

First of all, because *life* and *death* are radically antithetical to each other, the qualifying adjective *eternal* or *everlasting* needs to be understood in a manner appropriate to each respectively. Everlasting life is existence that continues without end, and everlasting death is destruction without end, that is, destruction without recall, the destruction of obliteration. Both life and death hereafter will be everlasting in the sense that both will be *irreversible*: from that life there can be no relapse into death, and from that death there can be no return to life. The awful negation and the absolute finality of the second death are unmistakably conveyed by its description as "the punishment of eternal destruction and exclusion from the presence of the Lord" (2 Thessalonians 1: 9).

Secondly, immortality or deathlessness, as we have said, is not inherent in the constitution of man as a corporeal–spiritual creature, though, formed in the image of God, the potential was there. That potential, which was forfeited through sin, has been restored and actualized by Christ, the incarnate Son, who has "abolished death and brought life and immortality to light through the gospel" (2 Timothy 1: 10). Since inherent immortality is uniquely the possession and prerogative of God (1 Timothy 6: 16), it will be by virtue of his grace and power that when Christ is manifested in glory our mortality, if we are then alive, will be superinvested with immortality and our corruption, if we are then in the grave, will be clothed with incorruption, so that death will at last be swallowed up in victory (1 Corinthians 15: 51–57; 2 Corinthians 5: 1–5). And thus at last we shall become truly and fully human as the destiny for which we were created becomes an everlasting reality in him who is the True Image and the True Life. At the same time those who have persisted in ungodliness will discover for themselves the dreadful truth of Christ's warning about fearing God, "who can destroy both body and soul in hell" (Matthew 10: 28).

Thirdly, the everlasting existence side by side, so to speak, of heaven and hell would seem to be incompatible with the purpose and effect of the redemption achieved by Christ's coming. Sin with its consequences of suffering and death is foreign to the design of God's creation. The renewal of creation demands the elimination of sin and suffering and death. Accordingly, we are assured that Christ "has appeared once for all at the end of the ages to put away sin by the sacrifice of himself" (Hebrews 9: 26; 1 John 3: 5), that through his appearing death has been abolished (2 Timothy 1: 10), and that in the new heaven and the new earth, that is, in the whole realm of the renewed order of creation, there will be no more weeping or suffering, "and death shall be no more" (Revelation 21: 4). The conception of the endlessness of the suffering of torment and of the endurance of "living" death in hell stands in contradiction to this teaching. It leaves a part of creation which, unrenewed, everlastingly exists in alienation from the new heaven and the new earth. It means that suffering and death will never be totally abolished from the scene. The inescapable logic of this position was accepted, with shocking candor, by Augustine, who affirmed that "after the resurrection, when the final, universal judgment has been completed, there will be two kingdoms, each with its own distinct boundaries, the one Christ's, the other the devil's, the one consisting of good, the other of bad." To this it must be objected that with the restoration of all things in the new heaven and the new earth, which involves God's reconciliation to himself of *all things*, whether on earth or in heaven (Acts 3: 21; Colossians 1: 20), there will be no place for a second kingdom of darkness and death. Where all is light there can be no darkness; for "the night shall be no more" (Revelation 22: 5). When Christ fills all in all and God is everything to everyone (Ephesians 1: 23; 1 Corinthians 15: 28), how is it conceivable that there can be a section or realm of creation that does not belong to this fullness and by its very presence contradicts it? The establishment of God's everlasting kingdom of peace and righteousness will see the setting free of the whole created order from its bondage to decay as it participates in the glorious liberty of the children of God (Romans 8: 21).

Fourthly, the glorious appearing of Christ will herald the death of death. By his cross and resurrection Christ has already made the conquest of death, so that for the believer the fear and sting of death have been removed (Hebrews 2: 14–15; 1 Corinthians 15: 54–57), the passage from death to life is a present reality (John 5: 24), and the resurrection power of Jesus is already at work within him, no matter how severely he may be afflicted and incommoded outwardly (2 Corinthians 4: 11, 16). We do not yet see everything in subjection to the Son (Hebrews 2: 8); but nothing is more sure than that every hostile rule and authority and power will finally be destroyed, including death itself. Hence the assurance that "the last enemy to be destroyed is death" (1 Corinthians 15: 24–26). Without the abolition of death the triumph of life and immortality cannot be complete (2 Timothy 1: 10). This is the significance of *the second death*: it will be the abolition not only of sin and the devil and his followers but also of death itself as, in the final judgment, not only will Death and Hades give up their dead for condemnation but Death and Hades themselves will be thrown with them into the lake of fire (Revelation 20: 13–15). Hence the clear promise that "death shall be no more" (Revelation 21: 4).

Though held by many, it is a hollow contention that if the death sentence pronounced at the final judgment against the unregenerate meant their annihilation the wicked would be getting off lightly and would be encouraged to regard the consequence of their sin without fear. (It may be interposed that far more does the expectation of the never-ending torment of finite creatures raise the question of the purpose that might be served by such retribution.) There is altogether no room for doubting that, first, at the last judgment God will mete out condign unishment in accordance with the absolute holiness of his being, and, second, the Scriptures allow no place whatsoever to the wicked for complacency as they approach that dreadful day when they will stand before the tribunal of their righteous Creator. This ultimate Day of the Lord is depicted as a day of indescribable terror for the ungodly, who will then be confronted with the truth of God's being which they had unrighteously suppressed and experience the divine wrath which previously they had derided. [. . .]

The horror of everlasting destruction will be compounded, moreover, by the unbearable agony of *exclusion*. To be inexorably excluded from the presence of the Lord and from the glory of his kingdom, to see but to be shut out from the transcendental joy and bliss of the saints as in light eternal they glorify their resplendent Redeemer, to whose likeness they are now fully and forever conformed, to be plunged into the abyss of irreversible destruction, will cause the unregenerate of mankind the bitterest anguish of weeping and wailing and gnashing of teeth. In vain will they have pleaded, "Lord, Lord, open to us!" (Matthew 25: 11–12.; cf. 7: 21–23). Too late will they then wish they had lived and believed differently. The destiny they have fashioned for themselves will cast them without hope into the abyss of obliteration. Their lot, whose names are not written in the Lamb's book of life, is the destruction of the second death. Thus God's creation will be purged of all falsity and defilement, and the ancient promise will be fulfilled that "the former things shall not be remembered or come to mind" as the multitude of the redeemed are glad and rejoice forever in the perfection of the new heaven and the new earth (Isaiah 65: 17–18; Revelation 21: 1).

Comment

This text represents an important statement of the concept of "conditional immortality" by an evangelical theologian who is otherwise noted for his conservative position on matters of controversy. The basic theme that underlies Hughes's book is that the traditional understanding of hell rests on rather less secure foundations than might be thought; Hughes sets out four major considerations which he feels demand a revision of the existing view.

Questions for Study

1 Set out clearly, in your own words yet citing from the passage as appropriate, four main considerations which Hughes believes call into question the traditional teaching on hell. Why does he single out Augustine so often?
2 What would be the effect of Hughes's ideas on Jonathan Edwards' views on everlasting hell, as set out in his famous sermon "Sinners in the Hands of an Angry God" (10.17)?

10.25
Kathryn Tanner on Eternal Life

Kathryn Tanner (born 1957) is presently Dorothy Grant Maclear Professor of Theology at the Divinity School, University of Chicago. Her 2001 book *Jesus, Humanity and the Trinity* set out a creative synthesis of Christian beliefs, rooted in tradition, yet orientated towards the future. Tanner's discussion of the concept of "eternal life" is of particular interest, and has been included in the present collection on account of its lucidity and clear sense of constructive engagement with the Christian theological tradition. See also 10.1, 10.10, 10.12, 10.13, 10.15.

Because it runs across the fact of death, life in Christ is eternal life. There is a life in the triune God that we possess now and after death, in Christ through the power of the Holy Spirit. Ante and post mortem do not mark any crucial difference with respect to it. Death makes no difference to that life in God in the sense that, despite our deaths, God maintains a relationship with us that continues to be the source of all life-giving benefit. Even when we are alive, we are therefore dead in so far as we are dead to Christ. Separation from Christ (and from one's fellows in Christ) is a kind of death despite the apparent gains that might accrue to one in virtue of an isolated, simply self-concerned existence. Eternal life, moreover, is one's portion or possession despite all the sufferings of life and death in a way that should comfort sufferers of every kind of tribulation. In all the senses of death, including the biological, we therefore live even though we die if we are alive to Christ. "If we live, we live to the Lord, and if we die, we die to the Lord; so then, whether we live or whether we die, we are the Lord's" (Romans 14: 8).

This understanding of eternal life follows the Old Testament suggestion, then, that all the goods of life ("life" in its extended senses) flow from relationship with God (the second biblical sense of life in relationship): "ye that did cleave unto the Lord are alive . . . this day" (Deuteronomy 4: 4, KJV). The effort to turn away or separate oneself from God has, in this understanding of things, the force of death, broadly construed. (It is literally the effort to unmake oneself.) Eternal life as *life in God* is a way of indicating this priority of the second biblical sense of life as relationship with God. It is also a way of specifying a character of relationship with God that might survive death. If the world, human society, and individual persons live in virtue of a relationship with God beyond the fact of their deaths, they must live *in* God and not simply in relationship *with* God. After death, the only powers of life our bodies have are God's own powers of life via the life-giving humanity of Christ in the power of the Spirit. *Eternal* life means a deepened affirmation that one's relation with God is not conditional; it is not conditioned even by biological death or the cessation of community and cosmos. The Bible maintains that God remains the God of Israel and the church, remains the God of the world that God creates and of all the individuals in it, whatever happens; the idea of eternal life is simply a way of continuing this affirmation of God's loving and steadfast faithfulness across the fact of death.

While continuing and consummating God's faithful commitment to the creature's good as that is manifest in creation, eternal life is itself a greater gift (and brings in its train greater gifts) than the relationship with God that creatures enjoy simply as creatures. The evident unconditionality of eternal life marks one such difference. With eternal life it becomes clear how relation with God as the source of all benefit cannot be broken by either sin or death (in all its senses including the biological); relations with a life-giving God are maintained unconditionally from God's side. Whatever might happen, God remains faithful to a life-giving relation to us and empowers us, through Christ, for faithfulness, too. The relationship is also unconditional, then, in that what we should be in it – the image of God's own relationship with us – is maintained or shored up from God's side (in virtue of the free favor and mercy of God in Christ) despite our own failings, sufferings, and sin. In the relationship of eternal life, God sets us in and upholds our position in relation to God, whatever we do, whatever happens to us. Despite the fact of human failing, faithlessness and death, we *are* alive in God.

Eternal life is, secondly, not the same sort of relationship as the rather external one that exists between God and creatures: our very identity as creatures is redefined so as to be essentially constituted by relationship with God. Separation from God is now impossible in a way it was not for us simply as creatures. The very meaning of this new identity is that our dependence upon God for our existence is now complete: in Christ we essentially *are* that relationship to God in a way that simply being creatures of God does not entail.

The model for this aspect of life in God is the incarnation. Jesus is the one who lives in God, the one who is all that he is as a human being without existing independently of God, the human being whose very existence is God's own existence – that is the meaning of the hypostatic union. Otherwise expressed, in Jesus God becomes the bearer of our very human acts and attributes. By grace – by virtue, that is, of a life-giving relationship with Jesus that is ours in the power of the Spirit – we enjoy something like the sort of life in God that Jesus lives. We (and the whole world) are to live in God as Jesus does, through him. In short, there is an approximation to the hypostatic union that the world enjoys through grace, most particularly after the world's death, when it transpires that, like Christ, the only life or existence we have is in and through God.

Eternal life is, in the third place, a greater gift than the relations enjoyed simply by creatures because of the gifts it brings with it. As a consequence of the incarnation, the powers and character of Godself shine through Jesus' human acts and attributes – giving Jesus' acts and attributes a salvific force (for example, so as to overcome and heal the consequences of sin) and eventuating in the manifest glorification of Jesus' own human being in the resurrection. So for us, life in Christ brings not just created goods but divine attributes such as imperishability and immortality, which are ours only through the grace of Christ in the resurrection of our bodies. When the fire of our own lives grows cold, we come to burn with God's own flame.

Comment

In this extract, Tanner sets out a strongly relational understanding of eternal life. Drawing on biblical roots, she points out how the covenantal relationship established between God and Israel, and subsequently the church, transcends the limits of earthly existence, temporal reality, and death. She also establishes an important connection between eternal life and Jesus Christ, particularly through her interpretation of the concept of the incarnation.

Questions for Study

1 Set out, in your own words, the three basic points that Tanner wants to make concerning eternal life. Notice how eternal life is something that we may be said to possess now – a present reality with future implications.
2 At several points in this extract, Tanner establishes a relationship between the concepts of eternal life and grace. Identity and explain these. What do you think she means by stating "eternal life is itself a greater gift (and brings in its train greater gifts) than the relationship with God that creatures enjoy simply as creatures"?

For Further Reading

John M. Baillie, *And the Life Everlasting* (London: Oxford University Press, 1934).
Richard Bauckham and Trevor A. Hart (eds), *Hope Against Hope: Christian Eschatology at the Turn of the Millennium* (Grand Rapids, MI: Eerdmans, 1999).
Carl E. Bratten, "The Kingdom of God and the Life Everlasting," in P. Hodgson and R. King (eds), *Christian Theology* (Philadelphia: Fortress Press, 1982), pp. 274–98.
David Fergusson and Marcel Sarot (eds), *The Future as God's Gift: Explorations in Christian Eschatology* (Edinburgh: T&T Clark, 2000).
Zachary Hayes, *Visions of a Future: A Study of Christian Eschatology* (Wilmington, DL: Michael Glazier, 1989).
Colleen McDannell and Bernhard Lang, *Heaven: A History* (New Haven, CT: Yale University Press, 1988).
Alister E. McGrath, *A Brief History of Heaven* (Oxford: Blackwell, 2001).
James Martin, *The Last Judgement in Protestant Theology* (Edinburgh: Oliver & Boyd, 1963).
Paul Minear, *Christian Hope and the Second Coming* (Philadelphia: Fortress Press, 1974).
Jürgen Moltmann, *The Coming of God: Christian Eschatology* (London: SCM Press, 1996).
H. Richard Niehbuhr, *The Kingdom of God in America* (New York: Harper & Row, 1959).
Henning Graf Reventlow, *Eschatology in the Bible and in the Jewish and Christian Tradition* (Sheffield, UK: Sheffield Academic Press, 1997).
J. A. T. Robinson, *In the End God* (London: Collins, 1968).
Jeffrey Burton Russell, *A History of Heaven: The Singing Silence* (Princeton, NJ: Princeton University Press, 1997).
John Sanders, *No Other Name: An Investigation into the Destiny of the Unevangelized* (Grand Rapids, MI: Eerdmans, 1992).
Hans Schwarz, *On the Way to the Future: A Christian View of Eschatology* (Minneapolis, MN: Augsburg Publishing House, 1979).
Krister Stendahl (ed.), *Immortality and Resurrection* (New York: Macmillan, 1965).

Details of Theologians

Abelard *see* Peter Abelard.

Alan of Lille (died 1203) Paris theologian with a special interest in the nature of theological language. See 6.24.

Alexander of Hales (c.1186–1245) An Englishman from Halesowen in the West Midlands, who took up a chair of theology at the University of Paris around 1220. He became a Franciscan in 1236, and did much to establish the distinctive features of Franciscan theology in the period of High Scholasticism. His *Summa Theologica* is a composite work, including material added after his death by writers such as William of Melitona. See 3.23.

Ambrose of Milan (c.339–97) A Roman civil servant who was ordained bishop of the northern Italian city of Milan in 374, despite being neither baptized nor ordained. He was a vigorous defender of orthodoxy, and made several fundamental contributions to the development of Latin theology. He was also instrumental in bringing about the conversion of Augustine of Hippo. See 6.8.

Ambrosiaster An unknown writer, who was first given this unusual name in the sixteenth century by Erasmus of Rotterdam. Initially confused with Ambrose of Milan, the distinctive character of this fourth-century writer, who is best known for his commentaries on the Latin text of the letters of Paul, is now recognized. See 6.9.

Anselm of Canterbury (c.1033–1109) Born in Italy, Anselm migrated to Normandy in 1059, entering the famous monastery of Bec, becoming its prior in 1063 and abbot in 1078. In 1093 he was appointed Archbishop of Canterbury. He is chiefly noted for his strong defense of the intellectual foundations of Christianity, and is especially associated with the "ontological argument" for the existence of God. See 1.7, 3.21, 5.13.

Apollinarius of Laodicea (c.310–c.390) A vigorous defender of orthodoxy against the Arian heresy, who was appointed Bishop of Laodicea at some point around 360. He is chiefly remembered for his Christological views, which were regarded as an overreaction to Arianism, and widely criticized at the Council of Constantinople (381). See 4.9.

Aquinas *see* Thomas Aquinas.

Arius (c.250–c.336) The originator of Arianism, a form of Christology which refused to concede the full divinity of Christ. Little is known of his life and little has survived of his writings. With the exception of a letter to Eusebius of Nicomedia, his views are known mainly through the writings of his opponents. See 4.7.

Athanasius (c.296–373) One of the most significant defenders of orthodox Christology during the period of the Arian controversy. Elected as Bishop of Alexandria in 328, he was forced to resign on account of his opposition to Arianism. Although he was widely supported in the west, his views were finally recognized after his death at the Council of Constantinople (381). See 4.8, 5.4, 5.5.

Athenagoras of Athens (second century) Little is known of this writer, who was one of the most able of the second-century apologists. See 3.1.

Augustine of Hippo (354–430) Widely regarded as the most influential Latin patristic writer, Augustine was converted to Christianity in the northern Italian city of Milan in the summer of 386. He returned to north Africa, and was made Bishop of Hippo in 395. He was involved in two major controversies: the Donatist controversy, focusing on the church and sacraments; and the Pelagian controversy, focusing on grace and sin. He also made substantial contributions to the development of the doctrine of the Trinity, and the Christian understanding of history. See 1.4, 2.8, 3.13, 3.14, 3.15, 5.10, 6.11, 6.12, 6.13, 6.14, 6.15, 7.6, 8.7, 8.8, 10.10.

Aulén, Gustaf (1879–1978) A Swedish Lutheran writer who was appointed to a chair of systematic theology at the University of Lund in 1913, and became Bishop of Strängnäs in 1933. He is chiefly remembered for his work on the doctrine of the atonement, and particularly his rehabilitation of the *Christus Victor* approach to the death of Christ. See 5.29.

Balthasar, Hans Urs von (1905–88) A Swiss Roman Catholic theologian who, despite never holding an academic teaching position, had a major influence on twentieth-century theology. He is chiefly noted for his emphasis on the need to relate theology to human culture, and for the strongly spiritual aspects of his theological reflection. See 10.22.

Barth, Karl (1886–1968) Widely regarded as the most important Protestant theologian of the twentieth century. Originally inclined to support liberal Protestantism, Barth was moved to adopt a more theocentric position through his reflections on World War I. His early emphasis on the "otherness" of God in his Romans commentary (1919) was continued and modified in his monumental *Church Dogmatics*. Barth's contribution to modern Christian theology has been immense. See 1.24, 2.41, 3.32, 6.51, 9.4.

Basil of Caesarea (c.330–79) Also known as "Basil the Great," this fourth-century writer was based in the region of Cappadocia, in modern Turkey. He is particularly remembered for his writings on the Trinity, especially the distinctive role of the Holy Spirit. He was elected Bishop of Caesarea in 370. See 3.10.

Bellarmine, Roberto (1542–1621) Roman Catholic theologian and controversialist, who served as rector of the Collegio Romano in 1592, as provincial of the Neapolitan province of the Jesuits in 1594, and papal theologian in 1597. He is best noted for his substantial engagement with post-Reformation controversies in his major work *Disputationes de Controversiis Christianae Fidei* (1586–93). See 2.25.

Benedict XII (died 1342) Originally named Jacques Fournier, this writer and scholar was elected as third Avignon pope in 1334. Although he was a significant theologian, few of his writings have survived. His most important writing is the papal constitution "Benedictus Deus" (1336), which deals with the beatific vision. See 10.13.

Bernard of Clairvaux (1090–1153) This French writer entered the Cistercian monastery of Cîteaux in 1112. In 1115 he was given the task of establishing a new monastery. He chose to do this at Clairvaux, which soon became established as a major center for spirituality. His writings are characterized by a deep personal devotion and love of God. See 2.11.

Beza, Theodore (1519–1605) Also known as Theodore de Besze, this French nobleman was attracted to Geneva in 1548, where he became an exponent of the ideas of John Calvin. He was appointed a professor at the Genevan Academy in 1558, and after Calvin's death in 1564 was recognized as a leading exponent of Reformed theology. See 6.40, 8.29.

Biel, Gabriel (c.1420–95) One of the most important German theologians of the fifteenth century, who was much admired as a preacher. A noted exponent of the theology of the *via moderna*, he was regarded with intense suspicion by Martin Luther, who viewed him as Pelagian in his soteriology. See 6.30.

Bloesch, Donald G. (born 1928) North American evangelical theologian, particularly noted for his contributions to discussions of the authority of Scripture. See 2.46.

Boff, Leonardo (born 1938) A Brazilian Roman Catholic theologian, chiefly noted for his contribution to the development of Latin American liberation theology, especially in relation to the Trinity as a model of society. Boff's views eventually led to his alienation from the Roman Catholic establishment. See 3.35, 7.28.

Bonaventure (1221–74). Franciscan theologian and spiritual writer, who did much to lay the foundations of early Franciscan theology. See 3.25.

Bonhoeffer, Dietrich (1906–45) A German Lutheran theologian, influenced by Karl Barth, with a particular interest in ecumenical work during the 1930s. He was arrested in 1943 and hanged by the Nazis in 1945. His letters and papers from prison include significant discussions on the suffering of God and the need for theology to relate to a "religionless society." See 1.28.

Boniface VIII (c.1234–1303) Pope from 1294. Italian church statesman, responsible for the bull *Unam Sanctam*, clarifying the relation of the church and state. See 7.10.

Bradstreet, Anne (1612–1672) American poet and Puritan religious writer, considered by many to be the first American poet. She was born in England, and emigrated to New England in 1530 with her husband, Simon, who went on to become Governor of Massachusetts. Many of her poems were written while her husband was away on colonial business. See 6.44.

Browne, Sir Thomas (1605–82) English scholar and antiquary, knighted by Charles II on the occasion of the king's visit to Norwich in 1671. See 2.27.

Brunner, Emil (1889–1966) A Swiss theologian who, while being influenced by his fellow countryman Karl Barth, developed ideas on natural theology which distanced them during the later 1930s. He is particularly noted for his strongly personalist idea of revelation. See 2.42, 6.50, 6.52.

Bucer, Martin (1491–1551) Also known as "Butzer." A German Catholic writer who was converted to Lutheranism around 1518, and became the reformer of the city of Strasbourg. In 1549 he moved to England at the invitation of Edward VI. He is chiefly noted for his work on biblical exegesis and his doctrine of the church. See 8.27.

Bultmann, Rudolf (1884–1976) A German Lutheran writer, who was appointed to a chair of theology at Marburg in 1921. He is chiefly noted for his program of "demythologization" of the New Testament, and his use of existential ideas in the exposition of the twentieth-century meaning of the gospel. See 2.43, 10.19.

Cabasilas, Nicholas (born c.1322) A Byzantine theologian, remembered especially for his "Concerning Life in Christ," which elaborates the way in which the believer achieves union with Christ. See 5.18.

Calvin, John (1509–64) Leading Protestant reformer, especially associated with the city of Geneva. His *Institutes of the Christian Religion* has become one of the most influential works of Protestant theology. See 1.13, 2.17, 2.18, 5.19, 6.36, 6.37, 6.38, 7.17, 8.26.

Candidus of Fulda (died 845) Benedictine scholar of the Carlovingian revival, known chiefly for his work *Dicta de imagine mundi*. He succeded Rabanus Maurus as head of the monastic school of Fulda when the latter was made abbot of the monastery in 822. See 8.12.

Cano, Melchior (1525–60) Spanish Dominican theologian and controversialist, whose reputation rests chiefly on his posthumous work *De locis theologicis* (1562). See 2.22.

Carr, Anne (born 1934) American Roman Catholic theologian, who spent much of her teaching career at the University of Chicago Divinity School. See 3.42.

Catherine of Genoa (1447–1510) A mystical Italian writer, who underwent a conversion experience at the age of 26. Her "Treatise on Purgatory" remains a major exploration of this theme. See 10.14.

Chrysostom, John (c.347–407) A noted preacher and theologian, who was appointed Patriarch of Constantinople in 398. Apart from his considerable gifts as a public speaker and preacher, he is remembered for his homilies on a number of biblical books, originally delivered at Constantinople during the period 396–8. See 10.9.

Clement of Alexandria (c.150–c.215) Alexandrian theologian, with a particular concern to explore the relation between Christian thought and Greek philosophy. See 1.2, 2.4, 5.3, 8.1, 8.2.

Coakley, Sarah (born 1951) Currently Edward Mallinckrodt Professor of Divinity at Harvard Divinity School, she is a systematic theologian and philosopher of religion, with particular interests in patristics, gender theory, and applied theology. See 3.43.

Cobb, John B. Jr. (born 1925) North American theologian, particularly noted for his commitment to process theology and the exploration of Christian–Buddhist dialogue. See 9.11.

Congar, Yves (1904–95) French Catholic theologian, associated with the emergence of *la nouvelle théologie*. His most important writings deal with the role of tradition, and issues of ecclesiology. See 7.25.

Cyprian of Carthage (died 258) A Roman rhetorician of considerable skill who was converted to Christianity around 246, and elected bishop of the north African city of Carthage in 248. He was martyred in that city in 258. His writings focus particularly on the unity of the church and the role of its bishops in maintaining orthodoxy and order. See 7.3, 8.3.

Cyril of Alexandria (died 444) A significant writer, who was appointed Patriarch of Alexandria in 412. He became involved in the controversy over the Christological views of Nestorius, and produced major statements and defenses of the orthodox position on the two natures of Christ. See 3.17, 4.13, 4.14, 4.15.

Cyril of Jerusalem (c.315–86) A writer noted especially for his series of 24 catechetical lectures, given at some point around 350 to those preparing for baptism, which are an important witness to the ideas which prevailed in the Jerusalem church. He was appointed Bishop of Jerusalem at some point around 349. See 2.7, 7.4, 8.4, 8.5, 10.7.

Denney, James (1856–1917) Professor of theology at the Glasgow Free Church College from 1897 until his death. Denney was a noted exponent of a traditional approach to the atonement. See 5.28.

Descartes, René (1596–1650) French philosopher noted for his emphasis on the role of systematic doubt, and the importance of "perfection" in discussion of the nature of God. See 1.16.

Donne, John (1571–1631) English poet, who was appointed Dean of St Paul's Cathedral, London, in 1621. See 5.21, 6.41, 10.15.

Dulles, Avery (born 1918) A noted American Roman Catholic with a distinguished record of writings, particularly on the doctrine of the church. See 7.29.

Duns Scotus, John (c.1266–1308) British scholastic theologian, noted for his exploration of faith and reason, and his emphasis on Aristotelian rather than Augustinian modes of reasoning. His emphasis on the doctrine of the immaculate conception of Mary was highly influential in the later Middle Ages. See 6.28.

Edwards, Jonathan (1703–58) American theologian in the Reformed tradition, noted especially for his metaphysical defense of Christianity in the light of the increasingly influential ideas of the Enlightenment, and his positive statements of traditional Reformed doctrines. See 2.31, 6.47, 10.17.

Ellul, Jacques (1912–94) A French Reformed theologian and sociologist, particularly noted for his analysis of the interaction between Christianity and culture. See 3.39.

Epiphanius of Constantia (c.315–403) Also known as Epiphanius of Salamis. A vociferous defender of orthodoxy, particularly against Sabellianism. His "Panarion," or "The Refutation of All Heresies," is an important witness to the controversies affecting the church at this stage. See 3.16.

Eriugena, John Scotus (c.810–c.877) A significant Irish philosopher and theologian, especially noted for his *Periphyseon*, which develops ideas concerning the four categories of nature. This work is often regarded as pantheistic. See 6.22.

Fackre, Gabriel (born 1926) North American theologian with a particular interest in the relation of narrative and systematic theology. See 10.23.

Feuerbach, Ludwig (1804–72) German Hegelian writer, whose ideas concerning the origin of religion had considerable influence on Karl Marx. His *Wesen des Christentums* ("Essence of Christianity"), which argued that Christianity was basically a projection of human needs and hopes, had considerable impact on its western European readership. See 9.2.

Forsyth, Peter Taylor (1848–1921) An English Protestant theologian with considerable interest in contemporary German theology, who abandoned his early theological liberalism. He is chiefly remembered for his *Person and Place of Jesus Christ* (1909), a vigorous criticism of liberal Protestant views of Christ. See 4.32.

Francis of Assisi (1181–1226) Although not traditionally regarded as a theologian, Francis had a considerable impact on the theology of High Scholasticism through his spirituality, particularly his emphasis on nature. See 6.25.

Franck, Sebastian (c.1499–c.1542) German radical reformer, noted for his commitment to the ideal of total freedom of thought in matters of religion. See 7.15.

Fulgentius of Ruspe (c.462–527) A Roman civil servant who became Bishop of Ruspe in north Africa around 502, and was a strong supporter of the theology of Augustine of Hippo. His theology mirrors the general pattern of the western thought of the period. See 3.18.

Gaunilo An eleventh-century Benedictine monk, who criticized Anselm's argument for the existence of God. Little is known of him. See 1.8.

Gerrish, Brian A. (born 1931) North American theologian with a particular interest in the history and contemporary exposition of the Reformed tradition. See 1.32.

Gore, Charles (1853–1932) English theologian of the late nineteenth and early twentieth century, who was appointed Bishop of Oxford in 1911. He is chiefly remembered for his Christological writings, including the 1891 Bampton Lectures, published as *The Incarnation of the Son of God*. See 2.38, 5.26.

Gregory the Great (c.540–604) Also known as Gregory I. He was elected pope in 590 and did much to establish the political power of the papacy, which reached its zenith in the Middle Ages. As a theologian, he is particularly noted for his pastoral and exegetical works. See 10.11.

Gregory of Nazianzus (329–89) Also known as Gregory Nazianzen. He is particularly remembered for his "Five Theological Orations," written around 380, and a compilation of extracts from the writings of Origen, which he entitled the *Philokalia*. See 3.11, 4.10.

Gregory of Nyssa (c.330–c.395) Cappadocian father, with a special interest in the relation of Christian theology and Platonic philosophy. See 3.9, 6.10, 10.8.

Gregory Palamas (c.1296–1359) A major Greek writer of the Hesychastic school, placing emphasis upon inner mystical prayer. He was elected as Archbishop of Thessalonica in 1347. See 4.23.

Gregory of Rimini (died 1358) Augustinian theologian of the fourteenth century, with a particular concern to re-establish the teachings of Augustine in the face of what he regarded as Pelagianism. See 6.29.

Gunton, Colin E. (1941–2003) British theologian, particularly associated with the exploration of the contemporary relevance of Trinitarian theology. See 5.35.

Gutiérrez, Gustavo (born 1928) Latin American liberation theologian, born in Peru. See 1.31.

Hampson, Daphne (born 1944) One of the leading contemporary representatives of feminist theology in Great Britain. See 4.39, 6.55.

Harnack, Adolf von (1851–1930) German liberal Protestant theologian and church historian, especially noted for his theories of the impact of Hellenism upon the Christian faith. See 1.23.

Hauerwas, Stanley (born 1940) American theologian and ethicist, based at Duke University Divinity School, with a particular interest in pacifism. Noted for his emphasis on the church as a community of character. See 7.30.

Hayter, Mary (now Mary Barr, born 1958) An English writer concerned to explore the relation between traditional Christian thought and aspects of feminism. Dr Barr now serves as chaplain to a hospital in Worcester, England. See 6.56.

Herbert, George (1593–1633) English religious poet of the seventeenth century, noted especially for his collection of poems entitled *The Temple*. See 5.22.

Herrmann, Wilhelm (1846–1922) German liberal Protestant theologian in the lineage of Schleiermacher and Ritschl, who held the chair of theology at Marburg from 1879. See 2.40.

Hick, John (born 1922) British theologian, based in the United States for the final stage of his career, noted for his commitment to a pluralist understanding of the relation of the world's religions. See 9.9.

Hilary of Poitiers (c.315–67) A noted Latin defender of orthodoxy, especially against Arianism, who was elected bishop of the southern French city of Poitiers around 353. See 3.12, 8.6.

Hildegard of Bingen (1098–1179) Abbess of Rupertsberg, near the city of Bingen, who established a reputation as a theological and spiritual writer with a particular interest in the spirituality of creation. See 6.23.

Hippolytus (c.170–c.236) Widely regarded as the most important Roman theologian of the third century. Writing in Greek, he devoted particular attention to the theological role of the Logos, and the relation of philosophy and theology. See 2.3.

Hodge, Archibald Alexander (1823–86) The son of the noted American Presbyterian writer Charles Hodge, who established himself as a defender of the "Old Princeton Theology" in the middle of the nineteenth century. He was called to a chair of systematic theology at Princeton Theological Seminary in 1877, and is particularly noted for his views on biblical authority and inspiration. See 2.35.

Hoen, Kornelius Hendriks (died 1524) A Dutch lawyer, active in the Hague, who developed the idea of a purely symbolic presence of Christ in the Eucharist. See 8.22.

Honorius of Autun (fl. c.1106–35) Although some suggest that Honorius was a native of Autun, in Burgundy, there is some evidence that he may have been active in southern Germany, possibly in the region of Augsburg. Honorius made significant contributions to the emerging synthesis of reason and faith, and is particularly noted for his discussion of the ultimate motivation for the incarnation. See 4.21.

Hooker, Morna D. (born 1931) Lady Margaret's Professor Emeritus of Divinity at Cambridge University, and the author of 13 books on the New Testament, with a particular interest in Christology. See 4.40.

Hooker, Richard (c.1554–1600) Anglican theologian during the period of the Elizabethan Settlement. He is noted especially for his *Laws of Ecclesiastical Polity*, significant for its defense of an episcopal form of church government. See 7.18.

Hopkins, Gerald Manley (1844–89) English Roman Catholic poet and theologian, whose poems remained unpublished during his lifetime. See 2.37.

Hugh of St Victor (died 1142) A theologian of Flemish or German origin, who entered the Augustinian monastery of St Victor in Paris around 1115. His most important work is *de sacramentis Christianae fidei* ("On the Sacraments of the Christian Faith"), which shows awareness of the new theological debates which were beginning to develop at this time. See 5.15, 8.14.

Hughes, Philip E. (1915–90) Anglo-American evangelical theologian, particularly remembered for his works of biblical exposition and systematic theology. See 10.24.

Hus, Jan (c.1372–1415) Also known as "Huss." A Bohemian theologian who was elected as dean of the faculty of philosophy at the University of Prague in 1401. He became noted for his views on the need to reform the church, which were given substance in his major work *de ecclesia* ("On the church"), published in 1413. He was burned at the stake in July 1415. See 7.11.

Ignatius of Antioch (c.35–c.107) A major early Christian martyr, noted for his letters to Christian churches in Asia Minor. Of particular interest is his vigorous defense of the reality of Christ's human nature and sufferings, in the face of those who wished to maintain that they were simply an appearance. See 4.1.

Innocent III (1160–1216) Pope from 1198, responsible for asserting the authority of the church over the state in western Europe, especially France. See 7.8.

Irenaeus of Lyons (c.130–c.200) Probably a native of Asia Minor, who was elected as bishop of the southern French city of Lyons around 178. He is chiefly noted for his major writing *adversus haereses* ("Against the heresies"), which defended the Christian faith against Gnostic misrepresentations and criticisms. See 2.2, 3.2, 3.3, 4.2, 5.1, 5.2, 6.1, 7.1, 10.1.

James I (1566–1625) King of England from 1603. Remembered chiefly for his commissioning of a new English translation of the Bible (the King James Version). See 2.24.

Jenson, Robert (born 1930) North American Lutheran theologian, noted for his major contributions to the doctrine of the Trinity. See 3.36.

Jerome (c.342–420) One of the most noted biblical scholars and translators of the early church, sometimes referred to as "Hieronymus." His most significant achievement was his translation of most of the Bible into Latin. However, he was also noted for his biblical commentaries and writings which discussed the place of the Bible in Christian thought and life. See 2.9.

Jewett, Paul (1919–91) North American evangelical writer, based for much of his career at Fuller Theological Seminary, with an interest in the restatement of evangelical ideas in a modern context. See 3.41.

John of Damascus (c.675–c.749) A major Greek theologian, whose work *de fide orthodoxa* ("On the Orthodox Faith") is of considerable importance in the consolidation of a distinctively eastern Christian theology. See 4.20, 8.9.

John Paul II (1920–2005) Polish writer and ecclesiastical statesman, born Karol Joseph Wojtyla, who became pope in 1978. See 8.36.

Jowett, Benjamin (1817–93) British classical scholar and educationalist, best remembered as Master of Balliol College, Oxford. He played an important role in English religious controversies of the 1860s on account of his views on the Bible. See 2.36.

Julian of Norwich (c.1342–c.1415) Little is known of the life of this English mystic, apart from the details she herself provides in her *Sixteen Revelations of Divine Love*. For at least part of her active life, she lived as a hermit in the city of Norwich. See 3.26.

Jüngel, Eberhard (born 1934) German Protestant theologian, presently professor of systematic theology at the University of Tübingen. His most significant work to date is *God as the Mystery of the World* (1977), which reclaims a distinctively Christian understanding of God in the face of its Cartesian rivals. See 3.38.

Justin Martyr (c.100–c.165) One of the most noted of the Christian apologists of the second century, with a concern to demonstrate the moral and intellectual credibility of Christianity in a pagan world. His *First Apology* stresses the manner in which Christianity brings to fulfillment the insights of classical philosophy. See 1.1, 9.1.

Kähler, Martin (1835–1912) A German Lutheran theologian with a particular concern for the theological aspects of New Testament criticism and interpretation. He was appointed to the chair of systematic theology at Halle in 1867. His most famous work is an essay of 1892, in which he subjected the theological assumptions of the "Life of Jesus Movement" to devastating criticism. See 4.29.

Kant, Immanuel (1724–1804) German philosopher, based at the University of Königsberg in East Prussia. His philosophical writings have been of major importance, especially to German Protestant theology. His critique of the "ontological argument" is generally regarded as being of decisive importance. See 1.19.

Kasper, Walter (born 1933) German Roman Catholic theologian and cardinal, who directed the Council for Promoting Christian Unity. Noted especially for his dogmatic works on Christology and Trinitarian theology. See 3.40.

Kierkegaard, Søren (1813–55) Danish existentialist philosopher and theologian, noted for his criticisms of contemporary Hegelian philosophy and the formalism of Danish Christianity. During his early period of writing, Kierkegaard frequently wrote under various pseudonyms that represented different ways of thinking and living. He is particularly associated with the idea of a "leap of faith," an image which emphasizes the limits of reason in theology. See 1.20.

Küng, Hans (born 1928) Swiss Roman Catholic theologian, noted for his contributions to many areas of theology. See 3.37.

Lactantius, Lucius Caecilius Firmianus (c.240–c.320) A Latin Christian apologist, professor of rhetoric at Nicomedia, especially noted for his *Divinae Institutiones* ("Divine Institutions"), which was intended to demonstrate the cultural and intellectual credibility of Christianity. See 6.7.

Lanfranc of Bec (1010–89) Leading thinker of the theological renaissance of the eleventh century, who was elected prior of the abbey of Bec in Normany in 1045. He was noted particularly for his intervention in the debate over the eucharistic views of Berengar of Tours. See 8.13.

Langton, Stephen (died 1228) An English theologian who achieved fame as one of the leading biblical scholars and interpreters of the University of Paris. He was noted particularly for his exegetical and homiletical works. In 1207 he was appointed Archbishop of Canterbury. See 2.12.

Lefèvre d'Etaples, Jacques (c.1455–1536) A noted humanist scholar, who acted as librarian at the Parisian monastery of St Germain-des-Prés. His writings on biblical translation and interpretation had a significant influence on the development of the Reformation. Although best known by his French name, he is also often referred to by his Latin name: Jacobus Faber Stapulensis. See 2.14.

Leo the Great (died 461) Also known as Leo I, who became pope in 440. He is remembered particularly for the "Tome of Leo" (449), a document which was intended to serve a diplomatic function in the midst of the fierce Christological disputes of the period. See 4.16, 7.7.

Lessing, Gotthold Ephraim (1729–81) A significant representative of the German Enlightenment, noted for his strongly rationalist approach to Christian theology. See 4.26.

Lewis, C. S. (Clive Staples, 1898–1963) Oxford literary critic and religious writer, noted for his popular works of Christian apologetics and the children's novel series "The Chronicles of Narnia." See 9.5

Lindbeck, George (born 1923) North American postliberal theologian, noted for his contributions to ecumenical theology, and more recently, his discussion of the nature of Christian doctrine. See 1.33.

Locke, John (1632–1704) A noted English philosopher, particularly associated with the empiricist doctrine that all knowledge derives from sense experience. Locke insisted that knowledge of God also arose through the senses, in contrast to Descartes, who argued that the idea was inherent to humanity. See 1.15.

Lombard, Peter *see* Peter Lombard

Lonergan, Bernard (1904–84) Canadian Jesuit theologian, best known for his discussions of theological method, especially his *Method in Theology* (1973). See 5.31.

Lossky, Vladimir (1904–58) Russian Orthodox theologian, who was expelled from his homeland in 1922 following the Bolshevik revolution. He settled in Paris and became a leading exponent of the ideas of Russian Orthodoxy in the west. See 1.27, 5.30.

Ludolf of Saxony (c.1300–78) Significant medieval writer, known to have entered the Order of Preachers and gained a qualification in theology before joining the Carthusians at Strasbourg in 1340. In 1343 he moved to the Carthusian house at Coblenz, becoming its prior. See 2.13.

Luther, Martin (1483–1546) Perhaps the greatest figure in the European Reformation, noted particularly for his doctrine of justification by faith alone, and his strongly Christocentric understanding of revelation. His "theology of the cross" aroused much interest in the late twentieth century. Luther's posting of the Ninety-Five Theses in October 1517 is generally regarded as marking the beginning of the Reformation. See 1.12, 2.15, 2.16, 4.24, 6.32, 6.33, 6.34, 7.12, 7.13, 8.17, 8.18, 8.19, 8.20.

Marx, Karl (1818–83) A highly influential left-wing Hegelian political thinker, whose ideas were developed in international Marxism and found their embodiment, in various forms, in socialist states such as the Soviet Union during the twentieth century. Marx regarded religion of any kind as the result of social and economic alienation, and argued that the coming of the revolution would eliminate religion altogether. See 9.3.

Maximus of Constantinople (c. 580–662) Also known as Maximus the Confessor. Widely regarded as one of the most significant Greek Christian writers, whose ideas continue to play an important role in modern Greek and Russian Orthodox theology. He is often thought of as the last great Christian Neoplatonist, and is particularly valued for his writings on the incarnation. See 5.11.

McFague, Sallie (born 1933) North American theologian, with a particular interest in the role of theological language and models in contemporary theological restatement. See 1.30.

Mechthild of Magdeburg (c.1210–c.1282) One of the most important women spiritual writers of the thirteenth century. She is remembered chiefly for one writing, whose full title (in the original north German dialect) is *Vliessende lieht miner gotheit in allu die herzen die da lebent ane valscheit* ("Light of my divinity, flowing into all hearts that live without falsehood"). See 6.27.

Melanchthon, Philip (1497–1560) A noted early Lutheran theologian and close personal associate of Martin Luther. He was responsible for the systematization of early Lutheran theology, particularly through his *Loci Communes* (first edition published in 1521) and his "Apology for the Augsburg Confession." See 6.35, 7.14, 8.21.

Methodius of Olympus (died c.311) A noted critic of Origen's theology, particularly the doctrines of the transmigration of souls and a purely spiritual resurrection body. His treatise on the resurrection develops the thesis of the continuity between the preresurrection and postresurrection bodies. See 10.6.

Meyendorff, John (1926–92) Orthodox theologian, who served as professor of theology at St Vladimir's Theological Seminary in New York State from 1959 until his death. See 2.47.

Mirandola, Giovanni Pico della (1463–94) Platonist writer and philosopher, who followed Marsilius Ficinus in reasserting the philosophical and theological authority of Plato against the prevailing scholastic Aristotelianism of his day. See 6.31.

Möhler, Johann Adam (1796–1848) Also "Moehler." Catholic theologian, cofounder of the Tübingen school, noted for his exploration of the confessional differences between Protestants and Catholics. See 2.33.

Moltmann, Jürgen (born 1926) One of the most influential of modern German Protestant theologians, particularly noted for his rehabilitation of eschatology and his exploration of the doctrine of the Trinity. See 3.33, 10.21.

Nestorius (died c.451) A major representative of the Antiochene school of theology, who became Patriarch of Constantinople in 428. His vigorous emphasis upon the humanity of Christ seemed to his critics to amount to a denial of his divinity. Nestorius's failure to endorse the term "Theotokos" led to him being openly charged with heresy. Although far more orthodox than his opponents allowed, the extent of Nestorius's orthodoxy remains unclear and disputed. See 4.12.

Newbigin, Lesslie (1909–98) British theologian, with substantial experience of the Church of South India and a particular interest in the relation of Christianity and modernity, and the issue of religious pluralism. See 9.12.

Newman, John Henry (1801–90) Roman Catholic theologian, who began his career as a member of the Church of England, and was initially involved in the reinvigoration of the catholic wing of that church. He is particularly associated with a theory of the development of doctrine. See 1.22.

Niebuhr, Reinhold (1892–1971) North American theologian (and brother of theologian Helmut Richard Niebuhr), whose early optimism concerning human nature gave way to a theology of human nature and society which is grounded in the doctrine of original sin. See 6.53.

Novatian (fl. 250) A third-century writer, noted especially for his work *de trinitate*, which is an important critique of Gnosticism. See 4.5.

Ockham, William of *see* William of Ockham

Oetinger, Friedrich Christoph (1702–82) Noted German Pietist writer, who reacted against the rationalism of Christian Wolff and came under the influence of the Pietist writer Johann Albrecht Bengel. His works emphasize the need for personal faith and renewal. See 6.46.

Origen (c.185–c.254) Leading representative of the Alexandrian school of theology, especially noted for his allegorical exposition of Scripture and his use of Platonic ideas in theology, particularly Christology. The originals of many of his works, which were written in Greek, have been lost, with the result that some are known only in Latin translations of questionable reliability. See 2.6, 3.5, 3.6, 3.7, 3.8, 4.6, 6.5, 6.6, 7.2, 10.5.

Orr, James (1834–1913) Scottish Reformed theologian, who became professor of theology at the United Presbyterian Theologian College, Glasgow. See 2.39.

Owen, John (1616–83) English Puritan writer, elevated to high office during the period of Oliver Cromwell's Commonwealth. He is particularly noted for his strong defense of a Reformed doctrine of grace against Arminianism. See 3.29, 7.20.

Packer, James I. (born 1926) Anglo-American evangelical writer, particularly noted for his writings on the doctrine of God and the Reformed theological and spiritual heritage. See 2.48, 5.33.

Paley, William (1743–1805) English exponent of natural theology and the argument from design. See 2.32.

Pannenberg, Wolfhart (born 1928) One of the most influential German Protestant theologians, whose writings on the relation of faith and history, and particularly the foundations of Christology, have had considerable influence. See 4.36, 5.32.

Pascal, Blaise (1623–62) An influential French Roman Catholic writer, who gained a considerable reputation as a mathematician and theologian. After a religious conversion experience in 1646, he developed an approach to his faith which was strongly Christocentric and experiential. His most famous writing is the collection known as the *Pensées*, first gathered together in 1670, some years after his death. See 1.17, 1.18.

Paschasius Radbertus (c.790–865) A Benedictine writer, who entered the monastery at Corbie in Picardy in 822 and was noted as a vigorous defender of the real physical presence of Christ in the Eucharist. See 8.10.

Pelagius (c.355–c.435) A British theologian who was active at Rome in the final decade of the fourth and first decade of the fifth centuries. No reliable information exists concerning the date of his birth or death. Pelagius was a moral reformer, whose theology of grace and sin brought him into sharp conflict with Augustine, leading to the Pelagian controversy. Pelagius's ideas are known mostly through the writings of his opponents, especially Augustine. See 6.16, 6.17, 6.18.

Peter Abelard (1079–1142) French theologian, who achieved a considerable reputation as a teacher at the University of Paris. Among his many contributions to the development of medieval theology, his most noted is his emphasis upon the subjective aspects of the atonement. See 5.14.

Peter Lombard (c.1100–60) Also "Abailard." A noted medieval theologian, active at the University of Paris, who was appointed Bishop of Paris in 1159. His most significant achievement was the compilation of the textbook known as the "Four Books of the Sentences," a collection of extracts from patristic writers. See 8.15, 10.12.

Petilian of Cirta (born c.365) Donatist Bishop of Cirta, and defender of a rigorist approach to the ministry. See 7.5.

Pinnock, Clark (born 1937) Canadian evangelical theologian, noted as a contemporary exponent of Arminianism, and more recently for his exploration of an inclusivist approach to religious pluralism. See 9.8.

Rahner, Karl (1904–84) One of the most influential of modern Roman Catholic theologians, whose *Theological Investigations* pioneered the use of the essay as a tool of theological construction and exploration. See 2.44, 9.6.

Rashdall, Hastings (1858–1924) English modernist theologian, noted especially for his emphasis upon the moral influence of Christ's death, and his criticisms of classic Protestant understandings of the atonement. See 5.27.

Ratranmus of Corbie (died 868) A ninth-century theologian, based at the monastery of Corbie in Picardy, who is noted chiefly for his doctrine of double predestination, and his rejection of any understanding of a real physical presence of Christ at the Eucharist. See 8.11.

Richard of St Victor (died 1173) A leading representative of the school of thought based at the Abbey of St Victor, in Paris. His most important work is *de Trinitate* ("On the Trinity"), which sets out an influential understanding of God as a person. See 3.22.

Ritschl, Albrecht Benjamin (1822–89) German liberal Protestant theologian, widely regarded as the successor to Schleiermacher, who became professor of theology at Göttingen in 1864. See 4.28.

Ruether, Rosemary Radford (born 1936) Feminist theologian and writer, based at Garrett Evangelical Divinity School, Evanston, Illinois. Among her books, the most influential has been *Sexism and God-Talk* (1983). See 4.38.

Rufinus of Aquileia (c.345–410) Although born in Italy, this writer eventually settled in Egypt, and was responsible for the translation of many Greek theological writings, including those of Origen, into Latin. He was also an original thinker in his own right. See 5.7.

Rupert of Deutz (c.1075–1129) Twelfth-century theologian and biblical commentator, who became abbot of Deutz, near Cologne. He is particularly remembered for a commentary on John's Gospel. See 5.16.

Sayers, Dorothy L. (1893–1957) English novelist and dramatist with a strong interest in Christian theology. See 4.34.

Schillebeeckx, Edward (born 1914) Dutch Roman Catholic theologian, who developed some aspects of the agenda of the Second Vatican Council. His *Jesus, An Experiment in Christology* (1979) was admired by many, although he is better known for his critique of traditional ontological approaches to eucharistic theology. See 8.32.

Schleiermacher, F. D. E. (1768–1834) One of the most influential German Protestant writers since the Reformation, noted especially for his emphasis on the role of "feeling" in theology in reaction against the rationalism of the Enlightenment. His most important work is *Der christliche Glaube* ("The Christian Faith"). See 3.31, 4.27, 5.24, 5.25, 7.21.

Schmemann, Alexander (1921–83) Orthodox theologian, for many years based at St Vladimir's Orthodox Theological Seminary, New York. See 8.34.

Schweitzer, Albert (1875–1965) This leading German Protestant theologian was noted particularly for his work on the historical Jesus, which led to a series of influential publications calling its validity and presuppositions into question. In 1913 he gave up his theological career to undertake medical work in Africa. See 4.31.

Scotus, John Duns *see* Duns Scotus, John.

Simeon the New Theologian (949–1022) A leading representative of Byzantine theology, who is widely regarded as one of the most influential writers within the movement. His writings develop characteristic Byzantine themes, such as redemption as deification, while laying the foundations of the movement known as Hesychasm. See 5.12.

Sölle, Dorothee (1929–2003) Also "Soelle." German-American Lutheran theologian, whose many interests included the theological legacy of Auschwitz. See 5.34.

Song, C. S. (Choan-Seng, born 1920) Taiwanese theologian with a particular interest in the relation of Christianity and Asian (especially Chinese) culture. See 9.10.

Spener, Philip Jakob (1635–1705) Widely regarded as the founder of German Pietism, Spener laid considerable emphasis upon the experiential and devotional aspects of faith, which he believed to be missing from contemporary Lutheran orthodoxy. See 2.29.

Spinoza, Benedict (1632–77) A Jewish philosopher, noted for his pantheism. Spinoza's most important work, the *Ethica* ("Ethics"), was published posthumously in 1677. See 3.30.

Staniloae, Dumitru (1903–1993) Romanian Orthodox theologian, rector of the Theological Academy in Sibiu and then professor at the Bucharest Theological Institute, best known for *Dogmatic Orthodox Theology* (1978). See 1.34.

Swete, Henry Barclay (1835–1917) English patristic scholar and theologian, sometime Regius Professor of Divinity at Cambridge University, particularly noted for his commentaries on Mark's Gospel (1898) and Revelation (1906). See 7.23.

Swinburne, Richard (born 1934) British philosopher of religion, especially associated with the theme of the "coherence of theism." See 3.34.

Tanner, Kathryn (born 1957) Dorothy Grant Maclear Professor of Theology in the Divinity School, University of Chicago. See 10.25.

Taylor, Jeremy (1613–67) Anglican theologian and spiritual writer of the seventeenth century. See 10.16.

Tertullian (Quintus Septimius Florens Tertullianus, c.160–c.225) A major figure in early Latin theology, who produced a series of significant controversial and apologetic writings. He is particularly noted for his ability to coin new Latin terms to translate the emerging theological vocabulary of the Greek-speaking eastern church. See 1.3, 2.5, 3.4, 4.3, 4.4, 6.2, 6.3, 6.4, 10.3, 10.4.

Theodore of Mopsuestia (c.350–428) Antiochene theologian, whose writings came into disrepute as a result of the Council of Ephesus (431), which associated him with the Christological views of Nestorius. See 4.11

Theodoret of Cyrrhus (c.393–c.460) Antiochene theologian, with a particular concern to defend the distinctive features of the Antiochene school of Christology. See 5.9.

Theophilus of Antioch One of the more significant Christian apologists of the second century. Little is known of his life, including the dates of his birth and death. Of his writings, the most significant to survive is the apology addressed to Autolycus. See 10.2.

Thielicke, Helmut (1908–86) German Lutheran ethicist and theologian, especially noted for his three-volumed *Christian Ethics*. See 10.20.

Thomas à Kempis (c.1380–1471) A leading representative of the *Devotio Moderna*, who is widely accepted to be the author of the classic work of spirituality known as the *Imitatio Christi* ("The Imitation of Christ"). See 3.28.

Thomas Aquinas (c.1225–74) Probably the most famous and influential theologian of the Middle Ages. Born in Italy, he achieved his fame through his teaching and writing at the University of Paris and other northern universities. His fame rests chiefly on his *Summa Theologiae*, composed towards the end of his life and not totally finished at the time of his death. However, he also wrote many other significant works, particularly the *Summa contra Gentiles*, which represents a major statement of the rationality of the Christian faith. See 1.9, 1.10, 3.24, 4.22, 5.17, 6.26, 7.9, 8.16.

Tillich, Paul (1886–1965) A German Lutheran theologian who was forced to leave Germany during the Nazi period, and settled in the United States. He held teaching positions at Union Theological Seminary, New York, Harvard Divinity School, and the University of Chicago. His most significant theological writing is the three-volumed *Systematic Theology* (1951–64). See 1.29, 4.35.

Torrance, Thomas F. (born 1913) Scottish theologian, particularly noted for his writings dealing with the relation of Christianity and the natural sciences, and the interpretation of Karl Barth. See 2.49, 4.37.

Trible, Phyllis (born 1948) North American feminist writer and biblical scholar. See 2.45.

Troeltsch, Ernst (1865–1923) A theologian and sociologist who was closely involved in the founding of the "History of Religions School," which placed an emphasis upon the historical continuity of the religions. His most important theological contributions are thought to lie in the field of Christology, especially his discussion of the relation between faith and history. See 4.33.

Turrettini, François (1623–87) Reformed theologian of Italian origin, who became professor of theology at the Genevan Academy in 1653. He is regarded as one of the leading representatives of Calvinist thought during this period. See 4.25.

Tyrrell, George (1861–1909) English Modernist writer, noted for his increasing hostility towards traditional Roman Catholic teachings, and his criticism of the liberal Protestantism of Adolf von Harnack. See 4.30.

Ussher, James (1581–1656) A noted Irish Anglican writer, who eventually became Archbishop of Armagh. He was strongly Calvinist in his theology. See 6.42.

Vincent of Lérins (died before 450) A French theologian who settled on the island of Lérins (now Isle St Honorat, off the southern coast of France). He is particularly noted for his emphasis on the role of tradition in guarding against innovations in the doctrine of the church, and is credited with the formulation of the so-called "Vincentian canon." See 2.10.

Watson, Richard (1781–1833) English Methodist theologian, best known for his *Theological Institutes* (1823), an attempt to give systematic presentation to the ideas of John Wesley, the founder of Methodism. See 6.49.

Wesley, Charles (1707–88) English theologian and writer of hymns, noted for his Pietist emphases and hostility to Calvinism. Along with his brother John, he contributed to a significant revival within eighteenth-century English Christianity. See 5.23.

Wesley, John (1703–91) English theologian, pastor and hymn-writer, remembered especially as the founder of Methodism. Like his brother Charles, he was deeply influenced by Pietism, which had a considerable impact on his early theology. His theology found its expression in hymns and sermons, rather than works of systematic theology. See 6.48, 8.30, 10.18.

White, Francis (c.1564–1638) Anglican theologian and divine, who served as bishop of Norwich, then Ely. See 2.28.

William of Ockham (c.1285–1347) Also known as William of Occam. An English scholastic writer who developed the teachings of his predecessor John Duns Scotus, and is particularly associated with the development of "nominalism" or "terminism" as a philosophical system. See 1.11, 3.27.

Williams, Rowan (born 1950) Welsh Anglican theologian and writer, who became Archbishop of Canterbury in 2003. His wide-ranging publications deal with many aspects of theology and spirituality, showing a particular interest in the Russian Orthodox tradition. See 8.35.

Wittgenstein, Ludwig (1889–1951) An Austrian philosopher, who studied and taught at Cambridge University, noted for his exploration of the relation of language and the structure of the world. See 1.25, 1.26.

Wojtyla, Karol Joseph *see* John Paul II.

Wright, N. T. (Tom) (born 1948) British New Testament scholar, presently Bishop of Durham, noted for his major series dealing with Christian origins and the question of God. See 4.41.

Zeno (c.450–91) Also known as Tarasicodissa or Trascalissaeus, who became Emperor of the eastern Roman empire from 474, noted for his attempt to reconcile the various factions involved in the Monophysite controversy. His *Henoticon*, which was intended to contribute towards the resolution of this debate, actually ended up by making things worse, causing a new schism between Rome and Constantinople. See 4.18.

Zinzendorf, Nikolaus Ludwig von (1700–60) A German writer who reacted against the rationalism of the theology of his day, and emphasized the emotional and experiential aspects of Christian faith. There is a clear connection between Zinzendorf's ideas and those of Pietism. He is remembered especially as the founder of a religious community at Herrnhut. See 2.30, 6.45.

Zizioulas, John D. (born 1931) Now Metropolitan John of Pergamon, a leading contemporary exponent of Greek Orthodox theology. See 7.27.

Zwingli, Huldrych (1484–1531) Also known as Ulrich Zwingli. Swiss reformer, particularly associated with the vigorous denial of the real presence of Christ at the Eucharist, a view usually designated "Zwinglianism." He died in battle, as a result of his attempts to spread his reforming ideas in his native Switzerland. See 8.23, 8.24.

A Glossary of Theological Terms

What follows is a brief discussion of a series of technical terms that the reader is likely to encounter in the course of reading texts which relate to Christian theology, many of which occur in the present collection of texts.

adoptionism The heretical view that Jesus was "adopted" as the Son of God at some point during his ministry (usually his baptism), as opposed to the orthodox teaching that Jesus was Son of God by nature from the moment of his conception.

aggiornamento The process of renewing the church, which was particularly associated with Pope John XXIII and the Second Vatican Council (1962–5). The Italian word can be translated as "a bringing up to date" or "renewal," and refers to the process of theological, spiritual, and institutional renewal and updating which resulted from the work of this council.

Alexandrian School A patristic school of thought, especially associated with the city of Alexandria in Egypt, noted for its Christology (which placed emphasis upon the divinity of Christ) and its method of biblical interpretation (which employed allegorical methods of exegesis). A rival approach in both areas was associated with Antioch.

allegory An understanding of how biblical texts are to be interpreted which sees certain biblical images as possessing deeper, spiritual meanings, which can be uncovered by their interpreters.

Anabaptism A term derived from the Greek word for "rebaptizer," and used to refer to the radical wing of the sixteenth-century Reformation, based on thinkers such as Menno Simons or Balthasar Hubmaier.

analogy of being (*analogia entis*) The theory, especially associated with Thomas Aquinas, that there exists a correspondence or analogy between the created order and God, as a result of the divine creatorship. The idea gives theoretical justification to the practice of drawing conclusions from the known objects and relationships of the natural order concerning God.

analogy of faith (*analogia fidei*) The theory, especially associated with Karl Barth, which holds that any correspondence between the created order and God is only established on the basis of the self-revelation of God.

anthropomorphism The tendency to ascribe human features (such as hands or arms) or other human characteristics to God.

Antiochene School A patristic school of thought, especially associated with the city of Antioch in modern-day Turkey, noted for its Christology (which placed emphasis upon the humanity of Christ) and its method of biblical interpretation (which employed literal methods of exegesis). A rival approach in both areas was associated with Alexandria.

anti-Pelagian writings The writings of Augustine relating to the Pelagian controversy, in which he defended his views on grace and justification. See "Pelagianism."

Apocalyptic A type of writing or religious outlook in general which focuses on the last things and the end of the world, often taking the form of visions with complex symbolism. The second half of the book of Daniel (Old Testament) and Revelation (New Testament) are examples of this type of writing.

apologetics The area of Christian theology which focuses on the defense of the Christian faith, particularly through the rational justification of Christian belief and doctrines.

apophatic A term used to refer to a particular style of theology, which stressed that God cannot be known in terms of human categories. "Apophatic" (which derives from the Greek *apophasis*, "negation" or "denial") approaches to theology are especially associated with the monastic tradition of the Eastern Orthodox church.

Apophthegmata The term used to refer to the collections of monastic writings often known as the "Sayings of the Desert Fathers." The writings often take the form of brief and pointed sayings, reflecting the concise and practical guidance typical of these writers.

apostolic era The period of the Christian church, regarded as definitive by many, bounded by the resurrection of Jesus Christ (c. AD 35) and the death of the last apostle (c. AD 90?). The ideas and practices of this period were widely regarded as normative, at least in some sense or to some degree, in many church circles.

appropriation A term relating to the doctrine of the Trinity, which affirms that while all three persons are active in all the outward actions of the Trinity, it is appropriate to think of those actions as being the particular work of one of the persons. Thus it is appropriate to think of creation as the work of the Father, or redemption as the work of the Son, despite the fact that all three persons are present and active in both these works.

Arianism A major early Christological heresy, which treated Jesus Christ as the supreme of God's creatures, and denied his divine status. The Arian controversy was of major importance in the development of Christology during the fourth century.

asceticism A term used to refer to the wide variety of forms of self-discipline used by Christians to deepen their knowledge of and commitment to God. The term derives from the Greek term *askēsis* ("discipline").

atonement An English term originally coined in 1526 by William Tyndale to translate the Latin term *reconciliatio*. It has since come to have the developed meaning of "the work of Christ" or "the benefits of Christ gained for believers by his death and resurrection."

Barthian An adjective used to describe the theological outlook of the Swiss theologian Karl Barth (1886–1968), and noted chiefly for its emphasis upon the priority of revelation and its focus upon Jesus Christ. The terms "neo-Orthodoxy" and "dialectical theology" are also used in this connection.

beatific vision A term used, especially in Roman Catholic theology, to refer to the full vision of God, which is allowed only to the elect after death. However, some writers, including Thomas Aquinas, taught that certain favored individuals – such as Moses and Paul – were allowed this vision in the present life.

Beatitudes, the A term used to describe the eight promises of blessing found in the opening section of the Sermon on the Mount (Matthew 5: 3–11). Examples include "Blessed are the pure in heart, for they shall see God" and "Blessed are the peacemakers, for they shall be called children of God."

Calvinism An ambiguous term, used with two quite distinct meanings. First, it refers to the religious ideas of religious bodies (such as the Reformed church) and individuals (such as Theodore Beza) who were profoundly influenced by John Calvin, or by documents written by him. Second, it refers to the religious ideas of John Calvin himself. Although the first sense is by far the more common, there is a growing recognition that the term is misleading.

Cappadocian fathers A term used to refer collectively to three major Greek-speaking writers of the patristic period: Basil of Caesarea, Gregory of Nazianzen, and Gregory of Nyssa, all of whom date from the late fourth century. "Cappadocia" designates an area in Asia Minor (modern-day Turkey), in which these writers were based.

Cartesianism The philosophical outlook especially associated with René Descartes (1596–1650), particularly in relation to its emphasis on the separation of the knower from the known, and its insistence that the existence of the individual thinking self is the proper starting point for philosophical reflection.

catechism A popular manual of Christian doctrine, usually in the form of question and answer, intended for religious instruction.

catharsis The process of cleansing or purification by which the individual is freed from obstacles to spiritual growth and development.

catholic An adjective which is used both to refer to the universality of the church in space and time, and also to a particular church body (sometime also known as the Roman Catholic Church) which lays emphasis upon this point.

Chalcedonian definition The formal declaration at the Council of Chalcedon that Jesus Christ was to be regarded as having two natures, one human and one divine.

charisma, charismatic A set of terms especially associated with the gifts of the Holy Spirit. In medieval theology, the term "charisma" is used to designate a spiritual gift, conferred upon individuals by the grace of God. Since the early twentieth century, the term "charismatic" has come to refer to styles of theology and worship which place particular emphasis upon the immediate presence and experience of the Holy Spirit.

Charismatic Movement A form of Christianity which places particular emphasis upon the personal experience of the Holy Spirit in the life of the individual and community, often associated with various "charismatic" phenomena, such as speaking in tongues.

Christology The section of Christian theology dealing with the identity of Jesus Christ, particularly the question of the relation of his human and divine natures.

circumincession See *perichoresis*.

conciliarism An understanding of ecclesiastical or theological authority which places an emphasis on the role of ecumenical councils.

confession Although the term refers primarily to the admission to sin, it acquired a rather different technical sense in the sixteenth century – that of a document which embodies the principles of faith of a Protestant church, such as the Lutheran Augsburg Confession (1530), which embodies the ideas of early Lutheranism, and the Reformed First Helvetic Confession (1536).

consubstantial A Latin term, deriving from the Greek term *homoousios*, literally meaning "of the same substance." The term is used to affirm the full divinity of Jesus Christ, particularly in opposition to Arianism.

consubstantiation A term used to refer to the theory of the real presence, especially associated with Martin Luther, which holds that the substance of the eucharistic bread and wine are given together with the substance of the body and blood of Christ.

contemplation A form of prayer, distinguished from meditation, in which the individual avoids or minimizes the use of words or images in order to experience the presence of God directly.

creed A formal definition or summary of the Christian faith, held in common by all Christians. The most important are those generally known as the "Apostles' Creed" and the "Nicene Creed."

dark night of the soul A phrase especially associated with John of the Cross, referring to the manner in which the soul is drawn closer to God. John distinguishes an "active" night (in which the believer actively works to draw nearer to God) and a "passive" night, in which God is active and the believer passive.

Deism A term used to refer to the views of a group of English writers, especially during the seventeenth century, the rationalism of which anticipated many of the ideas of the Enlightenment. The term is often used to refer to a view of God which recognizes the divine creatorship, yet which rejects the notion of a continuing divine involvement with the world.

detachment The cultivation of a habit of mind in which the individual aims to abandon dependence upon worldly objects, passions, or concerns. This is not intended to imply that these worldly things are evil; rather, the point being made is that they have the ability to enslave individuals if they are not approached with the right attitude. Detachment is about fostering a sense of independence from the world, so that it may be enjoyed without becoming a barrier between the individual and God.

Devotio Moderna A school of thought which developed in the Netherlands in the fourteenth century, and is especially associated with Geert Groote (1340–84) and Thomas à Kempis (1380–1471), which placed an emphasis on the imitation of the humanity of Christ. The *Imitation of Christ* is the best-known work emanating from this school.

dialectical theology A term used to refer to the early views of the Swiss theologian Karl Barth (1886–1968), which emphasized the tensions, paradoxes, and contradictions in the relationship between God and humanity and the absolute gulf fixed between the human and the divine.

Docetism An early Christological heresy, which treated Jesus Christ as a purely divine being who only had the "appearance" of being human.

Donatism A movement, centering upon Roman North Africa in the fourth century, which developed a rigid view of the church and sacraments.

doxology A form of praise, usually especially associated with formal Christian worship. A "doxological" approach to theology stresses the importance of praise and worship in theological reflection.

Ebionitism An early Christological heresy, which treated Jesus Christ as a purely human figure, although recognizing that he was endowed with particular charismatic gifts which distinguished him from other humans.

ecclesiology The section of Christian theology dealing with the theory of the church.

Enlightenment, the A term used since the nineteenth century to refer to the emphasis upon human reason and autonomy, characteristic of much of western European and North American thought during the eighteenth century.

eschatology The section of Christian theology dealing with the "last things," especially the ideas of resurrection, hell, the Last Judgment, and eternal life.

Eucharist The term used in the present volume to refer to the sacrament variously known as "the mass," "the Lord's Supper," and "holy communion."

evangelical A term initially used to refer to reforming movements, especially in Germany and Switzerland, in the 1510s and 1520s, but now used of a movement, especially in English-language theology, which places especial emphasis upon the supreme authority of Scripture and the atoning death of Christ.

exegesis The science of textual interpretation, usually referring specifically to the Bible. The term "biblical exegesis" basically means "the process of interpreting the

Bible." The specific techniques employed in the exegesis of Scripture are usually referred to as "hermeneutics."

exemplarism A particular approach to the atonement, which stresses the moral or religious example set to believers by Jesus Christ.

fathers An alternative term for "patristic writers."

fideism An understanding of Christian theology which refuses to accept the need for (or sometimes the possibility of) criticism or evaluation from sources outside the Christian faith itself.

Filioque A Latin phrase, literally meaning "and from the Son," found in western versions of the Nicene Creed. On this view, the Holy Spirit originates and proceeds from both the Father and the Son, rather than (as in the Eastern church) from the Father alone. The phrase had its origins at the third council of Toledo (589). By the ninth century, it was regularly in use within the western church. After the 1054 schism, it became one of the major theological points of difference between the Orthodox and Catholic churches, and a subject of intense debate and polemic on both sides.

Five Ways, the A standard term for the five "arguments for the existence of God" associated with Thomas Aquinas.

Fourth Gospel A term used to refer to the Gospel according to John. The term highlights the distinctive literary and theological character of this gospel, which sets it apart from the common structures of the first three gospels, usually known as the "Synoptic Gospels."

fundamentalism A form of American Protestant Christianity, originating in America, which lays especial emphasis upon the authority of an inerrant Bible.

hermeneutics The principles underlying the interpretation, or exegesis, of a text, particularly of Scripture, and particularly in relation to its present-day application.

Hesychasm A tradition, especially associated with the eastern church, which places considerable emphasis upon the idea of "inner quietness" (Greek: *hēsychia*) as a means of achieving a vision of God. It is particularly associated with writers such as Simeon the New Theologian and Gregory Palamas.

historical Jesus A term used, especially during the nineteenth century, to refer to the historical person of Jesus of Nazareth, as opposed to the Christian interpretation of that person, especially as presented in the New Testament and the creeds.

historico-critical method An approach to historical texts, including the Bible, which argues that their proper meaning must be determined on the basis of the specific historical conditions under which they were written.

history of religions school The approach to religious history, and Christian origins in particular, which treats Old and New Testament developments as responses to encounters with other religions, such as Gnosticism.

homoousion A Greek term, literally meaning "of the same substance," which came to be used extensively during the fourth century to designate the mainline Christological belief that Jesus Christ was of the same substance as God. The term was polemical, being directed against the Arian view that Christ was "of similar substance (*homoiousios*)" to God. See also "consubstantial."

humanism In the strict sense of the word, an intellectual movement linked with the European Renaissance. At the heart of the movement lay, not (as the modern sense of the word might suggest) a set of secular or secularizing ideas, but a new interest in the cultural achievements of antiquity. These were seen as a major resource for the renewal of European culture and Christianity during the period of the Renaissance.

hypostatic union The doctrine of the union of divine and human natures in Jesus Christ, without confusion of their respective substances.

icons Sacred pictures, particularly of Jesus, which play a significant role in Orthodox spirituality as "windows for the divine."

ideology A group of beliefs and values, usually secular, which govern the actions and outlooks of a society or group of people.

Ignatian spirituality A loose term used to refer to the approach to spirituality associated with Ignatius Loyola (1491–1556), based on his *Spiritual Exercises*.

incarnation A term used to refer to the assumption of human nature by God, in the person of Jesus Christ. The term "incarnationalism" is often used to refer to theological approaches which lay especial emphasis upon God becoming human.

justification by faith, doctrine of The section of Christian theology dealing with how the individual sinner is able to enter into fellowship with God. The doctrine was to prove to be of major significance at the time of the Reformation.

kenoticism A form of Christology which lays emphasis upon Christ's "laying aside" of certain divine attributes in the incarnation, or his "emptying himself" of at least some divine attributes, especially omniscience or omnipotence.

kerygma A term used, especially by Rudolf Bultmann (1884–1976) and his followers, to refer to the essential message or proclamation of the New Testament concerning the significance of Jesus Christ.

liberal Protestantism A movement, especially associated with nineteenth-century Germany, which stressed the continuity between religion and culture, flourishing between the time of F. D. E. Schleiermacher and Paul Tillich.

liberation theology Although this term designates any theological movement laying emphasis upon the liberating impact of the gospel, the term has come to refer to a movement which developed in Latin America in the late 1960s, which stressed the role of political action and orientated itself towards the goal of political liberation from poverty and oppression.

liturgy The written text and set forms of public services, especially of the Eucharist. In the Greek Orthodox church, the word "liturgy" often means "the (liturgy of the) Eucharist."

logos A Greek term meaning "word," which played a crucial role in the development of patristic Christology. Jesus Christ was recognized as the "word of God"; the question concerned the implications of this recognition, and especially the way in which the divine "logos" in Jesus Christ related to his human nature.

Lutheranism The religious ideas associated with Martin Luther, particularly as expressed in the Lesser Catechism (1529) and the Augsburg Confession (1530).

Manicheism A strongly fatalist position associated with the Manichees, to which Augustine of Hippo attached himself during his early period. A distinction is drawn between two different divinities, one of which is regarded as evil, and the other good. Evil is thus seen as the direct result of the influence of the evil god.

meditation A form of prayer, distinguished from contemplation, in which the mind uses images (such as those provided by Scripture) as a means for focusing on God.

Middle English literature Literature produced in the English language from the Norman invasion of 1066 to c.1485.

modalism A trinitarian heresy, which treats the three persons of the Trinity as different "modes" of the Godhead. A typical modalist approach is to regard God as active as Father in creation, as Son in redemption, and as Spirit in sanctification.

monophysitism The doctrine that there is only one nature in Christ, which is divine (from the Greek words *monos*, "only one," and *physis*, "nature"). This view differed from the orthodox view, upheld by the Council of Chalcedon (451), that Christ had two natures, one divine and one human.

mysticism A multifaceted term, which can bear a variety of meanings. In its most importance sense, the terms refers to the union with God which is seen as the ultimate goal of the Christian life. This union is not to be thought of in rational or intellectual terms, but more in terms of a direct consciousness or experience of God.

neo-Orthodoxy A term used to designate the general position of Karl Barth (1886–1968), especially the manner in which he drew upon the theological concerns of the period of Reformed Orthodoxy.

Old English literature The English literature of the period from 750 until the time of the invasion of the Normans in 1066.

ontological argument A term used to refer to the type of argument for the existence of God especially associated with the scholastic theologian Anselm of Canterbury. It claims that as God is greater than any other being that is conceivable, God must be greater than any being who exists only as an idea, so God must necessarily exist in reality.

orthodoxy A term used in a number of senses, of which the following are the most important: orthodoxy in the sense of "right belief," as opposed to heresy; Orthodoxy in the sense of the forms of Christianity which are dominant in Russia and Greece; Orthodoxy in the sense of a movement within Protestantism, especially in the late sixteenth and early seventeenth century, which laid emphasis upon the need for doctrinal definition.

parousia A Greek term, which literally means "coming" or "arrival," used to refer to the second coming of Christ. The notion of the *parousia* is an important aspect of Christian understandings of the "last things."

patripassianism A theological heresy, which arose during the third century, associated with writers such as Noetus, Praxeas, and Sabellius, focusing on the belief that the Father suffered as the Son. In other words, the suffering of Christ on the cross is to be regarded as the suffering of the Father. According to these writers, the only distinction within the Godhead was a succession of modes or operations, so that Father, Son, and Spirit were just different modes of being, or expressions, of the same basic divine entity.

patristic An adjective used to refer to the first centuries in the history of the church, following the writing of the New Testament (the "patristic period"), or thinkers writing during this period (the "patristic writers"). For many writers, the period thus designated seems to be c.100–451 (in other words, the period between the completion of the last of the New Testament writings and the landmark Council of Chalcedon).

Pelagianism An understanding of how humans are able to merit their salvation which is diametrically opposed to that of Augustine of Hippo, placing considerable emphasis upon the role of human works and playing down the idea of divine grace.

perichoresis A term relating to the doctrine of the Trinity, often also referred to by the Latin term *circumincessio*. The basic notion is that all three persons of the Trinity mutually share in the life of the others, so that none is isolated or detached from the actions of the others.

Philokalia A Greek term (literally meaning "a love of that which is beautiful"), which is generally used to refer to two anthologies of Greek spiritual works: extracts from the works of Origen, or the collection of writings assembled by Macarius of Corinth and Nicodemus of the Holy Mountain in the eighteenth century.

Pietism An approach to Christianity, especially associated with German writers in the seventeenth century, which places an emphasis upon the personal appropriation of faith, and the need for holiness in Christian living. The movement is perhaps best known within the English-language world in the form of Methodism.

postliberalism A theological movement, especially associated with Duke University and Yale Divinity School in the 1980s, which criticized the liberal reliance upon human experience, and reclaimed the notion of community tradition as a controlling influence in theology.

postmodernism A cultural development, starting in the late twentieth century, which resulted from the general collapse in confidence of the universal rational principles of the Enlightenment. It is characterized by a rejection of absolutes and of objective and rational attempts to define reality.

praxis A Greek term, literally meaning "action," adopted by Karl Marx to emphasize the importance of action in relation to thinking. This emphasis on "praxis" has had considerable impact within Latin American liberation theology.

Protestantism A term used in the aftermath of the Diet of Speyer (1529) to designate those who "protested" against the practices and beliefs of the Roman Catholic church. Prior to 1529, such individuals and groups had referred to themselves as "evangelicals."

Quadriga The Latin term used to refer to the "fourfold" interpretation of Scripture according to its literal, allegorical, tropological moral, and analogical senses.

radical Reformation A term used with increasing frequency to refer to the Anabaptist movement – in other words, the wing of the Reformation which went beyond what Luther and Zwingli envisaged, particularly in relation to the doctrine of the church.

Reformed A term used to refer to a tradition of theology which draws inspiration from the writings of John Calvin (1510–64) and his successors. The term is now generally used in preference to "Calvinist."

Sabellianism An early trinitarian heresy, which treated the three persons of the Trinity as different historical manifestations of the one God. It is generally regarded as a form of modalism.

sacrament A church service or rite which was held to have been instituted by Jesus Christ himself. Although Roman Catholic theology and church practice recognize seven such sacraments (baptism, confirmation, Eucharist, marriage, ordination, penance, and unction), Protestant theologians generally argue that only two (baptism and Eucharist) were to be found in the New Testament itself.

schism A deliberate break with the unity of the church, condemned vigorously by influential writers of the early church, such as Cyprian and Augustine.

scholasticism A particular approach to Christian theology, associated especially with the Middle Ages, which lays emphasis upon the rational justification and systematic presentation of Christian theology.

Scripture principle The theory, especially associated with Reformed theologians, that the practices and beliefs of the church should be grounded in Scripture. Nothing that could not be demonstrated to be grounded in Scripture could be regarded as binding upon the believer. The phrase *sola scriptura*, "by Scripture alone," summarizes this principle.

Socinianism A form of Christian heterodoxy especially associated with the Italian writer Socinus (Fausto Paolo Sozzini, 1539–1604). Although Socinus was noted for his specific criticisms of the doctrine of the Trinity and the incarnation, the term "Socinian" has come to refer particularly to the idea that Christ's death on the cross did not have any supernatural or transcendent implications. On this view, Christ died as an outstanding moral example, to encourage humanity to avoid sin, not to make satisfaction for human sin.

soteriology The section of Christian theology dealing with the doctrine of salvation (Greek: *sōtēria*).

Synoptic Gospels A term used to refer to the first three gospels (Matthew, Mark, and Luke). The term (derived from the Greek word *synopsis*, "summary") refers to the way in which the three gospels can be seen as providing similar "summaries" of the life, death, and resurrection of Jesus Christ.

Synoptic problem The scholarly question of how the three Synoptic Gospels relate to each other. Perhaps the most common approach to the relation of the three Synoptic Gospels is the "two source" theory, which claims that Matthew and Luke used Mark as a source, while also drawing upon a second source (usually known as "Q"). Other possibilities exist: for example, the Grisebach hypothesis, which treats Matthew as having been written first, followed by Luke and then Mark.

theodicy A term coined by the German philosopher Gottfried Wilhelm Leibnitz (1646–1716) to refer to a theoretical justification of the goodness of God in the face of the presence of evil in the world.

theopaschitism A disputed teaching, regarded by some as a heresy, which arose during the sixth century, associated with writers such as John Maxentius and the slogan "one of the Trinity was crucified." The formula can be interpreted in a perfectly orthodox sense and was defended as such by Leontius of Byzantium. However, it was regarded as potentially misleading and confusing by more cautious writers, including Pope Hormisdas (died 523), and the formula gradually fell into disuse.

Theotokos Literally, "the bearer of God." A Greek term used to refer to Mary, the mother of Jesus Christ, with the intention of reinforcing the central insight of the doctrine of the incarnation – that is, that Jesus Christ is none other than God. The term was extensively used by writers of the eastern church, especially around the time of the Nestorian controversy, to articulate both the divinity of Christ and the reality of the incarnation.

transubstantiation The doctrine according to which the bread and the wine are transformed into the body and blood of Christ in the Eucharist, while retaining their outward appearance.

Trinity The distinctively Christian doctrine of God, which reflects the complexity of the Christian experience of God as Father, Son, and Holy Spirit. The doctrine is usually summarized in maxims such as "three persons, one God."

two natures, doctrine of A term generally used to refer to the doctrine of the two natures, human and divine, of Jesus Christ. Related terms include "Chalcedonian definition" and "hypostatic union."

typology A way of interpreting the Bible which sees certain Old Testament figures and events as anticipating aspects of the gospel. Thus Noah's ark is seen as a "type" (Greek *typos*, "figure") of the church.

Vulgate The Latin translation of the Bible, largely deriving from Jerome, upon which medieval theology was largely based.

Zwinglianism The term is used generally to refer to the thought of Huldrych Zwingli, but is often used to refer specifically to his views on the sacraments, especially on the "real presence" (which for Zwingli was more of a "real absence").

Sources of Readings

Note that unless otherwise indicated, all translations are my own.

Chapter 1

1.1 Justin Martyr, *Apologia* I.xlvi.2–3, II.x.2–3, II.xiii.4–6; in *Saint Justin: Apologies*, ed. A. Wartelle (Paris: Etudes Augustiniennes, 1987), 160.6–9, 210.3–7, 216.11–18.

1.2 Clement of Alexandria, *Stromata* I.v.28; in *Die griechischen christlichen Schriftsteller der erste Jahrhunderte*. Clemens Alexandrinus: Zweiter Band. Stromata Buch I–VI, ed. O. Stählin and L. Früchtel (Berlin: Akademie Verlag, 1985), 17.31–18.5.

1.3 Tertullian, *de praescriptione haereticorum*, 7; in *Sources chrétiennes* vol. 46, ed. R. F. Refoulé (Paris: Editions du Cerf, 1957), 96.4–99.3

1.4 Augustine of Hippo, *de doctrina Christiana*, II.xl.60–61; in *Florilegium Patristicum*, vol. 29, ed. H. J. Vogels (Bonn: Peter Hanstein, 1930), 46.7–36.

1.5 H. Denzinger (ed.), *Enchiridion Symbolorum*, 39 edn (Freiburg im Breisgau: Herder, 2001), §125–6; 62–4.

1.6 H. Denzinger (ed.), *Enchiridion Symbolorum*, 39 edn (Freiburg im Breisgau: Herder, 2001), §30, 36.

1.7 Anselm of Canterbury, *Proslogion*, 3; in *S. Anselmi Opera Omnia*, vol. 1, ed. F. S. Schmitt (Edinburgh: Nelson, 1946), 102.6–103.9.

1.8 Gaunilo, *Responsio Anselmi*, 6; in *S. Anselmi: Opera Omnia*, vol. 1, ed. F. S. Schmitt (Edinburgh: Nelson, 1946), 128.14–32.

1.9 Thomas Aquinas, *Summa Theologiae*, Ia q. 2, aa. 2–3.

1.10 Thomas Aquinas, *Summa Theologiae*, 1a q. 13, aa. 5–6.

1.11 William of Ockham, *Quodlibetal Questions* I, q. 1; *Opera Philosophica et Theologica* vol. 9 (New York: St Bonaventure Publications, 1966), 1.1–3.59.

1.12 Martin Luther, Heidelberg Disputation, Theses 19–20; in *D. Martin Luthers Werke: Kritische Gesamtausgabe*, vol. 1 (Weimar: Böhlaus, 1911), 354.17–21.

1.13 John Calvin, *Institutes* III.ii,7; 17; in *Joannis Calvini: Opera Selecta*, ed. P. Barth and W. Niesel, vol. 4 (Munich: Kaiser, 1931), 16.31–5, 27.25–36.

1.14 Heidelberg Catechism, Questions 96–8; in E. F. K. Müller (ed.), *Die Bekenntnisschriften der reformierten Kirche* (Leipzig: Böhme, 1903), 710.8–27.

1.15 John Locke, *An Essay Concerning Human Understanding*, ed. P. H. Nidditch (Oxford: Clarendon Press, 1975), 314.25–315.24.

1.16 René Descartes, *Meditations on First Philosophy*; in *Mediationes de Prima Philosophia* (Paris: Librarie Philosophique J. Vrin, 1944), 65.7–15, 66.8–28.

1.17 Blaise Pascal, *Pensées* 110, 188, 190, 449; in Blaise Pascal, *Pensées* (Paris: Editions du Seuil, 1962), pp. 66, 99, 100, 196–7.

1.18 Blaise Pascal, *Pensées* 232, 242, 446, 449; in Blaise Pascal, *Pensées* (Paris: Editions du Seuil, 1962), pp. 117, 120, 195, 198.

1.19 Immanuel Kant, *Kritik der reinen Vernunft*, 2 vols (Frankfurt am Main: Suhrkamp Verlag, 2000), vol. 2, pp. 533–4.

1.20 Søren Kierkegaard, *Unscientific Postscript*, translated by David F. Swenson and Walter Lowrie (Princeton, NJ: Princeton University Press, 1941), pp. 182–3.

1.21 First Vatican Council, session 3, on faith and reason; in H. Denzinger (ed.), *Enchiridion Symbolorum*, 39 edn (Freiburg im Breisgau: Herder, 2001), §§3015–20; 818–20.

1.22 John Henry Newman, *Essay in Aid of a Grammar of Assent*, 2nd edn (London: Burns & Oates, 1870), pp. 159–60.

1.23 Adolf von Harnack, *Outlines of the History of Dogma*, translated by Edwin K. Mitchell (Boston, MA: Beacon Hill Press, 1893), pp. 2–7.

1.24 Karl Barth, "Theology," in *God in Action*, translated by E. G. Homrighausen and Karl J. Ernst (Edinburgh: T&T Clark, 1936), pp. 39–57.

1.25 Ludwig Wittgenstein, *Philosophical Investigations*, translated by G. E. M. Anscombe (Oxford: Blackwell, 1968), pp. 31–2.

1.26 Ludwig Wittgenstein, *Culture and Value*, ed. G. H. von Wright, translated by Peter Winch (Oxford: Blackwell, 1980), pp. 82–6.

1.27 Vladimir Lossky, *The Mystical Theology of the Eastern Church* (London: James Clarke, 1957), pp. 27–8.

1.28 Dietrich Bonhoeffer, Letter to Eberhard Bethge, dated 16 July 1944; in Dietrich Bonhoeffer, *Letters and Papers from Prison*, ed. E. Bethge, translated by Reginald Fuller (New York: Macmillan, and London: SCM Press, 1971), pp. 359–61.

1.29 Paul Tillich, *Systematic Theology*, vol. 1 (Chicago: University of Chicago Press, 1951), pp. 59–64.

1.30 Sallie McFague, *Models of God: Theology for an Ecological Nuclear Age* (Philadelphia: Fortress Press, 1987), pp. 32–4.

1.31 Gustavo Gutiérrez, *A Theology of Liberation*, 2nd edn, translated by Sister Caridad Inda and John Eaglson (Maryknoll, NY: Orbis Books, and London: SCM Press, 1978), pp. 9–12.

1.32 Brian A. Gerrish, *The Old Protestantism and the New: Essays on the Reformation Heritage* (Chicago: University of Chicago Press, and Edinburgh: T&T Clark, 1982), p. 175.

1.33 George Lindbeck, *The Nature of Doctrine* (Philadelphia: Westminster Press, 1984), pp. 32–5.

1.34 Dumitru Staniloae, *The Experience of God: Orthodox Dogmatic Theology*. Brookline, MA: Holy Cross Orthodox Press, 1998, pp. 81–3.

Chapter 2

2.1 E. S. Buchanan, "The Codex Muratorianus," *Journal of Theological Studies* 8 (1907), pp. 540–3.

2.2 Irenaeus, *adversus haereses* II.ii.1–iv.1; in *Sources chrétiennes*, vol. 211, ed. A. Rousseau and L. Doutreleau (Paris: Editions du Cerf, 1974), 24.1–32.29, 44.1–7

2.3 Hippolytus, *de antichristo*, 59; in J. P. Migne, *Patrologia Graeca* (Paris, 1857–66), 10.777C–779A.

2.4 Clement of Alexandria, *Stromata* I.xxviii.3; in *Die griechischen christlichen Schriftsteller der erste Jahrhunderte*. Clemens Alexandrinus: Zweiter Band. Stromata Buch I–VI, ed. O. Stählin and L. Früchtel (Berlin: Akademie Verlag, 1985), 17.31–18.5.

2.5 Tertullian, *de praescriptione haereticorum*, xx, 4–xxi,4; xxxii.1; in *Sources chrétiennes*, vol. 46, ed. R. F. Refoulé (Paris: Editions du Cerf, 1957), 112.17–115.15, 130.1–8.

2.6 Origen, *de principiis* IV.ii.4–5; in *Sources Chrétiennes*, vol. 268, ed. H. Crouzel and M. Simonetti (Paris: Cerf, 1980), 310.111–312.125, 316.147–320.176.

2.7 Cyril of Jerusalem, *Catechesis* V, 12; in *Opera quae supersunt omnia*, ed. W. C. Reischl (Munich: Keck, 1849), p. 150.

2.8 Augustine, *de utilitate credendi* III, 9; in *Oeuvres de Saint Augustin*, vol. 8, ed. J. Pegon (Paris: Desclée, 1951), pp. 226–8.

2.9 Jerome, *Letter* LIII, 4–6, 10; in *Corpus Scriptorum Ecclesiasticorum Latinorum*, vol. 54, ed. I. Hilberg (Vienna: Tempsky, 1910), 450.4–452.7, 463.13–464.6.

2.10 Vincent of Lérins, *Commonitorium* II, 1–3; in *Florilegium Patristicum 5: Vincentii Lerinensis Commonitoria* ed. G. Rauschen (Bonn: Hanstein, 1906), pp. 10–12.

2.11 Bernard of Clairvaux, *Sermones super Cantico Canticorum* XL.vi, 2; in *Sancti Bernardi Opera*, ed. J. Leclerc, C. H. Talbot, and H. M. Rochais (Rome: Editiones Cistercienses, 1958), 56.22–57.7.

2.12 Stephen Langton, unpublished manuscript B.II.26, Trinity College, Cambridge, as cited by Beryl Smalley, "Stephen Langton and the Four Senses of Scripture," *Speculum* 6 (1931), pp. 60–76; Latin text at p. 73, note 1.

2.13 Ludolf of Saxony, *Vita Jesu Christi Domini ac salvatoris nostri* (Paris: Gering & Rembolt, 1502), praefatio. Note that this edition uses a variant title: the more common title is *Vita Jesu Christi redemptoris nostri*.

2.14 Jacques Lefèvre d'Etaples, *Quincuplex Psalterium* (1508), preface; in *Quincuplex Psalterium* (Paris, 1509), α recto–α verso.

2.15 Martin Luther, *Dictata super Psalterium*, preface; in *D. Martin Luthers Werke: Kritische Gesamtausgabe*, vol. 3, ed. G. Kawerau (Weimar: Böhlau, 1885), 11.3–35.

2.16 Martin Luther, *Commentary on Galatians*; in *D. Martin Luthers Werke: Kritische Gesamtausgabe*, vol. 40 (Weimar: Böhlaus, 1911), 602.18–603.13, 607.19–609.14.

2.17 John Calvin, *Institutes* I.iii.1, 2; in *Joannis Calvini: Opera Selecta*, ed. P. Barth and W. Niesel, vol. 3 (Munich: Kaiser Verlag, 1928), 37.16–46.11.

2.18 John Calvin, *Institutes* II.x.1, 2; in *Joannis Calvini: Opera Selecta*, ed. P. Barth and W. Niesel, vol. 4 (Munich: Kaiser Verlag, 1931), 403.5–404.22.

2.19 Council of Trent, Session IV; in H. Denzinger (ed.), *Enchiridion Symbolorum*, 39 edn (Freiburg im Breisgau: Herder, 2001), §1501, 496.

2.20 *Confessio Gallicana*, 1559, articles 3–5; in E. F. K. Müller (ed.), *Die Bekenntnisschriften der reformierten Kirche* (Leipzig: Böhme, 1903), 222.5–44.

2.21 *Confessio Belgica*, 1561, article 2; in E. F. K. Müller (ed.), *Die Bekenntnisschriften der reformierten Kirche* (Leipzig: Böhme, 1903), 233.11–21.

2.22 Melchior Cano, *De locis theologicis* XII.v.5–14; in Melchior Cano, *De locis theologicis praelectiones* (Louvain, 1569), pp. 719–27.

2.23 *Epitome*, 1–8; in *Die Bekenntisschriften der evangelisch–lutherischen Kirche*, 2nd edn (Göttingen: Vandenhoeck & Ruprecht, 1952), 767.14–769.34.

2.24 James I, *Basilikon Doron; or His Majesties Instructions to His Dearest Son, Henry the Prince* (London, 1603), pp. 10–11.

2.25 Roberto Bellarmine, *Prima Controversiae generalis, lib. iii, de interpretatione et vera sensu scripturae*; in *Disputationes de controversiis Christianae Fidei, adversus huius temporis Haereticos* (Cologne, 1619), pp. 139–43.

2.26 *The Bible: Authorized King James Version* (Oxford: Oxford University Press, 1997), pp. lvi–lvii.

2.27 Sir Thomas Browne, *Religio Medici* I, 16. Text in Thomas Browne, *Religio Medici*, ed. Jean-Jacques Denonain (Cambridge, UK: Cambridge University Press, 1955), pp. 21–3

2.28 Francis White, *A Treatise of the Sabbath Day* (London: Richard Badger, 1635), pp. 11–12.

2.29 Philip Jakob Spener, *Pia Desideria* (1675); in P. J. Spener, *Pia Desideria*, edited and translated by T. G. Tappert (Philadelphia: Fortress Press, 1964), pp. 87–9.

2.30 Nicolas Ludwig von Zinzendorf, *Der deutsche Sokrates* (1732); in *Nicholas Ludwig von Zinzendorf: Hauptschriften* vol. 1, ed. E. Beureuther and G. Meyer (Hildesheim: Georg Olms Verlagsbuchandlung, 1962), pp. 289–90.

2.31 Jonathan Edwards, *The Images of Divine Things*, paras 57, 70, 156, 211; in Jonathan Edwards, *The Images of Divine Things*, ed. Perry Miller (New Haven, CT: Yale University Press, 1948), pp. 61, 69, 109, 134.

2.32 Willliam Paley, "Natural Theology"; in *The Works of William Paley* (London: William Orr, 1844), pp. 25–8.

2.33 Johann Adam Möhler, *Symbolism: or Exposition of the Doctrinal Differences between Catholics and Protestants* (New York: Dunigan, 1844), pp. 349–52.

2.34 John Henry Newman, *Lectures on the Prophetical Office of the Church*; in Eugene R. Fairweather, *The Oxford Movement* (Oxford: Oxford University Press, 1964), pp. 116–18.

2.35 A. A. Hodge, *Outlines of Theology* (1879; reprinted Grand Rapids, MI: Eerdmans, 1948), pp. 66–9.

2.36 Benjamin Jowett, "Essay on the Interpretation of Scripture"; in William Temple (ed.), *Essays and Reviews*. (London: Parker, 1860), pp. 330–433; extract at p. 404.

2.37 "God's Grandeur"; in *The Poems of Gerald Manley Hopkins*, ed. W. H. Gardner and N. H. Mackenzie (London: Oxford University Press, 1948), p. 31.

2.38 Charles Gore, *The Incarnation of the Son of God*, 2nd edn (London: John Murray, 1892), pp. 96–7.

2.39 James Orr, *The Christian View of God and the World as Centering in the Incarnation* (New York: Charles Scribner's Sons, 1908), pp. 75–7.

2.40 Wilhelm Herrmann, *The Communion of the Christian with God* (Edinburgh: T&T Clark, 1906), pp. 57–63.

2.41 Karl Barth, *Church Dogmatics*, I/1, edited and translated by G. W. Bromiley and T. F. Torrance (Edinburgh: T&T Clark, 1975), pp. 191, 193–4.

2.42 Emil Brunner, *Truth as Encounter*, 2nd edn, translated by Amandus Loos and David Cairns (London: SCM Press, 1964), p. 109.

2.43 Rudolf Bultmann, "New Testament and Mythology"; in H. W. Bartsch (ed.), *Kerygma and Myth*, translated by R. H. Fuller (London: SPCK, 1953), 1–16.

2.44 Karl Rahner, *Foundations of the Christian Faith: An Introduction to the Idea of Christianity*, translated by William V. Dych (New York: Crossroad, and London: Darton, Longman and Todd, 1978), pp. 371, 373–7.

2.45 Phyllis Trible, "Feminist Hermeneutics and Biblical Studies," *Christian Century* 3–10 (February 1982), pp. 116–18.

2.46 Donald G. Bloesch, "A Christological Hermeneutic: Crisis and Conflict in Hermeneneutics"; in R. K. Johnson (ed.), *The Use of the Bible in Theology: Evangelical Options* (Atlanta: John Knox Press, 1985), pp. 78–84.

2.47 John Meyendorff, *Living Tradition: Orthodox Witness in the Contemporary World* (Crestwood, NY: St Vladimir's Seminary Press, 1978), pp. 7–8.

2.48 J. I. Packer, *God has Spoken*, 2nd edn (London: Hodder & Stoughton, 1979), pp. 80–2.

2.49 Thomas F. Torrance, *The Ground and Grammar of Theology* (Charlottesville: University Press of Virginia, 1980), pp. 87–91.

2.50 *Catechism of the Catholic Church* (Collegeville, MN: The Liturgical Press, and other publishers, 1994), paras 75–82.

Chapter 3

3.1 Athenagoras of Athens, *Apologia*, X, 1–4; in *Athenagoras: Legatio and De Resurrectione, ed. W. R. Schoedel (Oxford: Clarendon Press, 1972), pp. 20–2.*

3.2 Irenaeus, *Demonstration of the Apostolic Preaching*, 12; in *Sources Chrétiennes*, vol. 62, ed. L. M. Froidevaux (Paris: Cerf, 1965), pp. 50–2.

3.3 Irenaeus, *Demonstration of the Apostolic Preaching*, 6; in *Sources Chrétiennes*, vol. 62, ed. L. M. Froidevaux (Paris: Cerf, 1965), pp. 39–40.

3.4 Tertullian, *adversus Hermogenem*, 2–3; in *Stromata Patristica et Medievalia*, ed. C. Mohrmann and J. Quasten. *Quinti Septimi Florentis Tertulliani adversus Herogenem Liber*, ed. J. H. Waszink (Utrecht: Spectrum, 1956), 16.10–18.7.

3.5 Origen, *de principiis*, II.i.4; in *Sources chrétiennes*, vol. 252, ed. H. Crouzel and M. Simonetti (Paris: Editions du Cerf, 1978), 242.118–244.156.

3.6 Origen, *Homilia in Numeros*, XIV, 2; in J. P. Migne, *Patrologia Graeca* (Paris, 1857–66), 12:677 D–678A; 678C–679A.

3.7 Origen, *Homilia in Ezechiel* VI, 6; in *Sources Chrétiennes*, vol. 352, ed. Marcel Borret (Paris: Editions du Cerf, 1989), 228.35–230.49.

3.8 Origen, *Contra Celsum* IV, 15; in *Sources Chrétiennes*, vol. 136, ed. M. Borret (Paris: Cerf, 1968), 220.18–27.

3.9 Gregory of Nyssa, *Ad Ablabium: quod non sint tres dei*; in *Gregorii Nysseni Opera*, ed. Werner W. Jaeger, Hermann Langerbeck, and Heinrich Dörrie, 3 vols. (Leiden: E. J. Brill, 1996), vol. 3/1, pp. 37–52.

3.10 Basil of Caesarea, *de spiritu sancto*, IX, 22–3; in *The Book of Saint Basil the Great on the Holy Spirit*, ed. C. F. H. Johnston (Oxford: Clarendon Press, 1892), pp. 51–4.

3.11 Gregory of Nazianzus, *Oratio theologica* V, 26 [= *Oratio* XXXI, 26]; in *Sources Chrétiennes*, vol. 250, ed. Paul Gallay and Maurice Jourjon (Paris: Cerf, 1978), 326.4–16

3.12 Hilary of Poitiers, *de Trinitate* XII, 52, 57; in *Corpus Christianorum: Series Latina*, vol. 62A, ed. P. Smulders (Turnholt: Brepols, 1980), 622.1–9; 627.1–11.

3.13 Augustine, *de Trinitate* IX.i.1–v.8; in *Corpus Christianorum: Series Latina*, vol. 50, ed. W. J. Mountain (Turnholt: Brepols, 1968), 293.33–301.31.

3.14 Augustine, *de libero arbitrio* II.xx.54; in *Corpus Scriptorum Ecclesiasticorum Latinorum*, vol. 74, ed. W. M. Green (Vienna: Hoelder–Pichler–Tempsky, 1961), 87.18–88.20

3.15 Augustine, *de Trinitate* XV.xvii.27–xviii, 32; in *Corpus Christianorum: Series Latina*, vol. 50A, ed. W. J. Mountain (Turnholt: Brepols, 1968), 501.34–508.32.

3.16 Epiphanius of Constantia, *Panarion* lxii, 1; in *Epiphanii Episcopi Constantiae Opera*, ed. W. Dindorf (Leipzig: Weigel, 1860), vol. 2, 572.20–573.17.

3.17 Cyril of Alexandria, *in Ioannis evangelium* XVI, 20; in *In D. Ioannis evangelium*, ed. P. E. Pusey (Oxford: Clarendon Press, 1872), 736.23–737.4.

3.18 Fulgentius of Ruspe, *contra Fabianum* XXVIII, 16–19; in *Corpus Christianorum* vol. 91A, ed. J. Fraipont (Turnhout: Brepols, 1968), 813.264–814.274.

3.19 John of Damascus, *de fide orthodoxa*, I, 8; in *Patristische Texte und Studien*, vol. 12, ed. P. Bonifatius Kotter, OSB. (Berlin/New York: de Gruyter, 1973), 25.172–26.194.

3.20 Council of Toledo, *Symbolum fidei de Trinitate et Incarnatione* 10–14; in H. Denzinger (ed.), *Enchiridion Symbolorum*, 39 edn (Freiburg im Breisgau: Herder, 2001), §§522–8, 242–3.

3.21 Anselm of Canterbury, *Proslogion*, 8; in *S. Anselmi: Opera Omnia*, vol. 1, ed. F. S. Schmitt (Edinburgh: Nelson, 1946), 106.5–14.

3.22 Richard of St Victor, *de Trinitate* III, 14; in *Richard de Saint Victor: De Trinitate*, ed. J. Ribaillier (Paris: Librarie Philosophique J. Vrin, 1958), 149.4–150.35.

3.23 Alexander of Hales, *Summa Theologica*, vol. 4 (Ad Claras Aquas: Collegii S. Bonaventurae, 1948), p. 197.

3.24 Thomas Aquinas, *Summa Theologiae*, la, q. 25, aa. 3–4.

3.25 Bonaventure, *Breviloquium* Pars III, cap. 1, 1–3; in Bonaventure, *Opera theologica selecta*, 5 vols (Florence: Editiones Collegii S. Bonaventuri, 1934–64), vol. 5, pp. 57–9.

3.26 Julian of Norwich, *Revelations of Divine Love*, 52, 62, 63; in Julian of Norwich, *Revelations of Divine Love*, translated by Clifton Wolters (Harmondsworth, UK: Penguin, 1958), pp. 151, 174, 176.

3.27 William of Ockham, *Quodlibetal Questions* VI, q. 1; *Opera Philosophica et Theologica*, vol. 9 (New York: St Bonaventure Publications, 1966), 585.14–586.24

3.28 Thomas à Kempis, *de imitatione Christi*, I, 1–2; in *De imitatione Christi libri quatuor*, ed. T. Lupo (Vatican City: Libreria Editrice Vaticana, 1982), 4.7–8.8.

3.29 John Owen, *Exposition of Psalm 130*; in *The Works of John Owen*, vol. 6, ed. W. Goold (Edinburgh: Johnson and Hunter, 1851), pp. 626–7.

3.30 Spinoza, *Ethics* V, 17; in *Opera: Lateinisch und Deutsch*, vol. 2, ed. Konrad Blumenstock (Darmstadt: Wissenschaftliche Buchgesellschaft, 1980), 526.31–528.6.

3.31 Friedrich Schleiermacher, *The Christian Faith*, translated by M. R. Mackintosh and J. S. Stewart (Edinburgh: T&T Clark, 1928), pp. 738–9.

3.32 Karl Barth, *The Epistle to the Romans*, translated by Edwyn C. Hoskyns (Oxford: Oxford University Press, 1933), pp. 28–9.

3.33 Jürgen Moltmann, "The 'Crucified God': God and the Trinity Today," in J. B. Metz (ed.), *New Questions on God* (New York: Herder & Herder, 1972), pp. 31–5.

3.34 Richard Swinburne, *The Coherence of Theism* (Oxford: Oxford University Press, 1977), pp. 126–31

3.35 Leonardo Boff, *Trinity and Society*, translated by Paul Burns (Tunbridge Wells, UK: Burns & Oates; Maryknoll, NY: Orbis Books, 1988), pp. 156–8.

3.36 Robert Jenson, "The Triune God," in C. E. Braaten and R. W. Jenson (eds.), *Christian Dogmatics*, vol. 1 (Philadelphia: Fortress Press, 1984), pp. 87–92.

3.37 Hans Küng, *The Incarnation of God*, translated by J. R. Stephenson (Edinburgh: T&T Clark, 1987), pp. 530–3.

3.38 Eberhard Jüngel, *God as the Mystery of the World*, translated by Darrell L. Guder (Edinburgh: T&T Clark, 1983), p. 13.

3.39 Jacques Ellul, *The Humiliation of the Word*, translated by Joyce Main Hanks (Grand Rapids, MI: Eerdmans, 1985), pp. 102–6.

3.40 Walter Kasper, *The God of Jesus Christ*, translated by Matthew O'Connell (London: SCM Press, 1983), pp. 267–9.

3.41 Paul Jewett, *God, Creation, and Revelation* (Grand Rapids, MI: Eerdmans, 1991), pp. 323–5.

3.42 Anne Carr, "Feminist Theology," in A. E. McGrath (ed.) *Blackwell Encyclopaedia of Modern Christian Thought* (Oxford: Blackwell, 1993), pp. 223–4.

3.43 Sarah A. Coakley, "'Persons' in the 'Social' Doctrine of the Trinity: A Critique of Current Analytic Discussion," in Stephen T. Davis, Daniel Kendall, and Gerald O'Collins (eds), *The Trinity: An Interdisciplinary Symposium on the Trinity* (Oxford: Oxford University Press, 2002), pp. 123–44; extract at pp. 123–5.

Chapter 4

4.1 Ignatius of Antioch, *Letter to the Trallians*, 9–10; *Letter to the Smyrnaeans*, 2–3; in *The Apostolic Fathers*, ed. Kirsopp Lake, 2 vols. (Cambridge, MA: Harvard University Press, 1902), vol. 1, pp. 220, 252–4.

4.2 Irenaeus, *adversus haereses* I.xxiv.1–2; in *Sources Chrétiennes* vol. 264, ed. A. Rousseau and L. Doutreleau (Paris: Cerf, 1979), pp. 320–4.

4.3 Tertullian, *adversus Praxean*, 1; in *Tertullian's Treatise against Praxeas*, ed. E. Evans (London: SPCK, 1948), 89.4–33.

4.4 Tertullian, *adversus Praxean*, 27; in *Tertullian's Treatise against Praxeas*, ed. E. Evans (London: SPCK, 1948), 123.24–125.3.

4.5 Novatian, *de trinitate*, 16; in J. P. Migne, *Patrologia Latina* (Paris, 1841–55), 3.915B–C.

4.6 Origen, *de Principiis* II.vi.3; in *Sources Chrétiennes*, vol. 252, ed. H. Crouzel and M. Simonetti (Paris: Cerf, 1978), 314.106–316.128.

4.7 A letter of Arius to Eusebius, Bishop of Nicomedia (c. 321). This letter is known, with slight variations, in two major sources, as follows: Theodoret of Cyrus, *Ecclesiastical History* I.v.1–4; in *Die griechischen Christlichen Schriftsteller der ersten Jahrhunderte*: *Theodoret Kirchengeschichte*, ed. L. Parmentier and F. Schweiweiler (Berlin: Akademie Verlag, 1954), 26.1–27.6; and Epiphanius of Constantia, *Pararion* lxix, 6; *Epiphanii Episcopi Constantiae Opera*, ed. G. Dindorfius (Leipzig: Weigel, 1861), 148.10–149.16.

4.8 Athanasius, *Epistulae ad Serapionem*, IV, 14; in J. P. Migne, *Patrologia Graeca* (Paris, 1857–66), 26:656C–657B.

4.9 Apollinarius of Laodicea, Letter 2; in *Apollinaris von Laodicea und seine Schule*, ed. H. Lietzmann (Tübingen: Mohr, 1904), 256.3–7.

4.10 Gregory of Nazianzus, Letter 101; in J. P. Migne, *Patrologia Graeca* (Paris, 1857–66), 37:177B–180A; 181C–184A.

4.11 Theodore of Mopsuestia, Catechetical Homily 8.13–14, as translated by Alphonse Mingana. *Woodbrooke Studies: Christian Documents in Syriac, Arabic, and Garshuni* (Cambridge, UK: Heffer, 1933), pp. 89–90, with slight alteration for clarity.

4.12 Nestorius, as cited in Socrates, *Historia Ecclesiastica* VII, 32; in *Socratis Scholastica: Ecclesiastica Historia*, ed. R. Hussey (Oxford: Clarendon Press, 1853), vol. 2, pp. 804–7.

4.13 Cyril of Alexandria, Letter XVII, 12 (Third Letter to Nestorius); in *Oxford Early Christian Texts*: *Cyril of Alexandria: Select Letters*, ed. L. R. Wickham (Oxford: Clarendon Press, 1983), 28.17–32.16.

4.14 Cyril of Alexandria, Letter IV, 3–5 (Second Letter to Nestorius); in *Oxford Early Christian Texts*: *Cyril of Alexandria: Select Letters*, ed. L. R. Wickham (Oxford: Clarendon Press, 1983), 4.22–6.28.

4.15 Cyril of Alexandria, *Homily at the Council of Ephesus*; in J. P. Migne, *Patrologia Graeca* (Paris, 1857–66), 77:991A–D; 996C.

4.16 Leo the Great, Letter 28 to Flavian (13 June 449); in J. P. Migne, *Patrologia Latina* (Paris, 1841–55), 54.758B–760A; 764A–768B.

4.17 H. Denzinger (ed.), *Enchiridion Symbolorum*, 39 edn (Freiburg im Breisgau: Herder, 2001), §§301–2; 142–3.

4.18 Zeno, *Henoticon*, cited by Evagrius, *Ecclesiastical History*, III, 14; in *The Ecclesiastical History of Evagrius*, ed. J. Bidez and L. Parmentier (London: Methuen, 1898), 113.2–15.

4.19 *The Petition of the Monophysites to the Emperor Justinian*; text according to Michael the Syrian, *Chronicle*, ed. J. B. Chabot, 3 vols (Paris: Leroux, 1899–1910), vol. 2, pp. 199–200, 202–3.

4.20 John of Damascus, *contra imaginum calumniatores* I, 16; in *Patristische Texte und Studien*, vol. 17, ed. P. Bonifatius Kotter, OSB. (Berlin/New York: de Gruyter, 1979), 89.1–4; 92.90–91. The text from which this citation is taken has no generally agreed title; it can also be found referred to as *pro sacris imaginibus orationes tres* as, for example, in the Migne edition.

4.21 Honorius of Autun, *Libellus octo quaestionum de angelis et homine*, 2; in J. P. Migne, *Patrologia Latina* (Paris, 1841–55), 172.1187A–C.

4.22 Thomas Aquinas, *Summa Theologiae*, IIIa q.1 a.3.

4.23 Gregory Palamas, *Homilia* 34; in J. P. Migne, *Patrologia Graeca* (Paris, 1857–66), 151.428D–429A.

4.24 Martin Luther, *On the Councils and the Church* (1539); in *D. Martin Luthers Werke: Kritische Gesamtausgabe*, vol. 50 (Weimar: Böhlau, 1914), 587.29–590.4.

4.25 François Turrettini, *Institutio theologiae elencticae*, topic 14, q. 5; in *Institutio theologiae elencticae*, 3 vols (Rome: Trajecti, 1734), vol. 2, pp. 424–7.

4.26 G. E. Lessing, "Über den Beweis des Geistes und der Kraft," in *Gotthold Ephraim Lessings sämtlichen Schriften*, vol. 13, ed. Karl Lachmann (Berlin: Göschen'sche Verlagshandlung, 1897), 4.11–8.20.

4.27 Friedrich Schleiermacher, *The Christian Faith*, translated by M. R. Mackintosh and J. S. Stewart (Edinburgh: T&T Clark, 1928), pp. 98–9.

4.28 A. B. Ritschl, *The Christian Doctrine of Justification and Reconciliation* (Edinburgh: T&T Clark, 1900), pp. 385–9.

4.29 Martin Kähler, *Der sogenannte historische Jesus und der geschichtliche, biblische Christus*, ed. E. Wolf (Munich: Kaiser Verlag, 1953), pp. 40–5

4.30 George Tyrell, *Christianity at the Cross-Roads* (London: Longmans Green & Co, 1909), pp. 46–9.

4.31 Albert Schweitzer, *Von Reimarus zu Wrede: Eine Geschichte der Leben–Jesu–Forschung* (Tübingen: Mohr, 1906), pp. 396–401.

4.32 P. T. Forsyth, *The Person and Place of Jesus Christ* (London: Independent Press, 1909), pp. 35, 41, 44.

4.33 Ernst Troeltsch, "Faith and History"; in Ernst Troeltsch, *Religion in History*, translated by James Luther Adams and Walter F. Bense (Edinburgh: T&T Clark, 1991), pp. 134–45; extract at pp. 134–9.

4.34 Dorothy L. Sayers, *Creed or Chaos?* (London: Methuen, 1947), pp. 32–5.

4.35 Paul Tillich, *Systematic Theology*, 3 vols (Chicago: University of Chicago Press, 1978), vol. 2, pp. 113–14.

4.36 Wolfhart Pannenberg, *Jesus – God and Man*, translated by Lewis L. Wilkins and Duane A. Priebe (Philadelphia: Westminster Press, 1968), pp. 22–5.

4.37 Thomas F. Torrance, *The Trinitarian Faith* (Edinburgh: T&T Clark, 1988), pp. 151–4.

4.38 Rosemary Radford Ruether, *Sexism and God-Talk: Towards a Feminist Theology* (Boston: Beacon Press, 1983), pp. 127–30.

4.39 Daphne Hampson, *Theology and Feminism* (Oxford: Blackwell Publishing, 1990), pp. 50–2.

4.40 Morna D. Hooker, "Chalcedon and the New Testament," in Sarah Coakley and David A. Pailin (eds.), *The Making and Remaking of Christian Doctrine* (Oxford: Clarendon Press, 1993), pp. 73–93; extract at pp. 86–8.

4.41 N. T. Wright, *Jesus and the Victory of God* (London: SPCK, 1996), pp. 4–8.

Chapter 5

5.1 Irenaeus, *adversus haereses* V.i.1; in *Sources Chrétiennes*, vol. 153, ed. A. Rousseau, L. Doutreleau, and C. Mercier (Paris: Cerf, 1979), 18.19–20.20.

5.2 Irenaeus, *adversus haereses*, III.xviii.1; in *Sources Chrétiennes*, vol. 211, ed. A. Rousseau and L. Doutreleau (Paris: Cerf, 1974), 342.1–344.13.

5.3 Clement of Alexandria, *Quis Dives Salvetur*, 37; in *Clement of Alexandria: The Exhortation to the Greeks; The Rich Man's Salvation*, Loeb Classical Library edition, ed. G. W. Butterworth (Cambridge, MA: Harvard University Press, 1960), p. 346.

5.4 Athanasius, *de incarnatione Verbi*, VIII, 4–IX, 1; in *Sources Chrétiennes*, vol. 199, ed. C. Kannengiesser (Paris: Cerf, 1973), 292.30–296.17.

5.5 Athanasius, *contra Arianos*, III, 33; in J. P. Migne, *Patrologia Graeca* (Paris, 1857–66), 26:393A–C.

5.6 An anonymous paschal homily inspired by the Treatise on the Passion of Hippolytus; in *Sources Chrétiennes: Homélies paschales*, vol. 1, ed. P. Nautin (Paris: Cerf, 1950), 177.8–179.9.

5.7 Rufinus of Aquileia, *Expositio Symboli* 14; in *Corpus Christianorum: Series Latina*, vol. 20, ed. M. Simonetti (Turnholt: Brepols, 1961), 151.9–152.22.

5.8 A homily for Holy Saturday, ascribed to Epiphanius of Constantia, but of uncertain authorship; in J. P. Migne, *Patrologia Graeca* (Paris, 1857–66), 43:440A; 452B–C; 461B.

5.9 Theodore of Cyrrhet, *de providentia*, 10; in J. P. Migne, *Patrologia Graeca* (Paris, 1857–66), 83.756B–760D.

5.10 Augustine, *Sermo* 261, 1; in J. P. Migne, *Patrologia Latina* (Paris, 1841–55), 38.10202D–10203C.

5.11 Maximus of Constantinople, *Quaestiones ad Thalassium*, 22; in *Corpus Christianorum: Series Graeca*, vol. 7, ed. C. Laga and C. Steel (Turnholt: Brepols, 1980), 137.4–139.46.

5.12 Simeon the New Theologian, *Hymns of Divine Love*, 7; in *Supplementa Byzantina: Texte und Untersuchungen*, ed. H. G. Beck, A. Kambylis, and R. Keydell (Berlin/New York, 1976), 71.29–42

5.13 Anselm of Canterbury, extracts from *Cur Deus homo* I.xi–xxi; II.iv–xx; in *S. Anselmi Opera Omnia*, ed. F. S. Schmitt, vol. 2 (Edinburgh: Nelson, 1946), 68.3–89.32; 99.3–132.6.

5.14 Peter Abelard, *Expositio in Epistolam ad Romanos*, 2; in J. P. Migne, *Patrologia Latina* (Paris, 1841–55), 178.832C–D; 836A–B.

5.15 Hugh of St Victor, *de sacramentis* I.viii.6–7; 10; in J. P. Migne, *Patrologia Latina* (Paris, 1841–55), 176.310B–D; 311D.

5.16 Rupert of Deutz, *Opus de gloria et honore Filii hominis super Matthaeum*, xiii; in J. P. Migne, *Patrologia Latina* (Paris, 1841–55), 168.1628B–D.

5.17 Thomas Aquinas, *Summa Theologiae*, IIIa q. 48 a. 2.

5.18 Nicholas Cabasilas, *de vita in Christo*, 3; in J. P. Migne, *Patrologia Graeca* (Paris, 1857–66), 150:572C–D.

5.19 John Calvin, *Consilium de peccato et redemptione*; in *Corpus Reformatorum*, vol. 10, part 1, ed. G. Baum, E. Cunitz, and E. Reuss (Braunschweig: Schwetschke, 1871), pp. 156–7.

5.20 *The Racovian Catechism* V, 8; in *The Racovian Catechism*, translated by Thomas Rees (London: Longman, 1818), p. 303.

5.21 John Donne, Holy Sonnet XV; in *Complete Poetry and Selected Prose*, ed. J. Hayward (New York: Random House, 1932), p. 285.

5.22 George Herbert, "Redemption"; in *The Works of George Herbert*, ed. F. E. Hutchinson (Oxford: Clarendon Press, 1941), p. 40.

5.23 John Wesley and Charles Wesley, *Hymns and Sacred Poems* (London: William Strahan, 1739), pp. 117–19.

5.24 Friedrich Schleiermacher, *The Christian Faith*, translated by M. R. Mackintosh and J. S. Stewart (Edinburgh: T&T Clark, 1928), pp.429–31.

5.25 Friedrich Schleiermacher, *The Christian Faith*, translated by M. R. Mackintosh and J. S. Stewart (Edinburgh: T&T Clark, 1928), pp.374–75.

5.26 Charles Gore, "Our Lord's Human Example," *Church Quarterly Review* 16 (1883), pp. 282–313; extract at 298.

5.27 Hastings Rashdall, "The Abelardian Doctrine of the Atonement"; in *Doctrine and Development: University Sermons* (London: Methuen, 1898), pp. 128–45; extract at pp. 130–43.

5.28 James Denney, *The Christian Doctrine of Reconciliation* (London: Hodder & Stoughton, 1917), pp. 181–4.

5.29 Gustaf Aulén, *Christus Victor: An Historical Study of the Three Main Types of the Idea of the Atonement*, translated by A. G. Hebert (London: SPCK, 1931), pp. 17–22.

5.30 Vladimir Lossky, "Redemption and Deification"; in *In the Image and Likeness of God*, translated by John Erickson and Thomas Bird (New York: St Vladimir's Seminary Press, 1974), pp. 97–8.

5.31 Bernard Lonergan, *The Collected Works of Bernard Lonergan: 6 – Philosophical and Theological Papers, 1958–1964* (Toronto: University of Toronto Press, 1996), pp. 8–13.

5.32 Wolfhart Pannenberg, *Jesus – God and Man*, translated by Lewis L. Wilkins and Duane A. Priebe (Philadelphia: Westminster Press, 1968), 38–9; 47–8.
5.33 J. I. Packer, "What did the Cross Achieve? The Logic of Penal Substitution," *Tyndale Bulletin* 25 (1974), pp. 3–45; extract pp. 16–22.
5.34 Dorothee Soelle, *Suffering* (Philadelphia: Fortress Press, 1975), pp. 162–4.
5.35 Colin E. Gunton, *The Actuality of Atonement* (Edinburgh: T&T Clark, 1988), pp. 62–5.

Chapter 6

6.1 Irenaeus, *adversus haereses*, IV.xxxviiii.1; in *Sources Chrétiennes*, vol. 100, ed. A. Rousseau (Paris: Cerf, 1965), 942.1–946.17.
6.2 Tertullian, *de patientia* V, 5–14; *Sources Chrétiennes*, vol. 310, ed. J.–C. Fredouille (Paris: Cerf, 1984), 72.15–76.49.
6.3 Tertullian, *adversus Marcionem* II.xv.2–3; in *Sources Chrétiennes*, vol. 368, ed. R. Braun (Paris: Cerf, 1991), 96.10–98.25.
6.4 Tertullian, *de baptismo* 5; in *Quinti Septimi Florentis Tertulliani: de baptismo*, ed. B. Luiselli (Turin: Paraviam, 1960), 12.166–172.
6.5 Origen, *de principiis* III.iv.1; in *Sources Chrétiennes*, vol. 268, ed. H. Crouzel and M. Simonetti (Paris: Cerf, 1980), 236.14–29.
6.6 Origen, *Homilia in Leviticum* xii, 4; in *Sources Chrétiennes*, vol. 287, ed. M. Borret (Paris: Cerf, 1981), 178.5–23.
6.7 Lactantius, *Divinae Institutiones* VI, 10–11; in *Corpus Scriptorum Ecclesiasticorum Latinorum* vol. 19, ed. Samuel Brandt and George Laubmann (Prague/Vienna/Leipzig, 1980), 514.6–515.8; 519.3–6.
6.8 Ambrose, *de sacramentis* V.iv.19; in *Corpus Scriptorum Ecclesiasticorum Latinorum* vol. 73, ed. O. Faller, SJ (Vienna: Hoelder-Pichler-Tempsky, 1955), 66.11–24.
6.9 Ambrosiaster, *Commentaria in Epistolam ad Romanos* v, 12; in *Corpus Scriptorum Ecclesiasticorum Latinorum* vol. 81, ed. H. J. Vogels (Vienna: Hoelder-Pichler-Tempsky, 1966), 165.9–15.
6.10 Gregory of Nyssa, *Commentary on the Beatitudes*, 3; in J. P. Migne, *Patrologia Graeca* (Paris, 1857–66), 44.1225C–1227B.
6.11 Augustine, *Sermo* 26, xii, 13; in J. P. Migne, *Patrologia Latina* (Paris, 1841–55), 38:177A–B.
6.12 Augustine, *de dono perseverantiae* XIV, 35; in *Oeuvres de Saint Augustin*, ed. J. Chéné and J. Pintard (Paris: de Brouwer, 1962), pp. 680–2.
6.13 Augustine, *de natura et gratia* iii, 3–iv, 4; in *Corpus Scriptorum Ecclesiasticorum Latinorum*, vol. 60, ed. C. F. Urba and J. Zycha (Vienna: Tempsky, 1913), 235.8–236.6
6.14 Augustine, *de civitate Dei* XXII.xxx.3; in J. P. Migne, *Patrologia Latina* (Paris, 1841–55), 41.802B–D.
6.15 Augustine, *de correptione et gratia*, XII, 34; in J. P. Migne, *Patrologia Latina* (Paris, 1841–55), 44:936D–937B

6.16 Pelagius, *Letter to Demetrias*, 16; in J. P. Migne, *Patrologia Latina* (Paris, 1841–55), 33:1110A–B.

6.17 Pelagius, *pro libero arbitrio*, as reported by Augustine, *De gratia Christi* IV, 5; in *Corpus Scriptorum Ecclesiasticorum Latinorum*, vol. 42, ed. C. F. Urba and I. Zycha (Vienna: Tempsky, 1902), 128.1–29.

6.18 Pelagius, *pro libero arbitrio*, as reported by Augustine, *de peccato originale*, XIII, 14; in *Corpus Scriptorum Ecclesiasticorum Latinorum*, vol. 42, ed. C. F. Urba and I. Zycha (Vienna: Tempsky, 1902), 175.22–27.

6.19 H. Denzinger (ed.), *Enchiridion Symbolorum*, 39 edn (Freiburg im Breisgau: Herder, 2001), §§222–30; 106–9.

6.20 Letter of Faustus of Rhegium to Lucidus (473); in *Corpus Scriptorum Ecclesiasticorum Latinorum* vol. 20, ed. A. Engelbrecht (Vienna: Tempsky, 1891), 165.20–166.2; 16–20. See also H. Denzinger (ed.), *Enchiridion Symbolorum*, 39 edn (Freiburg im Breisgau: Herder, 2001), §§330–42; 154–7.

6.21 H. Denzinger (ed.), *Enchiridion Symbolorum*, 39 edn (Freiburg im Breisgau: Herder, 2001), §§371–7; 176–8.

6.22 John Scotus Eriugena, *Periphyseon* IV, 15; in J. P. Migne, *Patrologia Latina* (Paris, 1841–55), 122:809B–D.

6.23 Hildegard of Bingen, *Liber Divinorum Operum* I.iv.100; in J. P. Migne, *Patrologia Latina* (Paris, 1841–55), 197.885B–C.

6.24 Alan of Lille, *contra hereticos*, I, 51; in J. P. Migne, *Patrologia Latina* (Paris, 1841–55), 210.356B.

6.25 Francis of Assisi, "Canticum fratris solis vel Laudes creaturarum"; in Kajetan Esser, *OFM, Die opuskula des hl. Franziskus von Assisi. Neue textkritische Edition*. (Rome: Editiones Collegii S. Bonaventurae ad Claras Aquas, 1976), pp. 128–9.

6.26 Thomas Aquinas, *Summa Theologiae*, Prima Secundae q. 110 a. 1.

6.27 Mechthild von Magdeburg, *Das flissende Licht der Gottheit*, 1.33–43; in *Mechthild von Magdeburg, "Das fliessende Licht der Gottheit", nach der Einsiedler Handschrift in kritischem Vergleich mit der gesamten Überlieferung*, ed. Hans Neumann, 2 vols (Munich: Artemis Verlag, 2001–3), vol. 1, pp. 26–7.

6.28 Johannes Duns Scotus, *In III. Sent*. dist. iii q. 1; in *Opera Omnia* (Rome: Vatican Press, 2003), vol. 20, pp. 123, 126, 129.

6.29 Gregory of Rimini, *In I Sententiarum* dist. Xl–xli, qu. 1 a. 2; in *Lectura super primum et secundum sententiarum* ed. D. Trapp, vol. 3 (Berlin/New York: de Gruyter, 1979–84), 326.17–26.

6.30 Gabriel Biel, *In II Sententiarum* dist. xxvii q. unica art. 3 conc. 4; in *Collectorium circa quattuor libros sententiarum* ed. W. Werbeck and U. Hofmann, vol. 2 (Tübingen: Mohr, 1973–84), 517.1–8.

6.31 Giovanni Pico della Mirandola, *Oratio de hominis dignitate*, 4.10–5.23; in Giovanni Pico della Mirandola, *Opera* (Bologna: Benedetto Faelli, 1496), fol. 132r–v.

6.32 Martin Luther, "Preface to the Latin Works (1545)"; in *D. Martin Luthers Werke: Kritisch Gesamtausgabe*, vol. 54 (Weimar: Böhlau, 1938), 185.12–186.21.

6.33 Martin Luther, *The Liberty of a Christian*; in *D. Martin Luthers Werke: Kritische Gesamtausgabe*, vol. 7 (Weimar: Böhlaus, 1897), 25.26–26.9.

6.34 Martin Luther, Lectures on Romans (1515–1516); in *D. Martin Luthers Werke: Kritisch Gesamtausgabe*, vol. 56 (Weimar: Böhlau, 1938), 269.25–30; 272.3–21.

6.35 Philip Melanchthon, *Loci Communes* (1521); in *Melanchthons Werke in Auswahl*, ed. H. Engelland (Gütersloh: Bertelsmann Verlag, 1953), vol. 2, 106.22–110.11.

6.36 John Calvin, *Institutes* III.xxi.1, 5; in *Joannis Calvini: Opera Selecta*, ed. P. Barth and W. Niesel, vol. 4 (Munich: Kaiser, 1931), 368.33–369.14; 373.33–374.17.

6.37 John Calvin, *Institutes* III.ii.29, 30; in *Joannis Calvini: Opera Selecta*, ed. P. Barth and W. Niesel, vol. 3 (Munich: Kaiser, 1928), 39.1–40.12.

6.38 John Calvin, *Institutes* III.xi.2, 23; in *Joannis Calvini: Opera Selecta*, ed. P. Barth and W. Niesel, vol. 4 (Munich: Kaiser, 1931), 182.25–183.10; 206.17–32.

6.39 Council of Trent, Session VI, chapter 4; in H. Denzinger (ed.), *Enchiridion Symbolorum*, 39 edn (Freiburg im Breisgau: Herder, 2001), §1524; 504.

6.40 Theodore Beza, Letter to John Calvin, 29 July, 1555; in *Correspondance de Théodore de Bèze*, ed. H. Aubert (Geneva: Droz, 1960), vol. 1, p. 171.

6.41 John Donne, *Holy Sonnet* XIV; in *Poems of John Donne*, 2 vols., ed. E. K. Chambers (London: Lawrence & Bullen, 1896), vol. 1, p. 165.

6.42 James Ussher, *A Body of Divinity*, 3rd edn (London: M.F., 1663), pp. 197–200.

6.43 Westminster Confession, X.1–2; in E. F. K. Müller (ed.), *Die Bekenntnisschriften der reformierten Kirche* (Leipzig: Böhme, 1903), 565.12–566.3

6.44 *The Works of Anne Bradstreet*, ed. Jeannine Hensley (Cambridge, MA: Harvard University Press, 1967), pp. 215–18.

6.45 Nicolas Ludwig von Zinzendorf, *Nine Public Lectures On Important Subjects in Religion*, translated by George W. Forell (Iowa City: University of Iowa Press, 1973), pp. 40–1.

6.46 F. C. Oetinger, *Biblisches Wörterbuch*, ed. J. Hamberger (Stuttgart: Steinkopf, 1849), pp. 55–6.

6.47 Jonathan Edwards, *Christian Doctrine of Original Sin Defended*; in *The Works of President Edwards*, ed. S. B. Wright, 10 vols (New Haven, CT: Yale University Press, 1929–30), vol. 2, pp. 309–16.

6.48 John Wesley, Sermon V "Justification by Faith"; in John Wesley, *Sermons on Several Occasions* (London: G. Whitfield, 1746), vol. 1, pp. 81–101.

6.49 Richard Watson, *Theological Institutes*, 4 vols. (New York: Hunt & Eaton, 1889), vol. 1, pp. 731–4.

6.50 Emil Brunner, *The Christian Doctrine of Creation and Redemption: Dogmatics, Vol. 2*, translated by Olive Wyon (London: Lutterworth Press, 1952), pp. 55–8.

6.51 Karl Barth, *Church Dogmatics* II/2, edited and translated by G. W. Bromiley and T. F. Torrance (Edinburgh: T&T Clark, 1957), pp. 103, 161, 164, 166–7.

6.52 Emil Brunner, *The Christian Doctrine of God: Dogmatics Vol. 1*, translated by Olive Wyon (London: Lutterworth Press, 1949), pp. 346–51.

6.53 Reinhold Niebuhr, *The Nature and Destiny of Man*, 2 vols (New York: Macmillan, 1941), vol. 1, pp. 256–9, 266–7.

6.54 Pastoral Constitution on the Church in the Modern World *Gaudium et Spes*, promulgated by His Holiness, Pope Paul VI on December 7, 1965, sections 12–17. Available from <http://www.vatican.va/archive/hist_councils/ii_vatican_council/documents/vat-ii_cons_19651207_gaudium-et-spes_en.html>.

6.55 Daphne Hampson, *Theology and Feminism* (Oxford: Blackwell Publishing, 1990), pp. 121–4.

6.55 Mary Hayter, *The New Eve in Christ* (London: SPCK, 1987), pp. 87–92.

Chapter 7

7.1 Irenaeus, *adversus Haereses* IV.xxxiii.8; in *Sources Chrétiennes*, vol. 100, ed. A. Rousseau (Paris: Cerf, 1965), 818.137–820.148.

7.2 Origen, *Homilia in Iesu Nave* III, 5; in J. P. Migne, *Patrologia Graeca* (Paris, 1857–66), 12.841B–842B.

7.3 Cyprian of Carthage, *de catholicae ecclesiae unitate*, 5–7; in *Corpus Christianorum: Series Latina* vol. 3, ed. M. Bévenot (Turnholt: Brepols, 1972), 252.117–254.176.

7.4 *Catechetical Lecture* XVIII, 23, 26; in J. P. Migne, *Patrologia Graeca* (Paris, 1857–66), 33.1044B; 1048A–B.

7.5 Petilian of Cirta, Letter to Augustine; in Augustine, *contra litteras Petiliani* III.lii.64; in *Corpus Scriptorum Ecclesiasticorum Latinorum*, vol. 52, ed. M. Petschenig (Vienna: Tempsky, 1909), pp. 462–3.

7.6 Augustine, *de baptismo* V.xxvii.38; in *Corpus Scriptorum Ecclesiasticorum Latinorum*, vol. 51, ed. M. Petschenig (Vienna: Tempsky, 1908), 293.19–195.15.

7.7 Leo the Great, *Sermo* 95 *de natali ipsius*; in *Sources Chrétiennes* vol. 200, ed. Dom René Dolle (Paris: Cerf, 1973), p. 266. Note that this sermon is numbered IV.1 in the Migne edition.

7.8 Innocent III, "Sicut universitatis conditor," as set out in Epistola I, 401; in J. P. Migne, *Patrologia Latina* (Paris, 1841–55), 214.377B.

7.9 Thomas Aquinas, *In Symbolum Apostolorum*, 9; in *S. Thomae Aquinitatis Opera Omnia*, vol. 6., ed. R. Busa (Stuttgart: Frommann-Holzboog, 1980), p. 20.

7.10 Boniface VIII, "De unitate et potestate Ecclesiae;" in H. Denzinger (ed.), *Enchiridion Symbolorum*, 39 edn (Freiburg im Breisgau: Herder, 2001), §§870–5; 385–7.

7.11 Jan Hus, *Tractatus de ecclesia*, 7; in *Tractatus de ecclesia*, ed. S. Harrison Thomson (Cambridge, UK: Heffer, 1956), pp. 44–5.

7.12 Martin Luther, *On the Councils and the Church* (1539); in *D. Martin Luthers Werke: Kritische Gesamtausgabe*, vol. 50 (Weimar: Böhlau, 1914), 628. 29–630.2.

7.13 Martin Luther, *Appeal to the German Nobility* (1520); in *D. Martin Luthers Werke: Kritische Gesamtausgabe*, vol. 6 (Weimar: Böhlau, 1888), 406.21–408.30.

7.14 Philip Melanchthon, *de appellatione ecclesiae catholicae*; in *Corpus Reformatorum* (Melanchthon) (Halle: Schwetschke), vol. 24, cols. 397–9.

7.15 Sebastian Franck, Letter to John Campanus, 1531; in B. Becker, "Fragment van Francks latijnse brief aan Campanus,"*Nederlands Archief voor Kerkgeschiedenis* 46 (1964–65), 197–205; extract cited at pp. 201–4. Only part of this letter exists in its original Latin; for the complete letter in German and Dutch translation, see *Quellen zur Geschichte der Täufer*, vol. 7, ed. M. Krebs and H. G. Rott (Gütersloh: Mohn, 1959), pp. 301–25.

7.16 The First Helvetic Confession, 1536, article 14; in E. F. K. Müller (ed.), *Die Bekenntnisschriften der reformierten Kirche* (Leipzig: Böhme, 1903), 101.25–37.

7.17 John Calvin, *Institutes* IV.i.9–10; in *Joannis Calvini: Opera Selecta*, ed. P. Barth and W. Niesel, vol. 5 (Munich: Kaiser Verlag, 1936), 13.24–16.31.

7.18 Richard Hooker, *Laws of Ecclesiastical Polity*, III.i.7–8; in Richard Hooker, *Works*, ed. J. Keble, vol. 1, 3rd edn (Oxford: Oxford University Press, 1845), pp. 342–3.

7.19 Westminster Confession, XXV, 1–5; in E. F. K. Müller (ed.), *Die Bekenntnisschriften der reformierten Kirche* (Leipzig: Böhme, 1903), 597.28–599.4

7.20 John Owen, *The True Nature of a Gospel Church*; in *Works*, ed. William H. Goold, vol. 16 (London: Johnstone & Hunter, 1853), pp. 11–15.

7.21 Friedrich Schleiermacher, *The Christian Faith*, translated by M. R. Mackintosh and J. S. Stewart (Edinburgh: T&T Clark, 1928), pp. 525–8.

7.22 First Vatican Council, *Pastor Aeternus*, First Dogmatic Constitution on the Church, chapters 1 and 4; in H. Denzinger (ed.), *Enchiridion Symbolorum*, 39 edn (Freiburg im Breisgau: Herder, 2001), §§3053–5, 3069–3075; 826–7, 832–3.

7.23 H. B. Swete, *The Holy Catholic Church: The Communion of Saints, A Study in the Apostles' Creed* (London: Macmillan, 1915), pp. 44–9.

7.24 "The Theological Clarification of the Present State of the German Evangelical Churches" (1934), 1–5; in *Bekenntnisschiften und Kirchenordnungen der nach Gottes Wort reformierten Kirche*, ed. W. Niesel (Zurich: Evangelischer Verlag, 1938), 335.25–31; 335.46–336.10; 336.21–38.

7.25 Yves Congar, *Lay People in the Church: A Study for a Theology of the Laity*, revised edition, translated by Donald Attwater (London: Geoffrey Cassell, 1965), pp. 111–13. Latin words italicized by editor for clarity.

7.26 Vatican II, *Lumen Gentium* ("Dogmatic Constitution on the Church"); in *Vatican II: Conciliar and Postconciliar Documents*, ed. Austin Flannery, OP (Northport, NY: Costello Publishing Company, and Dublin: Dominican Publications, 1975), pp. 353–8.

7.27 John D. Zizioulas, *Being as Communion: Studies in Personhood and the Church* (New York: St Vladimir's Seminary Press, 1985), pp. 257–9.

7.28 Leonardo Boff, *Ecclesiogenesis: The Base Communities Reinvent the Church*, translated by Robert R. Barr (Maryknoll, NY: Orbis Books, 1986), 11–15.

7.29 Avery Dulles, *The Catholicity of the Church* (Oxford: Clarendon Press, 1985), p. 185.

7.30 Stanley Hauerwas, *A Community of Character: Toward a Constructive Christian Social Ethic* (Notre Dame, IN: University of Notre Dame Press, 1981), pp. 91–2.

Chapter 8

8.1 Clement of Alexandria, *Paedagogus* I.vi.38; in *Sources Chrétiennes*, vol. 70, ed. H.–I. Marroli (Paris: Cerf, 1960), p. 180.

8.2 Clement of Alexandria, *Paedagogus* I.vi.26; in *Sources Chrétiennes*, vol. 70, ed. H.–I. Marroli (Paris: Cerf, 1960), p. 158.

8.3 Cyprian of Carthage, *Epistle* LXXI, 1; in *Saint Cyprien: Correspondence*, ed. Le Chanoine Bayard, 2nd edn (Paris: Société des Belles Lettres, 1961), pp. 256–7.

8.4 Cyril of Jerusalem, *First Address on the Mysteries*, 1–3; in *Sources Chrétiennes*, vol. 126, ed. A. Piédagnel and P. Paris (Paris: Cerf, 1966), 82.1–86.13.

8.5 Cyril of Jerusalem, *Fourth Address on the Mysteries*, 2–6; in *Sources Chrétiennes*, vol. 126, ed. A. Piédagnel and P. Paris (Paris: Cerf, 1966), 136.1–138.6.

8.6 Hilary of Poitiers, *in Matthaeum* ii, 5; in *Sources Chrétiennes* vol. 254, ed. Jean Doignon (Paris: Cerf, 1978), 110.9–13.

8.7 Augustine, *de baptismo* IV, 16, 18; in *Oeuvres de Saint Augustin*, vol. 29, ed. G. Finaert (Paris: Desclée, 1964), pp. 270–2, 280.

8.8 Augustine, *contra Cresconium* IV.xxi.26; in *Oeuvres de Saint Augustin*, vol. 31, ed. G. Finaert (Paris: Desclée, 1968), pp. 522–4.

8.9 John of Damascus, *de fide orthodoxa* IV, 13; in *Patristische Texte und Studien*, vol. 12, ed. P. Bonifatius Kotter, OSB, (Berlin/New York: de Gruyter, 1973), 194.81–83; 195.97–99.

8.10 Paschasius Radbertus, *de corpore et sanguine Christi* III.1; III.4; IV.1; in J. P. Migne, *Patrologia Latina* (Paris, 1841–55), 120.1275A; 1276D–1278A.

8.11 Ratranmus of Corbie, d*e corpore et sanguine Christi* 2, 9–11, 16; in J. P. Migne, *Patrologia Latina* 121.128A; 128D–129A; 131A–C; 132A; 135A.

8.12 Candidus of Fulda, *de passione domini*, 5; in J. P. Migne, *Patrologia Latina* (Paris, 1841–55), 106.68D–69A.

8.13 Lanfranc of Bec, *de corpore et sanguine Christi*; in *Beati Lanfranci archiepiscopi Cantuarensis opera*, ed. J. A. Giles, vol. 2 (Oxford: Clarendon Press, 1844), p. 167.

8.14 Hugh of St Victor, *de sacramentis* IX, 2; in J. P. Migne, *Patrologia Latina* (Paris, 1841–55), 176.317C–318B.

8.15 Peter Lombard, *Sententiarum libri quatuor* IV.i.4; ii.1; in *Sententiae in IV Libris Distinctae* (Rome: Editiones Collegii S. Bonaventuri, 1981), vol. 2, 233.9–20; 239.18–240.8.

8.16 Thomas Aquinas, *Summa Theologiae*, IIIa q. 75, aa. 2–5.

8.17 Martin Luther, *The Babylonian Captivity of the Church* (1520); in *D. Martin Luthers Werke: Kritische Ausgabe*, vol. 6 (Weimar: Böhlau, 1888), 509–12; 513–14.

8.18 Martin Luther, *The Babylonian Captivity of the Church* (1520); in *D. Martin Luthers Werke: Kritische Ausgabe*, vol. 6 (Weimar: Böhlau, 1888), 509.22–512.4.

8.19 Martin Luther, *The Babylonian Captivity of the Church* (1520); in *D. Martin Luthers Werke: Kritische Ausgabe*, vol. 6 (Weimar: Böhlau, 1888), 513.14–514.21.

8.20 Martin Luther, *The Lesser Catechism* (1529); in *D. Martin Luthers Werke: Kritische Gesamtausgabe*, vol. 30, part 1 (Weimar: Böhlaus, 1910), 255.20–257.24.

8.21 Philip Melanchthon, *Loci Communes* (1521); in *Melanchthons Werke in Auswahl*, ed. H. Engelland (Gütersloh: Bertelsmann Verlag, 1953), vol. 2, 140.25–144.19

8.22 Kornelius Hendriks Hoen, *Epistola christiana admodum* (published 1525); in *Corpus Reformatorum: Huldreich Zwinglis sämtliche Werke*, vol. 91 (Leipzig: Heinsius, 1927), 512.30–513.32.

8.23 Huldrych Zwingli, *On the Lord's Supper* (1526); in *Corpus Reformatorum: Huldreich Zwinglis sämtliche Werke*, vol. 91 (Leipzig: Heinsius, 1927), 796.2–800.5.

8.24 Huldrych Zwingli, *On Baptism*; in *Corpus Reformatorum: Huldreich Zwinglis sämtliche Werke*, vol. 91 (Leipzig: Heinsius, 1927), 217.14–218.24.

8.25 The First Helvetic Confession, article 20; in E. F. K. Müller (ed.), *Die Bekenntnisschriften der reformierten Kirche* (Leipzig: Böhme, 1903), 106.25–43.

8.26 John Calvin, *Institutes* IV.xiv.1, 3; in *Joannis Calvini: Opera Selecta*, ed. P. Barth and W. Niesel, vol. 5 (Munich: Kaiser Verlag, 1936), 259.1–261.3.

8.27 Martin Bucer, d*e regno Christi* I, 7; in *Martini Buceri Opera Latina: De regno Christi libri duo* (Paris: Presses Universitaires de France, 1955), pp. 66–8.

8.28 Council of Trent, Session XIII, chapters 1, 4; in H. Denzinger (ed.), *Enchiridion Symbolorum*, 39 edn (Freiburg im Breisgau: Herder, 2001), §§1636–7, 1642; 528, 530.

8.29 Theodore Beza, *Confessio Christianae Fidei*; in *Tractationes Theologicae*, 3 vols (Geneva: Jean Crispinus, 1570–1582), vol. 1, pp. 26–7.

8.30 John Wesley, *Hymns on the Lord's Supper*, 116; in John and Charles Wesley, *Hymns on the Lord's Supper* (London, 1786), pp. 86–7.

8.31 Vatican II, "Dogmatic Constitution on the Eucharist"; in *Vatican II: Conciliar and Postconciliar Documents*, ed. Austin Flannery, OP (Northport, NY: Costello Publishing Company, and Dublin: Dominican Publications, 1975), pp. 16–19.

8.32 Edward Schillebeeckx, *The Eucharist* (London: Sheed & Ward, 1968), pp. 108–19.

8.33 *Baptism, Eucharist and Ministry*. Faith and Order Paper 111. Geneva: World Council of Churches, 1982, pp. 2–3.

8.34 Alexander Schmemann, *The Eucharist: Sacraments of the Kingdom* (New York: St Vladimir's Seminary Press, 1988), pp. 224–7.

8.35 Rowan Williams, *On Christian Theology* (Oxford: Blackwell Publishers, 2000), pp. 203–4.

8.36 Pope John Paul II, Encyclical letter "Evangelium Vitae": To the Bishops, Priests and Deacons, Men and Women Religious, lay Faithful, and all People of Good Will, on the Value and Inviolability of Human Life. 25 March 1995. Available at < http://www.vatican.va/edocs/ENG0141/_INDEX.HTM>.

Chapter 9

9.1 Justin Martyr, *Apologia* I.xlvi.1–3; in *Saint Justin: Apologies*, ed. A. Wartelle (Paris: Etudes Augustiniennes, 1987), 160.1–10

9.2 Ludwig Feuerbach, *The Essence of Christianity*; in *Gesammelte Werke*, ed. W. Schuffenhauer, vol. 5 (Berlin: Akademie Verlag, 1973), pp. 46–7.

9.3 Karl Marx, *Theses on Feuerbach* (1845); in *Marx–Engels Gesamtausgabe*, vol. 1, part 5, ed. A. Adoratskii (Berlin: Marx–Engels Verlag, 1932), 533.14–555.35.

9.4 Karl Barth, *Church Dogmatics*, I/2, edited and translated by G. W. Bromiley and T. F. Torrance (Edinburgh: T&T Clark, 1956), pp. 280, 297–300.

9.5 C. S. Lewis, "Is Theology Poetry?"; in *C. S. Lewis: Essay Collection* (London: Collins, 2000), pp. 1–21; extract at pp. 15–16.

9.6 Karl Rahner, *Theological Investigations*, vol. 5 (London: Darton, Longman and Todd, and New York: Crossroad, 1966), pp. 115–34.

9.7 Vatican II, *Nostra Aetate*, 28 October 1965; in *Vatican II: Conciliar and Post-conciliar Documents*, ed. Austin Flannery, OP (Northport, NY: Costello Publishing Company, and Dublin: Dominican Publications, 1975), pp. 738–42.

9.8 Clark H. Pinnock, *A Wideness in God's Mercy* (Grand Rapids, MI: Zondervan, 1992), pp. 64–9.

9.9 John Hick, *The Second Christianity* (London: SCM Press, 1983), pp. 82–7.

9.10 C. S. Song, *Third–Eye Theology: Theology in Formation in Asian Settings*, rev. edn (Maryknoll, NY: Orbis, 1990), pp. 109–13.

9.11 John B. Cobb Jr., "Beyond Pluralism"; in G. D'Costa (ed.), *Christian Uniqueness Reconsidered: The Myth of a Pluralistic Theology of Religions* (Maryknoll, NY: Orbis, 1990), pp. 81–95; extract at pp. 81–4.

9.12 Lesslie Newbigin, *The Gospel in a Pluralist Society* (Grand Rapids, MI: Eerdmans, 1989), pp. 159–61, 168–170.

Chapter 10

10.1 Irenaeus, *adversus Haereses* V.xxxii.1; V.xxxiii.1; in *Sources Chrétiennes*, vol. 153, ed. A. Rousseau, L. Doutreleau, and C. Mercier (Paris: Cerf, 1969), 396.1–398.20; 406.9–408.21.

10.2 Theophilus of Antioch, *ad Autolycum* II, 27; in *Sources Chrétiennes*, vol. 20, ed. G. Bardy (Paris: Editions du Cerf, 1948), p. 164.

10.3 Tertullian, *Apologeticus*, XLVII, 12–14; in *Tertullian: Apology*, Loeb Classical Library, ed. T. R. Glover (Cambridge, MA: Harvard University Press, 1960), p. 210.

10.4 Tertullian, *adversus Marcionem* III.xxiv.3–6; in Oxford Early Christian Texts: *Adversus Marcionem*, ed. E. Evans (Oxford: Clarendon Press, 1972), pp. 246–8.

10.5 Origen, *de principiis* II.x.3; in *Sources Chrétiennes*, vol. 252, ed. H. Crouzel and M. Simonetti (Paris: Cerf, 1978), 380.82–382.119.

10.6 Methodius of Olympus, *de resurrectione* I.xlii.1–xliii.4; in *Methodius*, ed. G. N. Bonwetsch (Leipzig: J. C. Hinrichs'sche Buchhandlung, 1917), 289.12–291.10.

10.7 Cyril of Jerusalem, *Fifth Address on the Mysteries*, 9–10; in *Sources Chrétiennes*, vol. 126, ed. Auguste Piédagnel (Paris: Cerf, 1966), 158.4–160.13.

10.8 Gregory of Nyssa, *de anima et resurrectione*; in J. P. Migne, *Patrologia Graeca* (Paris, 1857–66), 46.156C–157A.

10.9 John Chrysostom, *Homilia in 1 Corinthos* xli, 5; in *Interpretatio Omnium Epistolarum Paulinarum*, vol. 2 (Oxford: Oxford University Press, 1847), pp. 525–6.

10.10 Augustine, *De civitate Dei* XIII, 20; in J. P. Migne, *Patrologia Latina* (Paris, 1841–55), 41.393C–394A.

10.11 Gregory the Great, *Dialogia* IV.xli.3; in *Sources Chrétiennes* vol. 265, ed. Adalbert de Vogüé (Paris: Cerf, 1980), 148.12–18.

10.12 Peter Lombard, *Sententiarum libri quatuor* II.xxx.15; in *Sententiae in IV Libris Distinctae* (Rome: Editiones Collegii S. Bonaventuri, 1981), vol. 1, 504.29–505.6

10.13 Benedict XII, *Benedictus Deus*, in H. Denzinger (ed.), *Enchiridion Symbolorum*, 39 edn (Freiburg im Breisgau: Herder, 2001), §1000; 406–7.

10.14 Catherine of Genoa, *Treatise on Purgatory*, iii, v; in *Edizione Critica dei Manoscritti Cateriniani*, ed. Umile Bonzi da Genova, vol. 2 (Genoa: Marietti, 1960), pp. 327–32.

10.15 John Donne, Holy Sonnet X; in *Complete Poetry and Selected Prose*, ed. J. Hayward (New York: Random House, 1932), p. 283.

10.16 Jeremy Taylor, *The Rules and Exercises of Holy Dying* (London, 1651), section 8, 1.

10.17 Jonathan Edwards, "Sinners in the Hands of an Angry God"; in *The Works of President Edwards*, ed. S. B. Wright, 10 vols (New Haven, CT: Yale University Press, 1929–30), vol. 7, pp. 163–77.

10.18 John Wesley, Sermon LXV: "The Great Deliverance," sections III.1–5; in John Wesley, *Sermons on Several Occasions*, vol 2 (London: Wesleyan Conference Office, 1874), pp. 61–3.

10.19 Rudolf Bultmann, *History and Eschatology* (Edinburgh: Edinburgh University Press, 1957), pp. 151–5.

10.20 Helmut Thielicke, *Theological Ethics*, 3 vols, ed. and translated William H. Lazareth (Grand Rapids, MI: Eerdmans, 1966), vol. 1, pp. 44–7.

10.21 Richard Bauckham, "Jürgen Moltmann," in D. F. Ford (ed.), *The Modern Theologians*, 2 vols (Oxford: Blackwell, 1989), pp. 293–310; extract at pp. 298–300.

10.22 Hans Urs von Balthasar, *Mysterium Paschale* (Edinburgh: T&T Clark, 1990), pp. 176–7.

10.23 Gabriel Fackre, *The Christian Story: A Narrative Interpretation of Basic Christian Doctrine*, rev. edn (Grand Rapids, MI: Eerdmans, 1984), pp. 223–5.

10.24 Philip E. Hughes, *The True Image: The Origin and Destiny of Man in Christ* (Grand Rapids, MI: Eerdmans, 1989), pp. 404–7.

10.25 Kathryn Tanner, *Jesus, Humanity and the Trinity: A Brief Systematic Theology.* (Minneapolis: Fortress Press, 2001), pp. 108–10.

For Further Study: Additional Collections of Readings

This reader is aimed to introduce you to the basic themes, issues, debates, schools of thought, and leading thinkers of the Christian tradition. By its very nature, it cannot hope to be comprehensive, although it will certainly act as a "taster" for the great themes of Christian theology. Happily, a wide range of theological readers has been published in the last 30 years, providing a rich range of resources for those with specialist interests. These often focus on particular topics or schools of thought. The following are recommended for further study.

Jeff Astley, David Brown, and Ann Loades, *Creation: A Reader* (Edinburgh: T&T Clark, 2003).

Jeff Astley, David Brown, and Ann Loades, *Evil: A Reader* (Edinburgh: T&T Clark, 2003).

Lewis Ayres, *The Trinity: Classic and Contemporary Readings* (Oxford: Blackwell Publishing, 2005).

John S. Bowden and James Richmond, *A Reader in Contemporary Theology* (London: SCM Press, 1967).

Ellen T. Charry, *Inquiring after God: Classic and Contemporary Readings* (Oxford: Blackwell Publishers, 1999).

Daniel B. Clendenin, *Eastern Orthodox Theology: A Contemporary Reader* (Grand Rapids, MI: Baker Books, 1995).

Dan Cohn-Sherbok, *Interfaith Theology: A Reader* (Oxford: Oneworld, 2001).

Dan Cohn-Sherbok, *Holocaust Theology: A Reader* (Exeter: University of Exeter Press, 2001).

Stephen E. Fowl, *The Theological Interpretation of Scripture: Classic and Contemporary Readings* (Oxford: Blackwell Publishers, 1997).

Robin Gill, *Theology and Sociology: A Reader* (London: Cassell, 1996).

Colin E. Gunton, Stephen R. Holmes, and Murray Rae, *The Practice of Theology: A Reader* (London: SCM Press, 2001).

Michael A. Hayes and Liam Gearon, *Contemporary Catholic Theology: A Reader* (Leominster, UK: Gracewing, 1998).

Edward Hindson, *Introduction to Puritan Theology: A Reader* (Grand Rapids, MI: Guardian Press, 1976).

William S. Johnson and John H. Leith, *Reformed Reader: A Sourcebook in Christian Theology* (Louisville, KY: Westminster John Knox Press, 1993).

G. Neil Messer, *Theological Issues in Bioethics: An Introduction with Readings* (London: Darton, Longman & Todd, 2002).

Michael S. Northcott, *Urban Theology: A Reader* (London: Cassell, 1998).

Ben C. Ollenburger, E. A. Martens, and Gerhard F. Hasel, *The Flowering of Old Testament Theology: A Reader in Twentieth-Century Old Testament Theology; 1930–1990* (Winona Lake, IN: Eisenbrauns, 1992).

Nelson Pike, *God and Evil: Readings on the Theological Problem of Evil* (Englewood Cliffs, NJ: Prentice-Hall, 1964).

Richard J. Plantinga, *Christianity and Plurality: Classic and Contemporary Readings* (Oxford: Blackwell Publishers, 1999).

Gesa Elsbeth Thiessen, *Theological Aesthetics: A Reader* (London: SCM Press, 2004).

Graham Ward, *The Postmodern God: A Theological Reader* (Oxford: Blackwell Publishers, 1997).

John B. Webster and George P. Schner (eds), *Theology after Liberalism: A Reader* (Oxford: Blackwell Publishers, 2000).

James Woodward and Stephen Pattison, *The Blackwell Reader in Pastoral and Practical Theology* (Oxford: Blackwell Publishers, 2000).

Three groups of readers may be singled out for special attention, in that they focus on areas of theology that became particularly significant during the second half of the twentieth century, and are often taught in college courses: feminism, liberation theology, and the theology of the emerging world. In what follows, we shall note some important collections of readings for those wishing to study these further.

Feminism

María Pilar Aquino, Daisy L. Machado, and Jeanette Rodriguez, *A Reader in Latina Feminist Theology: Religion and Justice* (Austin, TX: University of Texas Press, 2002).

Elisabeth Schüssler Fiorenza, *The Power of Naming: A Concilium Reader in Feminist Liberation Theology* (Maryknoll, NY: Orbis Books, 1996).

Ursula King, *Feminist Theology from the Third World: A Reader* (Maryknoll, NY: Orbis Press, 1994).

Prasanna Kumari, *A Reader in Feminist Theology* (Madras, India: Gurukul Lutheran Theological College, 1993).

Ann Loades, *Feminist Theology: A Reader* (Louisville, KY: Westminster John Knox Press, 1990).

Liberation Theology

Curt Cadorette, *Liberation Theology: An Introductory Reader* (Maryknoll, NY: Orbis Books, 1992).

Elisabeth Schüssler Fiorenza, *The Power of Naming: A Concilium Reader in Feminist Liberation Theology* (Maryknoll, NY: Orbis Books, 1996).

Arvind P. Nirmal and V. Devasahayam, *A Reader in Dalit Theology* (Madras, India: Gurukul Lutheran Theological College, 1990).

Theology in the Non-Western World

Ursula King, *Feminist Theology from the Third World: A Reader* (Maryknoll, NY: Orbis Press, 1994).

John D'Arcy May (ed.), *Living Theology in Melanesia: A Reader* (Goroka, Papua New Guinea: Melanesian Institute for Pastoral and Socio-Economic Service, 1985).

John Parratt, *A Reader in African Christian Theology*, rev. edn (London: SPCK, 1997).

R. S. Sugirtharajah and C. Hargreaves (eds), *Readings in Indian Christian Theology* (London: SPCK, 1993).

Index